MONKEY BUSINESS

The Lives and Legends of
The Marx Brothers

MONKEY BUSINESS

The Lives and Legends of The Marx Brothers:
Groucho, Chico, Harpo, Zeppo
with added Gummo

SIMON LOUVISH

THOMAS DUNNE BOOKS
St. Martin's Press
New York

THOMAS DUNNE BOOKS.
An imprint of St. Martin's Press.

Photographs and illustrations courtesy of Bill Marx, Glen Mitchell, Paul
Wesolowski, Joel Finler, the Kobal Collection, New York Public Library for the
Performing Arts, author's collection, Robert Marx, Armond Fields, and Film
World, Australia.

ISBN 0-312-25292-7

First published in Great Britain by Faber and Faber Limited

First U.S. Edition: June 2000

10 9 8 7 6 5 4 3 2 1

Contents

Preface

No book about the Marx Brothers can be written without reference to the magnificent resource of America's most notorious Marxist, Paul Wesolowski, Number One Fan, diligent Marx Brothers historian, and Editor of the *Freedonia Gazette*. Wesolowski's personal archive of over 40,000 clippings of Marxiana, collected over a twenty-five-year period, as well as his enthusiasm and generosity in sharing his research with others, has earned him the accolade of honorary membership of the Marx clan, under the nickname of Wesso. As such he will be often referred to anon. Researcher First Class mention also goes to genealogist David Rothman, zealous debunker of oral mythologies. Many others, Marx family members, archivists, fans and film buffs, have given generously of their time and sanity, and are fully acknowledged in the caboose of my rickety and inevitably old-fashioned vehicle. The reader is invited to take a seat, pull up a spittoon, and settle down to enjoy the ride.

Noxis on the Conoxis

It was a dark and stormy night in Columbus, Ohio, in the month of January 1915. This town was not the hub of the universe. A rail centre for the industrial heartlands of America, Columbus also produced coal, iron ore, steel castings, cement mixers and fire engines. It had, withal, an eccentric and concealed side which would, some years later, be chronicled by an awkward local youth named James Thurber who, in 1915, was experiencing some of the events he would record as *The Night the Bed Fell* and *The Night the Ghost Got In*. It was one of the Thurber family maids, Juanemma, who was so susceptible to hypnotism that, while in the audience, she was put under by a stage hypnotist at B. F. Keith's theatre, and joined the sucker on the stage in floundering about with loud cheeping noises, having been convinced she was a chicken.

A decade further on, this gawky Thurber will have a small role in our story, as a contributor to the one and only *New Yorker* magazine. But B. F. Keith's theatre in Columbus plays a more direct part in our tale.

On that night of 9 January, one of vaudeville's greatest luminaries, the juggler and 'Silent Humorist' W. C. Fields, arrived at the Columbus railway station. Shaking the snow off his boots and coat and unfurling his already bulbous proboscis, he proceeded towards Keith's theatre to begin his engagement for the week's vaudeville programme. Fields was, by this time, aged thirty-five, at the top of his profession, having completed a long tour of Australia the previous summer, but was impelled to return to the American stage by the outbreak of the Great War in Europe. He had, legendarily, travelled forty-nine days for a one-night stand in Syracuse, New York, where he was hoping to begin a long run with a 'legit' stage musical, *Watch Your Step*. But Fields's part of the show was axed after the opening night, and he returned for a while to his old vaudeville routine, pending his new career as a Ziegfeld *Follies* star, due to commence in June 1915.

W. C. Fields fully expected to star in Columbus. After all, he was a veteran headliner. His massive stage prop, the trick billiard table which had accompanied him around the world, was being readied for the Keith stage. The entire world had resounded with laughter at the Great Man's

1

deft tricks. But when Fields arrived at the theatre, he was due for a disturbing surprise. Backstage, he faced more than the accustomed bedlam. An entire forty minutes of the two-hour show was to be taken up by one act. Stage hands were struggling with its three major sets, a disembarkation dock just off an arriving ocean liner, the garden of a New York mansion and a giant boat to be carried down a river scene in the finale. A dozen young girls, in the familiar flimsy chorus costumes, were dashing about, shrieking and laughing.

Orchestrating this mayhem, four young men, in their mid-twenties, talked and wisecracked wildly, as they donned their own costumes, in the intervals between chasing and goosing the girls.

Once the show got going things got even worse. The Great Man fumed in the wings as the extravaganza entitled 'Home Again' unfolded. The four men, who were apparently brothers, and who seemed so interchangeable off-stage, took on absurdly differing characters. One, dressed as an old German paterfamilias, cracked a row of corny sea-voyage jokes: 'Next time I cross the ocean I'll take the train . . . then I'll know when I eat something I'll never see it again . . .' Another played an Italian comic with a highly hostile relationship to the English language. The third brother worked entirely in pantomime, dressed in a tattered raincoat and a horrendous bright red wig, characteristic of old German comedians. His handshaking routine with a stock Irish policeman, which involved a load of dinnerware cascading from his coat, had the audience rolling in the aisles. The fourth brother played the love interest, the old German's son, who has fallen for a flirtatious soubrette. The comic stuff proceeded at a breakneck pace, interspersed with songs and dances, piano solos by the comic Italian and a zany harp performance by the mute. By the time the Great Vaudevillian came on to do his billiard tricks, the patrons of Keith's were totally wrung out, unable to provide the customary acclaim for the star of the show.

The Great Man suffered through this humiliation for two nights, and then threw in the towel. Many years later, he was to write about this trauma: 'Never saw so much nepotism or such hilarious laughter in one act in my life. The only act I could never follow . . . I told the manager I broke my wrist and quit.'

Groucho Marx, the 'German' father, confirmed this confession in his own later years: 'He said: "You see this hand? I can't juggle any more because I've got noxis on the conoxis and I have to see a specialist right away."'

Within three months, the famous juggler had quit the vaudeville stage to clamber up the Ziegfeld ladder, leaving the Four Marx Brothers, Leonard, Arthur, Julius and Milton, to hungrily survey their kingdom, moving on, from Keith to Keith, from Bijou to Majestic, travelling with their wild caravan from town to town, city to city, pursuing their uphill struggle to conquer the variety stage. Switching brothers, as Milton dropped out and the youngest brother, Herbert, joined, the foursome proceeded to Broadway and then on to the creaky sound-stages of the early talkies, and the glamour of the Hollywood screen, to become the most well-known and, to many, the best-loved comedians of the twentieth century, their act disseminated by every modern medium: television, videotapes, and on into the digital age, and beyond –

But let us rewind the reel, and start again:

'What is your first number, Signor Bordello?'

'Nomber one!!'

ACT I

'Love Me and the World is Mine'

Our Father's *Kugel*

PROSECUTOR: Chicolini, when were you born?
CHICOLINI: I don't remember, I was only a little baby.

Duck Soup (1933)

The year is 1900. Dawn of a new century. New York City is in the midst of a new building boom, though more than one and a half million people in the city are estimated to be living in slums. Thirty-seven per cent of the city's inhabitants are foreign-born. In the East Side of New York, the mass of migrants, attracted by the promise of a new life in a Golden Land, remain trapped in some of the most overcrowded districts in the industrialized world. Some migrants, though, have managed to squeeze north, in search of relative breathing space.

On 8 June 1900, the Enumerator of the Federal Census records the residents of 179 East 93rd Street, in the Borough of Manhattan, between Lexington and Third Avenues. The street is part of the district known as Yorkville, inhabited mostly by new German and East European arrivals. The Enumerator, one John J. Conway, diligently interviews the resident families at Number 179. There are the Roplands, immigrants from Russia, with five sons and two daughters, all except the youngest born in the old country. There are the Schonfelds, husband, wife, grown daughter, teenage sons, father's place of birth: Germany. There appears to be a large family of Rumanians, whose name is illegible on the census form. And there is the Marks family: Samuel, born October 1860, in Germany; Minnie, his wife, born November 1864, in Germany; mother-in-law Fanny Schönberg, born May 1829 in Germany; and four sons, all born in New York City – Leo, born March 1887; Adolph, born 23 November 1888; Julius, born 2 October 1890; and Milton, born 23 October 1892. As well as these fine specimens of male juvenescence, a fifth child is listed: Pauline, a 15-year-old daughter, also born in New York, in January 1885.

In the fullness of time, the four sons would become known to us as Chico (Leo, or Leonard); Harpo (Adolph, nicknamed 'Ahdie' and later renamed

Arthur); Groucho (born Julius Henry); and Gummo (born Milton). The fifth son, Herbert, later known as Zeppo, would arrive in 1901.

Archival documents are strange beasts, and often upset long-revered versions of history and family tales. Both Groucho and Harpo Marx have written accounts of their childhood in Yorkville. Harpo, for his part, remembered 179 East 93rd Street as a 'tenement'. The Marxes, he wrote, were poor, and numerous: 'But thanks to the amazing spirit of my mother and father, poverty never made any of us depressed or angry. My memory of my earliest years is vague but pleasant, full of the sound of singing and laughter, and full of people I loved.'

Groucho wrote about their crowded apartment: 'In addition to the five brothers . . . there were my father and mother (in fact, they got there before we did), my mother's father and mother, an adopted sister and a steady stream of poor relations that flowed through our house night and day.'

The fifth brother, Herbert (Zeppo), was born on 25 February 1901, so he was just about to be conceived at the date of the census man's visit. Neither Zeppo nor Gummo nor Chico have left us direct accounts of their childhood, though Chico's daughter, Maxine, has written about her father's early life.

Memories are shaky at best, and show people's memories tend towards the shoring up of old legends. As Chico demands once, of the Brothers' screen foil, Margaret Dumont: 'Well, who you gonna believe, me or your own eyes?' Poor census man Conway might be forgiven for some perplexity in the face of the denizens of the Marx/Marks abode. By 1900, Leo-Chico would have been thirteen years old, and just past his bar mitzvah, or old enough to know better than to cavort with street idlers and gamblers, whose acquaintance he was already supposed to have made. Julius-Groucho, aged ten, was already a serious child for his age and a precocious reader. Milton-Gummo, aged eight, may have been too young to be the one delegated by legend to open the door whenever the landlord loomed and pipe out in a thin, stuttering voice: 'I've been sick.' And twelve-year-old Adolph-Harpo might or might not have offered the visiting official his leg.

The fact that Fanny Schönberg (or Schoenberg) is listed is a little surprising, since previous Marx Brothers annals have listed her as having died in 1896, aged 66, rather than being alive and kicking at 71. Another surprise is the omission of Louis Schoenberg, her husband and Minnie's father, who lived on until 1920. Perhaps he had a good reason to dive under the bed, though the New York City directory of 1900 lists him as a clerk working at a different address, 13 East 118th Street.

But who the heck is the fifteen-year-old Pauline?

Harpo wrote: 'There were ten mouths to feed every day at 179: five boys, from Chico down to Zeppo; cousin Polly, who'd been adopted as one of us; my mother and father, and my mother's mother and father. A lot of the time my mother's sister, Aunt Hannah, was around too. And on any given night of the week, any number of relatives from both sides of the family might turn up, unannounced but never unwelcome.'

One of these would have been Hannah's husband, Julius Schickler, whom Groucho claimed to have been named after, owing to Minnie's misconception that Schickler was a man of means, and might provide, although, as Groucho later claimed, it turned out that he was not only without funds, but owed Sam Marx thirty-four dollars. When he died, Groucho wrote: 'His estate, when probated, consisted of a nine ball that he had stolen from a poolroom, a box of liver pills and a celluloid dickey.' But Groucho, who changed a host of names in his autobiography, *Groucho and Me,* so as not to libel the dead as well as the living, calls Hannah's daughter 'Sally', and claims she was abandoned at birth by Hannah's unnamed first husband, who had taken one look at the babe and fled to Canada.

Groucho's 1979 biographer, Hector Arce, concluded that this tale was apocryphal, and that 'Sally' or Polly – our Pauline – was Aunt Hannah's illegitimate daughter, from a loose liaison that predated Julius Schickler. The archival record, however, now reveals that there was indeed a previous husband, one Max Lefevre, a grocer, whom Hannah married in 1881. Lefevre was certainly the father of Hannah's first child, Louis, who was destined for a brief career as Leo-Chico's stage partner in a piano and violin act, *circa* 1911, under the monicker of Lou Shean. The paternity of Pauline is still unclear, as Hannah, under the name Joanna Lefevre, is listed as a widow in the Manhattan City Directory of 1890–91, resident at the Samuel Marx home. If Max was proclaimed dead after the standard vanishment of seven years, this would preclude him from having fathered Pauline. Perhaps Groucho was named after Julius Schickler in the hope he would take Aunt Hannah out of the house. In the event, she did marry Julius Schickler (listed profession, 'driver') in 1892, under the name of Johannah Lefever.

The switching and changing of first names is, in fact, a staple of this oft-confusing family tale. It is a characteristic of Jewish first names, for many generations, that they often alternated between traditional forms and versions appropriate – and less conspicuous – in the land of present residence. The 'Henry' added to baby Julius's name was probably in honour of Minnie's brother Heinie, a.k.a. Heinemann, as he is named upon immigration. 'Adolph' was another Schoenberg brother, of great significance tale. The origins of the names Milton and Herbert are not known. Leo, later to mutate into Leonard, was, I suspect, another Americanization of grandfather Levy, or Lewi, alias Louis, Schoenberg.

Peering myopically over the archival documents, we find another discrepancy, with Samuel Marx and Minnie Schoenberg's marriage revealed as 18 January 1885, instead of the stated year of 1884. Clearly Minnie and Sam moved their marriage back a little, to accommodate Pauline's birth in January 1885, as they were passing her off as their own; a necessary protection, if Pauline was illegitimate, in an age when that stigma could destroy lives.

The facts tell us, therefore, that the Marx Brothers grew up from their early childhood with an elder sister, albeit adopted, who has been largely written out of the tale. We know nothing about her thoughts, her temperament and her dreams, although Groucho recorded that she had 'a pretty good shape, as we called it in those innocent days'. In true Groucho style, he told a cock-and-bull story about how she married a plumber named Applebaum, whom Minnie ensnared by having husband Sam cook him one of his lip-smacking meals, telling Applebaum 'Sally' had cooked it with her own dainty hands. In fact Pauline married a tailor named Muller, in 1903 – still registered as Pauline Marx – and was expunged from the annals, but not before Julius and Adolph had managed to disgrace themselves at her wedding by pulling a urinal out of the wall.

In the Marx family, boys were boys, and girls were in the story as matriarch, loyal wife, girlfriend, or comic relief. We are left to speculate whether Polly/Pauline, a solemn and older foil, might have been an embryonic Margaret Dumont for the growing mischief makers. But this is a veil no archive shaft can pierce, and even Doctor Hackenbush has left us no clues. Pauline had four children with tailor Simon Muller, and was still in the family fold in 1932, when a panoramic photo-portrait of a major family reunion in New York shows her present with her husband and her eldest daughter, Beatrice.

More solid clues concern the sixth Marx Brother, Manfred, unmentioned until the late 1970s. Family lore told privately of the firstborn son, Manny, born in 1886 but surviving for only three months, and carried off by tuberculosis. Even some members of the Marx family wondered if he were pure myth. But Manfred can be verified. A death certificate of the Borough of Manhattan reveals that he died, aged seven months, on 17 July 1886, of 'entero-colitis', with 'asthenia' contributing, i.e., probably a victim of influenza. He is buried at New York's Washington Cemetery, beside his grandmother, Fanny Schoenberg, who died on 10 April 1901.

It was because of Manfred's death, Maxine Marx records in her book *Growing Up With Chico* (1984), that the eldest surviving son was showered with his parents' frustrated love. Leo (Chico-to-be), was by all accounts a fiercely protected child, favoured over and above the others, and particularly over Julius, whom, Maxine relates, Minnie often referred to by the uneasy term *der Eifersuchtige* – 'the jealous one'.

Julius Henry's birth, in fact, is the only one recorded of Minnie's first five children – on 2 October 1890. His father is registered under his original first name of Simon, the parents then living at 239 East 114th Street. The birth might have been recorded because of complications that forced it to occur outside the home; a tribulation that might have caused Minnie to view her third-born with mixed emotions. Perhaps Groucho was grouchy from the first, with good reason – though the origin of his stage nickname is a matter of some controversy, as will be discussed in due course. Adolph and Milton both had an easier ride into the world, while Herbert came along much later, leaving him with the unhappy status of the afterthought, a burden he felt well into his adult life.

To make keeping track of things even more tricky, if not downright infuriating, a later city census of 1905 confuses all the ages of the Marks children resident at 179 East 93rd Street, listing Milton as nine years old and Julius as eleven, calls the elder Schoenberg Nathen and the head of the household Julius instead of Samuel, and records a younger Marks child after Herbert as 'Sam – age three'!

Not the most diligent search, nor the consulting of seers, mediums or soothsayers has managed to come up with any other trace of this new child. Birth and death certificates have been pored over for the requisite years, to no avail. One must conclude that either the census taker was drunk, or the family listed one of the neighbours' children who happened to have wandered in the apartment, as a prank, or that they were fed up with being asked official questions and took New York City's frazzled Enumerator for a ride. Only the shadowy ghost of a seventh Marx Brother chuckles in the fog of might-have-beens . . .

Samuel Marks, the head of this anarchic family, is listed, in the more reliable 1900 census, under Occupation, Trade or Profession, as 'Merch. Taylor'. His birthplace is entered as Germany. The family tradition places his birth in the French province of Alsace (Groucho at one point names the town of Strasbourg), annexed by Germany after the Franco-Prussian war of 1870–1. Hence his affectionate family nickname of 'Frenchy'. The family tale gives him the original name of Marrix, and claims his change to Marx occurred to give him a spurious family relationship to another Samuel Marx, a powerful Tammany Hall politician in New York. Since Samuel was still calling himself Simon in 1890, the year of Julius's birth, it's difficult to make a good fit here, even if one takes the leg in a bit. The Jewish Yiddish cognomen of Shimen, for Simon, might have mutated into 'Shmuel', or Samuel. Of the name 'Marrix' there is no verifiable trace, and the marriage certificate of Samuel and Mini (*sic*) names the groom Marks, and lists his father as Mark Marks and his mother as Hanne. (The worthy who entered these names on the certificate had a strange take on the spelling of names in English, as he listed Sanuel(*sic*)'s place of birth as 'Elsas Fransh'.)

One version of the family story has Simon/Samuel leaving his native land to avoid conscription into the German army. Harpo, on the other hand, tells us that his father was proud of the German side of his heritage, and delighted in the *plattdeutsch* dialect spoken by some of his Yorkville neighbours. In 1900 Samuel Marks listed the year of his immigration to the United States as 1880. In fact, there are so many Marxes, not to speak of Markses, listed in New York at the time, that it is difficult to distinguish 'Frenchy''s real kin from his coincidental namesakes. There was said to be a relationship with another Samuel Marx, who was to become a prominent Hollywood story editor and producer for MGM Studios in the 1930s, and claimed to be a distant relative of the Marx Brothers in his own book, *A Gaudy Spree*, published in 1987. As this Sam Marx was born in 1902, the possibility that he was the missing ghost brother is delicious but, alas, unsupported by the facts, which record his father as a Broadway theatrical tailor, Max Marx. There is no real evidence of any blood relationship between these Marxes at all. If it were so, a simpler, though still speculative, explanation of the phantom Sam might be that, as a distant cousin, baby Sam was visiting 'Frenchy''s household on that census day of 1905, and got caught up in early Marxian mischief.

This whole imbroglio of names and identities was summed up perfectly by Groucho, in the Brothers' 1946 movie, *A Night in Casablanca*, when, as Ronald Kornblow, the new manager of the Hotel Casablanca, he breezes in to inform his employers brusquely: 'The next thing we're gonna do is change all the numbers on all the rooms!' 'But the guests! They will go into the wrong rooms! Think of the confusion!' protest the hotel owners. 'Yes,' Groucho rolls his eyes, 'but think of the fun!'

I have found no hotel room numbers or verifiable immigration records for

'Frenchy', although the closest fit might be a Simon Marx who arrived in New York, aged twenty-three, aboard the steamer *Elbe* from Bremen, on 6 November 1882. The record shows he claimed to have a return ticket to Germany, though that might have been discarded. The profession of this twenty-three-year-old Simon is 'Merchant', a title which could cover any multitude of sins.

Samuel 'Frenchy' Marx has entered into history as a legend nurtured by his offspring. Despite his entry as 'merchant taylor' in the records, his sons all insisted he was the world's worst tailor, the original 'Sammy made the pants too long'. All his customers, Groucho related, could be recognized in the street, as they all walked 'with one trouser leg shorter than the other, one sleeve longer than the other or coat collars undecided where to rest'. Apocryphal stories abound: how the gargantuan Stookfleisch burst into the house in fury, wearing only the top part of the giant suit Frenchy had carefully tailored him, because Leo had pawned the pants to pay for his gambling; how Frenchy courted disaster by never using a tape measure, how he had to roam far afield, outside the city, for clients, because no one ever came back a second time.

But if Frenchy were so fickle a provider, it is difficult to figure out how the family was living on East 93rd Street, in 1900 – an apartment they occupied, it appears, from 1895 until 1909. The census is particularly useful at revealing the professional profile of the street. Despite Harpo's memories of the house as a 'tenement', this was not the poor part of town. The architectural shape of the street has in fact been preserved to this day, with its four-storey blocks and corner mansions. The neighbours at the adjoining addresses included butchers, clerks, civil engineers, a fur manufacturer, musicians, cigar makers, a dry-goods merchant, a real-estate broker. Some of the households in the street list a servant resident, although a maid could often be afforded by even lower-middle-class families well into the 1930s. Harpo does write about the south side of East 93rd Street as a row of brownstones, telling the tale of the elegant retired attorney, Mr Burns, who would tip his hat even to the children. Or the dashing young tennis player Marie Wagner, who would hand the little 'Ahdie' an old ball as a reward for an afternoon of ball retrieval at the Central Park tennis courts. Later on, Ahdie would start chasing the Miss Wagners, rather than the balls, but this was as yet but a gleam in the eye . . .

From the time Simon/Samuel married Minnie Schoenberg, in 1885, the family lived at Upper East Side addresses, first at 354 East 82nd, then at 217 East 78th Street, at 239 East 114th Street, where Groucho was born, then for two years at 137 East 119th Street, and briefly at 234 East 122nd and 703 East 135th, even further uptown than Yorkville. Legend has them vacating these premises one step ahead of enraged landlords. But this was hardly the slum of the Lower East Side, where most immigrants touched down after passing through Ellis Island, and where Minnie's parents, Louis and Fanny, had met the Promised Land.

Groucho claimed that other luminaries-to-be lived just across the street, citing Ira and George Gershwin, and Ehrich Weiss, alias Harry Houdini. But they can't have been very close, in 1900, unless Houdini spirited them all away for the census. Both Groucho and Harpo were recalling their childhood from palatial California homes, in the late 1950s. Naturally the old times appeared harsh and deprived. And indeed those were the days before social security and welfare, when none but the blind economic forces of the market were there to rescue the weak. Nevertheless, Frenchy could hardly have been a near-bankrupt failure if he could sustain his family in this milieu for over a decade, before the youngsters were old enough to get out and earn.

The saving grace of 'Misfit Sam' – as he was dubbed for posterity – lay, however, in another department. It was for his cooking that Frenchy was idolized. Harpo wrote: 'Frenchie always managed to put a meal on the table. With food he was a true magician. Given a couple of short ribs, a wilting cabbage, a handful of soup greens, a bag of chestnuts and a pinch of spices, he could conjure up miracles . . .' And Groucho told, in an affectionate tribute to his father written in 1933, how Frenchy used his culinary skills later in their career to charm theatrical agents: 'What a cook he was! His *Kugel* (plum pudding, our favorite dish) became the talk of the booking offices . . . for when a booking manager was only half-sold on the potentialities of the Marx Brothers, Mother invited him over to dinner. And as he sat purring over the ambrosia that was Frenchy's pudding, Mother found her job easy. Before the dinner was over, she usually got us the assurance of a few weeks' work.'

A dapper man, always well dressed and handsome, perhaps Sam's sin was that he was no workaholic. His other passion, apart from food, was pinochle, a trait which he perhaps passed on to his eldest son, Leo, with disastrous results. But Frenchy enjoyed playing cards for the love of the game and the company of his *plattdeutsch*-speaking partners. Gregarious to a fault, he was prone to trying out half-baked business schemes, like his partnership with a man Groucho named Jefferson, to buy a pants-pressing machine, with a down payment of fifty dollars won for him by Leo at a crap game, using Pop's original thirteen bucks as his stake. But people preferred to press their pants close

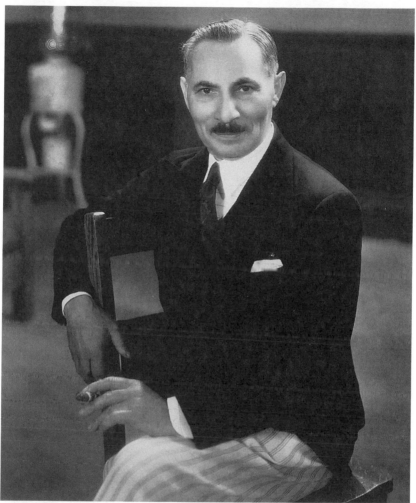

Paterfamilias: Samuel 'Frenchy' Marx.

to home, and the Marx-Jefferson alliance foundered, with the partner going back to his previous job as a porter, and Frenchy going back to the kitchen.

The real power, the true energy, of the household lay elsewhere. Not in the kitchen, but in the parlour. Not in the easygoing nature of Alsace Sam, but in the restless disposition and the unique family heritage of the unshakeable Minnie Schoenberg.

2

The Heart and the Harp

GROUCHO: Ah, this is the only way to travel, boys . . . the only way . . . I
was going to bring along the wife and kiddies but the grocer couldn't
spare another barrel.
CHICO: I was going to bring my grandfather, but there's no room for his
beard.
GROUCHO: Why don't you send for the old swine and let his beard come
later?
CHICO: I sent for his beard.
GROUCHO: You did?
CHICO: Yeah, it's a-coming by hair mail.

Monkey Business (1931)

When Groucho died, in 1977, Robert Dwan, co-director of his long-
running TV show, *You Bet Your Life,* wrote an appreciation of his friend, in
the *Los Angeles Times*, which included the tale of a shared journey to his
mother's birthplace. Groucho wanted to take his third wife Eden and his
daughter Melinda to see it in 1958. Dwan wrote:

We drove from Amsterdam, behind the dikes of the lowlands, over the
great causeway that crosses the Zuider Zee, into Hanover in
Northwestern Germany.
Dornum is in the flatlands between Essen and Wilhelmshaven, larger
than I had expected, six or eight blocks of brick and stone houses. A
church was on a low hill at one end, and what looked like a small castle
at the other. The streets were narrow and cobblestoned, so we left the
car and walked. The one-story houses backed blank walls against the
street. There were no cars, no bicycles and no people. Two children
scampered out of sight around a corner.
We found an inn. Groucho spoke with confidence and fluency in
what he called Plattdeutsch. The proprietor was delighted. His wife, as
large and friendly as himself, brought a most wonderful chicken soup,
summer sausage, Muenster cheese, black bread and beer. As his com-

16

mand of the language grew more flexible, Groucho had them laughing. 'I wonder if he knows who you are?' Melinda asked. But, 'nein', they had never heard of the Marx Bros., never seen the movies. Groucho tried to explain. One had a mop of hair and played the harp; another was a short Italian fellow who played the piano – with an orange. 'Nein.' Then Groucho did himself. He put his cigar in his mouth, glided around the room in his lope. They laughed. He wriggled his eyebrows. They laughed again, but they did not recognise.

In 1958, Groucho found no record of the Schoenbergs, his maternal ancestors, no headstones in the cemetery, no whisper of a memory. But another pilgrim, two and a half decades later, was luckier. In 1984, an eager German film historian, Ulrich Hoppe, published a slim book, *Die Marx Brothers*, in which he chronicled his own findings at the Marxian roots. Groucho, it appears, was looking in the wrong place, like Hoppe himself, who soon realized the folly of looking for Jewish ancestry in the churchyard. He found the Jewish synagogue in Dornum, which had become a shop in the village, though it still preserved the Hebrew writing on the portal. The Jewish chronicles of the village had survived the World War and the Holocaust, and were available in the Aurich State Archive of Lower Saxony. The secret is out:

Here are the marriage lines of Levy Schönberg, aged 28, son of Abraham Schonberg and Schontje Weiler, and Fanny Sophie Salomons, aged 22, parents unknown. The groom was born in Dornum, the bride in Bruchhausen, a village south of Bremen. Levy's occupation is given as 'ventriloquist', and the register also records an alternative, working or stage surname for him: Levy Funk. The date is 15 January 1851. The birth dates of their children, the first five all daughters: Schontje, registered as Schontje Weiler, 16 May 1850; Sara, 20 January 1858; Jette, 14 October 1859; Hanchen, 8 March 1862 (in the same year, three-year-old Jette dies, on 15 August); Miene, 9 November 1864. The couple's first son, Abraham Elieser Adolph, is born 14 May 1868. On 1 April 1870, an unnamed girl is born dead. Another daughter, Celine, and a second son, Heine, are also listed.

Once again, the mystery of facts. Family lore tells a romantic story: how the oddly named 'Lafe' Schoenberg and his wife Fanny and their children roamed the German countryside, 'Lafe' performing magic and ventriloquism while Fanny strummed upon her harp. Once again incompetence was the reigning theme, as exemplified in a 1932 *Photoplay* article culled from another of Groucho's embellishments:

There are some people who swear the Marx Brothers were pulled out of a silk hat along with two white rabbits and a soiled dove. For their grandpappy, as a magician, toured Europe for fifty years in a covered wagon that carried his wife, innumerable children, together with his scenery, and a harp. He could just as easily have been a sewing machine agent for all the magic he knew. But he got by. For each night at the end of a dubious performance, grandpappy very generously offered to cut off anyone's head and put it back on again . . .

For some reason no one ever hastened to take up grandpa's offer of a head amputation . . . Until one eventful night when a huge German yokel decided grandpa knew his business and volunteered.

Grandpa was flabbergasted. He produced an ax. Hoping the victim would back out. He never flinched. Deciding the ax was too easy, he came on with a saw. Rusty round the edges. The yokel thought he saw a big improvement . . . Grandpa was stumped. Finally he came on carrying a basin and towel. And the yokel loved it . . . So grandpa stepped quietly out the back door and somewhere else, his career as a magician considerably damaged in places.

But one of the little girls beneath the cover of that wagon, felt the call, the lure of the theatre even after she grew up, came to America and married Sammy Marx, the tailor . . .

(Sara Hamilton, *Photoplay*, July 1932)

Groucho biographer Hector Arce characterized 'Lafe' Schoenberg as akin to the Magician of Lublin of Isaac Bashevis Singer's story, portraying him as a man of Herculean strength who, driven out of his home town by the sexual scandal arising from his youthful indiscretions, roamed about, performing his magic, until 'he met his future wife Fanny, at the fairgrounds in Dornum, Germany, a desolate, lowland town of eight hundred inhabitants off the sandy North Sea shore'.

The family tale, related by Maxine, Chico's daughter and the keeper of the flame, goes that Fanny's family were religious, and wouldn't allow her to marry the handsome philanderer, until he got her pregnant and they had to yield. The record shows, indeed, that the first child, Schontje, was born one year before the marriage. The rest of the record sits at an angle from the myth. The name 'Lafe', in the first place, appears a 'gentilization' of 'Lev', for Levy, a common Jewish cognomen, which translates as 'Heart'. Levy was born in Dornum, and so had not wandered far, by 1850, or was otherwise loyal to his home base. Since the baby had been taken in as Levy's mother's child – a common practice with illegitimacy – Levy was not cut off from his family. The distance and disdain of Fanny's own family might account for the listing, 'parents unknown'. By the time Levy and Fanny's third child, Jette, is born, in 1859, a new profession of the father appears in the records: 'Umbrella maker'. And so the days of travelling have been curtailed. By the time Miene, later to be Minna, and then Minnie, is born, in 1864, Levy Schönberg is a hard-pressed artisan.

One poignant clue might be gleaned from a story told to film-writer Hoppe by a Dornum policeman: an ancient tale told to him when he was a child by his grandmother, who died aged eighty in 1939. She used to tell him about the travelling ventriloquist who once asked a farmer's wife for milk from a cow. When she refused the man, he made the cow speak: 'Come on, give him a cup!' If this is our only oral memory of Lev, the Heart, then perhaps he did continue to travel in the 1860s, and perhaps the story of the brood of children in the wagon and the little girl peering from under the canvas flap is a true one, rather than one of Minnie's fond fantasies.

Ulrich Hoppe unearthed other potent facts about the life of the Jews of Dornum, culled from the synagogue records. The Emancipation that lifted some of the burdens endured by Prussia's Jews in previous centuries brought citizenship to the Jews of Dornum in 1828. Nevertheless, until 1850, they were obliged to pay contributions to the Christian Church, an onerous humiliation. Hoppe reveals that in 1852, a Rabbi Hamburger, from nearby Emden, reported on the dire poverty of Dornum's Jews, who had to be supported by community funds. It is in these trying circumstances that Levy and Fanny Schönberg married.

The gap that follows is particularly puzzling, if indeed the next child was not born until 1858. Since children followed regularly thereafter, the mores and customs of the age suggest some kind of separation rather than modern-style family planning. What romantic drama might be hidden here behind the bald statistics? The disgraced Fanny, reclaimed perhaps by her family in Bruchhausen, over a hundred kilometres away, for a Biblical seven years before she can be reunited with her husband? Or sheer poverty, forcing her back to the fold? Did Levy Schönberg roam the countryside, alone, with his axe and basin, for seven years, till he could reclaim his bride? And what role did the alias of Levy Funk, noted in the Dornum synagogue records, have in the affair? Might there be, in some obscure Prussian stage journal, a record of this legendary performer? The past often retains its secrets, despite the stubborn searches of today.

Whatever occurred, it was not relayed to future generations, unless

Minnie, and her brothers and sisters, knew more than they were willing to tell. Certainly 'Opie' and 'Omie' – Grandpa and Grandma Schoenberg – enjoying Samuel Marx's fry-ups in the apartments of Upper East Side New York, kept well clear of so much past pain. The Marxes remember 'Omie' as a strict keeper of the Jewish faith, and 'Opie' as the grizzled magic maker, performer of tricks with coins and coacher of the boys in their Hebrew bar mitzvah lessons. As for Minnie, in her adult life she was to become an expert in the denial of bad news, the dressing-up of facts, the hype, the building of castles in the sky.

Minnie's greatest ambition, to make of her five sons a monument to her vision, became her one spectacular success, far beyond her wildest dreams. But this could not have been even the merest gleam in the eye for the young girl growing up in the ventriloquist-umbrella maker's family in the Prussia of the 1860s and 1870s.

Those were troubled and turbulent times. From 1862 to 1890, Otto von Bismarck, Minister-President of Prussia and then Chancellor, pursued, with an iron will, his life's project of a unitary and all-powerful German State. In 1866 Prussia fought a war against Austria and other German states, including Hanover and Saxony. From 1870 to 1871 the new North German Confederation fought a major war with France, resulting in the founding of the German Empire with Wilhelm I proclaimed Emperor at Versailles. Alsace-Lorraine, home of eleven-year-old Simon Marx/Marrix, was annexed. The decade that followed was marked by a cultural battle Bismarck declared against the Catholic Church in the name of German secular nationalism, a conflict known as the *Kulturkampf*. At the same time the German State fought to suppress the newly formed Socialist parties first founded by Ferdinand Lassalle and later influenced by the followers of the exiled Karl Marx. In October 1878 the Reichstag passed the Anti-Socialist Law. We do not know if Levy Schönberg harboured any socialist sentiments, though if heredity has anything to do with it, the social attitudes of his grandchildren, and particularly Groucho's later politics, might suggest some early rumblings in the umbrella makers' guild.

Be that as it may, Levy Schönberg did not in fact wait for oppressive laws to be passed. Along with many of his compatriots and co-religionists, soon to become a flood of émigrés, he rustled up the $30-a-head ticket, embarking with as many of his family as he could afford to pay for, to the New World, and a new life.

In fact, the record shows that Levy Schönberg took ship to the United States not once, but twice. On 4 August 1877, the passenger list of the SS

Rhein, docking at New York from the port of Bremen, includes Levi Schönberg, aged fifty-four, profession 'merchant', and his daughter Hannchen, aged sixteen – both travelling steerage. But two years later, on 9 August 1879, aboard the same ship, arriving again from Bremen, Levi – this time spelled Lewi – Schönberg, aged fifty-seven, is listed again, with four more family members: wife Fanny, aged forty-nine; daughter Minna, aged fourteen; and sons Adolph, nine, and Heinemann, six. Lewi/Levi Schönberg's profession this time is 'farmer'! Even more intriguingly, some years earlier, on 12 September 1873, again on board the *Rhein* from Bremen, another Schönberg, Sara, aged sixteen, arrived alone in New York City. While there were, of course, unrelated Schönbergs arriving, the pattern of events seems clear. Emigration to the United States was a long-term plan, which the Magician of Dornum and his family embarked upon with determination and tenacity.

The US census of 4 June 1880 reveals the family ensconced at 376 East 10th Street, square in the centre of the teeming Lower East Side, at the cusp of another New York turning-point – the building of the adjacent Brooklyn Bridge. Here they are: Louis Schomberg (*sic*), profession 'Huckster', aged fifty; wife Fanny, 'keeping house', aged forty-nine; Minnie, daughter, profession 'fur pointer', aged fifteen; sons Adolph and Henry, aged twelve and seven, 'at school'. All born in Prussia. In an odd discrepancy, Fanny Schönberg, mother-in-law of Samuel Marks, listed her parents, in the 1900 census, as having been born in France. In the 1880 census, she struck two years off her age, if the Aurich State Archive records, listing her date of birth as 1829, are to be considered the last word. Louis, *né* Levy, Schönberg altered both his name and his age, as his birth records reveal him to be fifty-seven years old in 1880.

The falsified age of Adolph, on the ship passenger manifests (he was eleven years old, not nine, on emigration) fits in with this confusing family pattern. It is, in fact, consistent with a common practice of emigrants of racking back the ages of sons in order to avoid the threat of army service. German port authorities, in particular, were known to question boys aged over ten, with the future draft in mind. Given the fresh memories of the Franco-Prussian War, Levy's eagerness to get his sons out of Europe was wholly understandable. And thus the family's continued suspicion of census-takers and government recorders can be seen in its abiding context, supplying the background to one of the conundrums of the century – the Great Marx Brothers Birth Date Scam.

The Schönbergs had arrived in the Promised Land, one tiny component

'Opie' and 'Omie' – Louis (Levy) and Fanny Schoenberg.

of those 'poor . . . huddled masses, yearning to be free'. Their closest neighbours at East 10th Street in 1880 are a Danish blacksmith, John Nelson; an American ship carpenter, born in Maine, William Drummond; another German, Henry Roth, car builder. Even here, not quite the poorest of the poor. Another neighbour, at number 378, John Kelly, an Irishman, has put himself down as 'politician'. Plumbers, machinists, bookbinders, printers,

The indomitable Minnie Schoenberg.

butchers, bakers, 'segar packers' and other 'hucksters' or street vendors abound; Irish, Swedes, Germans, Russians, all the shades of the immigrant rainbow.

Groucho wrote: 'Since neither my grandfather nor my grandmother spoke any English, they were unable to get any theatrical dates in America. For some curious reason there seemed to be practically no demand for a German

ventriloquist and a woman harpist who yodelled in a foreign language . . .'
Lafe, Groucho wrote, in brash fallacy, decided to mend umbrellas, although
he had never repaired an umbrella in his life. In one year he had made exactly
$12.50 from this trade. 'Licking his wounds,' Groucho continues, 'Lafe
decided to retire from the umbrella-mending business and embark on a new
career. The new career consisted of never doing another day's work until he
died, forty-nine years later.'

O calumnious grandchild! In fact, Levy-Louis's hard grind to make ends
meet would lead him through various trades: 'Pedlar' in 1883, 'cloth' in
1884, 'clerk' from 1885. Hannah having married her grocer, Max Lefevre,
it was Minnie who took up the burden of augmenting the family income,
serving her term in one of the district's many sweatshops, laboriously setting the white hairs in fur clothing. Fanny's harp had to be set aside, to
await the role it would play in a future twist of our tale.

Family lore has Minnie working in a straw hat factory when she was res-
cued by Samuel Marx. According to one version, told by Groucho to Hector
Arce, they met at a dancing school run by a Mr Engelhart on Second
Avenue, and Sam was already in the tailoring trade at this time. According
to Arthur Marx, Groucho's son, Sam was a dancing instructor at the school,
and chatted up the ebullient blonde while on a Sunday boat trip to North
Beach. Groucho loved to tease with alternate tales. Howsoever, Levy and
Fanny Schoenberg were obviously relieved to find a good match for their
younger daughter, given the troubles that, most likely, were already
attending Hannah's marriage.

But of Levy's offspring, it was not his daughter Minnie who was to
become the primary successor of Levy Schoenberg's theatrical past. It was in
fact the eldest son, Minnie's younger brother, who was to follow in his
father's footsteps: Abraham Elieser Adolph Schoenberg, aged twelve in
1880, soon to be sent out to labour, too, as a pants presser, would be the first
of the family to fall to the lure of the American stage. And when he discovered the gaudy world of Variety, he would also change his name, from that
foreign mouthful, and call himself simply – Al Shean.

3

Kidding the Captain: 'Was has gesachta?'
– Uncle Al, the Original Marx Brother

CHICO: My father was a-partners with Columbus.
GROUCHO: Well, what do you think of that, eh? Your father and Columbus
were partners?
CHICO: You bet.
GROUCHO: Columbus has been dead for four hundred years!
CHICO: Well, they told me it was my father.

Monkey Business, 1931

American variety in the late 1880s was in a process of transition. The 'honky-tonks', burlesque and the 'dime museums' were mutating into a new, soon to be industrialized entertainment which was to be known as 'vaudeville'. The progenitor of this type of show was Tony Pastor, born in 1837 and initially a circus ringmaster, whose dream was to turn the rough-and-ready world of variety into a spectacle fit for all the family. His opening show in this vein, in a theatre in 14th Street's Tammany Hall, was held on 7 February 1881. In 1885, two ex-grifters, Edward Franklin Albee and Benjamin Franklin Keith, inaugurated their first 'continuous perfor-mance' theatre in Boston, admission one dime, with an extra nickel for a chair.

In New York City below 14th Street, down the Bowery, on the Lower East Side, variety theatres were already booming. The most common enter-tainment was the 'museum' or freak show, featuring such wonders as the Wild Man of Borneo, the Leopard Children, the Double-Brained Child and a host of bearded ladies, tattooed people, albinos, and Old Zip, the missing link between ape and human. The fabulous Houdini began his career in one of these theatres as the 'Wild Man of Mexico'. In another vein, the prolific playwright Ned Harrigan and his partner Tony Hart wowed audiences with the muddled antics of the 'Mulligan Guards'.

Almost all the comedy in early variety was ethnic. Harrigan and Hart excelled in the satirizing of Irish immigrant follies, though their humour ran the gamut of the New York mix:

It's Ireland and Italy, Jerusalem and Germany,
Oh, Chinamen and nagers, and a paradise for rats,
All jumbled up together in the snow or rainy weather,
They represent the tenants in McNally's row of flats . . .

Another famous duo, Joe Weber and Lew Fields, were building their knockabout, rough-house act on the hard training grounds of the Bowery's stages. In 1887 they inaugurated their 'Crazy Dutchmen' routine as Mike and Meyer: 'I am delightfulness to met you.' 'Der disgust is all mine.' And Mike would say: 'I receivedid a letter from mein goil, but I don't know how to writtenin her back.' Meyer: 'You mean rottenin her back. How can you answer ven you don't know how to write?' Mike: 'Dot make no nefer mind, she don't know how to read.'

Perhaps two Chicos are better than one . . . The 'Dutch' act, the 'German' act, and the 'Hebrew' act were fairly interchangeable, though the Yiddish comics confused their English more thoroughly. Through the 1880s the comedy team of Burt and Leon sang 'The Widow Rosenbaum':

Was has gesachta? Zu klein gemachta,
A gang of suckers, around the town.
The kleine kinder, looks in the winder,
Dot was sung by the widow Rosenbaum.

In 1900, the *New York Dramatic Mirror* acclaimed the Jewish comic Joe Welch with a paraphrased ditty:

He knows apoudt der Yiddish man
Mit viskers red ant vireish,
But how he loined it, I know not,
Because Choe Velch is Irish.
But nefer mind – he maigs us crin,
Ant I haf hold a rumor –
Besides his chokes, he also maigs
A lot of real 'mazooma'.

The prospect of 'maiging real mazooma' was clearly tempting to anyone with a gift of the gab or some other talent who could escape the poverty trap of the sweatshops and survive his or her fifteen minutes on the stage. Audiences could be rough but also generous, and in many of these theatres a mug of beer brought down the aisles would aid conviviality. All you needed was something of your own to offer.

AL.SHEAN.

Abraham Elieser Adolph Schoenberg at the start of his career.

In the case of Al Shean, it was his voice. The pants presser of the Lower East Side had a fine baritone, and legend has him entertaining his fellow workers in the *shvitz* of hot irons and steaming fabrics. But this voice would not remain a private entertainment for long.

The real facts of Abraham Elieser Schoenberg's earliest years in show business have been particularly hard to pin down. As Al Shean lived to the age of eighty, and was performing both on stage and screen almost up to the end, he tended, when talking of his long career, to emphasize its later, successful phases. He told journalists celebrating his eightieth birthday in 1948 that he had begun his working life as a butcher's boy, messenger, tailor's apprentice and pants presser, but had always yearned for the theatre. To another correspondent, in 1934, he stated that he had been an usher at the Fourth Avenue Theatre when at the age of twelve, in 1881, he organized the Manhattan Comedy Four, his first known theatrical outfit, 'a variety and music hall turn that lasted for fifteen years'. Not a very likely story, particularly as the Manhattan Comedy Four, as a brand name, doesn't turn up until 1895.

What does turn up, as early as 1888, is a group calling itself the 'Manhattan Quartet'. Quartets were a standard act in vaudeville. You could not hang about the backstage of any variety theatre without falling over at least four of them. Joe Laurie, chronicler of early vaudeville, lists a couple of dozen, among them: the Bison City Quartette, the Avon Comedy Four, the Empire City Quartette, the Empire Comedy Four, the Arlington Comedy Four, the Bootblack Comedy Four, the New York Newsboys Quartette, the Quaker City Four, the Eclipse Quartet, the Twilight Quartet and so on. To columnist Danton Walker, in 1947, the elder Shean provided some further titbits:

'My first role was in a drama called *Apple Orchard Farm*, at the Windsor Theatre in the Bowery . . . We were promised forty weeks and played two – and without salary at that. I didn't think dramatic work could be so profitable, so I organized a quartet with Charley Harris, George Brennan and Sam Curtis, and we sang in all the music halls of the Bowery . . .'

In his 1934 interview, Al talks of his first big break, at Tony Pastor's, on 14th Street. This performance can be traced to the original Manhattan Quartet. In the week of 7 to 12 May 1888, they appear, sandwiched between the San Francisco Minstrels and a bevy of other minor luminaries. Unfortunately, Tony Pastor's theatre caught fire a short time later, a circumstance that seemed to run in the Schoenberg family, as a later tale of Harpo Marx will testify. The Manhattan Quartet then repaired further south, to Zipp's Casino in Elm Place, Brooklyn, an obscure venue which tripled as a beer hall and gambling parlour, where they shared the honours with the Five Tyrolean Yodlers, the Kossuth Hungarian Gypsies, Samson the Strong Man and Minnie Schult, a plump blonde Teutonic singer whose local popularity was not matched by critical acclaim.

Apple Orchard Farm existed too, a sentimental rural drama, staged at the Windsor Theatre the week of 8–13 June 1891, but promptly executed by

28

the critics: 'A weaker, more incoherent play has not been seen for some time,' growled the *New York Herald*. 'The interpolated songs and dances were . . . below mediocrity,' added the *New York Clipper*, woefully. The cast, led by Loduski Young and Maggie Barton, got off more lightly, and there, in the smallest type of the also-mentioned, is one Lawyer Crane, played by Alfred Shean – a somewhat cavalier rendition of his adopted first name, which he also enters, in city directories, as Albert.

Undaunted by this early flop, Shean – and, I assume, the rest of the Quartet – soon switched to another, more successful rural drama, a sleeper called *The County Fair*. Running for over three years, this stage hit starred its co-writer, Neil Burgess, in cross-dressing mode, as one Abby Prue, 'unable to pay off the mortgage of the farm, with a horse of unexpected speed in the barn, a horse which won the race and enough money to bring the play to a happy conclusion'. The nimble of mind will have discerned a strange psychic connection to Our Heroes' 1936 film, *A Day at the Races*. Plots that survive down the ages . . . The big attraction of *The County Fair*, which really wowed them in the 1890s, was the final racetrack scene, set on a treadmill – state of the art – with real horses, a real waterfall, and a real tree, eighteen feet high, on the stage.

'We got a job with Neil Burgess in *The County Fair*,' Shean told Danton Walker. 'I sang a solo in the corn husking scene . . . rode a horse in the third act, and handled props between times. We got $125 a week for the four of us.'

Al's mentor in this period was an overweight young actor, only one year his senior, Sam J. Curtis, who reminisced in 1916 about his career: 'I started the famous Manhattan Comedy Four, which was a singing quartet, and remained with it five years.' Sam added: 'My weight is about the same, holding around 320 pounds and it is pretty good weight for a tenor.'

In 1894 the Manhattan Quartet disappears, and in January 1895 the Manhattan Comedy Four appears, with Sam Curtis, Al Shean, Arthur Williams, and a veteran who had come from Ned Harrigan's troupe of actors, Ed Mack. Their faces, grinning through some outlandish, long-haired make-up, appear in the oldest photograph in Maxine Marx's collection of family snaps, dated 1896.

At this time, Sam and Minnie Marx's boys, and Pauline, were still the littlest of rascals. Leo-Chico was nine years old, and already a compulsive gambler, according to his daughter Maxine, although what his collateral was apart from his collection of marbles it might be hard to imagine. Milton-Gummo was four, and little Julius-Groucho was six years old, just beginning, according to Harpo's book, to struggle with phrases like 'This is a Cat, See the Cat.' Adolph-Harpo himself was eight, an age at which he later claimed to be finished with school altogether. Anyone who has seen Harpo's practically indecipherable scrawl and atrocious spelling in his later years might conclude he was telling no lies. True, he did quote a written statement that 'Harpo attended lectures at Hamilton College in Clinton, New York, for six years, was given the freedom of the campus, and was celebrated as the youngest student ever to enter a classroom in the history of that hallowed old institution.' But, he revealed, this referred to a poodle, also named Harpo, given for adoption by Hamilton graduate Alexander Woollcott, Harpo's latter-day mentor.

Harpo remembered being the only Jewish kid in a classroom of Irish boys, run by one Miss Flatto, who was inexplicably out of the room whenever the Irish kids chose to throw him out of the window. Luckily, recalls Harpo, it was on the first floor, only eight feet above the ground. A tumble that, we might surmise, would serve young 'Ahdie' well in his later cavortings on the stage. This kind of treatment was also the only solid grounding the boys had in the reality of their ethnic origins. As Bill Marx, Harpo's son, told me in conversation: 'The boys . . . were really not creatures of the Temple and didn't practise in a formal manner. What happened in those days, you sensed you were a Jew or an Italian or Irish based upon who tried to beat the crap out of you going home . . .'

Since Harpo also relates, in his tale of Miss Flatto, that Polly's boyfriend came to sort out the classroom, smelling of the herring he peddled on the street, and as Pauline was eleven when Adolph was eight, we must conclude that he stayed at school some time longer. But Harpo admits in his book, *Harpo Speaks*, that he had a hopeless memory for dates, which is obvious as, in keeping with his brothers, he moved his own birth date forward a full five years, to 1893, with consequences which we will explore anon.

The memory that was most vivid for both Julius and Adolph was that of Uncle Al's visits to their home. The kids would be rushed out to buy kummel cheese and huckleberry cake, and Leo would go for the beer. Groucho, in *Groucho and Me*, described Uncle Al breezing in sporting a frock-coat and gold cane, with a silk hat over his flowing long hair. When he left, he gave the boys a dollar each, and tossed a handful of nickels to the neighbourhood kids who gathered on the stoop outside to see the famous man.

Harpo also recalled being taken to the theatre to see Uncle Al perform. He doesn't say whether this was in Al's quartet days or during his later alliance with Charles Warren. Certainly the five years from 1895 to 1900 were the age of Al Shean's ascension from the shabbier stages to the first-rank vaudeville halls. Already in April 1895 the *New York Dramatic Mirror* singled out the act for special praise when it played at Keith's, Union Square: 'The hit of the evening was made by the Manhattan Four, an excellent male quartette who not only sing but are original in both make-up and costume.' On 31 August, again at Keith's: 'The Manhattan Four, one of the funniest and cleverest quartets now before the public, were obliged to respond to real encores.'

The Manhattan Comedy Four now toured the country, making a 'favorable impression' in San Francisco, and being 'the feature of the bill' in Chicago. They began introducing, along with songs like 'Sweet Molly Morin' and 'After the Ball', comic sketches, which 'kept their audience in an uproar'. This was the heyday of vaudeville, and competition was fierce, with acts having to achieve a high enough standard to impress the Keith and Albee bookers. There was also a new, mechanical rival: The Lumiere Cinematograph, introduced in July 1896, was packing them in at Keith's, Union Square. Audiences and even hardened newspapermen thrilled as 'the pictures . . . were thrown upon a screen. Some of them were so life-like that the blasé scribes were moved to applaud . . . The best picture was "the Arrival of the Mail Train." The train came into the station, passengers alighted, met their friends and walked about, and all the bustle incident to affairs of this kind was shown to perfection.'

Did the short-panted Marx kids see this early precursor of the engine that would impel them to immortality? If so, they forgot to record it. On 12 December 1896, the Manhattan Comedy Four appeared at Hammerstein's Olympia on the same bill as the Veriscope, another new moving picture machine – but it was the Four who were the hit of the show.

By 1899, Al Shean had progressed from singer to writer and was providing longer and longer skits, not only for his own foursome but for the companies they toured with as a whole. One such piece, entitled 'A Tin Wedding – A Musical Burletta in One Act', is listed proudly in a billing for 'Weber's Big Olympia Company', 11 December 1899, featuring the kind of characters which we might find not unfamiliar: one Odacia Prim, played by Nan Engleton; Mr Johnson Peanut, played by M. T. Bohannon; Dr X. Y .Z. Curem, 'a dealer in chills, pills and kills', played by R. Anderson, and Lightning Jack, 'a messenger boy', played by Ed Mack. The playlet concerns the fortunes of the Mulligan family of typical ne'er-do-wells, and Al Shean himself plays Julius Krautzmaul, 'Mrs Mulligan's uncle from

31

Milwaukee' – though why the good Celtic lady has a German dialect uncle is a secret lost in the sands of time. For good measure, Shean is listed as rendering 'Mein Liebes Maidchen' together with Bert Howard & Company.

Clearly wishing to move on from ethnic yodelling, Al Shean left the Manhattan Comedy Four in 1900, though the act soldiered on a while with other performers. Sam Curtis went on to his own career in vaudeville, and Al Shean found a new partner, Charles Warren. Two of their earliest sketches, entitled 'Quo Vadis Upside Down', dated 1901, and 'Kidding the Captain', 1902, are the first texts involving Levy Schoenberg's offspring to have survived down the ages. As Al Shean wrote the Marx Brothers' seminal show, 'Home Again', and was reputed to have been involved in both their previous stage pieces, 'Fun in Hi-Skule' and 'Mr Green's Reception' – all of which have resisted the stubborn efforts of researchers, including your frustrated servant, to unearth them – it is worth looking at his early prose style, shaky as it may be. None of the Manhattan Comedy Four sketches were preserved, not even 'The Tin Wedding', although, even in the trivialities of vaudeville, writers did send their scripts in for formal copyright at the Library of Congress in Washington. Al Shean entered six scripts, of which only three, the two above mentioned and a later sketch, 'Summer Time' (1912), can be found.

Harpo, in his autobiography, remembered seeing 'Quo Vadis Upside Down' and imitating it at home with his brothers. It was a spoof of a then current play of the eponymous Roman era saga, and provides the earliest echo of the Schoenberg-Marx agenda:

FIRST ACTOR: Nero was the Emperor of Ancient Rome. Nero the blood-thirsty, at the mention of whose name there arises scenes of the blood-soaked arena –
SECOND ACTOR: I had it for breakfast.
FIRST ACTOR: Had what?
SECOND ACTOR: Soaked farina . . .

And plenty more in that vein. In 1902's 'Kidding the Captain', the fearsome Captain Kidd is bearded (*sic*) on his desert island by a rapacious debt collector:

CAPTAIN KIDD: A ship! . . . She looks like a man-o'-war, but I cannot make out her country. (*Business – noises off . . . 3 golden balls slowly fired through the sky . . .*)
KIDD: A Hebrew man-o-war! I am lost, lost! I have defied all but now it is useless!

Collector enters . . . boat on shoulder, anchors, chains, etc. . . . reading aloud from note book: Capt. Kiddinsky, #28 Atlantic Ocean. *(Also amount due his form, mention name of firm, with interest.)*
KIDD: Traitor!! Installment house blood hound! . . .
COLLECTOR: Kidd, Kidd, you're big enough to be a man!
KIDD: At the mention of that awful name nations tremble!
COLLECTOR: And you want me to tremble? How many times?
KIDD: This is no time for trifling! Fool, fool, you shall tremble 10,000 times!
COLLECTOR: At 12³/4 cents a tremble? How much is that, 2¹/2 off?

George S. Kaufman it is not. When this skit was revived in 1906, how-ever, the *New York Dramatic Mirror* noted that 'Al Shean and Charles Warren were excruciatingly funny in their new act . . . Kidding the Captain. Shean has a number of original oddities in this act, and Warren helps materially in bringing out the fine points.' It is difficult to figure what the fine points might have been of such exchanges as 'Stand ready!! All heave the anchor!' – 'They were so sick, all heaved the anchor?' But never-theless, through the sea-mist and schlock, we can make out the bare skeleton of later Marx Brothers routines:

KIDD: The Captain swore a round oath –
COLLECTOR: If he was a square captain he'd swear a square oath! . . .
KIDD: A castaway, a cast-off!
COLLECTOR: Yes, I know a cast-off, 2nd hand.

In the later sketch, 'Summer Time – a Comedy in One Act', Shean fea-tures an exchange between a gentleman rider, Klotz, and the Commodore of a boat club:

COMMODORE: Now listen. A lady here has lost a jewelled garter.
KLOTZ: A Jewish garter?
COMMODORE: A jewelled garter – and we must find the thief that took it.
   Behold the jewelled garter. Of course I could not trust you with this
   garter.
KLOTZ: No, I'm too damn dumb.
COMMODORE: But, I will give you the measurements – *(pulling out tape measure)* behold the size of the calf.
KLOTZ: That's almost a cow.
COMMODORE: Remember, I am giving you the right steer.
KLOTZ: I hope you are not handing me a lot of bull.

We are on more familiar territory here, reminiscent of some of the Groucho–Chico routines in *The Cocoanuts* and *Animal Crackers* – and those *are* George S. Kaufman! Within three years of this piece of theatrical bric-a-brac, Shean was writing and staging 'Home Again' for his upwardly mobile nephews. But in later years, he grew more and more reluctant to discuss this relationship, and kept his distance from their professional progress. At the age of eighty, in his interview with the *New York Post-Dispatch*'s Virginia Irwin, he even managed to omit mentioning the Marx Brothers altogether! The kids to whom he had imperiously handed his dollar bills had outstripped him and overshadowed his glory. Maxine Marx remembers him as an old man, rehearsing his role as a Catholic priest in *Father Malachy's Miracle*, leching and groping after the girls in the show, protesting, as they ran shrieking, 'But I only want to fondle your breasts!'

Today, his long career is a footnote. He starred, after his days with Charles Warren, in many stage plays and musicals, creating the specialty of a comic German, with names like Schwattermagon, Schmaltz, Schmuke and Schniff. But his big break occurred because of a single comic song, performed together with his next partner, Ed Gallagher, in the *Ziegfeld Follies* of 1922. 'Oh, Mr Gallagher, Oh Mr Shean' made Uncle Al famous after a stage career that had already lasted thirty-four years. Its catch-phrase became so popular that Shean ordered it inscribed on his tombstone, in anticipation of his death, in 1948 –

Born May 12, 1868.
I could have lived longer,
but now it's too late.
Absolutely, Mr Gallagher,
Positively, Mr Shean.

Without Al Shean there would have been no Marx Brothers, at least not in show business. Minnie would not have been galvanized to thrust them towards the stage, and we might have had five unknown juvenile delinquents or, on another path, perhaps five somewhat psychopathic dentists causing a rush of malpractice suits throughout the 1920s and '30s. Or even, perhaps, a genuine shyster law firm – Marx, Marx, Flywheel and Marx?

Horatio Alger and the Tin Can Swinger

DETECTIVE: (*to Chico*): Who is this fellow?
CHICO: That's my brother.
DETECTIVE: (*to Harpo*) Is that your brother? (*Harpo business with head*)
GROUCHO: Figure that out.
DETECTIVE: (*to Chico – pointing at Groucho*) Who is this fellow?
CHICO: That's my father.
GROUCHO: How long has this been going on?
DETECTIVE: (*to Groucho*) Are these your sons?
GROUCHO: Yes
DETECTIVE: Are you their father?
GROUCHO: I object!

I'll Say She Is (1923)

When Ahdie and Julius pulled the urinals out of the wall at Pauline's wedding, at Schaeffer's Casino in the Bronx, Julius was a few months short of his bar mitzvah. Leo had already 'become a man' in 1900, and Adolph ('Ahdie') a year later. According to Groucho's colourful account, the irate Casino owner broke into the Rabbi's Hebrew blessing at the bridal canopy to cry: 'Stop the wedding! Stop the wedding!' Groucho reported a ray of hope in the groom's eye, but the indomitable Minnie promptly raised a collection to pay the thirty-eight dollars' worth of damage.

All the accounts of the Marx Brothers' childhood portray their family life as a non-stop rush of madcap escapades. When the brothers co-operated with Colliers associate editor and showbiz profiler Kyle Crichton in 1949, he produced the only book-length account to date of the Brothers' early days, from childhood to Broadway success. Crichton's book *The Marx Brothers*, long out of print, provides a heavily fictionalized portrait of the family home as a wild Katzenjammer Kids-type cartoon. On Frenchy shmoozing an angry customer: '"Schupkie!" he cried, with feigned delight. "Sitting on der schteps yet. Tsch! Tsch! Sun on der haid, you get a schtroke. Come up and have somesing."' *Oi vei!*

When *The Marx Brothers* was published in 1950, after serialization in several newspapers, the Brothers were unhappy about the book's many cavalier departures from reality, although it was in fact copyrighted to Harpo, Groucho, Chico, Zeppo and Gummo Marx, in that order. Harpo and Groucho's own versions, published in 1961 and 1959 respectively, contain their own quota of pitfalls, as is only to be expected from showmen. Of course, the chief pleasure in reading these personal accounts is in the authentic voice of our heroes, the sheer exuberance of these inside stories. And for many, this might be enough. When the legend becomes the truth, print the legend.

Fiction, despite the cliché, is mostly stranger than truth. But the truth has its own, often peculiar mixture of genuine craziness and disillusion. Our main problem, in dealing with Harpo and Groucho's tales of their earlier years, relates to their habit, previously mentioned, of bringing forward their birth dates, which has confused generations of scholars and fans. In a 1966 booklet, *The Marx Brothers, Their World of Comedy*, by Allen Eyles, the birth dates of the Brothers are given as follows: Leo-Chico, 22 March 1891; Adolph-Harpo, 23 November 1893; Julius-Groucho, 2 October 1895; Herbert/Zeppo, 25 February 1901; and Milton-Gummo bringing up the rear. Apart from Herbert's date, the rest is nonsense. The days and months are right, but Chico has become four years younger, and Harpo and Groucho both five years younger than in fact they were. And of course Milton preceded Herbert, by eight years.

Groucho writes: 'Give or take a few years, I was born around the turn of the century. I won't say which century. Everyone is allowed one guess.'

Indeed we are. From 1890 to 1900! That's more than a few ticks of the clock. But the result of the subterfuge is not just a pedantic or academic matter. It has real consequences for the life story of the Marx Brothers – from childhood through their first decade on the stage – but this has escaped serious notice up to now, despite the fact that the real dates have been on record since researches by Joe Adamson, Hector Arce and Paul Wesolowski teased them out in the mid-1970s.

So what of the real story? The earliest proper record is in the photographs: early snapshots of the boys, in a New York winter, wrapped in somewhat ill-fitting winter clothing – the sleeves perhaps taken in by Frenchy? A portrait of bar mitzvah boy Adolph shows him in a dark coat, with his right gloved hand clutching the other glove, a bowler hat on his head, ears sticking out at either side of a pale moon face. A dreamy stare is fixed somewhere on the street in front of him; a high white collar is constricting his neck. 'Today I am a man!' is the caption to this shot in *Harpo*

Speaks. Another picture, from the family files, shows an older Adolph, holding a black and white dog, with a bar mitzvah-age Julius by his side, hands in his coat pockets, with a tilted cap, and a face that can only be described as typically European Jewish. He looks oddly like the child in the famous Holocaust photograph who is being hustled away by German soldiers, with his hands up. But the Marx boys were vastly more fortunate than their co-religionists two generations down the line . . .

An earlier photograph, the earliest ever of Julius, depicts him and Leo with

Two boys and a dog: Julius and Adolph – teenage dreamers.

two cousins, Hattie and Edna Wolfenstein, while accompanying Minnie on the only visit she ever made to her native Dornum, in 1895. The trip was paid for by the girls' father, Henry, a distant relative who worked in the menswear business. As legend has it, since the money could only cover two accompanying Marx children, Adolph and Milton were bribed by Leo and Julius to stay behind. In one version of the story the bribe is an extra sweet roll; in another version, toy wagons. In the photograph little Leo looks rather awkward between the two girls. Five-year-old Julius, standing bashfully behind them, with his thumb poised as if he hasn't decided whether to suck it or not, sports an unexpectedly thick shock of black hair. Soon after this trip Leo and Adolph enrolled at school, PS 86 at 96th Street and Lexington.

Indeed, the census of 1900 lists all four boys 'at school'. Harpo's own tales of his tearaway childhood as 'Ahdie', following his defenestration by the Irish mafia, take on a new perspective when the birth date change is factored in. We can now realize that many of the stories Harpo relates as the adventures of a twelve- and thirteen-year-old are in fact the experiences of a much older teenager, as the seminal tale of Mrs Schang, Ahdie's rite of passage, can be verifiably dated to 1907, when he was nineteen – not fourteen, as hitherto assumed.

But we have not yet reached Mrs Schang, of whom more later. Let's remain with school, or with the lack of it. A certain amount of confusion, in Harpo's case, might be put down to ghost writer Rowland Barber's struggles with Harpo's dizzy time-scales. But you can't mistake your teens for your childhood. Groucho was a renowned teller of tall tales, but accusing Harpo of deception is akin to accusing Mother Teresa of having had multiple abortions, as Harpo was always considered a saint in the Marxian canon, a man of impetuous truthfulness.

The origin of the Great Birth Date Scam might be as simple as the gut response of a family obsessed with the prospects of army draft for their sons, even in the New World, and Minnie's schemes to keep her sons out of the war that loomed fifteen years into the new century lend credence to this suggestion. There were also other advantages, in the early vaudeville days, of understating the boys' ages, as we shall see, though the continuation of this subterfuge into later years is more puzzling. In Harpo's case I think we can sense, under the robust charm of his narrative, an underlying discomfort about the way he was perceived during those formative years by both his family and his peers. It's clear that Ahdie did leave school quite early, a matter he writes about with his customary good humour but with a certain bitter flavour:

'School doesn't teach you what to do when you are stopped by an enemy gang – when to run, when to stand your ground. School didn't teach you how to collect tennis balls, build a scooter, own a dog, go for a swim . . . School didn't teach you which hockshops would give you dough without asking where you got your merchandise, or how to shoot pool or bet on a poker hand or where to sell junk or how to find sleeping room in a bed with four other brothers. School simply didn't teach you how to be poor and live from day to day. This I had to learn for myself . . .'

The personal tutor at hand to coach Ahdie in these vital skills was his elder brother, Leo. Of all the brothers, Leo was, and remained, the favourite first son, the one who could get away with anything. In looks, he was the closest to Minnie, with his blue eyes and light hair. He inherited from Minnie a seductive quality, which made friends, strangers, women and, later, audiences fall in love with him. When we look at Chico on the screen we are looking at a palimpsest of Minnie Schoenberg. His daughter Maxine used the Yiddish word *schmeikel* to describe his special quality, that alluring demand to be adored. Unfortunately, wrote Maxine, 'His "street smarts" developed rapidly, and . . . by the time he was eleven, he was staying out all night with a tough neighborhood gang, spending his time hustling pool and getting into fights.'

Eleven may be a little premature, but certainly by his early teens Leo was through with school. Physically strong and mentally determined where Ahdie was on the timid side and wary of confrontation, Leo was well able to hold his own. According to legend, he had beaned Augie Hartzfeld, son of the local cop, with a water-filled bag, knocking the little bully cold. At the age of twelve, says Maxine, he took his first job, at a lace factory, keeping track of the employees' work records. A floating crap game on the premises was his new training ground, but he was fired when it was discovered. Other jobs followed, and more crap games, and more money lost to the bad run of the dice than he could bring back home to the family.

Eventually Minnie and Sam decided to do something about their way-ward eldest son. They bought a second-hand piano. Minnie hired a proper Viennese piano teacher to tutor both Leo and Ahdie. Her name has not been preserved, but Harpo remembered her as a rather hefty lady with a moustache. Alas, the story goes, she was a one-handed player, and taught all her pupils accordingly to favour the right hand, and idle with the left. Legend has not related whether she also tended to punch the keys with her right forefinger, or whether Leo developed this trick on his own. Ahdie, the tale continues, could only manage to learn two tunes: 'Waltz Me Around Again, Willie', and 'Love Me and the World Is Mine'.

As they grew up, Leo and Adolph – Chico and Harpo – resembled each other physically more and more until, in their early twenties, only their slightly differing haircuts allowed people to tell them apart. Leo was always a fraction of an inch taller than Adolph, which sparked a running gag between them of challenging each other to a measuring contest, to see which one was the taller. Chico always won, until one day, well into their Broadway period, Harpo, astonishingly, proved to have a slight advantage. It turned out he had spent the day at a chiropractor's, who had stretched him for hours on a bench.

It was obvious that Leo was a bad influence on Ahdie, and Ahdie's contempt for school was at least in part due to his idolization of his elder brother. While Leo branched out into the world, using his new-found skill to get jobs playing in movie nickelodeons, and spending more and more time away from home, Ahdie caught balls for Miss Marie Wagner, stacked wood at Goodkind's Bakery on Third Avenue, worked for Geiger's Dairy and Dried Fruits, did a spell as a bellboy at the Seville Hotel, and as a cigarette boy at the German Freundschaft Club for twenty-five cents a day plus as many hamburgers as he could put away – which was plenty. He worked as a delivery boy for Edwards, Engel and Lefkowitz, a cash boy at Siegel and Coopers, and a do-everything for F. M. Haverhill's office, obtaining customs permits to ship goods overseas. He became, in his own words, a 'working man'. If we take the missing five years into account, we must conclude that this phase of his existence lasted throughout his teenage years. The closest he came in this period to show business was a job, perhaps apocryphal, walking dogs for an English vaudeville star, Cissie Loftus. According to Groucho, this ended when another dog killed one of the lady's mutts, leading her to give him the air. (In another version of this story Groucho changed the mutt into a baby leopard which escaped, killed a neighbour's dog, and was shot by a customer 'just emerging from Abercrombie and Fitch', in case you wanted to really pin this down.)

In short, although he declared himself 'a man' on his bar mitzvah, in 1901, Ahdie was going nowhere. This must have seemed much less funny at the time than when it was being recalled sixty years later. Perceived as unschoolable, trudging from one dead-end job to another, interspersed with various dud money-making schemes set up by Leo, like the pawning of discount cuckoo clocks for an ephemeral profit, or selling stray cats with Julius, Ahdie looked for ways out of his rut. At one point, he fell in with a con man, whom he names Seymour Mintz, who almost landed him in jail. Mintz's racket was obtaining advances from haberdashers for goods he didn't have and couldn't deliver. Hopping from town to town, Ahdie kept being puzzled at his partner's constant disappearing acts, leaving him with unpayable hotel bills, only to appear as suddenly as he had gone, with wads of dough. Eventually, Frenchy rescued his son from this worthy, who had been simply using Adolph as a decoy.

As he wandered, Ahdie observed the life of the city. With those wide, dreamy eyes, he took in the wonders and follies of everyday existence, the roots of the character he was eventually to play on stage and screen: the loafer, the layabout, the urchin without prospects, the ageless sprite for whom all life is both marvellous and absurd. Above all the brothers, it was Adolph, eventually changing his name to Arthur, then to become Harpo, who saw the world invariably through a child's eyes. As his son Bill told me, discussing his father's last years: 'My Dad never went through his second childhood, because he never got out of his first.'

Typical of the child's-eye view was his lifelong use of the mannerisms of the cigar maker, Gehrke. Labouring in the window of his store on Lexington Avenue, with a collarless striped shirt, leather cuffs and elastic armbands, the Teutonic tobacconist always muttered to himself when he worked, and was so wrapped up in his labours he would be unconscious, as Harpo writes, 'of the comic face he was making. His tongue lolled out in a fat roll, his cheeks puffed out, and his eyes popped out and crossed themselves.'

Peering in the glass, young Ahdie would practice 'doing a Gookie' until the unwitting subject would look up and chase him down the road, shaking his fist, as the boy yelled out 'Gookie! Gookie!'

Most kids do this, but few store it up and transmute it, against all the odds, into a gainful profession.

The third brother, Julius, was a very different person. Unlike the two elder boys, he was not physically active, apart from the urinal-pulling episode. He had a slight cast in his left eye, which never quite mended, and which can't have helped his early self-confidence. A contemplative boy, he discovered the joys of reading, and devoured pulp novels, first brought to the house by Leo, which starred dashing heroes like George Patten's Frank Merriwell, all-in sports hero and campus idol. He told his mother, according to *Groucho and Me*: '"I've been reading a book called *Julius, the Street Boy*. It was written by Horatio Alger, and it told all about how a poor young boy with nothing but grit and determination worked his way from nothing to the presidency of a bank. I've got the same name he has, so why can't I get a job and help support the family?"'

41

Minnie had no objections to her son becoming a bank president, so she allowed him to take a job as an office boy. This involved sitting in the office to take in the mail for his absent boss and answer the phone which almost never rang. Reducing his hours of attendance day by day, Julius was caught out eventually when he ran into his employer in the street during working hours. This cut off the road to financial stardom.

Of all the boys, it was Julius who was the most influenced by Uncle Al's stage career. Early fancies of studying to be a doctor had been sparked by admiration for an uncle he named Dr Carl Krinkler, a chiropodist who tended Frenchy's feet. According to Groucho, this worthy of the Hippocratic tradition disappeared and then turned up in jail, having been nabbed in his more lucrative sideline of burning down resort hotels for the insurance. Whether Dr Krinkler was real or an invention, the medical attraction soon faded, as in any case it was not financially feasible. Uncle Al's profession, on the other hand, made sense. It was, after all, the family heritage.

Kyle Crichton, unreliable as he may be, does state at one point that Minnie, rather than being keen on the stage life, feared the theatre, remembering it as the cause of her father's long hard grind. This may well have been a truth one of the Brothers let slip, in a rare moment when they were not nursing the myth. Harpo, on the other hand, claims even Al Shean's career was part of Minnie's theatrical Grand Plan. But Minnie's life was constantly preoccupied with bringing up the kids, encouraging Sam, protecting Pauline, entertaining the hordes of relatives, playing pinochle and klabiasch, worrying about Leo and Adolph, and of course tending baby Herbert, who arrived in 1901. Discipline in the house was left to the father, who couldn't bear to inflict more than a few token licks of a whisk broom to the rears of his errant brood.

Milton, the fourth son, was still at school, though he was spending long periods at home due to illness, real or imagined. Diagnosed as having a weak heart, he was the one delegated to open the door to the landlord when that scourge of civilization called. Milton had developed a stutter, which was to plague him throughout his years on the stage. But, as a teenager, he became a skilled dancer, a talent he maintained all his life, though it was of an eccentric kind, earning him the designation of 'the world's slowest whirlwind dancer'.

When they were smaller, the boys lived as most kids did – they took summer trips to the park, to North Beach, to Coney Island, stealing free rides on the cable cars and the trolleys. As they grew older, and developed different likes and dislikes, it seemed as if they would, as in most other families, take separate roads, and drift apart. In fact, this was largely the case in their teens, when the two older boys seemed lost to semi-delinquency, and the younger ones were just finding their feet in the city's harsh push and shove.

In 1901, Grandma – 'Omie' – died, leaving her harp to gather dust in a corner. 'Opie', retired in his promised land, cultivated his memories. On election day, as a naturalized citizen doing his democratic duty, he could enjoy a fat stogie from Samuel's namesake cousin, the Tammany Hall *macher*, and mutter, 'Ah, lucky to be in America!' Surrounded by his brood, he would never be lonely. Strasbourg and Dornum swarmed in his parlour. This was more than a family. It was, in Jewish parlance, *mishpocheh,* a clan, almost a veritable tribe. Its members might break soup plates over each other's heads, but in tribulation they hung together, and it would still be a long time before good times pulled them apart. Despite their adoption by the land of the huddled masses, they were still strangers in the *goldeneh medina,* the land paved with gold – though not yet for them.

At times, to escape the horde – or, according to Harpo, when the family was broke – Opie would take up the umbrella business again. On his rounds, Harpo wrote, he carried his tool kit and a tin can with charcoal coals to heat his soldering iron: 'The can would be swung round to fan the fire. My special job with Grandpa was Tin Can Swinger.' But the umbrella business soon petered out as, in the early dawn of a consumer society, it was cheaper to buy new brollies than fix the old ones.

'I was sorry,' wrote Harpo. 'Tin Can Swinging was one occupation I could have stuck at permanently. It was fun.'

But it was Levy Schoenberg's original profession that was to be his grandsons' destiny.

5

'Impersonations of the Yiddisher' – from the
Whangdoodle Four to Mrs Schang

(– *As the boys walk on to the stage, they pass a large old-fashioned wagon parked by the curb. Sitting on the tailboard is a cigar-smoking gent in a frock-coat, black moustache and silk high hat* – S. QUENTIN QUALE.)

QUALE: So you two hombres is a-headin' west, eh, podner?

JOE (Chico): Not me – just my brother. I gotta no money – so he's-a going west, and when he gets off the train he'll pick up some gold and mail it to me. (*Pokes Rusty knowingly.*) They say it's laying all over the streets, hey, Rusty?

(*Rusty {Harpo} snaps open his valise and pulls out the only thing it contains, a large iron shovel. Quale eyes these gullible New Yorkers greedily.*)

QUALE: Of course, the streets are paved with gold . . . but they won't let *him* take any – he's a tenderfoot.

JOE: You wear those shoes – you'd have tender feet too.

QUALE: Oh, are those shoes? I thought they were fungus – with buttons.

TRAIN ANNOUNCER: Western express leaving in eight minutes!

from vaudeville routines for *Go West* (1940)

The first of the Marx Brothers in show business was Leo, now calling himself Leonard. He was not performing on the stage, but off screen, playing piano at the nickelodeons, dance halls and saloons. Occasionally, the story goes, he would call in Ahdie to substitute for him, as few could tell them apart. However, Ahdie's limited repertoire of 'Waltz Me Around Again, Willie', and 'Love Me and the World Is Mine' soon palled on the audience, and he was fired. Spoilsport as I am, I must pour cold water on this fond legend, given the evidence of Harpo's later instinctive genius for music. He could not read notes throughout his stage and screen career, but his performances on harp, piano and clarinet were impeccable. So if Adolph didn't stick to the nickelodeons, it was probably because he hadn't found his *métier* – one might say his voice, if that weren't an ironic paradox. We tend, of

44

course, to see 'The Marx Brothers' full blown, in hindsight, rather than the four struggling youths they were then.

The next candidate to shimmer in the ghostly air of legend as First On the Stage is Milton. As the tale is told, Uncle Heinie, jealous at his brother Al Shean's vaudeville success, decided to revive the old family trade of ventriloquism. Unfortunately, he had no talent in this field and thus conceived an ingenious subterfuge. He would use a hollow dummy, with little Milton inside. According to Kyle Crichton, the act was supposed to open in York, Pennsylvania. During the act Uncle Heinie planned to thrust a long pin into the dummy's leg to prove it was really inanimate. Milton's legs were both to be stuffed into one wooden leg so that Heinie could jab the other. Unfortunately Uncle Heinie jabbed the wrong leg and Milton leapt off his lap and off the stage.

Alas for verisimilitude, Crichton sets this story at a point when Milton would have been aged fifteen, a most unlikely story. But Milton himself, alias Gummo, did verify a version of this tale, in an article for *Variety's* twentieth-anniversary issue, where he claimed the whole point of the act was to make use of his brother Julius's cast-off coachman uniform, in which Julius had performed in some unspecified role. What the point was of a ventriloquist's dummy dressed as a coachman is not explained. In a later interview, with writer Richard Anobile for *The Marx Brothers' Scrapbook* (1973), Gummo repeated the tale, again setting it at a later point, when Julius was already on stage:

'I did an act with my uncle, Harry Shean. He was Al Shean's brother and insisted on being in show business due to his brother's success. The fact that he was completely deaf didn't make a difference! . . .

'We concocted an act which consisted of a ventriloquist's dummy, in which I was inside. The head was over my head and I operated the mechanical part as well as speaking. Uncle Harry just stood there. That the act lasted only a couple of weeks is evidence that it was not a success.'

Even the indomitable Paul Wesolowski, keeper of the vaudeville archives, has been unable to turn up the merest woof of this old shaggy hound in print form. But clearly it did not predate Julius, who therefore retains the honours:

'The first real job I ever got was on Coney Island,' he wrote in *The Groucho Phile* (1976, co-authored with Hector Arce). 'I sang a song on a beer keg and made a dollar. Later I sang in a Protestant church choir, until they found out what was wrong with it. For that I got a dollar every Sunday . . . I began my show business career at the age of fifteen, in 1905, by answering a classified ad in the *New York Morning World*. The job called for a boy singer for a vaudeville act, room and board and four dollars a week. When I saw the ad, I ran all the way from our house on 93rd Street to 33rd Street. The man's name was Leroy, and I looked for his name on the mailbox. Then I ran up five flights of stairs and knocked on the door. A man answered. He was in a kimono and wearing lipstick. This was the profession I wanted to get into?'

At last, a tale that scans! Leroy's Touring Vaudeville Act is factual, if the details are still anecdotal. Up on the roof Julius joined thirty other 'gamins' ready and waiting to display their wares, many with dancing taps on their shoes which raised an unruly racket. Julius sang – of course – 'Love Me and the World Is Mine', and got the job, along with a tough East Side dancing kid called Johnny Morris. Carrying a shoebox containing pumpernickel, bananas and hard-boiled eggs, Julius departed upon the long train journey to Grand Rapids, Michigan. Groucho recalled:

'The show opened with four colored performers dressed as Chinamen, which he (Leroy) called the Whangdoodle Four. I wore a sweater that said The Leroy Trio. Later I wore a fake altar boy's outfit as I sang a song called "The palms" . . . "la-la-la Jerusalem . . . lift up your gates and sing . . ."' A religious fanatic, who rose and shouted 'Hallelujah!' at this point, was ejected by the manager. 'Then Leroy would come out dressed in a short skirt and high-heeled shoes and sing, "I wonder what's the matter with the mail, it never was so long before . . . I've been up since seven bells and nothing's slipped under my door." Finally Morris did a tap dance.'

In an earlier description of this act, given to the *Saturday Evening Post* in 1931, Groucho wrote: 'Leroy hadn't told us that our first jump would be to Denver, and that we'd have to sit up for three nights in day coaches. But we didn't much care. It was worth a few discomforts to become an actor. Nor had Leroy told us that we were going to be female impersonators.' Indeed, the fact that Julius's first appearance on stage was in drag was never mentioned again, and was tactfully expunged from all later accounts.

At the opening show – Groucho related in *Groucho and Me* – Morris's shoe came off and hit a member of the audience, which caused the manager to fine them twenty dollars, one third of their total fee. They moved on to Victor and Cripple Creek, Colorado, where Leroy eloped from their boarding house with Johnny Morris, leaving young Julius stranded, with only eight dollars in his 'grouch bag', a purse that actors carried strung about their necks. Seeing an ad for a job delivering groceries in a horse-drawn cart, Julius had his first encounter with the Western mustang, beasts he recalled later as being as big as elephants, with 'the most malevolent expressions this side of Fu Manchu'. This was only a terrifying stopgap until Minnie could wire him money to go back home to New York.

Leroy and Morris drop out of our tale, and perhaps lived happily ever after, though Groucho wrote, in 1931, that Johnny Morris was 'an actor now in Hollywood'. The Whangdoodle Four certainly never made it to Tinseltown, and may well be trapped in Cripple Creek to this day. Julius returned to New York City, shaken but unbowed. Far from being deterred by this farcical first step, he now saw himself as a fully fledged actor. It was at this point, Groucho recounts, that Minnie, convinced of his zeal, if not of his sanity, took over, and began peddling him about the theatrical agencies. A few nights singing at a beer garden ensued, but real stage work was still elusive. Eventually, in one of her forays, Minnie met an English singer who was looking for a juvenile boy to fill in during her costume changes.

Cue Lily Seville, and the first-known mention of a Marx Brother in the printed annals. For, as Paul Wesolowski's incomparable archive reveals, on Christmas Eve, 1905, the *Dallas Morning News* advertised, for the Majestic Theatre: 'Lily Seville and Master Marx, "The Lady and the Tiger," direct from Paris.' And the *Dallas Daily Times Herald*, waxing even more expansive on this earth-shaking début, wrote: 'Lily Seville is a directly imported English act. Miss Seville, being a born and bred Yorkshire lass who will give impersonations of the London "coster." She is assisted by Master Marx, a boy tenor.'

A photograph of la Seville, dated 16 February 1906, shows a rather buxom lass of uncertain years, with a whangdoodle dress and what appears to be a few bay leaves in her upswept hair, described as 'a pale proud English beauty, with 107 times more ginger and go in her than you might think by looking at a picture of her in repose. She is a "coster singer and comedienne," so billed, and made her first appearance at Tony Pastor's Theatre "with instant success." We have to quote the last three words, because we weren't there, but her manager says it's a fact, and he ought to know. Lily is good to gaze upon.'

A fact with which young Julius heartily concurred. Stricken with the lady, if not the tigers – which presumably referred to the accompanying act of Martha Florrine and her trained lions and leopards – he embarked on his second and longer-lasting odyssey across the United States, with his shoebox and pumpernickel sandwiches, to Texas. The rest of the bill of his first proper vaudeville engagement was composed of the Musical Goolmans, Leo & Munroe, clog dancers, and the seventy-four-year-old tenor singer, Samuel B. Holdsworth. The *Dallas Morning News* reported, on Christmas Day:

Miss Seville is a typical Yorkshire lass and speaks that elusive but delightful twang of that shire in England . . . Her 'Costermonger' song, a genuine one which she sings at the close of her performance, is a delightful bit of melody . . . Master Marx is a boy tenor, who introduces bits of Jewish character from the East Side of New York. The act is a novelty and will be appreciated by the Majestic audience.

From Dallas the act moved on to Houston, where the critics, perhaps grumpy and hungover after the New Year's Eve binge, were unkind enough to remark that 'another act below the standard of the Majestic's bookings is that of Lily Seville and Julius Marx. The performers show a disposition to please, but their voices are of poor quality and their vehicle, "The Lady and the Tiger," a poor one.'

The following week, the critic of the *San Antonio Light* was better disposed towards Lily's act, calling it 'very high class as a study of human types . . . She sings several coster ballads, and is assisted in the act by Master Marx, a juvenile soprano singer and impersonator of the Yiddischer.'

Note that, as Julius progresses through Texas, his voice changes, at least in the ear of the beholder, from tenor to soprano, but the substance of his little act remains the same. Not just sentimental songs but the old tried and true *shtik* of Jewish patter, taken, in all probability, from Uncle Al Shean's repertoire. And so, from the beginning, the comedy is very much a part of the act.

Groucho's recollections of this second western adventure are that the act broke up in Waco, when the coster singer handed him his return ticket to New York and ran away with the lion tamer. Since the clippings identify the lion tamer as a Mademoiselle, not a Monsieur, this suggests either a second encounter by young Julie with theatrical gay life, or yet another tall tale. The Wesolowski clippings do place them at Waco, on 27 January, but then at Fort Worth, on 12 February. By 10 March Lily Seville is back east, in Massachusetts, but there is no mention of Master Marx.

These first glimmers of the Marxian career suggest another possible clue to the origins of the Great Marx Brothers Birth Date Scam. Throughout the clippings, the impression is given of the boy singer as much younger than his actual fifteen years, and Julius was said to have looked young for his age. Certain subterfuges might have been born on the spur of the moment, and Minnie Marx might well have shaved a couple of years off Julius's age when she proposed his act to Lily Seville. The dialogue might have run something like this:

LILY: *I want a young boy to go with me on the tour. A real nipper. I don't want some grown-up hulk who might get ideas. Know what I mean, luv?*
MINNIE: *You von't haff any problems. Mein poy, he is only tirteen years old. Only chust bar mitzvah. And vot a tsatskeh!*

This speculation would fit in with later stories, like that of Minnie buying the boys half-price tickets for the train, some years later, and the conductor coming round and finding them puffing on cigars and shaving in the rest room. Indeed, a review of the Brothers' 1907 act, The Nightingales, in the *New York Dramatic Mirror* of 28 September, comments that this turn 'pleased those who like to encourage precocious children'. Not so precocious, since Julius was already sixteen and even Milton, his partner at that point, was fourteen years old. Not to speak of the fact that Adolph, a.k.a. Arthur, a.k.a. Harpo, who joined the juvenile Nightingales on stage for the first time at Henderson's, Coney Island, in June 1908, was in fact, at that point, twenty years old, and not fifteen, as he mischievously claims.

But we have just returned from Texas, and can follow young Julius, now a seasoned actor, to his next job, with a much more bona fide outfit. Step forward, Gus Edwards' School Boys and Girls. Now, for the first time, Julius came in contact with one of vaudeville's most experienced talent scouts. Gus Edwards, born Gustav Hohensalza in Germany in 1879, and an immigrant of 1891 vintage, had been discovered as a boy singer by Tony Pastor, and later formed a partnership with one Will D. Cobb to write a series of song hits. Their early fame was sealed with 'School Days', which became the centrepiece of Edwards's long-running series of kid acts. The original song went like this:

School-days, school-days,
Dear old golden rule days,
Read-in' and 'rit-in' and 'rithmetic,
Taught to the tune of a hick-ry stick . . .

Tiddle-dum, tiddle-dum. It was in fact Will Cobb who wrote Harpo's perennial 'Waltz Me Around Again, Willie', as well as 'I Can't Make My Eyes Behave' for the risqué singer Anna Held. Gus Edwards, in later years, would be the discoverer of such young talents as Eddie Cantor, George Jessel, Harry Ruby and one Walter Winchell, not yet the news column mogul. But in 1906, Edwards was forming one of his many spin-off acts, to be called 'Gus Edwards' Postal Telegraph Boys'. Eight boys in Postal Telegraph uniforms would indulge in 'boyish pranks at one another's expense, ever and anon breaking into song, using Mr Edwards' latest compositions' in a telegraph office setting, with one girl, Grace Emmons, playing an operator. On 28 April 1906 the act opened at the Alhambra in New York, with the boys listed as: Charles De Haven, Jack Sidney, Charles Lewis, Lewis Corn, Harry Bloom, Dave Goodwin, Eddie Raymond and Julius Max (*sic*).

Ten days before, on 18 April, the city of San Francisco was devastated by an earthquake and its consequent fires. Stage people everywhere rallied to benefits for the disaster victims. Gus Edwards sent his Postal Telegraph Boys to sing in fashionable Broadway restaurants to raise donations for the relief funds. At the Café des Beaux Arts, Café Martin and Churchill's Restaurant, young Julius exercised his larynx for the cause. He then had his first taste of the big-time, when the Telegraph Boys were included in the all-day Metropolitan Opera House Benefit on Friday, 3 May, alongside such luminaries as Ethel Barrymore, Yvette Guilbert, Elsie Janis, Joe Weber and Lillian Russell.

'I went on stage with a seventy piece orchestra and sang "Somebody's Sweetheart I Want to Be,"' Groucho recalled, in *The Groucho Phile*. The Messenger Boys appeared just after the overture, and one can imagine Julie's awe at the grand auditorium, with its 3,000 seats, packed to the rafters, applauding his song. This, he must have felt, was the theatre to which he aspired.

For the first time, also, young Julius's picture appeared professionally, as a vignette on the cover of sheet music for Edwards's 'Farewell Killarney'. Edwards chose to use an old snapshot, of Julius aged eleven or twelve, rather than of the sixteen-year-old he was then – more evidence that the boy's official age was being set back.

Julius appeared to have a good run with the Postal Telegraph Boys, but Edwards was constantly turning over the cast. By August 1906 we find Julie elsewhere, in the cast of a regular play, called 'Man of Her Choice', which embarked on a long East Coast tour. On 8 September, the *New York Dramatic Mirror* reported from New Haven, Massachusetts: 'W. F. Nugent . . . did well as Heinrich Heimindlinger . . . Julius Marx made quite a hit in a "kid" part as Jimmy Armstrong, the office boy. Some incidental vocal solos by Elizabeth A. Chester, Mabel Mordant, and Julius Marx were well received.'

The play was a piece of prime ham, by Edward M. Simmonds, involving a love triangle, stolen bonds, a jealous lover who burns down the house, and a self-sacrificing heroine who offers the skin from her arm to the badly burned fallen lady. The presentation of the skin-grafting operation on stage was considered novel and bold at the time. The play ran through the winter of 1906–7, travelling from New Jersey up New England to Canada. 'Should a woman yield even her honor to "the Man of Her Choice"?' burbled the ads. Groucho remembered his opening line, according to Hector Arce, as 'Stop! Move one step and I'll blow you to smithereens!' But this doesn't quite sound like Jimmy-the-office-boy dialogue. There is reference, in one of the reviews, to 'four comedians', who rescue the hero from a watery death, but it is not clear who these comedians are. There is certainly only one Marx Brother upon the stage at this point . . .

Meanwhile, back in New York City, not all was well with the Marx clan. Milton was still at school, and young Herbert was five, but the eldest sons were still unsettled. Leo was hustling from job to job, and details of his progress are sketchy. He continued to play the nickelodeons and odd jobs at resorts, hotels and beer gardens. Groucho mentions Leo taking a job as a lifeguard who couldn't swim much more than one hundred yards. Maxine Marx reports a one-time job as a wrestler with a small, unnamed, touring circus troupe. Maxine wrote, in *Growing Up With Chico*:

'After betting his earnings on himself and losing, he switched to prize-fighting and boxed as a flyweight. Having won a series of bouts, he began to get cocky, and started thinking along the lines of a world championship. This idea was knocked into oblivion when he was K.O.'d by a lightly regarded opponent.'

Leo's talent as a gambler and card player was never enough to ensure that he won. All the Brothers, and Maxine, attest to the fact that young Leo had a phenomenal grasp of numbers. He amazed his teachers at school with his aptitude for maths. He was later regarded as one of the top pinochle players in the country. He could figure the odds, but he couldn't beat them. He was restless, and indecisive. Groucho mentions another job Leo took as a wrapper of blotting papers in a wholesale paper factory. Continually losing his salary by the throw of the dice, he brought home four thousand blotters to the family. He recommended them to his weeping mother as 'better than handkerchiefs, and it will cut the laundry bills in half.'

Adolph was still fetching and carrying, and occasionally substituting for Leo on the piano. But his realization that art could pay more than peanuts was due, he later claimed, to a delivery job to a Brooklyn house where an Irish wake was in progress. Spotting the piano and assaying his usual repertoire of 'Waltz Me Around Again, Willie', he was showered with coinage by the tearfully inebriated mourners. Considering that music might be his *métier* after all, he answered an ad for 'Piano Player Wanted'. This led him to a saloon in the Bowery, and to the redoubtable Mrs Schang.

Verification of the existence of Mrs Schang is due to Harpo's 1920s mentor, Alexander Woollcott. As a gift to his favourite comedian, Woollcott dug out from the morgue of the *New York Times* an actual cutting of the aftermath to this seminal Harpo tale:

August 2, 1907:

INDICTED AS BURGLAR GANG.

27 Charges Against Woman and Three Men Who Robbed Long Island Homes.

MINEOLA L. I., Aug. I. – Fourteen indictments charging burglary and grand larceny were found by the Nassau County Grand Jury to-day against August Van Fehrig, alias Luckner, leader of the gang of burglars that robbed more than twenty houses . . . cleaning up at least $50,000. Eleven indictments charging the same crimes were found against Christopher Schang, 19 years old, a member of the gang, and two indictments for receiving stolen goods were returned against his ageing mother, Mrs Alma Schang. Morris Belkowitz, another member of the gang, was indicted on three counts for burglary.

When the prisoners were brought into court before County Judge Jackson for pleading, Mrs Schang, who had to be supported by Sheriff Foster, suddenly screamed and fell fainting to the floor. She was carried back to the jail unconscious.

As well she might. Mrs Schang, about six foot two and all bone and muscle, ran a brothel called 'The Happy Times Tavern' in Freeport, Long Island. As Harpo told the tale, in *Harpo Speaks*, he first encountered the formidable Madame when he answered an ad for a piano player, at a Bowery saloon. Mrs Schang, waiting for her prospective employee in the back room, took one look at him, cried out, 'Get out of here, you little Jew son-of-a-bitch!' but then changed her mind and hired him. Adolph was to play the piano in Mrs Schang's Long Island establishment, while the girls chatted up their clients. When the fights started on Saturday nights, he was to play louder. Eight bucks a month, and expenses. And, one might figure, special extras. All this seemed a secure niche to Adolph, who was under no pressure to extend his repertoire. But he became anxious when Mrs Schang, her son

Christopher and their surly sidekick, Max, began disappearing regularly, of nights, to some unknown business outside. One day Max disappeared completely and the Schangs took to heavy drinking. A week later Madame roused the piano player and told him to drive her and her son in their horse-drawn buggy. 'Keep driving east until we get to the Pot O' Gold,' she said, 'I'm going to kill Louis Neidorf.'

Excited by the prospect of real-life mayhem, Adolph waited with the two brothel-keepers at another seedy dump for several hours, but Louis Neidorf fooled them. He no show up. On their way back the horse got sick and then died. Perhaps affected by the animal's tragedy, Adolph got the measles, in the midst of his next night's piano playing, and the girls took him out and shoved him on the train home.

So much for Adolph-Harpo's story. Later, he said, he saw the news cutting and realized what the Schangs had been up to on their nights off, and, still later, realized why Mrs Schang had first greeted him with such hostility. It seemed his brother Leonard had already played at The Happy Times Tavern, and been fired. Due to the brothers' resemblance, Mrs Schang had thought at first that Leonard had returned.

Harpo wrote: 'I now regarded myself, after the events of the summer, as more of a man than a boy.' This is fine, if one accepts Adolph's age, in 1907, as fourteen, in keeping with his chronology. A fourteen-year-old playing the piano in a brothel is funny. But since we now know Adolph was nineteen at the time, the whole story takes on a more seedy veneer.

Although Frenchy's chicken soup soon cured Adolph of the measles, Minnie still had no solution for her second eldest son. Leonard, at least, seemed to have found a steady job, with a song publishing firm, Shapiro, Bernstein & Co., of Philadelphia. Sticking to his last, for a change, he was soon managing the company's Pittsburgh office. Adolph seemed destined to take over as the family's nickelodeon player. But the fortunes of the two teenage brothers, Julius and Milton, were about to take a decisive turn.

6

The Incubator and the Chicks – from Wayburn's Nightingales to Minnie's Mascots

PROFESSORS: But, Professor, where will the students sleep?
GROUCHO: Where they always sleep – in the classroom!

Horse Feathers (1932)

In the early spring of 1907, two Marx Brothers went to vaudeville school. This without doubt was Minnie's idea. Having seen how Gus Edwards, combined with an earthquake, could get one son into the Metropolitan Opera House, imagine what another mentor might do for two! Leo was on the road, Adolph in the clouds, but Julius and Milton were available.

The chosen Svengali for the next phase of the Marx project was impresario Ned Wayburn. The New York *Sunday Telegraph*, in 1904, enthused about this distinguished citizen thus:

NED WAYBURN IS THE PRINCIPAL INSTRUCTOR OF BUDDING
DRAMATIC TALENT THAT SEEKS FAME AND POSSIBLE PROFIT.

By Lincoln Ramsay.
  Having been appointed a committee of one to seek out and analyze
. . . the theatrical bee, I knocked on the door of the New Amsterdam
Theatre.
  'I seek an interview with Ned Wayburn,' I said to the attendant.
  'Mr Wayburn is very busy. His incubator is in session.'
  'His what?' I exclaimed.
  'His incubator. He is engaged in working ideas into a hundred and
fifty young chicks.'
  'Then I have called at an opportune time.'
  The 'finest theatre in the world' is a somber place when the lights are
out. Through the skylight of the roof of the stage a sickly light finds its
way. The stage is bare and yellow. The curtain is up.
  Behold, the stage is alive! . . . One hundred and fifty trilbies lift in
the air. The dance is on . . .

Born in Woodlawn, Illinois, in 1874, Edward Claudius Rossiter Wayburn was another stage-struck boy, who got his break doing a blackface dance and monologue in the Minstrel shows. He was paid a $15 advance for a song called 'Syncopated Sandy', which eventually made a fortune for the man who bought it from him. Opening in New York at, where else, Tony Pastor's, he linked up with musical comedy star May Irwin, and decided at an early stage that producing was a better bet than performing. But as well as producing, he began setting up a string of theatrical teaching institutes. The first and most famous was Ned Wayburn's Institute of Dancing, at which pupils were directed to adhere to a stern set of rules and regulations. To wit: 'All pupils (except boys and men) must wear the Ned Wayburn Standard Studio Rompers in all classes and private lessons', and 'all pupils who are studying for a stage career are required to procure Ned Wayburn's Own Book, THE ART OF STAGE DANCING, A Manual of Stage-Craft.' Another newspaper special recounted the scene at Wayburn's 'squab farm' as the man himself led the instruction:

> He uses a whistle now to stop and start the dancing. He had a bell one time. One ring, stop; two rings, go ahead; but the girls going home from rehearsals and the theatre used to cause confusion on the street-cars, when tired and distraught, by bursting into song and dance, and as suddenly stopping, when the conductor signalled to the motorman . . .

In early 1907, Wayburn issued his prospectus for a new venture, Ned Wayburn's College of Vaudeville. Minnie had probably already met the impresario, who had co-produced Gus Edwards's School act. She must have hot-footed it over to his offices because, by April, Milton and Julius were firmly in the clutches of the proto-Pavlovian guru. The *New Jersey Sun*, 14 April:

> Yesterday was commencement day at Ned Wayburn's Vaudeville College, 143 West 44th Street . . . [the] catalogue reads: 'Ned Wayburn, producing stage director, past master of stagecraft, and greatest living exponent of the Delsarte system of expression, the true science of acting, who personally supervises every department of instruction in the institution which bears his name, is accredited with more successful dramatic, musical, vaudeville and spectacular productions than any other theatrical producer of modern times . . . Of unimpeachable integrity, and operating at all times with the highest

standard of morality, his original methods, wonderful inventive faculty, marvellous mastery of detail . . . vast stores of nerve force and physical energy, all generated by an exceptional executive ability and directed by a master mind, have established him a veritable genius standing alone at the head of his calling . . .

The evening show, said the report, 'showed what the college has done and was an earnest of what it will do. Leslie Power, the soon to be well-known singing comedian, led off, followed by Marie Gerard, the international chanteuse . . . the Astaire children, Miss Burnley, Jeanette Mozar, Kathryn Schuyler, Bertha May Mann, Laura Estelle Ellis, the Marks boys and little Mabel O'Donnell, Rice and Weimers and Frank Farrell. They were all "perfectly fine" and you'll hear from them some day, don't you think?'

Note, piquantly, the Astaire children, Fred and Adele, then eight and ten years old!

Curiously, Groucho chose, in his reminiscences, to forget Ned Wayburn entirely, probably wishing to expunge the whistling martinet from his life. With his crookhandled cane, which he used to hammer ominously upon the stage, Wayburn was the terror of many of his 'chicks' and 'squabs'. But at least Julius and Milton were not obliged to wear Ned Wayburn's Standard Studio Rompers. Groucho's version is that Minnie, emboldened by his own burgeoning stage stardom, decided to recruit Milton-Gummo to the stage. Milton, the shy, retiring one, the stutterer, the pale ghost to repel the landlords – how was this going to be achieved? 'Sailors and sex!' was Minnie's answer. (Not that such a three-letter word would ever pass her lips.) She had found a couple of sailor-boy costumes going cheap at Bloomingdale's, and planned to recruit a girl singer for whom she would arrange a suitable dress.

The girl singer, Mabel O'Donnell, was, as we can see above, already cast in the act, by Ned Wayburn, who was going to take it on the stage as 'Wayburn's Nightingales'. It does not seem that Minnie had much to do with the act, at this point. It opened in Atlantic City, in June, wedged in among a full vaudeville programme of such standards as The Aerial Rogers, Blanche Bishop, The Three Gilden Sisters, Mantel's Marionettes, and Clark's Dogs and Ponies.

Quite what Wayburn's Nightingales did on stage is obscure, though the *New York Clipper* called it 'a spectacular singing novelty' when it played at Tony Pastor's, in September. The *New York Dramatic Mirror* wrote: 'Two clean-cut, good looking boys and a little mite of a girl with a voice that seems about ten times too large for her make up a most pleasing singing trio . . . The act was a solid hit at Pastor's, and will please anywhere through the youthfulness and the good singing of the trio.'

Paul Wesolowski told me that when he had shown this review to Groucho, in the mid-1970s, Groucho was delighted even in his eighties at this evidence of his melodic prowess, after dining out for a lifetime on his own disparagement of the Nightingales as an act that only survived on sheer *chutzpah* and Minnie's determination. Apart from the singing, another review, from *Variety*, suggests that Julius was still doing a patter, noting: 'The larger of the youths does not announce the "Dutch" imitations as formerly, though he sings one song with a distinct German dialect. The three children have splendid voices that blend beautifully . . . The white costumes worn at the opening should be sent to the cleaner.'

But all was not well, despite this success, at Ned Wayburn's College of Vaudeville. The stage guru had overextended his empire, and was getting deeper into debt. In January 1908 he declared bankruptcy, owing $28,252, with assets of $135. A hundred and sixteen creditors, realtors and advertising companies closed in, and closed down all his enterprises. He was to bounce back, and become, ten and twenty years later, one of the foremost producers on the New York stage, with several *Ziegfeld Follies* and numerous revues, plays and musicals to his name. But Wayburn's Nightingales were no more.

Family lore tells a different story of this demise. An ad in *Variety*, on 30 November 1907, had already announced: THE THREE NIGHTINGALES, BIG HIT EVERYWHERE – MINNIE MARX, MANAGER.

A rift had developed, so the story goes, between the guru and Minnie; the battle of the titans, for control of the act. Given the fact of Wayburn's financial problems, this seems a little unlikely. Wayburn, until that point, was doing good for his charges. They were set to play top New York halls and then tour. Wayburn had two other concurrent attractions: 'Phantastic Phantoms', an act with skeleton costumes played against a black background, and something called 'The Side Show', featuring girls with elastic inflatable rubber costumes. 'It is a foolish thing, but it is a scream,' said Wayburn. So it is possible he may not have been paying his Nightingales as much attention as their mama bird considered their due. At any rate, his plunge into bankruptcy sealed the act's fate. From now on, it was Minnie's own show.

The Mythical Minnie is born at this point – the Matriarchal Manager and Maker of the Marx Brothers. In future accounts, she would be practically deified, as the all-purpose, archetypal Jewish mama. A typical description can be found in a 1933 article, in *Liberty* magazine, by Clara Beranger:

> How those boys love to talk about her! If you say 'your mother' to any of them, you are immediately deluged with paeans of praise and a flood of anecdotes to prove that she was not only the most remarkable woman that ever lived, but the best mother. They give her full credit for making them 'what they are today.' For teaching them to act, to sing, to clown. For helping them write their stuff and booking it with managers. For going with them on the road, selling them to any manager who had a vaudeville house and would give her brood a chance. She stayed by them, settling their disputes, arranging their financial affairs, scolding, browbeating, directing but not restraining their crazy irresponsibility on and off the stage.

Debunking a Jewish Mother could be a heinous crime, and Minnie was without doubt a remarkable woman, totally dedicated to her family. But she was also dedicated to constructing her own myth. As time passed, she became determined to carve out her own identity, not only through her sons, but in her own right, as a theatrical entrepreneur. In this she was only partially successful, as we shall see. But her impact on her sons' career as the Nightingales was, the record shows, quite ambiguous. By pushing Milton, and later Adolph, into the act she laid the basis for the immortals of the future. But her control of their day-to-day management was to have a dire impact. First under the guidance of Gus Edwards, then of Ned Wayburn, Julius and Milton had set foot on the lower rungs of the prestigious New York stage. When Minnie took over, they stepped off the ladder completely, and began their retreat to the boondocks. A couple of turns at the starting post of Tony Pastor's, one awesome glance at the big lights of the Met, and then down, towards Trenton, New Jersey; Henderson's, Coney Island; Glen Haven Park, Rochester NY; the Howard, Boston; Mansfield, Ohio, and off to points west, jostling for space, attention, bookings, and survival with several hundred other standard acts, condemned to crowded and roach-ridden boarding-houses in an endless succession of split-weeks and one-night stands. They did not return to the front rank Manhattan stage until seven years later, when they played the Palace, in 1915.

In short, being Minnie's Boys was a bad career move.

Minnie's first act as Nightingale manager was to get rid of Mabel O'Donnell. Groucho was not entirely kind to Mabel in his reminiscences, remarking, to Richard Anobile, compiler of *The Marx Brothers' Scrapbook*:

'We played some pretty good theatres because basically Mabel O'Donnell was a pretty good singer in spite of the fact that she was cockeyed. Her big problem was she always went off key. That's why we finally had to let her go and ended up getting some boy to take her place.'

Of course, there might have been other reasons for Minnie to prevent the youngsters from haring around the country with this strabismal siren, though she did not stand in the way of future hanky-panky. The boy Minnie engaged to replace Mabel was Lou Levy, about whom the Brothers have said very little. In fact, they have said almost nothing. Groucho told Hector Arce: 'He was from Brooklyn, and had a wonderful voice. Minnie was lucky to get him.' And she had to find a third sailor suit to fit him. In his autobiography, Groucho omits to mention Lou Levy at all. And yet he remained with the act until the summer of 1909. One year and a half of being an honorary Marx Brother, and then oblivion. The most stubborn searches yield nothing more. He came, he sang, he dropped out when the family moved west. We honour his memory, whoever he was, or was to become. There are two Lou Levys mentioned in showbiz dispatches: one a manager at Universal Pictures in Des Moines, who died aged sixty-nine in 1967, and another who discovered and managed the Andrews Sisters, and was involved with Bob Hope. Neither can be positively traced to the Nightingales. Mabel O'Donnell, too, disappears from the record, having had enough, perhaps, of show business. *Requiescite in pace*, troupers.

In June 1908, at Henderson's, Coney Island, the next link in the Marxian chain was forged. Let Harpo tell the tale:

'While I was working at the nickelodeon . . . one afternoon, in the middle of the movie, my mother marched down the aisle of the theatre to the piano. She ordered me to leave at once and come with her. Minnie's face was set with desperation and determination. She was in some kind of a jam, and from the look of her, it could be serious trouble. Minnie had never come to me for help in a crisis before . . .'

Groucho, of course, tells the tale differently:

'"I have a great idea," she said. "Instead of calling the act the Three Nightingales, we'll call it the Four Nightingales! Its a great name! I'll go over to Bloomingdale's this afternoon and get two more white outfits. And you, Harpo," she added, "while I'm gone, you practice singing, bass."

'"Mom," he pleaded, "you know I can't sing."

'"Keep your mouth open and no one will know the difference!" she replied.'

And so the Fourth Nightingale was born. Minnie's crisis was said to be that she had concluded a deal with the United Booking Office for the act at Henderson's, but discovered that the manager required a quartet. Thus the silent-movie pianist was dragooned. Harpo himself recounts that, when he first set foot on the stage, he was so terrified that he disgraced himself by wetting his pants. Since, in Harpo's chronology, he was just fourteen at the time, that can pass. However, as we now know that he was in fact twenty years old, and had pluckily survived his *contretemps* with Mrs Schang the year before, holding his bowels throughout the long night of Louis Neidorf, we are once again in the embarrassing and pedantic position of doubting our hero's sacred word.

But, hey, this is show business! 'A sea of hostile mocking faces across the footlights,' relates Harpo. 'And there I was, with nothing to hold onto . . .' The performer's eternal stage fright. But Adolph sang. 'A voiceless swan song', he called it, to his days of street hustling and wandering from job to job; to the days of Mrs Schang and Marie Wagner and Miss Flatto and the Irish gangs who beat him up, and the nickelodeons at which he'd perfected the art of playing endless permutations of 'Waltz me Around Again, Willie', and 'Love Me and the World Is Mine'. So Harpo sang, and spoke, and learned the patter, as he joined his two brothers, from town to town: Philadelphia; Lancaster; Lima, Ohio; Atlanta; Mobile; Little Rock; Fort Worth; Dallas; Houston; Galveston. Pushing further west and south than even Julius had ventured in his first outing with the Leroy Trio, the Brothers were discovering the rough and tough music halls of what was not quite yet the fully tamed west.

Let alone the east. August 14, White City, Dayton, Ohio: 'Minnie Marx and her Four Nightingales.' Was this Minnie's own début on the stage? What on earth possessed her, the ventriloquist's daughter, who had found the perfect substitutes to throw her voice, to face the uncertain mercies of the audience in person? But face them she did. Six months later, the act would have a new name: The Six Mascots, with Minnie joined on the stage by Aunt Hannah – Pauline's mother – the women aged forty-two and forty-four respectively. Groucho made his mother fifty and her sister fifty-five, in telling the tale of these alarming additions to the ageing juveniles on the stage. But this was yet another phase of the Schoenberg-Marx saga, for, following the famous maxim of Horace Greeley, the family had uprooted itself, lock, stock and barrel – or four barrels, if one leaps forward to the famous movie scene of *Monkey Business* – from the immigrant capital of New York City, and gone west, to the windy city of Chicago.

The Nightingales: Julius (Groucho), Adolph (Harpo), Milton (Gummo) and Lou Levy.

ACT II

The Road from Nagacdoches

'Ah Poosh, Ah Poosh, Ah Poosh!'

CHICO: Hey, Rusty, I no like-a the west. I like-a the west better if it was in the east . . .

Go West (1940)

I can remember playing a movie and vaudeville house in the business section of Jacksonville, Florida. It was a long, dark, narrow hall, filled with folding yellow chairs, the kind that are used by undertakers to make the mourners more uncomfortable . . . It wasn't really a theatre, but a gent's furnishing store that had been converted into a theatre simply by removing the counters, shelves and some of the rubbish, and by installing an electric piano.

There was no stage. There was, however, a long, narrow platform about as wide as the scaffolding used by painters and stone masons, and it was on this precarious ledge that most of the performance was given . . . The dressing room was large and roomy and had perfect ventilation. It was, in fact, a trifle too roomy, as it comprised the whole backyard and was shared alike by a grocer, a butcher and a blacksmith. It was not much for privacy but great for congeniality and comradeship. One had for companions a crate of chickens, three pigs that were about to be slaughtered, some horses waiting to be shod, two girls who later became known as the Dolly Sisters and a covey of the largest rats that ever gnawed at an actor's shoes . . .

The first performance began at noon and then every hour on the hour until midnight, or longer if the business warranted it. The manager was a Greek who had been in the theatrical business only a few months – just long enough to master such a childish profession – and he had therefore set himself up as critic, censor, master of ceremonies, stage manager, ticket chopper and, frequently, bouncer . . .

The opening performance (as the Nightingales) had us Marxes singing lustily to what we imagined was a spellbound and enraptured throng. We had just arrived at the point in the chorus where we hit the big harmony chord, the chord which was supposed to put the song over with a bang, when we heard a terrific noise which might have come from a wild bull, but which turned out to be the manager running down the aisle, waving arms, head and hands, and shouting: 'Stop it! Stop it, I say! It's rotten. Hey, you fellers, you call that singing? That's terrible. The worst I ever heard. My dog can do better than that. Now you go back and do it right or you don't get a nickel of my money, not a nickel . . .'

While we cowered in the corner, the Florida Belasco announced to an audience which was entirely too sympathetic to suit us that these hams – pointing to us – could sing rotten in Tampa, could sing rotten in Miami and, if they so desired, could sing rotten in St. Petersburg, but when they sang in Jacksonville, the biggest and best town in the state, they would have to sing on key or they wouldn't get any money. Ordering us back to the stage, he jumped off the ledge and ran up the aisle to hearty applause and vocal encouragement from the local music lovers. Apparently there was no more than the usual amount of discords on our second attempt, as there were no interruptions, except the customary jeers and catcalls which always accompanied our musical efforts.

Julius Marx: 'Up From Pantages',
first published *New York Times*, 10 June 1928

Giant blood-hungry mosquitoes of the bayous, wormy boarding-houses, fiery breakfast chilli, apathetic or downright hostile audiences, all featured prominently, according to the lore, in the Marx Brothers' (and Lou Levy's) sweep through Florida, Mississippi, Louisiana and Texas in the portentous summer of 1909. The mosquitoes were even bettered by the ants which, Groucho recalled in 1939, 'crawled right up the legs of the beds, despite the tin of poison in which the bed legs rested. We'd get up two or three times a night to brush all the ants off . . .'

As for the performances, Groucho recalled:

We usually went on during the lull periods in those continuous vaude-ville bills. Most times, the ushers took the opportunity to fill up those nickel chocolate bar machines they used to have on the backs of seats. I'll never forget the time we sang accompaniment for a prize fight film. I doubt if anyone heard us above the shouts from the audience.

One night in Nagacdoches, Texas . . . the entire audience ran out of the theatre to see a mule running away, right in the midst of our perfor-mance. They came back and we waited until they returned.

Ah! Nagacdoches, Texas! The birth of the Brothers' distinctive brand of anarchy was supposed to have derived from that one inspired moment in this obscure Texan town, named after an even more obscure Indian tribe. Other accounts of the event place it in Marshall, Texas. Harpo's book locates it in Ada, Oklahoma, at a later date, during the Brothers' 'School Act'. At any rate, the familiar story goes like this: as the audience trickled back into the dingy hall where the Nightingales had been so rudely upstaged and abandoned, the Brothers were so miffed that they let fly with a barrage of unrehearsed mayhem, commencing with Julius's immortal jibe at the town's less hygienic attributes: 'Nagacdoches is full of roaches.'

When the legend becomes truth, print the legend. Scholars have since descended on the remote Texan pueblo, searching for tangible clues. The intrepid archivist and Number One Fan, Paul Wesolowski, cutting a swath through the west and south in his zealous quest for Marxian hoofprints during the 1970s, found no evidence in the Nagacdoches newspaper morgue that the Marx Brothers had ever played there. Another fan, Michael P. Cahill, visiting the town in 1985, also found no direct traces, except for the mysterious presence of a Fredonia Hotel – an occult signal of the future *Duck Soup*. The only evidence of their showbiz fame the townspeople of Nagacdoches could produce were Marx Brothers books relating the old legend in their public library. But Cahill unearthed elsewhere some old 1930s cuttings which named the witnesses to this momentous occasion. A conglomeration, one imagines, of grizzled baccy-chewing Walter Brennans, these were allegedly the audience of Julius Marx's very first ad-lib: Head Usher Ernest W. Spradley, citizens Giles M. Halton, Willie Bowdon, Guy Blount and L. I. Muller (plus, I suspect, Hugo Z. Hackenbush).

In fact, the Nightingales were featuring their own brand of comedy at least from their opening night as a foursome, as *Variety*'s review of the act in June 1908 at Henderson's, Coney Island, reveals:

A quartet of youngsters who, for individual merit as singers, attain a high degree of excellence. They are nice looking, fresh boys and there is a certain agreeable youthfulness about their singing that places it apart from the conventional music of male quartets . . . The harmony is true and appealing . . . The boys, however, are wasting a good deal of valuable time in the exploitation of ineffectual comedy and dialogue. The talk is far from funny and makes the turn seem to lag. The greater part of it could be dropped altogether, and the precious moments thus saved devoted to more singing. As a straight singing number 'The

Nightingales' can be made into a sure winner with very slight eliminations.

And so are the pundits confounded. In 1985 the travelling fan Michael Cahill recounted his disappointment that he had 'spent a day in legendary Nagacdoches and didn't see a single roach'. But the three Marx Brothers were less fortunate in that area, as they continued their trek through the hinterland . . .

Concerned by her distance from her far-flung offspring, Minnie redoubled her efforts to move the Marxian base of operations away from the East Coast, and closer to a central hub, from which these thespian ventures could be more properly organized. And so, in the autumn of 1909, Minnie, Sam, and the five boys, together with Julius and Hannah Schickler, arrived in Chicago to start a new chapter in their lives. 'Opie' Louis Schoenberg stayed behind for a year or so longer in New York, dossing down with Al Shean and his wife Joanna, before he too made tracks west, relocating, reluctantly, at the age of eighty-eight.

Chicago was the major vaudeville centre outside New York. Three major circuits – the Orpheum, Sullivan & Considine and Pantages – and the smaller Gus Sun circuit, all operated out of the city. Chicago was big, boisterous and booming, and was yet to experience the consequences of Prohibition that were to mark it as a capital of gangsters and crime. Major forces in the newly born film industry, such as the Essanay Studios, were based in Chicago. It had a thriving theatrical and literary life, with major bookstores which would soon be discovered and frequented by Julius, the family bookworm.

The Marxes' first port of call was an apartment at 4649 Calumet Avenue, where the city directories find them ensconced in 1910 and 1911. Both Julius and Arthur are listed mysteriously as 'foremen', while Leo and Samuel are both 'commercial travellers'. (They just could not resist kidding officials!) Late in 1912 the family moved to a three-storey brownstone house at 4512 Grand Boulevard. This was the first self-contained home that the boys, and their parents, had ever known. The house had a large kitchen for Frenchy and a pool table in the basement, necessary now that Leo was back home. Minnie's ideal was to have enough room for all the other members of the Schoenberg tribe who were expected to follow the ox carts west. With a loan from Uncle Al, Minnie and Sam made a thousand-dollar down payment and committed themselves to a $20,000 mortgage, introducing a new

The Four Nightingales on stage: Milton, Lou Levy, Julius and Adolph.

bogeyman to the Marx legend: the dreaded mortgage holder, Greenbaum. On the road, whenever the Brothers were slack, or below par, or simply disillusioned, Minnie would whisper in their ear the magic word, synonymous with the danger of debt, degradation and eviction: 'Greenbaum!'

But Minnie lost no time, at Calumet Avenue, in schmoozing the city's booking agents. She had a new master plan. Very soon after her arrival in Chicago Minnie Marx underwent a miraculous identity transplant, and a wholly new theatrical entrepreneur was born, the euphoniously named Minnie Palmer.

The only problem about this new gentile monicker was that it was already occupied. The original Minnie Palmer was a well-known singer and actress who had first appeared on the 'legit' stage in 1874. Born in Philadelphia in 1860 (or 1857, take your pick), she had appeared in countless musical and dramatic plays and sketches such as *The Day After the Wedding*, *The Little Rebel*, *The Cricket on the Hearth*, and *My Sweetheart* in 1883. She became one of the best known soubrettes in the country, and married her manager, John Rogers, who took her on long world tours. Then she divorced Rogers, married a rich Englishman, Francis Jerrard, and left the American stage to become a country wife in a sumptuous mansion in deepest England. She returned briefly to the USA in 1906 but then decamped again, and thus was not present to protest at the appropriation of her name by a German-Jewish mama in Chicago.

Whether Minnie Marx adopted Minnie Palmer's name in ignorance or guile is a matter on which the Grand Jury has never been convened. But it is clear she was not averse to critics and audiences jumping to their own conclusions. In October 1916 the reporter of the *Columbus Evening Dispatch* wrote, in an article about the Marx Brothers: 'To the younger generation (the theatre going crowd of the last ten years) the name of Minnie Palmer may not mean so much, but going back a bit further, there are thousands of vaudeville fans all over the country . . . who remember the winsome Miss Palmer, who in later years has conducted a booking office in Chicago.' According to the reporter, the Marx Brothers 'have been accosted, at the stage door, by a number of older people who remember their talented mother . . .'

To this day, the existence of two Minnie Palmers confuses archivists, who continue to include both in the same files. But the famous name certainly did Minnie no harm, despite her ignominious début in Chicago in February 1910, with 'Minnie Palmer's Six Mascots'.

This was not an act that set the world on fire, although *Variety* noted, in its Chicago news, that: 'The German comedian [i.e. Julius] is exceptionally clever and keeps things stirring.' At one performance, Groucho reports, there was only one chair to accommodate the two matrons, Minnie and Aunt Hannah, who were trying to add their impersonation of young schoolgirls to the Nightingales' male trills, only to collide and hit the floor in a heap. At another performance, at an all-black theatre, the Pekin, on 21 March, Julius barely survived the evening, having prepared a song about the impending world heavyweight championship fight between Jim

Jeffries and Jack Johnson, predicting the victory of Jeffries, only to find that Johnson was in the audience.

A photograph of the Six Mascots shows the ersatz juveniles attired in white, with Julius in a butcher's boy apron pointing at the picture of what seems to be a cat on an easel. Arthur is at the right edge of this photograph, which also features a boy named Freddie Hutchins, a short-lived replacement for Lou Levy. The butcher boy or grocer boy get-up, alias Hans Pumpernickel, stood Julius in good stead throughout the run of these shows, and was probably the origin of the comic song: *'Ist das nichts ein Schnitselbank? Ja, das ist a Schnitselbank!'* which Groucho was performing at the piano for his guests well into his eightieth year. The sillier the patter, the more it seems to stick in the mind – and we haven't even got to 'Peasie-Weasie' yet!

Aunt Hannah, who at some point had become converted to Christian Science, soon decided that show business was not really her *métier*. But her son, Pauline's brother (or half-brother?), was about to go on the boards as Lou Shean, performing not with the Nightingales – but with the elder Marx brother, Leo.

Leo's activities and whereabouts, between 1908 and 1910, are not precisely known. He continued working for a time in Pittsburgh with the song-publishing firm of Shapiro, Bernstein and Company. Office life, how-

'Ist das nichts ein Schnitselbank?' The Six Mascots: (left to right) Aunt Hannah, stand-in Freddie Hutchins, Julius, Milton, Mama Minnie, Adolph at the piano.

71

ever, could not appeal to him for long. Together with an assistant, Arthur Gordon, he began planning his own career in vaudeville.

Arthur Gordon was still a teenager, with a good singing voice. Leo, having passed twenty without stopping, was never a prospective Nightingale. Schooled in the saloons and pool halls that fed his gambling habit, he began, some time in this period, to adopt the Italian accent that, legend has it, he borrowed from his barber. If you had one Italian, you needed two Italians, and so Gordon became Gordoni. Gordoni and Marx hit the road with a piano and singing act leavened with bursts of ethnic ribaldry, recalled by Maxine Marx as something like this:

'Where do you work-a, John?'
'On the Delaware-Lackawan.'
'And what do you do-a, John?'
'Ah poosh, ah poosh, ah poosh.'

As Maxine wrote, 'inevitably . . . push came to shove.' Even the immortal Chico couldn't make a living out of this kind of material. Arthur Gordon later told Maxine that Leo collected their meagre salary, paid for his food, rooming costs and laundry and fifty cents a week for a haircut, but the rest of the money was invariably swallowed up by the dice and the cards. They resorted to various scams, with Gordon acting as the disinterested stooge to trick people into betting on anything appropriate, such as the afternoon's ball game. Leo would then collect the bets, they would rush back to the boarding-house, pay the outstanding bills, or not, collect their luggage and hightail it for the next town. This could not keep the duo going for long. Chico told his daughter Maxine that Gordon had been with him for two years, which would qualify the young singer for a top place in the pantheon of Marxian saints. Gordon did remain a lifelong friend – more proof, if proof were needed, of Leo's ability to charm and seduce everyone he came in contact with – whether worn-out partners or, later, betrayed girlfriends and wives. But Arthur Gordon could afford to look back in languor, after he achieved a certain fame in vaudeville by becoming the fourth husband and, briefly, stage partner, of one of variety's brightest stars, the comedienne Nora Bayes.

According to Maxine, Leo made a brief attempt at a solo act, but this did not prosper either, and we have no record of it. In the summer of 1911, he re-enters our field of vision, teamed up with Lou Shean, in a new venture, described as a 'rathskeller act' by *Variety*, on 7 October:

Shean and Marx are quite new and . . . good. The only mystery surrounding the offering is Shean's makeup. The comedian essays the

German character closely resembling the one made popular by his brother (*sic*) Al Shean. But aside from the opening number, 'Chile Chile Bean' taken from 'The Big Banner Show,' this Shean does not dabble in German at all. After Marx has offered 'Glow Worm' with variations and encoring with 'Oceana Roll,' Shean returned to deliver a medley of parodies. This as easily the best number. Finally Shean rendered one or two Italian songs (still in the Dutch makeup, but with Italian dialect) . . . Marx is an exceptionally good piano player with a certain personality that stands out, while Shean can warble with the best . . . (Wynn)

At this point, Shean and Marx were operating out of Chicago, as Leo had returned to the fold, although he was still functioning on his own, not as part of the Minnie Palmer Grand Plan. For, by this time, the Six Mascots had been safely mothballed and, like a phoenix from its own ashes, a totally new act had been devised.

This was, at last, the vehicle which would shape the Three, then the Four Marx Brothers into the mutating form in which they were later to advance and conquer vaudeville, Broadway, Hollywood and the universe: the one and only – well, one among several dozen – 'School Act', otherwise known as – 'Fun In Hi Skule!'

8

Sex, Life and Vaudeville

GROUCHO: Why were you smoking opium in a Chinese joint?
BEAUTY: Because I wanted to get a new sensation.
GROUCHO: Did you ever eat a bowl of rhubarb in a ferris wheel?

I'll Say She Is (1923)

The roll call in 1911:

Leo, on the 'rathskeller' trail, is twenty-four years old; Adolph, now calling himself Arthur, is twenty-three; Julius is twenty-one (and now officially a man!); Milton is nineteen; little Herbert is still only ten years old. They are still a good four years away from the happenstance that would provide them with the nicknames we now know so well: Chico, Harpo, Groucho, Gummo, Zeppo. But the playful demons were already astir.

Leo has left us no record of his sexual awakenings. Arthur/Adolph has been pretending he was fourteen years old at Mrs Schang's bawdy house. Milton is the whirlwind dancer, so we assume he had someone to dance with. Julius, lovelorn after being dumped by Lily Seville without so much as a goodbye, or even a hello kiss, has left us a record of one of his first encounters with the Other Sex, at about the turn of the century.

Writing in *Memoirs of a Mangy Lover*, Groucho recalls a visit by his most beautiful aunt to the Marx ménage: 'She had red hair, high heels, and a nice, tight shape that bulged where all desirable shapes were supposed to bulge.' This was, no doubt, his Aunt Joanna, Jo Davidson, Uncle Al's vivacious wife. Says Julius:

When she sailed into our flat, the whole area began to take on a tanta-lizing, exotic fragrance that later in life I recognized as the standard odor of a bordello. Of course I had no idea what I was inhaling. For all I knew it was embalming fluid . . . In our moth-eaten flat I was accustomed to the combined odors of four generally unwashed brothers, bean soup, and a kerosene stove that smoked. Now, here I was, breathing the heady perfume of the ages: a fragrance that made strong men tremble with desire and weak men whimper in despair.

When Aunt Joanna told little Julie's mother: 'You know, Minnie, Julius has the loveliest big brown eyes I've seen', the smitten mite spent hours walking in front of her, bulging his eyes and panting for more compliments. None was forthcoming, and later investigation in the bathroom mirror confirmed that his eyes were in fact grey.

A few years later, aged twelve, his eyes were still grey, and his relationships with the other sex just as misinformed. Relating his first outing with a girl next door, named 'Lucy' in *Groucho and Me*, he relates how he invited her to Hammerstein's Victoria music hall, having carefully stockpiled the necessary fifty cents for two tickets and two streetcar rides. 'Lucy', however, invested in unbudgeted-for candy, leaving them with just one nickel between them for the fare home. It was a dark and stormy night, and young Julie, incensed at his companion's selfish financial mismanagement, suggested they toss the coin to see who would ride home. Having won the toss, he left her to walk. This provided Julius with his first romantic débâcle, if not the last. Julius was definitely not the Lothario with women that Leo, and even Arthur, were effortlessly. In the male Marxian pecking order, he came out a poor third.

Just as Uncle Al learned, and was determined never to forget, the first rule of gender in vaudeville – the men are predators, the women merely prey – so the Marx Brothers grew up with the credo of the *droit de seigneur*. An early portrait of Julius, on the make at seventeen, in *Groucho and Me*, is captioned: 'A hot sport in New Orleans. Notice the 10 cent cheroot. Cigar and me both burning furiously, on the prowl for the not-so-elusive female.'

First sighting of the Groucho cigar. A pretty meagre stogie it is too, at this point, compared to the Cuban 'La Preferencia' cigars he would be smoking later, but a start. As the Brothers honed their act, their personal philosophy of chasing *les femmes*, even over overturned sofas and in and out of state rooms, was woven into their routines. Like many other quirks, these personality differences between the brothers became the warp and weft of the characters that were to emerge from the vaudeville mill.

Milton, of course, remains the elusive one, the one who never made it to the screen. His son Robert told me that 'Gummo . . . did not like the stage. He was very nervous on stage, and stammered, to the point that he made himself a student of the dictionary as a result of that.' In order to force himself to speak his lines without failing, Milton built up a mental list of

75

synonyms: 'He had every innuendo of every word that he could possibly do, because he needed other words to get out, to get the line out, so the show would go on, in normal timing.'

In a cartoon drawn for *The Show World*, illustrating the July 1911 programme for the Lyda Theatre in Chicago, 'The Three Marx Brothers' are portrayed in their characters in the 'Hi Skule' act. Milton Marx is the derby-hatted Jewish dandy, with a speech balloon saying: 'Some-one stuck me in the back of the stomach!' Arthur Marx, as the Irish boob – a generic character known as a Patsy Brannigan, after a real-life Irish comic of that name active in the 1890s – is seated at a school desk with short breeches and a yokel's hat, saying nuttin'. Beside him, Julius Marx, as the old Dutch schoolteacher, is saying: 'Take that thing off your head! Don't think because I am a fool I am a Dutchman!' A broomstick and apple lie before him. A slight blond youth named Paul Yale plays what Groucho called 'the nance'. Groucho wrote, in *The Groucho Phile*, about these characters:

The frock coat was borrowed from Uncle Julius (Schickler), and the German accent . . . was borrowed from Opie. Gummo . . . played a young Hebrew boy . . . We Marx Brothers never denied our Jewishness. We simply didn't use it. We could have safely fallen back on the Yiddish theatre, making secure careers for ourselves. But our act was designed from the start to have a broad appeal. If, because of Chico, a segment of the audience thought we were Italian, then let them . . .

But Leo was not yet with the show, and didn't join the act until mid-1912. Minnie recruited some more talent, including female support, for the dancing and musical numbers. A surviving photograph shows one Lucille Textrude, an unidentified partner, and Aunt Hannah, still apparently a trouper, if a Christian one. Minnie remained wisely behind the scenes.

The School Act was based around the many imitations of the original Gus Edwards show. These sketches, whose popularity is a bit mystifying to us today, when adults playing at juveniles are mostly confined to government circles, were a standard act, with standard characters given names like Ikey Mulligan, Katzenjammer and Tony Spaghetti, who would come through with such lines as 'Shut up-a Jimmy, I break-a you face!' The humour was relentlessly ethnic. One of the Marx Brothers' later collaborators, Herman Timberg, began his career with Gus Edwards's 'School Boys and Girls' as Izzy Levy, a Russian immigrant boy who tries to help an outcast girl in the city. The Marxian twist was to present 'a burlesque side of a small country school that aspires to the dignity of "High School."'

The original script of the Marx Brothers' School Act, like its subsequent spin-offs, 'Mr Green's Reception' and 'Home Again', has not been found, as I have mentioned, and we do not even know who wrote it. Reports that it was the work of Uncle Al Shean are not borne out by the references of the time. It seemed to have been cobbled together from bits of every other School Act. Harpo has left us a descriptive chunk, though his story includes Minnie on stage as the 'Not-So-Bright Little Girl', possibly a mismatched memory of 'The Six Mascots'.

'My Patsy Brannigan costume was a delight,' writes Harpo, 'Minnie got out the wig she'd made up for Jenny, our ex-singer, cut off the piece that used to cover Jenny's cockeye [presumably Jenny is Mabel O'Donnell here] and dyed the wig red for me. She sewed bright patches onto my travelling pants, which were pretty well shot anyway, and I used a piece of rope for a suspender. The rest of the costume was my beloved turtle-neck sweater and a decrepit beaver hat.'

The old 'Dutch' teacher would stand up and whack his slapstick – a pair of wooden barrel staves – calling out: 'Patsy Brannigan . . . give the alphabet!'

PATSY: The alphabet – the alphabet – ? Gimme a start, teacher.
TEACHER: All right, dumkopf, I'll give you a start – Ah – ah - ah!
PATSY: Ah!
TEACHER: Not Ah! – A!
PATSY (heading for his seat): That's the alphabet – A.
TEACHER: That's not the alphabet. Come back here.
PATSY: There's more?

As Groucho later comments in an *Animal Crackers* routine, this could go on for ever. Joe Adamson recounts another hearsay part of the routine:

GROUCHO (*Teacher*): What is the shape of the world?
PATSY: I don't know.
TEACHER: Well, what shape are my cufflinks?
PATSY: Square.
TEACHER: Not my weekday cufflinks, the ones I wear on Sundays.
PATSY: Oh. Round.
TEACHER: All right, what is the shape of the world?
PATSY: Square on weekdays, round on Sundays!

The astute reader will note that this is, in later Marxian repartee, the dialogue usually deployed between Groucho and Chico. But this is Arthur/Harpo speaking, a phenomenon that has not been preserved. In February 1912, the major showbiz magazine *Variety* reviewed the School Act thus:

> When Gus Edwards' 'School Boys and Girls' recently appeared at Hammerstein's, it was mentioned in a criticism in this paper that there were 'school acts' on the 'small time' much better than Mr Edwards' played out turn. The act arrived sooner than expected. It is the Marx Brothers, from the west, with seven people . . . A lively set of youngsters, with four comedians. One is the school teacher doing 'Dutch.' The other three are a 'Patsy Bolivar' [*sic*], Hebrew and 'Cissy.' The Patsy boy is like a Clarence Wilbur in work, and a natural comedian. Also he is a harpist, and a good one. Introducing the harp into the center of the turn, he scored an unusually large success, deservedly so, besides giving a classy touch to the whole . . . There is little rough stuff in this school act, and it will be liked on almost any bill . . . It is the best 'school act' since the Edwards turn had Herman Timberg in it.

The harp! A monumental step in show business, revealed by this small review. As the pianist of the family was still absent, plying his trade in separate form, some kind of music was necessary. Minnie must have calculated that not all audiences would be enamoured of endless renditions of 'Waltz Me Around Again, Willie' and 'Love Me and the World is Mine'. Harpo relates that one day in Aurora, Illinois, he received a telegram from Mama: 'DON'T LEAVE TOWN UNTIL YOUR SHIPMENT ARRIVES BY FREIGHT. PAYMENTS ON IT ONE DOLLAR PER WEEK. DON'T GET IT WET. MINNIE.' Arriving puzzled but intrigued at the depot, what should emerge from the monstrous box in the freight car but 'the biggest musical instrument I had ever seen'.

If the legend becomes truth . . . This was not, it seems, Fanny Solomons-Schoenberg's harp, although that had, according to lore, been shipped from New York to Chicago, but a new one, costing forty-five dollars. Omie's harp, it appears, was not in working condition, but it does seem odd to the point of incredible that Minnie would have obtained and crated the big monster up with only the hope and the prayer that Arthur could learn to play it. He certainly never claimed to have shown any interest in it before. A family heirloom, the only living artefact of Grandpa and Grandma's legendary days on the road in the Old Country, it mouldered away at 179 East 93rd Street, a memory of long-forgotten tunes: the mythical days of the Covered Wagon, and little Minnie peeking out from under the flap; Grandpa with his axe, offering to cut off and resurrect heads.

78

It took Arthur a year to learn to play his first solo on the harp – 'Annie Laurie' – which makes it certain he must have started training much earlier, in Nightingale times. At St Joseph, Missouri, he says, he saw a display in a ten-cent Woolworths shop window of an angel playing the harp, with the instrument leaning against the right, not the left shoulder, which he had been using. In Muskogee, Oklahoma, he learned a further lesson. A harpist, unlike a tuba or string player, needed total silence to play the soft tones of the harp. At one performance, a fellow vaudevillian, a Hungarian escape artist, went to the toilet just offstage in the small theatre they were playing. In the *pianissimo* part of the sextet from *Lucia* Arthur looked round to see the man sitting on the can, with the toilet door open. Just as he paused in amazement the escape artist flushed. The audience, assuming the harp was producing an unusually astounding effect, applauded. Angel harpists, Arthur noted, never had to put up with this.

In fact, Arthur's aptitude for the instrument was completely instinctual. In later life, his son Bill related, he hired a famous harp instructor to teach him how to play 'properly', but the maestro kept prompting him to do it his own way, watching and marvelling and taking notes all the while. No one in the world, it appeared, played the harp like that. In the end the maestro departed, having taught Harpo nothing, but having jotted down all his unwitting secrets. Bill, who is a musician and composer himself, told me, about the later Harpo: 'His great loves in music were Gershwin; the impressionists, Ravel, Debussy . . . He took those basic elements, but they were both very harmonically interesting at that time. [Later, in] the thirties, forties and fifties he loved Prokofiev and Stravinsky, he loved to listen to that stuff and it was pretty unconventional . . .'

But we're still in vaudeville in 1912 and Arthur has just about mastered 'Annie Laurie', not to speak of *Lucia*. Before the harp, Arthur and Julius made do with strumming on mandolins, as they went into the umpteenth chorus of their closing School Act song ('Always leave 'em with a song,' Minnie admonished) – the crazy doggerel of 'Peasie Weasie', written, according to Groucho, by Charlie Van, half of the Charlie and Fannie Van vaudeville team:

My mother called sister downstairs the other day,
I'm taking a bath, my sister did say,
Well, slip on something quick, here comes Mr Brown.
She slipped on the top step and then came down.

Peasie Weasie, that's his name,
Peasie Weasie, what's his game?
He will catch you if he can,
Peasie Weasie is a bold, bad man!

This seemed to have had about ten thousand verses. The Brothers bought the song for twenty-seven dollars. It stood them in good stead, for several decades, as its rendition chased all but the most stalwart family members out of the room at tribal Marxian gatherings well into the 1960s.

Meanwhile Minnie was continuing to build her empire, quite separately from 'Fun in Hi Skule'. She teamed up with John J. O'Connor, a vaudeville playwright, who was *Variety*'s Chicago reviewer, code-named Wynn. Several of his sketches from 1912 are listed in the Library of Congress, with titles such as 'Busy Afternoon', 'Caught with the Goods', and 'Midnight Appeal'. The main text he wrote for Minnie, 'The Duke of Durham', an English drawing-room satire, actually copyrighted by Minnie Palmer, is unfortunately missing. On 19 May 1912, Wynn wrote in *Variety*:

> Shean and Marx have separated as a vaudeville team and Leonard Marx, who played piano in the former offering, has doubled with George Lee, ex-comedian with the Arlington Four. Marx occasionally writes a song hit and incidentally is one of the several children of Minnie Palmer, who is represented in vaudeville with several acts, among them being the Marx Brothers, a 'school act' made up practically of one family.

On 25 May Wynn reported that 'Minnie Palmer, Chicago's only woman producer, will shortly establish headquarters and produce several new acts, at the same time looking after vaudeville productions she now has on her books.' On 1 June, he noted further that Minnie Palmer 'has arranged to look after the interests of a new summer park in Gary, Indiana, where she will make her headquarters during the hot months managing the project and arranging for several vaudeville attractions'.

Old Minnie Schoenberg was really cooking with gas. Later in the year, the first of these much-vaunted 'attractions' would emerge as 'The Golden Gate Girls'. Wynn, of course: 'A new tabloid production being produced by Minnie Palmer. The troupe numbers eighteen with the Popular Four and the Lewis Sisters featured. It opens at Michigan City next week. Al Shean wrote the book.'

So Al Shean has been roped in as well. Chicago was a key spot for him too, as this was the place where he would team up, for the second time, with his most famous partner, Ed Gallagher. By November 1912 the 'Golden Gate Girls' were booked on the Pantages Circuit, while something called 'Palmer's Cabaret Review' was playing the West Coast, Seattle and Vancouver. Later in November the 'Six American Beauties', produced by Minnie Palmer, turn up in San Diego, and in Tacoma, in December, Minnie Palmer's 'After Midnight' – possibly O'Connor's 'Midnight Appeal', is on. Minnie Palmer was now a definite force on the circuits.

By this time, another crucial revolution had occurred on the home front, as Marx and Lee fizzled out in the summer of 1912 and both Leo Marx and George Lee were featured in September in the latest mutation of the Marx Brothers' School Act, now renamed and revamped as – 'Mr Green's Reception'.

9

Down by Pantages

Knock on door.

MANAGER: Come in! Come in!

ZEPPO: My name is Sammy Brown and I just got into town. Saw your ad, you're Mr Lee. Say you could make a mint on me.

MANAGER: What do you do?

ZEPPO: Dance, sing.

MANAGER: Play a role?

ZEPPO: Anything! I'm a find for guys like you, cause there's nothing I can't do! . . .

MANAGER: Who told you you could dance and sing?

ZEPPO: For money I'd do anything. Why don't you try me. You might as well.

MANAGER: You might be great.

ZEPPO: Who can tell.

MANAGER: What do you call your speciality?

ZEPPO: You mean my big sensation? I knock them cold when I pull off my Frisco imitation!

On the Mezzanine (1921)

The Pantages Circuit in 1912 was a step up from the hardships and squalor of the Marxes' 1909 trail, but not a leap. Its founder, an eccentric Greek, but not the manager portrayed by Julius in his earlier essay, could never read or write, and his wife and employees would read his correspondence to him and act as his scribes. He claimed not to know where he was born, except to indicate some island off the Greek coast, and to say that he had run away from his father at the age of nine, in Cairo. He was next spotted prospecting for gold in the Klondike, before operating the ten-cent theatre in Seattle which was the basis of his great wealth. At its height, the Pantages Circuit had theatres all the way from Birmingham, Alabama to Niagara Falls; in Dallas, Denver, Detroit, Kansas City, Portland, Salt Lake, San Francisco and in a string of Canadian cities: Edmonton, Toronto, Winnipeg and Vancouver. *Variety* estimated that at one point Pantages was 'the most important independent vaud circuit in the country in amount of weeks offered and territory covered. It was booked out of New York and Chicago on a circuit basis, with acts travelling in road-show fashion.'

Later, in 1929, Pantages sold out to RKO, and in the same year he was charged with the statutory rape of a seventeen-year-old chorus girl in one of his theatres, sentenced to fifty years, but then released after a retrial in 1931.

A salutary tale of American immigrant ups and downs. Fred Allen, in later years close friend and recipient of some of Groucho's famous letters, has left us his description of the Pantages road shows in that era. The Pantages shows would have their own railway Pullman car, which would be dropped off on a siding at the various booked towns. Show people, like Schoenbergs, were a clan, bickering but binding together in support. In his autobiography *Much Ado About Me,* Allen writes:

> On a Pantages trip, there were certain cities in which each show caught up with the show ahead of it. If you knew an act with the preceding unit, that act would leave a note at the theatre, telling you the best hotel, the better eating places, and any other information that might be helpful in a strange town. If the act ahead was a single man, and he met any girls in the town, he would leave the girls' names and phone numbers, and any suggestions that he felt were vital to further his successor's conquests. In most of the towns there were girls who made it their business to meet vaudeville actors. If they bestowed their favors on the town boys, they risked gossip. The girls felt secure with the actors, who were gone at the end of three days or a week. Like dead men, actors told no tales.
>
> Many good-looking vaudeville actors, after each matinée, dressed hurriedly and rushed out to stand in front as the audience left the theatre. As the girls came out, the male peacock preened himself. This practice was called 'three-sheeting.' (A three sheet is a large sheet of paper used on billboards to advertise an attraction or a show.)

The Marx boys became experts at this practice, if not always competent at securing their prey. In was in Muncie, Indiana, Groucho claimed, that he was caught out in the classic predicament when he chatted up a young girl with a baby carriage, who told him she was only walking the tot for her sister. Repairing to her boudoir, and securing her in a preparatory arm lock, Julius was shaken loose by a knock on the door and the inevitable 'Oh, my God! It's my husband!' Retiring to the closet, Julius just evaded the prying fingers of the jealous husband, and escaped with his life out of the window, surviving the fifteen-foot jump only by landing in a clump of bushes.

Another story, with a more ethnic tinge, has Leo and Arthur accepting an invitation to a local rabbi's home for the Friday night eve-of-Sabbath meal, only to be caught on Thursday by the enraged worthy sampling his nubile daughter upstairs. 'Is Friday night still on?' calls out Chico as the two defenestrate nimbly.

Indeed, since we are on the subject of religion, we should note that, in Mobile, no less, according to the *Clipper* of 24 May 1913, 'Milton Marx, one of the Marx Brothers, sang "Alexander's Ragtime Band" in Yiddish for the benefit of Rabbi Moses of the Mobile synagogue, when "Mr Green's Reception" company appeared there recently. It pleased the Rabbi so much that he visited the boys in their dressing room and extended an invitation to attend the Saturday morning service.'

Could this have actually been the setting for Leo and Arthur's *Shabbes* eve disgrace? The prayer shawl of time, alas, conceals this from our gaze. Milton's son, Robert, was amazed at this evidence of his father's knowledge of Yiddish which, he said, was never deployed at any other time.

By this date, however, the revamped Marx show had been on the road for over nine months. Unlike the more modest 'Fun in Hi Skule', this was a larger-scale, extravagant piece with an on-stage crew of twenty-one: fifteen pretty girls, four Marx Brothers, Paul Yale and George Lee. Vera Bright, Dot Davidson and Saba Shephard became stalwarts of the stock Marx Brothers troupe for several years to come. Although not directly credited, it seems that Al Shean was drafted in by Minnie to write new material and gags, though the wonderfully named *Battle Creek Enquirer* claimed that 'the musical piece was written by the four boys, each contributing to the book, music and lyrics. Two of the boys staged the dancing and singing numbers and one of the youthful brothers designed the scenery and costumes.' Some people would print anything Minnie told them.

It certainly seems that Leo's entry into the act galvanized the Brothers into more ambitious efforts. The last appearance of Marx and Lee was on 9 August 1912, and in September, Leo was on board the new vessel. The basic idea was to expand the School Act into two sections: the original fun in the classroom and a sequel, set ten years later, at a garden reception given by the old Dutch teacher, Mr Green. This featured, according to the *Kalamazoo Gazette:* 'the smart doings and sayings of his precocious pupils of whom there are a dozen or more, mostly pretty girls, with short skirts, yaller hair and pink stockings.' As copied out by the inimitable Paul Wesolowski sixty years later, the 'Kazoo Gazette' announced the opening of the new extravaganza thus, on 12 January 1913:

If there is any style of entertainment not represented by the Four Marx Brothers' big beauty review in 'Mr. Green's Reception,' it is yet to be discovered. Farce, musical comedy and vaudeville have all contributed towards making this entertainment, which comes to the Majestic theatre for three days, starting tomorrow. [It] is arranged along the lines of musical comedy, but in reality it is a big vaudeville show with a gorgeous 'girlie' setting.

Among the variety contingents will be found Arthur Marx, long a favorite harpist in the realm of variety. Marx and Lee, noted for their syncopated melody; the Harris Brothers, rightly dubbed 'the boys with the Elgin movement feet'; Vera Bright, a recent recruit to musical comedy, who heretofore has delighted thousands in concert with her rich soprano voice.

'Mr. Green's Reception' is in three acts and is described as a 'modern mixture of mirth, melody and motion.' In it are an unusually large number of tuneful melodies, the principal ones of which are 'When I Met You Last Night,' 'Circus Day,' 'Roll Me Around Like a Hoop, My Dear,' 'Yittsky College Boy,' 'Days of Boys and Girls,' 'Hello Mr Stein,' 'Beautiful Nights, Beautiful Girls,' 'Robert E. Lee,' and other tuneful triumphs.

Among the special features that will be introduced are the lazy levee slide, the spectacular ship scene, the big cabaret entertainment and fun in a country school, each of which is said to be a winner as a pleasing musical comedy contribution.

Mrs Minnie Palmer, who is responsible for the production of this big beauty revue, has a novel method of recruiting and keeping chorus girls. It seems to be the general opinion of the public, which, however, is to a great extent erroneous, that there is a plethora of chorus girls, despite the enormous flood of stage-struck misses to the musical comedy field. It is almost impossible for producers to obtain sufficient girls who can really sing, dance and look beautiful.

The present venture is Mrs Palmer's first in the musical comedy field, for heretofore she devoted herself to the presentation of 'Girl acts' in vaudeville. She has applied her various methods to the present production and from all reports it appears that the infusion of new blood in the musical comedy field comes as a welcome innovation.

Mrs Palmer maintains what she calls her 'chicken farm' on the exclusive north shore of Chicago's suburban residence district. She has a lease on a large mansion. Here during the 'off season' may be probably the greatest gathering of beautiful young women ever housed under one roof.

'I would not have a professional chorus girl working for me,' declared Mrs Palmer to a representative of The Gazette. 'All of the girls working in my acts and shows have previously had no stage experience. I take most of them from their parents and give them an education in the art of singing, dancing and the dramatic art. In return for this I pay a liberal salary, but according to the contract with their parents they must stay with my attraction until I have completed their education.'

There is a department in deportment, which is presided over by Walter Meekin. The young women are taught to dance by Signor Antonio Marconi.

Bravo maestro! This is a very different Minnie from the Yiddischer mama we have been led to embrace. The idea of the house at 4512 Grand Boulevard bulging with 'chicks' seems taken straight out of the Ned Wayburn school of exploitation. It certainly must have driven Opie mad, as he was reputed in any case to have spent his latter years chasing the household's coloured maid. Or perhaps they were all being harvested for the Brothers themselves and Al Shean. In any case, the little girl from Dornum was certainly enjoying having the hick scribblers of deepest Michigan eat out of her hand, inflating her modest operation into a major enterprise.

Back to the *Kalamazoo Gazette* of 13 January:

Tabasco hasn't even one little squirt of 'pep' on this jolly entertainment . . . The fair young persons in the piece impersonate Eva Tanguay, Gertrude Hoffman, Adele Ritchie, Lillian Russell, Anna Held, Sarah Bernhardt and Rose Stahl and they are a cute, piquant and sassy lot, not strong on the vocal thing, perhaps, but good enough to get by with it. And that's more than can be said for the chorus with the average tabloid musical tinktum . . . The comedy harp playing by Arthur Marx is a winning card. He is not only a really good performer on this instrument, but he can make it do some laughable stunts, too. It's worth hearing and seeing, especially the way he hypnotises the members of the company to do all sorts of freak movements to his accompaniment.

Three of the Mark brothers do a snappy piano and singing act that pleases immensely. Two of them play the piano, singly and duetically, as 'twere – none of your highbrow stuff, just common, everyday, grotesque comedy playing that gets the cachinatory goat of the hearers with a vengeance. The vocalist of the family comes in for his share of the honors as a contributory cause to the merriment of the hour. And then there are a whole lot of circus things that happen that lack of space forbids even mentioning . . .

A whole lot of circus things indeed. Clearly this was no longer the belt-and-braces, slapstick-and-apple-sauce stuck together by Minnie and the boys just to survive the road. Although the Kazoo *Gazette*, the *Saginaw Daily News* and the *Flint Daily Journal* were not the *New York Dramatic Mirror*, they might not have known about art, but they knew what they liked. As the *Flint Daily Journal*'s 'Jimmy the Office Boy' column put it: '"Mr Green's Reception" is a Prime Pippin. "Dese Four Marx Brothers dat's in the show are the real frosting off the chocolate cake . . . Dat chorus is the classiest pack of dames dat kicked up their toes on the Bijou stage . . ."'

The *Lansing State Journal* names some of the high-kickin' dames as Laura Lawrence, Carlen (?) Fleming, Gan Tobbena, Elsie Moore and Clara Shaw. The 'Hebrew' comedy of George Lee, in particular, came in for high praise. Here was another potential 'sixth' Marx Brother who came, did his tour of duty and then went off into the shadows. Groucho, naming him 'Moe' Lee in *The Groucho Phile*, commented, on his role in the later 'Home Again': 'Moe was the singer of the group. He had a little piece of business that always got a laugh: he'd stick his chin out. Each of us was getting twenty-five dollars a week; Moe felt he deserved thirty. He didn't get it, and left the act. I don't think he ever worked in show business again.'

Harpo, in his book, remembered Kalamazoo, Michigan, but claimed the act only played there for the one night. He recalled coming on after the intermission, as a ten-years-older Patsy Brannigan, 'with the same ratty red wig, turtle-neck sweater and blacked out teeth, but with long pants on, carrying a trash can'.

MR GREEN (*who has miraculously lost his German accent somewhere during the intermission*): And who might you be, my good fellow?
PATSY: Why, Patsy Brannigan, the Garbage Man.
MR GREEN: Sorry, we don't need any.

This piece of repartee got them fired, says Harpo, because, unbeknownst to them, the current local scandal in Kalamazoo was that the theatre owner's wife had just run off with a city garbage collector. But an immortal exchange had been born.

Or maybe that didn't happen in Kalamazoo after all, because in February

Spot the Marxes competition: the full cast of 'Mr Green's Reception' on tour.

Minnie was back there, at the Majestic, with her *Duke of Durham*, the musical play by John J. O'Connor, about 'a foolish aristocratic mamma who insists upon her daughter marrying a "furrin" nobleman when she loves a husky Yankee yachts-man'. The actors were Kathryn Allen, Frank Smith and Mabel LaConver, and the featured songs, 'First Train to Tennessee', 'Carolina', 'Schlitz' and 'That Old Girl of Mine'. The Kazoo *Gazette*, thorough as always, noted on 18 February that the supporting motion picture on the bill, *The Life of a Frog*, showing the growth of the amphibian from spawn to adult, was of particular interest.

Like the amphibian, Minnie continued to grow, putting on 'Running For Congress' at Knoxville, Tennessee, playing *The Duke of Durham* in Hamilton, Ohio when the floods came (19 April) and something called 'The Seven Orange Blossoms', co-produced with Harry Shean (the last gasp of Uncle Heinie in show business?), in Chicago in May. Not to speak of Minnie Palmer's 'Parisian Violets', another offshoot of the 'chicken farm'. On 19 July, the *New York Clipper* reported from Chicago that:

> The Four Marx Bros. are shaking hands with their numerous friends after a long tabloid tour covering forty-six weeks. For a time only three of the boys were with the company, as one of the brothers underwent an operation here. The quartet was intact for the final engagements at

Springfield Mo., Coffeyville, Hutchinson and Wichita, Kan. A party at Minnie Palmer's newly acquired mansion, on Grand Boulevard, was attended by Leonard, Arthur, Julius and Milton. Herbert Marx, a younger brother, cut out for show business too, George Lee, Paul Yale, Prof. [*sic!!*] Lou Schoenberg, Lou Shean, J. Schickler, Sam Marx, Fred Phillipson, E. E.Meredith, Saba Shephard, Lillie Brown, Mr & Mrs Proval, Eileen Murphy, Dot Davidson, Ten Bennet, Dot Bennet, Marie Lawrence, Harris Bros. and Minnie Palmer.

Note, again, Minnie's mastery of press hype here, a simple family and cast get-together becoming what we would today call a media event, with the modest if comfortable brownstone elevated to a much grander status.

Herbert was now twelve years old, and just below the age when Milton first stepped on the stage (barring the ventriloquist's dummy). He must have been experiencing a great deal of frustration watching his elder brothers making good, and travelling along with fifteen beautiful girls, while he stayed at home, tied to Frenchy's apron strings (though he may well have had the run of the 'chicken farm'!). In his old age, interviewed for BBC TV by Barry Norman about his early life, Herbert/Zeppo belittled the Chicago days:

My mother was always trying to get the boys – Gummo, Groucho, and Chico and Harpo – jobs, playing vaudeville. Cheap vaudeville, really, four or five shows a day and maybe three days' work and then get laid off for a week or two or something. She was always downtown where the theatrical district was, where the agents and the managers were hanging out, so she would always try to get us [*sic*] bookings. If some act was cancelled some place, she'd try to shove us in there.

Zeppo was, like the others, confusing his dates, bringing in later times after he'd joined the act – in 1919, in quite different circumstances – and making the whole scene look more precarious than it was, since Minnie was no beggar at the door well before Herbert was bar mitzvah. On 30 August 1913, the *Clipper*'s 'Chicago News' column reported Minnie as treasurer of a consortium of producers which included Charles A. Sellon, Ned Alvord and James A. Galvin, set up to offer high-class shows at popular prices for longer runs, eliminating the one-night stands and expensive railroad costs. She had, of course, a new act raring to go – 'The Society Sextette', which was 'good enough to play the best houses in Chicago'. The chicken farm was at full stretch.

The Four Brothers were themselves fully occupied, alternately on the Pantages, then on the Butterfield circuit. In August they were in Canada, breaking all records in Edmonton, and doing well in Calgary. Moving down to San Francisco, Oakland. On 13 November the *Salt Lake Telegram* noted the entire chorus of 'Mr Green's Reception' sang 'Apple Blossom Time in Normandy' in the 'beautiful garden scene'. About the school sections the good Mormon scribes noted that 'among the boy scholars are a Hebrew, an Italian, an Irishman, a German and a couple of "sissies."' Mercifully, they did not name them.

By Thanksgiving, the troupe was in Denver, joining in on a mobile stage, set on 'a big motor truck filled with vaudeville artists, including the usual number of pretty girls with stunning costumes, [which] will go up and down Sixteenth and Seventeenth Streets from Lawrence to Broadway, and give open-air perfomances of fifteen minutes in length at frequent intervals . . .' Proceeds were to go to the Craig colony for consumptives, 'mindful of these unfortunates to whom Thanksgiving brings little enough cheer'. At Christmas the Brothers were back home with the tribe, and ready for their first big opening in Chicago itself, at the Colonial, on 17 January 1914: 'Cold weather could not keep back the immense throng that came . . . for the opening performance. The house was packed to the doors.'

Once again, the act was getting too small for Minnie's ambitions. She wanted it to be bigger, better, louder. In any case, the schoolroom format was beginning to lag behind the actual ages of the cast. Leo was after all twenty-seven, and even Milton was over twenty-one. Minnie kept promising that 'Herbert Marx, youngest of the Marx Brothers, will change the title of the act from the Four Marx Bros. to the Five Marx Bros. as soon as he completes school. He appeared at the Willard one night recently, and scored . . . big.' But this event was to be postponed for a while. The company was reported to be hit by illness, Julius down with kidney trouble and one of the girls, Saba Shephard, out with appendicitis, though this was in fact a ruse to give the players some breathing space while Minnie considered their future. Nevertheless, the *Lansing State Journal* reported that 'having nine men and one to spare, the Marx Brothers carry a regularly organized baseball team with them, playing local teams whenever possible . . .' According to the *Flint Daily Journal*: 'The Marx Brothers show is known as the "Show of youth and laughter," as every member of the company is youthful, good to look upon and entirely capable . . .'

The Marx Brothers seemed to have arrived. But they were still in exile. New York, and Broadway, were still far away. And then Al Shean came to wave his wand and mutate the show, once more, into another format with, yet again, a new name.

'An Elaborate Disorder of Amateur Antics'

> MR GREEN: This must be the Far Rockaway boat.
> MRS GREEN: How do you know?
> MR GREEN (*twitching his nostrils*): I can smell the herring.
>
> *Home Again* (1914)

'Home Again' – and we can smell an Al Shean joke four thousand miles and eighty-five years away. As Harpo wrote, the above exchange did not go down very well in Kankakee, Illinois. But the whole thing, square on week-days, round on Sundays, wowed them well enough at its big city opening. From *Variety*, 26 September 1914, Lincoln Hippodrome, Chicago:

This merry little musical short gives the Four Marx Bros. opportunity to do some very effective work in their several lines. They all have talent, and they shine in this piece which allows them time to display their own brand of rollicking humor in which they excel. But there is little plot to the piece. The story concerns Henry Schneider (Julius Marx) who is returning with his family and friends from a voyage across the ocean. The scene opens in 'one' with the party on the dock after disembarking. There is a flirtatious soubret mixed up in the affair who has been on the boat, and Schneider, who is susceptible, has fallen for her charms, much to the anger of Mrs Schneider. Milton Marx is seen as Harold Schneider whose chief work is to look handsome, which he does without question. Leonard Marx is seen in an Italian character, and his specialty at the piano, in which he does comic things with his hands and fingers, is one of the best features. He gets a laugh about every minute, is at ease and graceful, and makes good all the time.

Arthur Marx is billed as a 'nondescript.' He is made up as a 'boob' and his makeup is not pleasant. He gets a good many laughs but a change should be made in his character. He plays the harp well, and does some comedy with the strings that is in a class by itself. Songs are interspersed and modern dances are introduced to round up the second part of the show where the people are engaged in a frolic at a house party at the home of the Schneiders. At the close, the young people all get into a boat and move off the stage with a rousing chorus. Then follows a pretty scene wherein the boat is seen going down the river in the distance. There are times when the members of the company do not seem to have quite enough to do but these things will doubtless be remedied in time. The chorus work is good, with many good voices in the ensemble.

Al Shean wrote and staged the piece, and Minnie Palmer presents it. At the Lincoln Hip., where it was the Sunday feature it went over very big with many encores demanded. It looks like a good piece of property. (Reed)

Once again, we have a missing script, all the more frustrating as Al Shean, as we noted earlier, did send some of his texts for copyrighting. The legend goes that Uncle Al came in at the last minute to jazz up a flagging show and wrote the whole thing in a couple of hours on the back of an envelope, as it were. Not so. Even more than 'Mr Green's Reception', this was a carefully crafted affair. The *New York Clipper* reported in its vaudeville notes of 4 July 1914:

Al Shean and the Four Marx Brothers will head a big vaudeville act of sixteen people, which will play U.B.O. (the United Booking Office) and Orpheum time next season. Mr Shean has been the guest of Minnie Palmer, his sister, in Chicago, for a few weeks, and a party consisting of Mr and Mrs Al Shean, Minnie Palmer and Arthur Marx moved on to Mt. Vernon, NY, last Saturday.

Mount Vernon was a well-known Catskills retreat for people wishing to escape the city bustle. The *Clipper* noted that 'the vaudeville act will have both Al Shean and Julius Marx in Dutch comedy roles, but their work is so entirely different that this will not detract from the offering. Saba Shephard, Katherine Fleming, Marigo Gano, Jack Laemle and Henry Randolph have already been engaged.'

Minnie's party remained out east until August and returned to continue planning the Big Show. In the sealed Schoenberg sanctum, for whatever reason, Uncle Al decided he would prefer not to go on stage with his nephews, a prudent decision, as W. C. Fields too came to realize a few months later, at his upstaging in Columbus, Ohio. But Al had already bequeathed to Julius the kind of role he himself had made a speciality, most recently as 'Schmuke' in the operetta 'The Rose Maid' – his pompous German routine.

'Home Again' established for the Brothers the roles they would more or less stick with from then on. Without a text it's difficult to figure out with any accuracy what went on upon the stage. A great deal is made, in the legend, of the extent of ad-libbing carried out by the Marx Brothers in their various acts and shows. The classic story is that of George S. Kaufman, co-writer of *The Cocoanuts* and *Animal Crackers*, pausing once in the wings of the theatre, during a *Cocoanuts* performance, to comment to his companion: 'Ssh! I think I just heard a line from the script!' Alas, a quick scan of the original play script of *The Cocoanuts* shows a huge amount of dialogue, gags and routines, assumed to be ad-libs, but actually written in the original and preserved, virtually unchanged, up to the movie version of 1929.

What is no doubt true is that the less script there was, the more unscripted mayhem was unleashed, and certainly the Brothers would have been less respectful of Uncle Al's *bons mots* than those of the Illustrious Playwright. Nevertheless, even the most anarchic team would have to plan, block, time, organize and rehearse. Good gags are not born without pain. The comic tries them, tests them, hones them, changes them, drops them if they fail to get a laugh. It's clear too that audiences were more prepared than critics to accept the 'elaborate disorder of amateur antics' which Percy Hammond of the *Chicago Tribune* lamented in January 1915. O. L. Hall of the *Chicago Journal* complained of 'lack of finished singing', and grumped: 'The young men are in need of a first class stage director, and some one to choose things for the young women to wear.' He meant someone other than Minnie, I presume.

Another reviewer, in *Variety* on 12 February, huffed about 'the expectoration by Arthur. That should go out immediately.' The *Brooklyn Eagle*, writing a year later in 1916, lamented, 'why a man, who can evidently play exquisite music on the harp, should waste his time in kicking the harp around, as does Arthur Marx, as the "nondescript," is inconceivable . . .' though it did concede that 'all the brothers are good actors . . .'

Thank goodness for small mercies. Both Arthur and Leo, as we have seen, had found the characters they were to play, unaltered, until the end of their show-business lives. Leo was already fixed in his wisecracking, piano-playing, Italian role, codified in 'Home Again' as the 'wop' Tony Saroni. Arthur, as the 'boob', had changed the turtle-necked sweater and blacked-out teeth of the Irish Patsy and adopted the striped shirt, torn raincoat, battered hat and red fright wig that were the stock signs of nineteenth-century

German comedians. But something more significant than the costume, and even the harp playing, had changed: Arthur had become a mute.

'Why Harpo Doesn't Talk' was the title of an essay by Groucho Marx in the *Los Angeles Times* of 12 December 1948. It was all supposed to be about the night – a week before Christmas, no less – when a boorish manager in one of the mid-west boondocks fined Julius ten dollars for smoking his cigar in the theatre. When Julius consulted his brothers about this dire insult, the Four (or was it the Three?) decided to go on strike, and refused to go on, just as the orchestra was tuning up for the show. The audience was restless, the manager, one Mr Wells, adamant, when Harpo suggested: 'We'll take ten dollars and you take ten, and we'll combine it and throw the whole twenty in the Salvation Army pot in the corner.'

A likely story. But, seven days later, as the Brothers prepared to move to the next town, two management stooges staggered up with four immensely heavy canvas bags containing the combined week's take of $112.50, in pennies. Wrote Groucho:

> We barely made the train, and as it pulled out of the depot, we stood on the back platform watching the town and theatre recede into the distance.
>
> Then Harpo, the pantomimist, raised his voice, and above the clatter of the train, bellowed:
>
> 'Good-by, Mr. Wells. Here's hoping your lousy theatre burns down!'
>
> We thought it was just a gag, till next morning – when we discovered that during the night, Jack Wells' theatre had been reduced to ashes. From then on we decided not to let Harpo talk – his conversation was too dangerous.

And that's the truth. Another tradition has it that Uncle Al, having hastily scribbled the text for 'Home Again' on that famous envelope, discovered at the end that he had written only three lines for Arthur. Therefore it was decided he should play the mute. This makes just as little sense as Groucho's story and is much less entertaining. Clearly the pantomime act was, like Leo's Italian accent, something that had developed deep in Arthur's gut, a feeling that he was far from his best at dialogue. He was having too much fun playing the harp, and the harp and Patsy Brannigan did not mix. He had to become his own person – the silent observer of all the world's 'Gookies', the purely physical element of the act. Bill Marx, Harpo's son, put it this way:

[In the old] commedia dell'arte . . . you had the authoritarian figure, you had the idiot and you had the mime, and it was a proven formula that has lasted through the ages. The Marx Brothers, through hit and miss, search and destroy, you name it, accidentally came upon it, with Groucho being the authoritarian figure, Chico being the idiot, and Harpo being the mime. Of course, their own personalities, on stage, became stage persona more or less based upon an extension of their real personalities . . . Groucho was always a pretty acerbic guy, Harpo was always a very impulsive liver, he did it without harm to other people, he was always looking in his own life, without knowing it, to just enjoy it. When he saw a pretty girl, he pursued her, when he heard a good piece of music, he would listen to it. He wasn't particularly concerned about rationalising his life . . . It just developed that way. And they never knew that they had fallen upon a formula that had existed years and years ago, but . . . they contemporised it [so that] people could really understand it and didn't view it as an art form.

Art?! Perish the thought! In an early sample of their mayhem Harpo reported on the night, in Alabama, when they were still the Four Nightingales, when the whole singing lark seemed just too boring: 'We stopped singing in the middle of "Mandy Lane" when we spotted a large bug walking across the stage. The four of us got down on our hands and knees and began to follow the bug, making bets whether it was a beetle, a cockroach, or a bedbug.'

What wouldn't we give, to be able to fly back in a time machine and watch the Marx Brothers' vaudeville act, live on stage, when they were in their vigorous twenties, rather than their movie forties! One later collaborator, who had the gift of description, recalled the show as it was in February 1916, on a cold winter night in Providence, Rhode Island. This piece, which first appeared in *The New Yorker*, was penned by S. J. Perelman, in memory of the afternoon when, as a mawkish twelve-year-old, he entered the portals of the Keith-Albee Theatre:

To recall with any degree of clarity the acts I saw on gaining my balcony perch would, of course, be impossible across the gulf of thirty-six years. Out of the haze of memory, however, I remember Fink's Trained Mules, Willie West & McGinty in their deathless housebuilding routine, Lieutenant Gitz-Rice declaiming 'Mandalay' through a pharynx swollen with emotion and coryza, and that liveliest of nightingales, Grace Larue. All these, however, were mere appetizers for the roast. The *mise en scène* of the Marx Brothers piece was the Cunard docks in New York, an illusion conveyed by four battered satchels and a sleazy backdrop purportedly representing the gangway of the *Britannic*. Garbed in his time-honored claw-hammer coat, his eyes shifting lickerishly behind his specs and an unlit perfecto in his teeth, Groucho irrupted onstage accompanied by his presumptive wife, a scraggy termagant in a feather boa. Behind him came Gummo, impersonating his cocksure son, and Harpo and Chico, a pair of shipboard cronies. Groucho's initial speech set the flavor of the proceedings.

'Well, friends,' he observed, stifling a belch, 'next time I cross the ocean, I'll take a train. I'm certainly glad to set my feet on terra firma. Now I know that when I eat something, I won't see it again . . .' Groucho began to expand on his trip abroad. Heckled at almost every turn by Gummo, he remarked waspishly, 'Nowadays you don't know how much you know until your children grow up and tell you how much you don't know.' According to Groucho, no pundit has ever been able to explain exactly what the foregoing meant or why it elicited cheers and applause . . . At any rate, after considerable horseplay in which Harpo disgorged the ship's cutlery from his sleeves and inspected the lingerie of several *zoftick* fellow-passengers, Chico approached Groucho with hand extended.

'I'd like-a to say goombye to your wife,' he proposed, in what was unquestionably the paltriest dialect ever heard off Mulberry Street.

'Who wouldn't?' riposted his brother. This boffo ushered in the second scene, laid without any tiresome logical transition at Groucho's villa on the Hudson. The plot structure, to be candid, was sheerest gossamer; vague reference was made to a stolen chafing dish, necessitating a vigorous search by Harpo of two showgirls drifting unaccountable about the premises, but on the whole there were few nuances. Following a rather soupy rendition of 'The World is Waiting for Sunrise' by Harpo, Chico played 'Chopsticks' on the piano with gruelling archness, and the pair exited rear stage left in a papier-mâché boat on wheels, knocking down three members of the troupe. Those who remained thereupon joined in a stylish chorale entitled 'Over the Alpine Mountains E'er So Far Away,' and, as the orchestra segued into von Suppe's 'Light Cavalry Overture' to herald the acrobats, I descended to Farcher's Drugstore for a double banana split with maxixe cherries.

The Four Marx Brothers: Arthur (Harpo), Milton (Gummo), Leo (Chico) and Julius (Groucho) during 'Home Again' years.

Perelman did not, he claimed, see or hear any more of Groucho and 'his tatterdemalion crew' until Groucho summoned him, in Hollywood, to discuss the writing of a script, which turned out to be *Monkey Business,* a story in which four tatterdemalion stowaways get off a boat and cause mayhem at a rich gangster's mansion. But we are running ahead of ourselves once again. 'Home Again' stood the Marx Brothers in good stead for almost four years, until the spring of 1918! Testing in the hinterland, and at Columbus, Ohio, where it nonplussed the veteran W. C. Fields, it hit New York City, where it played the prestigious Palace Theatre in the week commencing 22 February 1915. After their seven years' exile, the Marxes were home again, in New York. But times had changed, and the rumblings of war across the ocean, in Europe, were heralding a new era which would change both the boys, and the society in which they moved and performed, in both subtle and profound ways.

The Kaiser, Art Fisher and the Rhode Island Reds

GROUCHO (*blowing out a puff of smoke*): Now – how many men you got in your army?
CHICO: Well, we gotta one hundred thousand men.
GROUCHO: That's not fair, we've only got fifty thousand.
CHICO: That's all right. We let you have twenty-five thousand men, and we both start even.
GROUCHO: That's the spirit – fifty-fifty . . . Now, how many battalions you got?
CHICO: Well, we gotta two battalions and one Frenchman.
GROUCHO: I wish you were still working for me, so I could ask you to resign. How're you fixed for cavalry?
CHICO: We gotta five thousand men but no horses.
GROUCHO: That's funny – we got five thousand horses but no men.
CHICO: That's all right – your men can ride our horses.
GROUCHO: Not a bad idea. If our horses get tired they can ride your men for a change. (*Chico nods agreeingly.*) Now I don't mind letting you have our horses but you must promise to put them through their maneuvers.
CHICO: Oh sure. We have horse maneuvers every morning.

'Cracked Ice', draft script for *Duck Soup* (1933)

Napoleon Bonaparte, no less, is credited with a saying that could be the Marxes' motto: 'From the sublime to the ridiculous is but one short step.' As a man who plunged his world into death and destruction in the cause of freedom and liberty, he knew whereof he spoke. The other Marx, who wrote of revolutionary change to free the world from the fetters of oppression, had less sense of irony. But he at least foresaw the conflicts that would tear the old empires apart. On 4 August 1914, just as Minnie Marx and her entourage were returning from Mount Vernon with the shining script (or envelope) of 'Home Again' tucked in her bosom, the German armies invaded Belgium.

The ensuing war in Europe was a hazy ghost in the attic of the Schoenberg household, which did not impinge on the family's show business life until the sinking of the passenger ship *Lusitania* by German Uboats in the Atlantic on 7 May 1915. The Marx Brothers were playing in Toronto, and the immediate impact was to change Julius's character temporarily from a German papa into a Yiddish one, and then permanently to a domiciled American. Henry Schneider metamorphosed into Henry Jones, and the crucial transformation that created the Groucho we know was effected, not by fantasy, but by reality.

The hundreds of American lives lost on the *Lusitania* must have struck a special terror into Minnie's heart. Always more German than Jewish, both Minnie and Sam had sentimental ties to their old homeland, its language, its music and its cuisine. Jews fought on both sides in the First World War, and many immigrant families were haunted, when America finally joined the war, by the spectre of brother fighting brother. There did not seem to be many related Schoenbergs left in the old country, but Minnie was definitely not happy with the idea of her sons being called up to fight 'the fatherland', or any land, for that matter. We have seen to what lengths the Schoenbergs had gone to alter their children's ages when they were a decade away from any possible army draft age. Certainly the propaganda depicting the Germans as Huns, murdering women and babies, was frightening. Al Shean came directly under fire for his innocent portrayals of comic Germans who could still be patriotic Americans, as attested by a clipping from an anonymous critic, questioning his loyalty over some unknown jibes:

> Mr Shean has the more credible impersonation, has he not – of the German born who is faithful and true to the nation that has adopted him and made him rich? Yes he has! But he is one of those happy, blithe, truculent, and secure citizens who are above the draft age, and who have no sons old enough to go to war . . . Yet he is comic, and he illustrates the ease with which it is possible to be star-spangled without discomfort other than the income tax . . . He is not quite right, this fellow, is he, since no one should be talkative for war unless he or his blood is in the war. Should we not have a lot of silence from those who have not undergone the great emotion? Something tells us that we should.

Yet show business continued, unabated. On 3 September 1915, the *Flint Daily Journal* recorded a unique event:

> The Four Marx Brothers, Julius, Milton, Leonard and Arthur, who have on many occasions delighted Flint patrons of vaudeville, opened another three days' engagement at the Majestic yesterday. For this

occasion, however, there is a fifth Marx brother in the company, Master Herbert Marx, a lad of about 14, who gives promise of becoming as much of a favorite as the rest of the family. Master Herbert added some four or five songs to the rest of the program last night in a manner which left no doubt as to his future . . .

But the *Battle Creek Enquirer,* announcing the Brothers' next engagement, on 5 September, mentions only the Four Marx Brothers. Flint, Michigan, remains the only venue where the Five Marx Brothers ever appeared together on the stage. It was around this period, according to the next enduring legend, that the Brothers gained the nicknames that were to be their labels from then on (though *The Groucho Phile* dates the year as 1914, and the Marxian historians offer a specific day, 15 May – as good a day as any for legends). In Galesburg, Illinois, at a backstage poker game, a fellow actor, one Art Fisher, a 'monologuist' – or what we today call a stand-up comic – dealt them the names as he dealt them their cards around the table: 'That's for you, Groucho (Groucho always carried the Brothers' grouch-bag, or money-bag); that's for you, Harpo (an obvious choice); that's for you, Chicko (the chick chaser, the 'k' dropping out a little later); that's for you, Gummo (of the gum-soled dancing shoes).'

Groucho claimed that all these 'o' names derived from a popular comic strip, 'Sherlocko the Monk' by Gus Mager ('No Mystery is Too Baffling For Him!'), featuring monkey-faced characters with names like Watso, Yanko the Dentist, Hamfatto, and a toothache-ridden 'Groucho' – described by Sherlocko as 'a red-faced man – very quick-tempered and carried a stout stick!' Of course, the scholars have ransacked this tale too. Paul Wesolowski ('Wesso') found a reference to the Marx Brothers' intended appearance in Galesburg, Illinois, in 1914, but no verifying record in the Galesburg press. Neither he nor I have been able to find hair nor hide of Art Fisher. Far from being a monologuist, he appears to have been an illusionist, vanishing himself out of history. The comic strip reference would suggest that the naming took place much earlier, during 'Mr Green's Reception', as 'Sherlocko' ran from 1911 to 1913 and then mutated, after threats of legal action by Sherlock Holmes author Arthur Conan Doyle's American agents, into 'Braggo the Monk' and then, dropping the 'o', into 'Hawkshaw the Detective'.

The trend for names ending in 'o' did however seem to linger on for some years, as Paul Wesolowski unearthed a piece from the *Louisville Times* of 22 February 1919, showing cartoons of the newspaper's own staff as 'Boosto the

Monk – editor and publisher; Helpo the Monk – managing editor; Hoppo – sporting editor; Scratcho – staff artist; Bettso – staff photographer; and Inko the Monk – chief galley boy'. That narrows us down to anywhere between 1912 and 1919, thank you very much. (Harpo, with his usual delinquency with locations, sets the seminal event in Rockford, omitting to say which Rockford: Illinois, Michigan, Minnesota or Idaho . . .)

The only fact in all this is that the first mention in dispatches of the Marx Brothers by their new names occurs in February 1919, in a *Variety* review of 'The Four Marx Brothers Revue', another revamp of the act, playing the Palace, Chicago. Julius is still Julius in this piece, but 'Harpo', 'Chico' and 'Zep', for Herbert, are named. In their professional life, the Brothers were using their original names right up to and including their first Broadway show, *I'll Say She Is,* in 1924. It was, in fact – leaping forward again – Alexander Woollcott, their mentor and discoverer, who witnessed them backstage calling each other by their nicknames and said: 'Wait a minute, you've got these great stage names and you're still billing yourselves as Julius, Arthur, Leonard and Herbert? Gedoutahere!' Or words to that effect. What is obvious to us was far from obvious to the protagonists themselves.

Despite this omission, the Brothers were bent on building their myth, in particular with regard to Mama Minnie. 'We Are Minnie Palmer's Sons' was the heading for a piece in the *Columbus Daily Dispatch,* 1 October 1916. The piece continued: '"Our mother expected us to make good – so we had to do it,"' said Arthur Marx. '"We never do anything on stage that we could not offer as parlour entertainment to our mother and her guests,"' said Milton disingenuously, omitting to mention the wild nature of the family ménage. The Columbus reporter gushed: 'If "a wise son maketh a glad father," surely such four boys must be the happiness of their mother.' Aah!

The newspaper continued to rhapsodize about the Brothers, alluding, intriguingly, to 'Milton and the athletic Billie de Rex in a whirlwind dance which the harpist finishes, dragging her off in the most approved male vampire fashion.' In November 1917, the *San Antonio Light* praised Arthur Marx, 'who plays "Nondescripty" [as] a comedian of unusual ability . . . He is a skilled harpist and a talented musician. He can play the piano and the clarinet with the same dexterity. Leo, who plays "Tony," is also an accomplished musician, and renders some snappy, catchy numbers.' The same report mentions that 'the boys were all in the draft registration and three of them volunteered, but were rejected on account of their eye sight. All the members of the company bought Liberty Bonds.'

We are very glad to hear that. In fact, the Marx Brothers' failure to go forward and participate in 'winning the war for democracy' in Europe is another fuzzy tale. Neither Groucho nor Harpo have a single word to say about the First World War in their autobiographies, although Groucho mentions the *Lusitania* tragedy in *The Groucho Phile*, telling the tale of his emergency switch to Yiddish. Standards of fitness were very rigorous in the War's call-ups, and Julius's old eye defect would have disqualified him, but it does stretch credibility a little far to see Leo and Arthur as health rejects. Both had the build of oxen. And Milton had no trouble getting accepted when he finally did join up – on 31 October 1918, eleven days before the Armistice!

Minnie's fears of her sons being taken off to the trenches did not cause her merely to weep and wring hands. As usual, she had a foolproof plan. The war, in fact, did not affect Americans until the spring of 1917. After a long period in which Germany tried to keep the United States out of the war, despite the continued attacks on Atlantic shipping, the United States declared war on Germany on 6 April. The draft boards convened soon after. The Four Marx Brothers – Julius, Leonard, Arthur and Milton – were playing the southern Interstate Circuit through May. Then the act disappears, to emerge again in Springfield, Illinois on 17 August. Between these dates lies a new and astounding transformation of the Marx boys – into gentleman farmers.

Minnie discovered that farmers, who fed the nation, could be exempted from the draft. She therefore bought a farm, in La Grange, south-west of Chicago, in an area far less built up then than it is today. (It was north of Joliet Road and east of La Grange, according to Wesolowski in his *Freedonia Gazette*. The farmhouse has long been replaced by development.) Groucho described the move to these rural surroundings to Hector Arce: 'The first morning on the farm, we got up at five. The following morning, we dawdled in bed until six. By the end of the week we were getting up at noon, which was just enough time for us to get dressed to catch the 1:07 to Wrigley Field, where the Chicago Cubs played.'

Pretty good, eh, boss? This was, according to legend, the place where the fifth brother, Herbert, got his nickname as he sat on a haystack with a straw in his mouth, as Chico passed by. 'Howdy, Zeke,' says Herbert. 'Howdy, Zep,' says Leo. And so Zeppo was born.

Of course, there is another story, something about World War One Zeppelins, but that is much too far-fetched. Harpo, as always, via his co-writer Rowland Barber, presents a totally different version, with Herbert named Zippo because he was constantly doing gymnastic chin-ups and acrobatics like 'Mr Zippo', a famous trained chimpanzee. Since Herbert thought this a little demeaning, Zippo became Zeppo. Take your pick. The nature of the farm is also shrouded in flimflam. The brothers – or possibly Minnie – bought several hundred chickens, which duly laid their eggs, but the rats on the farm always ate 'em. When buyers came for eggs the new farmers had to rush to the store to buy some to put under the chickens. The buyers were amazed to see Rhode Island Reds, which laid brown eggs, produce white ones, by Marxian mutation. We might call this a shaggy duck story. An attempt to raise guinea pigs for research labs also came to nought, as the labs preferred to use rabbits. The cumulative contribution of La Grange farm to the war effort appears to have been to keep the Marx Brothers from reducing the European 'theatre' to the level of the finale of *Duck Soup* or, worse, to deprive us of their performances entirely.

The only surviving evidence of the agricultural Marxes is a photograph in *The Marx Brothers Scrapbook*. Harpo, Gummo, Zeppo and Groucho stand sheepishly in soiled overalls, Gummo with shovel over his shoulder; all are wearing turned-up sombreros, and looking like rejects from the cast list of a Hal Roach production of *The Grapes of Wrath*.

The Marx Brothers continued to own the farm until Kaiser Wilhelm's decisive setbacks in the trenches led to the victory of the Allies. On the brink of peace, the brothers lost a Gummo and gained a Zeppo, but before then they continued to tour 'Home Again' on the Orpheum Circuit. From the Houston Press on 17 November:

> It's a comfort to go into a theatre, guide a dainty little heart breaker down the aisle, flop into the choice 'down front' seats and see a show that is strong enough to even make you forget all about the li'l lady beside you. That's precisely the way the Four Marx Brothers in 'Home Again' affect me . . . The act is one long laugh from start to finish . . .

In San Francisco, Julius notched up a wholly different achievement, managing to get a hole in one at the golf links at Lincoln Park: 'The hole is 153 yards, par 3. Responsible witnesses saw the play and are prepared to make affidavit it was accomplished. Marx at the time was playing a match, but refused to continue, fearing to besmirch his brilliant record.'

On 9 March, at Salt Lake, the Brothers presented a rare glimpse of the inner workings of the construction of their act to a reporter from the *Utah Democrat*:

> A few short years ago when the Four Marx Brothers . . . decided to go on

the stage they agreed among themselves that they must have an act which would be sure to please at least 99 per cent of their audience. 'But how are we going to do it?' inquired Milton, the youngest. 'Ha!' exclaimed Leonard, the oldest, and the last of the four brothers to succumb to the lure of the calcium; 'that's the rub, and I've got it!' The other three – Milton, Julius and Arthur – hitched their chairs closer and listened attentively to brother Leonard's idea. It was as follows: Since some people like one style of comedy and don't care for another, it behooved the Marx boys, if they wanted to stick to their agreement, to offer every style of comedy known to the stage; if one of the brothers did not please, one of the other three would be sure to; and thus the four brothers, individually and collectively, would be credited with being a 'hit.' Accordingly, they divided up the field of comedy among themelves thus: Julius took up eccentric comedy; Milton, light comedy; Arthur, nut comedy; and Leonard, boob comedy. Each of them went to work hard to perfect himself in his particular forte and the result was that the Four Marx Brothers are today considered vaudeville's superior entertainers and their offering is one of the most successful on the Orpheum circuit.

There is no doubt that by this time Leo was the guiding hand behind the Brothers' show. He had also, it appears, written some of the songs: one sheet crediting Leonard Marx as the author of 'Walking Thru Lovers Lane', music by Leonard Marx and Harry de Costa, is headed 'Songs Introduced and Sung by the Four Marx Brothers in their own musical comedy, Home Again'. So the Brothers were definitely still singing, even though all those Nightingale timbres were gone. Leo himself was singing a new song in 1917, as a result of the momentous change in his status, which we shall trace in the next chapter, from confirmed bachelor to properly married man.

Minnie, too, underwent her own transformation, as her management status – in fact, all of her stage empire – had collapsed some years before. In October 1914, Jones, Linick and Schaeffer of the McVickers Theatre sued Minnie Palmer for breach of contract for the non-appearance of the Marx Brothers at their venue. Intriguingly, one 'Adolph Marks' represented the three appellants, but it could not have been Harpo, because the appellants won the case and were awarded $350. It tells us something of the fragility of Minnie's business ventures that she could not, or would not, raise the money. On 19 December 1914, the *Clipper* noted that 'Minnie Palmer . . . was served with an execution by the bailiff but evaded payment by filing a schedule'.

That is, in effect she declared her bankruptcy. There is no further mention of Minnie Palmer's many enterprises in the annals from that point on.

It is ironic that, of all her 'chicken farm' ventures, the only show of Minnie Palmer's that had any success was her home-grown Four Marx Brothers. All the other shows were flops. If she had any thoughts of an eventual comeback as a major theatrical *macher,* these were dashed by the return to the United States, in 1918, of the original Minnie Palmer. Having divested herself of her English husband, Jerrard, she remarried her manager, John Rogers, and reappeared, on the stage of the Gaiety, New York, as Mrs Jordan in the hit play *Lightnin'*, which ran for over 300 performances. To confuse matters further, she set herself up as a bona fide producer of her own musical shows.

The original Minnie Palmer died in 1936, at the age of eighty, having outlived her usurper by seven years.

Farewell to the Old Five-and-Dimes . . .

GROUCHO: Many years ago, I came to this country without a nickel in my pocket. Today – I have a nickel in my pocket.

The Cocoanuts (1925)

The bad old, bad old days. The vaudeville tales: Groucho, on those boarding-houses, the bedrooms which contained 'an iron bed, a lumpy mattress, a thin rug and a bowl and pitcher. Draped over the pitcher would be two sleazy face towels and two threadbare bath towels. By the end of the week the towels would be so dirty you would usually by-pass them and fan yourself dry . . . Room and board, seven dollars single per week. Two in a room, six dollars each. Three in a room, five-fifty apiece. One act I knew never patronized either a hotel or a boarding house. They slept on army cots in their dressing room and cooked all their meals on a Sterno stove . . .'
Harpo:

In Laredo [Texas] we shared the bill with one of the saddest vaudeville acts I ever saw – 'The Musical Cow Milkers.' It was a team. The guy led a live cow onstage; while his wife, in sunbonnet and pinafore, squatted on a stool and milked the cow, they sang duets.

After opening night the manager fired them. They would be replaced on the bill, he said, with a second solo by the 'Marx boy who wears the red wig and plays the big zither or whatever you call it.'

The musical half of the Musical Cow Milkers was very bitter about being fired. He walked across the border to Mexico and mailed a dead rabbit to the Laredo theatre manager . . .

Mr and Mrs Musical Cow Milker had three small children. Minnie went to bat for them. She yelled and wept and begged for the couple to be rehired. At length, her eloquence swayed the theatre manager.

'All right, all right,' he said. 'I'll take 'em back . . . I'll put 'em in place of the Marx Brothers. You're closed.'

There was the time Julius, standing in for the announcer, introduced a female impersonator billed as 'The Creole Fashion Plate' as 'The Queer Old Fashion Plate', and was fired.

Or 'Swayne's Rats and Cats': the rats dressed as jockeys riding on the cats round a miniature racetrack. One day, Groucho claimed, a rat from the sewer crawled up, scaring the pants off fellow performer Fanny Brice, and became the star of the show.

Groucho: 'We played towns I would refuse to be buried in today, even if the funeral were free and they tossed in a tombstone for lagniappe.'

All that sustained the Brothers, often, in these dismal surroundings, was the solidarity of the family. During the Chicago days, Frenchy began travelling with them, as accommodations manager and to arrange their posters and publicity with the theatre. Sometimes, Groucho and Harpo have reported, he would take over the boarding-house kitchens, though I would take this with a pinch of paprika. Groucho, in his aforementioned essay in *Redbook* magazine (1933), wrote about Frenchy's take-away services:

When we were living in Chicago, and playing . . . the five-a-day houses, Frenchy would come into our dressing room after the final matinées, with a big basket of food . . . no restaurant could provide roast chicken or kugel like Frenchy's.

After dinner was over and it was again our turn on the stage, Frenchy would pack his basket and rush out into the audience to provide his 'prop' laugh, which nearly always proved infectious   The prop laugh was designed not only to lead the rest of the audience into laughter, but to fool the managers, who unfortunately soon became as familiar with Frenchy's mechanical merriment as we were . . .

Frenchy, according to Julius, was then instructed by Minnie to go out and hire 'boosters', a whole claque of applauders to arouse a despondent audience. One apocryphal story has him sent out, as an advance scout, to a Midwest venue, getting on the wrong train, and calling long-distance back home to Minnie, asking plaintively: 'Minnie, vere am I?'

Early in the Chicago days, Frenchy had tried to return to the tailoring business – for example, his failed pants-pressing enterprise – according to Groucho. But city directory entries in this period invariably list him as 'commercial traveller', and in 1916 he is listed as 'salesman'. During the tour of the Interstate Circuit, Groucho claimed, Frenchy tried to open a cafeteria back in New York, but became lonely, joined the boys and closed the café, by long-distance phone call, from Dallas. The 'travelling salesman' gambit apparently involved selling cardboard boxes to grocery stores. But these were just ploys to keep Frenchy occupied, as the earning power of the family lay elsewhere.

Opie, on the other hand, enjoyed his idle old age, becoming more and more eccentric as he slid into his nineties, skating in the park and ogling the hired help. Having, in the family tradition, creatively altered his birth date, he was pretending to be a sage of one hundred years when he was in fact a mere stripling of ninety-six. Omie's harp had long mouldered away, and even Harpo's first replacement had been smashed up, in a train accident north of Mobile, Alabama, necessitating a brand new purchase.

It is an ironic twist to the saga that Leo was the first Marx Brother to marry. Of all the brothers, promiscuous Chico was the least likely candidate. But some years earlier, in 1914, his compulsive 'three-sheeting' had attracted a young girl who was, at that time, only sixteen. The place was Pittsburgh, and Leo was meeting Sophie Miller, a colleague from his Shapiro-Bernstein office days, who brought along her teenage friend, Betty Karp.

Leo persuaded young Betty, as he could persuade even a marble statue, to agree to a date. But, wisely wary of actors, she stood him up. Three years later, she turned up with another girlfriend at the Marxes' stage door, in Brooklyn. This girlfriend was always dropping famous names, and Betty wanted to show her she too knew a 'celebrity', a genuine Marx Brother.

As Chico and Betty's daughter Maxine tells the tale, Leo remembered: 'Hey, you're the little girl who stood me up in Pittsburgh.' Betty was nineteen, full of verve and spirit, with 'an exquisite figure, great legs, curly blue-black hair, and lovely olive skin.' Coming from a proper Jewish family, she was not one of the local yokels the Brothers could love and leave. If Leo wanted the goods, he had to pay the price. The knot was duly tied, in Chicago, by a properly accredited rabbi. Neither Minnie nor the other brothers were called to the ceremony, so urgent was Leo's need. Groucho, in particular, was so insulted he failed to invite Chico to his own wedding, three years later.

Betty was, according to Maxine, immediately inducted into the Grand Boulevard tribe:

It seemed as if an army was living under that one roof! Chico and Betty shared a room, the boys were doubled up . . . Then there was Opie . . . still incredibly vigorous at ninety, he went figure skating in the park. In the evenings, a mob of show business people would descend on the house to eat and make merry. Frenchy had bought a huge kettle – the kind they use in restaurants to boil soup – and there was something bubbling in it all day.

At first, Betty was intimidated by Minnie, who would come sweeping down to dinner in a chiffon dress and blonde wig designed to make her look far younger than her fifty-three years. Betty likened her to the Queen of Sheba. Leo had to caution his new wife about the intense solidarity and clannishness of the Dornum family. She learned her own lessons pretty rapidly when the other brothers each made advances to her. 'Their code of honor was nonexistent,' writes Maxine, 'nothing ventured, nothing gained.' Leo had to read them the rules of marriage: hands off! Writes Maxine: 'Years of touring the hinterlands, seeing the uglier side of people and life, made the boys callous and insensitive. In the world known to the Marx Brothers, only the fittest survived . . . If Betty couldn't take care of herself, too bad.'

Betty and Leo's marriage took place in March 1917, and was probably the reason for Leo's absence from the 'yokel' photograph at La Grange farm He obviously spent little time there, attending to his new bride at Grand Boulevard. When the Brothers recommenced their 'Home Again' tour in August, Betty was pregnant. She spent the months of her pregnancy at the farm, in the care of Frenchy, Herbert and assorted Schoenbergs. Her daughter, Maxine, was born in January 1918. Maxine was the first Marx grandchild, and the only Marx vaudeville baby, so far, toddling on the show business path.

As Maxine and Betty joined the Marx circus, another momentous change was occurring in the family: the departure of Milton-Gummo from the Marx Brothers' act and his replacement by Herbert – Zeppo.

Seventeen-year-old Herbert had, in addition to his talent for chinning up like 'Zippo' the chimp, developed an expertise with motor cars and machines. This was to stand him in good stead later in life but was, for the present, leading him down hazardous paths. Groucho, who omitted the Great War in Europe from his book, nevertheless spends quite a few pages on Zeppo's mechanical skills and his own love affair with automobiles – beginning with a hundred-and-fifty-dollars'-worth Scripps-Booth, and progressing to Studebakers, and beyond. This was, of course, the vaudevillians' grand prize – the American ideal of personal, individual mobility.

Both Zeppo and Gummo feature, in the Marx legends, as the funniest of the brothers off-stage. Groucho always used to say that Zeppo creased him up, and in private life had the wickedest gift for repartee. Zeppo's public life, unlike that of his brothers, was almost non-existent, and for any detailed descriptions in his own voice we have to turn to his recollections in his old age, as this, in Richard Anobile's *The Marx Brothers Scrapbook*:

> I never did care about show business. But my mother called me up to tell me that Gummo was leaving for the army and that she wanted to keep the name THE FOUR MARX BROS. intact. She insisted I join the act and that's what I did. I did have a bit of experience in that I had done a little singing and dancing as part of a cheap boy and girl act.

No trace of such an act can be found. But later still, in 1979, Zeppo gave more details of his reluctant transition, in his BBC interview with Barry Norman:

BBC (Barry Norman): You came into the act . . .
ZEPPO: Good thing I did, else I'd have gone to jail – really. I was working as a mechanic for the Ford Motor Company and I was a really bad boy. I was a kid, but I carried a gun and I stole automobiles. I was real bad and there was an older boy . . . about twenty and we were pedalling around. I loved to be with him because he was so tough and I sort of felt that if I got into any trouble he'd protect me, you know, so we both carried guns all the time.

Many years later, in Las Vegas, Zeppo came across a man who recognized him and introduced himself as the younger brother of that older boy, Louis Bass. Zeppo's youthful colleague had become a San Francisco dope dealer and had been killed in a shoot-out with the cops. 'That story', said Zeppo, 'shows how close my life would have been . . . like his.' But Minnie had called him to the flag – just as she had summoned 'Ahdie' from the nick-elodeon ten years earlier – and Herbert was saved from a life of crime. 'Gummo had danced and did some straight lines, so I ad libbed some of the lines . . . and the dancing I didn't do because I didn't know the routines.'

Milton, in fact, had long been growing weary with his role, as his son Robert explains:

'Gummo felt that he was the most dispensable of the group . . . the act was changing . . . becoming less of a song and dance act, and more of a comedy act, and he became the straight man. So when the opportunity came for him to go in the service he did that and left the act and that was his way of breaking out.'

Becoming the straight man had involved Milton in more dialogue than his continuing stutter allowed him to handle with any degree of comfort. He had been on the stage for thirteen years, a long time for a man with a speech impediment! A couple of years earlier, he had already expressed his unhappiness with the vaudevillian's life in two poems, which were published in *Variety*, in December 1915 and April 1916. The first reads:

The Wise Drummer
BY MILTON MARX

In these unenlightened days an actor doesn't seem to know
Just what his salary is going to be or where he is going to go;
But if he wants to find out, tho' his agent's in the air,
He walks into a smoking car and plumps down in a chair.
In walks a smart young travelling man with a 'cinco' in his mouth,
And greets you with, 'Hello, old chap! I met you in the south.
Say, that's too bad about that date in Ipswich being canned,
How can I fix your act so the finish gets a hand.
How'd that cut week strike you when you got six-sevenths pay?
It's a shame the way you actors have to lose a day.
I hear that Pam. has got a week or two around St. Paul.
Say, that guy had better stay out west, or he's in for a fall.
I guess you go to Chi next week. But those guys don't pay much,
And I would rather pay for less than jump and get in Dutch.
Well, here's my stop. Some rotten burg! So-long,' you'll hear him say,
And you have learned how much you get and where you're going to play.

Milton had, in fact, a hankering for the writing game, and took another recorded stab at it, in June 1919. A sketch preserved in the Library of Congress, entitled '"Adam's Apple" By Milton Marx', is a somewhat un-Marxian parody of a Cook's Tour of Paradise and the other place, featuring Adam, Eve, the Devil, Methuselah, Noah and the Kaiser, no less, as the new King of Hell. One Professor Masters and his two daughters enter the Garden of Eden to do biological research, but not, alas, to herald any quality lines:

DEVIL: What's the matter, Adam, where are you going?
ADAM: Going home. I'm sick of this life.
EVE: And me, too.
DEVIL: Well, if you wait a while I'll go with you . . . But first we must fix these young people up . . . (*Enter rest of company. Song.*)

This sketch is the very first Marx Brother play script I have found. It was obviously never performed, and although Milton dabbled with a typewriter afterwards it was not where his main interest, or talent, lay.

Milton never returned to the stage. Having joined the army at the brink of the armistice, he was assigned to the Chicago University Training Detachment, where a friendly captain who recognized him as a Marx Brother made him an 'acting corporal'. The appropriately farcical aftermath was described by Gummo in *The Marx Brothers Scrapbook*:

Groucho and Harpo bought second hand cars and they would loan their cars to me . . . The captain and I would be using the cars to pick up all the dames in the various shows in Chicago. I'd go out with these dames and have a hell of a good time . . . After six weeks I was sent for by the captain who told me he had room for a top sergeant or a supply sergeant and asked me which I'd like to be. I said that I'd like to be a supply sergeant and he said that that was very wise since we didn't have any supplies . . . Well, this was a great life. I had soldiers cleaning my cars for me! This went on for quite some time when all of a sudden the captain is made a major and sent overseas. [A second captain, named Thurston, took up where the first one left off.] Thurston eventually fell in love with a girl, one of two beautiful sisters. Both of them wanted to go on stage so I taught them to sing and dance and got some friends of mine who had theatres to book them. The girl he fell in love with ended up marrying a songwriter.

This was Gummo's first act as an agent, the role that would be his mainstay in later years. Meanwhile, he was soon released from the army in 1919, Germany having been vanquished without his assistance, and went back to New York. Relates Robert Marx:

'[Gummo] came out of the army and ended up in the dress business, but he was doing some other things. Gummo had an inventive mind. He invented this cardboard . . . concept of, here's a box right here, like the old laundry boxes, and they were wasting all the sides, and he created a machine that you would put the laundry on the machine and it would automatically size it in the right size and it would save all that cardboard.'

After an initial success this great enterprise foundered, but Milton had other ideas, such as his invention of the first skidless tyre. Robert Marx:

'He had this prototype manufactured, put on a car, and I think it was in Akron, Ohio . . . he got the heads of the tyre companies come out and watch a demonstration of this skidless tyre, and he had Zeppo drive the car. The car was up on a great big hill, and Zeppo came down the hill, and when he got to where all the luminaries from the tyre company were standing he hit the brakes . . . The tyres stopped, grabbed the road, but the car went right on through, and the tyres were just laying there on the ground, and that was the end of the skidless tyre.'

Shades of W. C. Fields's Samuel Bisbee, in the 1934 film, *You're Telling Me!*

By 1919, The Marx Brothers' 'Home Again' was played out, and required a transfusion of new material, not just a younger Brother. In October 1918, the Brothers had their first stab at a 'legitimate' musical, commissioned from veteran writer Jo Swerling and songwriters Gus Kahn and Egbert Van Alstyne. This was probably the last show Milton appeared in, but it was closed almost before it opened. The première, in Grand Rapids, Michigan, coincided with the arrival in town of the great flu epidemic which was killing people in their thousands throughout the country. It was a uniquely terrifying epidemic in that it appeared to target the young and hale rather than the old, whom medical scholars have speculated might have been immunized by a previous, less lethal strain in the 1880s (perhaps the strain that carried off Manfred?). No one wanted to congregate in crowded, closed spaces, and those courageous or foolhardy enough to attend the theatres sat far from each other in the empty halls. By 8 November the show was dropped, and the old material revived, renamed as 'The Four Marx Brothers Revue'. This version opened at the Palace in Chicago on 7 February 1919, when the epidemic had begun to abate, as rapidly and mysteriously as it had started.

Variety's review awarded Julius special notice:

Julius Marx is developing into an actor. He shows flashes of Louis Mahn, at least a chemical trace of David Wakefield and at times reflects the canny technique of Barney Bernard. Julius has a strongly defined sense of humour. His asides are more funny than the set lines. He is a confirmed ad-libber, and claims he had a right to interpolate, he having written the material for the act.

Once again, we have no text to show this. But the act was adapting further. Within a few weeks it had yet another new name, 'N'Everything'. The writing was credited, still, to Al Shean:

Julius has the role of Henry Hammer, who makes a lot of acquaintances on shipboard, many of whom do not appeal to his 'high-browed' wife, son and daughter. He invites them to a party at his villa on the

Hudson. Arthur Marx . . . never says a word, but as a comedian, he is an artist . . . Leonard Marx as Chico Baroni, an Italian, boobs the part and is a splendid piano player. Herbert Marx, the fourth of the brothers, takes the part of a 'sissy' son of Hammer.

Zeppo can't have liked this at all. According to the *Louisville Herald*, 'There are several comely girls in the company, but their singing is offered without dancing. The dancing is done by Julius Marx, who is surprisingly agile . . .'

The act flowed on, into winter 1919. In November, *Variety* noted that the Brothers had signed a three-year contract with Broadway producer Charles Dillingham. By January they were back in New York, playing major houses, Keith's Alhambra and the Colonial. Then they toured again. While they were on tour in Winnipeg, Canada, on 13 February 1920, Grandpa Louis, Levy Schoenberg, died in New York City. The newspapers announced that he was 101 years old. As he was in fact only ninety-seven, he had left himself the last laugh. And so the ventriloquist of Dornum passed away, taking with him the secrets of his life on the road, in a world far off in place and time, but having passed on, to the next but one generation, the echoes of his craft and his sardonic and mischievous spirit . . .

Levy's death marked the end of an era in more ways than one. The Marx Brothers were a standard act, at the top of a profession that, as a genre, was slowly dying. Vaudeville was in terminal decline. The golden years, from 1900 to the eve of the First World War, could not be revived. A new popular art, the cinema, was replacing it. The Brothers had, they claimed, met its emperor, Charlie Chaplin, while he was still a boy actor with the Fred Karno company, touring Winnipeg and Vancouver. He is reputed to have told the Brothers he had been offered $500 a week from Mack Sennett to make movies, but had declined, thinking the work wouldn't last. The year was 1912. Chaplin was making his living spitting oranges and crackers at the soprano on the stage. Groucho remembered him as wearing a dirty white collar and a black bow tie, 'like a pale priest who had been excommunicated, but was reluctant to relinquish his vestments'.

By 1920, Chaplin was the Pope of comedy. But the Marx Brothers were still, at most, bishops.

At least they had graduated from pawns.

ACT III

The Four Horsemen of the Apoplexy

There Is No Chapter 13 in This Book

'Washington with a Mustache'

GROUCHO: Pardon me while I have a strange interlude . . .

Animal Crackers (1930)

On 11 November 1918, President Woodrow Wilson sat down at his desk to write, in pencil, the following message to the American People:

'My Fellow Countrymen: The armistice was signed this morning. Everything for which America fought has been accomplished. It will now be our fortunate duty to assist by example, by sober, friendly counsel, and by material aid in the establishment of just democracy throughout the world.'

Three and a half million Americans had been inducted into the war effort, and now they were all to come home and, it was to be hoped, find jobs. While Europe stood aghast over the mass graves of a generation bled to death in the trenches, America, while mourning her own losses, girded up for a ticker-tape celebration. The leadership, speaking of a sober aftermath, took steps to ensure this would be so literally, by prohibiting the sale and manufacture of alcohol. The National Prohibition Act, or Volstead Act, was passed on 28 October 1919, and came into effect at the birth of the new decade (although the puritan President himself opposed the bill). Overnight, an entirely new culture of illegal boozing sprang up. It was the speakeasy age, and everybody had to know the password: Swordfish!

The establishment's watchword at the beginning of the 1920s was 'Normalcy'. Its perfect proponent was Warren G. Harding, a small-time Ohio politician who became President in 1921, and was promptly bogged down in a swamp of allegations of mismanagment and graft. The year before, female suffrage was granted, one of Woodrow Wilson's last legacies. Minnie Marx, among America's hundred million women, could vote, though her preferences remained, as ever, domestic.

With the enemy without vanquished, an enemy within was discovered: the Communists, alleged followers of the Workers' Revolution that had grabbed Russia in 1917. Only one week after the 1918 Armistice, New York's Mayor

Hylan outlawed the red flag in his city. A Socialist mass meeting in Madison Square Garden was broken up by police. All labour activists were tarred with the red brush and all strikes seen as Bolshevist tricks. Patriotism ran riot. In Indiana a jury acquitted in two minutes a man who had shot a foreigner for shouting: 'To hell with the United States!' Blacks, Jews and Catholics also felt the ire of the whipped-up search for agitators. The Ku Klux Klan was revitalized. The conservative *Christian Science Monitor* published an editorial in June 1920 decrying 'The Jewish Peril' and quoting segments of the forged 'Protocols of the Elders of Zion'. In Massachusetts, in April that year, two Italian anarchists, Sacco and Vanzetti, were arrested, then tried and sentenced to death, on flimsy evidence, for a double murder during a payroll robbery, a case that sparked off widespread outrage and protest.

Julius Marx must have mopped his brow in relief that he had dropped the German Henry Schneider from his repertoire as early as 1915. Leo was still imitating his Italian barber, but Arthur, wisely, was keeping stum. Herbert had not many lines anyway. Like most show business people, they were zealously non-political in public, satisfied to provide an entertainment that had literally 'everything – numbers, sets, riotous comedy, every kind of instrumentalism, pretty girls, versatility, good-natured frolicking, lighting effects'. And they were still decidedly Mama's boys. *Variety*, 16 June 1920:

> It was Mothers' night at the Majestic. Jack Osterman and the Marx Brothers came down into the house and kissed their mothers, the same going to riotous applause. The acts that had no mothers were out of luck. There were one or two others, though, that could have had their mothers in, because this bill, like most of them, had a goodly percentage of Chicagoans . . .

Momism apart, there were other cultural strands in the air. A different view of family and home was implicit in the dramas of Broadway's newest hero, Eugene O'Neill, whose Pulitzer Prize-winning play, *Beyond the Horizon*, opened at the Morosco Theatre in February 1920. The war, distant as it had been, had nevertheless shaken loose old certainties, and new voices of social criticism were being heard. Between women's suffrage and the 'flapper' – the girl of newly defined desires and independence – and her predators – the young men with the hip flasks and sports cars – morality was being redefined, and old mores contemptuously discarded. Youth was in, age was out. The automobile brought a new mobility. The cinema provided an escape into other lives, into the central dynamic of America's machine age and the growth of a new, consumers' society. There was an exciting new medium, radio, which broadcast the national election on 2 November 1920 and would soon reach into almost every home. The mail could now be delivered, coast to coast, by aeroplane.

This was the golden age of the American city, and of the greatest American city, New York. No longer the immigrant station for those huddled masses, it was firmly installed as the country's commercial and cultural centre. As cultural historian Ann Douglas put it, New York was 'trendsetter to the nation and the world. New York finds its job in the commercialization of mood swings: the city translates the shifting national psyche into fashions of all kinds, from ladies' frocks and popular music to Wall Street stocks, ad layouts, and architectural designs.'

In this city which was constantly on the move there was nurtured a new élite, not the business giants of the nineteenth century like J. P. Morgan or Andrew Carnegie, but a coterie of writers, journalists, columnists, commentators, playwrights and musicians. Foremost among these were the people who could wield the awesome opinion-forming power of the modern press: the newspaper columnists, the men – still always the men – who decided what was new and what was old, what was art and what was trash, who was in and who was out.

Perhaps paradoxically, the most influential among these new opinion-leaders was a man who spurned New York for his native Baltimore, the iconoclastic H. L. Mencken. Descended from a long line of learned Germans through his grandfather, who settled in Baltimore in the mid-nineteenth century, and was in the cigar-making trade (no, he was not Harpo's 'Gookie'!), young Henry Louis Mencken was a precocious reader who discovered Mark Twain at the age of nine, and read voraciously after. But, in his late teens, he decided to spend his life not in an academic field but in the 'real world', and chose the life of a journalist. As he described his choice: 'To lay in all the wordly wisdom of a police lieutenant, a bartender, a shyster lawyer, and a midwife.' Mencken developed a prose that was shrewd and observant, unwaveringly critical of received wisdoms. In writing on 'The Art Eternal' of lying, in 1918:

> For the habitual truth-teller and truth-seeker . . . the world has very little liking. He is always unpopular, and not infrequently his unpopularity is so excessive that it endangers his life . . . Especially in the United States is his whole enterprise viewed with a bilious eye. The men the American people admire most extravagantly are the most daring liars; the men they detest most violently are those who try to tell them the truth . . .

From 'The Artist', 1924:

It is almost as safe to assume that an artist of any dignity is against his country, i.e., against the environment in which God hath placed him, as it is to assume that his country is against the artist. The special quality which makes an artist of him might almost be defined, indeed, as an extraordinary capacity for irritation, a pathological sensitiveness to environmental pricks and stings . . . He is, in brief, a more delicate fellow than we are, and hence less fitted to prosper and enjoy himself under the conditions of life which he and we must face alike . . .

The artists cited by Mencken were Dante, Tolstoy, Shakespeare, Mark Twain, Goethe, Heine, Shelley, Cervantes, Swift, Dostoevsky and the like. But other fellow critics and columnists would soon extend this category further, into the less exalted realms of popular art, which they would raise up, by the awesome power of the press, into an intellectual domain far removed from The Musical Cow Milkers, The Creole Fashion Plate, the Whangdoodle Four and Swayne's Rats and Cats. And foremost among these critics, these shakers and movers, was the rotund, eccentric and unstoppable figure of Alexander Woollcott, writer, raconteur, *bon vivant*, who will soon make his grand entrance on to our stage.

Our humble heroes, meanwhile, although still whirling in Whangdoodleland, were not unaware of the ferment that gripped the big city after the war. Their social circle was far removed from the dining rooms of the élite, or even, at this time, from the soon-to-become-famous 'round table' at the Algonquin Hotel. Leonard still preferred the gambling rooms and pool halls where he could fraternize with such luminaries as 'Nick the Greek' and other sharp operators. Together with his brother Arthur, he also consorted with show people and sports personalities like the boxer Benny Leonard, who often toured conducting exhibition bouts.

But Julius was still the family bookworm. While in Chicago, he had frequented the central Covici-McGee book shop, where many well-known writers could be encountered. Luminaries such as Carl Sandburg, Sherwood Anderson, even Theodore Dreiser, might be found there, not to speak of upcoming smart-mouths like Ben Hecht, already carving a unique career in journalism. These were people who represented a world of fine art and fresh thinking well outside the confines of the vaudeville show and its daily, repetitive grind. It was a world Julius Henry Marx looked up to with great enthusiasm.

But he was, as yet, a reader, not a writer. The great writing talents who would shape him as an author in his own right had not yet got their scalpels into his brain. The character he was to become, on stage and screen, was only partly formed as he approached the age of thirty. He was still, in 1920, the quickfire gagster of that earlier age of Uncle Al Shean.

This much is evident from Julius's first known piece of writing, a hitherto unknown sketch, lying dormant in the Library of Congress, entitled 'Art in Vaudeville: An Original Vaudeville Idea in One Act, Billed as Two Separate Acts, by Herbert Ashley and Julius H. Marx'. The four-page skit was registered for copyright on 24 May 1920.

Herbert Ashley, co-writer of this piece, was 'a comedian of the Jewish type', who plied his trade as a double act, first with Al Lee in an act called 'Chinatown' and then with Jack Allman, as a Jew and an Irishman duo. 'Art in Vaudeville' was intended as a vehicle for Ashley and one 'Madame Vici, in a cycle of melodies'. It was probably never performed. The sketch is a dialogue between a vaudeville actor and a stuck-up dame – note the similarity to the society lady later to be personified in the Marx Brothers' shows and movies by the peerless Margaret Dumont:

– I am Madam Vici, they call me the woman without a soul.
– You may be without a sole, but you're vici on top.
– I have studied for ten years in Europe under the best directors.
– Yes, but someone gave you the wrong directions . . .
– In my mind's eye, I can see myself now, as I strode on the stage, there was no scenery up, everything was bare.
– Weren't you ashamed to go on the stage like that? . . .
– This was the very gown I had on.
– I should say you was bare! . . .
– After I left Paris, I went . . . through every Court in Europe.
– Say, you haven't anything on me, I've been in a few courts myself. Say, I've been arrested for bigamy, non-support and spitting.
– I didn't know that you had an Auto?
– Not speeding, spitting . . .

Simple stuff, no doubt, but we can see the roots of things to come. Prohibition, of course, also figures in the wisecracks: 'A jail ain't such a bad place, it's about the only place left you can see any bars.' And some lines are pure Groucho-and-Maggie:

– I'll never forget how the Greeks fell at my feet.
– I had a couple at my feet this morning, but fifteen cents is too much for a shine.

The sketch is unfinished, suggesting, at the end, that it would introduce 'an original dialogue idea, consisting of popular songs, immediately followed by an original parody on each song'. In other words, much as the Brothers had been proceeding in their earlier shows.

But 'Art in Vaudeville' was clearly not going to solve the problem of the Marx Brothers' urgent need for new material. In the uniquely hot and sweltering summer of 1920, Minnie and her sons put on their thinking caps and tried to figure out a way forward. Al Shean, the usual crutch, was not available, as he was away building his act with Ed Gallagher.

Step forward, a new collaborator: Herman Timberg. Fellow graduate of Gus Edwards's academy, Timberg had played the little Russian immigrant boy Izzy Levy in Edwards's original 'School Boys and Girls'. He was known in the trade as 'the pint-sized humorist'. Song writer, composer, fiddler *extraordinaire*, one of his 'foremost contributions' to show business, said his *Variety* obituary in April 1952, was 'the Timberg "crawl-off"', a comic movement in which he went offstage on all fours. Not quite Eugene O'Neill, but it got a laugh. Timberg's mission now: to boldly crawl forward and provide for the Marx Brothers a new vehicle which would propel them from the diminishing returns of vaudeville into the world of the fully-fledged revue.

The vessel constructed for this journey was entitled, initially, 'The Mezzanine Floor'. A few months later it was renamed 'On the Balcony'.

Here at last is a text, also yielded for the first time by the Library of Congress, which enables us to chart how far the characters created and performed by the Brothers in the past decade had evolved, before their encounters with the big guns, or typewriters, of George S. Kaufman and other top-drawer writers.

'On the Balcony' opens with the now famous scene in the office of the theatrical manager, which was repeated in the later show *I'll Say She Is*, and filmed, in 1931, as a publicity short for Paramount Pictures: 'My name is Sammy Brown and I've just got into town . . .' Each of the Brothers enters for his own rhyming sequence, Chico following Zeppo on the stage (the only one of the Brothers to be described by his nickname here is Chico):

MANAGER: Come in, you want to talk to me.
CHICO: I want to talk to Mr Lee.
MANAGER: I'm Mr Lee.
BOBBY (Zeppo): That's him.

CHICO: I see – you want a very good actor – yes? I'm the guy you want, I guess. I no speaka da very good English, but I'm fulla da pep and I gotta da ambish.

MANAGER: What do you do?

CHICO: Acrobat!

MANAGER: What's your name?

CHICO: Zbysko – but the best thing that I do is to give the imitation of [Joe] Frisco.

Chico does the imitation, which does not do him much good. The next to knock on the door is Groucho:

(*Enter Mr. Hammer*)

HAMMER: I want to speak to Mr Lee. I'm a dramatic actor.

CHICO: Oh, I see, that's Mr Lee.

HAMMER: Lend an ear to me.

MANAGER: Can you play a role?

HAMMER: Can I play a role? Do you know who you're looking at? I'll play any kind of role . . . And I'll eat it up like that (*snaps fingers*). I played a part in *Ben Hur* once.

MANAGER: What part did you play?

HAMMER: The Girl, she played the part of Ben.

MANAGER: And you?

HAMMER: And I played her.

MANAGER: When you go out, don't slam the door.

HAMMER: You are kidding me, are you not?

MANAGER: Kidding you? Say, I've been her[e] all day – now show me what you got.

HAMMER: I want to play a dramatic part – the kind that touches a woman's heart. To make her cry – for me to die –

CHICO: Did you ever get hit with a custard pie? . . .

HAMMER: I'll give a recitation – or would you prefer to see me give my Frisco imitation?

Harpo, next, breezes in, holding his hand for a handshake and walking past. Business with his cane and horn. He hands Manager his card, which Mr Lee reads out: 'My name is What-do-you-care. My address is anywhere. The people say I'm very dumb, so I thought to you I'd come.' Hammer: 'Wait a minute, maybe he is crazy . . .' To Harpo: 'Do you want to get on the stage?' Harpo nods gleefully. Hammer: 'Crazy.'

BOBBY: I have a manuscript for a one act musical comedy, you put these boys in it and they will be a knock-out.

MANAGER: Any Frisco imitations?

BOBBY: No, sir, not a one.

MANAGER: Sit down, my boy. I'm always willing to listen to new material (*as he says this business of boys moving desk and chairs and generally upsetting office*).

MANAGER: Say, what is this?

BOBBY: Well, my first scene takes place in a hotel – there are a lot of pretty girls –

MANAGER: You're not going to explain the plot to me, are you?

BOBBY: I was just going to –

MANAGER: (*interrupts*) Give me a show with lots of comedy, with pretty girls and a few fast comedians, and you can't miss. With a plot you are taking a chance, and when you give the audience a chance to concentrate it makes them think and when you give the audience a chance to think that's the time they get wise to you, and the result is that you have to do your business through the cut rate ticket office (*as he says this he slams his hand on desk and misses hat and boys do business of grabbing hats and putting them on their heads*).

BOBBY: Well my story has no plot and means absolutely nothing.

MANAGER: That's what I want!

This Manager's credo is not in the short film version. The script continues on to Part Two, the curtain going up on the Mezzanine Floor, and the girls coming out to sing, 'What would become of the musical show if it weren't for beautiful girls?' What, indeed? This segues into a step-dance including Bobby and Hammer – Zeppo and Groucho. As the House Detective enters, Hammer throws his coat over his head. This introduces the plot, which involves the *ingénue*, Dorothy Gould, whose father made an agreement with Hammer fifteen years earlier that his daughter and Hammer's son would be married when they came of age –

DETECTIVE: Well you know Mr Gould was sick two years before he died.

HAMMER: I guess that's vot killed him.

DETECTIVE: He left this hotel to his daughter. She is his sole possessor and beneficiary.

The Detective being the girl's guardian, a long argy-bargy ensues between him and Hammer over the legal documents. The Detective was played by Ed Metcalfe, who had played the cop in 'Home Again' for several years, and had settled into the role. He was the stooge who shook Harpo's hand on the dock, precipitating the long cascade of stolen silverware from Harpo's coat – a part he was to carry forward into the Brothers' movie version of *Animal Crackers*.

Enter Mrs Gould, another embryonic Margaret Dumont. She will only consider marrying off her daughter to a good musician, since her deceased husband adored music. But Hammer's only son is Bobby, who is a musical dunce. To overcome this obstacle, Hammer calls the Musicians' Union to engage two unemployed candidates:

HAMMER (*business of telephone*): Hello, Gumchewer, give me two wrong numbers, then give me the Musicians' Union. 'Union,' u-n-u-n. Hello Une. Say, have you got a couple of men who are out of work? Oh, they're all out of work? Oh, it's a union. Well, send me a couple of men that look like me. What do I look like? Did you ever see Lincoln without a beard? Well, I look like Washington with a mustache.

The two engaged musicians are, of course, Chico and Harpo, the latter causing complete consternation when introduced to Mrs Gould:

MRS GOULD: What a queer looking object – who brought it here?
HAMMER: Quinine, go ahead and give your future wife a kiss.
MRS GOULD: What?
HAMMER: She's got to be his wife. (*Shows her the agreement*)
MRS GOULD: Don't you think I ought to be consulted in this matter?
HAMMER: I'll insult you later.

Chico is also introduced with some flimflam:

HAMMER: Mrs Gould, I want you to meet my son Geshveer.
CHICO: My name is Chico.
DETECTIVE: I thought his name was Geshveer.
HAMMER: That's what I always call him, but his mother calls him Chico. Put them together they spell Zweibach . . .

A note for linguists: *Geshveer* is Yiddish for an ulcer or abscess, and *Zweibach*, apart from being a toasted cracker, can literally translate as 'two bangs', or even 'two rivers', if you want to be poetic. Harpo proceeds, as he did in 'Home Again,' to hypnotize the girls in the show, while Chico hypnotizes Harpo to the piano. 'Business of turning stool and bending down until it comes up to him, then plays a few chords and spits on his hands . . .' All stuff recognizable to fans of the Marx Brothers' later incarnations. There follow more high jinks with Mrs Gould on the sofa:

HAMMER: You won't believe it, but from the first time that I set eyes on you there is something I'm ashamed of and I think it's you. Oh, dear, when I'm with you I'm so lonesome – won't you please let me alone?

Cue various musical specialities, with imitations, à la 'Mr Green's Reception', of famous stars like Ann Pennington, Marilyn Miller, and Groucho doing the blackfaced Eddie Leonard:

HAMMER: These are the Four Horsemen of the Apoplexy. Now since they all have relations of their own, that makes me a nephew to George M. Cohan . . .

The script then gets awfully confusing, as Mrs Gould seems to want to marry her daughter Dorothy off to Harpo, leading to a wedding ceremony with Harpo unable to say 'I do' as he is busy eating a banana. Hammer remonstrating – 'Now all is lost – now we ain't got a quarter of a million – no estate – no girl – all you got now is a banana . . .' Harpo shows him a bottle of whisky. Hammer: 'Well, maybe it ain't so bad after all.'

But all is well. Bobby and Dorothy, now betrothed to each other, and the chorus girls, come out for the finale, to the strains of the wedding march:

GIRLS: Mr Hammer, Mr Hammer, we have some news for you. Mr Lee has packed his trunk and said that he was through. He leaves for home today.

HAMMER: Are you sure he went away? Well, believe me when I say he was the worst one in the play.

GIRLS: Mr Hammer, Mr Hammer, he doesn't like the plot –

HAMMER: No one's going to worry about the little plot we got.

Detective enters –

HAMMER: Goodbye, goodbye. I hate to see you go.

DETECTIVE: Goodbye, goodbye, and what a terrible show.

(Enter Bobby and Dorothy)

BOTH: What's the matter? What's the matter?

HAMMER: He doesn't like our act.

DETECTIVE: I like the patter.

BOTH: Well, what's the matter?

DETECTIVE: I didn't like the way your story ended.

BOTH: What did he say?

DETECTIVE: And I don't like your dialect.

(Chico enters)

CHICO: For twenty a week, what do you expect?

DETECTIVE: It sounded good when first you read it to me – Now here's the only remedy that I can see – You'll have to go into a great big dance and they'll forget about the rest.

COMPANY: Give us a chance and we'll do our best . . .

COMPANY: We thank you, Mr. Lee.

HAMMER: What do you think of me?

DETECTIVE: I don't use that kind of language. (*Harpo enters*) Who is this guy who plays the harp? He should have more to say.

HAMMER: Once we let him speak two words and they pinched us right away.

DETECTIVE: You'll have to go into a great big dance and I'll come up and help you out.

COMPANY: Thank you, Mr Lee. Play a dancing melody and we'll go over with a shout.

(*Company do finale dance*)

CURTAIN.

Humor Risks

GROUCHO: I love you! Why don't you marry me?
MRS TEASDALE: Why, marry you?!
GROUCHO: You take me and I'll take a vacation. I'll need a vacation if
we're going to get married! . . . Married! I can see you right now in the
kitchen, bending over a hot stove, but I can't see the stove . . . come,
come, say the word and you'll never see me again . . .

Duck Soup (1933)

The first year of the 1920s was marked, apart from the Great Red Scare, by
two other vital Marxian events – Groucho's first marriage, and the Brothers'
first, little-known stab at the production of motion pictures.

On 4 February 1920, Julius Henry Marx married Ruth Johnson,
daughter of a Swedish immigrant, Oscar Johnson. Johnson was described as
a journeyman carpenter with two daughters, neither of whom had any
dowry. The Chicago city directories, on the other hand, identify Oscar
Johnson as variously 'manufacturer's agent', 'salesman' and 'commercial
traveller' (same profession as Samuel 'Frenchy' Marx) and list his address as
5249 Calumet Avenue, a stone's throw from the Marx family's own first
Chicago abode in the same street. This suggests the families might have
known each other for some time, which is at odds with the description of
Ruth's entry into the saga as set out by Zeppo in his 1979 BBC interview:

ZEPPO: I never considered Groucho a very great lover. Chico was all right
and Harpo and Gummo were fine.
BARRY NORMAN: Groucho was rather romantic about women, wasn't he?
ZEPPO: He would get a girl and she would be very stupid and he would
talk to her, oh, about Gilbert and Sullivan. He would try to impress
'em that way where the rest of us would just get right to it . . .
B. N.: Ruth Johnson joined your act as your dancing partner, then she
married Groucho, didn't she?
ZEPPO: She was stupid and she was very pretty and I really got stuck on

her just by seeing her. And . . . I said, 'Would you like to go into show business,' and she said 'Yes.' I said, 'Can you dance?' and she said 'No.' I said, 'Well, I'll teach you,' so I got her the job. And of course Groucho eyed her immediately . . .

Zeppo's unkind characterization of Ruth must be put down to his pique at being upstaged by his intellectual brother; a rebuff that still rankled, up to the last year of his life! Ruth clearly preferred being swept off her feet by Julius to being hurled about the stage by his youngest sibling. Julius, at the ripe age of thirty, was a mischievous and witty catch, though already cloaked in a choking cloud of cigar smoke. Grace Kahn, wife of songwriter Gus Kahn, who wrote the songs for the influenza-plagued 'Street Cinderella', remembered the puckish Groucho of that period, in an interview with film historian Anthony Slide:

> I was working for Remick & Company, that was a big music publisher, and they sent me as a song-plugger, to go to Grand Rapids and get Groucho to sing this song when he came to Chicago . . . I rapped at the door and he said, Come in . . . sit down. And I said, I'm from the publisher and I'm here about a song. He said, have a cigar! I said, No thank you. We started to talk about the song, and he said, You want to take a shower? That was my first meeting with Groucho.

But far from the last, as, in the twists and turns of fate, Grace Kahn's daughter, Irene, was to marry Groucho's son, Arthur. It is not on record whether Julius offered his own wife-to-be, Ruth, the above form of ablutionary bonding on their first date.

Much has been made, above all by Groucho himself, of young Julius's sexual mores, not to speak of old Julius, the 'Mangy Lover' of Groucho's second book of essays, published in 1963, with chapter headings such as 'Horsing Around With My Hormones', 'L'Amour the Merrier', 'Social Notes from a Social Outcast', and 'The Unnatural History of Love':

'I must point out that the anthropologists fail to tell us how the earliest man learned the facts of love. My own deductions are that the amoeba and the oyster got their knowledge, just as you did, from the stories of flowers and their pollen and an exhaustive study of *The Tropic of Cancer* and *The Carpetbaggers*.'

The real sexual education of Homo Grouchomarxus appeared, according to more unguarded confessions, to have had much more to do with black chambermaids at various hotels. We have noted his singular lack of prowess at 'three-sheeting'. Whorehouses were another staple, according to his outpourings to Charlotte Chandler in *Playboy* Magazine, in 1974:

PLAYBOY: What was your first physical relationship with a woman?
GROUCHO: Going to bed.
PLAYBOY: We're going to be more careful about how we phrase things.
How did you lose your virginity?
GROUCHO: In a hook shop in Montreal. I was 16 years old and I didn't know anything about girls. Before I left town, I had gonorrhea.

Groucho loved telling those tales in his old age, but in his mid-eighties he had a shaky grasp of the consequences. When, in 1973, Richard Anobile published *The Marx Brothers Scrapbook*, based on several long, uncensored taped interviews, Groucho furiously tried to stop publication, having realized, too late, the full extent of his four-lettered tirades: 'I was trying to fuck a girl who worked in a bakery shop in LaGrange. Chico was also trying to fuck her. He did pretty good. Anyway it was a lousy bakery!' Anobile: 'Now where were we?' Groucho: 'I think we were talking about cunt!'

As the man himself might have said: 'Love goes out the door when sex comes innuendo!' The Marx Brothers were unashamed predators, in an era when women were expected to adjust to this habit of the common male, as a fact of life. But even a gentleman always kept double standards, and an actor triple or quadruple ones. The underlying reality, in Julius's young adulthood, was his intense shyness, despite his strong urge to perform. It took some time for Julius Henry Marx to develop his armoury – his ten-cent cheroots, his dancing eyebrows and his non-stop patter – to face down the world.

Groucho wrote, in *Memoirs of a Mangy Lover*: 'A poor man's pet is definitely not a chorus girl, but nevertheless some day I hope to own one.' This may well have said more than might have been intended about his marriage to Ruth Johnson, long-term neighbours or not. In the hazy glow of 1920, however, Ruth and Julius's troubles lay in the future. The marriage duly took place in Chicago, despite the obstacles caused by their different religions, and the fact that Ruth's mother, Josephine, was, according to Groucho, a serial Christian – having dabbled in Mormonism, Christian Science, Baptism and Seventh Day Adventism, before settling for the straight Protestant ticket. Ma Johnson was not keen on her daughter marrying a Jew, went the tale, until she saw his salary slip.

According to Groucho's son, Arthur, Julius heckled the Justice of the Peace throughout the ceremony (Arthur, of course, wasn't there, but quoted his namesake uncle, Harpo), responding to 'We are gathered here to join this couple in holy matrimony' with: 'It may be holy to you, Judge, but we have other ideas.'

Justice of the Peace: 'Do you, Julius, take this woman to be your lawful wedded wife?'

Julius: 'I've gone this far, I might as well go through with it.'

Like all good troupers, bride and groom repaired back to the theatre for the night's orchestrated mayhem. Their firstborn, Arthur, made his grand entrance on 21 July 1921, and promptly joined three-year-old Maxine on the road.

Two Marxes down and three to go.

In 1920, the Brothers were still presenting their pot-pourri, 'N'Everything'. By the autumn, however, they had made a decision to move back east, to New York City. Leo was the first to move back there, setting up base in a West 55th Street apartment with Betty and Maxine. During their latest western tour, meanwhile, in Los Angeles, the Brothers had renewed their acquaintance with the little 'excommunicated priest' they had first met in Vancouver, in 1911, Charles Chaplin. Maxine has a pithy tale to tell about that 1911 meeting. When the Brothers invited the still unknown Chaplin to see their act, he sat through it pointedly reading his newspaper. Writes Maxine: 'They, in retaliation, sent four Orthodox Jews to a performance, who arrived wearing the traditional Hassidic garb: long black coats, broad black hats, and long, flowing beards. Chaplin outdid himself, but got no reaction from his guests, who he assumed were the Brothers in disguise. Finally, Chaplin's pantomime grew so outrageous that the four men in black stood up and silently filed out.'

It is unlikely that Hassidic Jews would attend a *goyisch* vaudeville performance, but why spoil a good story with logic? Two decades later, the 'little tramp' had a more satisfying method of upstaging his rivals. Chaplin's lavish dinner table completely overwhelmed the Brothers with its display of the fruits of Hollywood stardom. 'He was so rich', Groucho told Hector Arce, 'that he had a butler behind each chair, and the dinner was served on solid gold plates.'

It was pretty clear where the real mazoomah beckoned – and it was not on the Pantages or B. F. Keith circuits. What was good for the boy from Fred Karno's roadshow was certainly good enough for the Marx Brothers. But theirs, Harpo apart, was a verbal comedy, basically unsuited to the silent cinema. Nevertheless, those solid gold plates! And so, in New York, the Brothers embarked on their first kinematographic enterprise.

Groucho ruefully told the tale in his 1931 *Saturday Evening Post* essay, 'Bad Days Are Good Memories':

> Chico, Zeppo and I each contributed $1,000; and similar amounts came from the author, Jo Swerling, and two friends who would rather be nameless, although their names are Al Posen and Max Lippman. To be sure, the art and business of making movies were profound mysteries to all of us, especially Jo, who, maybe because of this, has since become a celebrated Hollywood author. But our lack of knowledge and experience did not keep us from going ahead. And go ahead we did, to Fort Lee, New Jersey, where somehow or other the picture got itself finished.

Several members of the 'N'Everything' cast, including Mildred Davis, co-star and soon to be wife of Harold Lloyd, joined in the mayhem, which began with Harpo, in a top hat, as the 'love interest', sliding down a coal shute, and Groucho as the old movie villain. The director, according to Marx compiler Allen Eyles, was Dick Smith, of whom there seems no record, and the plot was equally obscure. Only the final shot of Groucho trudging off dragging a ball and chain has been dignified by a mention. No daily rushes were screened, and the denouement was described by Groucho, *ibid.*:

> So the seven cheerless producers gathered in the projection room with notebooks, cigars and heavy hearts. None of us was very hopeful about the proceedings, but we said, without really believing our words, that 'You can't tell until an audience sees it . . .' None of the theatre managers shown the concoction would take it, until Chico found a weak-willed exhibitor in the Bronx who was willing to let us show our picture in the afternoon, when the audience consisted mostly of backward children . . . When the picture began Benny, in the fourth row, would recognise Sammy sitting in Row L, and the two would shout hello's, and then join in running up and down the aisles. Unless it was wholly imagination on my part, I think the manager ran with them.

In short, there were more Marx Brothers antics in the audience than on the screen, and the première, and closing show, of 'Humor Risk' was over. Four years later, after the Marx Brothers had been adopted by the *habitués* of the Algonquin 'round table', their mentor, Alex Woollcott, demanded a screening of this elusive artefact. The aforementioned Al Posen came up with a can of film which, the projectionist discovered upon cracking it

133

open, contained only the negative. This should not, in theory, have deterred such luminaries as Robert Benchley, Dorothy Parker, Herbert Bayard Swope et al., who were allegedly present, but the projectionist was having none of it. Shamefacedly, the Brothers slunk off, forgetting the can of negative film in the projection booth, from whence it promptly vanished, leaving not a trace, not a frame, not a single perforation of the Marx Brothers' screen début for posterity.

'We tried to forget "Humor Risk,"' wrote Groucho, 'but it remains one of those memories . . .'

Back, then, to the stage, and *On the Mezzanine*. This piece of theatrical bric-a-brac served the Brothers for almost two years, through 1921 and 1922. It was, as we have seen, a transitional vehicle, harking back to tried-and-true routines but beginning to search for another kind of structure. Gus Edwards would have felt at home with it, and proud of his pupils' progress.

The 'Mezzanine' was a family affair in more ways than one. Hattie Darling, the star, was the stage name of writer Herman Timberg's sister, and her mentor and admirer, the boxer Benny Leonard, was one of the show's primary 'angels'. He also made guest appearances on stage, telling his tales of the ring and jousting, only partially in jest, with the Brothers on the stage, resulting in black eyes, as well as the usual high jinks, as reported by *Variety*, June 1921, from Chicago: 'Leo Marx slipped in on skates . . . supplied laughs and came in on the finish. If he forgets to wear a hip flask, it will be fatal . . .'

Groucho told Richard Anobile about more playful pranks in *On the Mezzanine*, which may have been the origin of the Brothers' puns on music titles bantered between Groucho and Chico: 'I'd make up parodies of song titles of the day . . . I'd say, "Chico, play Slipshod Through the Cowslips!" That was a parody of "Tiptoe Through the Tulips." Or I'd say, "Chico, play I'm a Dreamer, Montreal . . ."'

The show was bringing in $2,750 a week for the Brothers, but they were not satisfied, and had the distinct feeling of treading water. The next move was, once again, proposed by Chico, as Minnie had by now retreated into a purely supportive role. With two of her sons now fathers themselves, it was time they made their own way in the world. Having signed on with Abe Lastfogel of the William Morris Agency, the Brothers were hungrier than ever for the big time. But no one could lay proper claim to the big time unless they had proved themselves in a much wider field. And so the Marx Brothers committed themselves to a new venture, if an apparently less hazardous one than their blind leap into movie oblivion. On 4 June 1922, they sailed for England, aboard the SS *Mauretania*, in their first – but not, they hoped, last – attempt to stretch their appeal beyond the borders of the United States.

The Marxian crew included Mrs Samuel Marx, wives Betty and Ruth with babies Maxine and Arthur, and a new *ingénue* to replace Hattie Darling: Helen Schroeder, who would later become Helen Kane, the 'Boop-Oop-a-Doop Girl', destined still later to enter immortality as the model of cartoon superstar 'Betty Boop'. Ed Metcalfe was still enrolled as the house detective, and the embryonic Margaret Dumont role of the *ingénue*'s mother was taken by Eleanor Riley.

The Marx Brothers opened at the London Coliseum on 19 June, sharing the bill with comedian Tommy Handley and impressionist Cecelia Loftus – the same Cissie Loftus whose dog (or leopard!) Harpo had unceremoniously walked to disaster on the streets of New York so many years before. Her response to meeting the dog-boy again has not, alas, been recorded. La Loftus's speciality was her impeccable imitations of theatrical luminaries such as Sarah Bernhardt, Vesta Tilley, Marie Lloyd, 'the late Signor Caruso', Sir Harry Lauder, et al. Also featured were Mademoiselle Ninette de Valois, and the Russian and Polish dancers Lydia Lopovka, Leonide Massine and company, in a 'New Divertissement'.

First notices were enthusiastic: 'Non-stop entertainment, and the audience are not allowed a moment's respite from laughter,' quoth *The Era*. *The Stage* review of 22 June, however, notes that the Brothers' rendition of *On the Balcony* lasted for half an hour, indicating that not all the play was performed. This may have accounted for the confusion of the audience later in the week, who only stirred from their hostile stupor to boo and throw pennies on the stage. Most readers may be too young to remember the old British penny, which was so heavy it was classified by the police as a lethal weapon. Groucho braved the storm and walked forward to the footlights to inform the audience that, since the Brothers had crossed the Atlantic Ocean at great expense, the least they could do was throw some shillings – the old 'bob' being a much lighter implement.

Later accounts provided a more soothing spin on this story, fingering the penny-hurling goons as a claque organized by Madame Lopovka and her acolytes, enraged at being denied the starring slot in the show. But it was clear that the act did not click with the audience, and by 26 June the Brothers had dropped the two scenes from *On the Balcony* and unfurled their old standard, 'Home Again'. This too, met with mixed success. *The Times* complained that the Marxian humour 'seems to be a little too trans-Atlantic for English audiences', adding snidely that the Brothers 'so obviously enjoy their own performance that it cannot be long before they persuade their audiences to do the same. Their playing and dancing, however,' *The Times* conceded, 'is so far above the average that nothing else matters very much.'

The act transferred in July to the Alhambra in London and then toured in Manchester and Liverpool, where it wrapped, and the Marx Brothers took ship back home to America, disembarking on home shores on 29 July.

It had been the unhappiest experience for the Marx Brothers since early 'Nightingale' days. Groucho omitted the whole tale from his autobiography and Harpo called the traumatic night at the Coliseum a fiasco: 'People began to hoot and whistle and throw pennies at us . . . We had never been so humiliated in public in all our professional years.' He consoled himself, as he always did, with the bright side, recalling the warmth of their reception after they had transferred to the Alhambra:

> We found that the English everywhere gave actors and vaudevillians special treatment . . . It was a far cry from the days of one-night stands at home, the days of stale bread pudding, bug-ridden hotels, crooked managers, and trudging from town to town like unwanted gypsies.
> Here there was genuine kindness and dignity in show business – even between the most eminent impresarios and the seediest performers.

The Marx Brothers did not return to England until ten years later, when they were immunized from any repeated indignities by their status as Hollywood stars.

Back home, however, the Brothers found themselves in more serious trouble than could be caused by amateur movie antics or disgruntled Slavic dance fans. They had embarked on their English tour without clearance from the all-powerful Edward Albee, co-founder and head muckamuck of the Keith-Orpheum circuit, and storm clouds were a-brewing.

Albee was a dictator who brooked no defiance, and crossing him was a much worse career move than abandoning Ned Wayburn. The Brothers found themselves barred from all the B. F. Keith theatres. Where were they now to go? The purported three-year deal with Broadway producer Charles Dillingham wasn't turning up a single offer. The only viable rivals to Albee were the Shubert brothers, Lee and J. J., who were trying to expand their productions beyond their home territory of New York. But they had just sued the Marxes' uncle, Al Shean, and his partner Gallagher, for their decision to forgo the Shubert vaudeville circuit for a lucrative – and, as it turned out, vital – slot in the 1922 *Ziegfeld Follies*.

The Schoenbergs were understandably not keen on the Shuberts, and Shubert vaudeville was widely regarded in any case as a foolhardy enterprise, given that all the leading acts in the field were committed to Keith. The Shuberts were sending out cut-rate shows to compete with their rival, organized into so-called 'Shubert Units', which had to manage themselves on the road.

These were dog days for the Marx Brothers – but they had more mouths now to feed. *Variety*, 22 September 1922:

MARX BROS. UNIT FEATURE: The Four Marx Brothers and their vaudeville act, of eight people in all, were engaged last week for a Shubert Unit show. It was expected early this week they would be assigned to the 'Hollywood Follies,' a unit production that is to be improved while on tour.

The 'improved' production turned out to be something named the 'Twentieth Century Review'. Quite what it consisted of is not very clear, but it was another *mélange* of old material. *On the Balcony* was dropped, but some of its material was incorporated into the new show. Harpo developed some new stunts, including the trick of blowing up a rubber glove to pretend to be milking a cow (a gag that can be seen on screen in the frantic hotel breakfast scene in *A Night at the Opera*). The cop shaking the silverware out of his coat was retained, with more 'Home Again' leftovers. A local paper, the *Hartford Daily Courant*, remarked in a feature about the show, on 22 November:

The Four Marx Brothers on the stage bubble with humor and music. Meet them off the stage and they are pretty much the same. Fun is their specialty in life, and they find plenty of it. Music is their delight and they are always plunking a piano or tooting a saxophone or strumming a harp.

'We are planning to become motion picture actors, comedians, stars or what have you,' said Groucho. 'Tests have been made by a big company. They have proved satisfactory. Then came this offer to appear on the stage. It was a chance to study motion picture audiences. So here we are. Why not?

'When this engagement is over we are going back East, to stage a big show. After that, you'll find us living in Hollywood with a private telephone number, a couple of pedigreed dogs and two or three separate addresses. The latter is in the event that our stuff doesn't go over with éclat on the screen. We can dodge the audiences.'

'To what do you attribute your whatever-it-is you possess?' he was asked.

'Ask Chico,' was the reply.

'Well,' mused Chico, 'you see, we didn't have anything whatever to begin with, and such being the case, we must have whatever-it-is.'

'Atsa telling 'em, boss. Groucho just could not let go of that gleam of Hollywood gold plates. But the Brothers did not, alas, have to do much to dodge the audiences, which were hardly flocking to the cause. Financial troubles were dogging the Shubert Units all the way, and even the 'Twentieth Century Review' could not save the ramshackle companies from their fate. *Variety* reported a flurry of managerial changes as various actors who had rashly put their money on the line tried to keep the show on the road (*Variety,* 1 December):

TEMPESTUOUS UNIT – Marx Bros. show reported changing once more –

It is reported the Marx Brothers and Kranz and White are to take over the Shubert unit often designated as the Finklestein & Rubin show, though put out by Jimmy O'Neil and W. R. Morganstern. Eugene Cox, who provided the scenery, left Chicago last week for the east with the announced determination to bring matters to a head.

The career of this unit has been tempestuous from the start. It had Joe Whitehead as principal comedian when first organized. He is now back in vaudeville. Kranz and White, who were in the original company, have stuck. The Marx Brothers came into the show when it was reorganized. Olga-Mishka company were with the show from the start until after it left Chicago, after playing the Englewood.

The Shubert Unit shows were losing money hand over fist. At the Majestic, Boston, the 'Twentieth Century Review' grossed a mere $5,000 for the week. On 8 December *Variety* reported: 'Actors take over unit and keep on operating the show: . . . the Marx Bros. and Kranz and White hold 40% of 20th Century Revue, sold 60% back to former owners, one of whom, Clarence Morganstern, now company manager, for $4,000 dollars, $2,000 in cash and the rest 'in debts of the company assumed by the purchaser.' The company was being pursued by costumier Maybelle Shearer, of Chicago, who sued to attach the show.

Like wounded buffalo, the actors staggered through Cleveland and Philadelphia over Christmas and New Year 1923, getting their usual good reviews as old favourites, but attracting less and less rears on seats. The *Cleveland Press* noted: 'Four Marx Brothers are headliners in this self-written and self-styled revue. They are excellent comedy makers. Two of the brothers play the piano well. The chorus is well-selected. What dancing is demanded of it is well done. Perhaps the best number is Hawaiian.'

There was worse to come. *Variety*, 8 February: 'The receipts of the "20th Century Revue" were attached at the State, Cleveland, Feb 1, by Al White (White and Kranz) as the treasurer of Betty Amusement Co. of Chicago, 60 per cent owner of the unit. The other 40 per cent is held by Kranz and White and the Four Marx Brothers equally.'

The Betty Amusement Company, named after Chico's wife, had been formed with the intention of putting the Marxes' business on a proper footing, but this was not how things were working out. The show limped through Cincinnati and St Louis, but on 23 February *Variety* estimated the overall Shubert vaudeville unit losses for the season at a staggering $1,550,000! The final act of the 'Twentieth Century Review' was as inevitable as Greek tragedy. *Variety*, 8 March:

UNIT SHOW WITH $60 IN BOX OFFICE, ATTACHED.

Kranz and White sued out the attachment in Indianapolis, where the unit was closing a three day run. Playing to $2 top, there was $60 in the box office Saturday night, when the attachment was served. The Marx Brothers ordered a refund and called off the performance, but the deputy sheriff refused to lift the attachment on the box office. Someone dug the money from somewhere and returned it to the few cash patrons . . .

INDIANAPOLIS MARCH 7 — Fifteen minutes before the curtain was scheduled to go up at the Murat Saturday evening a deputy sheriff arrived and attached the box office, scenery and costumes of 'The Twentieth Century Review.' The performance was called off and the Four Marx Brothers, owners of the Betty Amusement Company, are trying to work out the indebtedness. Harry Kranz and Al B. White, former comedians with the show, caused when they filed suit for $1,490 in alleged back salary . . .

While the audience waited in wonder the deputy sheriff went about the front of the theatre and back stage appraising whatever he could find that belonged to the company. One by one the drops and props were exhibited to the officer and an assistant who valued them. Chorus girls were trotted out and their costumes appraised on them. Sixteen Hawaiian outfits were valued at 25 cents each . . .

Seven years after Minnie Palmer's bankruptcy over a paltry $300 debt, the Marx Brothers seemed to be all washed up.
Would they have to kiss their fond dreams goodbye?

16

Cometh the Hour, Cometh the Men – the Four Horsemen Meet the Round Table

GROUCHO: Tell me, my comely wench, have you any liquor on your hip?
RUBY: No, but I have suppressed desires.

I'll Say She Is (1923)

In the summer of 1919, a group of like-minded friends – newspaper columnists and editors, critics, playwrights, actors and aspiring writers – began meeting at the Pergola Room of the Algonquin Hotel in New York, on 44th Street, between 5th and 6th Avenues, to reminisce about their experiences of the Great War that had ended in November 1918, to discuss their thoughts on art, music, plays and life in general and just to shoot the breeze. Most of them were, in fact, not native New Yorkers, but free spirits who had been drawn to the city from places such as Pittsburgh and Chicago, McKeesport PA., New Jersey and other barbarian stations. Their names were to become a roll call of the 'opinion makers', the arbiters of New York culture and art: Franklin P. Adams, Heywood Broun, Robert Sherwood, George and Beatrice Kaufman, Marc Connelly, Harold Ross, Frank Crowninshield, Edna Ferber, Dorothy Parker, Robert Benchley, Ring Lardner, Herman Mankiewicz, Charles MacArthur, Herbert Bayard Swope, Tallulah Bankhead, Alice Duer Miller, Donald Ogden Stewart, Ruth Gordon, Helen Hayes, Deems Taylor, Peggy Wood.

But the doyen of these worthies, these rebels without a cause, who were to become the gatekeepers, was the roly-poly, 'arsenic and old lace' figure of Alexander Woollcott.

At the time of the founding of the Round Table (which was only a couple of oblong tables put together, initially) Woollcott was the drama critic of the *New York Times*, master of the acid attack: 'The suffering of the audience was beyond words,' he would write, or 'Mrs Patrick Campbell is an aged British battleship sinking rapidly and firing every available gun on her rescuers.' But he was also capable of explosive enthusiasms which could make, as well as break, actors and plays.

Woollcott was a man with a curious history. Born in 1887 in Red Bank, New Jersey, he was the grandson of the founder of a communal sect known as the Phalanx which attracted, among others, the famous Horace Greeley – who, despite his advice to young men to 'Go West', only got as far as the Red Bank commune himself. The commune had failed before Alexander was born, but his father inhabited its house and kept its precepts, despite his genteel poverty. Woollcott grew up in an atmosphere of 'plain living and high thinking', which would today be categorized as 'New Age'. He also manifested, in his adolescence, an extreme uncertainty about his sexuality, which some have attributed to a hormonal imbalance, and which led him to seek out women's roles in school plays, to dress up in women's clothes off-stage and to prepare personal cards that read 'Alexandra Woollcott'. He tried to read Krafft-Ebing's *Psychopathia Sexualis* but found no solutions there, as he wrote to a friend: 'I've been flowing through Krafft-Ebing but the tide simply isn't in . . . I am more wild about Wilde.'

The elegance and style of the great English dissimulator was a model for Woollcott's art, but not his life. To allay fears of homosexuality in a homophobic world, young Aleck chose a 'proper' man's profession: like his contemporary, H. L. Mencken, he turned his back on the aesthetic or academic life, and became a jobbing newspaperman. One of his early assignments, in April 1912, was to go down to Halifax to view the mounds of corpses taken out of the water after the sinking of the *Titanic*. Twenty years later he looked back on this time and wrote, of himself as the young rookie reporter:

His name is Woollcott. Alexander Humphreys Woollcott. Later he'll throw that middle name overboard as too darned heavy to carry . . . He's suffering from an inferiority complex but he's never heard of one. He's never heard of daylight-saving. Nor rayon. Nor Soviets. Nor jazz. Nor insulin. Nor G-men. Nor broccoli. He's never seen a one-piece bathing suit nor read a gossip column . . . He's never heard a radio nor seen a talking picture . . . You see, he does live in a world quite different from the one to which you and I must soon return. His very ideas are different. Take two as a sample. What does he think a job is? He thinks a job is something any man can get who's willing to work. And a war? Why, war is a practice still carried on only by remote, comic opera countries in Central America and the Balkans. How much he had to learn!

But learn he did. When the United States entered the war in Europe, Woollcott volunteered, despite his physique, which was already manifesting the flabby pear shape that was to characterize him all his life. His eyesight was abysmal. Nevertheless, still determined to prove his manhood, he persuaded the draft board to enlist him as an orderly. In training, he cut a sorry sight, one officer calling out at boat drill: 'For God's sake! Who's the pregnant mermaid?' But Woollcott served, and found his niche, in an army newspaper, produced for the enlisted men, entitled *Stars and Stripes*. The editorial board was another roll call of future notables: Captain Franklin P. Adams, Lieutenant Grantland Rice, and Private Harold Ross, who was later to found *The New Yorker*. Sergeant Woollcott was a frontline correspondent, portrayed in cartoons as a mincing figure tripping along the trenches, oblivious to incoming fire.

In 1919, Woollcott returned to the *New York Times*, to take up his pre-war post as a drama critic. Among the assistants waiting for him was a skinny man of quick wit named George S. Kaufman, who had just had his first play, *Someone In the House*, produced at the Knickerbocker Theatre. Kaufman, then aged thirty, had already cut his teeth as a writer for columnist Franklin P. Adams (F. P. A.), and as the author of his own daily column for the Washington *Times*, entitled 'This and That'. That position ended when Kaufman collided one day with publisher Frank A. Munsey, who picked himself painfully off the floor and complained to an assistant, 'Who is that Jew in my composing room?'

Woollcott had no problems with a Jew in his composing room, or anyone of any race or creed, as long as they were talented, and could amuse and entertain him. He loved the challenge and the banter of like-minded souls, and deified this idea of an endless intellectual tournament with the Algonquin Round Table.

Kaufman himself was to debunk the pretensions of the Algonquinites in an article written in 1945, for the *Saturday Review of Literature*, in which he claimed:

> The truth is . . . that the Round Table was made up of a motley and
> nondescript group of people who wanted to eat lunch, and that's about
> all. They had no power at all over the literature of the day, and it seems
> to me that the least thought on the part of the accusers would convince
> them of that fact . . . The Round Table members ate at the Algonquin
> because Frank Case was good enough to hold a table for them, and
> because it was fun.

It was quite true, as Dorothy Parker later commented, that the real giants of American letters, like Hemingway, Faulkner or Fitzgerald, flourished well away from Frank Case's table. But Kaufman was being defensive about the fact that so much press power was concentrated in that small circle. Herbert Bayard Swope edited the New York *World*; F. P. A. was the doyen of all columnists; John Weaver was literary editor of the Brooklyn *Eagle*; Harold Ross was soon to be the most 'in' of the in-crowd; Robert Benchley wrote for *Vanity Fair*, the *World*, and *Life*; Heywood Broun and Woollcott reigned over the theatre, Woollcott leaving the *Times*, first for the *World*, then on to become the drama critic of the *Sun*. It was in this capacity, on the evening of 19 May 1924, that Alexander Woollcott attended the New York opening, at the Casino Theatre, of an extravaganza starring an act he had allegedly never heard of before: The Marx Brothers, in *I'll Say She Is*.

As legend has it, *I'll Say She Is* was born at another round table, the poker table of Chico's nocturnal exploits. The 'Twentieth Century Review' had crashed in Indianapolis, and the Marx Brothers were all out of jobs. Harpo describes himself walking about the streets of Indianapolis, depressed and confused. He was remembering the stern admonitions of his schoolteacher, Miss Flatto – 'Someday you'll realize, young man! Someday you'll realize!' He felt he had hit rock bottom. He was thirty-five years old (in his book he claims thirty, remember?) and unemployed again, with no skills except the harp and the pantomime. Wandering aimlessly, he stopped short outside an auction sale. The inventory of a small grocery store which had gone bust was being sold off, and soon nothing was left except one solitary scrub brush, with an elderly couple hovering about, gazing at the brush wistfully, but silent. The auctioneer, desperate, called out: 'One last desirable item! What am I offered?' Harpo called out: 'One cent!' The auctioneer whacked his gavel. Harpo picked up his brush and handed it to the couple. With tears in their eyes, and floods of Italian, they thanked him, took the brush, and toddled off into the sunset.

Harpo obviously did not take Chico's advice, as given some years later, in *The Cocoanuts*, to 'Bid 'em op! Bid 'em op!'

As he rejoined his brothers and Minnie, Harpo was apprised of the miracle: Uncle Al had come up with a loan, again. The family had decided that the act should split up. Groucho would audition as a single, Chico as a piano player, and Zeppo would go back to Chicago with Minnie. To which, Harpo reports, he had one word: 'Nuts!'

And so the family repledged its unity.

Great yarn. And one part of it is undoubtedly true: the Brothers were blessed with a miracle. The angel this time round, rather than Uncle Al, was a Pennsylvania coal magnate, one James P. Beury, who had a crush on a chorus girl, and was looking for a show to back. Chico, coincidentally, was looking for a backer, as well as a better run of luck with the cards. The two met over the card table and clicked. 'You want-a your girl in a show? 'Atsa no problem, boss! Hey, but we put on a show, itsa run into cash . . .'

The archive, on the other hand, as is its wont, paints a more mundane picture. *Variety,* 3 April, less than a month after the Indianapolis débâcle, reported from Philadelphia:

MARX BROS. IN STOCK:

The stock musical company, Charles Wanamaker (manager) and Jos. M. Gaites (producer) are to place in the Walnut Street (theatre) for a summer run, will be headed by the Four Marx Brothers. It is expected the company will open around May 21.

The Shuberts, after all their travails, were still in the picture. Loath to allow their investment in the Marx Brothers to go to waste, they proposed a marriage between them and one of their other properties, an ailing show called *Love For Sale.* This prime turkey had been commissioned by Shubert producer Joseph Gaites from newspaper cartoonist and writer Will B. Johnstone and his composer brother Tom, as a vehicle for a British actress, Kitty Gordon. The show's renaming as *Give Me a Thrill* had failed to fool the audience, and its costumes and props now languished in the Walnut Theatre warehouse.

Another account has Chico and Tom Johnstone meeting in New York and clicking, over this project: 'You wrote-a this show, but you no have-a the stars? Hey, we have-a the stars, but we no gotta the show! It's-a poifect!'

Somehow producer, angel, chorus girls, stars and theatre came together, and the Marx Brothers were in business again. *Variety,* 3 May:

The Four Marx Brothers will head Philly's first summer revue, aimed for the Walnut Street Theatre, May 29. Will and Tom Johnstone are writing the show, which is produced by Joseph M. Gaites and J. M. Beury. The attraction may be called 'You Must Come Over.' Gaites favors four word titles, they having been lucky for him with his 'Take It From Me,' and 'Up In the Clouds.' Both the latter shows were by the Johnstones.

So, alas, the poker tales are probably apocryphal. We can but imagine the titling conferences, as all the four-word combinations were thrown about in the air. The words that finally came down were as nonsensical as any others, but are now history – *I'll Say She Is.*

Harpo's scrub-brush miracle was still working for the show's opening – it was one of the hottest summers on record and many unventilated theatres were closed. The Philadelphia *Public Ledger* reviewed the show on 5 June:

'I'LL SAY SHE IS' HAS PROPITIOUS OPENING.

Summer Revue at Walnut is Lively, Tuneful Affair, with Remarkable Dancing.

There is little doubt that 'I'll Say She Is' will make ideal hot weather entertainment . . . It is not particularly subtle, and the comedy skits are pretty elementary stuff, and the scenes, while often striking, are not always in the most delicate and artistic of taste, but who cares when the thermometer is 90 degrees or thereabouts and entertainment is the only requirement . . .

The Four Marx Brothers are inimitable in all that they have to do. Occasionally one wishes that they were given more leeway, but when Arthur did remarkable things on a harp and Edward [sic] Marx performed on a piano with unbelievable dexterity there was little to complain of; and Julius Marx, impersonating Napoleon, had moments of gutsy humor . . .

'I'll Say She Is' has all the earmarks of a sturdy success, a success it will win by aid of jazz and plenty of dancing and pretty girls, and not by amazing novelty, really funny comedy or any degree of subtle imaginative material . . .

I'll Say She Is ran at the Walnut in Philadelphia for a solid three months. It was a smash hit. Groucho bought his first new car, a Studebaker, and was so delighted with it he took it on the road outside the theatre during the intermission and got stuck in traffic. This meant he had to run through the streets dressed as Napoleon, to be in time for the second act. Or so he told the tale.

There were other glitches, of course. The play flopped in Boston, in September, and later in Washington, in April 1924. But in between were successful runs in Chicago, Kansas City and Buffalo. By May the Brothers were ready for their big break, their first 'legit', all-singing, all-dancing, all Marx Brothers Broadway Show, at the Casino – and their date with Aleck Woollcott.

Just before the opening night, the play's good luck was sealed by the actors' mother breaking her leg. Minnie was being fitted for a gown to wear for the occasion and slipped off the measuring chair. Carried into the theatre – much, one imagines, like Groucho's celebrated entry as Captain Spaulding in *Animal Crackers* – she was deposited in triumph in a front row, box seat. This was, Groucho wrote, 'her personal victory . . . the culmination of twenty years of scheming, starving, cajoling and scrambling'. And Frenchy, too, could finally celebrate. No more the need to travel feverishly across country, getting on the wrong trains and being shunted off to sidings, arguing with boorish theatre managers and jealous boarding-house cooks, kick-starting hesitant audiences into applause . . .

According to myth, the front-rank critics attended the Marx Brothers show only because another show they were due to attend was postponed at the last minute. Hector Arce diligently researched and reported that the post-poned show, *Innocent Eyes*, with the French star (and lover of Maurice Chevalier) Mistinguette, was also at a Shubert theatre, the Winter Garden, and the wily Shubert brothers decided not to open both at the same time. The story that Woollcott attended the show by chance, thinking he was going to see a 'troupe of acrobats', does not hold water anyway. Woollcott was brought to the show by Charles MacArthur, friend and writing partner of the mercurial Ben Hecht, who had known the Brothers since their Chicago days. Harpo wrote, in *Harpo Speaks*, that both he and Groucho were fans of Hecht's regular column, '1001 Nights in Chicago'. Hecht's robust and contrary opinions about everything under the sun (his list of the world's twenty two worst books included works by Shakespeare, H. G. Wells, D. H. Lawrence, Robert Louis Stevenson and Karl Marx) were made to order for the Marxes, and both he and McArthur were to become firm friends and doting fans.

Another reason to doubt Woollcott's reluctance to see the 'acrobats' was that within a few weeks of his attendance at *I'll Say She Is* he was discovering another vaudevillian turned legit star – W. C. Fields in the stage musical *Poppy*. 'His jaunty and shameless old mountebank', wrote Woollcott, 'has the flavor of someone astray from one of Mark Twain's riverboats or one of Mr Dickens' groups of strolling players.' The new breed of highbrow critics were quite deliberately picking their chosen highlights out of popular culture for the attention of the mainstream. They would continue to do so throughout the decade of the 1920s, most significantly with their adoption and co-option of black American jazz. This was not, as it appeared on the surface, merely a frivolous exercise: it represented a crucial shift in the spirit of the times, the reflection of a war-shocked generation which disdained the class divisions of the past, and the set categories and divisions of culture into 'fine' as against 'vulgar' art.

Whether Woollcott was really out of the Hecht-McArthur 'loop', or whether he had known of the Marxes as vaudevillians but had not seen them perform before, which is more likely, it's clear the show was a revelation to him. His review, in the next day's *Sun*, was an anointment:

HARPO MARX AND SOME BROTHERS:

Hilarious Antics Spread Good Cheer at the Casino.

By Alexander Woollcott.

As one of the many who laughed immodestly throughout the greater part of the first performance given by a new musical show, entitled, if memory serves, 'I'll Say She Is,' it behooves your correspondent to report the most comical moments vouchsafed to the first nighters in a month of Mondays. It is a bright colored and vehement setting for the goings on of those talented cutups, the Four Marx Brothers. In particular, it is a splendacious and reasonably tuneful excuse for going to see that silent brother, that shy, unexpected, magnificent comic among the Marxes, who is recorded somewhere on a birth certificate as Arthur, but who is known to the adoring two-a-day as Harpo Marx.

As Groucho said, years later, when trying to deal with Woollcott's androgynous sexuality, 'Woollcott fell in love with Harpo.' Indeed, the famous critic raved:

Surely there should be dancing in the streets when a great clown comic comes to town, and this man is a great clown. He is officially billed as a member of the Marx family, but truly he belongs to that greater family which includes Joe Jackson and Bert Melrose and the Fratlini Brothers, who fall over one another in so obliging a fashion at the Cirque Medrano in Paris.

Woollcott did not omit the other brothers, but was less incandescent about them: 'The speaking is mostly attended to by Julius H. Marx . . . a crafty comedian with a rather fresher and more whimsical assortment of quips than is the lot of most refugees from vaudeville . . . Leonard Marx is more or less suppressed until the property man remembers to leave a piano on the stage. As for Herbert Marx, he is probably the property man . . .'

Harpo tells how he went to bed after the show to be awakened the next morning by Groucho's phone call, reading out Woollcott's review. Harpo's reaction was annoyance: 'Didn't the son-of-a-bitch say anything about you or Chico or Zeppo? What did he think – I was doing a single?' Groucho's assurances failed to satisfy. Then the phone rang, at ten o'clock, with a surprise call from Woollcott. The new admirer wanted to meet his new idol. Somewhat reluctantly, Harpo agreed.

After the show that night, the critic literally barged into the dressing room. As Harpo described the scene: 'I had no idea what a "big New York critic" ought to look like, but I didn't expect this. He looked like something that had gotten loose from Macy's Thanksgiving Day Parade.'

Woollcott was by that time an even more grotesque figure than the 'pregnant mermaid' of World War One. He had a voice that, Harpo said, 'could have been reproduced by letting the air out of a balloon', with a squeaky and whining tone. Harpo did not know what to make of this phenomenon at first, especially as the man praised him so highly: 'You are the funniest man I have ever seen on the stage.' 'What about my harp solo?' asked Harpo. 'Consider yourself fortunate, Marx,' said Woollcott, 'that I am not a music critic.'

Harpo began to warm to this joker, and Woollcott confessed to his social disease. He always spoke whatever came to his mind. What came to his mind now was a summons, for the Great Clown to join the magic circle of Camelot at the Algonquin Hotel. Specifically, to join the late-night poker game at what Woollcott had dubbed the Upper West Side Thanatopsis and Inside Straight Club.

This invitation may not have come as promptly as related by Harpo, though we must accept that, in true fashion, he handed the big New York critic his leg. It was not long, however, before Harpo was ensconced as a full member of the Algonquin Round Table. Lucky for the members that it was Harpo who joined their poker table and not Chico, who might have cleaned them out. Chico did play some hands at the Table, but his usual circles were much more downmarket.

At first, Harpo relates, he could not tell these upper-echelon fellows apart, and could only remember them as 'a bunch of guys named "Benson."' But he soon learned their names and their foibles. None more than Harpo could appreciate the irony of the least educated of the Marx Brothers, the class dunce and despair of Miss Flatto, being accepted into the inner circle of New York City's most prestigious intellectuals. But Harpo was Harpo, he could no more be awed by the concatenation of brain power than he could be disdainful of the old couple to whom he had handed the one-cent scrub brush in Indianapolis. In life, as on stage, and later on the screen, Harpo was the world's elemental democrat: he treated kings, commoners, millionaires, paupers, the famous and the obscure with the same wide-eyed curiosity – and often made them the butt of the same practical jokes. Harpo was still the child, ambling about the streets, stealing the fruit from the forbidden gardens, sampling the sights, odours and sounds of the city, and handing his leg cheerfully to anybody who might come along . . .

Vive la France! *or* Opening Sardines with a Sword

RICHMAN: Have you had any theatrical experience?
GROUCHO: I was with the Covered Wagon last season. I played the axle grease.

I'll Say She Is (1923–4)

Of the Marx Brothers' three Broadway shows, *I'll Say She Is* was the only one that was not subsequently filmed. Reason enough for us to linger awhile with this vehicle that carried the Brothers to stardom and Harpo to the status of New York's mute mascot, and take a look under the hood.

I'll Say She Is was in many ways a jalopy, an inspired rejigging of spare parts. Even the sets, in its first run, were bits and pieces left over from 'The Squaw Man', 'Way Down East' and even 'Uncle Tom's Cabin', according to Groucho – whatever debris was found backstage at the Walnut. The score, he wrote, 'was probably the most undistinguished one that ever bruised the eardrums of a Broadway audience'. We cannot tell if this slur on poor Tom Johnstone is justified, but it was probably no more tuneless than other scores of its ilk. The fact that the show was not filmed may have been due to the relative obscurity of the Johnstones, compared to the prestige of George S. Kaufman, who wrote both the Brothers' later Broadway hits. But it may well have had more than a sniff to do with the play's central plot line, which has the 'Thrill Girl', Beauty, standing trial for stabbing a Chinaman in an opium den.

Most of the original, pre-Marxian script clearly disappeared in a hail of gags and diversions, but the central theme, of the bored heiress promising to marry the man who could give her the greatest thrill, was unchanged. The main characters, Merchant (later changed to Doctor), Poorman, Lawyer, Beggarman, were played by Zeppo, Chico, Groucho and Harpo, respectively, still billed to the outside world as Herbert, Leonard, Julius and Arthur – a gaucherie Woollcott was soon to correct. Other characters, Chief and Thief, were played by Lloyd Garrett and Edgar Gardiner, with Carlotta, alias Lotta Miles, as Beauty. The opening scene, however, was an action replay of the opening of *On the Balcony*, with stalwart Ed Metcalfe playing the theatrical agent, Richman, confronted in his office by the Four Musketeers, each presenting a Gallagher and Shean imitation in place of the less topical Joe Frisco. Cue Zeppo:

> Our songs are a lot of junk,
> And as actors we are punk,
> Positively, Mr Gallagher,
> Absolutely, Mr Shean.

Chico's contribution is: 'My name is Sebastian Chicolino and the best thing I do is give the imitation of Gallagher and Shean –

Courting habits of the Marxmen, with Lotta Miles in *I'll Say She Is* (Zeppo on bended knee).

'Oh Mr Gallagher, oh Mr Gallagher,
One day I take a street car ride,
And a lady big and fat, she sat right on my hat,
And when she gets up I nearly cry –
Christopher Colombo – what do you think of that?'

Clearly not much. Groucho's contribution is a typically acid swipe not only at his successful Uncle Al but at another current stage idol:

'Oh Mr Gallagher, oh Mr Gallagher,
I can do just what you do,
I can't sing but neither can you,
So I'll do it like an Eddie Cantor nance . . .'

Groucho wraps up with an enigmatic comment: 'That's the beauty of moth-balls – you don't have to eat them.' Then the agent introduces the boys to the thrill-seeking heiress:

RICHMAN: She is a victim of suppressed desires. She has complexes because she has never been in love.
GROUCHO: Is she married?
RICHMAN: Will you please keep quiet. What do you know about love?
GROUCHO: Nothing. I've been married four times. I'm not getting the mileage I used to.

Prescient words. Chico arrives: 'Did you come by appointment?' 'No me, I come by the subway.' The Thief, Edgar Gardiner, takes Beauty to the opium den for the thrill of a lifetime, but she becomes mixed up in a stabbing. Groucho: 'You are going to be convicted of murder.' Beauty: 'What makes you so confident?' Groucho: 'I'm going to be your lawyer.'

This ushers in one of the most tantalizing scenes in *I'll Say She Is*, in view of the play's unfilmed status – the trial, with Chico as Attorney for the Defence, Groucho as Prosecutor, and Harpo as Judge.

Enter Harpo as Judge, in robe –

CHICO: Good morning Judge. (*To officer*) Don't let anyone in. The Judge has something important he wants to talk to me about. (*To Judge*) Little draw poker, eh? All right. All the time you want to play with your cards . . . Say Judge, nobody's looking – give me one from the bottom. You think you're smart, eh? We cut for the deal. The low card deals. What you got? Two? You lose . . . How many cards you want? None?

You got to take some – it's draw poker. Four? You got openers? I take one. It's no good. Take another. I'll bet you five bucks. You raise me? I raise you. You call? Oh, you raise . . . All right, I call. What you got? Aces? . . . How many aces? 1 aces? That's good, I thought you were bluffing. Let's see the aces. What's the matter – you call that aces? That's 8's. Tell me you got aces when you got 8's. What's the matter? You cheat like that? Cut the cards. *(Harpo cuts cards with hatchet)*

OFFICER: Court's in order. Make way for my learned District Attorney.

(Chico plays solitaire as the Prosecutor proceeds –)

GROUCHO: Your honor, as you know I am here to try a woman for murder. I realise you are a busy man, and I don't suppose you have given much thought to the case. You don't look as though you would give much thought to anything. *(To officer)* Officer, get this judge a banana – this is the Court of Appeals . . . I am sure it is very gratifying to be before a judge who is not only unbiased and unemotional but practically unconscious. Officer, bring in the prisoner. *(Beauty is brought in)* Young lady . . . you are charged with murder, and if you are convicted you will be charged with electricity . . . Why were you smoking opium in a Chinese joint?

BEAUTY: Because I wanted to get a new sensation.

GROUCHO: Did you ever eat a bowl of rhubarb in a ferris wheel? . . . Were you ever in love?

BEAUTY: That's my business.

CHICO: How's business?

Of course, reading a script of a Marx Brothers show is like making love through an industrial-strength condom: we're missing the whole flavour of the performance, the manic speed, the relentless ad-libbing and adding of new jokes, the sudden bursts of unplanned activity on stage – as when Harpo would goose one of the chorus girls, or chase her for no reason all over the stage – the nightly variations on Chico's piano and Harpo's harp solos. Gaining confidence from their new status, the Brothers felt able to stretch their wings and draw their audience into their world. We can see, from these lines, that the brothers Johnstone were working with tried-and-tested routines, and that Groucho, and probably Chico too, had a great deal to do with the writing. Herman Timberg's 'Mezzanine' input has been cannibalized, and the tit-for-tat puns of Al Shean embedded. Finally, Groucho has discarded the last vestiges of Pa Schneider or the venerable teacher, Mr Green. All that remains of the grey hair and wrinkle greasepaint is the painted moustache, which was born, according to legend, one night when Groucho had not enough time to put the real one on – early tales attributing the change to a few days after Arthur's birth, when Groucho rushed back from the hospital just in time to grab a brush and dart on stage.

This completed the development of the Four Brothers into the figures that we recognize today. The key to the Brothers' eternal appeal: as with Chaplin's tramp, or Keaton's stone-face, or Harold Lloyd's bespectacled All-American boy, we want them to remain just as they are; we want them fixed in time, but not tied to any specific period or age. They must never grow old, indeed never grow up, but stay unchanged, to mirror the child within us all.

A pretty feckless child, at that, and with a precocious sexuality that would have alarmed even Sigmund Freud: Groucho, the eternal lecher; Chico, the pied piper of the keyboard; Harpo, the impulsive girl chaser. Zeppo remained in an awkward limbo, the straight man, the butt of jokes, the amiable and occasional love interest, a sounding-board for the others, but mainly Groucho's stooge.

These characters were already set in their mould by the time the stage writers came on the scene. Old routines continued to be recycled, with *I'll Say She Is* including the 'Home Again' favourite of Harpo, the detective, and the endlessly dropping knives:

GROUCHO: I don't understand what's delaying the coffee pot. (*Clang*)
DETECTIVE (*to Harpo*): Well, you certainly surprise me!
GROUCHO: Me too. I thought he had more than that.

The only new element in the show seems to have been the Napoleon and Josephine number. This is presented as yet another 'thrill' set up for Beauty, to make her think she is 'Empress of the World':

RICHMAN: You see while Napoleon is at the front –
CHICO: They come in at the back.
RICHMAN: While Napoleon is fighting at the front, he suddenly remembers his Josephine.
CHICO: While he is fighting . . .
RICHMAN: Then he comes a rushing . . .
CHICO: He went away a Frenchman and came back a Russian. That's what you call hypnotism.
RICHMAN: You know where hypnotism comes from?
CHICO: No.
RICHMAN: Hypnotism was taken from the Greeks.

CHICO: Oh no, you can't take anything from the Greeks. You can't even get your right change back.

Indeed, this is pure Al Shean! Enter Napoleon and Josephine, with Groucho crying out: 'My sword! I lost my sword!'

JOSEPHINE: There it is, dear, just where you left it.
GROUCHO: How stupid of me! I'm as dumb as a Congressman . . . I wish you wouldn't open sardines with my sword. My troops are beginning to smell like the Lenox Avenue local. Farewell, my queen! Farewell! I am going any minute now! Farewell! I run on the hour and the half hour . . . If my laundry comes, send it General Delivery, care of Russia. And count it, I was a sock short last week. And you might sew on a button hither and yon. Hither is not so bad, but yon is terrible. Farewell, my queen! Vive la France!

The Napoleon–Josephine scene became a legendary centrepiece of 'Lost Marxism': gags and lines never captured on film. *The Groucho Phile* includes a whole segment that differs wildly from the version above, which is the original Will Johnstone script. The later version brings in a character called François, played by Chico, who introduces lines that will later be expropriated by Groucho:

FRANÇOIS: Why don't you marry me?
EMPRESS: What about Napoleon?
FRANÇOIS: I'll marry him too. He's got money. He's the guy I'm really after.
EMPRESS: Why, that's bigamy!
FRANÇOIS: Yes, it's big-a-me too!

Neither version includes the legendary line, the classic ad-lib: 'It's the Mayonnaise! The army must be dressing!' But the original version has its own share of twisters:

GROUCHO: Forgive me my queen, I don't doubt your love. When I look into your big blue eyes, I know that you are true to the army. Fortunately, France has no navy. (*Business with hat*) . . . But then, I must not tarry . . . I must be off to make Russia safe for French pastry.
BEAUTY: Napoleon, fight as you have never fought.
GROUCHO: I shall not fire until I see the whites of their eyes. That's a good yolk.
BEAUTY: Napoleon, don't forget your flannels.

GROUCHO: Josephine, when one wears flannels, one can't forget . . .
Farewell my queen. Beyond the Alps lies Peter's milk chocolate. I will
bring you home a hunk. Vive la France!

Finally, Napoleon discovers Josephine has been hiding her lovers, Chico
and Harpo, behind her couch, prompting the riposte:

GROUCHO: Do you think that you can stand there and make a Schimmil
out of Napoleon? I'm no kibitzer . . . I know women of your elk. I'm an
elk myself. I'll smoke out those Siberian jackrabbits . . . You minx eyed
wastrel, traitress!
BEAUTY: Napoleon!
GROUCHO: Do you know what I am going to do to you? (*Business of sharp-
ening sword*)
BEAUTY: Napoleon! You're not going to kill me!
GROUCHO: Kill you, I should say not! I'm going to sell the couch!
(*Two pierrots skip on, closing curtains, and exit*)

If we picture Alexander Woollcott and the other Round Tablers he
brought to this performance rolling in the aisles we can begin to realize that
it was, at this stage, not so much the New York intellectuals who were
changing the Marx Brothers, as the Marx Brothers changing the intellectuals. With hurricane force, they were sweeping the uncouth world of the
vaudeville entertainers on to the 'legitimate' stage, enabling the upper
crust to enjoy what 'downmarket' mass audiences had been delighting in
since the mid-nineteenth century. When the Marx Brothers performed on
the stage of the Casino, and later in theatres across America, many ghosts
were cavorting beside them: the shadows of Joe Welch, Weber and Fields,
Duffy and Sweeney, Williams and Walker, Collins and Hart, and many
long-forgotten clowns, dancing out of neglected graves. Like their great co-
survivor, W. C. Fields, the Brothers were reconstituting the best of the old
days to entertain the audiences of the new.

But, having reached the top, they had to go further, and find new
backers, new collaborators, new media, to keep those audiences laughing,
and coming back for more.

From Coolidge to Cocoanuts
– 'Do You Want to be Wage Slaves?'

CHICO: He say five, I say six. He say eight, I say nine. He say ten, I say
eleven. I no stop-a for nothing. I bid 'em op. I go higher, higher, higher!

The Cocoanuts (1925)

I'll Say She Is made the Marx Brothers rich. As Groucho titled the relevant
chapter in his book, *Groucho and Me*, RICH IS BETTER. Groucho wrote:

My father acknowledged our success sartorially. He began cutting a
fancy figure on the Great White Way . . . He gave all his old clothes to
my grandfather, who had been dead for seven years. His new outfit
consisted of a pearl-grey derby, pearl spats, pearl vest, a cutaway coat,
diamond horse-shoe stickpin, pearl gloves and a cane.

Fully assembled, Pop looked like something that would have been
rejected by Madame Tussaud's Wax Works. He began affecting a faint
English accent and larded his conversation with fruity 'pip pip's and
'what-ho's. Nobody understood him, but nobody had ever understood
him, so it didn't make too much difference.

Sam and Minnie bought a new house in Little Neck, Long Island, a new
Chevrolet, with a hired chauffeur, and set themselves up as the pinochle
king and queen. Minnie organized her own ladies' poker club, and spent
her time, according to Harpo, shuttling back and forth to the pawnshops
with her jewellery, to pay off her debts. Another tale told by Harpo has
Frenchy setting off in style to the grocery shops with his chauffeur,
sweeping back into the new car with his bundles, and then finding the
chauffeur reluctant to carry the bundles into the house and clean the car,
and loudly demanding his money. Minnie, called to deal with the disgruntled chauffeur, discovered he was in fact a cab driver, and Frenchy had got
in the wrong car.

Harpo described himself as 'more the hot-sport type'. He favoured 'golf
caps or straw skimmers, blazers, and white linen knickerbockers'. The more

outlandish the gear, the more it embarrassed his new friend Aleck Woollcott, which was of course the purpose of the exercise. Harpo delighted in playing practical jokes on Woollcott, who was always susceptible to any leg-pulling, though his annoyance soon fizzled out. Announcing to Harpo that he was bringing the Grand Lady of the American Theatre, Minnie Maddern Fiske, to the show, Woollcott was taken aback to find a fake poster in the lobby of the theatre, showing himself in his academic robes, retouched to appear among the high-kicking chorus. Woollcott cut Harpo for a week after that, until all four brothers wooed him, at another première, with mandolins.

Harpo rented an apartment on East 57th Street, but spent most of his off-stage time at the Algonquin or at Woollcott's own town house on West 47th, which was shared with an old college buddy of Aleck's named Hawley Truax and with Harold Ross and his wife, Jane Grant. Harold Ross was at that point in advanced planning for a new type of weekly magazine which would be unveiled in 1925 as *The New Yorker*. A figure as tall and awkward as Woollcott was fat and awkward, Ross made himself even taller by cultivating his hair in a great vertical coif, a kind of pompadour style, which inspired actress Ina Claire to exclaim once: 'I'd like to take off my shoes and wade in Ross's hair!' Harpo characterized him as 'a cowhand who'd lost his horse', while Woollcott's contribution was: 'Ross looks like a dishonest Abe Lincoln.' The house at 412 West 47th had been a wreck revitalized by Truax, and visitors were often greeted by Woollcott in dressing gown and pyjamas, or Ross stretched out asleep on the floor. This atmosphere suited Harpo fine.

The first *New Yorker* appeared on Tuesday, 17 February 1925, and did not change the world overnight. Its cover portrait of a Regency dandy looking through his monocle at a butterfly was puzzling, and its cartoons were strange: a man and his flapper niece are looking at a theatre poster titled 'The Wages of Sin'; the Uncle says, 'Poor girls, so few get their wages!'; the Flapper says, 'So few get their sin, darn it!'

Not, of course, if they were dating Chico. Marriage had not tamed the pied piper of the keyboard. He made an effort to adapt himself to the obligations of wedlock and fatherhood but considered his role as husband and father to be merely one compartment of his life. The closeness of the brothers meant that, in a sense, Chico's daughter Maxine grew up with several fathers, as both Groucho and Harpo were a boon to have around. Maxine called Groucho 'Uncle Gaukee', and wrote in her book: 'I loved him almost as much as Daddy because his love was offered unconditionally,

159

coming as spontaneously as it does from a child.' It would be many years before Maxine would discover that Groucho's unconditional love turned more complex when his own children – Miriam, his daughter, was born 19 May 1927 – became teenagers and began to act like adults, competitors in his embattled world. But Harpo was a child's dream uncle, picking her up one day backstage and piggy-backing her across the stage, to audience applause.

Maxine wrote:

> I would watch him during intermissions, his flaming red wig on a stand, furiously plucking on a harp he always kept in the corner of his dressing room so his fingers would stay tough (they would bleed if he didn't practice every day). He would have a big Turkish towel wrapped round his head because he perspired a lot under the wig and was always worried that he would get a chill.
>
> Daddy most likely would be doing a crossword puzzle, muttering obscure words to himself. Groucho would be seated in the adjoining dressing room with his copy of *The Nation*, composing obscene letters to the editor, while Zeppo would be on the phone trying to get a date.

Of all the brothers, Zeppo was the most distant to Maxine. The age difference between himself and the other three brothers never ceased to be a barrier, and his role as straight man never satisfied him. According to Groucho, Zeppo used his part of their new earnings to buy a forty-foot cruiser and tear up and down the Long Island Sound. He became renowned as quite a playboy around town, hitting the night spots and indulging to the hilt in his old love for motor cars.

Chico responded to his new-found wealth by squandering it, as he had squandered his meagre vaudeville earnings, at the card tables, poolrooms and, increasingly, at the racetrack, where he could now play for higher and higher stakes. As Groucho wrote, once Chico got through with the prosperous racetracks they were even more prosperous. By the end of the Brothers' first Broadway season he was thirty-seven weeks behind in his salary.

Maxine recalled that Chico always possessed the most boundless and unfettered energy. She wrote of her earliest memories of her father:

> Running, always trying to keep up with him, finally begging him to slow down . . . running down a snow-covered street in Chicago, trying to catch snowflakes on our tongues . . . his reading the funnies to me

every week, each comic strip in a different accent . . . weaving in and around the posts holding up the Third Avenue el train, Daddy at the wheel, me standing on the seat next to him, hearing him say, "Daddy will bet you that before you count to five the light will turn green . . ." Daddy at his dressing table, darkening his eyebrows, daubing his lip rouge, putting on the black, curly wig to cover his fine brown, thinning hair; and always the excited shouts and patter of the showgirls, who were all nude flesh and spangles.

Not something even a married Chico could resist . . .

'Uncle Gaukee', always the most frugal of the brothers, used his increased bank balance to lease a pleasant two-bedroom apartment at 654 West 161st, at Riverside Drive, and to begin what he was advised would be a sober but lucrative series of investments in the stock exchange. His idea of a good time, to curl up with a book whenever possible, was a matter of some frustration for Ruth, who was a social animal and a party lover, but the storm clouds that were to gather over their marriage were still beyond the horizon.

Friday nights, whenever possible, the boys were still expected to attend the family eve-of-Sabbath table. This was a new version of the Chicago Grand Avenue headquarters, much more genteel now, less raucous and chaotic. After all, Minnie Marx was a woman of means, and no longer needed to scrape a living for her brood. Al Shean was a frequent live-in visitor. Tante Hannah, mother of Pauline, now with her own grown-up daughter, Beatrice, would occasionally turn up, a devout Christian Scientist, ever ready to pray over her nephews' lost souls.

Minnie herself, however, was not quite ready to hang up her spurs. She had several business plans, none of which came to much: first to set up a ginger ale business, then to manage new showbiz talents. But concentrating on the pinochle and klabiasch evenings turned out to be much too tempting. She would still turn out for dinner dressed to the nines, in a blonde wig which she thought would make her look twenty years younger. Chico's wife Betty had stopped commenting on the actual results. Maxine's future husband, animator Shamus Culhane, wrote in his memoirs that Betty Marx, whom he met in the 1940s, was 'the best originator of malapropisms that I have ever heard . . . She worried about "the autumn bomb," was "knocked from pillow to post," and loved to hear the "Moonlight Sinatra."' Conversation at the Little Neck dinner table must have been very 'simulating' . . .

The Friday evenings were also an opportunity to catch up on the missing brother, Gummo. Having left the army and tried his luck with his various inventions, the cardboard laundry boxes and the W. C. Fieldsian skidless tyre, he had gone into the garment business with a partner, registering in 1922 as President of Marx and Moses Inc., and living close to Minnie, in Richmond Hill. Samuel Marx might have felt at least a twinge of satisfaction that one of his sons thought the old schmutter business worth taking up.

Maxine remembers that Frenchy's dapper attire was often flecked with food stains, as he became less meticulous in his mid-sixties. He was colour blind, and would put on mismatched socks. But he was closer and more attentive to Maxine than her grandmother, who was still preoccupied with so many little schemes. As she grew older, Frenchy took Maxine to the movies, and she was once terribly embarrassed when he stood up with tears streaming when the 'Marseillaise' was played at one film. When he took Maxine to the movie *The Scarlet Letter*, starring Lillian Gish, she embarrassed him by asking why they had put the letter 'A' on the lady's dress. 'Pshaw,' he said, dismissively, and then: 'Don't tell der Mamma vhat you saw, yah?'

They were the best of times, they were the worst of times: the 'Roaring Twenties'. The lacklustre Calvin Coolidge had become President in August 1923 after the sudden death of Warren G. Harding, and in November 1924 he was re-elected for a full four-year term. This was despite the infamous 'Teapot Dome' scandal which involved numerous kickbacks on oilfield leases. An immigration bill signed in May 1924 severely restricted immigration; each country was allowed an inflow of 2 per cent of the nationals of that country according to the census of 1890. America was turning inwards, to self-celebration. On 20–21 May 1925, Charles Lindbergh flew solo over the Atlantic, in the first non-stop New York to Paris flight, igniting a patriotic frenzy. A few weeks later a teacher, John Thomas Scopes, was being tried in Dayton, Tennessee, for teaching the doctrine of evolution to high-school students. It was apparently too much to suggest that Americans might be descended from monkeys, though the Marx Brothers might have embraced this idea warmly.

Coolidge believed in the Great God Business. In domestic policy he preferred to do nothing that would upset the rolling bandwagon of Prosperity. He knew and understood little of foreign policy. For most Americans, he was the perfect expression of the age. The New York Stock Exchange was booming, though it was yet to experience the acme, and nemesis, of its popularity. As Frederick Lewis Allen wrote: 'The country had bread, but it wanted circuses.' And Broadway was there to supply the demand.

It was probably inevitable that, Round Table or no Round Table, like would meet like in this environment, and George S. Kaufman would team up with the Marx Brothers. The matchmaker was producer Sam H. Harris, a Broadway veteran who had worked with George M. Cohan. The Brothers had an enormous respect for Sam Harris, not only because of his track record – over thirty shows produced, most of them hits – but also his reputation as a good friend to actors: he had taken their side in the watershed Equity strike of 1919, a conflict in which Cohan had sided with the employers. After the success of *I'll Say She Is*, the Brothers were wooed by other Broadway producers, but favoured Harris, though he was not sure he wanted to preside over their playground. Kaufman too was reluctant, though he had met Harpo, Groucho and Chico, if not Zeppo, at the Thanatopsis poker nights. But there was another matchmaker: Irving Berlin.

Beginning as a singing waiter at 'Nigger Mike's' in 1904, Israel Baline, alias Irving Berlin, had written, since he was nineteen years old in 1907, over four hundred songs – and was to go on to top 1,500 titles. By 1911 he was known as the Ragtime King, the conduit by which black Americans' syncopation was made popular to white audiences. By the end of the First World War he had graduated from the hustle of Tin Pan Alley and become a force in the legitimate theatre, composing seven numbers for the Ziegfeld *Follies of 1919*, for which he wrote 'A Pretty Girl Is Like a Melody'. Two years later his alliance with Sam Harris produced the *Music Box Revue of 1921*, which encapsulated the spirit of the new Jazz Age. All of New York was singing Irving Berlin songs. It was inevitable that he would gravitate to the Algonquin Round Table, though his natural shyness, and his concentration on work, kept him aloof from Woollcott's inner circle. Nevertheless, he and Harpo became mutual fans, and Berlin matched up Harris and the Brothers. Presenting their routines in his office, they soon reduced it to bedlam, and the great producer to Marxian putty. The next stage was to convince the popular playwright of the age to join the popular songsmith of the age in the venture.

In 1925, Kaufman was riding high. Ten of his plays had already been produced, and the eleventh, *The Butter and Egg Man*, was to open in September. This was the first play Kaufman had written by himself, having previously collaborated with Marc Connelly (in nine plays) and Edna Ferber, with *Minick* (1924). Kaufman and Connelly's first collaboration, *Dulcy*, in 1921, was constructed around a wide-eyed young girl whose well-intentioned meddling leads to a string of mishaps, which gave the young playwrights an opportunity to demonstrate their skills with characters, quick repartee, sly social observation, and sharp, sophisticated wit. A young and awkward aspiring writer from Columbus, Ohio, James Thurber, saw the play and realized the direction his own quirky satire might take.

Kaufman himself would deride the word satire, as against straightforward comedy. His definition was 'satire is what closes Saturday night'. But Kaufman was notoriously nervous, indeed paranoid, about his own powers and talent and would pace about at first nights even when he was famous, gloomily convinced that his work was a failure, and only the audience's obtuseness prevented them from seeing the manifold flaws that he, Kaufman, sensed clearly. 'The play's artificial,' he would moan, 'it's too long. It's a failure. Well, at least we tried . . .' He would only let go reluctantly when the applause was echoing in his ears.

Kaufman was reluctant to write a play for the Marx Brothers, and was said to have remarked, when approached by Sam Harris: 'I'd as soon write a show for the Barbary Apes.' He had built up a skill in creating characters, working out situations that the playwright could develop from scratch. What was the point of working with characters that were already set, and owned, by a group of men who were notoriously undisciplined, and whose entire appeal lay in their ad-libs, in the spontaneous madness that would erupt on the stage? 'And how do I write for Harpo?' he protested. But Sam Harris had set his sights on Kaufman, having previously struck out on a completely different concept – hiring a sketch writer, or 'blackout' man, to develop the Marxes' material. This anonymous worthy had turned up at the Brothers' dressing room, only to be challenged by muscle man Zeppo to a wrestling bout. Another account has all four Marxes stripping the poor man of all his clothing, a gambit the Brothers were said to be especially fond of, inflicting it even on Aleck Woollcott. (The great critic merely gathered his togs and, in his underwear, invited them to walk out with him. In Woollcott the Marx Brothers always met their match.)

At least Harris was – reasonably – sure that the Marx Brothers would not gang up on George S. Kaufman and rip off his clothes. In fact, Groucho had already tangled verbally with Kaufman, having read the *Herald Tribune* critic, Percy Hammond's, claim that he (Groucho) and Kaufman were very similar both in appearance and temperament. Kaufman had apparently expressed some pique at this comparison, and Groucho responded with one of his earliest, but already inimitable, letters:

I have never seen Mr Kaufman in the flesh, or the rough, or whatever you call it. I have seen a number of his plays, and I am not sure whether he had a mustache or not, although some authors find it advisable to wear something on the opening night . . . If you can suggest any humorous get-up that wouldn't look like the aforementioned gentleman I would be only too glad to adopt it . . .'

What the critic might have been referring to was not only the playwright's dark and handsome semitic looks but, in the words of his biographer, Scott Meredith: 'His habit of walking in his office with his hands behind his back, his head bent forward, and his body slightly stooped in deep concentration. His concentration was so intense that one day he banged his head, with a clang, against the fire extinguisher.' Scholars have debated long into the night whether Groucho adopted this characteristic pose from Kaufman, or whether it was there from time immemorial, in the act, perhaps a left-over from Mr Green. This physical peculiarity was but a part of George S.'s many quirks when deep in his creative processes. Others were washing his hands obssessively before beginning the day's work; prowling about the room picking up and examining every piece of paper; and swooping down on pieces of lint on the carpet and dropping them in the wastepaper basket. In striving to perfect every line and plot twist, Woollcott said of him, 'in the throes of composition, he seems to crawl up the walls of the apartment in the manner of the late Count Dracula'.

Whatever the physical similarities, it is clear from any examination of Kaufman's own prose style that he and Groucho were in many respects two soul mates, clawing their way, in the thick fog of history, slowly but surely towards each other. One of the abiding puzzles of this period in the Marxian tale is that it was Harpo, the 'inarticulate', rather than Groucho, the bookworm, who became a formal member of the Round Table. This had much to do with the emotional spasm of Aleck Woollcott's 'love affair' with Harpo. Perhaps, if one takes a more critical view of that period, Harpo was easier for the 'Wasp' grandee to patronize. If there was anyone who appeared the very image of the smart-ass, 'pushy' Jew, in this context, it was surely Groucho. But Groucho, too, had his inhibitions. He felt too keenly the gulf between himself and this sophisticated, college-educated circle. As he himself described them: 'The admission fee was a viper's tongue and a half-concealed stiletto. It was a sort of intellectual slaughterhouse, and I doubt if this country will ever see its like again.' Even as trained a sophisticate as Clare Boothe Luce could find the Algonquin lunches too competitive. 'You couldn't say, "pass the salt," without somebody trying to turn it into a pun or trying to top it.' It is significant that W. C. Fields, the other Woollcott discovery, and no mean slouch either at the *bons mots* or the cards, not to speak of the speakeasy, never sat around the Round Table. These 'highbrows' were too smart for mere show people. Only Harpo, who sat, listened and played cards, and who was at ease anywhere, could survive unscathed. As Woollcott wrote about him in 1928, in one of his *New Yorker* pieces entitled 'Portrait of a Man with Red Hair':

Harpo Marx belongs to the company of those who, by the talisman of some secret in their hearts, could be dropped out of a parachute into any town at dawn and be among its oldest inhabitants by noon. Harpo would certainly be a crony of the village padre by noon and a mighty entertainment to all the adoring children. By sundown he would have an engagement to play dominoes at the café in the corner, this contest to be followed by a tryst with a pretty wench at the river's edge and, at sunup, by a solemn engagement to go out with the village fisherman in his boat.

But not Groucho. He would be too painfully aware of his status as a stranger in town. Above all, Groucho envied writers. He knew that no actor could open his mouth on the stage and wow an audience unless someone had sat down and painstakingly put words on paper. And here was Kaufman, spoofing *Life* magazine's famous 'Calendar' for October 1922:

October 17, Tuesday: Burgoyne surrenders to Gates, 1777. Last New York delicatessen store begins using colored paper sauerkraut for window decoration, 1922.

October 21, Saturday: Edison produces first incandescent light; 'Don't-blow-out-the-gas' joke begins to fight for its life, 1879. First composite photograph of presidential timber, 1892.

October 23, Monday: First boat on Erie Canal, 1819. Ten-cent tip for ice water becomes obsolete, 1914.

October 25, Wednesday: New York subway opens; James L. Gleep, 1675 Amsterdam Avenue, being first man to have back broken while pushed into car, 1904.

This man was born to write *The Cocoanuts*. In the spring of 1925, he duly set to work, recruiting, as his own reinforcement against the onslaught of the Foursome, a young collaborator, another ex-contributor to the 'Conning

Tower' columns of Franklin P. Adams, one-time assistant for his *New York Times* pieces – Morrie Ryskind. The pencils were sharpened; the typewriter unhooded; the papers shuffled and the lint picked carefully off the carpet. Irving Berlin would write the songs. The Marx Brothers would star. There would be some young, fresh talent for the love interest and the dances. And there would be a new member of the cast, to play the straight role of a stuck-up society lady, an actress absent from the stage for some years but now eager for a comeback. Her name, she claimed, was Margaret Dumont.

The Mystery and Mystique of Daisy Dumont
– Staying at a Bum Hotel

MRS POTTER: Remember that in two hundred years, the Potters have
   never been involved in a single scandal!
POLLY: I know, mother. Except for Uncle Dick.
MRS POTTER: Polly, it is a well known fact that your uncle was drunk at
   the time!

The Cocoanuts (1925)

The Marx Brothers without Margaret Dumont are like chicken soup
without the matzo ball, like a bagel without the cream cheese, or like Laurel
and Hardy without Jimmy Finlayson. Every comedy act needs some kind of
foil, some example of the world they are lampooning, or struggling to tear
down, or to join. Margaret Dumont was the perfect society lady, the wealthy
widow who was foolish or generous enough to allow such dangerous wastrels
as the Brothers Marx to get through her gossamer-thin defences. Sometimes
she is an *arriviste*, as in *A Night at the Opera* where, for some unfathomable
reason, she has engaged the useless manager, Otis P. Driftwood, to insert her
into society. Another time she is Mrs Teasdale of Freedonia, the piggy bank
of an imaginary country. Then again, as in *Animal Crackers*, she parades herself in the grand manner as the patroness of the arts.

   She died in 1965, still lamenting the fact that the Marx Brothers had set
her career in aspic, frozen her for ever in that typecast role, which she could
never escape; for ever the butt of jokes, the figure of fun, the fairground
Aunt Sally at whom one throws all the brickbats, insults and gibes. All
Marx Brothers fans are familiar with her statuesque shape, an Aphrodite
who got away from the dietitians, dressed in her flowing evening gowns,
suggesting both a kind of supercilious distance and a come-and-get-me to
the nearest social climber; that look of bemused tolerance with which she
accepted every Grouchoesque shaft, and even the physical insults visited
upon her by Chico and Harpo, who often adopted her as a kind of human
Everest, to be scaled with full mountain gear.

Off screen, as on, she was the Brothers' favourite victim. Stories abound of how the Brothers tormented her, from the earliest rehearsals for *The Cocoanuts*, hitting her with a billiard cue when she asked for her acting cue, tripping her up, stepping on her train, and Harpo – who else? – sticking his hands up the sleeves of her dress, and snatching off her stage wig. She was not the only one whom the Brothers tormented on stage, as actress Maggie Irving, who appeared alongside Dumont in *Animal Crackers*, found out to her cost. Being hit with a rolled up painting or batted with oranges and apples were the least of the hazards of the Marx *femme*. Like all small boys, the Marxes had to beat up the girls. This was, we can safely assume on the evidence, the way they had treated their 'big sister', Pauline.

The prevailing legend of Margaret Dumont was that she never understood any of the Marx Brothers' jokes. 'What are they laughing at, Julie?' she was supposed to have asked Groucho. Groucho always insisted that she really was the character she played on the stage. The whole point of the fun was that she was authentic, a genuine foil, not a made-up one.

But how true is this? Who was Margaret Dumont, behind that fine marble exterior? The reference books suggest a straightforward answer: she was born as Margaret, or Marguerite, Baker in Brooklyn on 20 October 1889. Her father was Irish and her mother French. She was a 'delicate child', and was brought up mainly in Europe by private tutors. She was trained as an opera singer and made her début aged seventeen or eighteen at the Casino de Paris, in Paris, where she was talent-spotted by J. J. Shubert, who brought her back to the US to join the Lew Fields company. (Other accounts have her touring London, Paris, Vienna and Berlin.) In her early stage career she was known as Daisy Dumont – Dumont, she claimed, being her mother's maiden name. After a distinguished career in Fields and Shubert shows, she married a millionaire, John Moller Jr., in 1910, and retired from the stage. She became a socialite, and a bona fide member of New York's élite 'four hundred'. When Moller died, she wished to return to acting, and appears to have had a credit as a background extra in a movie version of *A Tale of Two Cities*, filmed in 1917 by Frank Lloyd. Her stage appearance as a society lady in *The Four Flushers,* a Sam H. Harris production, led the producer to suggest her for the *grande dame* role in *The Cocoanuts*. And the rest, as they say, is movie history.

A more intriguing variant of the Dumont tale was proposed by Charlotte Chandler in her long book on Groucho's table gossip and old-age reminiscences, *Hello, I Must Be Going*, published in 1978, a year after Groucho's death. Born as Daisy Baker in 1889, in Atlanta, Georgia, Dumont was

Daisy Dumont in showgirl days (1909).

brought up in the home of her godfather, Joel Chandler Harris, 'creator of Uncle Remus, Br'er Rabbit, and Br'er Fox . . . Opera-trained, she had served her apprenticeship for two years as a show girl in the music halls of England and France . . .'

One does wish people would source their tall tales. The only sources for the generally accepted version are a combination of Maggie Dumont's stories told to her friends in Hollywood, and a biographical profile in *Collier's* magazine of May 1937, penned by Kyle Crichton – author-to-be of the semi-fictional *The Marx Brothers*. The prosecution rests. As Dumont never remarried, and had no children, the trail she left is pretty thin. Flimflam prevails. The *New York Herald Tribune*, 20 January 1937, wrote of Dumont:

> Groucho Marx, in fact, has proposed to her so many times on the screen that the public now believes she is actually his wife.
>
> 'Once,' Mrs Dumont declares, 'a newspaper actually printed that I was

Groucho's wife. I told Groucho that the announcement was embarrassing.'

'Embarrassing,' he cried, 'I have just written an article about my wife, and the magazine is running her picture. When that article comes out, I'll be arrested for bigamy!'

But it is now possible, owing to the stubborn digging of our indefatigable genealogist Dave Rothman, in Family History archives, to present, at last, the real Maggie Dumont.

Charlotte Chandler, in one aspect, was right: she was born Daisy Baker – Daisy Juliette Baker – not in Atlanta, but in Brooklyn, on 20 October 1882, not 1889 – a full seven years to add to her stated age. Her father was William F. Baker, described variously as 'seaman', 'sea captain' and US Navy pilot. Her mother was Harriet Anna Baker, maiden name Harvey. Daisy was her mother's second child, but we have no record of the first. Soon after Daisy's birth, William F. departed the ménage, and we next find Harriet Baker, listed as 'widow of William F.', ensconced as a 'vocalist' in the Manhattan directory of 1893–94. (Though William F. can still be traced, very much alive, until 1899, living down by the port on Fulton Street. Separated women often listed themselves as 'Widow'.)

Harriet Baker's trail goes cold after this, and the circumstances of young Daisy's childhood must be left to her future biographer. An early clipping, from the Shubert company archive, dated from her earliest comeback stage role, as Mrs Cornwallis in the 1920 musical comedy *Fifty Fifty*, playing at the Chestnut Theatre in Philadelphia, casts doubt on the later tales of early European tours, as Dumont enthuses: 'It was on this very stage I made my professional début. I was in "The Beauty and the Beast." You may imagine my feeling then, for only a little while before I had left the Loretta Academy, in Toronto, Canada . . .' No sign here of the Casino de Paris.

The Loretta Academy was a Catholic finishing school of some repute, so we might surmise that Harriet Baker was not keen for her daughter to follow her into show business. But as early as August 1902, aged twenty, we find 'Daisy Dumont' in a vaudeville act at Atlantic Gardens, New York, billed as a 'vocal comedienne'.

Even in her earliest days, 'Margaret Dumont' told the Philadelphia press, her stage partners were 'always joking with me and playing practical tricks, which got on my nerves to the extent that I was constantly bordering on hysteria. I was nicknamed among my associates, "Daisy, the Leading Lady . . ."' Clearly the Marx Brothers, in tormenting their Maggie, were following in much earlier footsteps.

From 1907, we can begin to trace Daisy Dumont's development in the Lew Fields company, formed after the break-up of the famous double act of Weber and Fields. She first turns up in a Lew Fields hit, *The Girl Behind the Counter*, playing 'Millie Mostyn, overlady at the "Universal," an American department store in London.' (One scene is set in 'a parvenue restaurant in Hammersmith', and may have been the closest to London that Daisy reached at that point.) The show starred Lew Fields, Connie Ediss and the eponymous Lotta Faust, but Daisy got to sing 'two comic songs with fine spirit' – 'Won't You Buy', and 'The Glow Worm'.

A slim archive file includes a handful of portraits of the young soubrette, in a variety of stylish costumes. Most of the portraits date from her supporting role in a Shubert comedy of 1909, *The Belle of Brittany*, described by its publicists thus: 'The Marquis de St. Gautier needs money and has mortgaged his chateau to Poquelin. He hopes to save himself by arranging a marriage between his son, Raymond, and his ward, Denise. But Denise loves one Compte Victoire.' Dumont, of course, is Denise. Her head is crowned with an immense dark coiffure, upgathered like a Japanese geisha. The reviewer in *Theatre* magazine wrote that 'Daisy Dumont is the statuesque beauty of the aggregation.' In another Lew Fields production, *The Summer Widowers*, staged by our old friend Ned Wayburn, and featuring a ten-year-old Helen Hayes, Daisy appears way down the cast list as 'Fritzi Fluff, an absent-minded Prima Donna', and sings 'Oh, You Summertime Romeo', with full chorus.

Later listings of *The Summer Widower*, which was a long-running hit, omit Daisy Dumont, and so this may be the period when she became hitched to sugar heir Moller. At any rate, she disappears abruptly from the stage. The first verified sighting of the new couple is from the New York census of 1915, which lists Moller, John J., and Daisy J., at 235 West 103rd Street, living with a domestic servant – Janoga Kiugo, Japanese, male, 'alien'.

The *New York Times*, 26 December 1918, obituaries: 'Died: Moller, at the Flower Hospital Tuesday Dec. 24 . . . John Moller, Jr., beloved husband of Daisy Baker, and son of John and the late Louise Moller . . . Interment private.' Poor Daisy was widowed on Christmas Eve, at a time when the rest of the nation was still celebrating the end of the Great War. Probably to soothe her grief, she lost little time in returning to the stage, with a string of Broadway productions: *Fifty Fifty*, George M. Cohan's *Mary* (1920), *The Fan* and *Go Easy Mabel* (both 1921), and another Cohan production, *The Rise of Rosie O'Reilly* (1922) – described as 'the first musical comedy to be set in Brooklyn'. The reviews noted 'handsome Margaret Dumont, looking every inch an aristocrat', as the wealthy 'dowager' widow, Mrs Montague Bradley.

Charlotte Chandler quoted Dumont as having said her husband's family 'didn't entirely approve of my return to the stage', though one might imagine they would hardly have approved of the magnate's marriage to a show girl in the first place. We do not know if he left her all his money, as Mr Teasdale did for Mrs Teasdale ('I held him in my arms, and kissed him!' Groucho: 'So it was moider!?'). We might even speculate that she did not in fact inherit much, and may well have been compelled to return to the stage for economic reasons. Her formal studio biography for Paramount Pictures, in 1930, states that:

> She returned to the stage because of a longing for something besides a round of teas and receptions to occupy her mind. As a result she is as much at home in the drawing room(s) of the élite as in the studios, and it is natural that she should be able to play a society matron with poise and distinction, or gently burlesque the role and still keep it real.

Note the word 'burlesque', for this indeed was the form for which Daisy was trained in her early roles in Lew Fields's musicals. She was, in fact, an accomplished comedienne, who found her character and then stuck to it for the next fifty-eight years. The more one examines her early record the less likely become all the later stories about her lack of humour or awareness of the Marx Brothers' jokes. Chandler quotes Maureen O'Sullivan as stating that Margaret Dumont actually believed that *A Day at the Races* was a serious picture. 'When we started, she told me, "It's not going to be one of those things. I'm having a very serious part this time."' This after ten years of playing comedy with Groucho, Chico, Harpo and Zeppo!! Some people are just too gullible for words.

George Kaufman's co-writer, Morrie Ryskind, was more sceptical, as he wrote of Dumont in his autobiography, nicely titled *I Shot an Elephant in My Pyjamas* (1994):

> I strongly suspect that she was convinced that great ladies weren't expected to have great intellects, and she responded accordingly . . . No one could have been a showgirl for as many years as she was without acquiring at least a modicum of street savvy. If my theory is correct, then she should be lauded for the longest running performance in show business history, for she never slipped from her character until her death.

It was in 'Daisy Dumont''s absolute interest to insist that her social origins matched her later status, particularly if this status evaporated on her rich husband's death. Born in very ordinary circumstances, to a professional family, she had learned a role in the theatre and then become, by marriage, the creature of her fantasy, for seven lucky years. We might, then, venture a quite different interpretation of that enigmatic screen smile, as we see her fielding Groucho's barbs and insults about her origins and bona fides: not so much a bemused failure to see the joke but, more likely, a Cheshire Cat simper, a hidden twinkle, mingled with a deep-seated anxiety over her well-buried secret.

By the time she returned to the stage in 1920 it was imperative that Daisy Dumont should be seen as an actress in the prime of life, a bookable thirty-one, rather than a more mature and probably less employable thirty-eight. And so she changed her name again, her age, her stage history, and her family annals. (Margaret, of course, is a version of the French *marguerite*, meaning daisy.) It is not therefore Margaret Dumont who failed to see the joke, but the Marx Brothers, their interpreters and biographers, who have been unwitting victims of a desperate practical joke played upon us for three-quarters of a century by that greatest of dissimulating comediennes, the finest 'straight' lady in the history of motion pictures – Daisy Juliette Baker.

Bravo!

'Margaret Dumont' was not the only token of the watershed nature of *The Cocoanuts*. Irving Berlin's music, which some critics nevertheless found mundane, and George S. Kaufman's text, which they certainly did not, marked this show as something different. The lavish sets, too, lifted the production from the rag-and-bone level of *I'll Say She Is*. Four merry monkeys garlanded the poster for the show heralded as 'A Musical Tornado', 'A Musical Laugh-quake' and 'Mirth, Melody and Dancing in Abundance'. The show previewed in Boston and Philadelphia and then opened on 8 December 1925, at the Lyric Theatre on 42nd Street. It ran on Broadway for 377 performances before going on the road in 1927, and playing well into 1928, until the second show Kaufman wrote for the Brothers (this time with the full acknowledged collaboration of Morrie Ryskind), *Animal Crackers*, opened, in October 1928.

Kaufman and Berlin were uneasy collaborators over *The Cocoanuts*, since, as Berlin soon discovered, Kaufman was 'not merely indifferent to music but actively hostile to it'. Irving Berlin's biographer, Lawrence Bergreen, quotes from Kaufman's own acid account of their encounter:

Irving woke me up at five o'clock one morning to sing me a song he had just finished. Now, Irving has a pure but hardly strong voice, and, since I am not very strong myself at five o'clock in the morning, I could not catch a word of it. Moving to the edge of the bed, he sat down and sang it again, and again I failed to get it. Just when it looked as if he would have to get in my bed before I could hear it, he managed, on the third try, to put it across. The song was a little number called "Always," and its easy-going rhythms were just up my street. I learned it quickly and as dawn broke we leaned out of the window and sang it to the Atlantic Ocean . . .

To this day, I do not quite know the difference between Handel's "Largo" and – well – Largo's "Handel." But I have always felt that I knew a little something about lyrics, and I was presumptuous enough then to question Irving's first line, "I'll be loving you always." Always was a long time for romance . . . I suggested, therefore, that the opening line might be a little more in accord with reality – something like "I'll be loving you Thursday." But Irving would have none of it.'

(Note the timbres of Kaufman's natural writing style – the clearest source of Groucho's own cadences when he began to dabble in prose.) The problem that Kaufman was facing was, quite obviously, that the songs were holding back the whiplash speed of the comedy dialogue scenes, making the whole thing far too long for consumption as the light, frothy confection it was intended to be. Pull and push between the writer and lyricist continued, until Kaufman offered Berlin, in irritation, 'I'll tell you what, you waive the songs and I'll waive the story.' In the end the melodious 'Always' was cut from the show, but went on to become one of Berlin's most enduring hits, while *The Cocoanuts* was left with 'The Monkey Doodle Doo', 'A Little Bungalow' and 'Florida by the Sea' performed by the Cocoanut Grove Ensemble and the Cocoanut Beach Octette.

The play that Kaufman wrote for the Marx Brothers was a brilliantly sustained attempt by the playwright to write into the heads of the characters, who had been presented to him ready made. Kaufman was smart enough to understand that there would be no point in trying to alter these characters, or reconstruct them, or dispense with certain characteristics in order to round up a preconceived plan. What he could do, despite his initial reluctance to tangle with these 'barbary apes', would be to perk up their naturally anarchic inclinations with a more focused, sharper satire (that stuff that closes Saturday night), and tap into those sociopathic tendencies with, quite simply, better jokes, better word-play, better punning than could be supplied by Herman Timberg, Will Johnstone, or Al Shean. Even the Margaret

Dumont character was already present, in embryo, as we have seen, in Groucho's own authored sketches and the dowager mother of *On the Balcony*.

Both *The Cocoanuts* and *Animal Crackers* are available to us in their later screen versions and so give us a glimpse, for the first time, into the world of the Marx Brothers in their Broadway revues. The prevailing legend, of Kaufman's extreme exasperation at the Brothers for virtually ignoring his script and launching forth into the cuckoo clucks of ad-lib-land, can't hold water, if we look at the script versions of both stage plays alongside the versions on the screen. Kaufman's famous comment to Ryskind, in the theatre, 'Hush! I think I just heard a line from the script!' may have expressed his ongoing battle with all interpreters of his lines, but the facts are that, give or take obvious departures and omissions, there are many scenes in both shows that are practically identical, on screen, to the original stage texts. Kaufman himself noted the *modus operandi* of the Brothers in a speech he gave at Yale University in 1939. He said:

> Morrie Ryskind and I once learned a great lesson in the writing of stage comedy. We learned it from the Marx Brothers. We wrote two shows for them, which, by the way, is two more than anybody should be asked to write. Looking back, it seems incredible that this was something we had not known before, but we hadn't. We learned that when an audience does not laugh at a line at which they're supposed to laugh, then the thing to do was to take out that line and get a funnier line. So help me, we didn't know that before. I always thought it was the audience's fault, or when the show got to New York they'd laugh.

This obvious method cut both ways. Once the boys got a good laugh from a line or scene, and that scene stayed funny with different audiences, then that scene was locked in place. There would be no point, beyond minor tweaking, in changing something that worked on stage. A typical case in point is the scene close to the opening of *The Cocoanuts* in which the bellboys rise up in mutiny against hotel manager Mr Schlemmer (who later became Hammer, as in *On the Balcony*) over their unpaid salaries:

BELLBOYS: We want our money!
SCHLEMMER: You want your money?
BELLBOY: We want to be paid.
SCHLEMMER: Oh, you want my money. Is that fair? Do I want your
    money? Suppose George Washington's soldiers had asked for money?
    Where would this country be today? . . .

Four hams on wry: Chico, Zeppo, Groucho and Harpo in the stage *Cocoanuts*.

SEVERAL BELLBOYS: We want our money!

SCHLEMMER (*quiets them with an upraised hand*)· Well, I'll make you a promise, if you all stick with me and work hard, we'll forget all about money. We'll make a hotel out of this place yet. We'll put in elevators and subways. I'll put in three blankets in all your rooms. That is, there'll be no cover charge. Think of the opportunities here in Florida. I came here with a shoe string, and now I've got three pairs of buttoned shoes.

BELLBOY: We want our wages.

SCHLEMMER: Wages? Do you want to be wage slaves? Answer me that.

SEVERAL BELLBOYS: No.

SCHLEMMER: Well then, what is it that makes wage slaves? Wages. I want you to be free. Strike off your chains. Strike up the band. Strike three, you're out. Remember, there's nothing like liberty. That is, there's nothing like it in this country. Be free. Now and forever, one and indivisible, one for all, and all for me and me for you, and tea for two. Remember, I have only my best interests at heart, and I promise you, that it's only a question of a few years before some woman will swim the English Channel. I thank you.

In the movie, there are some minor tweaks of the monologue, such as 'Remember, there's nothing like Liberty, except Colliers and the Saturday Evening Post. Be free my friends, one for all and all for me and me for you and three for five and six for a quarter.' But generally there's little change. Structurally the bellboy scene comes earlier in the movie, whereas Schlemmer doesn't turn up till page twelve of the first stage script. Both screen and stage versions open with the 'Lovely Florida' chorus number, as the stage text goes:

> So this is Florida, where flow'rs are booming,
> The sunny land where everybody thinks they're swell . . .
> So this is Florida, the land of sunshine,
> Its not so lovely – stopping at a bum hotel . . .

The plot centred round the very current Florida land boom, in which greedy and gullible New Yorkers shelled out cash for lots, many of which proved worthless, as they were more fit for the accommodation of alligators than of entrepreneurial householders looking for a 'lovely paradise by the sea'. The idea of an America made safe for speculators was an old one for Kaufman. It even figures in one of his very early columns for 'This and That' – from 14 August 1913: 'AMERICA FOR AMERICANS – Land where a mon-eyed ring / corners a certain thing / Ev-e-ry bit, / Land where the clever trust / has the inhabs nonplussed; / Land where we simply must / Pay up or quit.'

The all-American sucker and his predator were a predominant Kaufman theme, and Groucho was a perfect vehicle for the quintessential huckster: 'Do you know that property values have increased 1924 since one thousand percent? Do you know that this is the greatest development since Sophie Tucker? Do you know that Florida is the show spot of America, and that Cocoanut is the sore spot of Florida?'

In fact, the great Florida Real Estate Rush was not much different in reality from the version shown by Kaufman in *The Cocoanuts*, as commentator Frederick Lewis Allen described in his book on 'The Fabulous Twenties' – *Only Yesterday*. Quoting a banker's paean in the local rag, *The Miamian*:

> Go to Florida, where enterprise is enthroned –
> Where you sit and watch at twilight the fronds of the graceful palm,
> latticed against the fading gold of the sun-kissed sky . . .

Where the silver cycle is heaven's lavalier, and the full orbit its glorious pendant . . .

Not for nothing did Groucho/Schlemmer tell Mrs Potter: 'The Chief Justice is just mad about this type of sewer.' Everybody who had any cash, and many who didn't, converged on Florida from the summer of 1924 to the autumn of 1925, wooed by the promise of huge Riviera-type condominiums rising on empty sand, in a state brought close to the East Coast conurbations by the new boon of the mass-produced motor car. Miami was set to grow from a sleepy town of 30,000 inhabitants in 1920 to a great city of over a million souls. This was Coolidge Prosperity with a vengeance, and anybody could cash in. But by 1925, Allen wrote, 'One had only to announce a new development, be it honest or fraudulent, be it on the Atlantic Ocean or deep in the wasteland of the interior, to set people scrambling for house lots. "Manhattan Estates" was advertised as being "not more than three-fourths of a mile from the prosperous and fast-growing city of Nettie"; there was no such city as Nettie, the name being that of an abandoned turpentine camp, yet people bought.' Cue Groucho's immortal auctioneer's spiel:

SCHLEMMER: You are now in Cocoanut Manor. One of the finest cities in Florida. Of course, we still need a few finishing touches, but who doesn't. This is the heart of the residential district. Every lot is a stone's throw from the station. The only reason we haven't got any station is because we haven't got any stones. Eight hundred beautiful residences will be built right here. They are as good as up. Better. You can have any kind of house you want to. You can even get stucco. Oh, how you can get stucco. Now is the time to buy while the new boom is on. Remember a new boom sweeps clean, and don't forget the guarantee. If these lots don't double themselves in a year, I don't know what you can do about it!

Writes Allen: 'In the height of the fury of building a visitor to West Palm Beach noticed a large vacant lot almost completely covered with bathtubs. The tubs had apparently been there for some time . . . The lot, he was informed, was to be the site of "one of the most magnificent apartment buildings in the South" – but the freight embargo had held up the contractor's building materials and only the bathtubs had arrived!'

The Marx Brothers' *The Cocoanuts* turns out to be a documentary! So solid was Kaufman's satirical base that he knew he should avoid confusing matters by anything more than the most rudimentary plot: Mrs Potter's

More Cocoanutty than this you can't get: 'Play I'm a dreamer, Montreal.'

daughter Polly's boyfriend Bob is framed by two crooks, Penelope and Harvey, for the theft of a pearl necklace belonging to Mrs Potter. Meanwhile, hotel manager Schlemmer and his lobby clerk, Zeppo, have to contend with the two bums, Chico and Harpo, who have turned up at the hotel having made 'reservache'.

CHICO: We want room and no bath.
GROUCHO: Oh I see. You're just here for the winter. Step this way.

Ripping up the manager's telegrams and drinking the ink from Zeppo's inkpot are but the beginning of the affair, which culminates in Chico's inspired trashing of Groucho's auction by continuing to 'Bid 'em op, bid 'em op.' Along the way comes Chico and Groucho's immortal screen exchange over the viaduct – 'Why a duck? Why-a no chicken?' which is not in Kaufman's original script and was developed in the course of the performances – though Morrie Ryskind, writing nearly seventy years later, laid his own claim to the scene. The whole shebang leads on to the final celebratory dinner, at which Sheriff Hennessy's lost shirt is found (new cop Basil Ruysdael leading the spoof *Carmen* chorus), and Groucho delivers a no-holds-barred speech which is much truncated in the film version:

GROUCHO (*as Harpo leaves*): They're dropping out early. When this Irishman died and he went to heaven and on the way to heaven – he met a Scotchman and a Swede and there wasn't room for all of them to get in bed so they had to stop overnight at a farm house and Little Willie had to stay up late. Well you can bet that the Minister never asked that question again. Well ten minutes later when the lady came back in the sleeping car, there was a foot sticking out of every berth. So St Peter said you can't come in here and the Irishman said, why not? Now stop me if you've heard it . . . Well the result was that my mother and father had to move to New York. So they took a little house in the Bronx. And it was in that very house that Abraham Lincoln was born. Much to my father's surprise . . . I am now going to call for a speech from Mrs Potter and keep it clean . . .
(*Follow Mrs Potter speech and Chico and Harpo specialties, then –*)
GROUCHO: And now ladies and gentlemen, you can have your choice of two things. You can either have a recitation of Gunga Din, or you can have Gunga Din without the recitation. I will now distribute the ballots.

The crooks are foiled, Mrs Potter announces the engagement of her daughter Polly to her chosen Bob, and Groucho offers everyone, in honour of the event, 'a free dinner. Admission four dollars.' Jiggled eyebrows at Mrs Potter. Margaret Dumont smiles her enigmatic smile back at Groucho. Girls and boys reprise 'Bungalow By the Sea' number. End of Scene, Curtain, End of Play.

20

Triumph of the Left-Handed Moths

ROSCOE W. CHANDLER: Ah, but after all, money isn't everything. Suppose
a man works hard, and makes eighty million dollars a year, after he has
paid his income tax, what has he left, seventy million.
MRS RITTENHOUSE: That's life.
CHANDLER: Anyway, if it is in you to be artistic, then it comes out of you
no matter what . . .

Animal Crackers (1928)

Whatever the solution to the mystery of Margaret Dumont, there is no mystery in the Marx Brothers' ascendancy between 1925 and 1929. During this same period their contemporary, W. C. Fields, 'discovered', as we have seen, by Alexander Woollcott in the same halcyon summer of 1924, was not faring quite so well. Still a star on Broadway, in the *Ziegfeld Follies*, he was trying his luck in the movie business with *Sally of the Sawdust* and *It's the Old Army Game*. Despite critical acclaim, he could not compete with the silent greats, Chaplin, Keaton and Lloyd. But the true key to the magic room, which he did not possess, was the jovial embrace of the Algonquin Round Table.

Nineteen twenty-five, as we have noted, was the year of the founding of *The New Yorker*, though it would take about a year for the magazine to find its distinctive voice and authority. The man whom Woollcott described as looking like a 'dishonest Abe Lincoln' was forging a unique combination of intellectual gossip and cultural iconoclasm. Intensely incestuous, its pages were used by the favoured élite to display their wit and wisdom, and highlight the books, plays and art of the day. Nineteen twenty-five was not only the year of *The Cocoanuts*, but also of Maxwell Anderson and Laurence Stallings's coruscating anti-war play *What Price Glory* (which opened in 1924), of F. Scott Fitzgerald's *The Great Gatsby*, of Theodore Dreiser's *An American Tragedy*. Five of Eugene O'Neill's plays were produced between 1924 and 1926 – and Groucho himself was to lampoon O'Neill's gloominess in a 'strange interlude' in *Animal Crackers*.

Apart from Harold Ross and *The New Yorker*, *Life* magazine, another influential weekly, was represented at the Table by its editor, Robert Sherwood. And we have noted the presence of other powerful newspapermen like F. P. Adams, Herbert Bayard Swope, and Heywood Broun. Harpo may have been sitting quietly at the table, playing his poker with the Thanatopsisites, listening and saying very little, but he was a pure conduit through which power flowed from the opinion leaders to their adopted quartet of clowns.

In short, the Marx Brothers were the New York élite's favourite sons, and their anointment with the holy oil of George S. Kaufman served to assure their position. Even before *The Cocoanuts* opened, Groucho had become the proud author of an early piece for Ross's *New Yorker*, inaugurating a series of 'casuals', under the heading of 'Vaudeville Talk', and still signed Julius H. Marx:

VAUDE: What is your opinion of the women of this generation?
VILL: I don't know. All those I have been out with have been of the last generation.
VA: You don't seem to get me.
VI: I don't want you, I don't even want your opinion.
VA: Well, why did you ask me for my opinion?
VI: Well, I didn't think you had one.

According to Robert Bader, editor of Groucho's collected essays, Groucho's first published piece appeared in Franklin P. Adams's *Conning Tower* column in 1923. But it was not till 1929 that he would begin to blossom in print, with a series of articles in *The New Yorker*. One year later, his first full-length book of humorous essays, *Beds*, would be published; an event that pleased the budding author no end. It was a source of great gratification for Groucho that he could be recognized in the same journal that published Aleck Woollcott, Wolcott Gibbs, Robert Benchley, Dorothy Parker, E. B. White, Ring Lardner, S. J. Perelman and that shy, blinking man from Columbus, Ohio, James Thurber. These were not quite the Himalayan peaks of literature – Hemingway wrote one piece for *The New Yorker* and Fitzgerald contributed three 'casuals' and two poems, but Faulkner, Dos Passos and Dreiser were conspicuous by their absence – Ross was not very strong on novelists. Thurber said of him that he hadn't read a novel since *Riders of the Purple Sage*: 'He doesn't read anything except what goes into his magazine.' But *Riders of the Purple Sage* would do very nicely for Groucho. The foothills were enough for Minnie's Boy who had had to start by scaling the hills of Denver with the Leroy Trio and the Whangdoodle Four.

Groucho's new-found security now enabled him to move out with Ruth and little Arthur from their apartment in Upper West Side New

York to a two-storey house in Great Neck, Long Island, at 21 Lincoln Road – genuine stucco, with ten rooms and a bluestone gravel driveway for his grand Lincoln car. Chico, Betty and Maxine also moved to a leased house close by. Groucho's house was the first he had ever owned. Great Neck had already become something of an artists' colony: Eddie Cantor, Al Jolson, Ruby Keeler, Sam Harris, Scott Fitzgerald and Ring Lardner were in the neighbourhood, and even W. C. Fields moved in, with his full supply of bottled succour. Groucho threw himself into his new home-owning life, planting a fruit orchard whose trees never reached fruit-bearing age before he had to move on. He also resolved to join one of the Long Island beach clubs, a venture which produced one of his most scathing comments, when he drew up at the gate of the Sands Point Bath and Sun Club with Arthur in tow. The manager, unimpressed by Groucho's celebrity, refused him entrance on the grounds that he was Jewish. 'What about my son?' retorted Groucho. 'He's only half-Jewish. Would it be all right if he went into the water up to his knees?' At the end of the day, he joined the even more expensive Lakeville Country Club, with all the other showbiz Jews.

Zeppo had continued to resent Groucho for stealing his girl, and Ruth's days on stage with the act had ended after an occasion when Zeppo had failed to catch her in the dance, precipitating her into the orchestra pit. Soon Betty, too, was out of the act and the new Marx girls became full-time housewives. This affected Ruth and Betty differently. Betty was a tough-minded trouper, who was determined to stick with Chico through thick and thin. Knowing his reputation, it came as no surprise to her that her husband never rested his roving eye. She knew he was following the Golden Rule: 'If you can get away with it, try; if you can't, try anyway.' In any case she had little choice in the matter in the hard days on the road. More imme-diately worrying was Chico's gambling, which escalated to higher and higher stakes as his income increased.

In one instance, Maxine reports, Chico absconded from the night's per-formance of *The Cocoanuts* while on tour in Detroit. It turned out that he had lost all his money at 'Nick the Greek''s in New York and, unable to pay his debts, took it on the lam, afraid his creditors were on his trail. This peep into Chico's relationship with the gangsters who controlled New York's gambling tables lifts a corner of a veil but not much more, at this point. The upshot of the Detroit scare was a flustered Chico returning a few days later to face a furious row, neither the first nor the last, with his brothers over his behaviour.

Maxine relates that Groucho confided in Betty: 'I'm not going to forgive him for this one . . . He should have said something to me. I knew the bastard needed some dough. Instead of trusting me, he makes everybody think he's wearing a block of cement at the bottom of a lake. I don't know how you can stand him, Betty, I really don't.' But Betty was still deeply in love with her incorrigible husband. Years later, she told Maxine: 'When I hear his step on the stair, my heart still flutters.'

The problem was when his step was absent, as it was all too often.

Ruth Marx turned out to be much more vulnerable to her husband's vices, although these did not include adultery and betrayal. Groucho's prime vice was, at the end of the day, his impatience. Like many people of sharp wit, he was prone to quick irritation at the fact that slower wits were not keeping up with him. Later on, of course, his talent for insults, innuendoes and put-downs became so legendary he felt compelled to give it free rein, though the person Groucho disparaged most, and before anyone else, was himself. Being dissatisfied with his own performance in the human drama, he felt perhaps more justified in being dissatisfied with everyone else's. It should be no surprise then that the person closest to him, his wife, should soon have become his chief target. Groucho had married Ruth for her good looks and good company, but she was not his intellectual equal. At an early stage in their marriage, she began to drink, while Groucho, despite many quips about being stewed at last night's party, was a very light drinker. None of the brothers seemed to have been captured by the boozing frenzy that accompanied Prohibition, and that sealed the fate of W. C. Fields and so many others. But as time went by, guests at Groucho's house would be shocked at how he would put Ruth down in their presence, insulting her cooking, and making her the butt of his quips.

To his children, on the other hand, he was inordinately attentive, at least as long as they remained kids. When his daughter Miriam was born on 19 May 1927, Groucho described this as the happiest day of his life. Now Great Neck had three small Marxes. There might be more expected, as Zeppo had married, on 12 April 1927, a bona fide Jewish actress, Marion Benda, née Bimberg. Gummo would marry, in March 1929, Helen von Tilzer, a young widow with a baby daughter, leaving Harpo the only Marx bachelor.

But Harpo was having far too good a time to get hitched. He was enjoying life both on and off the stage. At one performance, he relates, he chose a cute blonde from the chorus, and promised her a bigger part, to run screaming across the stage as he leapt after her, honking his beloved horn.

This gave Groucho the opportunity to throw up some quip to cover the unscripted chase: 'The nine-twenty's right on time; you can always set your clocks by the Lehigh Valley!' Later, Harpo discovered the blonde's boyfriend was Jack 'Legs' Diamond, who didn't want his baby 'mixed up in no monkey business with them loony actors'. Swiftly, Harpo found another blonde to pursue.

At some point in 1925, just before the opening of *The Cocoanuts*, Harpo landed a small part in a movie, entitled *Too Many Kisses*. A romantic comedy in a Spanish setting, it starred Richard Dix, Frances Howard and William Powell. No one can quite figure out how this came to be, and Harpo doesn't mention it in his memoirs. The lore is that he was visiting friends on the set, at Astoria, Long Island, and ended up in the picture. The film was considered lost for many years, but has recently turned up, looking somewhat the worse for wear. Harpo is seen, dressed in a peasant smock, in a courtyard, taking a drink from a pitcher. He saunters over to a trussed-up heavy, who calls to him (intertitle): 'Untie me, you pig! I can't move!' To which Harpo responds (intertitle): 'Are you sure you can't move?' Checking his bonds, and then knocking him out with an uppercut, he saunters off screen. It is, of course, only fitting that Harpo's only words on screen are silent. Just an intriguing glimpse of another might-have-been . . .

At the Algonquin, Harpo continued to star. At the Thanatopsis poker games, his most consistent partners were Aleck Woollcott and Heywood Broun, and he remained close friends with both. Broun was a shambolic giant of a man, and the most overtly radical of the Algonquinites. His long association with the New York *World* ended in 1928, when he clashed with the publisher over his emphatic defence of the anarchists Sacco and Vanzetti. In 1930 he ran for Congress on the Socialist ticket. Needless to say, he didn't make it. His personal behaviour was no less rebellious. Having been invited once by Broun to meet Mabel Normand, Harpo turned up in a suit and tie, 'something I hadn't done since Zeppo's wedding', only to find the beautiful screen star in Broun's bedroom, the host languishing in bed in his pyjamas, 'swatting a punching bag that hung from the ceiling'. His doctor had ordered him to get both rest and exercise.

Another time, on a freezing January night, Harpo relates, he shared a taxi with Broun and Woollcott when they were arguing with each other about some obscure literary matter. When Harpo's stop arrived, Woollcott told him condescendingly: 'Tell the driver where to drop us off, like a good boy, Harpo.' Harpo told the driver to drop the two gentlemen off at 'Werba's Theatre, Brooklyn', a remote burlesque house in Flatbush. The two intellectual giants were way over the Brooklyn Bridge before they realized their fate. Two hours later, Harpo was woken by a furious phone call from Woollcott, who had got stuck after their cab had stalled in the snow: 'You Jew son of a bitch!' This seemed to be Woollcott's favourite epithet for Harpo, borrowed from Harpo's old tale of his adventure in Mrs Schang's brothel.

With Herbert Bayard Swope, editor of the *World,* and a man described by Woodrow Wilson as having 'the fastest mind with which I have ever come into contact', Harpo took a slightly different tack, arriving in his old raincoat for a dinner jacket banquet of forty. At Swope's behest, all the men then removed their jackets in solidarity.

Harpo was besotted, as many men were, with Neysa McMein, a talented cover artist who drew all the famous people, and counted among her admirers George Gershwin, Charlie Chaplin, Fyodor Chaliapin, and the famous Times Square priest, Father Duffy. Harpo does not tell us if he struck gold, but claims that she introduced him to the joy of painting, which was to enliven his retirement years. 'You'll never be alone, Harpo,' she told him, 'as long as you have some paint, a brush, and some canvas.' The only problem with their art soirées, wrote Harpo, was her passion for fires, which caused her to down tools and rush out into the street whenever fire-engine alarm bells sounded.

To be near his brothers, and their parents, Harpo too took what he termed 'a bachelor-size summer estate' on Long Island Sound, close to Great Neck. His flatmate, at this time, was 'a retriever disguised as a black poodle'. Harpo wrote: 'I bought me a kite and fixed up a special rigging so the string could tickle the bottoms of my feet while the kite flew and I stretched out and snoozed on the grass.' But the call soon came for him to down kite and poodle and hie to Alexander Woollcott's summer residence in Neshobe Island, in Lake Bomoseen, Vermont. This was a heavily wooded and isolated paradise with initially primitive accommodations including hand-pumped water and an outdoor toilet. There was no gas, electric light or telephone. Woollcott's New York aesthetes just loved it.

Transport to the lake was a motor launch provided by a lakeside innkeeper called William Bull. The most delicate transport job, Woollcott's biographer, Howard Teichman, wrote, 'was to get Harpo Marx's harp into the boat, across the lake, and onto the little pier that jutted out from the island. From there it was carried by hand into the house, which was in reality a painted shack. Set in the middle of the cluttered room the harp looked like a jewel, and after dinner, on the nights he felt like it, Harpo would play for the distinguished guests', to wit: George and Beatrice Kaufman, Alice Duer Miller, Neysa McMein, Ruth Gordon, Harold Ross, Charlie Lederer, Howard Deitz and other Broadway stalwarts. Writes Teichman:

> Harpo Marx pulled up to the boat landing in an old broken-down jalopy that he had taken to a mechanic to make look even more dilapidated. Woollcott was invited to inspect the automobile.
> 'What do you call that?' he asked.
> 'My town car,' Harpo replied.
> 'What was the town?' Woollcott asked, 'Pompeii?'

The dress code at Neshobe was ultra-casual. Both Woollcott and Heywood Broun would gallivant about in shorts weighed down by their massive paunches. At one point Harpo, having been informed by a distressed Alice Miller that tourists had infiltrated the island, broke in upon them in the nude, smeared with mud, wearing his red fright wig, brandishing an axe and unleashing his Gookie. This was the end of mass tourism at Neshobe Island. Here, Aleck's friends could disport themselves as babies, answering their host's squeaky call to come 'buckety-buckety' down to the lawn for his favourite game of croquet. Harpo soon became a croquet fanatic too, looking, probably, extremely sane and staid before the esteemed New York drama critic who would 'dance around the court on his toes, kicking his heels together (unaware that his shorts were falling down), and singing in the exuberant soprano of a cherub in a Sunday-school play: *I'm des a 'itto wabbit in de sunshine! I'm just a 'itto wabbit in de wain!'*

In the summer of 1928 Harpo and Aleck went one better than Neshobe Island, embarking, in May, with Alice Duer Miller and Beatrice Kaufman, aboard the SS *Roma*, on a trip to the French Riviera. This vacation was the acme of Harpo's social rise. The coast was teeming with Anglo-Saxon celebrities. Called up from the beach one day with nothing but a towel to cover his crown jewels, Harpo found himself confronted by 'a tall, skinny, red-faced old geezer with a beard, decked out in a sporty cap and knicker suit', who called out, 'Where the devil's Woollcott? Who the devil are you?' Told that the water sprite facing him was none other than Harpo Marx, the bearded geezer extended his hand, said, 'I am Bernard Shaw', and then immediately whipped away Harpo's towel and introduced him *au naturel* to the lady accompanying him: 'And this is Mrs Shaw.'

Shaw had long been on record as admiring vaudevillians, whom he thought beat straight actors any time for their emotional and physical energy. He cannot ever have seen Harpo perform, but the fame of the

Brothers was already widespread. Harpo became the Shaws' unofficial driver, chauffeuring them about with his customary lunatic verve. Noël Coward, Somerset Maugham, Scott Fitzgerald, and the King of Spain were also summering at the Cap that *saison*. The King of Spain was tone deaf and travelled with a special stooge who gave him the high sign whenever the Spanish Anthem was played. But everyone was equal before Harpo. Introduced to the venerable H. G. Wells, he remarked that, in his days on the Pantages circuit, there was a Wells, Fargo office in every town. Denied entry to the Casino at Monte Carlo because of his usual casual attire, Harpo backed off, removed one of his black socks and arranged it around his neck, reappearing proudly. An early run of luck was followed by miserable losses. One might speculate what would have happened had Chico been around. But one Marx Brother was probably enough for the Riviera to handle.

Perhaps Harpo's strangest adventure was with the visiting Ziegfeld goddess, Peggy Hopkins-Joyce. The beautiful star invited him for a fun-filled dinner at her villa, raising Harpo's expectations to fever pitch. Then, when both were seated on her nest of silk cushions, she rang for the butler and told him, 'You may bring the books now.' The books were a stack of comics, bound in hand-tooled leather – *Mutt and Jeff*, *Bringing Up Father*, *Krazy Kat*, and so on. Harpo had to sit and read to Peggy Hopkins-Joyce from the comic books, complete with all the 'Bam! Bang! Sock! Pow!' parts. Deprived of any hope of Bam, Bang, Sock, Pow of his own, he soon beat a rueful retreat.

Harpo returned to the US in time for rehearsals for Kaufman's second Marx Brothers show, *Animal Crackers*, which opened at the 44th Street Theatre on 23 October 1928.

Once again, George S. K. and his co-writer Morrie Ryskind had come up with a confection that was light enough for popular consumption but full of sharp, unexpected tastes. Some critics, like Robert Littell of the *Evening Post*, were sceptical, acclaiming Harpo the Silent but saying of Groucho: 'There is a little too much of him, and a good many of his lines sound like the glib, wisecracking patter of almost any professional humorist.' Of the rest of the show Littell morosely stated that it 'might just as well not be there, and one often wishes it weren't'. But most critics were kinder. Gilbert W. Gabriel raved that *Animal Crackers* 'is the most steadily, unflaggingly funny show I've ever dedicated my sore ribs to . . . It is a wild-eyed satire of Long Island social climbers. It includes such recognisable curios as Wally Winston, scandal twitterer for The Daily Traffic, and Roscoe W. Chandler, ex-rabbinical millionaire and patron of the arts . . .'

Captain Spaulding – bagged elephants in his pyjamas.

Brooks Atkinson, heavyweight critic of the *Times*, wrote:

They are nihilists – these Marx boys. And the virtue of their vulgar mountebankery is its bewildering, passing stinging thrusts at everything in general, including themselves. Burlesquing their own comedy, the show occasionally resolves itself into a vicious circle that is less amusing than it deserves to be. But their stock in trade has other ruffian advantages. They make a good deal of their ludicrous costumes – Groucho in the sun helmet of an African explorer and the morning coat of a floor walker; Harpo in evening dress that slides off and leaves him hideous in trunks and a tall hat; Chico in the ungainly attire of an immigrant . . . There is another rude card game full of chicanery, and a loud, thumping robbery scene in which they steal a portrait in the darkness during a thunderstorm . . . Whatever the plot or the background may be these scurrilous mimes remain very much themselves . . .

This was the first work for which Morrie Ryskind received a full stage credit. Probably the most long-lasting of the Marxian collaborators, Ryskind lived to the age of eighty-nine (he died in 1985), and tested Groucho's loyalty to his friends to the limit by flip-flopping from his early socialist views to the outer shores of right-wing conservatism, becoming one of Richard Nixon's staunchest defenders. Born in Brooklyn to Russian immigrant parents, Ryskind was brought up in Manhattan, and enrolled at Columbia University's School of Journalism, only to be expelled six weeks before his graduation for publishing, in the school's own journal, a pacifist poem against American involvement in World War One. Having cut his teeth, even before college, on Franklin P. Adams's 'Conning Tower' column, he later worked for Herbert Bayard Swope at the *World*. In 1921 a book of his poetry, *Unaccustomed As I Am*, led to some Hollywood film assignments, after which he returned to New York. A rejected Algonquinite, he tried unsuccessfully to form his own rival table, named, for some pungent reason, the Cheese Club, but it was not flavoured.

Ryskind's collaboration with Kaufman continued after *Animal Crackers*, and resulted in the Pulitzer Prize for Ryskind, Kaufman and George Gershwin for their 1931 musical satire on the Presidency, *Of Thee I Sing*. Ryskind would later be nominated twice for Academy Awards, for his scripts of *My Man Godfrey* in 1936, and *Stage Door* in 1937.

Ryskind's passionate pacifism, in the 1920s, clearly clicked both with Kaufman and with Groucho, who considered uniforms, quite properly, as funny costumes to be used for getting laughs on stage. It is of course difficult to figure out who wrote what in a collaboration, and Ryskind came in on *The Cocoanuts* only after the plot and structure had already been worked out. In *Animal Crackers*, however, his influence seems stronger in the more zany and less logical aspects of the play. Kaufman's puns and games were always socially based, whereas Ryskind, in his heyday, was more of an anarchic Groucho-clone.

Did Ryskind initiate Captain Spaulding? In his posthumously published memoir, *I Shot an Elephant in My Pajamas*, Ryskind wrote that 'in a collaboration, ideas get batted back and forth so many times that it would be impossible to assign any sort of proprietary authorship'. The African Explorer, who does not seem to have come from anywhere further than the Carnegie Deli, via Central Casting, to pick up his African bearers, is the most inspired of Grouchoesque creations. There was a real Captain Spaulding, a vaudeville fire-eater ('The Man Who Was Hotter Than Vesuvius'), so perhaps the actual name might have come from Groucho, rather than either of his eager scribes. Ryskind himself told Richard Anobile, for *The Marx Brothers Scrapbook*, that the Brothers had no formal approval over Kaufman's texts – 'They wouldn't have questioned George's stuff' – but, certainly after the success of *The Cocoanuts*, we can assume some give and take between writers and performers, even before the on-stage ad-libs.

'Groucho's great gift is in timing and feeling,' Ryskind told Anobile. 'My sister read the script for *Animal Crackers* the afternoon before it opened. She said if she hadn't read it she would have sworn that Groucho was making up every word of it on the stage. Which is, of course, the great test of an actor.'

Except in this case the Act preceded the Word. Once again the writers had got into the Brothers' heads and once again when a scene worked and got the laughs it was locked in place and left unchanged. A perfect example, in *Animal Crackers*, is the scene where Harpo and Chico sneak off to steal the famous painting around which the plot vaguely revolves, fumbling about for their tools in a dark room:

CHICO: You got everything? The shovel, the axe, the dynamite, the
    pineapples. Where you got the flash? The flash.
(*Harpo indicates his own flesh by pinching his own cheek*)
CHICO: No, no the flesh. The flash.
(*Harpo takes out fish from pocket*)
CHICO: That's a-fish. I no wanna a fish. Flash. When you go out in the
    night time you gotta have a flash.

(Harpo takes out large silver flask)
CHICO: That's a flisk.
(Harpo takes out flute and plays it)
CHICO: That's a flutes. I no wanna the flutes. Flash. When you wanna see somebody, you gotta have the flash.
(Harpo takes out five playing cards)
CHICO: That's a flush. When it's light and you wanna make it dark, you gotta have the flash.
(Harpo takes out blackjack)
CHICO: No, I make a mistake. When it's dark and you wanna make it light, then you gotta have the flash.
(Harpo finally brings out flashlight . . . thunder and lightning puts light out –)

There it is, in black and white, in the original script, almost to the letter as it is performed in the screen version, two years later, in 1930. The same goes for Chico as Ravelli's immortal verbal pyrotechnics in discussing who in the house might have stolen the painting:

SPAULDING: Suppose nobody in the house took the painting?
RAVELLI: Then we go to the house next door.
SPAULDING: Well, suppose there isn't any house next door?
RAVELLI: Well, then of course we got to build one.
SPAULDING: Well now you're talking. What kind of a house do you think we ought to put up?
RAVELLI: Now look, I tell you what my idea is. I think we build something nice and small and comfortable.
SPAULDING: That's the way I feel about it. I don't want anything elaborate. Just a little place that I can call home and tell the wife I won't be there for dinner.
RAVELLI: I see, you just want a telephone booth . . . *(Etcetera, till:)*
RAVELLI: Hey Cap, it came to me like a flash. You know what happened to this painting? This painting wasn't stolen. This painting disappear. And do you know what make it disappear? Moths. Moths eat it. Left-handed moths. That's my solution!
SPAULDING: I wish you were in it.

Of course, there are some later embellishments, but the main thrust is all there. Once again, Margaret Dumont did her sterling best as art moneybags Mrs Rittenhouse, subjected to all the usual indignities. She appeared to have recovered from her torments on *The Cocoanuts* tour, in which Chico and Harpo set alarm clocks to go off hourly in her berth on the night train, not to speak of Harpo stealing her costume to wear 'for a fancy dress ball'. This scene was described by actress Margaret Irving, who was allegedly a direct descendant of Margaret of Navarre, wife of French King Henry II, although she was born in Paducah, played with vaudevillian Fred Stone, and featured in the *Ziegfeld Follies* 1919 to 1922. She described the scene to Hector Arce as she repaired to producer Sam Harris's office to sign her contract for the show:

> Girls were coming out of his office, screaming at the top of their lungs. There was a policeman on horseback on the street. 'What's going on?' I asked him. He said, 'They're auditioning for the new Marx Brothers' show and the boys are goosing the girls.' That was for starters. When I talked to Sam, he said, 'Dress yourself in tin drawers and have some fun.'

Extremely sound advice, as the boys proceeded to wrestle with her on the sofa in the Du Barry scene as, fully dressed in French court regalia, she was upended and thrown by all four brothers, wedging her dress hoop between the divan and the flats. Being a woman in a Marx Brothers show was much like having to be the patsy in an equatorial ocean-crossing ritual every single night.

The Du Barry scene, a kind of reprise of the Brothers' favourite Napoleon and Josephine sketch from *I'll Say She Is*, did not survive into the movie version. Maggie Irving, 'Mrs Whitehead' in the 'real' section of the story, enters to remark to Groucho/Spaulding, moonlighting as the King of France:

DU BARRY: Sire, I fear for me to come here is indiscreet.
GROUCHO: Nonsense, you'll be in the street sooner or later. You come from good stock, you'll probably be on the curb. Ah, Du Barry, you look wonderful in that French dressing . . . May I call you Du, Du?
DU BARRY: As you will, milord.

And on to similar frippery, involving Groucho calling for champagne and musing: 'What do you think, do you think we'll ever get the saloon back? . . . And if we do, what's going to become of the bellboys in the Hotel Astor?' In a later version of the script, the scene culminates with the butler, Hives, introducing the French Premier, Doucet, who announces: 'Compliments, Your Majesty. Herzegovina has declared war upon us.' To which Groucho replies: 'If you think I'm going to let my army fight with a Pullman car, you're crazy.'

But all this is, alas, lost to posterity. What we have, unaltered, is the sem-

Animal Crackers: the Du Barry scene, with Margaret (Daisy) Dumont.

inal Captain Spaulding himself, and his immortal song, lyrics and music by Bert Kalmar and Harry Ruby, '*Hooray for Captain Spaulding / The African Explorer / Did someone call me schnorrer? / Hooray hooray hooray!*' There were six other songs in the stage show: 'Who's Been Listening to my Heart?', 'The

195

Long Island Low-Down', 'Go Places and Do Things', 'Watching the Clouds Roll By', 'When Things Are Bright and Rosy', and 'Cool Off'. But only Captain Spaulding's ditties and a plaintive lament from Lillian Roth, 'Tell Me Dear, Why Am I So Romantic', remain to brighten future generations. Although the movie omits, by means of the crudest cut, the following underlined line from the Captain's warble:

MRS RITTENHOUSE: He is the only white man who covered every acre.
SPAULDING: I think I'll try and make her.
OMNES: Hurrah, hurrah, hurrah!

Animal Crackers' other great creation is the pretentious art expert Roscoe W. Chandler, who is unmasked by Chico and Harpo as Ivan Pilsudski, the fish-peddler from Czechoslovakia, and made the butt of several of Groucho's best verbal barrages. Chandler was played both on stage and screen by Louis Sorin. At one point he was 'Rabbi Cantor', but on screen he ended up as the ethnically neutral Abe Kabiddle. Cue the sly exchange:

CHANDLER: All right boys, I confess, I was Ivan Pilsudski.
CHICO: How did you get to be Roscoe W. Chandler?
CHANDLER: Say, how did you get to be an Italian?
CHICO: Never mind, whose confession is this?

Precisely. The original Chandler was supposed to be an attack on the art-loving mogul Otto Kahn who, somewhat implausibly, had taken to playing down his humble Jewish origins. But he could stand in for every kind of social imposture that the Marx Brothers were sworn to unmask – if necessary, by trumping it with even more blatant imposture, as in Groucho's riff on being told by Chandler that he is about to depart to Uruguay, which went through several script versions:

Version One:
SPAULDING: Where are you going?
CHANDLER: Uruguay.
SPAULDING: Uruguay? Well, you go Uruguay and I'll go mine. Say, how did this ever start anyhow? Let's talk about something else. Take the foreign situation. Take Abyssinia. I'll tell you, you take Abyssinia and I'll take a butterscotch sundae on rye bread. (*Both exit*)

Version Two:
SPAULDING: Well, you go Uruguay and I'll go mine.
CHANDLER: What about Guatemala?

SPAULDING: Well, that's a totally different problem. Guatemala every night or you can't take Mala at all. Of course, that takes a lot of Honduras. How did this ever get started anyhow. Let's talk about something else. Take the foreign situation. Take Abyssinia. I'll tell you what, you take Abyssinia and I'll take plain White Rock. No, make mine the same. Let's see what the boys in the back room'll have. (*Both exit*)

Third version and film:

SPAULDING: Well, you go Uruguay and I'll go mine. Say, how long has this been going on? Let's change the subject. Take the foreign situation. Take Abyssinia. I'll tell you, you take Abyssinia and I'll take a hot butterscotch sundae on rye bread. Let's go see what the boys in the back room will have . . .

Presumably champagne, because *Animal Crackers*, while not as big a smash as *The Cocoanuts*, ran a respectable 171 performances in New York before going on tour, despite the storm clouds of financial disaster that, unbeknownst to the rosy-eyed, were gathering and finally burst on 24 October 1929. In the shadow of the Wall Street Crash, not only the Marx Brothers blithely capered, but all of Broadway danced what would turn out to be, in economic terms, a dance of death.

But, by this date, two other seismic shifts had occurred in the Marx Brothers' fortunes. Two years before, Al Jolson had opened his mouth on screen in *The Jazz Singer* to utter the immortal words: 'Wait a minute! Wait a minute! You ain't heard nothing yet!' – consigning the silent cinema to the archive of history. A new art form – the Talking Picture – finally opened the door for the Marx Brothers to leap from the ephemeral stage to the more solid state of the movies. Their first film, the screen version of *The Cocoanuts*, was shot at the Astoria Studio in Queens, concurrently with the stage run of *Animal Crackers*.

The Cocoanuts premièred at the Rialto in New York on 3 May 1929, in the absence of the stars, who were performing at the Riverside Theatre. Initial responses were lukewarm, but the movie picked up as it went on release. The Marx Brothers were on top of the world. Then, on 13 September, Minnie suffered a seizure in the car while being driven, with Frenchy, home from Friday night dinner at Zeppo's house. According to Harpo, his parents were driving across the Queensboro Bridge when Minnie slumped over. Frenchy jumped out, stopped the traffic on both lanes of the bridge and ordered the chauffeur to turn round. Back at Zeppo's house, the entire family gathered round their stricken mother. She had suffered a stroke, and died about two in the morning of 14 September. At the age of sixty-five, the indomitable Minnie Schoenberg had left the stage for good.

Alexander Woollcott penned his heartfelt tribute, for *The New Yorker*:

A short history of the magician's daughter who was the managing mother of the Four Marx Brothers . . . Last week the Marx Brothers buried their mother. On the preceding Friday night, more from gregariousness than from appetite, she had eaten two dinners instead of the conventional one, and, after finishing off with a brief, hilarious game of ping-pong, was homeward bound across the Queensboro Bridge when paralysis seized her. Within an hour she was dead in Harpo's arms. Of the people I have met, I would name her as among the few of whom it could be said that they had greatness.

She had done much more than bear her sons, bring them up, and turn them into play actors. She had invented them. They were just comics she imagined for her own amusement. They amused no one more, and their reward was her ravishing smile . . . She was in this world sixty-five years and lived all sixty-five of them. She died during rehearsals, in the one week of the year when all her boys would be around her – back from their summer roamings, that is, but not yet gone forth on tour. Had she foreseen this – I'm not sure she didn't – she would have chuckled, and, combining a sly wink with her beautiful smile, she would have said, 'How's that for perfect timing?'

ACT IV

The Magician's Grandsons
and the Magical Lens

The Marx Brothers hit Hollywood: cartoon by Will Johnstone for the pressbook of *Monkey Business*.

PROLOGUE

Get the Marbles Out of Your Mouth!

'About the end of 1928,' writes S. J. Perelman, in a 1961 article in *Show* magazine, 'my work was appearing in some profusion, and Horace Liveright, whose daring as a publisher verged on audacity, brought out a collection of it called *Dawn Ginsberg's Revenge* . . . The dust-jacket bore a blurb from, coincidentally, Groucho Marx. It read: "From the moment I picked up your book until I laid it down, I was convulsed with laughter. Someday I intend reading it."'

The enterprising young humorist, whose childhood memories of the Marx Brothers' vaudeville show 'Home Again' we have chronicled afore, was delighted with his idol's characteristic accolade, and even more delighted three years later when, in the depths of the Depression, both nationally and personally, he received a summons from Groucho to work on a proposed radio series. Groucho suggested a collaboration with Will Johnstone, saying: 'I can't imagine two people worse equipped for the job, but there's one thing in your favor. You're both such tyros you might come up with something fresh.'

Writes Perelman:

Johnstone turned out to be a jovial, exuberant chap in his late forties, with a fund of newspaper stories. We put in a couple of enjoyable sessions that got nowhere, except for a misty notion that the Marxes might be characterized as stowaways aboard an ocean liner. On the day designated to report our progress, the two of us met outside the Astor, resolved to confess our inadequacy and throw in the towel. Luncheon with the troupe was as disorganized as my colleague had predicted it would be. Groucho expatiated at length on his stock-market losses, Chico kept jumping up to place telephone bets, and Harpo table-hopped all over the dining room, discomposing any attractive lady who gave him a second glance.

Gathering their courage, the two scribes confessed their failure, only to find the Brothers enthusiastic about their tiny kernel of an idea. 'You fellows have stumbled on something big,' Groucho told them, 'this isn't any fly-by-night radio serial – it's our next picture!'

'Pinioning our arms,' resumes Perelman, 'they hustled us across the street into the office of Jesse Lasky, the head of Paramount Pictures. There was a short, confused interval brimful of references to astronomical sums of money, contracts, and transportation to the Coast, inexplicably for our wives as well. We were to entrain for Hollywood within the week, it was tempestuously agreed, to write the screenplay . . .'

On the train – relates Perelman – Johnstone, fortified by illegal libations, dashed off over fifty strip cartoons for his paper, as well as a sheaf of water-colours of the remarkable passing landscapes. But Hollywood Boulevard, even in those halcyon days, failed to impress the New York wordsmiths and their wives: 'Viewed in full sunlight,' writes Perelman, 'its tawdriness is unspeakable; in the torrential downpour of the rainy season, as we first saw it, it inspired an anguish similar to that produced by the engravings of Piranesi. Our melancholy deepened when the mem and I took an exploratory walk around the hotel. As we sat in a Moorish confectionary patterned after the Alcazar, toying with viscid malts and listening to a funereal organ rendition of "Moonlight in Kalua," the same thought occurred to each of us, but she phrased it first.

'"Listen," she said. "Do we really need the money this much?"'

The answer, of course, was 'Yes'. Settling into their laxative nirvana, with its plethora of health-food stores and dry-cleaners, the two merry easterners found themselves 'quartered in a ramshackle warren of tan stucco that housed thirty or forty other scribes . . . all in various stages of gestation, some spawning gangster epics and horse operas, others musical comedies, dramas and farces.' The ordeal by fire continued up until the date of delivery, when Perelman and Johnstone were summoned to read the script to the assembled quartet, who were accompanied by their progenitor, Sam. Zeppo and his wife brought two Afghans they had purchased during a trip to England, Harpo brought 'two blonde civilians he had dined with', and Chico brought Betty and a 'scrappy wire-haired terrier that immediately tangled with the Afghans. In the midst of the tohubohu, Groucho and his wife entered; I supposed that thirteen constituted a quorum and made as if to start but was told to desist – other guests were due. These, it proved, were three gagmen the Marxes had picked up in transit . . . their wives, sweethearts and an unidentified rabble I took to be relatives, and last of all, several cold eyed vultures obviously dispatched by the studio.' These, together with the producer, Herman Mankiewicz, and his little brother, Joe, made up an audience of twenty-seven humans and five dogs. After reading this assemblage the 126 pages of accumulated wit and wisdom masquerading as the script for *Monkey Business*, Groucho said, 'It stinks', rose and led the exodus from the room.

Five months later, nevertheless, *Monkey Business*, the Marx Brothers' first Hollywood film, hit the screens, to universal applause. Perelman was engaged to write a second script for the Brothers, with another collaborator, a young man named Arthur Sheekman, whom Groucho had promoted from the ranks. The new production, *Horse Feathers*, was to be, once again, supervised by the mercurial Herman Mankiewicz, whose stormy character and gargantuan appetite for food and drink were legendary long before he achieved fame as the screenwriter of *Citizen Kane*. Perelman relates:

He had a tongue like a rasp, and his savage wit demolished anyone unlucky enough to incur his displeasure. I myself was the recipient on various occasions, but one, which Groucho delighted to recall many years later, deserves repetition.

On a very hot midday in July, it seemed, Mankiewicz betook himself to a celebrated restaurant in Hollywood called Eddie Brandstatter's, much frequented by gourmands, where he treated his palate to two whiskey sours and a gargantuan lunch consisting of lentil soup with frankfurters, rinderbrust with spaetzle, red cabbage and roast potatoes, and noodle pudding, irrigating the mixture with three or four flagons of Pilsener Then, eyeballs protruding, he lumbered painfully to his car and drove to his office in Paramount. [There to be confronted by Perelman and Sheekman, knocking timidly at his door, and stammering their apologies.]

'What the devil do you want?' Mankiewicz barked. 'Get the marbles out of your mouth!'

'Well, it's like this,' I squeaked, moistening my lips. 'In this sequence we're working on, we're kind of perplexed about the identity of the Marx Brothers – the psychology of the characters they're supposed to represent, so to speak. I mean, who are they? We – we wondered if you could analyze or define them for us.'

'Oh, you did, did you? he grated. 'OK, I'll tell you in a word. One of them is a Guinea, another a mute who picks up spit, and the third an old Hebe with a cigar. Is that all clear, Beaumont and Fletcher? Fine,' he concluded, forcing a poisonous smile. 'Now, back to your hutch, and at teatime I'll send over a lettuce leaf for the two of you to chew on. Beat it!'

But let us rewind the reel, from Arcadia to Astoria, early in 1929 . . .

Before Hollywood *or* 'Why Are You So Concerned with Having Real Backgrounds When One of the Leading Characters Wears an Obviously False Moustache?'

'Nobody could be at ease with the Marx Brothers . . .'
George Folsey, cinematographer on *The Cocoanuts* (1929)

The early sound cinema was an unwieldy and uncomfortable affair, with its massive cameras encased in glass soundproof boxes, and its inability to post-mix different tracks. For a musical such as *The Cocoanuts*, the orchestra had to be accommodated and recorded in the studio. Even having Irving Berlin come down to conduct the musicians in person failed to compensate for this problem. The film was one of the first sound movies to be shot at Paramount's east-coast studios at Astoria, Long Island (now the American Museum of the Moving Image), which had just been reopened after a two-year closure, during which all Paramount's silents were relocated to Hollywood. The first all-talking feature made at Astoria was *The Letter,* co-directed by Monta Bell, who was assigned to produce *The Cocoanuts*.

The deal to bring the Marx Brothers to the screen without further 'humor risks' was arranged through the William Morris Agency, negotiating with Paramount executive Walter Wanger. Studio head Adolph Zukor, who was then only fifty-six years old but was to live to the age of 103, balked at the asking price of $75,000. He was disarmed, according to the lore, by Chico who, putting on his most seductive demeanour, oiled the mogul's ego by telling him what a great man he was for practically founding the motion-picture industry, and pledging all the Marx Brothers' hard-worked talent for a mere $100,000. 'Well, Walter,' Zukor said to Wanger, 'that doesn't sound unreasonable.' (In a previous version, this story was told about Zeppo, but he was not in the agency game at that time.)

The cinematographer, George Folsey, was an experienced lensman who had shot his first film, *His Bridal Night*, in 1919, and was soon to shoot

Rouben Mamoulian's ground-breaking talkie *Applause*, also at Paramount's Astoria studios. He was to go on to be one of MGM's top lensers, shooting *Meet Me in St Louis* (1944), *Adam's Rib* (1949) and *Seven Brides for Seven Brothers* (1954). So at least somebody knew what they were doing, despite the Brothers' infuriating failure to hit their marks and stay in the camera frame.

For the director, producer Bell engaged a Frenchman, Robert Florey, who had not seen the Marx Brothers perform, and, when taken to see *Animal Crackers*, did not find them particularly funny. He was hired, apparently, because he had proved rigorous in handling modest budgets and the producers were fearful that the Marx Brothers' *Cocoanuts* would far surpass the peanuts level. Florey's initiation into films was watching the fantasies of Méliès, and the shooting of a stage play was not his idea of a good time. It should, however, be noted that he had worked as a gag writer in movie silents for Sunshine Comedies, starring Al St John, and was a close friend of Chaplin. (He was to be Chaplin's associate director, in 1946, on *Monsieur Verdoux*.) Groucho's later complaint about him that he spoke virtually no English is a typical *soupe de canard*.

But Florey had his work cut out. First of all, he failed dismally to convince the producers to move some of the shooting to locations in Florida. Monta Bell asked him: 'Why are you so concerned with having real backgrounds when one of the leading characters wears an obviously false moustache?' As Florey commented later: 'With that kind of logic, what could I say?' Instead, the Florida backdrop was a shaky canvas which moved whenever somebody opened a door. Proper rehearsals were impossible. 'What was there to rehearse with the Marx Brothers?' Florey moaned. 'They had performed the show a thousand times!' Normal direction was out. 'You couldn't direct the Marx Brothers any more than you could a Chaplin or a clown who had been doing the same number for many years. They did what they did and that was that. Aside from directing traffic, which turned out to be my main function, I photographed it to the best of my ability.'

The Brothers' complete lack of respect for the camera frame and the difficulty of moving the camera, or even panning, led to Florey developing the use of multiple cameras, as he related to Richard Anobile, in *The Marx Brothers Scrapbook*: 'I had five cameras going at all times. One for a long master shot, one for a medium shot and three for close-ups. If one or even two of the brothers went out of range I could always cut to a close-up to compensate for the missing member.'

Close examination of *The Cocoanuts* bears out the use of multiple cameras, though I, for one, can see no sign of five. Two seems to have been the norm. But Florey had enough trouble corralling the Brothers on to the set in the first place: 'The Marx Brothers gave me a great deal of trouble,' he related. 'You could never catch them all together. Harpo . . . spent his time making gags and running after the girls. We found Chico on the roof of the studio or in the basement . . . Zeppo . . . came late and Groucho delivered interminable speeches.' Ad-libs would proceed as on stage, as the Brothers 'would start to talk about things that didn't make any sense and couldn't be edited off – on account of the recording on disc.'

To compensate for his frustration, Florey got to experiment with the music and dance scenes. Forced to accept a co-director, Joseph Santley – a song-and-dance man brought in to set up the musical numbers – Florey made 'at least an attempt to make the play a film', and add 'some imagination to what was happening'. An early example is the credit sequence, with the dancing girls in negative, like the carriage scenes from Murnau's *Nosferatu*. Placing two cameras in soundproofed booths, one on top of the other, Florey was able to alternate with higher angles. Dance scenes were shot with silent cameras, enabling a more fluid movement and patterned sequences which were later claimed to be the progenitors of Busby Berkeley's extravagant numbers. Folsey wrote: 'Florey . . . had an eye . . . he was an artist, with a good sense of balance and composition . . . He knew it was interesting to shoot down on a bunch of chorus girls unfolding like flowers – we hadn't done that before.'

But all to no avail. Hands up all those who want to watch *The Cocoanuts* for Florey's innovative staging of the ballroom scene? No takers? I didn't think so. What we want is our first glimpse of the Marx Brothers, all together, in the prime of life – or at any rate not too long in the tooth – doing their act.

Groucho is now thirty-nine years of age, Chico forty-two, Harpo forty-one years young, Zeppo twenty-eight. The missing Gummo, aged thirty-seven, is getting married at this point and somewhat embroiled in his wife's battle for custody of her eighteen-month-old baby daughter from her deceased first husband's family. He is also in a bit of a bind because while honeymooning in the Île-de-France, his new partner in the rag game, Charlie Drapkin, cut all the goods wrong and took him to the cleaners, so that he left the United States on holiday as a garment mogul and returned as a pauper, to start all over again. And this even before the stock-market crash which was to make all Florida land scams look like small potatoes.

Cocoanuts on celluloid: 'This can go on all day.'

Groucho himself, as he springs to life on the screen, has not yet been affected by the economic meltdown. Brash and confident, he faces the rebellious bellboys – 'Three years ago, I came to Florida without a nickel in my pocket; now, I've got a nickel in my pocket' – seeing off their brief wage rebellion in a hot-shoe shuffle of 'Hooray's. We get a brief glimpse of Zeppo as Jamison, not having much to say except 'Yes, Mr Hammer.' No wonder that he was already chafing at the bit, and dreaming of some kind of neat exit.

Our first view of Chico and Harpo is delayed for a while by the plot, involving the two thieves, Penelope and Yates, and the love interest, represented by Mary Eaton and Oscar Shaw as Polly Potter and Bob Adams. These two replaced Jack Barker and Mabel Withee from the stage version, and although Mary Eaton is fey and pretty, Oscar Shaw is not; to modern eyes, he suffers from his startling resemblance to the young Richard Nixon. (Shaw and Eaton were, believe it or not, past stars of the Ziegfeld *Follies*, as well as of a hit Broadway musical of 1928, *The Five O'Clock Girl*.) A rendition of 'The sky will all be blue / when my dream comes true' is enough to convince us that the 1920s had their down side, but eventually the star-crossed lovers mercifully vacate the stage. A short introductory scene between Maggie Dumont, as Mrs Potter, and her daughter Polly gives way to Hammer in reception: 'Hallo, yes, ice water in 318? How did it get there? Get some onions, that'll make your eyes water.' And cue Chico and Harpo.

For the first time we have all four brothers in frame, chasing each other with hands outstretched in a circle round and over chairs and sofas. As Harpo, with evident joy, eats the buttons off the bellboy's jacket, Chico and Groucho indulge in their first on-screen bout: 'Would you like a suite on the third floor?' 'No, I'll take a Polack in the basement.' Harpo tears up the letters in the pigeon-holes, as Groucho obligingly hands them to him. Groucho: 'Would you like a single room?' Chico: 'We like to double up.' 'Well, eat some green apples.' Groucho breaks off for another phone query: 'You want to to know where you can get hold of Mrs Potter? I don't know, she's awfully ticklish!'

None of this business is in the original stage script, and was obviously developed in performance. And so we wend our merry way, through Harpo eating the telephone and drinking from the ink-well, to the first on-screen love scenes between Groucho and Maggie: 'Your eyes – they shine like the pants of a blue serge suit . . .' And Harpo's first film harp solo: the dropping of the mask, as Harpo transforms back into Ahdie, the grandson of fairground harpist Fanny Schoenberg. Comedy halts, to pay tribute to an even older element – the fusion between the musician and his music. Always, in his harp solos, Harpo drops back into this deeply serious moment. And then the comedy, as ever, resumes.

Cocoanuts, the movie, suffers considerably from its rough-edged production values, and can seldom be seen in anything approximating a good, clean, sharp 35-mm print. Some segments, such as the crucial auction scene, appear to have survived only as fuzzy dupes, which inevitably create a distance between a modern audience and the film. More than any other Marx Brothers film, it presents itself to us as an artefact, glimmering out of cinema history. Even its vintage exchanges, like the immortal 'Why-a-duck, why-a-no chicken' routine, appear like miracles from another age. And then: 'Signor Pastrami will play a cup of coffee, a sandwich and you, from the opera *Aïda*.' – 'Signor Pastrami, what is the first number?' – 'Nomber One!' And Chico's miraculous pistol finger roams across the keyboard under that bewitching smile.

Despite this, the Marx Brothers do not look totally at ease in *The Cocoanuts*. Their first sojourn before the cameras was obviously a fraught affair, for them as well as for their innocent victims, the director and the crew. For twenty years, the Brothers had performed before an audience, gauging from the instant response across the footlights whether their act was going over or dying the death of a sea of straight faces. Now there was no audience, except for a bevy of camera grips and electricians and sound men attending to their own work, and a maze of cables and lights. The gaping vacancy of the camera lens replaced the fat man in the third row falling over and choking on his guffaws. There were not even hecklers to liven up a faltering scene; just the deadening cry of 'Silence!' and the faces inside the great glass booth. The material was tried and true, but it would take time before the Brothers would trust the camera to do its mysterious job. In 1929, even veterans were new at this 'talkie' business, and it shows.

The Brothers' next film, *Animal Crackers*, in comparison, survives as a much more assured piece. By the time it was shot, in the summer of 1930, the Astoria studios had considerably more experience in handling sound. The camera is not necessarily locked in place, and the services of a more determined, disciplinarian director, Victor-Heerman, were engaged.

But before *Animal Crackers* could go on the set, the adapted stage script had to be sanitized by the guardians of the cinema's morality squad: the censors of the Motion Picture Producers and Distributors Association, led by the appropriately named Colonel Joy. Morrie Ryskind, who adapted the screenplay from the stage script he co-wrote with George Kaufman, incorporating Bert Kalmar and Harry Ruby's lyrics, had not reckoned with the strange puritanical obsessions of the watchdogs of the silver screen. An initial letter, from the MPPDA to Mr J. W. Fingerlin, at Paramount Famous Players Lasky, on 29 April 1930, laid out the key topics at issue:

'The underlined word "the women *hot*, the champagne cold,"' in Captain Spaulding's speech, did not conform to the Motion Picture Code, nor did the dialogue, 'I'll wash your mouth out with gin', not to speak of Arabella's reply to Mrs Rittenhouse: 'Don't worry, mother, I won't disgrace you, I can hold my liquor with any of them.' Furthermore, 'Sequence B, pages 13–15: We suggest that instead of having Chandler called a peddler from Czechoslovakia, you have the name of the country changed to some fantastical kingdom. While the story is a comedy, any country mentioned specifically would be sure to object to the use of its name in this way . . .

'Sequence E, page 1: Story about farmer's daughter – it is our experience that censors generally cut out that kind of reference . . . Sequence G, page 18: Any reference to Mussolini is bound to be resented by the Italian people. We suggest that you eliminate the name entirely . . . In casting and treating the Spaulding part there are several references in the script that

Abie the Fishman's Czech bounces: Harpo and Chico with Louis Sorin.

lead us to suggest that you treat this role with care, having in mind Section II, No. 4 of the code which relates to sex perversion.'

Warnings like this were routine in motion pictures, but signified the problems the Code guardians were having in dealing with the new phenomenon of talkie scripts. It is difficult to imagine what in Captain Spaulding's dialogue alerted them to the possibility of what the censor was later to call 'pansy' tendencies, apart from the African Explorer fainting at the discovery of a caterpillar on his collar just as he is relating his exploits with Big Game. Perhaps the censors thought the very loquaciousness of the character was a sign of less than total manliness. At any rate, the complete confusion of the censors when faced with a Marx Brothers script was echoed in another letter to Paramount, from one S. F. Harmon, setting out the law in regard to the script of 28 April, which had been summed up by a reader, E. Tschudi (*sic?*) in the stern warning: 'There are a considerable number of double meaning lines in the script and other violations of the Code.' To wit:

1. Eliminate the word 'make': in the second verse of Harpo's song, when, turning to the hostess, he sings, 'I'm going to try to "make" her.' [Harpo's song??!!]

2. Cut the business of Zeppo pulling an intimate undergarment out of the woman's bosom with his teeth, and the following scene on the couch with the girl throwing her legs in the air and exposing her crotch after he bites her. [Well, we certainly lost that!!]

After the film was shot Colonel Joy wrote to producer B. P. Schulberg: 'Cut out the following dialog by Groucho – "we took some pictures of the native girls but they weren't developed. We are going back in a couple of weeks."' Also: 'Cut out the underlined words of dialog by Groucho – "Somewhere my love lies sleeping <u>with a male chorus</u>."' Also, the dialogue between Groucho and Chico about getting to the maid's room through his own room: 'You can't keep the maid in your room.' 'What makes you think you can't?' 'There's going to be a lot of traffic in that room.'

A later report informs Schulberg of censor cuts in various territories, British Columbia deleting 'vulgar and rough usage of woman', 'close-up where man pulls girl's lingeries out by his teeth', and the aforementioned 'traffic in the maid's room' dialogue. In Finland they took out 'Harpo pumping leg of old lady', and in Singapore the local scout commented on 'an excellent production but lost out with Chinese and Native audiences. Characters speak much too fast and are not understood by the names [sic] section of our public.'

A look at the film reveals that Paramount did not pay much heed to the MPPDA's advisories (though they were obliged, as noted, to chop 'I think I'll try and make her' out of the print), but they constitute a wagging finger at the kind of comedy the studio was about to unleash – with the Marx Brothers, Mae West and W. C. Fields – upon a receptive public. What had convulsed theatre audiences would soon convulse film fans throughout the country, and haul Paramount out of the financial pit the studio, like so many businesses in the United States, had found itself in due to the collapse of the Age of Prosperity and the advent of the Great Depression. Comedy was, if not a solution, at least a brief escape from the fear and despair caused by economic hardship and the disappearing act performed by so many enterprises and jobs.

In fact, the Marx Brothers had switched to the cinema in the nick of time. Broadway took the brunt of the early impact of the Wall Street crash in October 1929, with theatres closing right and left. Five thousand actors were soon to lose their jobs. Even a successful show, which *Animal Crackers* certainly was, could sustain itself for only a limited period, with its 171 performances, as against *The Cocoanuts*' 377 nights.

Both Groucho and Harpo lost heavily in the stock market crash, though the impact on Groucho was far more profound. Chico, too, had participated in the great buying bonanza that preceded the fall, but money never stuck to Chico very long. The horses or his fellow card-sharpers galloped away with it long before the Big Bad Wolf closed in. Groucho was being shepherded along the road to perdition by his close friend, producer Max Gordon, né Mechel Salpeter, who would call him up collect and urge him to rush out and buy this or that stock: 'Marx, this is a fast rider. It will jump like a kangaroo. Get in now before it's too late.' Everybody around was jumping in the same merry dance, with Groucho's friends and collaborators, George Kaufman, Morrie Ryskind, Sam Harris and Irving Berlin all investing like crazy in sure things. What they were all doing, along with the rest of the country, was buying on margin, i.e., putting up as little as 10 per cent of the cost of any deal, and owing the broker the other 90 per cent later, when of course the stock would appreciate, and could be sold off at a profit. As Groucho wrote: 'It was like stealing money.'

Except that the victims of the theft turned out to be themselves. Nobody ever seemed to sell a stock, but everyone was buying. Groucho's stage colleague, Eddie Cantor, was allegedly a prime perpetrator, urging Groucho to run down to his broker's first thing in the morning to snap up a couple of hundred shares of Goldman Sachs: 'Don't tell me you've never heard of Goldman Sachs? It's only the most sensational investment on the board!'

When the bubble burst, market jitters escalated at a terrifying rate, as stockholders began to sell, and brokers, panicking, called for more margin, and began calling in their clients' debts. Stocks were dumped for fractions of their original price and all the 'invested' money began shrinking away. The day of the crash, Groucho was on tour with *Animal Crackers*, when Max Gordon phoned from New York: 'Marx, the jig is up!'

It was five weeks after Minnie Marx's death. Groucho, like thousands of others, scrambled to sell his stock to pay for the additional margin he was required to put up. Within two days, he had lost $250,000, his entire accumulated savings. According to his son, Arthur Marx, he also had to borrow from his bank, and mortgage his house, plunging deep into debt. Arthur wrote:

'All his life he had been striving for complete financial security, and berating others – principally his brother, Chico – for spending their money on ridiculous luxuries, instead of putting some away for the future, as he was doing. *He* had known the value of money . . . Now it was gone.'

From that point on, Groucho became an insomniac, a condition he would never quite shake off. In three days' time, *Animal Crackers* was due to open in Baltimore, and it took all the persuasive powers of Harpo, Chico, Zeppo, Sam Harris and all the stage crew to buck him up enough to step out on to the stage. But it was Groucho's family – Ruth and the kids, Arthur and Miriam – who had to bear the weight of the continual anxiety and penny-pinching which were to characterize Groucho's private life even after he had rebuilt his wealth, painstakingly, with his work on stage and screen. Daily instructions on how to conserve food, water, electricity, heating oil, poured out in a continuous stream. The shadow of the poorhouse, imaginary as it might have been, haunted his nights. Wrote Arthur:

> He tried sleeping on his back, on his stomach, on his right side, on his left side; with one pillow, two pillows, three pillows, no pillows; with the windows open, with them shut; with the lights on, with them off; alone, not alone; sitting up in a chair, lying on the floor; with the radio on, with it off; with pyjamas, with no pyjamas; and with a night-coat. He finally settled for the bed, one pillow, a night-coat and bed-socks. (He had heard that no one could hope to fall asleep with cold feet, but in his case it didn't make any difference.)

Harpo, too, lost all his holdings, approximating to a quarter of a million dollars, and was in hock to the tune of $10,000 required to avoid a legal suit. Having begged, borrowed and sold everything except his harp and his croquet set, Harpo related, his assets were 'probably worth a medium-sized bag of black jelly beans'. Which may not have been so negligible in value, given Harpo's obsessive love for jelly beans. 'I was flatter broke than the day the Shubert unit died in Indianapolis,' he wrote. But, he related, Zeppo came to his rescue, dragging him off to a riverboat in Pittsburgh, Pa., to play a childish game of 'Pinchie Winchie' with the card-dealers, which consisted of each man pinching the other in the same spot in turn. Harpo put some burnt cork on his finger so that his victim would end up completely smudged. For some unknowable, and perhaps occult reason, playing 'Pinchie Winchie' with Harpo became the most prized activity for riverboat gamblers in Pittsburgh on the night of the Wall Street crash. The boat's operator, one Milt Jaffe, pinchie-winchied to the gills, came up with ten thousand dollars for Harpo on spec. In consequence, wrote Harpo: 'I was one of the luckiest citizens in all of America. My Great Depression lasted exactly four days, the last four days of October 1929. When times got so rough that, as Groucho said, "the pigeons started feeding the people in

Central Park", headliners in show business kept on working. I was lucky enough to be one of them.'

But Harpo's carefree world of the 1920s was over. The fun and games of the Thanatopsis card table, the 'buckety buckety' croquet games with Alexander Woollcott, the easy pranks and quips of the Algonquin Round Table, were done. 'Our million-dollar playground', wrote Harpo, 'had been condemned.'

Thank heaven, then, for Victor Heerman who, according to the legend, had four police cells built on the set of *Animal Crackers*, so that the Brothers could be locked in to be on tap for their takes. Heerman doesn't verify this, but does talk about the Brothers' dressing room as: 'The Crazy House – they'd lock each other up in there, so you'd know where to find them.' It was, of course, the Brothers themselves who had the keys. But Heerman's troubles started long before he got on set. English born, but raised in New York City, Heerman was already a veteran director in 1930, having begun directing short comedies for Mack Sennett and his first feature films in 1920. His titles included *The Poor Simp*, *A Marriage of Convenience*, *Love Is An Awful Thing*, *Rupert of Hentzau*, *Modern Matrimony*, *Irish Luck*, and so on. His previous project had been the multi-director hodgepodge *Paramount On Parade*, which had driven him and everyone else involved in it to distraction, but had actually turned out quite well. He was a cinch, therefore, to take over the Marx Brothers. Heerman told film historian Anthony Slide:

'I said, "Hell, I've seen the Marx Brothers a hundred times, and look at the picture they made – it was lousy. They're tough to handle. Joe Santley and Bob Florey, they're people who know their business. If they run through like this . . ."' However, the studio heads prevailed on him to see the play in Cleveland, and then meet the Marx boys at their hotel. 'My introduction to Groucho was, he said, "So you're Victor Heerman?" I said, "Yes." He said, "I expected a long, thin Jew, and you sent us a little, fat gentile." So then I met Ryskind – a very clever guy. Now on the other picture, they had timed it, so that every laugh they had in *Animal Crackers*, they would count, and the stage director would take a stop watch, and time how long the laugh would be, so they would delay, as they figured laughs were stepped on in the other one. That part, I didn't argue there.'

But Heerman ruthlessly cut out the stage journalist character's scenes, much to the Brothers' chagrin – a director was only a technician, after all! 'I pulled the whole thing out,' said Heerman, 'and took each comedy scene all the way down, and one after another said, "Are you crazy? We've been in this business for so-and-so." And I said, "And I've been making comedies for that long, and I think I know a little bit, and this is pictures and not the theatre." I said, "This is very funny, and I wouldn't touch one line of it, but I certainly am not going to have choruses come in that don't mean a damn thing, and cut my picture in half.'" The Marxes mutinied, through Ryskind, protesting that, in the movie *Cocoanuts*, 'we stepped on each other's laughs'. Heerman told them: 'That's because the timing was wrong. If a laugh is there, we'll hang on to it, and you'll get it.'

This stand-off between stage and screen wisdom lasted for some time, with studio boss Walter Wanger trying to pacify the combatants. Eventually Heerman suggested try-outs, shooting four or five trial scenes and testing them with an audience at Paramount. The audience, which included stalwart professional fans like George Jessel, howled with laughter. Heerman: 'We went back upstairs to the office, and Groucho said, "Now look here, you know your business, and we don't know your business. We know our business. Now any son-of-a-bitch that argues with you, send him to me." Now each of those fellows came round separately to tell me not to put up with any talk from the other one . . . I never had a bit of trouble all the way through. We made the picture in four weeks – we would have in four weeks, but Harpo got something in his throat. Didn't talk, but still they took him to the hospital . . .' So the crew waited three more weeks, just to shoot Harpo's harp solo, after the picture had wrapped.

The 'police cells' were not used after all. Like all stars, the Brothers had doubles, to set up the scenes, till they were required. Chico was the main absentee: 'We'd finish a scene, and then, "Where's Chico? He was right here a minute ago." . . . At last the stage manager said, "Let's try the bridge club." Now we're in Long Island, and this is over on Riverside Drive, so we'd call up, and sure he was there. "Just as soon as the hand is over, I'll be right over." You just had to be very gentle, and say, "Now listen, this is all charged up against me, and that's not fair . . . Anytime you want time off, I'll try and arrange to be taking something else, but let's be fair to each other." And all those fellows were just marvellous. You know, you make a test at the end of each scene, and Harpo was in it, and . . . he drops his trousers and he hasn't got a goddamned thing on. I just walked up, and said, "Don't you ever do that again." He said, "What's the matter?" I said, "You know those girls will see this." He said, "It'll give them a laugh." I said, "You put the laughs in the picture, not in the tests."'

And indeed they did. *Animal Crackers* is the Marx Brothers' first indisputable film masterpiece, despite its openly theatrical setting. Victor

Heerman's insistence on the Brothers rethinking their comic timing for the particularities of the motion picture made it a much more cinematic work than Florey's juddery *Cocoanuts*. And, as noted, the musical numbers were ruthlessly cut, leaving the musical high note not the 'Monkey Doodle-Doo' but Captain Spaulding:

> Hello, I must be going.
> I came to say, I cannot stay, I must be going . . .
> I'll do anything you say,
> In fact I'd even stay —
> But I must be – go-ing . . .

Not much notice, indeed, was taken of the censor's disapproval of Captain Spaulding's risqué policies, as outlined by his secretary, Jamison – Zeppo with a few more lines this time:

> JAMISON: I represent the Captain who insists on my informing you of these conditions under which he camps here. In one thing he is very strict. He wants his women young and picked. And as for men, he won't have any tramps here . . . The men must all be very old, the women warm, the champagne cold. It's under these conditions that he camps here!

Cue Captain Spaulding's own credo and chorus: 'The Captain Is a Very Moral Man!'

The 'morality' of Captain Spaulding, following on the 'morality' of hotelman Hammer, established the character that Groucho was to play in all the films the Marx Brothers were to make together; brash, arrogant, self-assured, but at the same time highly conscious of his own, and everyone else's, lowly origins, he is a social climber who loves to saw the rungs off the ladder – even if these are the rungs still above him. Like ancient oracles, he is a man who speaks the truth in riddles; a man of the world, as familiar with the park bench at night as with the silk sheets of the Waldorf-Astoria – for which he can never, or will never, pay. A huckster ever ready to fleece the rich, he is a soft sentimentalist at heart, a Cupid for young lovers, and a sucker for a real con man, such as Tutsi-Frutsi man Chico. No longer the paterfamilias Henry Schneider, he remains in some undefined patron status to the two scamps Chico and Harpo, who are constantly undermining his plans. The Marx-Schoenberg family history is never far from the surface. True to the hierarchy, Groucho also keeps a tight rein on his kid brother Zeppo, the amanuensis, the straight man, the stooge:

GROUCHO: Jamison, take a letter to my lawyers: Honourable Charles H. Hungerdunger, care of Hungerdunger, Hungerdunger, Hungerdunger, Hungerdunger and McCormick. Gentlemen question mark . . . In re yours of the fifth inst, yours to hand, and beg to rep, brackets, that we have gone over the ground carefully and we seem to believe, i.e., to wit, e.g. in lieu, that despite all our precautionary measures which have been involved, we seem to believe that it is hardly necessary for us to proceed, unless we, uh, receive an ipso facto that is not negligible at this moment quote unquote and quote, hoping this finds you . . . Now read me the letter, Jamison . . .

ZEPPO: Honourable Charles H. Hungerdunger . . . in care of Hungerdunger, Hungerdunger, Hungerdunger and McCormick . . .

GROUCHO: 'You've left out a Hungerdunger! You left out the main one, too! Thought you could slip one over me, didn't you, eh? All right, leave it out and put in a windshield wiper instead . . . Make it three windshield wipers and one Hungerdunger. They won't be all there when the letter arrives, anyhow. Hungerdunger, Hungerdunger, Hungerdunger . . .

ZEPPO: And McCormick . . . Gentlemen question mark . . .

GROUCHO: Gentlemen question mark! Put it on the penultimate, not the diphthongic. You want to brush up on your Greek, Jamison. Well, get a Greek and brush up on him.

ZEPPO: In re yours of the fifth inst . . .

GROUCHO: I see.

ZEPPO: Now, you said a lot of things here that I didn't think were important, so I just omitted them . . .

GROUCHO: You just omitted them, eh? You've just omitted the body of the letter, that's all! . . . Yours not to reason why, Jamison! You've left out the body of the letter . . . All right, send it that way and tell them the body'll follow.

ZEPPO: Do you want the body in brackets?

GROUCHO: No, it'll never get there in brackets; put it in a box.

Pricking Groucho's pretensions, his brothers are always there, in their proletarian cast-offs, to remind him, and us, of where we came from. If we may view Groucho as a rampaging Freudian super-ego, Chico is his immigrant reality-principle, and Harpo his unconscious id. They are, in this sense, different parts of the same personality, and therein, perhaps, lies their secret – and also their Achilles heel, as we shall see. Zeppo keeps notes, and could therefore, in due course, become expendable, leaving the great Hungerdunger ding-dong as a sample of what might have been.

Animal Crackers retained most of the supporting cast of the Broadway play, apart from the love interest – Alice Wood as Arabella Rittenhouse and Milton Watson as John Parker – who were replaced by Lillian Roth and Hal Thompson.

Robert Greig as Hives, the butler with the knockout drops, Louis Sorin as Roscoe W. Chandler, Margaret Irving as Mrs Whitehead and Margaret Dumont as Mrs Rittenhouse, reprise their well-rehearsed roles. At times, Maggie Dumont almost corpses at Groucho's flood of innuendoes or the social gaucheries of Chico and Harpo's card game – Harpo slamming ace of spade after ace of spade on the table. (Chico: "Atsa what you call a finesse!")

Continually receiving Harpo's thigh in her grip, Maggie Dumont maintains the highest sang-froid, just as Daisy Dumont had, in real life, when being ribbed by her young co-actors in her earliest pre-war shows. Even the disappearance of the famous Beaugard painting, whose unveiling is to be the high point of her high-society party, only fazes her for a short while.

The police are called – Ed Metcalfe returning in his traditional role as Inspector Hennessey – allowing us the only filmed sighting of Harpo's famous knife-dropping act, the cascade of silverware falling out of his coat while the uncomprehending cop shakes his hand. The other Brothers settle down to watch a routine they must have watched, literally, more than a thousand times. Groucho gets to perform his 'Strange Interludes', direct to camera, with a swipe at the foul fortunes of the Market:

'Living with your folks, the beginning of the end . . . Drab dead yesterdays shutting out beautiful tomorrows . . . Hideous stumbling footsteps creaking along the misty corridors of time . . . And in those corridors I see figures. Strange figures. Weird figures: Steel 186. Anaconda 74. American Can 138 . . .'

But these are surmountable nightmares. Inexorably, the Brothers get to trash 'polite' society, stripping it of its pretensions and conceits. Abie the Fishpeddler is exposed, the police are confounded, and the sweet hopes of youth are realized.

Only Maggie Dumont, the main target of the onslaught, survives every offence and indignity – even the physical assault by Harpo, egged on by Chico to punch her right in the stomach ('Oh, she can't take it there!'), which is followed directly, as if nothing has happened, by the ace-of-spades-rich bridge hand. For somewhere in the story is the idea that society

– despite, or even because of, its absurdities – will triumph, in the end, against the revolutionaries, who are not, at the end of the day, out to destroy it, but to join it, under their own quirky terms. As Harpo, having put the entire assembly of party guests to sleep with his flit-spray of Hives's chloroform, spots a luscious blonde in the slumbering pile and, spraying himself in the face, gently lies down beside her, in anaesthetized bliss . . .

Stowaways in the Forward Hatch

OFFICER (*saluting*): Sorry to report there are four stowaways in the forward
  hatch!
CAPTAIN: Stowaways? How do you know there are four of 'em?
OFFICER: Why, they were singing 'Sweet Adeline'!

Monkey Business (1931)

One encounter during the filming of *Animal Crackers* was to have a long-lasting influence on one of our heroes: Lillian Roth, who played Arabella, the *ingénue* of the piece, brought along her younger sister, Ann, who was then fourteen years old, to the set. Chico's roaming eye settled quickly on this new teenage admirer. Time would pass before much came of this, but when it did, it would blow his marriage to Betty apart.

Chico's nuclear family was experiencing a brief period of 'normality' following Minnie's death, though storm clouds were already gathering. Twelve-year-old Maxine was enrolled in the Ethical Culture School on Central Park West in New York City, close to her parents' new apartment. Maxine learned to shut out the constantly raised voices and slamming doors, immersing herself in books. The war behind the doors was mostly about Chico's gambling. Betty might have been able to live, for a while, with human rivals, but not with the demon dice and the cards. After one bad fight Chico packed and left, but returned, some days later, to collect Maxine from school. Maxine became a tool for Chico to use in order to become reconciled with Betty without facing their root problems. Maxine had her own problems at school, having to work out which of her classmates were seeking her friendship for her own sake and which just because of her famous father. One happy moment came when he turned up to star at the Ethical School's mid-term assembly show, though ethics were presumably not discussed.

Groucho, living in his ten-room house at Great Neck, found a form of therapy, and perhaps a use for his sleepless hours, in expanding his occasional magazine essays into a full-length book, entitled *Beds*. This was initially conceived as a series of short pieces, for the magazine *College Humor*, about the amusing things people could do in beds, while leaving out the most obvious topic. As Groucho told Hector Arce: 'It was about people not fucking.' The book was published by Farrar and Reinhart in the autumn of 1930, with a four-part serialization in September. Hector Arce wrote that *Beds* was ghost-written by Groucho's new young gag writer, Arthur Sheekman, but this does not seem to hold much water, given the similarity of the writing to Groucho's other essays of the later 1920s. The book sold about 25,000 copies but Groucho, as ever, disparaged that in his later writings: 'Instead of buying my *Beds*, people took to their own. During the next forty years people refused to have anything to do with *Beds*. Whole families slept standing up.'

The book was indeed out of print for decades, until 1976. But Groucho was immensely proud at the time: 'The thrill of my life, a fellow with little education and a tall blonde stenographer joining such immortals as Shakespeare, Tolstoy and Longfellow.' Perhaps so, with prose such as this: 'Some of us are greatly indebted to the bedbug. I'm referring to his famous silence. How many more divorces and murders would there be, and how many beautiful actresses would be fired in Hollywood, if these little reticent creatures were to talk and tell all they knew? Think that over carefully the next time you try to slaughter the little cimex.'

'Tis not quite Macbeth, but 'twill serve. It was the precursor of much more to come, later.

At the end of the run of *Animal Crackers*, and with the film version in the can, the Marx Brothers returned briefly to their vaudeville roots with a short stage tour presenting a version of the Napoleon sketch from *I'll Say She Is*, entitled 'Napoleon's Revenge' or, according to Groucho, '*Schweinerei*' (another term for 'monkey business'). The act opened at New York's Palace and then moved west. During one of these shows, in November, at Chicago, Groucho was rushed to the hospital with appendicitis and Zeppo appeared in his place, greasepaint moustache, cigar and all, to give what *Variety* termed 'a credible performance Saturday Matinée, with the public unaware of the missing member. Seemingly it was Zeppo who was absent.' A perfectly understandable error.

Groucho was sufficiently alarmed at Zeppo's success in supplanting him to rush back to the stage within two weeks, minus his extracted organ. Zeppo had been chafing at the bit for some time at his minor role in the act. As early as January 1929 he had told *Theatre Magazine*'s Sylvia B. Golden, in an unusually revealing outburst:

My career on the stage is practically ruined, because I am afraid of my brothers. I'm the youngest, and from the moment I first went on I would look over at them, who had already been established as comedians, and if I caught them smiling, even good-naturedly, over what I was saying or doing, I would become self-conscious to the point of unhappiness. For quite a while I've been in the real estate business, on the side, and that's to what I'm going to devote myself when this show closes. I won't even go on tour. I'm not suited to the musical comedy stage; should have been in straight comedy, and not with my brothers. They make me feel so self-conscious that I suffer. It's developed an inferiority complex in me.

The real estate line can't have been bringing much in, because Zeppo persevered in the act, nevertheless, for another five years. He went on tour, smiled, spoke his few lines, and bore the slings and arrows. At Christmas 1930, he joined his three brothers on a six-week trip to England. The Brothers had been invited, by British impresario Charles B. Cochran, to reprise their vaudeville act on the London stage. Cochran planned to inaugurate a run of old-time variety shows at the Palace Theatre, and he wanted the Brothers to add an international dimension. And so, on Christmas Eve 1930, all four Brothers, with wives Betty, Ruth and Marion, and Groucho's children, nine-year-old Arthur and three-year-old Miriam, embarked on the SS *Paris*, accompanied by old stalwarts Ed Metcalfe and Maggie Dumont. Maxine stayed at the Ethical School, and Harpo followed separately, a little later.

As far as one can gather, none of the events later chronicled in *A Night at the Opera* took place on this Marxian ocean voyage, though Groucho was often laid low by seasickness. Arthur Marx recalled Groucho's Christmas Eve ode at sea:

Twas the night before Christmas
And all through the house,
Not a customer was stirring,
Not even a louse,
Because Christmas week has always
Been a drop dead week in the theatre . . .

Groucho was probably recalling with dread the Brothers' first, ill-starred tour of England in 1922. In the event, after a sneak preview in a suburban cinema, the first night at the Palace was a triumph, on a bill shared with

Miss Okabe, Novelty Japanese Juggler; George Dormond, in Scientific Nonsense; Duffin and Draper, Animated Rag Dolls; Ivy St Helier, imitator of such stalwarts as Sophie Tucker and, note, Maurice Chevalier. The Marx Brothers would have had no trouble shining among this assemblage of second-raters, especially as they were no longer unknown Chicagoans with bizarre behaviour and incomprehensible dialogue, but international movie stars. They performed selected episodes from their Broadway hits and also from *On the Balcony*, with Margaret Dumont as Mrs Gould, celebrating her daughter's marriage, in this case, to Zeppo.

Reviews and responses were mixed. Some critics raved about 'this delightful quartette of true comedians', and spoke of the house 'rocking with laughter which continued for forty minutes'. But some, like Gilbert Wakefield, sniffed about 'the almost insolent carelessness with which the screen-show has been adapted for the stage [*sic*!]' and noted, 'I could not help feeling that the actors were heartily sick of their familiar wise-cracks, and that much of their old virtue was gone out of them.' An unkind but possibly perceptive comment.

In an echo of 1922, the initial enthusiasm of audiences wore off, and business began to slacken. England was still not quite at home with the Marx Brothers, although the Marx Brothers felt at home in England; not the home of their own humble and raucous origins, but the more refined dining rooms of their illustrious hosts: the Duke of Manchester (whoever he might have been), and writers Groucho admired and was keen to meet – J. B. Priestley, Somerset Maugham, A. P. Herbert and Noël Coward, familiar from the New York stage – Shakespeare and Longfellow being out of reach. After London, Groucho and family stayed two weeks in Paris, at the swanky Hôtel Georges Cinq, lapping up the tourist attractions, from Versailles to the Eiffel Tower, where Groucho got sick in the lift.

Harpo has not left us any memories of this New Year trip, allowing a discreet veil to fall over the Anglian conquests of the only remaining Marx bachelor. Zeppo purchased the Afghan dogs that were so to annoy S. J. Perelman. Chico, by all accounts, behaved impeccably, becoming a bridge buddy of the 'Dook', though, Maxine recalled, he was not very impressed by the gracious gloom of English manors.

According to Maxine, Chico was instrumental in closing the crucial contract for the Brothers' next project, aboard ship, with a group of Paramount lawyers. A facsimile of this seminal document, reproduced by Paul Wesolowski in *The Freedonia Gazette*, shows, intriguingly, that it was signed, by all four brothers and by Jesse Lasky for Paramount Publix

Corporation, on 24 December 1930, the very day the brothers sailed from New York. To wit, i.e., e.g., in lieu, quote unquote:

> FIRST: The Corporation hereby engages the Artists (the Marx Brothers), to act, to perform, play and take part (in that order) in three motion-picture photoplays of feature length, with which music, songs and/or dialogue recorded synchronously by mechanical and/or electrical means are intended to be reproduced, said three motion-picture photoplays to be produced at the Studios of the Corporation in the City of New York or Los Angeles, California, and on such locations as may be selected by it.
>
> SECOND: The Artists hereby accept the said engagement and agree to give their time and attention and devote their best talents and abilities to portraying the roles assigned to them by the Corporation in the said productions and in rendering musical, comedy, pantomime and dancing numbers and specialties, together with such dialogue and other business as the respective parts shall require, during the production thereof, for photographing by the motion-picture camera and for synchronized recording by such mechanical and/or (ipso facto) electrical means as may be employed therefor.

And nary a Hungerdunger in sight!

The four Marx Brothers were to receive an advance of $200,000 on 50 per cent of the net profits of each of the prospective photoplays. This was no bad deal, even if $50,000 per brother did not yet put them on millionaires' row. Groucho had no real reason to be seasick on his Atlantic trip, and it is no surprise that he was frisky enough on the return to New York to declare his occupation blithely to customs officials as 'smuggler'. This was not one of his more successful jokes. Poor Ruth Marx became increasingly agitated as the customs officers went through every item of baggage. The last straw was when Groucho whispered loudly to her, 'What did you do with the opium?' This led, according to Arthur, to a total strip-search of both parents and children in the Customs' inner office. Innocent days! But this, too, would find its way into art . . .

While the Astoria Studio on Long Island continued to turn out Paramount productions, it was very much the number two studio and, from 1931 onwards, the number of feature films shot there declined. If the Marx Brothers were going to be big stars they would have to relocate, to the West.

Groucho wrote: 'We piled aboard the *Santa Fe* and set off to stake a tentative claim in movieland . . . When we stepped off the train at Los Angeles the air was sweet with a heavy blend of orange and lemon blossoms. The rush to California had not yet begun, and Hollywood still had that quiet, pastoral air about it . . .'

Nostalgia ain't what it used to be! As we have seen, S. J. Perelman had quite a different take on the 'unspeakable tawdriness' of Hollywood Boulevard and the 'hayseed's idea of the Big Apple'. The Mecca of show business had its many down sides, even then. But this was the age before the freeways, and the sun shone, and the air was pure. The Marxes' first port of call was the Garden of Allah, an exclusive enclave of bungalows and apartments grouped around a great kidney-shaped pool, once the estate of silent star Alla Nazimova. Here they could feel at home, despite the palm trees, owing to the presence of newly arrived Algonquinites like Robert Benchley and, later, Dorothy Parker et al. Many scandals centred around this oasis, which Aleck Woollcott described as 'the kind of village you might look for down the rabbit-hole', though Looking-Glass Alice might have had something else in mind when faced by the bottles marked 'Drink Me'.

Harpo claimed that he slept through it all, once he had to keep the rigorous film studio schedule, up at six and on the set by eight. It was not a place for the kiddies though, and Groucho and Ruth soon moved out to a rented house in Beverly Hills, near the schools that Arthur and Miriam could attend, along with other film stars' offspring. Chico and Betty found a three-bedroom house in Malibu, between the homes of Joan Bennett and John Gilbert, so Maxine could beachcomb with the élite. Zeppo and Marion settled in Hollywood and promptly bought a Rolls-Royce and a yacht.

The gold rush, in fact, was on. In the same summer that the Marxes settled in paradise, W. C. Fields arrived, after his cross-country car trip, rapping his cane on the reception desk of the best hotel and demanding the bridal suite. Eddie Cantor had been in town for a year, having arrived in the spring of 1930 to shoot his first sound feature, *Whoopee*. Broadway was decanting its stars from the land of bust and bankruptcy to the land of milk and honey. The queen bee, Mae West, was to arrive in 1932, to get the hive really buzzin'.

The talkies were drawing them in: actors, directors, writers who could write spoken dialogue, the Ben Hechts, the Charlie MacArthurs, the Charles Lederers, Gene Fowlers and all. Three out of these four named had already worked for the doyen of Broadway/Hollywood transplantees, S. J. Perelman's nemesis – Herman Mankiewicz.

Mankiewicz – 'Mank' to his friends, and to his enemies – has been a relatively unsung hero of maverick Hollywood; a poacher turned game-keeper *par excellence*. An Algonquin Round Table regular and *The New Yorker*'s drama critic, Mank was a celebrated Prohibition boozer in a city of drunken lunch-addicts. Born in 1897, a son of German-Jewish immi-grants, he was a pacifist in the World War who enlisted just in time to catch the last week of the war in devastated France. He had spent three years between 1920 and 1922 living in Berlin with his just-married wife, Sara – who was to stick with him through thick and thin till his death – writing articles for *Women's Wear Daily* about the new sin capital of the world.

In a population of entrenched parochialists, whether in New York or Los Angeles, Mank was a man whose horizons stretched past Coney Island or the Santa Monica pier. His gargantuan appetites for food and drink were only part of his lust for life and knowledge. He was a political radical, despised Coolidge and Hoover, was passionately pro-union and an early supporter of the American Civil Liberties Union. In many ways, he was a perfect candidate for the cultural swirl of 1920s New York, but he lacked the discipline to be what he most wanted, a playwright who would set the world on fire. A facilitator more than a creator, he was perfectly cast for script-hungry Hollywood. In mid-1925, offered $500 by MGM to write a scenario based on an idea he had allegedly had on the toilet, he quit *The New Yorker* and went West. His first assignment – not the rest-room-inspired one – was a script for Lon Chaney, called *The Road to Mandalay*. The leg-endary production chief B. P. Schulberg took Mank under his wing at Paramount. He engaged a secretary, Rachel Linden, whose experience with the mercurial Mankiewicz was to equip her perfectly for her later post, as the Marx Brothers' official Girl Friday.

Mankiewicz's telegram to Ben Hecht, in 1925, inviting him west, summed up Mank's delight in his new role: 'Will you accept three hundred per week to work for Paramount Pictures? All expenses paid. The three hundred is peanuts. Millions are to be grabbed out here and your only com-petition is idiots. Don't let this get around.'

But the news did spread. Silent films, of course, required a special skill from the writer. The only dialogue was in the intertitles. Both Mankiewicz and Ben Hecht excelled at these, which could pep up even flagging vehi-cles. One of Mank's early unsung pieces was the now lost W. C. Fields circus freak movie, *Two Flaming Youths* (1927). He also intertitled a string of movies for the maverick director Josef von Sternberg, *The Drag Net*, *Thunderbolt* and *The Last Command*. The talkies came to Mank as a perfect boon, and he returned to New York to trawl for more writers, where else but at the Algonquin, where, he said, 'Writers are so thick they get in your hair.' Charles MacArthur, Charles Lederer, Nunnally Johnson, were swept up, to become a key part of Hollywood's script talent. Between them they would account for *The Front Page, His Girl Friday, Twentieth Century, The Grapes of Wrath, Tobacco Road, Gentlemen Prefer Blondes*, et cetera, et cetera, et cetera. And Mank himself would fulfil his ambition to set the world alight, in suitably controversial mode, ten years on, with his script for *Citizen Kane*.

In 1931, however, he was put in charge of the Marx Brothers. Studio boss Schulberg knew that the two sides had been acquainted since Algonquin days, and surmised that Mank was both ruthless and crazy enough to survive and even, perhaps, control the lunatics. Who better than the King of the Asylum! We should not be surprised, then, at the hardline tactics he adopted with the hapless writers.

In fact, Perelman and Johnson were only the tip of the iceberg of the Marxian writing team. Arthur Sheekman was a young columnist for the *Chicago Times*, who had come to interview the Brothers during their run of *Animal Crackers*, but ended up with his column guest-written by Groucho. Soon after, they collaborated on a number of sketches for a Broadway revue entitled *Three's a Crowd*. Sheekman became one of Groucho's closest friends and edited the 1967 compilation book, *The Groucho Letters*, which includes a large chunk of their correspondence.

Nat Perrin was a young law graduate just about to take his exams when he inveigled his way backstage at the Albee Theatre, Brooklyn, where the Brothers were promoting *Animal Crackers*, the movie. He had tried to get an official introduction from Broadway writer Moss Hart, so as to present the Brothers with a sketch he had written for them but, failing to do so, faked a letter from Hart's agent, introducing him as a 'bright young man'. Impressed by his *chutzpah*, Groucho collected him as a gag man for Hollywood and Perrin duly trekked west, the day after his bar examinations.

Hector Arce tells the tale of Bert Granet, a young protégé of Kaufman and Ryskind, who was already working for Paramount as an assistant director and sound engineer, but yearned for a more creative role. His ploy to reach Groucho was to call at his dressing room with a pretty blonde and ask, 'May I come in?' 'No,' said Groucho, 'but she can.' Arce claims that Granet submitted ideas for two films, one about antics on a cruise ship, entitled 'The Seas Are Wet', and another set on campus, called 'College Daze' – the nuclei of *Monkey Business* and *Horse Feathers*. This is at odds with Perelman's tale of the genesis of these movies, but Arce found that Granet had sued Paramount when he discovered his ideas had been made into movies without his knowledge or any acknowledgment. Paramount settled by hiring him as a screenwriter, to work with Arthur Sheekman on a Bing Crosby picture.

So all the pieces were in place, in that golden summer of 1931, in the pleasure gardens. Out in the rest of the country, however, things were dire. The Depression was biting harder and harder. Herbert Hoover was President and Franklin D. Roosevelt was just a dissenting voice on the horizon. The number of the unemployed was rising towards fourteen million, and many cities were blighted with new shanty towns, the 'Hoovervilles' of the increasing homeless. This was an America no one wanted to see, far less to be a part of.

Behind Hollywood's brash façade, in the offices of the studios' accountants, the figures were bad, and getting worse. Jesse Lasky called for the saving graces of comedy, lashings of comedy.

The Four Horsemen of the Apoplexy were only too glad to oblige.

The Pleasure Principle and the Poetic Seal

> I don't care what you have to say,
> It makes no difference anyway,
> Whatever it is, I'm against it!
> And no matter how you changed it or condensed it
> I'm against it!
>
> *Horse Feathers* (1932)

The Hollywood the Marx Brothers set out to conquer in 1931 was, in the words of a contemporary journalist, Anne O'Hare McCormick: 'The remotest place in the world, set apart from reality, concentrating on the literal and missing the truth, and yet it is ourselves in the mass: America's self-portrait.' Writing from within the movie crucible in a series of long articles for the *New York Times* at the end of 1931, McCormick dissected the factory mood and ethos of Hollywood long before it became a staple of 'post-modern', present-day analysts:

> The studios are large enclosures, like walled towns, kremlins which in these days it is not so easy to enter. The gates are guarded and some sort of passport is required. The outsider stands in a little entry in front of a grille like a bank teller's and states his name and business . . . The efficiency engineer has come to Hollywood. He is one of the evils of the depression . . . With him arrive the time clock, the inspection system, these copious reports from the ushers of the country, carefully card-indexed, on the remarks they overhear as picture audiences leave the theatre. Hollywood is being speeded up and pared down, the pace of production is being quickened . . .

Although the talkies were barely four years old, and – McCormick wrote – perhaps because of this, the fact was that:

> Hollywood is very unsure of itself. It has no settled policy, no sense of direction; it tries one thing and then another, buys talent it is afraid to

use, flies trial balloons it is afraid to follow up, advances and backs down with jolts that make the Stalin regime in Russia look like a straight line. It gallops like the famous mechanical horse of Mr. Coolidge, standing violently in one spot because it cannot turn, or does not know where to turn . . . It is so universal in scope, technically so sophisticated, commercially such a giant, that it is easy to forget that it represents the development of a single generation . . . Motion pictures are first and last a business. Two billion dollars have not been invested here as a Medicean gesture, with the idea of encouraging an infant art. It happens however . . . that the business shows faint, unhappy signs of developing into an art. Observe that it is criticized now not only for its ethics but its esthetics. As it presents more and more photographed stage plays, employs those who have figured as artists in other fields, inherits the conventions and pretensions of the theatre.

This is not art worried by business, the classic complaint, but business beginning to be worried by art . . .

Indeed, the Marx Brothers, like almost everyone else, did not go to Paramount studios to make art, but money. To both their and our delight, they made both.

The three movies the Brothers made at Paramount – *Monkey Business*, 1931; *Horse Feathers*, 1932; and *Duck Soup*, 1933 – are, to many, the acme of their cinematic art, though their first two MGM movies, *A Night at the Opera*, 1935, and *A Day at the Races*, 1936, jostle for a place on the podium. Here are the Marx Brothers unbound, freed from the limitations and necessities of the stage and unleashed upon an unsuspecting mankind.

These movies did not emerge, *extempore*, out of the performers' psyches, but out of a long process of collaboration with their coterie of writers, served, if only as traffic wardens, by their assigned directors and the noble complement of cameramen, sound engineers, art directors, electricians and other technicians without whom all would be crackling and dark. In Billy Wilder's 1950 classic *Sunset Boulevard*, narrator William Holden's character bemoans the fact that audiences don't think about the screenwriter, they believe the actors make the lines up as they go along. Today's audiences are far more cine-literate, even fanatic in their attention to the details and minutiae of film creation yet, still, the grand old image persists: the Marx Brothers as complete lunatics, uncontrollable loons who did what they wanted on screen, to the despair of colleagues, crew and producers.

But, as we have seen, the Marx Brothers were nothing if not professionals, paying the most serious attention to their craft, worrying endlessly about lines and gags, working to perfect their art, and then to disguise all that hard work, as all best artists do, under the veneer of a spontaneous ease.

The Marxian writers, that band of brothers – Perelman apart, who peeled off at an early opportunity, and later became heartily fed up with his early identification with the Marx Brothers – knew, by 1931, what was required of them as shapers of the Marxes' dialogue and stories. They became adept at the creative game of 'What would Groucho say here?' or 'How would Chico respond to this?' or 'What would happen if we put the Marx Brothers (a) on board an ocean liner; (b) in an ivy league college; (c) in charge of a Ruritanian-style country? It's less clear how much they had to do with Harpo's pantomime gags, and Zeppo remained the writers' weak spot. But the scribes knew enough to work, in our latter-day argot, 'minimally', to draw on the Marxian routines, experiences, their long-fixed character personas, within the jokes and idioms of the time.

Kaufman and Ryskind had set the tone and moved on to sterner stuff: in 1931 they embarked on their most successful stage collaboration, a musical satire (music by Ira Gershwin) on the United States Presidency, *Of Thee I Sing*. The powerful lampoon of the Presidential candidate, John P. Wintergreen, his ineffectual Vice-President, the ramblings of the Senate and the gullibility of the great American Public was premièred in December 1931 and was, as noted, to win the Pulitzer Prize, the first time the award had been given to a musical. The play, with its torchlight chorus of Wintergreen sycophants: 'He's the man the people choose, loves the Irish and the Jews', must have had some effect, if only indirectly, on the writing of the Brothers' 1933 movie, *Duck Soup*. The Brothers would, in fact, explore the possibility of appearing in a film version of *Of Thee I Sing*, but this was one project that was left on the producers' floor.

The team that would replace Kaufman and Ryskind as chief Marxist writers – once S. J. Perelman had succumbed to the regular two falls or a submission and vacated the Paramount dungeon – were the songwriters Bert Kalmar and Harry Ruby.

Kalmar and Ruby had been collaborating since their early days in vaudeville in 1919, and had written the lyrics and music for the stage *Animal Crackers*. Harry Ruby, né Rubinstein (1895–1974), was a New Yorker brought up in the hard school of the Bronx, escaping by the skin of his teeth from a life of petty larceny. As a teenager he teamed up in a song-and-dance act with Harry Cohn, later to become the most hated of Hollywood's moguls. At the age of seventeen, Ruby was taken on by Gus Edwards and soon wrote his first song hit, 'When Those Sweet Hawaiian Babies Roll Their Eyes'. He 'plugged songs with George Gershwin, played the piano for Irving Berlin and accompanied Walter Winchell, who was singing at the time in a Woolworth 5 & 10 cent store on 14th Street'.

Bert Kalmar (1884–1947), the elder of the duo, was a boyhood magic enthusiast. He claimed to have played in vaudeville with Houdini when the great man lived in New York, and made the acquaintance of other famous magicians such as Herman the Great and his successor, Harry Keller. He had visited Egypt and Japan, pursuing his hobby, and used to enjoy telling how he had stolen his parents' clothes-lines to practise the old Indian rope trick.

Groucho had known Kalmar and Ruby from their earliest collaborations, and the earliest letter in his collection, *The Groucho Letters*, is a missive from Ruby dated 16 August 1923, replying to Groucho's best wishes for his show, *Helen of Troy*: 'I'm sorry you asked how the show opened out of town, but I'll answer your question as soon as I can stop crying.'

Ruby did not need to cry for long, as his song-writing career took off with *Good Boy*, starring Boop-Oop-a-Doop girl Helen Kane, and *Top Speed*, which introduced a very young Ginger Rogers. While working on *Animal Crackers*, Kalmar and Ruby had received their baptism of fire with the Marx Brothers during a party in their hotel suite, in the course of which the brothers began throwing plates out of the window on to the roof of the hotel's garage. Harpo arrived late and began manoeuvring the room's piano out of the window to join the rest of the flotsam, until the song-writing duo managed to stop him. At three in the morning, so Ruby told Richard Anobile for *The Marx Brothers Scrapbook*, Groucho, who was not immediately recognizable without his painted moustache, went down to the lobby to complain about 'the rowdies and bums up in room so-and-so . . . something should be done about them . . . Imagine!' said Ruby. 'They tried to get Bert and me thrown out of our own suite! But that's what it was like all the time, with the Marx Bros.'

Showing exemplary courage in the face of the enemy, or foolhardiness beyond the bounds of reason, Kalmar and Ruby nevertheless signed on in 1932 to join Perelman, Johnstone and Sheekman as the script team for *Horse Feathers*. They were to remain to pen the immortal *Duck Soup*, with Nat Perrin and Arthur Sheekman as additional gagsters.

Monkey Business, *Horse Feathers* and *Duck Soup* are so well known that I will assume the reader's acquaintance with these photoplays. For the benefit of any readers who might not have the entire Marx *oeuvre* committed to

'This is the only way to travel': fishy stuff in *Monkey Business*.

Professor Quincy Adams Wagstaff with senior colleague (Robert Grieg).

memory, here is a brief summary of the first two of these movies – *Duck Soup* rates its own chapter.

Monkey Business: the Marx Brothers are discovered as stowaways aboard a ship bound for home shores. Evading the infuriated Captain, the Brothers expropriate his quarters and his lunch, while causing havoc among the passengers. They become entangled with gangster Alky Briggs and his wife Lucille, played by the peerless Thelma Todd. Briggs, impressed by their daring, takes Groucho and Zeppo on as bodyguards while a rival gangster, Joe Helton, engages Chico and Harpo. (Chico: 'You pay little bit, we little bit tough; you pay very much, we very much tough; you pay too much, we too much tough . . .' Helton: 'I pay plenty!' Chico: 'Well, we're plenty tough.') None of this leads to very meaningful action, not even for Lucille, though Zeppo, as the love interest this time, becomes enamoured of Helton's daughter, Mary. When the ship docks, the Brothers try to get off by producing, in turn, a passport Harpo has stolen from (an off-screen) Maurice Chevalier. In an echo of the theatre agent scene from *On the Balcony* and *I'll Say She Is*, they each do a Chevalier imitation. An added bonus is the only appearance on film of the Marxes' father, Frenchy, in a bit part, both as a passenger on board and in the crowd waiting on the dock, so that he seems to be meeting himself. In the confusion, the Brothers manage to disembark.

Act Two: gangster Helton's palatial residence, a coming-home party for his daughter Mary. The Brothers attend, while rival gangster Briggs plots to kidnap Mary Helton. Folderol between Groucho and Lucille; Chico and Harpo piano and harp specialities. Mary is kidnapped to the barn and the Brothers follow to effect her rescue. Groucho in the hay: 'Where's all these farmers' daughters I've been hearing about for years?' Mary is rescued, Helton is grateful, and Mary and Zeppo exit to a chorus of cow bells and animal noises.

Note the close structural resemblance to the Brothers' primal 'Home Again' sketch, witnessed goggle-eyed by the young S. J. Perelman in the halcyon days of 1915.

Horse Feathers: Huxley College is appointing a new President, Quincy Adams Wagstaff, alias Groucho. In a song-and-dance speciality (partly on the table), he announces to the assembled bearded professors and the students his credo: 'Whatever it is, I'm against it.' His son, Zeppo, a student, is in love with the College Widow, Thelma Todd again. (No, I have no idea what a College Widow is either.) Huxley College is badly in need of a winning football team. Zeppo tells Groucho two expert players can be bought at the local speakeasy. They have already been snapped up by the rival college, Darwin

Serious legwork with the College Widow (Thelma Todd).

(geddit?) but Groucho engages Chico and Harpo, who hang out there, by mistake. At College, Harpo feeds the fireplace with the Professors' books, and all present try hanky-panky with the College Widow, who seems for some reason to be shacked up with the rival college's fixer, Jennings. Groucho, finding out his mistake, engages Chico and Harpo to kidnap the real football stars. Chico and Harpo cause havoc in the classroom. Some flap-doodle with the buying of the college's football signals from the team's coach,

Chico. Pause for song, on piano, harp and Groucho with guitar in canoe: 'Everyone Says I Love You'. Chico and Harpo get kidnapped while trying to kidnap the rival players, but escape by sawing through the floor. (Famous dialogue: 'Tie on-a bed, throw the rope out of the window.') They arrive at the game by bicycle and horse-drawn garbage cart, in time to win the game with an endless supply of footballs. Wedding ceremony of Zeppo and College Widow descends into scrum involving all four brothers. The End.

Plot, of course, means very little in these films, and the opportunities for fun and games are paramount. The director of both movies was Norman Z. McLeod, a World War One pilot with the Royal Canadian Air Force who had begun his film career as an animator in 1919, later becoming a gag writer for Al Christie Comedies, a lesser-known rival of the Mack Sennett and Hal Roach studios. He had been assistant to director William Wellman on the air war epic, *Wings* (1927). *Monkey Business* was his fourth feature as a director, and he was to go on to direct W. C. Fields's classic *It's a Gift* in 1934, two *Topper* movies, and films with comedians Bob Hope and Danny Kaye. Unlike Victor Heerman, he was no disciplinarian, and this won him, during the shooting of *Horse Feathers*, the ultimate Marxian accolade of being pounced on en masse and debagged, with the Brothers running through the studio waving his pants aloft like a captured enemy flag. McLeod described his own low-key directing approach as 'I'm quiet as a mouse pissing on a blotter', but he knew how to time and pace comedy. In both movies the central comic scenes move verbally and visually like greased lightning. The exchanges, and even Groucho's crackerjack delivery, in *The Cocoanuts* and *Animal Crackers*, were languid by comparison. Take the following scene with Joe Helton in *Monkey Business*:

GROUCHO: Now, there are two fellas trying to attack you, aren't there? And there are two fellas trying to defend you.

HELTON: Why . . .

GROUCHO: Now that's fifty per cent waste. Now why can't you be attacked by your own bodyguards? Your life will be saved, and that's . . . that's a hundred per cent waste . . . Now what have you got? You've still got me and I'll attack you for nothing.

HELTON: Say, what are you getting at?

GROUCHO: I anticipated that question. How does an army travel? On its stomach. How do you travel? On a ship. Of course you're saving your stomach. Now that same common sense will . . .

HELTON: I don't think you realize . . .

GROUCHO: Oh I realize it's a penny here and a penny there, but look at me. I've worked myself up from nothing to a state of extreme poverty. Now what do you say?

HELTON: I'll tell you what I say. I say . . .

GROUCHO: All right. Then it's settled. I'm to be your new bodyguard. In case I'm gonna attack you, I'll have to be there to defend you too. Now let me know when you want to be attacked, and I'll be there ten minutes later to defend you.

Or check out the schoolroom scene in *Horse Feathers*:

GROUCHO: What is a corpuscle?

CHICO: That's easy. First is a captain, then is a lieutenant, then is a corpuscle.

GROUCHO: Why don't you bore a hole in yourself and let the sap run out? We now find ourselves among the Alps. The Alps are a very simple people living on a diet of rice and old shoes. Beyond the Alps lies more Alps and the Lord alps those who alp themselves. We now come to the bloodstream: the blood moves down to the feet, gets a look at those feet, and then rushes back to the head again. This is known as auction pinochle . . . Now, in studying your basic metabolism, we first listen to your heart's beat, and if your hearts beat anything but diamonds and clubs, it means your partner is cheating, or your wife . . .

And so on, until the peashooting starts. Without any surviving script of the Marx Brothers' early 'Hi-Skule' act, we don't know how much of these schoolroom squitters are reprises of the boys' early material, or new imaginings dropped in by Perelman and co. We do have Perelman and Johnstone's original treatment for *Monkey Business*, dated 28 February 1931, which may well have been the very text that the two scribes read out to the congregation of Marxes and dogs at the Roosevelt Hotel in Hollywood, and it is indeed no wonder that Groucho led the walkout with 'It stinks.' It is quite a clumsy concoction, with the opening barrel scene on the ship consisting of a meandering Groucho monologue:

Now that you know the way, Mrs Feibleman, you must come over and have tea in our barrel someday. On the other hand, you take the Captain. He's a fur bearing animal . . . That goes for you too Mrs Feibleman. And all the little Feiblemans. Oh dear, there goes Jim's dinner bubbling over on the stove. Here I am gabbing away and Fred's cup-cakes half-baked in the pan . . .

One can imagine the Afghans beginning to howl already. There is no Maurice Chevalier routine in this version, but a rather confusing sequence with foreign reporters on the ship, who are confronted by Groucho:

GROUCHO: Are you one of those two heart balms shot in prominent mid-town penthouse lovenest during fatal midnight booze orgy? Grilled by cops, did you ask probe of vice-squads frame-up of Broadway butterfly, the Woman of a Thousand Loves?

REPORTER: No comprisc inglese, signore!

GROUCHO: Trying to muzzle the press, are you? You can't mussolini all of us!

(*The Brothers escape off the boat by stealing the reporters' press cards, and the foreign news corps are nabbed as the stowaways.*)

This is an example of the kind of thing S. J. Perelman reports Groucho objecting to on the basis that it would not be understood by 'the barber in Peru', by which he meant Peru, Illinois (or it could have been Peru, Nebraska). This kind of humour was predominantly urban and New York, and the Brothers, mindful of their long mid-American experience, were very wary of limiting their appeal. On the other hand, this principle did not stop them from inserting any number of contemporary references and in-jokes into their material – not to speak of the College Widow.

A great deal of printer's ink has been spilled describing the Marx Brothers' humour as 'surreal', This has a certain amount to do with the announcement by various surrealists that the Marx Brothers' movies were, inadvertently as they may be, in the surrealist canon, but mostly with the ignorance of the surrealists of the origins and roots we have spent so much time digging up in these pages. Joe Adamson quotes both Antonin Artaud and Philippe Soupalt on adopting the Marxes as exemplars:

Soupalt: 'They are exactly like ordinary people and act just as we should act if social regulations did not prevent us from behaving in that way.'

Artaud: 'The poetic quality of a film like *Animal Crackers* would fit the definition of humor if this word had not long since lost its sense of essential liberation, of destruction of all reality in the mind.'

Mon dieu! But the most prominent of the surrealists who embraced the Brothers, and especially Harpo, was the Spanish painter Salvador Dalí. This did not occur until 1936, when Dalí briefly met Harpo in Paris, and then sent him a typically Dalían Christmas present – a harp with barbed-wire strings, strung with spoons. Perhaps he misremembered the knife-dropping act. Dalí arrived in California in February 1937, and promptly visited Harpo, having decided that he wanted to make a Marx Brothers film. Communication between the two was limited by the unfortunate fact that they did not share a common language, though Dalí was very taken with California, enthusing about '*muchos desiertos, indios congelados, excursiones a caballo entre los cactos mas artisticos del mundo*'. In an interview to the American press Dalí stated, with his usual flamboyance: 'The Marx Brothers are the typical Americans, and Americans have the greatest thirst for irrational things.'

The Americans certainly had developed a great thirst for Dalí paintings, which they were buying up by the crateful, so Dalí was delighted to heap on the praise. 'The Americans . . . are irrational, because they are for the fulfilment of the pleasure principle, for doing the things they want to do and for letting others do the same. If an American woman wished to take off her clothes on the street she would be more likely to do it than would any other kind of woman.' Not in Kansas City she wouldn't! But Dalí was exhibiting in Madison Avenue titles such as 'Design for a Coat with Window Shades', 'A Chemist Lifting with Precaution the Cuticle of a Grand Piano', 'Soft Construction with Boiled Beans', 'The Aphrodisiac Smoking Jacket', 'Suburbs of the Paranoiac Critical Afternoon', and 'Autumnal Cannibalism'. These were the days of the Spanish Civil War and the painter, infuriatingly neutral, was eager to express his preference for Marx Groucho over Marx Karl. He was probably the first to articulate this euphonious concept, which has grown ever more appropriate.

Dalí's flirtation with the cinema was a continuing hope of recovering the passion of his two early film productions, the twenty-minute short, *Un Chien andalou*, made in 1929, and *L'âge d'or*, 1930, both directed by Luis Buñuel. *L'âge d'or*, a celebrated scandal, was taken off the screen soon after its first showing in Paris in October 1930, due to violent protests by French fascists, who lit up smoke bombs and spattered the screen with violet ink. None of the Marx Brothers would have seen either movie, nor would they have recognized any affinity to their own concept of art. Buñuel said that the ruling principle in conceiving *Un chien andalou* was the 'refusal of any rational image, or any image that referred to any memory or recollection'. The dark comedy of the Dalí–Buñuel movies emerges out of outrage, and the depiction of the frustration of unrequited love by mad images, such as the hero of *Un chien andalou* pulling two priests tied to a grand piano with a horse's bleeding cadaver upon it, or Gaston Modot, in *L'âge d'or*, throwing a cornucopia of objects out of the window of a mansion – a burning Christmas tree, an archbishop, a plough, a load of feathers and a stuffed giraffe.

The problem of the surrealists, as Buñuel defined it, was that their main aim was to change society, by affecting a revolution of perception, rather than behaviour, for their personal pranks were rather tame. The result of their revolution was that they became famous, their books were garlanded with praise, and their paintings hang in museums and increase in cash value every year – but this was not the purpose of the exercise for André Breton, Louis Aragon, Eluard, Max Ernst and Magritte. Dalí, alone, embraced fame and money above all else, but in a manner that the Marx Brothers, and most contemporary – and much more puritanical – American showbiz people, would have considered vulgar and extreme.

The last thing on the Marx Brothers' minds was any notion of changing society. They liked it just as it was – a sitting target. Like the clown from time immemorial, they needed the patronage of kings and princes to enable their attacks on the ruling classes' self-esteem. Harpo arriving at Rittenhouse Manor with a cloak hiding only his underwear is the eternal revealer of the Emperor's new clothes. Chico is ever the hired help who does what he damn well pleases, and Groucho reveals that anybody can become the President, and not only of Freedonia . . .

The admiring intellectuals were astute enough to realize, perhaps, that it was the Marx Brothers and their fellow clowns, not the novelists and painters of Paris, who were the true surrealists, who stripped away the veneer of hierarchy to show that we are all idiots under the skin. The intellectuals knew they were straining for an effect that was mother's-milk to the inheritors of the traditions of Grock, of Dan Leno, of Weber and Fields, Al Shean and Harrigan and Hart. And it wasn't just the clowns. Who could be more surreal than Houdini, who chained himself upside down from bridges or released himself from bondage under water?

Harpo as Dogcatcher, catching the policeman in his cage, is playing with an image as old as Punch and Judy. When he pulls from his trousers a dead swordfish as his password to the speakeasy, or a barking seal to place on a contract, when he unzips a banana, eats the horse's oats, and raids the public telephone for a miraculous shower of coins into his hat, Harpo lives a life much freer than Dalí's flaccid dreams. The fulfilment of the pleasure principle is indeed a Marxian birthright. And what more fitting image for Depression America, witnessing in real life the collapse and futility of great institutions, banks, companies, centres of scholastic excellence, than Groucho's usurpation of the professors' robes, or Harpo producing, from those magical trousers, a steaming cup of coffee for a passing tramp?

Dalí's screenplay for the Marx Brothers, entitled *Giraffes on Horseback Salad*, has been considered lost since Harpo extracted its sketches, to hang in his living room, and then, at some point, mislaid the text. The sketches portray an eyeball with twenty-three arms, a couch shaped like a pair of lips, flowers blooming from an armchair and Groucho as Buddha answering telephones with six arms. The script has, however, now turned up in Dalí archives. It consists of sixty-five handwritten pages in Dalí's pidgin French (he keeps writing 'la fame surréaliste' instead of 'la femme', a perfect Dalífreudian slip), illustrated with doodles of nude women with huge nipples, an erect penis growing flowers and another sofa, with sheep for arms.

The plot concerns 'Jimmy, a young Spanish aristocrat living in America because of political circumstances in his own country', and his stuck-up fiancée Linda, whom he wishes to abandon in favour of the aforementioned 'femme surréaliste', a woman of extravagant and mad desires who is accompanied by Groucho and Harpo, and sometimes Chico (or Beppo, as Dalí mistakenly calls him, an error apparently common in Europe, where an 'Italian' clown was expected to have an Italian name). Dalí notes: 'The general idea of the scenario consists in the transposition to the present of all the imaginative pomp, splendour and epic character of historical films as typified by Cecil B. de Mille.' In further grand style, Dalí imagined the film being scored by Cole Porter. The 'Surrealist Woman', in Dalí's narrative (probably imagined as his wife, Gala), would preside over an equally surrealist cabaret, with the mouth-shaped sofa, and mirrors with holes out of which girls' arms would snake out to entangle Groucho and Harpo in their caresses. Musicians with roast chickens fixed to their heads would play, 'with chicken legs on their shoulders as epaulettes'. Writes Dalí:

Groucho gives a series of orders, each more absurd and incomprehensible than the other, to his three brothers who answer the telephone, and rush from one end of the town to the other carrying out his orders. For instance, Groucho tells Harpo: 'Bring me the eighteen smallest dwarfs in the city.' Harpo, armed with a large butterfly net, goes out, finds the dwarfs in a circus and on the street and catches them.

These he piles into a car, and takes to the best hairdresser where their hair and whiskers are arranged in the most fantastic way possible, and beauty masks are applied.

Groucho asks his brothers to fetch a herd of goats, a dead ox, a sixty-foot long bed, trombones with fair hair, platinum blonde beauty queens. Money and sometimes violence get for the brothers in typical Marx Brothers style all that Groucho asks them. During the telephoning, his face disappears and reappears, each time covered by the tell tale marks of kisses . . .

Later scenes include Dalí's trademark soft watches and lobster-telephones, troupes of cyclists with rocks on their heads and a fifty-foot loaf of bread wrapped in newspapers. Burning giraffes wearing gas masks stampede, and Chico, dressed in a diving suit ('en scaphandier') plays the piano next to Harpo's harp. In one scene the Brothers are to be installed in 'a hideous villa bought by Groucho. One evening Groucho invites the former proprietor and his wife to a picnic, during which he brings up a gun and fires on the villa. After the first shot, Groucho hands a large pair of field-glasses to the old man so that he can more easily watch its destruction. His wife faints at this sight.'

The whole extravagance is based on 'the continuous struggle between the imaginative life as depicted in the old myths and the practical and rational life of contemporary society'. God knows what the movie, like other unfilmed Dalí scripts, might have looked like, but it was clearly an impossible project for the Marx Brothers. Dalí may have grasped the under-lying anarchism of their comedy, but he didn't understand he had to write from within their characters outwards, rather than from his own familiar obsessions. Nor did he understand that American comedy was based on lampooning the external world, not the internal world of pure fantasy. Of course, Salvador Dalí could function no other way, but it would not have done at all for the barber in Peru, Illinois.

The surrealists' ideal was the principle of mad, spontaneous love. But the only spontaneous love the Marx Brothers would countenance was Groucho's insulting wooing of Margaret Dumont, or their communal assaults on for-ward blondes, most preferably Thelma Todd. One can discount the mushy romantic interludes, even if they involved poor put-upon Zeppo. The only true, mad love in a Marx Brothers movie is Harpo's pure passion for his horse. And that, my dears, was platonic.

An authentically surrealist footnote must be added about Thelma Todd – the perfect Dalían 'platinum blonde beauty queen'. Having joined the Hal Roach studios a day before becoming Miss Massachusetts, she had become a leading lady for comedians Charley Chase and Laurel and Hardy. Among her likes, in a Hal Roach press sheet, she listed 'autobiographies, riding, jelly beans' and 'to make people laugh'. This should have endeared her to fellow jelly bean lover Harpo. Soon after completing *Horse Feathers* she was injured in a car crash with her husband, Pasquale de Cicco, an 'intimate' of

'Lucky' Luciano, whom she soon divorced on charges of cruelty. (The Judge: 'Did he call you harsh and opprobrious names?' Miss Todd: 'Yes.' Judge: 'Did he nag and quarrel until your highly nervous temperament was affected?' Miss Todd: 'Yes.') Miss Todd, no slouch, became involved in the restaurant business in Santa Monica, but was soon embroiled in a blackmail racket allegedly run by Los Angeles bodyguards.

On 16 December 1935, a few days after being heard arguing against the setting up of a gambling casino in her restaurant, Thelma Todd was found dead, slumped beneath the steering wheel of her car in a garage at 17531 Positano Road. Her death, of carbon monoxide poisoning, became a celebrated unsolved Hollywood mystery, inspiring countless magazine articles, a book, and – as late as 1991 – a TV movie. The coroners' verdict on her demise was 'accidental death', but Lucky Luciano departed Los Angeles soon after, for lucrative affairs elsewhere. Much speculation centred on a 'mysterious foreigner' with whom she had been seen hours before her death. (A 'well-informed' and impeccable Hollywood source informs me, however, that the entire affair had been a cover-up from the start: Thelma had been giving her lover, director Roland West (1887–1952), oral attention in the car after a rumbustious night, but nipped his organ with her teeth, causing him to depart in high dudgeon and shut the garage door after him. She fell asleep in the car with the engine left running, and suffocated in her drunken stupor. The police, at the time fiercely protective of LA's celebrities, kept the sordid details of this accident secret, thus fuelling six decades of conspiracy theories.)

The Marxian irony of Thelma Todd's sad fate lies in the line, spoken by Groucho, to Thelma as Lucille Briggs, the gangster's wife in *Monkey Business*: 'You're a woman who's been getting nothing but dirty breaks' (close-up of Groucho, with Lucille's bosom over him) '– well, we can clean and tighten your brakes, but you'll have to stay in the garage all night.'

24

'Hey, Where's Your Brother?'

OFFICER: Say, this picture doesn't look like you.
GROUCHO: Well, it doesn't look like you either.
OFFICER: This man has no moustache!
GROUCHO: Well, the barber shop wasn't open this morning . . .

Monkey Business (1931)

The Marx Brothers' fame, as established Hollywood stars, rocketed to new heights. On 15 August 1932, they made the cover of *Time* magazine, all four together in football gear, bunched up in the garbage cart from *Horse Feathers*. Somebody was really handing out the molasses though, because their life story, told within, included such gems as both Gummo and Harpo having enlisted in the army, and Harpo working as a reporter for *Stars and Stripes* in France, with the 7th Regiment, as well as becoming a founder member of the Algonquinites with Harold Ross and F. P. Adams. The Marx Brothers now had more formal assistance in getting out their press puffs, in the shape of ace Paramount publicist Teet Carle, who was also busily reinventing W. C. Fields as the misogynous curmudgeon we all know today.

Major press books were issued by the studio, announcing of *Monkey Business*, that 'The 1931 Nut Crop Is Ready, Sir!' and proposing contests in which theatre owners were invited to build 'your own "monkey island," a little barred enclosure with a stubby tree or perch, swing and bars . . . a novel, effective and inexpensive lobby or street float ballyhoo.' A 'laff-o-meter of gigantic proportions' was also a favoured lobby proposal, or wax models of the Brothers. For *Horse Feathers*, Paramount proposed an audience contest for the zaniest curriculum for a Marx Brothers college, with debates such as 'History: Lecture on subject, "Did Nero Fiddle While Rome Burned; or Was Rome Burned to Stop Him Fiddling?"' Another game was 'Name Fifth Marx Brother! $10 reward and free tickets'. The meaningless nature of the movie's title prompted a 'Name Next Marx Brothers Picture' contest; a 'Survey for Longest List of Goofy Similes', such as 'Snakes' Hips' or 'Bee's Knees!' – 'Make it goofy. Make it wild. The nuttier the title, the better your chance of winning this contest. It should be short and snappy and it must not transcend the bounds of good taste.' Harpo's vocation in the movie set off a Town's Biggest or Smallest Dog contest: 'All you need to do to enter this contest . . . is to leash your dog next Saturday morning and bring him or her, as the case may be, downtown to the front of the . . . Theatre.' History has not recorded the outcome.

At about this time, too, the Marx Brothers began to be part of Hollywood's ubiquitous merchandising. In their Broadway days, they had already begun endorsing cigarettes and other products, but now there would be Marx Brothers dolls, statuettes, cigarette cards and bottle stoppers, which would, in the fullness of time, become collectors' items. Not to speak of the cigar and eyebrow images . . .

The Marx Brothers' lives continued to mesh together on screen, but off-screen, they were inevitably drifting apart. In the summer of 1932, following the release of *Horse Feathers*, this was the state of play:

Harpo: apart from judging dogs, Harpo had been settled for over a year at the Garden of Allah, renewing old friendships. Harold Ross turned up outside his window soon after he arrived, shaking a cup of dice and offering a game of backgammon. This was a foolhardy act on Ross's part, as a press cutting of 7 July 1931 reveals that 'Harpo Marx is now a sizeable stockholder of the "New Yorker," which holdings he won at backgammon and cribbage from Harold Ross and Alexander Woollcott . . . Big killing occurred in between Woollcott's stopoff from his Oriental tour and his departure from New York.' Whether this stock was real or imaginary is not so clear, but a later Hollywood directory of 1933 shows Arthur H. Marx as Treasurer of the Harpo Realty Company, so the silent clown would soon be hiding talents other than his voice.

Another member of the Woollcott mob, Charles Lederer, introduced Harpo to the west coast equivalent of the Algonquin Round Table, the circle buzzing about publishing magnate William Randolph Hearst. Hearst, as is well known, was determined to advance the career of his mistress, Marion Davies, by buying into the Hollywood crowd. Davies's Santa Monica beach house was a favoured celebrity hangout, and Harpo's initiation was at a fancy dress party to which he came dressed as Kaiser Wilhelm. Accompanying an unnamed drunken couple home from this beano, he became stranded in Beverly Hills, in full costume, with the visor of his helmet jammed. Never mind, pedants, that a Kaiser Wilhelm costume doesn't include a visor, this is Harpo's tale! Arrested for stopping the traffic on Sunset Boulevard in the guise of a European potentate, and held for identification, Harpo called Chico, who issued a description of his brother: 'Big mop red curly hair. Cross-eyed. Mute. Can't talk.' This did not fit the culprit. In the end, Harpo had to be rescued by Lederer.

The next thing Harpo knew, he was being invited to the Hearst castle at San Simeon. Harpo was impressed, like any visitor to this vast private demesne, the grand folly of the age. He got on very well with Marion Davies, though, we must assume, not too well, given his status as the only Marx bachelor. Another old acquaintance, George Bernard Shaw, was also slumming at the castle. And, though Harpo does not mention this, Herman Mankiewicz was lurking among the medieval bric-a-brac too, already weaving the threads of the web that would in due course become *Citizen Kane*. Harpo, therefore, was snug as a bug in a rug.

Groucho: after a brief swing at the Garden of Allah, Groucho settled down for the homebody life in California. He fell in love with the climate and soon formed his own circle, the 'West Side Writing and Asthma Club', founder members S. J. Perelman, Ben Hecht, Charles MacArthur, Robert Benchley, Charles Butterworth and other old regulars. Groucho was inaugurated as President in the summer of 1932. The Brothers had still not completely severed their links with the theatre. Soon after their arrival in Hollywood, they were summoned back east, for a brief guest appearance in

Zeppo.

Chico.

Gummo.

Groucho.

Harpo.

a show sponsored by the Round Tablers, put on by Heywood Broun. The show was called *Shoot the Works!* and was a forlorn attempt to save Broadway from the big bad wolf by getting an all-star cast to appear without pay. Dorothy Parker, E. B. White and Nunnally Johnson joined Eddie Cantor, George Jessel, Al Jolson and the Marx Brothers, who appeared for two nights on 20 and 21 August. This, it seems, was the first time Groucho, Chico and Harpo appeared without Zeppo, and it was their swansong together on Broadway, which, by this time, was beyond saving.

At about the same time Groucho and co. formed the 'Writing and Asthma Club', he and Ruth purchased a thirteen-room, seven-bathroom mansion house in North Hillcrest Road in Beverly Hills; a palatial residence where the family lived for ten years and in which Arthur and Miriam grew up. Groucho wrote that it cost him $44,000 and was sold eventually for $200,000. The Wall Street Crash was well and truly behind him now, but Groucho could still not sleep soundly.

Lack of sleep certainly did not faze Chico, who as usual had his own ideas about the uses of money. California certainly opened up for him fresh opportunities to squander his new wealth by gambling. Apart from the dens of LA, there were places like Agua Caliente, across the border, just outside Tijuana, in Mexico, where the high rollers of Tinseltown found the dice, and the women, even hotter.

For Chico's wife Betty, life continued to be a long-drawn-out strain, while young Maxine enjoyed her technicolour summers, hobnobbing with the sons and daughters of the stars, but always aware that all was not well at home. Between Tijuana and Hollywood, Chico's opportunities for indulgence were legion. Apart from the one-night stands, the longer-term affair with Ann Roth, now blossoming in her late teens, was continuing behind the scenes. And there was the extra worry, given the nature of the place and the times, of the dangers of entanglement with serious mobsters in the seedy Hollywood underworld. Under the glittering surface, the upright denizens of Hollywood had to make their peace with the shadowy forces that stretched their tentacles over the restaurants, the night spots, and the business of Hollywood itself. Lucky Luciano was but a harbinger of the hard men of the Chicago mob who, during the 1930s, moved into positions of power in the technicians' union, IATSE, and into the heart of the motion-picture industry. By all accounts, the Marx Brothers kept their noses clean, and none so clean as Chico, whose nostrils were so close to the smell. Even Luciano or Bugsy Siegel, or Sydney Korshak, the uncrowned mob king of Hollywood for over forty years, might balk at the public impact of rubbing out a Marx Brother! So Chico was reasonably safe from the mob, if not from his own carousing and folly.

Maxine was at school in New York when, in April 1932, she read in the newspaper: 'Chico Marx Seriously Injured in Auto Crash.' In fact he had smashed his knee and fractured a number of ribs, midway through the shooting of *Horse Feathers*. Production had to be halted for ten weeks before the shooting of the climactic football game. The accident cramped Chico's style just for a short period, but nothing could keep the man down. He managed to keep sufficient money from the card dealers to rent a succession of homes in Beverly Hills and Hollywood, the first of which, an enormous hillside property with an Olympic-size swimming pool and a tennis court, was handed over to Harpo, and later became the home of George Burns and Gracie Allen. The second house was a slightly more modest residence, on Rexford Drive, north of Sunset. Maxine, by then enrolled at Beverly Hills High, remembers her family's itinerant lifestyle as 'gypsies with a difference, taking with us trains of servants, cars, furs and jewels . . .'

The fourth brother, Zeppo, was still bringing up the rear. He consoled himself by living the high style too, with an apartment in Hollywood, at Havenhurst Drive, and a beach cottage in Malibu. His uneasy status within the clan seemed to be exacerbated by a succession of unlucky events and annoyances. In August 1932 he and his wife Marion were victims of a robbery at their apartment, losing $37,500-worth of clothes and jewels. In the same month, the *Herald* and the *Examiner* reported, Zeppo was sued by the Sunset Laurel Market for the non-payment of a grocery bill amounting to $52.37, incurred for 'certain necessities of life, to wit, foodstuffs', the accused having 'failed, neglected and refused' to pay the bill, which had been outstanding since 31 August 1931. This was only the first in a line of lawsuits and petty complaints that were to dog Zeppo for many years. To cap this, he and his wife were robbed again, in June 1933, by two armed men who locked them in their closet and took $30,000-worth of diamonds. Being the youngest Marx Brother seemed to be a regular hoodoo.

According to Paul Wesolowski, Zeppo tried his hand, during this period, at scriptwriting, offering a screenplay entitled 'Tom, Dick and Harry' to Paramount, which considered it and then turned it down. It was offered to Universal, under the title 'Muscle Bound', as a possible vehicle for Slim Summerville and Zasu Pitts, but nothing came of this offer either.

It was, however, Zeppo who had taken in the Brothers' father in Los Angeles, when they had transferred from the east. Frenchy, despite his continuing grief at Minnie's death, still cut a dapper figure in the background.

Even in his last days he was searching out new pinochle pals, and taking on that brief double appearance in *Monkey Business*, greeting himself off the boat; a tiny but symbolic contribution to the Marx Brothers' schizophrenic canon.

In his *Redbook* article in 1933, Groucho wrote, about Frenchy: 'He is seventy-two years old now, but his hair is still thick and black; his moustache is still trimmed in the sprightly Menjou manner, and his gay Chesterfieldian wardrobe remains the envy of all his five sons . . .'

When this affectionate portrait was written, Frenchy had only a few months left to live.

But if Frenchy was Marx number six (if not number one), what news of number five, Gummo? At the same time that *Horse Feathers* opened in Hollywood, Gummo Marx, separated from the band but still fighting fit, was inaugurating his own show in New York. His new dress business, Gummo Marx Inc., opened at 1375 Broadway, in mid-August 1932. Journalist A. J. Liebling, for the *New York World-Telegram*, caught him at the opening in an ebullient mood, ready and willing to talk about his brothers:

> 'I attribute their success entirely to me,' said the eldest [*sic!*] Marx brother, as he observed the gyrations of a mannequin in front of a resident buyer. 'I quit the act. That is No. 923, a burgundy crepe with full bell sleeves; $10.50 wholesale. You couldn't buy it for fifteen in a larger house.
>
> 'Were the Marx Brothers always funny? I don't know – we never gave me a laugh. That is a black afternoon dress with erminette cape. Sure there's a nice dress, but there's nothing in it for you,' following the direction of the buyer's glance.
>
> 'Harpo was in this morning to chase the model, but she wouldn't run. He got scared and went home. I'm glad somebody thinks they're funny. Maybe I can make a touch.'

Gummo's later career, as his brothers' agent, was yet to come, but even then he rarely opened himself up to the world. A unique self-portrait, published by *Daily Variety* on its twentieth anniversary, shows him somewhat injured by the lack of attention paid to his role in the Marx saga, and his excision from history:

The Fifth Marx Brother
BY GUMMO MARX.

There is a story about two brothers who went fishing. One brother caught all the fish. They changed positions on the boat, changed rods, but the fish always came on the line of the same brother. So the next day the brother who hadn't caught any fish decided to go out alone, and in the early morning he baited his hook, threw his line in the water and waited expectantly. A fish rose out of the water, looked at the fisherman and said, 'Hey, where's your brother?'

I mention this story because I seem to be in the same boat with the second fisherman.

I am the fifth Marx Brother. My name is Gummo. I was once the fourth Marx Brother. In fact I was once the third Marx Brother, and, to be exact, I was once the second Marx Brother. This is how it came about.

Groucho is two years older than I, and whatever age Groucho says he is, I am still two years younger. Groucho was the first of the Marx Brothers to go on the stage. The part he played is hazy to me, but it called for a coachman's uniform. Up to this point in my life I could always tell what color and style of clothes I was going to wear the succeeding year because Groucho was breaking them in for me. I always succeeded to Groucho's cast-off clothing, so what was more natural when I turned to a career on the stage but that I should inherit the coachman's uniform.

[Here Gummo relates the tale of his appearance as the ventriloquist's dummy.]

. . . Things have happened to me through the years which were humorous, interesting or tragic, as they have happened to most other people. But whenever it gets into print, these things which have happened to me strangely happen to Groucho, or Harpo, or Chico, and sometimes Zeppo, but they never happen to me.

Years ago Irvin S. Cobb wrote a story called 'The Thunder of Silence' which has left a great impression on me. It was a story about a flaming-haired senator from the west who was a pacifist during the first World War, and how the newspapers and magazines conspired to omit his name from all the papers and print as he was threatening the war effort. This flaming-haired senator was soon forgotten. I don't know why this has happened to me as I didn't interfere with the war effort, though my commanding officers may disagree with this.

There are many people in the world who would like to hide, and they go to all means of disguise such as changing their names, dying their hair, growing beards and moustaches, or shaving them off; even as far as having surgery performed to change their features. They are wasting a lot of time. Just let them become the sixth Marx Brother . . .

A fifth is always a mark of opprobrium. For example, a fifth wheel is always hidden in the back of a car. When a golf game is arranged and there are five players, one of them is eliminated. Even in a bridge game, or gin, a fifth is unnecessary.

As the Marx Brothers became more popular my position became a little more difficult. I was rapidly dropping into obscurity. This wouldn't have bothered me very much as I realized what a bad actor I was. For many years after I quit the stage people referred to me as an actor, but during my career most people vehemently denied this.

One of the most difficult things for me in the past, and even in the present, is for me to get a reservation in a hotel or restaurant. When I call and give my name they would question me suspiciously. 'I never heard of Gummo Marx,' some would say. 'How do you spell it?' And I would spell it for them. They would want to know which one of the Marx Brothers I was, and I would patiently explain. While I generally got the reservation, they treated me as though I had cheated the income tax department or forged a check. On other occasions I would call and be accepted with alacrity. However, upon arriving at the hotel or resort and they found out that I was not Groucho, or Harpo, or Chico, the look of disappointment on their faces could not be obliterated even though I tipped more lavishly than they did . . .

When my son [Robert] first started school, he came home one day and told his mother that he stood up in class and said he was one of the Marx Brothers. He was instantly challenged by the other students who thought he was a bit too young for that. He thereupon defiantly told them that he wasn't one of the Marx Brothers but that he was Harpo's son. When his mother heard this story she said, 'Why did you say you were Harpo Marx's son? Why didn't you say you were Gummo Marx's son?' he turned to her and said, 'Who ever heard of Gummo Marx?'

I have been toying seriously with the idea of changing my name to Smith, but I am afraid if I do someone will say, 'Which one are you – the one on the left or the one on the right?' And that would be the last straw. Say, Straw – that's not a bad name. Gummo Straw. Then if they ask me which straw I am, I can say, 'the one who broke the camel's back.'

This Program is Coming to You from the House of David!
– the Short and Snappy Life of Waldorf T. Flywheel

MISS DIMPLE: Here comes a lady. She looks like a client.

MRS. JACKSON: Aw . . . pardon me. Are you Mr. Flywheel?

GROUCHO: Am I Mr. Flywheel? Before I answer that, there's one thing I want to know. Are you Mrs. Flywheel?

MRS. JACKSON: Certainly not.

GROUCHO: All right, then I'm Mr. Flywheel. And I bet I can guess who you are.

MRS. JACKSON: Well then, who am I?

GROUCHO: I give up. Who are you?

CHICO: I give op, too. And I wasn't even playing.

Radio show, 16 January 1933

S. J. Perelman's call to think up a radio play for the Marx Brothers was just a premature squawk of spring. But by 1932 the airwaves were a-buzz with entertainers rushing to escape the bankruptcy of the Broadway stage. Eddie Cantor was an early beneficiary of radio's ability to reach the widest possible audience, broadcasting on the 'Chase and Sanborn Hour' from September 1931. Radio seemed ready-made for the Marx Brothers, or at any rate for Groucho and Chico's dialogues, if not for Zeppo nor, obviously, Harpo. An unrecorded and untitled wireless sketch, written by Morrie Ryskind and Will Johnstone and dated 22 September 1931, does, however, include scenes for both Zeppo and Harpo, complete with honking horn and plonking harp. The dialogue was pretty plonking, too, and that project came to nought. (Sample lines: Chico's explanation to the real-estate agent of why he's Groucho's brother: 'Look, I explain it to you. My mother is a-scared by spaghetti two years before she was born, so that make-a me an Italian, and make-a you a landlord. So that make Groucho my brudda. Understan'?')

The phenomenal box office success of *Horse Feathers* led to Paramount bringing forward their plans for a third Marx film, per contract, though no one had figured out what it might be. While various plots were cooking, Chico, once again, came up with an interim project, having tootled off to

New York City to arrange a sponsorship deal with Standard Oil in the autumn of 1932. A rival oil company, Texaco, was doing well with comedian Ed Wynn on the airwaves, and Standard Oil couldn't lag behind.

Groucho recorded his tongue-in-cheek approach to radio in a piece in the magazine *Tower Radio*, a couple of years later, in 1934:

> I suppose I ought to begin with Marconi. I seldom do begin with Marconi, though. I prefer to start with antipasto, follow that with a plate of Minestrone, and work up to Marconi gradually. Marconi, DeForest and I were all sophomores together at old Gorgonzola for six years. I was always inventing things for which those boys got the credit. But I'm wiser now. I get credit everywhere . . .
>
> One day with my grind-organ – I was doubling for an Italian street pianist – I wandered idle and ill at ease. Suddenly a sign caught my eye – a nasty crack. I stepped back and read: 'GINSBERG'S BOWLING ALLEYS, pin-setter wanted.' I hesitated about going in and applying, for I hadn't eaten for three days and I was a little shaky on my pins.
>
> At last I mustered up my courage and fell through the revolving doors. I found myself inside a radio station. Still numb with surprise, or just numb, I said to the bouncer: 'Where may I find Ginsberg's Bowling Alleys?' He replied: 'This is a radio station, young mugg. That was only a blind ad. We're looking for a crooner.'

Well, they certainly had to look no further. The programme was called 'Five Star Theatre', and it aired under the patronage of the Standard Oil Companies of New Jersey, Pennsylvania and Louisiana (no tickets will be sold after the train leaves the depot!!) and the Colonial Beacon Oil Company: Tuesday night, Joseph Bonime's Symphony Orchestra; Wednesday, a dramatization of a Rex Beach story; Thursday, Franz Lehar's *The Merry Widow*; Friday, *Charlie Chan* by Earl Derr Biggers. But Monday – the inimitable Marx Brothers, Groucho and Chico, in a series of comedies entitled 'Beagle, Shyster and Beagle, Attorneys at Law'!

S. J. Perelman was already elsewhere, presumably getting out of the way of Herman Mankiewicz and his spaetzle and sauerkraut binges. Kalmar and Ruby were working with Arthur Sheekman and Nat Perrin on the tentative screenplay of Paramount Film Number Three, but Perrin and Sheekman were able to spread themselves thin and form the backbone of the writing team for the radio show. Other writers reported to have contributed gags – unacknowledged by Groucho – were Tom McKnight, George Oppenheimer, Benny Ryan, Richy Craig Junior, and – blast from the past – Herman

Timberg. The supporting cast included Mary McCoy as the secretary, Miss Dimple, with Broderick Crawford alleged to have played some bit parts.

The first episode of 'Beagle, Shyster and Beagle' was broadcast on 28 November 1932, on the NBC Blue network. But this title soon had to be changed. A real lawyer named Morris Beegle filed a lawsuit for $300,000, alleging gross slander of his good name. He calculated his damages at $50,000 per episode. Rather than suffer a running headache and compounding liability, the producers changed the title to *Flywheel, Shyster and Flywheel*.

The last episode of *Flywheel* was aired on 22 May 1933. The shows were recorded on disc, but the discs were not preserved. *Flywheel, Shyster and Flywheel* remained an unknown chapter in the Marx Brothers' career until a young scholar, Michael Barson, found the texts hiding among the multitudinous stacks at the Library of Congress.

Barson found twenty-five episodes of the show out of twenty-six aired. Episode twenty-one was missing, or never submitted for copyright. The scripts represent an invaluable workshop of verbal routines and comedy ideas. Shorn of the necessity for economy and structure required of a film or play script, the whole collection, published by Barson in 1988 in over 300 pages of dialogue, echoes to the hammer blows and chainsaw buzz of gag-writing uncut; a cannonade of hit-and-miss projectiles:

JUDGE: Counsellor Flywheel, are your witnesses ready?
GROUCHO: No, your honor, and that's my complaint. There are only three of my witnesses here and I paid for eight.
JUDGE: So, you were tampering with witnesses? Did you give them anything?
CHICO: Sure. He gave 'em tamper.
JUDGE: He gave them what?
CHICO: Tamper. Tamper cent of what dey asked.

(Episode 6)

Flywheel, Shyster and Flywheel abounded with lines and bits of business taken from earlier Marx scripts, like the entire musicians' dialogue from *Animal Crackers* in Episode 1: 'What do you get an hour?' 'Well, for playing I get ten dollars an hour.' 'What do you get for not playing?' 'Twelve dollars an hour.' . . . 'Now for rehearsing I make a special rate – fifteen dollars an hour.' 'What do you get for not rehearsing?' 'Oh, you couldn't afford it.' *Animal Crackers* also provided material for Episode 17: 'This is either a left-handed painting or a vegetable dinner . . .' and the return of philanthropist

Roscoe W. Chandler, alias one Baldwin, in Episode 23: Chico: 'Let me see, I met you some place. Were you ever in Sing-Sing? . . . Joliet?' Of course, it's 'Peter Palooky', the fish-peddler from Czechoslovakia. But the series also served as a testing ground for new dialogue, scenes and plot lines that would find their way into later Marx Brothers pictures:

JONES (*the client*): Ravelli, then you didn't shadow my wife?
RAVELLI (Chico): Sure, I shadow her all day.
JONES: What day was that?
RAVELLI: That was Shadowday. I went right to your house –
JONES (*anxiously*): What did you find out?
RAVELLI: I find your wife out.
JONES: Then you wasted the entire two weeks?
RAVELLI: Aw no. Monday I shadow your wife. Tuesday I go to the ball game – she don't show up. Wednesday she go to the ball game – I don't show up. Thursday was a doubleheader. We both no show up. Friday it rain all day – there's-a no ball game, so I go fishing.

(Episode 1)

All this turns up, only slightly changed, and in a different context, in *Duck Soup*. Also appearing in *Duck Soup* – a version of the court scenes that run through several of the radio scripts, such as the 'jury tampering' lines quoted above, in Episode 6, with its splendid denouement:

JUDGE: Gentlemen of the jury, I find your verdict most unsatisfactory. I discharge you without thanks.
GROUCHO: Just a minute, judge. You can't discharge these jurors. I hired them.
(*Signature music, end.*)

Episode 12, transmitted on 12 February 1933, while the early drafts of what was to become *Duck Soup* were still being cranked out, includes another exchange that has become familiar in a somewhat modified form:

GROUCHO: Emanuel Ravelli, where were you born?
CHICO: I wasn't born. I had a stepmotter.
JUDGE: Come, come, Ravelli. Tell the court your birthday.
CHICO: What you wanna know for, Judge. You ain't gonna buy me nuttin.
GROUCHO: He's right, your honor. You haven't bought a thing since you bought your place on the bench.
JUDGE: See here, Mr. Flywheel, the court considers that remark most unnecessary and vicious.

CHICO: Hey, Judge, dat's what I got for my birthday.
JUDGE: You got what?
CHICO: Vicious – I got a telegram with very best vicious. (*Laughs.*) Some joke!
(*Judge pounds gavel.*)

Chico's brilliant mangling of the English language is nowhere more evident than in the flood of crazy puns unleashed by Sheekman, Perrin, et al., in the name of Standard Oil. Some of them have entered the pantheon as jokes even separate from their recycled movie use: 'Taxes? Hey, I got a brudder living in Taxes.' 'Quiet, we're talking about taxes – money, dollars.' 'Well, dat's where my brudder lives, Dollas, Taxes.' (Again, *Duck Soup.*) Others were born, sputtered and died on the ephemeral airwaves: 'I know how to make a pair of pants last.' 'All right, Ravelli, just how do you make a pair of pants last?' Chico: 'Make the coat first.' One, undoubtedly, for Frenchy! Some might well have deserved immortality:

GROUCHO: Ravelli, what are you singing?
CHICO: 'Home Sweet Home.'
GROUCHO: It sounds terrible.
CHICO: Well, my home is terrible . . .
GROUCHO: What are you singing for anyhow?
CHICO: Just to kill time.
GROUCHO: Well, you've certainly got a swell weapon. What have you been doing here all week?
CHICO: Chasing ice wagons . . .
GROUCHO: I thought I sent you out to chase ambulances.
CHICO: You did, but ambulances go too fast.

(Episode 2)

'Atsa good, eh, boss? The writers continued their strip mining for seven and a half months. Episode 7, on 9 January 1933, introduced a Mrs Carraway, who receives a nerve-wracking examination by Doctors Perrin and Flywheel, the seed of Margaret Dumont's mistreatment in the yet unconceived *A Day at the Races*. Episode 15, aired 6 March, has Flywheel and Ravelli brought in as advisors to a big department store, an idea that will lie fallow for eight years until it will sneak up upon the unsuspecting public under the title of *The Big Store*.

At the end of each episode the boys had an 'afterpiece' which had to promote the product: 'Chico, will you stop muttering!' 'I won't stop muttering.

Muttering is-a very nice when I use Essolube, dat famous hydrofined mutter oil.' 'Chico, your dentist must have a pretty tough time when he gives you gas. How can he tell when you're unconscious?' 'I don't go to a dentist for gas. I go to a filling station for Esso, which is better than any gasoline.' (Episode 13.) As Chico remarks, at the end of Episode 5, at Christmas 1932: 'If we don't sell the Essolube, we no got the job.'

Or, to top the lot, from the do-gooding Mrs Van Regal, visiting Chico in jail in Episode 6: 'Mr Ravelli, your case interests me. Do you think you've inherited your criminal tendencies from your father?' Chico: 'No, lady, my father still got his.'

As Groucho might have said: 'That's my answer: restrict immigration!' But the Marxist tide couldn't be stopped.

The first six episodes of the radio series were recorded in New York City, but after Christmas 1932 Frenchy suffered a mild heart attack in California, and Groucho and Chico headed back west. From 9 January (Episode 7), the show was recorded on a sound stage at RKO, though it was still heard only on the east coast because of legal arguments over whether the sponsor, Standard Oil, would be in violation of anti-trust laws by the supposedly independent regional companies co-sponsoring the same show. On 18 January, the co-writers of the Marx Brothers' next movie, now entitled 'Cracked Ice', submitted their draft to Paramount. The culprits were Harry Ruby, Bert Kalmar and Grover Jones, a noted Paramount script troubleshooter. Shooting was supposed to begin in February. But things were not going well at Paramount, and the Marx Brothers became increasingly anxious.

Paramount Pictures began feeling the bite of the Depression late in 1931, when dwindling audiences ate away at company profits. Jesse Lasky, Paramount's co-founder and renowned as the only proper *mensch* among the moguls, was taking the brunt of the blame. Early in 1932 he was fired from the company he had formed in 1916 with Adolph Zukor, Shmuel Gelbfisch (alias Samuel Goldwyn) and Cecil B. de Mille. Soon after he left, his protégé B. P. Schulberg was also forced out. Since these were the people who had taken on the Marx Brothers in the first place, their departures were cause for alarm.

Paramount had already been causing the Brothers grief by trying to weasel out of certain conditions of their Christmas Eve 1930 three-film contract, by reducing the advance due for *Horse Feathers*. Max Gordon, representing the boys in this affair, stood firm on their behalf. But while the

Flywheel shows were being broadcast, Paramount Publix Corporation, the signatory of their contract, had transferred its assets to a new company, Paramount Productions. The Marx Brothers, through their attorney, Nathan Burke, filed notice of termination of contract, claiming that it had been assigned without their consent, and that the company had failed to account for the profits from their first two films.

The ins and outs of this dispute have been examined in great detail by the zealous Paul Wesolowski (Wesso) in the pages of *The Freedonia Gazette* which, I confidently expect, every self-respecting Marx fan keeps by his or her bedside. For those unfortunates who have neglected their subscription, I need only summarize the dispute in Chapter Headings:

Chapter One: Marx Bros. junk Paramount contract, but still declare their readiness to make 'Cracked Ice'.

Chapter Two: *Variety* reports Marx Bros. left Paramount to form new company with Sam Katz, Sam Harris and Max Gordon.

Chapter Three: Marx Bros. not going to shoot 'Cracked Ice', but not signed up with Max and the two Sams.

Chapter Four: Marx Bros. form own company, Marx Bros. Inc., to produce their own films. Harpo is President; Chico, Secretary; Groucho, Treasurer; Zeppo, Vice-President. Negotiations begin with United Artists.

Chapter Five: a distribution agreement drawn up between the new company and United Artists. A 'hypothecation agreement' was also drawn up to cover the financing of the movie to be made in this deal. Neither of these agreements was ever signed.

Chapter Six: the Marx Bros. Inc. drew up a five-year contract with the Katz-Gordon-Harris company, Producing Artists, involving a movie version of the Kaufman-Ryskind hit, *Of Thee I Sing*. Since this, unlike the titles of all other achieved or prospective Marx Bros. productions, was a comprehensible title, rather than one that was completely meaningless ('Ooh-La-La' was another working title of the 'Cracked Ice' project), this proposal was, of course, doomed to failure. Meanwhile, Standard Oil announced that it was terminating *Flywheel*, presumably because Chico's weekly promotions were not dispensing enough Essolube. Groucho and Chico recorded the last four episodes in New York, where Harpo joined them for a company pow-wow.

On 11 May 1933, Frenchy died in Los Angeles. Of his sons, only Zeppo was by his side. The same night, Zeppo and Marion took the body by train to New York, for burial by Minnie's side, at the New Mount Carmel Cemetery in Queens.

Maxine Marx, who was at school in Beverly Hills at the time, was also at

Frenchy's side in his last days. She recalled that as he lay slipping away, he spoke a few words in French, having floated off to the earliest days of his childhood, in Alsace. As Maxine leaned towards him to hear, he whispered: 'Regarde, papa . . . les lapins . . . dans la forêt . . .'

But the forests and the plains of Europe were far away. And demons were soon to walk there, cutting off heads that no magician could reattach.

The *New York Herald Tribune* marked the patriarch's passing thus:

Samuel Marx, 72, Dies; Father of 4 Comedians. Retired Clothing Retailer Succumbs in Los Angeles.

Samuel Marx, father of the four Marx Brothers, comedians of the motion pictures and the musical comedy stage, died of heart disease yesterday at his home in Los Angeles, according to word received here by his fifth son, Gummo Marx, of 697 West End Avenue.

Mr. Marx, who was seventy-two years old, retired a few years ago as proprietor of a men's retail clothing store in lower Broadway. He had planned careers for his sons in the cloak and suit industry, but the boys, encouraged by their mother, Minnie Palmer Marx, slipped away from their home at Third Avenue and Ninety-third Street, to become actors. Of the five sons, only Gummo, President of Gummo Marx Inc., women's dress firm, of 1375 Broadway, settled down to business.

Mrs. Marx died two years ago. Surviving, besides Gummo Marx, are Groucho, Harpo, Chico and Zeppo Marx, known off-stage as Julius H., Arthur, Leonard and Herbert Marx.

Yehi zichro baruch.

Cracked Ice: Freedonia to Moscow Express

The last man nearly ruined this place,
He didn't know what to do with it,
If you think this country's bad off now –
Just wait till I get through with it!
President Rufus T. Firefly's credo,
Duck Soup (1933)

Statecraft in Freedonia: Firefly and Mrs Teasdale in *Duck Soup*.

On 4 March 1933, Franklin Delano Roosevelt was installed as the thirty-second President of the United States. On 22 May, Flywheel and Ravelli closed their last broadcast for Standard Oil with a chorus of 'Good night, ladies', their quarrel with Paramount having been miraculously patched up, within a week of Frenchy's death. On 17 November the Marx Brothers' new movie, now entitled *Duck Soup*, was released. Three days before, on 14 November, Harpo took ship, on his own, for Hamburg, Germany, aboard the SS *Albert Baline*, en route for Leningrad and Moscow, in the Union of Soviet Socialist Republics.

A fiendish skein of circumstance and calculation led to this chain of events. The facilitator, as usual, was Alexander Woollcott, a passionate advocate, among passionate advocates, of Roosevelt's much-vaunted New Deal. To an arguable extent, and through a fairground mirror, the Roosevelt administration could be seen in some sense as the Algonquin Round Table in office, minus the *bons mots*, and with doers rather than talkers, and real power to affect events and change lives. The new administration also signalled a new direction in foreign affairs, which would include the resumption of diplomatic relations with Moscow's Bolshevik bogeymen.

Woollcott, however, was ahead of the game. Having established close ties with the brainy set of Europe, he had just discovered the rest of the world. A close friendship with Harry Yuan, son of Yuan Shi-Kai, China's Republican President from 1912 to 1916 – Woollcott was sponsoring the young man's US studies – led to an invitation from Yuan, who had returned to China, for a visit to the Far East. Woollcott's trip to China and Japan influenced him deeply, not least as his immense bulk was carried about the Great Wall, prompting mutterings about 'the Yellow Man's Burden'. In the autumn of 1932, Aleck followed up this tour with a visit to Russia, a rare event for a 'bloated American capitalist', especially one as bloated as he. In Russia, a small boy ran up to Woollcott and rubbed his great belly, as if in awe and appreciation of all the food that had gone in there. As a noted drama critic, Woollcott went to every play in Moscow and Leningrad, met the actors and directors, and was fêted wherever he went, even in those dismal, Stalinist days.

It may be noted that Woollcott was following the lead of another fêted worthy, none other than the bearded 'geezer' and Harpo fan, George Bernard Shaw, who had visited the Soviet Union in the summer of 1931, met Stalin, and lauded the socialist utopia, give or take a few temporary flaws. Shaw strongly advised all his friends and western intellectuals in general to go east and see the future of mankind for themselves. Whether he had the nude bather of the Cap Antibes in mind at an early stage is an intriguing prospect. Note Shaw's presence at the San Simeon revels – from Stalin to Hearst in one easy somersault . . .

It is significant, however, that when Woollcott returned from his own pilgrimage, the first person he approached to follow in his footsteps was Harpo Marx. Entertainers often like to present themselves not only as political neuters, but as political idiots, and mainly for safety's sake. It was fine to be a Roosevelt New Dealer, as many stars were, or even an opponent, like the ever-contrary W. C. Fields. But any hint of more left-leaning, Socialist sympathies could alienate the mainstream audience. The days of Red Scares were not that far past, and the execution of Sacco and Vanzetti, in 1927, was an event still fresh in the mind. Any kind of sympathy for the Soviet Union was way beyond the pale.

The most prominently political of showmen was Chaplin, whose heart was worn not only on his sleeve but in his feature films, from *The Kid* to *City Lights*. The Marx Brothers, however, with their immigrant roots and their overt display of ethnic types, their verbal gags deriving from Weber and Fields and Al Shean's Germanic mangling of the English tongue, had all the more reason to fear stereotyping, to eschew any hint of 'foreign' or unpatriotic ideas. Groucho, the most intellectual of the brothers, had developed his ideas under the influence of social commentators like H. L. Mencken, with his passionate defence of freedom of speech and of thought, and contempt for the American 'booboctacy', the criers of a flag-waving conformity. Mencken's maxim: 'It is almost impossible to find any trace of an artist who was not actively hostile to his environment, and thus an indifferent patriot' might well be echoing in Groucho's mind. But he would be the last person to repeat it. Instead, he had Captain Spaulding, Professor Quincy Adams Wagstaff, Rufus T. Firefly, et al., to utter these sentiments for him. As ever, the Clown could speak, where the man would not.

More than a decade later, Groucho would bare his core social and political beliefs in the poignant letters he sent his daughter Miriam, when she was nineteen years old. Unlike the letters he sent to friends, and sometimes enemies, these letters reveal his more serious side. Here, discussing the Hollywood strike of 1946:

> I am certainly happy that the strike is over. I always felt kind of squeamish driving through the line of pickets at our gate. Whether right or wrong, they all looked rather pathetic pacing up and down with those signs. They only make a living and not a particularly luxurious one,

and some day both sides – Capital and Labor – are going to have to sit down and work out a more sensible formula for labor problems than any they have yet devised. Don't forget, the big industrialists are always rich and the little guy is fighting for a few extra bucks . . . None of them die with twenty-eight million dollars in the bank or have yachts in Sheepshead Bay . . .

In another letter, in the same year, Groucho writes enthusiastically to Miriam about a book he is reading called *Sixty Families*, by Ferdinand Lundberg:

This is the most devastating and revealing book on America that I have ever read. I know I am quite emotional politically so after I finished it, I lent it to [Norman] Krasna, who is stone cold about such things. He was tremendously impressed with it. When you come home, you can read it. It's not a new book – it was published in 1937. I had been planning on reading it for many years but just got around to it.

Groucho always described himself as a man who believed in America but also in justice for the ordinary citizen. In one letter he congratulates Miriam for ending her flirtation with 'the Stalinites', though he abhorred the McCarthy witch-hunts. In this liberal outlook he had a soul mate in Harpo, though Chico was quite another matter. One magazine profiler, Mary Morris, caught Chico and Harpo with their guard down at one point, while she was lunching at Harpo's house in late 1945, in the period of the filming of *A Night in Casablanca*:

He [Chico] lay down on the couch, looked at a newspaper, began complaining about strikes. They were gangster led, and should be prevented, he said, whereupon Harpo spoke up.
    What he said was not terribly original or brilliant, but it sounded as if he had read the papers and knew what he was talking about. He said the General Motors workers – in fact all workers – deserved a raise and that the fair way to decide how much the raise should be was in relation to company profits. He thought the companies ought to show their books. He told Chico to stop complaining about the recent Hollywood strike and comparing it to all strikes. The Hollywood strike wasn't typical, he said, and the issues were complex, whereas the GM strike was easy to understand and there was nothing to be said for the company . . . I asked Harpo about his Russian tour, with wig and harp, in 1933, the first tour of the USSR by an American entertainer. He'd had a lot of

fun, he said, stayed in Moscow with Maxim and Ivy Litvinov. Mme. Litvinov had returned the visit to Harpo in Hollywood a few years later when her husband was Ambassador to the U.S.A. . . . .

But there was more to this fun than met the eye. Woollcott had clearly canvassed the idea of Harpo's trip to Russia while on his own visit in 1932, as evidenced by a newspaper clipping of 18 November 1932, headlined: 'Reds Invite Harpo Marx To Act Dumb at Moscow'. Comrade A. M. Dankman, 'Director of the state organization which controls all music halls and circuses' was inviting the American actor for a month's engagement in Moscow for the following spring:

> Russia has never seen any of the Marx Brothers' motion pictures, but their reputation in Europe and America is widely known here. It is felt that Harpo would be particularly adaptable to Russian audiences because his type of pantomime comedy would eliminate the language difficulty usually experienced by a foreign performer. Dankman said he would like to hear from any American actors or actresses who might be interested in engagements here. In this connection it is understood that Paul Robeson already has contracted to play Othello and other roles here next year.

In Los Angeles, Harpo Marx was said to be 'crazy to go' to appear on the Moscow stage. Paul Robeson, at that time, was based in London, involved in working-class politics and closely influenced by both Aleck Woollcott and the ubiquitous Bernard Shaw, though his own Soviet trip did not take place until 1934.

But Woollcott's idea was a stroke of genius: it was typical of him to realize the potency of the name of 'Marx' coupled with Harpo's clowning. As a mute, of course, Harpo could communicate, but he could not be accused of saying the wrong thing: even if he spoke up, all was deniable, since everyone knew Harpo did not speak. He was a perfect candidate to 'break the ice', as it were, between ordinary Americans and their supposedly implacable enemy.

In November 1932, however, Roosevelt had just been elected, but Herbert Hoover was still in the White House. The only Marx in Moscow was still the man on the red banners. The only breaking ice was in the imagination of the writers beavering away at the next Marx Brothers script, 'Cracked Ice', delivered in January 1933 to supervisor Herman J. Mankiewicz.

The genesis of 'Cracked Ice' is suitably foggy, not to speak of the meaning of the title. (Another working title for this project was, for equally unknown reasons, 'Grasshoppers'.) The eventual director of the movie, Leo McCarey, was not yet in the picture. Mankiewicz himself had just supervised the shooting of another Paramount crazy comedy, *Million Dollar Legs*, co-starring W. C. Fields. (Its top-billed star was Jack Oakie.) Herman's younger brother Joe Mankiewicz, eventually to become one of Hollywood's top directors, had written the original story. It was the tale of an imaginary country, Klopstokia, a bankrupt Ruritania in which every citizen is an Olympic-level athlete, including the weightlifting President, Fields. Ben Turpin is a spy who hides everywhere, even in a mounted painting. The President is constantly arm-wrestling his Prime Minister, and the cabinet is endlessly plotting against him. The President's daughter, Angela (every woman in Klopstokia is called Angela, and every man George), was played by a young actress named Susan Fleming. Two years later, she would marry Harpo.

The similarities between *Million Dollar Legs* and *Duck Soup* are so striking that conclusions cannot be avoided. There is no connection between Kalmar and Ruby's previous Marx Brother screenplays and this project except through the magic mirror of Mankiewicz. How this magic was worked I do not know, and no one seems to have marked the process. Perhaps it emerged over one of Mankiewicz's gargantuan dinners (*Duck Soup* as a metaphor or result of indigestion . . .?). Groucho, for one, did not like Mankiewicz, and described him, in *Groucho and Me*, as a monster, whom he named Delaney: 'A large, soggy man with a drooping belly, which he constantly kept pushing up with both hands as though fearful it might fall on the floor and get stepped on. He had a loud, angry voice which he only employed when he was absolutely certain he didn't know what he was talking about. Long ago, this producer had a fine mind, but by the time they slipped him to us he had dissipated it and was now just a huge, hollow shell. He ate like a pig, guzzled his booze, and played the dames relentlessly.'

Not a flattering portrait, but nevertheless, I insist there is a resemblance . . . Another possible influence on the emerging script was more noble. *Of Thee I Sing*, Kaufman and Ryskind's satirical play on the non-Ruritanian US Presidency, was first performed in December 1931. It, too, includes elements that have a resonance, when compared to the eventual *Duck Soup*. Note, for example, the scene with the French Ambassador, who enters President Wintergreen's quarters with a formal message from his government:

FRENCH AMBASSADOR: You will pardon this intrusion, Monsieur, but I have received another note from my country.

266

WINTERGREEN: That's all right. We've got a lot of notes from your country, and some of them were due ten years ago.

FRENCH AMBASSADOR: But this is not a promise to pay – this is serious.

This exchange caused ruffled feathers among some Gallic diplomats in Washington, but the lines remained in the play. Familiar stuff? *Of Thee I Sing* was certainly preying on the Marx Brothers' minds throughout this period, as the constant rumours and pronouncements of their intention to film it, which came to nought, suggest.

Whatever the hocus-pocus and the influences, Kalmar, Ruby, and studio appointee Grover Jones banged away at their typewriters, and 'Cracked Ice' was duly born.

The early draft of 'Cracked Ice' is, in most essentials and structure, the *Duck Soup* that we all know, set in the Ruritanian country where the gift of the Presidency is in the hands of the richest woman in Freedonia, the unflappable Mrs Gloria Teasdale. But in one important element it differs from the final version – in the character of the newly appointed Freedonian President, named in this draft Rufus T. Firestone. (The 'T', by the way, as revealed in *Flywheel*, is Tecumseh!) In 'Cracked Ice', he has a proper, or very improper, profession which has disappeared in the eventual movie.

TRENTINO: My dear Mrs Teasdale, this, uh, Mr Firestone . . . I understand he is merely an ammunition salesman.

MRS TEASDALE (*proudly*): What of it? Poland had a Prime Minister who was a piano player!

Welcome back, of course, Margaret Dumont, absent through unpardonable neglect from the Brothers' first two Hollywood movies. Thelma Todd, on the other hand, had moved on, towards her tryst with tragedy. But Groucho's new profession, as proposed by the writers, is a rude shock, suggesting a much more sinister and hard edge to the satire, and enabling an entire extra level of banter between himself and Chico, recent appointee to the Freedonian Government:

GROUCHO: Now that you're secretary of War, I want to ask your advice. I've been running this country for two weeks, and I haven't sold one piece of ammunition. How do you account for it?

CHICO: That's easy. You no gotta war – how you gonna sell ammunition if you no gotta war?

GROUCHO: You've got a brain after all, and how you get along without it is amazing to me. (*Deep study*) So you got to have a war to sell ammunition.

(*He begins to pace the floor*) Why hasn't somebody told me about this before? . . . How do you start a war?

CHICO: Well, the best way is to insult somebody.

(*Groucho suddenly slaps Chico across the face with his gloves, then as quickly brings to light a card – *)

GROUCHO: My card?

CHICO: (*laughing*) That's a no good. You gotta insult somebody from another country. (*Illustrating with the desk top, dividing it into two imaginary halves*) Look, I come from one country. You come from another country. I say something you don't like. You say something I don't like – and I'm insulted.

GROUCHO: Why wasn't I insulted?

CHICO: You was insulted, but you don't know it.

Of course, the solution is to insult Ambassador Trentino, as occurs on the screen. But other lunatic exchanges follow:

GROUCHO: Where do you think we ought to hold this war?

CHICO: I've been thinking about that too.

(*Business with drawing board and pegs. {They} begin removing men like checkers – Chico jumps all Groucho's men – *)

CHICO (*as he gathers up his men*): Do you want to play another game?

GROUCHO: No, that's enough. How much do I owe you?

CHICO: Thirty-six dollars.

GROUCHO: All right. Now look, you need ammunition to fight the war, don't you?

CHICO: Yes.

GROUCHO: You buy your ammunition from me and I'll forget about the thirty-six dollars.

CHICO: That's fair enough. What kind of ammunition you got?

GROUCHO: Let me show you some samples.

(*Harpo enters dragging innumerable samples of ammo with rope, like a Volga boatman . . . *)

GROUCHO (*to Chico, reading from catalogue*): That's our latest number – 417 line 8 – new 16 inch Horowitz gun.

(*Business with Harpo ramming powder in and firing gun, with target on wall, but the gun fires backwards, blowing a hole through the back wall. Groucho turns to Chico – *)

GROUCHO: With a gun like that you can kill some of your own men.

CHICO: That's a-pretty good. I'll take a dozen of them. (*Groucho begins to write order on pad*) You got any Gatling guns?

GROUCHO: Yes, but I won't sell them to you. They're not fresh. What about some nice shells?

CHICO: I can't afford them, but I'll take some on the half-shell.

GROUCHO (*writing order down*) Anything else?

CHICO: (*mentally figuring*): Yes, one gross of bullets, two dozen hand grenades, three kegs of powder, and throw in some matches . . .

GROUCHO: I'll go right out and write this order to my firm, so you can get the ammunition in time for the war . . . Oh by the way, how are you fixed for spies?

CHICO: Fine. We gotta him. (*indicating Harpo*)

GROUCHO: So he's on your side too.

CHICO: Sure.

GROUCHO: With you two fellows on the other side I ought to have no trouble keeping the wolf from the door.

None of this appears in *Duck Soup*, which has replaced the armaments bazaar with an anarchic denouement involving uniforms of all ages, Harpo putting out a sign, 'HELP WANTED', and various stock shots of police motorcyclists, firemen and Tarzan's jungle elephants rushing to the rescue. There is spy business with Chico and Harpo (out of *Flywheel*), a court scene (out of *Flywheel*) with Chico tried for treason ('Isn't it true you tried to sell Freedonia's secret war code and plans?' 'Sure. I sold a code and two pair of pants. Atsa some joke, eh boss?'), and an original scene – all four Marx Brothers leading the entire court in a rousing chorus of 'We got guns, they got guns, all God's chillun got guns!' – which could have been arms dealer Firestone's sales motto. All these elements liven up the movie while removing the first draft's harshest salvo.

Verbal fireworks, sight gags, digressions and slapstick stuff – the memorable scene with old stalwart Edgar Kennedy as the lemonade seller – turned *Duck Soup* into the cornucopia of sheer anarchic craziness that has made it into most fans' favourite Marx Brothers movie. But I can see Groucho turning his nose up at the prospect of donning the mask of a bona fide Merchant of Death. One can only imagine the impact of the quoted dialogue, that gruesome haggling, on screen.

The production itself was not without its own quota of haggling and disputation. The chosen director was comedy veteran Leo McCarey, supervisor and director of some of Laurel and Hardy's best short films, and later director for W. C. Fields, Mae West and Harold Lloyd, as well as of other comedy classics such as *Ruggles of Red Gap*, 1935; *The Awful Truth*, 1937; *Going My Way*, 1944. He was not an eager bridegroom, as he told an interviewer in 1967:

> I don't like it [*Duck Soup*] so much, you know . . . In fact I never chose to shoot this film. The Marx Brothers absolutely wanted me to direct them in a film. I refused. Then they got angry with the studio, broke their contract and left. Believing myself secure, I accepted the renewal of my own contract with the studio. Soon, the Marx Brothers were reconciled with the company in question and I found myself in the process of directing the Marx Brothers. The most surprising thing about this film was that I succeeded in not going crazy, for I really did not want to work with them: they were completely mad. It was nearly impossible to get all four of them together at the same time. One was always missing! Yes, they were the four battiest people I ever met, which didn't stop me from taking great pleasure in the shooting of several scenes in the film. As my experience in silent films had very much influenced me, it was Harpo that I preferred. But this film wasn't the ideal film for me. It is in fact the only time in my career, to my knowledge at least, that I made the humor rest with the dialogue: with Groucho; it was the only humor you could get. Four or five writers furnished him with gags and pleasantries. As for me, I didn't do any of them.

Interview in *Cahiers du cinéma*, January 1967

Once again, the director directed the traffic, though McCarey increased its speed exponentially and ruthlessly excised the usual piano and harp solos. The resulting film came in at a mere seventy minutes, two minutes ahead of *Horse Feathers,* the Brothers' shortest movie (apart from the lost *Humor Risk*).

The movie opened to mixed reviews, *Motion Picture Herald* heralding 'another truckload of hilarious nonsense from the irrepressible comedy four . . . plenty of related fun interluding, all of which is noticeably clean'. (I suppose you know this means war!) *Variety* purred: 'Practically everybody wants a good laugh right now and *Duck Soup* should make practically everybody laugh.' Not, alas, critic John S. Cohen, who wrote: 'The Marx Brothers take something of a nosedive in *Duck Soup* . . . This new film at the Rivoli just doesn't happen to be very amusing in comparison with their previous films.' Audiences manifested the same mixed feelings, though business was strong enough at first. The Paramount press department went to town on *Duck Soup*, emphasizing all-round zaniness to the extent of featuring a contest,

'Name the Four Marx Sisters', and showing Groucho, Harpo and Chico's heads over female figures and garb (Groucho in ball gown, Harpo in naughty briefs): 'Chico now a Chickie! Can you suggest an appropriate and humorous name for this lovely creature? If you can, a pair of guest tickets to Paramount's *Duck Soup* opening . . .' blah-blah-blah. 'Marxmen Invent Country! Populate it, Print Money, Found Army, Build Cities!'

In a desperate gambit to excuse the movie's incomprehensible name (which encyclopaedist Glenn Mitchell suggests was a carry-over from a previous Leo McCarey/Laurel and Hardy short with the same title), Paramount proposed a duck-hunting contest, in which the hunters would bring back their catch to be cooked in a grand duck dinner, beginning with duck soup, to be tendered to local newsboys. Even better: 'Try a duck parade! . . . dig up four boys, dress them appropriately (as the Brothers) . . . let them lead the parade. Promote the ducks from a poultry market or farmer. Tie them together on a long string. The ducks will not stay in line but that will only add to the confusion and the excitement.'

In another press puff, Paramount tied together Freedonia and Moscow:

Harpo Marx is on his way to Russia. The pantomime member of the
Four Marx Brothers, whose latest picture, 'Duck Soup' coming on . . .
to the . . . Theatre, is off to appear in theatres throughout the Soviet
Union . . .

'I want nothing for the work,' Harpo declares. 'I am anxious to see
Russia and to make the experiment of presenting pantomime performances in a non-English speaking country.'

The offer was accepted before 'Duck Soup' was started at the
Paramount Studios. After the picture's completion, Harpo left with the
cheers of his brothers ringing in his ears.

'Good luck,' said Groucho. 'The Russians will probably start another
revolution as soon as they get a look at you.'

'You Moscow up,' said Chico, 'and see US some time.'

'When in Russia,' cautions Zeppo, 'don't let the Russians Russia.'

'It isn't Russia any more,' insisted Harpo, 'it's the Soviet Union.'

'We don't have no onions,' quoth Chico, 'soviet matzas . . .'

No wonder they're called gag writers. But the *Duck Soup* Soviet link was exemplified by the official resumption of US–USSR diplomatic relations on the very day of the movie's release – 17 November 1933. It seems clear that Roosevelt's new deals, foreign as well as domestic, cracked the ice for Aleck Woollcott's one-year plan.

A week later, Harpo was in Germany, witnessing at first hand the real, rather than the imaginary, face of despotism: walking around the port city of Hamburg, he was horrified, he later wrote, to see the shop windows painted over with stars of David and daubed with the word '*Jude*' for Jew. 'Inside,' wrote Harpo, 'behind half-empty counters, people in a daze, cringing like they didn't know what hit them and didn't know where the next blow would come from. Hitler had been in power only six months, and his boycott was already in full effect. I hadn't been so wholly conscious of being a Jew since my bar mitzvah. It was the first time since I'd had the measles that I was too sick to eat.

'I got across Germany as fast as I could go.'

In Warsaw, Harpo met an American who loaned him a hundred rubles so that he could pay his excess baggage in Moscow. Harpo was unaware that importing Soviet currency into Russia was a grave crime, indicative of high treason, espionage and other felonies meriting several lifetimes in a labour camp. Matters were not improved when the border guards, at Negoreloye, opened the suspicious visitor's trunks to find 'four hundred knives, three stilettos, half a dozen bottles marked POISON, and a collection of red wigs and false beards, mustaches and hands'. Ambassador Trentino could not have been more nonplussed. Not even the great harp, redolent of culture, could mollify them, until Harpo's Warsaw pal, who turned out to be a favoured businessman, got off the train and explained matters, in Russian. The mad artist could go on his way.

Harpo's visit to Russia is described in great and entertaining detail in the 1961 *Harpo Speaks*. He was assigned a lady interpreter and guard, Comrade Mal-e-kee-noff, whom he called Melachrino, after the cigarettes, but she was most assuredly not the model for Greta Garbo's Ninotchka, sporting, according to Harpo's description, bushy eyebrows, blue rings under her eyes and a patch of whiskers round a mole on her chin. Harpo marvelled at the lack of traffic in Moscow and the quiet, patient queues. He tells the tale of his meetings at the Moscow Art Theatre, with stony-faced Russians nonplussed at his 'Gookies' and knife act. Eventually, the ice was broken by Ivy Litvinov, the English-born wife of the Soviet Foreign Minister, Maxim Litvinov. At last, Harpo met smiling Russians.

In fact, Harpo's visit to Moscow and Leningrad was a major diplomatic breakthrough in a cold war that was as icy as it would be in the crisis-ridden late 1940s and '50s. Only fourteen years before, American soldiers had been fighting, with the British and French, against the Red Army in northern Russia, in an intervention designed to crush the Soviet State at birth.

Unions and workers' organizations were still castigated in America as Bolshevik-inspired. It is in fact surprising to me that, two decades later, Harpo was not summoned to the queue of alleged Communist sympathizers called before the House Un-American Activities Committee in the McCarthyite heyday. Perhaps they too, confused by his legend, could not countenance the idea of sitting there trying to get a sensible answer to the question, 'Mr Harpo Marx, Are You or Have You Ever Been . . .?'

The US press, at the time, reported Harpo's Russian tour favourably. 'Russians Wildly Applaud Antics of Harpo Marx,' reported the *Los Angeles Examiner* on 19 December:

> Leningrad: In Broadway's own parlance, Harpo Marx knocked 'em cold here tonight. Making his first appearance before a Russian audience in his celebrated knife dropping act, the American comedian literally brought down the house in the Music Hall as a capacity crowd of usually phlegmatic Soviet theater-goers applauded, cheered and whistled for 25 minutes during and after his six-minute act.
>
> He wore a wig, played a harp and preserved his usual waggish silence, and was assisted by two members of the cast of the Moscow Art Theater, with whom he had rehearsed ten days. He will play here six days and afterward will open in the Moscow Music Hall Theater.

The newly established American Ambassador, William C. Bullitt, telephoned his congratulations. In Moscow, Minister Litvinov himself attended the performance after 'a strenuous day in which he had told the All-Union Central Executive Committee – the Russian parliament – of the international outlook for the soviet and his hope for continued friendly relations with the United States'. (*LA Times*, 31 December.) It was at this performance, according to Harpo, that Litvinov appeared on stage at the end of the show, to shake his hand, dropping, as he did so, a cascade of knives from his own sleeve on to the stage. 'The only time I ever played the straight man,' wrote Harpo, 'I got my biggest laugh. And my comic was the Foreign Minister of the Soviet Union.'

In a contemporary news report, soon after his return from Russia, Harpo described this incident a bit differently, saying that Litvinov came on stage and simply helped him gather his knives together, amid much resulting clatter. However it was, the opportunity to laugh lawfully at a Soviet Minister was too good a chance for any Moscow audience – something that came but once in a lifetime.

Comrade Litvinov himself, the People's Commissar for Foreign Affairs, would have had good reason for keeping at least some knives up his sleeve. He remained in his post throughout the next terrible decade when Stalin's purges intensified – first in the army, then the Communist Party itself, then throughout society – extracting a dreadful toll in mass executions and the imprisonment of millions. From 1937 to the end of his life, in 1951, Litvinov always kept a revolver at hand, 'so that if the bell rang in the night, he would not have to live through the consequences'.

But how could a mere clown foresee all those terrible things that would come to pass? When he returned to America, Harpo enthused about his trip, and the warm welcome he had received in the land of frozen smiles and bleakness:

> 'Bourgeois or proletarian,' he said, 'they're just the same – they like it and they laugh . . . I think I will go back. It was a great experience. The audiences are appreciative. I don't know what they would do if they didn't like you.
>
> 'Actors are important people over there, too. It's one of the few professions in which good salaries can really be made . . . I was knee deep in caviar all the time . . .'
>
> (*LA Times*, 20 January 1934)

'I suppose a good ballet star gets a hundred times as much as Litvinov,' Harpo told another reporter. 'The most impressive play he saw, he said, was "The 14th Division Goes to Heaven," an anti-religious work showing a group of soldiers debating with the Holy Trinity. The second act setting represents Heaven and the characters go through their parts while suspended on wires.'

On his last day in Moscow, Harpo writes, Ambassador Bullitt called him in for a secret mission – to take a package of letters back to the United States, strapped to his right leg. According to Harpo, he carried this burden, underneath his sock, through Poland, Germany and France, and throughout the slow ocean voyage back home, until he was met, just before docking at New York, by three bulky goons who introduced themselves as US Secret Service, and took charge of his precious cargo.

All that time and no bath? As Groucho said, in *The Cocoanuts*: 'Oh, so you're only staying for the winter?'

Whether this tale is true, or a nice embellishment to shore up Harpo's patriotic credentials in the post-McCarthyite, Eisenhower age, is a secret the FBI files have not disclosed.* But he might well have reflected, as he

---

*See Appendix: The FBI and the Marx Brothers.

crossed the gloomy winter solstice of a dictator-torn Europe, on the last
routine of 'Cracked Ice', dropped from the final script of *Duck Soup*, in
which Freedonia's diva, Mrs Teasdale, hails Groucho's victory in the war
with Sylvania, with a song urging his coronation:

MRS TEASDALE:
This man is too great for his position,
Without a question.
I'd like to offer this with your permission,
As a suggestion:
I really think he should be King!
ALL: We really think he should be King!
And wear a crown and everything! He should be King!
GROUCHO: Although it would please me to govern the throng –
Suppose I were King and everything went wrong?
MRS TEASDALE: The King can do no wrong!
(*The war begins, shells fly – Groucho calls:*)
GROUCHO: We must unite against the common enemy and concentrate
   our forces! Now is not the time for political temporizing. Now is not
   the time for disintegrated loyalty. All interests must be sacrificed to the
   common weal!
(*Groucho running madly on table, which Chico and Harpo are rotating, Groucho
   getting nowhere:*)
GROUCHO: Rags are royal raiment when worn for virtue's sake. It is far
   better to give than to receive. I say give all we've got! It's war! Let's give
   the enemy no quarter! *It's War!*

Fade out.

Make That Three Hard-Boiled Eggs!

CHICO: This contract is-a no good. He's got-a no loopholes.
GROUCHO: You sign it and we'll put the loopholes in later.

From vaudeville routines for A Night at the Opera (1935)

One of the most cherished scenes in *Duck Soup* is the mirror gag. Chico and Harpo, spies for Ambassador Trentino of Sylvania, have infiltrated President Groucho's abode, and have dressed to look like him in night-shirts, cigars and moustaches. Groucho, in his nightshirt, is roused by the noise. Running to hide, Harpo breaks a large wall-length mirror and, as Groucho rushes in, has to mimic his movements so that Groucho will be fooled into thinking his reflection is real. This is, in fact, a classic silent routine, famously achieved by the French comedian Max Linder in *Seven Years Bad Luck* (1921). The astonishing tricks, as the suspicious Groucho bounds from side to side and twists around, trying to fool his 'reflection', matched with Harpo's efforts to keep up with him, are given added force by the fact that, made up the same, the Brothers are practically indistinguishable from each other. Harpo and Chico were the most similar, physically, while Zeppo was usually thought more like Groucho. The scene ends, as a topper, with Chico, as the third 'Groucho', entering the frame to spoil the symmetry.

The dysfunctional reflection was a perfect metaphor for the Four who were perceived as One. In real life, as we have noted, the brothers were drifting more and more apart, until finally the chain snapped, at its weakest link, in 1934. The New York *Herald Tribune* reported on 31 March:

> The Four Marx Brothers took a 25 per cent cut yesterday and will henceforth be the Three Marx Brothers. Zeppo, the youngest of the quartet, whose real name is Herbert, has resigned to become a theatrical agent.
>
> In the following letter to Brother Groucho, he explained his defection from the comedy team:
> 'I'm sick and tired of being a stooge. You know that anybody else

would have done as well as I in the act. When the chance came for me to get into the business world I jumped at it.

'I have only stayed in the act until now because I knew that you, Chico and Harpo wanted me to. But I'm sure you understand why I have joined Frank Orsatti in his theatrical agency and that you forgive my action. Wish me luck. Love, ZEPPO.'

'It's going to complicate things terribly for us, particularly on sleeper jumps,' Groucho replied. 'In the old days there were four of us. Then we could split up peacefully, two to a berth. Now we're three, and there's bound to be bad feelings.'

Zeppo, as we have seen, had been looking for alternatives since 1929, if not even earlier. In July 1933 he had bought a part interest in fighter Bob Perry's Brass Rail Café, which featured 'singing waiters with red noses and phony handlebar mustaches', and Zeppo tending the bar. But tending bar beside the singing waiters probably felt too much like old times for comfort. The Bren-Orsatti Agency was another stopgap, which lasted only until Zeppo realized that Bren and Orsatti were not on speaking terms. The next stop was the Small & Landau agency, but Zeppo Marx Inc. was soon born, with offices in the New Amsterdam Theater building in New York.

Gummo, whose dress business had foundered in March 1933, hied west, serving a brief apprenticeship at Universal Pictures' distribution arm, to learn the motion picture business. But 1935 saw him back in New York, working for Zeppo and his new partner, Allan Miller. In 1937 the agency would formally become a triangular partnership, Marx, Miller and Marx. The persistent tale, that Zeppo quit acting to become his brothers' agent, is inaccurate. Zeppo and Gummo, at first, were agents not for their brothers but for a range of both stage and screen writers and actors, who included, over the coming years, George S. Kaufman, Moss Hart, Dorothy Parker, Norman Krasna, Al Boasberg, Lucille Ball, Fred MacMurray, Barbara Stanwyck, Jean Harlow and Lana Turner. It was Gummo who eventually became the Marx Brothers' formal agent. The only deal Zeppo ever brokered for his brothers was with RKO Pictures, for the 1938 movie, *Room Service*.

So here were the Three Marx Brothers, left to bicker over who would get to sleep on his own in the Pullman car – just as they might have bickered, as children, over who got to be two to a bed, and who three. What the Brothers preferred, however, was not to bicker among themselves, but as a group, with others. It was no wonder they were the terror of studio executives and their appointees. In the eternal war between employer and employee, artist and patron, creative personnel and the managerial money-bags, the soldiers of Hollywood were perpetually in dispute with the gen-erals. Among the comics, Mae West and W. C. Fields' battles against the studios exhausted both stars, leading Fields to successive bouts of despair. The Marx Brothers, at least, had an advantage in numbers. Together – and Four were better than Three – they were the most formidable force in the business, capable not only of ferocious defence of their interests but, as we have seen, of physically ganging up on their opponents – and even their friends – and leaving them in their underwear. Even within the extended Marx family, Gummo's son Robert told me, when the Brothers met they were a tightly bound clique, like the bunched fingers of one hand, excluding even their wives and their children. This should hardly surprise us when we recall that, as a stage foursome (give or take Gummo and Zeppo), they had shared most of their working days, and nights, for almost twenty years of their teenage and adult lives.

No surprise either, then, that Paramount, like the defeated Russians in the First World War, sued for a separate peace. *Duck Soup*, contrary to legend, was not a flop, but it was not as big a hit as *Horse Feathers*, being 'merely' the company's fifth largest grosser of 1933. The studio, however, was Marxed out, and neither side wished to discuss a new contract.

In the spring of 1934, Groucho and Chico made an attempt at a radio comeback, with CBS, signed for seven weeks on Sunday nights. Neither the name nor the content of this show has come down to us, only a press release, touting Groucho as Ulysses S. Drivel, 'eagle-eyed news hound', and Chico as his trusty assistant Penelli. Later that summer, Groucho appeared for a short run in his first role in a 'legit' play, Ben Hecht and Charles MacArthur's *Twentieth Century*, performed in stock in Maine. Groucho played the lead part of Jaffe, a theatrical producer loosely based on the erratic Broadway mogul, Jed Harris. This was Groucho's first performance without a moustache since The Four Nightingales, and perhaps for this reason, he was barely noticed by the critics. In a letter to *Variety*, on 23 August, he complained about the showbiz journal's blind eye to his feat: 'The important fact that I was keeping the drama alive in the Maine woods wasn't even in the obit column,' he peevishly demurred.

The Brothers, however, were expending most of their energy in looking for a new Hollywood deal. It was not long in coming. Between the House of Algonquin in exile, and the Hearst crowd, the Marx Brothers were exceedingly well connected. Harpo clocked in first, with Samuel Goldwyn in tow, vaguely suggesting he might produce their next movie, though there was no clear suggestion what this might be. But Chico trumped him, with an even more powerful contact from his bridge-playing circle: MGM's wunderkind, Irving Thalberg.

Thalberg's meteoric progress has been charted often: appointed to run his uncle Carl Laemmle's Universal Studios in 1919, at the age of twenty, he established a reputation for ruthless control by sacking the movie business's most autocratic director, Erich von Stroheim, from his movie, *Merry-Go-Round*, in 1922. Two years later, aged twenty-five, Thalberg joined with Louis B. Mayer to become Vice-President and head of production at the new giant among studios, Metro-Goldwyn-Mayer. In the next decade Thalberg was to oversee and produce dozens of movies without requiring a screen credit. This deceptive modesty was typical of Thalberg, to whom the power of creation, and its end result, were far more important than public recognition. In an era when the director was still considered the prime moviemaker, Thalberg established, for good or ill, the producer-led picture. Thalberg would originate, cast, rewrite, and edit many of the classic films that bore the MGM trademark lion. These included the silents *The Big Parade* (1925), *Ben Hur* (1926), Greta Garbo in *Flesh and the Devil* (1927), King Vidor's *The Crowd* (1928) and *Hallelujah* (1929), and the talkies *Freaks*, *Strange Interlude* (1932), *The Merry Widow* (1934), *Mutiny on the Bounty* and *China Seas* (1935). Always in frail health, he suffered a heart attack in December 1932, but this intimation of fragile mortality only made his whirlwind life even more intense. His flamboyant lifestyle, and his ambition to make his wife, Norma Shearer, into the screen's greatest star, was to inspire F. Scott Fitzgerald's short story *Crazy Sundays* and his unfinished novel, *The Last Tycoon*.

Thalberg's forte was drama, but he was a Marx fan, and despite Louis B. Mayer's reluctance – possibly caused by Mayer's loathing of anything in pictures that might draw attention to his Jewish immigrant origins – the Brothers were signed up for the studio that had 'more stars than there are in heaven'.

The result was *A Night at the Opera*.

A great many stories have been told about the relationship between the Brothers and Irving Thalberg, which began with him telling them how lousy their last picture was. 'I was a little annoyed by this,' Groucho told Richard Anobile, 'as I thought *Duck Soup* was a very funny picture and I told him so. "Yes," he said, "that's true, but the audience doesn't give a damn about you fellas. I can make a picture with you that would have half as many laughs as your Paramount films, but they will be more effective because the audience will be more in sympathy with you."'

The Brothers cannot have been very pleased with this young Jew telling older Jews how to suck eggs. But Thalberg was the best catch there was. They swallowed their pride and got to work. They had a kind of revenge some time later when, left waiting in his lobby for hours as Thalberg attended to some other business until well past closing hours, so that even his secretary had left for the day, they pulled the mogul's steel cabinets over to the door and trapped him in his own office. At a later meeting, when he left them in mid-conference for a meeting elsewhere, the Brothers sent off to the studio commissary for potatoes and lit the log fire in his inner sanctum. Groucho recalled: 'When Thalberg returned he found us all sitting naked in front of a roaring fire, roasting mickeys over the flames. He laughed and said, "Wait a minute, boys!" He then phoned the commissary and asked them to send up some butter for the potatoes. He never walked out on us again.'

There are a dozen different versions of this seminal event, some of which even have the Brothers debagging Thalberg, a *lèse-majesté* they would never have dared. What all these stories reveal is the suppressed frustration of the Brothers at having to accept, for the only time in their careers, a final arbiter of their scripts and performances who outranked them, and to whom they had to defer. They swallowed their pride and accepted this because, when Thalberg smiled on you, you were going to end the day with much more than a nickel in your pocket.

A Night at the Opera is the first Marxian opus whose progress, owing to MGM's archival zeal, we are able to trace from the earliest treatments to the final product, with one crucial caveat: a mysterious and infuriating omission which we will note en route. Unlike the Paramount records, which mostly include three sample scripts of different stages, plus an outline or treatment, MGM provided the Library of the Academy of Motion Picture Arts and Sciences with great piles of script versions and documents. This enables us to explore a case history of development, to appreciate the sheer weight of effort and energy, not to speak of confusion, that Thalberg put into arriving at a Marx Brothers screenplay.

The crucial innovation, which made all the difference, was the decision to test selected episodes and drafts of the script versions in front of live audiences, on an old-style vaudeville tour. Groucho claimed it was the Brothers' own idea but, according to Joe Adamson, Thalberg himself had experimented with live audiences on sound stages during rehearsals of early talkies. Whoever initiated the concept, it was swiftly put on the drawing board, with the first 'vaudeville sketch' rolling off the typewriters on 28 December 1934.

Three authors were credited with 'Vaudeville Sketch No. 1': Bert Kalmar, Harry Ruby and James K. McGuinness, an MGM staff writer assigned by Thalberg to ensure a proper formula structure. McGuinness alone was the author of the first 'Marx Bros. Story Outline', tendered to MGM as early as 9 October. In that outline, 'Groucho, a fly-by-night promoter, arrives in Milan on the eve of the opening of the opera season. He has been commissioned by the group controlling wrestling in the United States to sign up a new crop of wrestlers . . . Groucho immediately contacts Pio Baroni, Italy's outstanding wrestler, and discusses terms with him.'

Baroni the wrestler invites Groucho to opening night at the Scala. At the opera, Groucho learns that Harpo, 'the greatest tenor in Italy, could earn in the United States three times as much money as Pio and his wrestlers ever could'. Chico, in this small acorn of the great oak to come, is 'the greatest voice coach in Europe'. The walls of the opera house are plastered with announcements that Harpo will sing Pagliacci the next night. The trick is that Harpo has – naturally – lost his voice.

There are no prizes for guessing James K. McGuinness's original vocation, which was that of sports writer. On 12 October, he reluctantly dropped the wrestling theme, in a new outline: Groucho is trying to leave the lobby of the Hotel Italia, Milan, without paying his bill, but his luggage is impounded. Groucho insinuates himself into the company of a Mrs Roanoke Webster, widow of a Texas steer king, and convinces her he is a talent scout from the Metropolitan Opera in New York. Chico is Baroni's voice coach, and Harpo is his faithful valet.

We are getting warmer, but then McGuinness veers completely off course: in an outline dated 19 October, Mrs Roanoke Webster has become Mrs Wharton Phelps, 'widow of the enormously wealthy inventor and manufacturer. Her late husband's most noted invention was the Household Silencer, a simple sound proofing device which gave to each room in the house the quiet and peace of a monastery cell. He labored years on the gadget – inspired, people said, by his wife's singing.' Groucho, in this version, was 'the bosom pal of the late Mr Phelps. Their friendship was based on a mutual fondness for snooker pool', and now he is executor and financial advisor to the widow.

These outlines were presumably funnelled to Thalberg, who promptly filed them, and sent the scribe back to his desk. By 24 October McGuinness had worked his way a little further into the story:

In the humbler quarters of Milan, three friends live together – two of them musicians, Harpo and Chico, the third, Pio Baroni, a young tenor of promise, who has sung in some of the provincial operas, but has yet had no chance to appear in the larger cities.

They live happy, carefree lives together. When one is in funds, all are supplied with money . . . The trio is preparing a typical Italian supper when the picture opens. They are cooking spaghetti, preparing sauce, putting huge hunks of bread and cheese on the table, setting out the bottles of Chianti. *(Buon appetito! ed.)*

Thalberg must have realized that this was not going anywhere, and began recruiting more writers. Kalmar and Ruby set to work and, by 31 October, turned in their first quick draft for a screenplay. This incorporated a gag that was not used in the film, but was utilized for a special trailer – replacing the MGM lion with Chico, Groucho and Harpo, roaring (Harpo's roar is, of course, silent). There follows a street scene in 'one of the humbler sections of Milan'. A street cleaner is humming Pagliacci, the tune taken up by more people, then by priests humming in front of Milan's cathedral.

This specifically Milanese milieu never made it into the final picture, though there is speculation that it was filmed and later dropped, due to the censor's concerns over Italian sensitivities – 1935 was of course still the era of Mussolini. But these troubles were yet to come. While Kalmar and Ruby toiled, Thalberg hired two other writers, George Seaton and Robert Pirosh, to pep up McGuinness and bash out their own version.

George Seaton's own recollection, as told to Richard Anobile, is embarrassingly at odds with the record. Seaton said: 'Irving Thalberg was not satisfied with a couple of scenes in the script as written by George Kaufman and Morris Ryskind. Kaufman had gone back to New York and Ryskind wasn't available, so Robert Pirosh and I were called in to do a little patchwork. The funny thing about this is that Bert Kalmar and Harry Ruby were in the next office working on the same scenes and none of us knew the other.'

This is a salutary lesson in the trustworthiness of oral history and the selective memory of senior citizens. According to the available, dated documents, Kaufman and Ryskind did not plunge into Thalberg's writing pool until several months later. Seaton and Pirosh's outline, dated 2 December 1934, is clearly another early draft:

In the huge office of a New York efficiency expert, an army of employees is engaged in card and dice games, ping pong, impromptu dances and other innocent pastimes. A warning bell heralds the entrance of a client, and suddenly typewriters start clacking and everyone looks as businesslike as possible. Guili-Guili, impresario of the Manhattan Opera Company, is ushered in . . .

He wants to see the boss, Groucho, who is engaged in a contest with the office boy with rubber bands and coloured tacks, shooting at a map on the wall . . . Chico and Harpo are part of a 'vagabond opera troupe . . . always out of funds but never out of spirits', back in Italy. Their star is Luigi, the aspiring singer.

On 10 December, another Seaton-Pirosh outline has Groucho interviewing his next client, 'Ruby Sitwell, a "dese and dem goil", whom the sanctity of marriage transplanted from Minsky's singing chorus to a Park Avenue flat. Now with her final divorce papers and a half million dollars in cash on hand, Ruby is all set to finance a Broadway musical in which she will be starred.'

Nothing more is heard of the 'dese and dem goil'. On 11 December, another Seaton-Pirosh outline introduces the name of Lassparri: 'Star of Milan's La Scala', signed by Groucho to sing at the Manhattan Opera Company.

By this time, Seaton–Pirosh and Kalmar–Ruby had managed to negotiate the office door and started to pool their resources. 'Vaudeville Sketch No. 1' of 28 December appears to have been the fruits of this labour, though credited, as we have seen, only to Kalmar, Ruby, McGuinness. Here we have arrived, more or less, in the ball-park of the movie as we know it today, with the rich widow and her upstart business advisor become the familiar Mrs Claypool and Otis B. Driftwood – Maggie Dumont and Groucho to be. The villain of the piece, impresario Guili-Guili, is still not the Herman Gottlieb-Siegfried Rumann whom we have come to know and hiss:

Open on drop representing lobby of the La Scala Opera House in Milan . . .
Mrs Claypool and Guili-Guili come from the interior of the opera house and pause at the door . . .
GUILI-GUILI: We have come thirty-two hundred miles to sign Lassparri, the greatest tenor in all Italy, and your Mr Driftwood isn't here yet.
MRS CLAYPOOL: Otis is a very busy man. Something must have held him up.
GUILI-GUILI: For twenty-five years I have been signing opera singers. Let me arrange the contract.
MRS CLAYPOOL: No, Maestro. I wouldn't think of making a move without Otis. I trust him implicitly.

As do we all. At this point, we switch to the exterior of the Opera House and a sequence which, in the movie, has been reduced to one line, as Groucho arrives by coach, berating the coachman for delivering him before the opera's over: 'Hey you, I told you to slow that nag down; on account of you I almost heard the opera!' The sketch provides an entire unfilmed scene which tantalizes us with another might-have-been:

GROUCHO *dashes up to the doorkeeper, calling*: Is the opera over yet?

DOORKEEPER: No. It won't be over for ten more minutes . . .

GROUCHO (*to carriage driver*): I told you to slow those horses down. On account of you, I nearly heard the opera. This is the narrowest escape I ever had in my life, and it's all your fault. Give me back my tip.

DRIVER: You no give me a tip, signor.

GROUCHO (*sweetly apologetic*): I didn't? I'm sorry, I meant to. Here. (*Hands tip to driver, who accepts with a 'gracia'. Groucho becomes indignant again.*) Now, give me back my tip. That's what I get for taking a carriage. Next time I go to the opera I'll take a turtle.

DRIVER (*amazed*): You no like opera, signor?

GROUCHO: Like it. The night Caruso sang 'Bohème' at the Metropolitan, I cried like a baby. I was at the dentist's having a tooth pulled out. You can't mention an opera ever written that I haven't stayed away from. I know all the plots backwards, and if they played them that way they'd make more sense. What's this one about?

DRIVER: Well, there's a man. He's a name Canio. He's a clown. He's a gotta beautiful wife.

GROUCHO: Why is it that all the clowns get beautiful wives? I've been clowning around for years and can't even get a telephone number . . .

DRIVER: Well, Canio's friend, he's-a steal his wife. Canio's a-find out. (*very dramatically*) He's-a go mad. He's-a go crazy. He's-a getta knife. He's-a kill his friend. He's-a kill his wife.

GROUCHO: That's what I like – an opera with a happy ending . . . (*turns from driver to doorkeeper*) What's the name of this place?

DOORKEEPER: La Scala – mother of all opera houses.

GROUCHO: Who's the father? (*the doorkeeper looks puzzled*) You might as well come clean. We'll find out. You're protecting somebody. Why should you be loyal to this beast? Did he think of her? No, he ran away, like the coward he was. Picture all those poor little opera houses all over the world not knowing who their father is. (*He dashes over to the astonished driver*) Are you a family man?

DRIVER: Yes, signor.

GROUCHO: Oh – so you're the father! Drive me to the police station! (*He grabs the Driver by the arms and starts leading him to the wings*) I knew I'd track this thing down . . .

At this point in the sketch Mrs Claypool comes over, with Guili-Guili, telling Driftwood that he must hurry and sign Lassparri right away. An immediate antagonism develops between Guili-Guili and Groucho, ending in the exchange:

GUILI-GUILI: This is intolerable. I am beside myself.

GROUCHO: Move over. You're in bad company.

The sketch continues, backstage at the Opera House, with Harpo and Chico rushing in, chasing girls. His friend Baroni is down in the dumps, and Chico promises to get him a contract to sing. Enter Groucho, and the contract scene roughly as familiar from the movie. ('The party of the first part shall be known in this contract as the party of the first part . . .') In celebration of the contract, Harpo produces several rows of bottles from his coat and unfurls a brass bar rail, to drink to the 'greatest tenor in all Italy', at which point Groucho realizes he's signed Chico's pal Baroni, and not the opera star, Lassparri. Familiar turf once more.

The next day, 29 December – Kalmar and Ruby worked almost as fast as Harpo – 'Vaudeville Sketch No. 3' was already delivered, with scenes at Mrs Claypool's house, including Chico's piano speciality.

On 31 December, George Seaton and Robert Pirosh produced another set of 'Story Points': 'The character Pio (Baroni), is to be changed according to Mr Thalberg's suggestions. In the first sequence, he will be a happy-go-lucky sort of fellow, fond of wine, women and song, but with an especially warm spot in his heart for Rosa. Far from being discouraged by his lack of success at La Scala, he feels only that the breaks have been against him . . .' Thalberg was evidently still playing divide and rule with his scribes.

Although the vaudeville sketches were written, Thalberg and the Marx Brothers were still not happy with the texts, and were not yet ready to try them out on the road. If too many cooks spoil the broth, what better remedy than to revert to the original chefs, the owners of the master recipe? Accordingly, George S. Kaufman and Morrie Ryskind received the siren call from MGM.

Kaufman, for his part, was reluctant to lie on the Marxian bed of nails again, and even more reluctant to leave New York for Hollywood, as he had already tangled with Samuel Goldwyn over his insistence on co-writing (with Robert Sherwood) an Eddie Cantor film, *Roman Scandals*, by long distance, without leaving Manhattan. Eventually a telegram from Groucho, 'COMING TO GET YOU', coupled with a $100,000 offer from Thalberg, did the trick. As Kaufman's biographer, Scott Meredith, described the occasion:

> Once he was established at the Garden of Allah . . . he immediately joined the 'Waiting for Irving' Club, the popular name for all those who spent hours sitting outside Thalberg's office. S. J. Perelman . . . once said that he had seen sitting there, all at one time, such literary lights as Sidney Howard, Robert E. Sherwood, Marc Connelly, S. N. Behrman, Donald Ogden Stewart, and Kaufman . . . 'On a clear day,' Kaufman once said, 'you could see Thalberg.'

When Thalberg started to demand a quick treatment from Kaufman, the playwright made a famous reply: 'Do you want it Wednesday, or do you want it good?'

Once again, Morrie Ryskind was roped in and, escaping 'the noise, laughter, music, and mating calls [which were] continuous each and every night at the Garden of Allah', decamped with Kaufman to the Beverly Wilshire Hotel, where they took adjoining suites and went to work.

Now here's the rub: we do not have the script that Kaufman and Ryskind wrote for Thalberg. (This is despite the fact that Viking Press, in 1972, published an 'Original Script' attributed to the duo, without providing any proof of the source.) This is the infuriating omission I remarked on earlier, amid the acreage of papers in the MGM boxes. Neither I nor the indefatigable Joe Adamson, who has spent large parts of his life combing Hollywood archives for these missing holy grails, have seen hair nor hide of it. What we do have is a 'Temporary Incomplete Screenplay', dated 20 February 1935, incorporating segments of the 'vaudeville sketches', which were to be revamped by Ryskind for their eventual stage tour. The archive also includes an even more intriguing but maddeningly undated treatment marked 'Suggested Changes by George S. Kaufman and Morrie Ryskind', typed, according to the stamp on the file, in New York, and containing references to a completely different script of *A Night at the Opera* from any that have survived on page or screen!

In this phantom version, Groucho was apparently down as 'a manufacturer of crooked dice' and Mrs Claypool seemed to have been encumbered by a daughter, since vanished from human sight. Kaufman and Ryskind suggest, in their undated 'changes', a plot in which Lassparri and the impresario Guili have missed the boat to New York, and are following on in a cattle ship. A cable from them is misread as 'battle ship', and Groucho cries: 'This means war!', while Harpo runs up a white flag. In a comedy scene with immigration officers, at disembarkation, the Brothers' 'artists' permits' are checked – shades of *Monkey Business*. On the night of the opera, in New York, it is Baroni who goes on, replacing the absent Lassparri, but he loses his voice and is booed off. Baroni 'disconsolately leaves opera house, followed by Chico and Harpo, then Groucho, fired by Mrs Claypool'.

At the end of this confusing document, Kaufman and Ryskind add: 'Notes: We would like to cut out some weak jokes, such as La Tuska and Samson and De-Lily. It is jokes like these that have imperilled the position of the Marx boys, both on stage and screen, and which will kill them absolutely in time. We would give them puns, but NEW ones, and, we hope, good ones.'

All this leaves us with the conclusion that the Marx Brothers, in fact, rejected Kaufman and Ryskind's screenplay, since the final result bears little resemblance to the above plot line. Having called for Kaufman and Ryskind in the first place, the Brothers, at this point, took on yet another chef for their endlessly churning spaghetti sauce: veteran gagster Al Boasberg.

Al Boasberg (born 1892 in Buffalo, NY) was a former tyre salesman turned jokesmith for various vaudevillians, who included Al Jolson, Eddie Cantor, Jack Pearl, and many others. Some of these jokes were printed in a book by Max Wilk, *The Wit and Wisdom of Hollywood*, but, in deference to Boasberg's memory, I shall not quote them. George Burns got him started as a comedy writer, and he moved on to write for Jack Benny, Bob Hope and, later, the less memorable Wheeler and Woolsey. He also worked as an intertitler for silent films, including *Battling Butler* and *The General*, for Buster Keaton. Keaton wrote about him: 'When the talkies came in, Al Boasberg became the best paid gagwriter in Hollywood, a walking marvel of verbal firecrackers and yak-getting wows. But he had a terrible flop when he tried to do sight gags for us.'

No one, of course, could have saved poor Buster's dire talkies, but the Marx Brothers, with their magpie eye for snapping up talent, recruited Boasberg to their team. And so the MGM vaudeville show finally took to the road, in mid-April 1935. Morrie Ryskind joined the tour, despite his dislike for Boasberg, his rival. By now the picture was cast, and the actors – Maggie Dumont, Allan Jones as Baroni, Kitty Carlisle as Rosa – went on tour with Groucho, Chico and Harpo.

Both Kitty Carlisle and Allan Jones were hired for the picture because they could sing, though some studio executives, as is their wont, initially wanted them to mime to Metropolitan Opera singers. Kitty Carlisle, RADA- and Paris-trained, was only twenty-one in 1935 but had sung in Broadway shows and appeared in two 1934 movies, *Murder at the Vanities* and *Here Is My Heart*. She might have achieved stardom in due course, but instead married playwright Moss Hart.

Allan Jones was born in 1907 in Pennsylvania, the grandson and son of Welsh coal miners. He could sing and dig coal at the same time, but preferred the former, although he worked in the mines to put himself through high school. A genuine opera tenor who studied in London and sang at Carnegie Hall in 1931, he was a regular for the Shuberts' opera companies, but Hollywood soon beckoned. He made his début with Jean Harlow in *Reckless* (1935), singing 'Everything's Been Done Before'.

Groucho, according to one tale, accepted Jones into the cast of *A Night at the Opera* with the greeting, 'Hello, Sloucho!' It was a big deal to replace the Fourth Brother, Zeppo, as the romantic lead, but at least Jones could sing. In an interview for *The Freedonia Gazette*, in 1979, he spoke about his experience on the road:

> We went to Salt Lake City and played movie houses. The movie would come on in the morning and then we'd come on and do an hour and fifteen minutes . . . Al Boasberg the gag writer and his secretary would sit in the back, and if the laughs would last a certain amount of time, we would have new lines to try in the next show. We did four shows a day.

Harry Guss, a reporter for *Variety*, described the feverish atmosphere backstage at Salt Lake when the Brothers performed: 'As soon as a show was performed they'd all go in a huddle and discuss what made it go, or didn't make it go . . .' After the performance, the huddle would break up. 'One thing I found curious,' Guss told Richard Anobile, in *The Marx Brothers Scrapbook*, 'was that Harpo and Chico would always pair off . . . Groucho was always by himself or with the writers. Harpo was always fooling around. One time I was standing with him outside the hotel and two beautiful girls, whom I happened to know, were coming down the street. One was the daughter of the President of the Intermountain telephone company . . . Harpo said, "Watch, I'm gonna do something," and as the girls came by, Harpo got hold of the president's daughter, threw her on the ground and said, "Where have you been, my lost love?"' Guss had a hard time convincing the hysterical girl, and then her irate father, that this was just a

Marx Brother goofing off. It was, after all, the city of Brigham Young, and all the other Latter-day Saints.

From Salt Lake City to Seattle, Portland, San Francisco, the troupe trooped, cutting and snipping the script as they went. It is difficult, with all these changes, to figure out who wrote what of the scenes in the film. A popular tale has Al Boasberg as the sole progenitor of the famous stateroom scene, in which everyone on the ship piles into Groucho's tiny cabin, amid the pervasive chorus of Harpo's beeps as Groucho orders breakfast – 'And two hard-boiled eggs . . . Make that three hard-boiled eggs . . . and one duck egg!' According to legend, Boasberg was so miffed at being rushed by Thalberg to rewrite his scenes that he told the producer and the Brothers he had left the sequence in his office, and went off for the day. When Thalberg and the Brothers rushed over, they found an empty office, with the immortal stateroom scene-to-be pasted on the ceiling, in tiny strips, each containing one line of dialogue. Groucho claimed it took them five hours to piece it all together. But they knew a classic scene when they saw it.

On the other hand, the stateroom scene exists, in fairly developed embryo, in one of the Vaudeville scripts, attributed to Morrie Ryskind, and dated 19 March 1935:

GROUCHO: And two hard-boiled eggs. And eight pieces of French pastry.
STEWARD: This is an Italian boat, sir.
GROUCHO: All right – what's the rate of exchange? Make it twelve pieces
    of Italian pastry, sixteen cups of coffee, and four demi-tasses.
CHICO: And two more hard-boiled eggs.
Two maids knock on door – We've come to make up the room.
CHICO: Are those my hard-boiled eggs?
GROUCHO: It's a little too early to know – this is my first day on the boat.
    (*To maids*): Come in, girls, and leave all hope behind.

Indeed, it was difficult to believe that there was any hope of anything but an overcooked turkey emerging from the crowded kitchen, despite the fact that the on-screen writing credit boiled down in the end – inaccurately, as we have seen – to George S. Kaufman and Morrie Ryskind alone for the screenplay, 'based on a story by James Kevin McGuinness.' Such were the realities of Hollywood power. But by May 1935, the patchwork text was deemed ready to shoot.

Thalberg, interventionist at every stage, now played his ace, appointing Sam Wood as the movie's director. Wood was an MGM employee who had already directed six talkies for the studio, including *Paid* (1930) with Joan

A Night at the Opera: with Sam Wood on the set.

The stateroom scene: four more hard-boiled eggs!

Crawford, and *Hold Your Man* (1933) with Clark Gable and Jean Harlow. He was a director who brought the film home on schedule and on budget. Later, in the 1940s, he would go on to direct a number of classic films: *Our Town*, *The Devil and Miss Jones*, *Pride of the Yankees*, *For Whom the Bell Tolls* and *King's Row*, with Ronald Reagan.

Groucho later claimed that he hated Sam Wood and told Thalberg, 'He's a lousy director.' Thalberg's response was that Wood was basically his puppet, and would do whatever reshoots he wanted. Groucho called Wood a 'fascist'. This is most likely hindsight in response to Wood's ultra-right-wing politics in later years. During the McCarthyite purges he founded the Motion Picture Alliance, aimed at expelling 'Communists' from the film industry. When he died, in 1949, his will specified that no heirs could inherit a penny unless 'they filed with the probate court an affidavit swearing that "they are not now, nor have they ever been, Communists"'. But by that time, Groucho's old friend Morrie Ryskind had also travelled a fair lick towards the politics of Attila the Hun, though he remained a pal. Groucho's long-term hostility may have had more to do with the fact that Sam Wood refused to take any Marx Brothers nonsense, and insisted on endless and exhausting retakes.

Walter Woolf King, who played Lassparri, had a very different memory of Wood:

Sam Wood was a hell of a nice guy, but they made his life miserable. I don't think he even wanted to do the picture. He was under contract to Metro and he had just a hell of a time with them, because they were never around when he wanted them or was ready to shoot. Chico would be over in the dressing room with a dame or Groucho would be some-place else . . .

The turmoil continued, with yet more script tweaking and cuts, one version – of a climactic fire at the opera – disappearing at some unspecified stage. (Harpo was to save the pompous impresario from the fire – a palpably ridiculous notion!) And we have not even mentioned the retakes, with Al Boasberg and even old stalwart J. K. McGuinness scribbling changes well into September.

Despite it all, and in the face of such chaos, *A Night at the Opera* lives as a triumph. Despite its multiple writers, outlines and scripts, it appears all of a piece, the only film in which the Marx Brothers' manic energy co-exists with a more humane pathos, a sense that the romance and sentiment are not just tacked on for appeasement's sake. Since the only guiding hand, in the

A Night at the Opera: Sig Rumann at work with two art lovers.

kingdom of divide and rule that made the movie, was Thalberg's, the credit for this miracle must accrue to him. Once again, as he had done with such hodgepodges as *Ben Hur* and *Grand Hotel*, as well as more coherent projects, he worked his magic, and knitted together all the scattered shards. From the opening restaurant scene in which Margaret Dumont discovers that her dinner date, Groucho, has been dining with a blonde right behind her at the next table ('Do you know why I sat with her? Because she reminds me of you!' – a ploy more appropriate in real life to philandering Chico), to the disruptive mayhem at the New York Opera House, with Verdi's *Il Trovatore* benefiting spectacularly from the addition of 'Take Me Out to the Ball Game' and a variety of descending modern backdrops, as well as serial frying pan knockouts – the world of art, culture and moneyed cultural pretension is made safe for the Marxism that Salvador Dalí lauded as the lure of the irrational and 'the fulfillment of the pleasure principle'.

But there is still more here than meets the eye.

From the movie's second sequence, in Lassparri's dressing room, when Harpo, as Lassparri's dresser, is caught playing around in his boss's costumes, and is cruelly whipped for his presumption, we are in a different Marx Brothers realm. For the first time Harpo is a victim, not an invulnerable sprite. The opera in this instance is *I Pagliacci*, Leoncavallo's saga of murderous passion among clowns ('Canio, he's-a go crazy, he's-a getta knife, he's-a kill his friend'). Harpo is temporarily rescued by Rosa, whom Lassparri is besotted by, only to be hammered again behind closed doors. Backstage, Harpo, as Tomasso, is embraced by his old pal Fiorello, Chico and Harpo having brought each other matching presents – a big stick of salami. Here Fiorello meets Baroni, recalling the times they studied together at the conservatory – a likely story, but this is a different Chico too, softer-edged, even sentimental. 'Whatsa matter, we both young, we got our health,' he berates Baroni. Not quite the Chico who 'bid 'em op!' so recklessly in *The Cocoanuts*.

Even Groucho has softened. Mrs Claypool, who is depending on Otis B. Driftwood to get her into society, clearly deserves all she gets for her foolishness. In his renewed role as Cupid, Groucho connives at drawing Baroni and Rosa together. These three Marx imps are no longer just the forces of retribution among the hypocrites. Thalberg has imbued them with an angelic flavour – happily, without diluting their destructive force.

Siegfried Rumann, as Herman Gottlieb (né Guili-Guili) is another welcome addition to the Marxian menagerie: a Teutonic volcano, ever threatening to erupt in an uncontrollable lava flow, but never quite making it; a kind of furioso interruptus. Born in Hamburg, Rumann cut his teeth on the German stage and began appearing in American movies in 1929, with *The Royal Box*. Like Margaret Dumont, his early horizons might have been broader but his bread and butter came from his narrow, one-dimensional energy. Appearing in over seventy films, his swansong, a year before his death in 1967, was the serendipitous role of the fearsome insurance doctor in Billy Wilder's Marxesque farce, *The Fortune Cookie* (1966). He went out fuming, and one can imagine standing by his grave, listening to the eternal, celestial splutter of 'Vot are you saying!!?? You *schweinhund . . .*'

Never has a man given so much pleasure just by being apoplectic. But Sig Rumann had, apart from his acting face, another life entirely, as a biologist specializing in desert snakes and spiders, specimens of which he would occasionally bring to the film set, to the alarm of his fellow performers. Behind the mask, as usual, another story beckons: the student who studied to be an engineer, then joined Hamburg stock companies; the man who served as a lieutenant in the First World War, wounded three times and captured by American troops, whom he found to be an enthusiastic audience for his shows. He came to America soon after the Armistice, and was discovered by Broadway star George Jessel, who initiated his fifty-year run of typecast German roles.

Walter Woolf King – Lassparri – was another actor who became stuck as a 'heavy'. A vaudeville alumnus and minor Broadway star, he joined the *hegira* to Hollywood and ended up a foil to the Marx Brothers, and later to Laurel and Hardy in *Swiss Miss* (1938). He had fond memories of the Brothers, who had cleaned him out in poker, and a poignant tale, when interviewed by David Koenig for *The Freedonia Gazette* in 1981:

> I remember one of the scenes of *A Night at the Opera*. My children are grown now . . . but at that time they were very little and my wife was just coming back from New York with the two children . . . I was working that day out at Metro . . . and they came out and were sitting in the audience because we had a big theatre there at the time and that was the scene in which they were throwing things at me. I was to start and sing the opera, and they would start to throw things and my kids were there and they started to scream. They got up and hollered 'They're hurting my daddy!' And poor Sam Wood was tearing his hair.

Wood need not have worried, the way things turned out. *A Night at the Opera*, given MGM's resources, was also the Brothers' most lavish film to date, with its great opera house set, quayside scenery for Allan Jones and Kitty Carlisle to warble 'Alone', and the steerage deck with its ebullient cast of dancing troubadours, in Hollywood-issue Italian peasant costumes, gambolling to Jones's fruity rendition of 'Cosi Cosa' – belting the stuff out as if he were really auditioning for a return to Carnegie Hall.

Raymond Durgnat, writing about the Marx Brothers ("Four Against Alienation", in his book *The Crazy Mirror*), commented upon 'the particularly American issue of immigrants versus conformism', stating that 'just under the surface of the Brothers' fantasy, a documentary is screaming to be let out.' This is most sharply felt in *A Night at the Opera*, where the hungry stowaways, Harpo, Chico and Zeppo-stand-in Jones (having eaten nothing but the caseful of hard-boiled eggs, devoured in one gulp, one assumes, by Harpo) emerge upon the dancing steerage deck to have a row of chefs thrust plates into their hands and pile them high with enough spaghetti and pineapples to sink the ship. By all accounts, the Marx Brothers were always hungry, and Maxine tells the tale of Chico being challenged at a farm, way back when, to gobble up as much duck as he could eat, and stopping only after the fourth duck. ('Your cheque, sir!' 'Nine dollars and forty cents?! This is an outrage. If I were you I wouldn't pay it.')

'Cosi Cosa' is followed by probably the best of Chico and Harpo's solo specialities, and certainly the best integrated of any into the surrounding plot. Chico is hemmed in by adoring children, and Harpo, approaching the piano to great cheers, manages to get both hands crushed by the lid. And then he spies the harp.

The piano and harp sequences in the Marx Brothers' movies were seen by some, like *Duck Soup*'s Leo McCarey, as a needless break in the funny business, but appear to me to stand at the centre of the Brothers' inner world. When Chico and Harpo play, their character masks drop, and what we are seeing, directly and without subterfuge, is Leo Marx, noodling at the nickelodeon, and 'Ahdie', finding his voice in his music. Chico's look is one of pure, mischievous enjoyment. Harpo's face, ever on the brink of a Gookie, relaxes, and a look of pure concentration takes over, the eyes dreamily fixed on a point that only he can see, somewhere in another dimension, as his fingers flail the strings. While Chico plays always for others, Harpo plays for himself, for his own inner fulfilment. It is the closest to a spiritual moment that we get to in any comedy, and a glimpse of both the absolute joy and the melancholy that lie beyond the laughs.

In this instance, Harpo's solo is played mostly in one long, frontal medium shot and, watching him, foreground frame left, is the facial silhouette of an old woman with close-cropped hair. She displays no reaction, and might as well be a ghost. Sam Wood and the cinematographer, one Merrit B. Gerstad, probably intended nothing more than a compositional ploy, to link the harpist to the on-deck scene but, as I watch it, I have the eerie feeling that the silhouette is that of Fanny Solomons-Schoenberg, the harpist grandmother, looking on from another place, at her bequeathed gift . . .

But hey! We haven't even mentioned the three bearded airmen, whose reception by New York's Mayor is usurped by Chico, Harpo and Jones, or the nonplussed detective Hennessy (Robert Emmet O'Connor taking over the old Ed Metcalfe role) being flimflammed by the disappearing campbeds – note the marvellous moment with Harpo sitting on Chico, swathed in a blanket, Gookie gawking over his pretence at knitting, Groucho as paterfamilias by the breakfast table – and several dozen other small gems of visual and verbal gags.

A Night at the Opera is by far the most densely packed of the Brothers' films with phrases and lines that stick in the mind: 'An outrage, if I were you I wouldn't pay it'; 'Waiter, have you got any milk fed chickens? Well squeeze the milk out and bring me a glass'; 'You're willing to pay him a thousand dollars a night just to sing? Why, you could get a phonograph record of Minnie the Moocher for seventy-five cents! For a buck and a half you can get Minnie!' Not to speak of the unsurpassable contract scene:

GROUCHO: The party of the first part shall be known in this contract as the party of the first part. How do you like that? It's pretty neat, eh?

CHICO: No, it's no good.

GROUCHO: What's the matter with it?

CHICO: I don't know, let's hear it again.

GROUCHO: The party of the first part shall be known in this contract as the party of the first part.

CHICO: Well, it sounds a little better this time.

GROUCHO: Well, it grows on you. Would you like to hear it once more?

CHICO: Just the first part.

GROUCHO: What do you mean? The party of the first part?

CHICO: No, the first part of the party of the first part.

GROUCHO: All right, it says, uh, the first part of the party of the first part shall be known in this contract as the first part of the party of the first part shall be known in this contract . . . Look, why should we quarrel about a thing like this, we'll take it right out, eh?

CHICO: Yeah, it's-a too long anyhow.

(Both tear a strip off their contracts.)

CHICO: Now whada we got left?

GROUCHO: Well, I got about a foot and a half. Now it says, the party of the second part shall be known in this contract as the party of the second part.

CHICO: Well, I don't know about that –

GROUCHO: Now what's the matter?

CHICO: I no like-a the second party either.

GROUCHO: Well, you should have come to the first party. We didn't get home till around four in the morning. I was blind for three days!

Joe Adamson writes about this scene:

The contract routine is one of the few great scenes in the history of film in which two people do nothing but stand and talk. The longer they stand and talk, the more hopeless becomes the idea of standing and talking, and the more hopeless becomes the idea of standing and talking, the longer they stand and talk. The scene consists of a pointless pyramid of perplexities, in which a lot of time and effort are involved in getting nothing accomplished.

On the other hand – Groucho has signed Ricardo Baroni, on false pretences, but nevertheless, a shrewd investment as it turns out at the end! For if one looks a little closer at the contract – taking into account the parties of all the parts – we might reflect that the Marx Brothers are not, after all, opposed to Art and Culture in themselves, but only to their usurpation by those who wish to use them merely as instruments of manipulation and power. Baroni is a better singer than Lassparri, and when he finally gets to sing, the Marx Brothers prevent all interruptions. They are, in fact, not the enemies of Art but the greatest defenders of its integrity.

The opera in *A Night at the Opera*, *Il Trovatore*, is Verdi's sumptuous tale of a wandering troubadour who, in his love for the Duchess Leonora, is pitted against the Count di Luna, who is, unbeknownst to both, the wandering knight's brother. A group of gypsies stand watch over this tale of jealousy and frustrated love. Verdi's Leonora preserves her honour tragically, with poison, whereas Thalberg's Rosa wins through, by comedy, to true love. What the gypsy Marxes have accomplished in the end is far from negligible – the triumph of *amore*, and the return of good art to its honest practitioners.

The most twisty, curvy path, the shredded social contract, turns out to be the shortest route, after all, to truth.

28

Get Your Tutsi-Frutsi Ice Cream!

QUACKENBUSH: I've won acclaim for curing ills
Both in the north and south,
You'll find my name, just like my pills
In everybody's mouth.
I've never lost a case —
ALL: He's never lost a case —
QUACKENBUSH: I've lost a lot of patients but I've never lost a case!

Kalmar and Ruby song for Vaudeville Sketch of *A Day at the Races* (1936)

A Night at the Opera still had two more hurdles to jump on its way to immortality. The first was the ubiquitous censorship of Joseph Breen, who tendered Louis B. Mayer a long list of objections to matters we would today see as child's play:

Care should be taken to avoid offense in the scene of Harpo masquerading as a woman. He should not be finally revealed in running pants – his person should be covered at all times. The girl who escapes from the closet should not be in underwear, but should be fully covered . . . The expression 'Lichee nuts to you' should be changed to delete 'nuts.'

Page 44: This entire gag of Groucho inviting Mrs Claypool into his cabin is open to grave question and should be changed to avoid all possible offense . . . delete: 'If I come here again, Mrs Claypool, there will be no beating about the bush.'

Page 54: The scene between Lassparri and Rosa is open to question on the grounds of being suggestive. Any suggestiveness should be deleted.

Page 69: The business of the girl under the shower being discovered by Harpo should be deleted.

And so forth. As later files reveal, idiotic censor cuts were not the sole

298

prerogative of the American Hays office, but were common and even more rigorous in other parts of the world. In Italy, still, in 1935, in the mid-term of Mussolini's fascism, release of the film was 'held up by the objection of the Italian government that it made fun of the Italian people. These objections were later withdrawn.' Despite the lifting of the ban, 'cuts were made to remove any inference that the characters were Italian'.

In Japan, the censors eliminated 'close shot of a girl whirling, showing her legs above knees' and 'Tomasso sticking his head through dancing girl's legs'. Also, 'eliminate dialog of Driftwood: "Call off that police dog."' In Australia, 'delete, after engineers say: "We've come to turn off the heat" – "you'd better start on him."' In Latvia they went one better: 'Eliminate scene of Marx Brothers eating at table, Tomasso making sandwiches of cigars, ties, etc.' Also, 'eliminate scene in which Gottlieb and Henderson are struck on their heads.' In England, 'eliminate: "for a buck and a quarter you can get Minnie."' Back home, in Kansas, 'eliminate all dialogue and views concerning beds.' (!!!!!) And, in Virginia, cut Groucho's line: 'Dispense with my services? Why she hasn't even had them yet.'

Before all that, there was the crucial hurdle of surviving the opening night. The first preview audience was lukewarm to cold, causing much brotherly despondency, but Thalberg, convinced he had a hit, had the film taken to another, adjacent theatre for a second viewing. This was, in fact, not much better, and Thalberg spent much of the next three days enclosed with editor William Le Vanway to tighten up the film in places where the gags were thought to be too far apart. The Brothers wanted him to cut out Allan Jones's 'Alone' song, but Thalberg left this item unchanged, and it became one of the hits of the year.

Thalberg's instincts were right. A Night at the Opera, despite some critical quibbles, became the Brothers' most successful picture. André Sennwald, of the New York Times, thought it 'below their best', but Variety predicted 'solid' box office, lauding 'laughs on a high frequency basis for an hour and a half'. The audiences certainly agreed. This was a new plateau for the Marx Brothers, and they buckled down for a second bout with Thalberg, although no one could quite figure out, for the moment, what this new picture would be.

Meanwhile the Brothers continued enjoying the good life in California, Groucho getting a little more sleep as he watched his money growing again, as well as his rising offspring. Arthur, at Beverly Hills High School, was becoming an ace tennis player, and Miriam, a precocious nine-year-old attending Hawthorne Grammar School, was trying to make sense of the crazy Hollywood world. Groucho's relationship with Ruth, however, was becoming more and more frosty and, according to Hector Arce, they were now sleeping in separate rooms. Ruth became a target for Groucho's daily barbs, as he insulted her cooking with comments such as 'What prison sent you the recipe for this?' The more Groucho doted on his son and daughter, the more he seemed to push Ruth away, towards the bottle which became her final refuge. Hector Arce theorized on Groucho's sexual inadequacy, speculating that his early rejection by his mother caused a later problem of premature ejaculation – a verdict that brought down the wrath of son Arthur upon the hapless biographer's head when his book hit the stands in 1979.

The above diagnosis seems to me a case of premature psychoanalysis. All I can conclude, at this distance from the events, is that for Groucho, there appeared to be no middle ground: adoration or derision seemed to be the poles between which his temperament veered. Another trait, which he shared with all his brothers – with the possible exception of Gummo – was the refusal to countenance failure. The Marx Brothers had fought against adversity all their lives, and had a mortal fear of weakness. Weakness, for immigrants, and the children of immigrants, meant falling by the wayside. One had to win through, to the promised land. To their children, who were born to this pot of gold which their parents mined with such toil and effort, they were equally loving and stern. Groucho, more than the others, would turn and attack at any sign of vulnerability. Perhaps he recalled how vulnerable he had been as the jealous middle son, *Der Eifersuchtige*. Naturally, as an adult, he fed on the adoration of others, and enjoyed to the full the opportunity fame gave him of meeting and hobnobbing with other famous people, like the pianist Artur Rubinstein, Charles Chaplin, and all his show business peers. To the outside world, he pretended to make little of it, as shown by the oft-told tale of his *faux pas* with Greta Garbo in the Thalberg building's elevator. Finding himself standing behind her, he playfully tipped her great hat over her face, saying, as she turned to him furiously: 'I beg your pardon, I thought you were a fellow I knew from Kansas City.' This explains, Groucho wrote, why Greta Garbo never appeared in a Marx Brothers picture.

Maxine Marx writes about her own delight and wonder at the Hollywood world of her teens. Life with Chico appeared mellow on the surface, with the lush houses, the swimming pools and servants. The MGM lot became Maxine's second home, as she rubbed shoulders with Clark Gable, Joan Crawford, William Powell, Jean Harlow and Greta Garbo (without tipping over her hat). She fell in love with Spencer Tracy, but learned to keep such feelings from Chico after he called out to the star when he and his daughter spotted him across the car park: 'Hey Spencer, my kid here's got a big crush on you!' Chico didn't believe in keeping his emotions hidden, except from his wife, who was just about to find out the true state of the long-running affair between her husband and Ann Roth.

'Our family', wrote Maxine, 'had fallen into a regular routine. It was arranged around Chico's need to be constantly involved in gaming of one kind or another. Tuesday and Friday were fight nights in Los Angeles and Hollywood. Mother and I usually went with him, though Daddy would get annoyed when I would take off my glasses at the bloody parts. Chico was a great fight fan and could call most of the winners, but his biggest thrill came from betting on the underdogs. He wanted the big win against the odds, and, as a consequence, lost his shirt.'

A gambling principle that would, in the end, lose him far more than metaphorical clothing. As Maxine tells the tale, Chico had made one of his periodic trips to New York, ostensibly to set up another Marx Brothers radio show, but more pointedly to meet his young lover. On his return, Betty finally challenged him openly about the Other Woman. Chico confessed and named Ann Roth. In the scheme of things, this open wound in the marriage was not something that could be kept hidden from the Other Brothers, who laid down the law to Chico. Philandering in wedlock was, if not kosher, at least acceptable if kept discreet. Dumping Betty for the mistress was not an option, even in Hollywood – not in this German-Jewish family with its powerful sense of tribal loyalties. Chico capitulated and, according to Maxine, broke off his relationship with Ann Roth by telephone, with Betty listening on an extension, to make sure. Chico's marriage was salvaged, but only temporarily. From then on, he and Betty were living a lie, which became more painful as it dragged on, with Maxine caught in the middle.

But these were the Marx Brothers, masters of comedy! On the surface, life was on the up and up. Zeppo and Gummo were firming up their creative agency, flitting about between Los Angeles and New York, though their business was still concentrated on Broadway. In *The Groucho Phile*, Groucho offered a tale of Zeppo's early days in business: the Brothers were in a Hollywood nightclub, with Groucho's friend, Norman Krasna, whom Zeppo was wooing for his agency. 'Norman was playing deaf to Zeppo's hard sell,' wrote Groucho. 'An obnoxious drunk came to our table and started pestering Krasna. Finally, Zeppo hauled off and hit the drunk on the chin. He turned to Krasna and asked, "Does the other agency give you that kind of service?"'

Grandpa Levy Schoenberg might well have applauded such a direct approach to life's challenges. As for his fifth grandson, the last remaining Marx bachelor, another crucial change was about to take place.

Harpo, having moved out of the Garden of Allah, had rented a huge furnished mansion in Beverly Hills which had room for his harp and plenty more besides, but was a pretty excessive pad for a single. He stocked the spacious grounds with his menagerie of cats, dogs and birds and began taking in guests: Sam Harris, Moss Hart, the Algonquin crowd – Kaufman, Ruth Gordon, Dorothy Parker from back east, and locals like Charles Lederer, Ben Hecht, George Burns and even, if Harpo can be believed on this, the Ritz Brothers, new rival comedians. Only Aleck Woollcott was missing, touring the country, on a high with his new role on radio as the 'Town Crier' (sponsored by Cream of Wheat). Woollcott was fulfilling a lifelong ambition of chatting to the entire nation about his obsessions in art, literature and politics. The crunch came when he denounced the fascist dictators, Mussolini and Hitler, in 1936. At that point Cream of Wheat had enough. But all this was yet to come. To console himself for the lack of Woollcott, Harpo took in Oscar Levant, obsessive and eccentric Broadway stage and film composer, whose insomnia could drive any host to distraction, but who was a soul brother in their shared realm of music. Harpo sailed through it all, until the lease on his property ran out, and he began scouting for a new residence.

But the inevitable was closing in: love, unplatonic, and not for a horse. At a party given by Samuel Goldwyn, as far back as 1932, Harpo had met an actress named Susan Fleming, co-star with W. C. Fields in Herman Mankiewicz's production of *Million Dollar Legs*. She reminded Harpo that from the stage he had once picked her out of the audience of *Animal Crackers*, as a stooge for his clowning. He had forgotten but she had not. Her name, though, had a resonance for Harpo, since he had been smitten, in his earliest Hollywood days, by a young girl named June Fleming. She was an amateur aviator, and was killed in a plane crash. Groucho used to say that Harpo had only been in love three times in his life, each time with a woman called Fleming. The second Fleming was an Anna, who was reported, in April 1916, to have sued Mr Arthur Marx for $50,000 in a breach of promise suit, but in the end settled for $50 for 'injured feelings'.

Harpo was not the marrying kind. He once told an interviewer: 'To me there are two common denominators for all movie actresses. All blondes are Thelma Todds; all brunettes are Lila Lee.'

Now the brunette was Fleming. But Harpo still hovered, for over three years. He took a new apartment at Sunset Towers, followed by a stint living in a wing of producer Joe Schenck's palatial mansion, waiting to move into a new house being built for him in Beverly Hills. He continued enjoying his friends, dating Susan, and making *A Night at the Opera*. A few months after the movie opened, MGM arranged a series of personal appearances in Europe for Harpo, to promote the film over the pond. The trip took place in the summer of 1936, and took in Rome, Milan – the real La Scala (the censors still mulling over the insults to the Italian fatherland) – Paris and London, where Harpo slummed it with the king-in-waiting, Edward VIII. According to Harpo, the King, at a reception, gave him his leg. As things turned out, Harpo should have kept it, but Edward went on to worse transgressions.

On his return, Harpo found Susan Fleming had remodelled his new dream house. They both decided they had waited long enough. On Sunday, 28 September 1936, without alerting anyone, the couple drove down to Santa Ana, rousted out a Justice of the Peace and two witnesses from the next-door firehouse, a fireman and his wife. Harpo was wearing, according to his own description: 'A squashed fedora, bright red tie, striped shirt dickie, swallow-tail coat, khaki pants and dark glasses.' His wife-to-be wore about the same. As Harpo was registered as Adolph Marx, nobody smelled a mute. The couple kept their secret until the night of Franklin D. Roosevelt's election for a second term, on 4 November.

'Mrs Marx', claimed the next day's news report, 'was happily confident that their marriage would be a success. So was Harpo.

'"He just acts crazy in the movies," the bride said.'

Lechayim.

While Harpo was still trying to make up his marital mind, and Chico and Betty were agonizing over their failing marriage, a troupe of gnomes was labouring mightily in the writers' dungeons of Metro-Goldwyn-Mayer to try and conceive Thalberg's second Marx baby.

Within days of *A Night at the Opera*'s preview, the first script proposal was logged by writers George Oppenheimer and Carey Wilson, the first an alumnus of *Flywheel, Shyster and Flywheel* and the second an MGM contractee. This was a tale of a travelling troupe of players who, organized by theatrical booking agent Cyrus P. Turntable, fetch up at a swank mansion and reduce it to chaos. ('Home Again' again?) Groucho performs as 'Vishnu the mind-reader', while Harpo has a dog-training act.

Like the Brothers' ship stateroom scene, more and more writers were piled in. A whole smorgasbord of scribes, recruited by Thalberg, churned out outlines, treatments and stories that could be hacked into a Marx Brothers vehicle. George Seaton and Robert Pirosh had done sterling work which had been ignored on *A Night at the Opera*. Will Johnstone, the oldest Marxian in the house, was also roped in like a prime steer. One 'Marx Brothers Story', dated 12 February 1936, is authored by 'Boratz, Dietz and Murra' (*sic?*). This has Groucho as patent attorney Otis B. Driftwood, and Allan Jones as an engineer with an anti-noise device to be presented at the World's Fair. The anti-noise device looks like a stubborn hangover from one of James K. McGuinness's rejected plans for *A Night at the Opera* (see previous chapter).

The studio had already pigeon-holed another Oppenheimer story (dated 26 November 1935), set in 'a fair sized town in that part of New England famous for its blue laws'. An old-fashioned hotel is owned by 'a lovable old gentleman, on the type of Al Shean, and his daughter Sylvia, our heroine. Business is terrible. Old Shean will make no compromise with modern trends and as a result the procession has passed him by.' If this was a ploy to get the real Al Shean to appear with his nephews for the first time, it didn't work. Perhaps Uncle Al thought business was not as terrible as all that, though indeed, despite a smattering of film and stage roles, the parade had left him behind. There was to be a Mrs Rittenhouse, her lawyer, Groucho, and the burlesque group, our boys, whom she is trying to ban.

Twenty-seventh December 1935: the first mention of 'Quackenbush', in an Oppenheimer-Seaton-Pirosh-Johnstone stew. But this is a 'Quackenbush Medical Building', and Groucho is still Cyrus P. Turntable. The New Year revels seem to have shaken something loose though, and by 15 January 1936, in a treatment entitled 'Peace and Quiet', we have a kind of sanatorium, the Redlands Hotel, and a bogus doctor, veterinarian Cyrus P. Quackenbush, prepared to do business. A parallel story by Will Johnstone, on 16 January, introduces a racetrack controlled by 'high powered gamblers', Allan Jones as a 'crooner in the orchestra' and Harpo as an 'eccentric trap drummer' who uses 'a surprising assortment of amusing traps and effects'.

On 7 February, 'Peace and Quiet' has become the tale of rich Mrs Standish, who has spent a fortune on an anti-noise campaign (they just won't let go of this anti-noise thing) to get absolute peace and quiet for her daughter Millicent. Sample lines – Mrs Standish: 'I have a good mind to call the police.' Groucho: 'What makes you think you have a good mind? I haven't heard you say anything smart yet.'

Well, we haven't written anything smart yet.

Well, that's why I haven't read it.

Groucho mentions eighteen scripts that went into the stew that became *A Day at the Races*. The archive contains thirty-seven items: six screenplays, fourteen outlines and treatments, and five vaudeville-act scripts. Once again, following the example of *A Night at the Opera*, the cast went on the road with its try-outs. Before that, we have once again the mystery of a George S. Kaufman intervention, though this time the playwright refused to come west and made his contribution out of New York City. We have no trace of Kaufman's contribution except a list, compiled by Seaton and Pirosh, on 29 April 1936, of all the scenes from different script versions, including a list of points attributed to a 'Kaufman script': 1. Lost and found routine at depot. 2. Mrs Standish takes Groucho on tour of sanatorium. 3. Harpo's routine in stable – equal division of everything between him and horse. 4. Touting scene at track – 'Chico touts Groucho of horse and before they have picked another one to bet on, the race is over and Groucho's horse has won.'

This is the first mention of perhaps the most famous scene in *A Day at the Races*, the 'Tutsi-Frutsi ice cream' scene, with Chico fleecing Groucho of dollar after dollar to buy a stack of breeding guides and code books. As the scene emerges later, in a succession of versions through June, it is credited to Seaton, Pirosh and Al Boasberg.

Boasberg's involvement with the script later became a bone of contention between the gag writer and the studio over the screenwriting credits: Boasberg, with Groucho's support, protested about his third placing after Pirosh and Seaton, and requested a special credit for 'Comedy Scenes and Construction'. When the studio ignored this, Boasberg demanded that his name be taken off the credits entirely, leaving Robert Pirosh, George Seaton and George Oppenheimer with the only on-screen credits for writing. The only comic element of this unfunny exchange of professional rancour was the names of Boasberg's attorneys, Gang and Kopp.

Another minor curiosity on the way to the racetrack is an outline, submitted by one Lew Lipton on 27 May 1936, of a proposed Marx story set in Russia, with the Brothers causing mayhem in a cheap boarding-house, followed by a scene with the police in a Soviet court. At the end they save the show for their friend Poliakoff's theatre, with a burlesque ballet, which Stalin, in his box, applauds wildly. A second version dated 29 May has the boys at Harpo's co-operative farm, then escaping in a sleigh over the frozen Volga. The two versions seem to indicate that rather than this being an unsolicited submission, it was another example of Thalberg farming out thinking caps in all directions, without even any unifying instructions as to the shape or nature of the result. Another synopsis attached to the above, inexplicably dated 6.1.30 (???) has 'the boys taken on a transatlantic liner Russia-bound; all are in irons, and are out into the steerage . . . Men Without a Country!'

Now there's a might-have-been to imagine . . .

In the summer of 1936, the Marx Brothers went on tour with the vaudeville sketches of *A Day at the Races*, ranging further afield than previously, and playing the centres of their old vaudeville triumphs, Minneapolis, Chicago, San Francisco. Every day the writers rewrote their scenes, and Groucho too spent hours changing lines, words, inflections, on every page. The final arbiter of what went in or out was the audience, which might roar with laughter at one combination of words but sit stone cold at another. In Groucho's line, 'That's the most nauseating proposal I've ever heard', Groucho variously tried 'obnoxious, revolting, disgusting, offensive, repulsive, distasteful, disagreeable'. But 'nauseating' got the biggest laugh. A crack by Groucho at Sig Rumann: 'Are you a fugitive from a mattress?' was thrown out, because the audience didn't seem to comprehend 'fugitive'.

After 141 performances, the Brothers were ready. Despite all Groucho's later fulminations, multiple-take Sam Wood was once again in the director's chair. Shooting began on 3 September 1936, on the MGM lot. On 8 September, Irving Thalberg went down with a bad head cold, followed by fever and a diagnosis of pneumonia. The long-fragile state of his health was taking its toll. He never recovered, and died on 15 September.

Sam Wood came on to the Marx Brothers set and said, 'The little brown fellow just died.' No one knows why Sam Wood used that phrase. Perhaps all Jews looked on the dark side to him. Irving Thalberg's burial took place on 17 September, with a ceremony at Wilshire Boulevard Temple, the Brothers joining dozens of stars who were watched sombrely by a crowd of several thousand. Within, the industry's giants, Louis B. Mayer, Adolph Zukor, the Warner brothers – Jack and Harry – sat contemplating the departure of the whirlwind that had swept them, temporarily, into the background. The producer who had refused all credits, but had consolidated the power of producers from that point on, was gone. But the machine was ready to grind on.

Production of *A Day at the Races* was shut down for three months. In the interim, as we have seen, Harpo took the opportunity to get married – perhaps it was Thalberg's death that had concentrated his thoughts on mortality and the notion of time running out. But this was the only cheerful note in the dirge. Louis B. Mayer reorganized the studio, dismantled Thalberg's production unit, took over his productions, and ordered various revisions and changes. The Marx Brothers were too valuable a commodity to be discarded, but they were to know who was the boss now.

Despite it all, once again the Marx Brothers pulled off a triumph, though not on the scale of *A Night at the Opera*. At 109 minutes in its original print, *A Day at the Races* is the Brothers' longest movie, and it certainly suffers from its *longueurs*. Allan Jones gets to sing again, in the grand water carnival sequence, but the main culprit is the carnival scene itself, with its lush fountains and dancing girls, in the manner, if not in the execution, of a Busby Berkeley routine. The double plot line combines the tale set in the sanatorium, with its star patient, Mrs Upjohn – Maggie Dumont of course ('Dr Hackenbush tells me I'm the only case in history: I have high blood pressure on my right side and low blood pressure on my left side!') – and the tale of a racehorse, Hi-Hat, which sanatorium owner Judy Standish's fiancé Gil has bought so that his winnings can save Judy from losing her life's work. It's a story oddly reminiscent of 'The County Fair', the nineteenth-century hit in which Uncle Al Shean made one of his first appearances on the stage. Serendipitous echoes. But the scenes that remain most memorable from the film are, as usual, incidental to the main plots: the 'medical' examination of Mrs Upjohn by Groucho, Chico and Harpo, in front of a fuming Siegfried Rumann (as Dr Leopold X. Steinberg); the Tutsi-Frutsiing of Groucho by Chico at the racetrack; the wooing by Groucho of siren Esther Muir (a somewhat chubby replacement for poor dead Thelma Todd), interrupted constantly by Chico and Harpo in a variety of disguises, as detectives and slapstick decorators; Harpo in Sherlock Holmes garb, led by a pack of yapping dogs. ('Who sent for these men?' Sig asks Groucho in the examination scene. 'You don't have to send for them,' Groucho replies, 'you just rub a lamp and they appear.')

The highlight of the film, however, is Dr Hackenbush himself, Groucho's second greatest creation after Captain Spaulding, forceps-born from Cyrus P. Turntable out of Quackenbush (the Q dropped allegedly because of a bevy of real-life Quackenbushes discovered hiding in the medical underbrush), conceived in writers' spit and polish. Groucho revels in the all-American quack: the hustling horse-doctor who is ready to take on all comers to claim his niche in a hierarchy of boobs and charlatans, but who can nevertheless be hustled by a transparently fraudulent race tout, in his rush to feed his greed with any available scraps. His battle royal with Sig

307

Rumann, in the examination room, is a stand-off between two hallowed American concepts: the power-mad professionalism of the medical establishment, and the small-timer, who hacks away at the roots of hypocrisy and dissimulation – 'I'm only an old country doctor with horse sense':

DR STEINBERG (Rumann): In all my years of medicine, I have never . . .
HACKENBUSH (Groucho): In all your years of medicine. Why, you don't know the first thing about medicine . . . And don't point that beard at me, it might go off!
WHITMORE: Dr Steinberg, do you remember your diagnosis?
STEINBERG: Certainly. To begin with, her pulse is absolutely normal.
HACKENBUSH: I challenge that!
STEINBERG: Challenge that? You take her pulse! . . .
HACKENBUSH: I – I don't do any pulse work. I'm an acute diagnostician! Take her pulse! Take her pulse!
Harpo snatches Mrs Upjohn's purse from her lap . . .

The other grand battle of the movie is the greatest of all screen wars between the favoured brother, Chico, and *der Eifersuchtige*, Groucho. This is another example of the way in which the Brothers, having found a routine that worked in front of an audience, locked it firmly in place. For here is the Tutsi-Frutsi scene, as written out by Al Boasberg, for the 'Marx Brothers Road Show', dated 19 August 1936, and performed, almost without change, and certainly with no risk of ad-libs, for the movie shot several months later:

Racetrack scene (Chico as Ice Cream seller):
CHICO: Get your ice cream. Your tutsi-frutsi ice cream.
(Groucho sneaks up)
GROUCHO *(to ticket clerk)*: Two dollars on Sun Up.
CHICO: Hey boss, you want something hot?
GROUCHO: No, I just had lunch. Anyhow I don't like hot ice cream.
CHICO: I don't sell ice cream. That's a fake to fool the police. I sell tips on the horses.
GROUCHO: Well keep on fooling the police and leave me alone. *(to ticket clerk)* Two dollars on Sun-Up!
CHICO *(tugging Groucho's coat)*: Sun Up is the worse horse on the track.
GROUCHO: I notice he wins all the time.
CHICO: That is just because he comes in first.
GROUCHO: I don't want him to come any better than first.

A Day at the Races: 'Get your tutsi-frutsi ice-cream!'

CHICO: Suppose you bet on Sun Up! What do you get for your money?

GROUCHO: It says up there on the board – Sun Up 10 to 1.

CHICO (*derisively*): That's the time he went home last night.

GROUCHO: Hey, that Lady Lou is no lady. She didn't get home till 8 to 5.

CHICO: What do you say? One dollar and you remember me all your life.

GROUCHO: That is the most nauseating proposition I've ever had.

CHICO: Come along, be a sport.

GROUCHO (*is tempted, wavers for a second, finally falls and pays Chico a dollar; examining envelope*): What's this?

CHICO: That's the horse.

GROUCHO: How did he get in here?

CHICO: Ice cream. Tutsi-frutsi ice cream!

GROUCHO (*reading slip inside of envelope*): ZVBXRPL – I had that same horse when I had my eyes examined.

CHICO: Ice cream! Tutsi-frutsi! Ice cream!

GROUCHO: Hey Ice Cream, come over here. What about this optical test you just slipped me here? I don't know – what does this mean?

CHICO: That's the name of the horse in code.

GROUCHO: Code?

CHICO: Look in your Code Book. That will tell you what horse you got.

GROUCHO: I haven't got a code book.

CHICO: You no got a Code Book? Just by accident I think I got one here. (*He takes a book out of the wagon*)

GROUCHO: Any charge for that?

CHICO (*shaking his head*): That's free.

GROUCHO (*happily*): Oh, thanks.

CHICO: Just-a one dollar printing charge.

GROUCHO: Well, give me one without printing. I don't care for printing. (*He throws the book back*)

CHICO (*He rehands it to Groucho*): You got to have it if you want to win. Ice cream! Tutsi-frutsi ice cream.

GROUCHO: I don't want to have the savings of a lifetime wiped out. (*He thumbs the book, mumbling*) Hey, Ice Cream, come here. I can't make head or tail out of this.

CHICO: Look in your Master Code Book . . .

(*Some more business with code books, for which there is no charge, except a delivery charge*)

GROUCHO: What do you mean, delivery charge? I'm standing right next to you.

CHICO: All right, for such a short distance I make it a dollar.

GROUCHO: Couldn't I move over here and make it fifty cents?

CHICO (*moves a couple of feet away*): Yes, but I'd move over here and make it a dollar just the same.

GROUCHO: Maybe I'd better open a charge account.

CHICO: You got references?

GROUCHO: The only one I know around here is you.

CHICO: That's no good. You'll have to pay cash.

GROUCHO: You know a little while ago I could have put two dollars on Sun Up and avoided all this. (*Fumbling for his money*)

CHICO: You better hurry or you won't get down there. Ice cream! Tutsi-frutsi ice cream!

Of course, Groucho has to buy a Breeder's Guide, and nine more books to figure out the number of the horse – 152, which of course has to be looked up in the Racing Register:

GROUCHO: I have no racing register and I'm not going to buy another book.

CHICO: You don't have to buy one. We have one down at the office in Philadelphia.

CLERK: They're getting ready to go! Boys, get your bets down.

GROUCHO (*to clerk*): Can you hold the race while I skip over to Philadelphia for a minute?

CHICO: You're a pretty good fellow. I'll look in my Racing Register. (*Chico takes out book size of postage stamp and reads*) 152 – that's Rosie!

GROUCHO: I'm lucky I met you. I would have bet on Sun Up. (*to clerk*) Two dollars on Rosie.

CLERK: Sorry, sir, but that race is over.

GROUCHO: Over? Who won?

CLERK: Sun Up. By a city block.

CHICO: Good! That's my horse.

(*The clerk pays him a wad of bills. Chico exits.*)

GROUCHO (*dejectedly*): What about Rosie?

CLERK: Can't tell you. She hasn't finished yet.

GROUCHO (*depositing his books in the wagon*): Get your tutsi-frutsi ice cream!

That voice you hear guffawing and calling out in *plattdeutsch* is Samuel Marx – Frenchy – applauding this trenchant vignette of life in the old homestead, when his sons were still in short pants. Betty Marx, on the other hand, might have seen a bitter-sweet irony in this display of Chico's familiar flair for seduction. At its deeper level, the Tutsi-Frutsi scene is a tremendous showdown between the two Great Dissimulators: Chico, the Outsider who can get away with anything, and Groucho, the Insider whose smart-cracking stratagems are a desperate attempt to conceal his essential fragility, the terrible fear of being revealed as a fraud. His suit-case, containing an old suit of clothes and a toothbrush, is ever packed, so that he can take off for the hills, for the next game of hide-and-seek with the world.

Harpo, not be outdone, has his own special scene in the movie, playing 'Gabriel' to a strange community of shack-dwelling blacks which seems to have sprung up on the other side of Sparkling Springs Lake, the unlikely locale of our story. This mawkish and bizarre scene features Ivy Anderson and the Crinoline Choir, and labours the point of Harpo as an elf for all races, a soul mate of all the dispossessed. One might rather have wanted to see the Brothers twinned with Eddie 'Rochester' Anderson, the only black actor allowed an *entrée* into white movies in any significant – if still stereotyped – role, but this was not to be.

Just as Mae West drew her singing style and much of her demeanour from black sources, so did all the jazz-hungry, dance-crazy, boogie-woogieing show people – first of Broadway, then of screen comedy – owe so much to the hot nights of razzle-dazzle away on the other side of the tracks. Only Harpo, the mute and innocent transgressor, could easily cross that line.

There was still a great deal in Hollywood that was silent – that heard, saw and spoke no evil. But in the movies, virtue always won, in the end.

'Step This Way' or How Long Can These Swans Keep Singing?

'I still think it makes a terrible play, but it makes a wonderful rehearsal.'

Chico, in *Room Service* (1938)

Groucho wrote: 'After Thalberg's death, my interest in the movies waned. I continued to appear in them but my heart was in the Highlands. The fun had gone out of picture making. I was like an old pug, still going through the motions, but now doing it solely for the money.'

Luckily for us, the fun had not gone out completely. The Marx Brothers – Groucho, Chico and Harpo – made four more movies in the next four years. *Room Service*, *At the Circus*, *Go West* and *The Big Store* have all survived as part of the canon and made the Brothers richer and more famous. Even their greatest fans, however, as well as the critics, had to admit that the best had gone before.

Critics and film historians have tended to neglect the long, arduous years of struggle, and the stage work, of comedians such as W. C. Fields, the Marx Brothers, or Mae West, which are often mentioned in passing, as prehistory. The result of this neglect is a failure to realize that, when these comedians finally came to make the movies that made them immortal, they were, to a great extent, past the prime of life; older, slower, less dynamic than they clearly were to the audiences who saw them on the stage. W. C. Fields was fifty-one years old when he made his first talkie feature, and the Marx Brothers were, Zeppo apart, passing the forty mark when they made their film débuts. By 1936, Groucho, Chico and Harpo had been performing together for nigh on thirty years, an astonishing time for siblings to remain on speaking terms, let alone so close. Now that even Harpo was married, they each had separate lives, in a Hollywood environment that, even in 1930s Los Angeles, favoured separateness, isolation and detachment.

Nineteen thirty-seven was a transitional year for the Marxes, as the implications of Thalberg's death slowly sank in. Harpo was settling in to home life with Susan, Chico continued to drive nails into the coffin of his marriage,

Zeppo and Gummo were happily hitched, and Groucho was brooding over a platonic crush he had developed for Maureen O'Sullivan, his co-star in *A Day at the Races*. She was, however, firmly married to director John Farrow, and Groucho, perhaps with Chico's example in mind, had no desire to break up his own home. Julius and Maureen went their separate ways.

For Groucho and Chico, in fact, much of the year was taken up by a depressing lawsuit over a radio sketch entitled 'Mr Dibble and Mr Dabble', broadcast the previous September.* It was the prototype of a pilot of another abortive series, 'The Marx Brothers Show', with Groucho and Chico as two shady Hollywood agents. Two other brothers, Garrett and Carrol Graham, claimed they were the authors of the skit and sued for $26,000 damages for copyright infringement. The suit was filed while Groucho and family were holidaying in Hawaii, and at first Chico was left to face the music alone. As the civil suit was buttressed by a criminal charge, Chico had to submit to being fingerprinted in the Federal Building in Los Angeles, a humiliation witnessed eagerly by the press. 'Do I have to get my head shaved too?' he asked. 'Are they going to slit one leg of my trousers?' But this was not his funniest moment. 'I've been on the stage and screen for twenty years,' he told *The Herald*. 'This is the first time I've ever been accused of stealing anything. Many other actors have used our stuff and we've never said a word.'

When Groucho returned, he and Chico settled the civil suit out of court for an undisclosed amount, only to find another suit, for $150,000, filed in August by Messrs. Henry Barsha and David Weissman, 'newspapermen and writers', for plagiarism involving material in *A Day at the Races*. In October, the criminal trial for the copyright infringement case was held. In court, Groucho and Chico claimed the sketch had been written for them by Al Boasberg but, by a stroke of ill fate, Boasberg had suffered a fatal heart attack on 18 June while walking upstairs in his house. To their dismay, the Los Angeles Federal Court jury found Chico and Groucho guilty of the copyright infringement charge. Maximum sentence could be a year in jail and a $1,000 fine. Groucho's quip of 'What's the limit we can get on a rap like this, and what's the best prison?' died in the courtroom's gloomy space. Groucho and Chico were fined the thousand dollars each, vowing to appeal. March 1938 saw the plagiarism suit in court, but the Marx Brothers were 'eliminated' from this imbroglio, which remained between the plaintiffs and MGM.

In April the Supreme Court in San Francisco upheld the conviction in the 'Dibble-Dabble' case. Groucho tried to joke that 'we might take it to

*See Appendix: The FBI and the Marx Brothers.

the United States Supreme Court, but it's pretty hot in Washington during the summer and they've got a rotten ball club there'. But he and Chico had to pay their fines. To cap a bad year, Chico got embroiled in a lawsuit brought by the widow of a gambler, Les Bruneman, who had been found shot dead in a café in Temple Street, with Chico's cheque for $2,000 in his possession. The widow claimed the cheque hadn't cleared. Chico sued in cross-complaint, asking for the return of the cheque, on the grounds that it represented a debt paid before the creditor's demise. This real-life tutsi-frutsing provided a glimpse of a part of Chico's life that further deepened his wife and brothers' anxieties. From this point on, protecting Chico from the consequences of debts to people who were in the cement overcoat business became a running concern.

Now that MGM were without Thalberg, the Brothers looked elsewhere for contracts, strengthened by the box office success of *A Day at the Races*, rated number fourteen in 1937, a respectable enough showing for a mid-budget movie. Zeppo, representing his brothers directly for the first and last time, brought in a $250,000 deal for them to appear for RKO Pictures in a version of a Broadway stage play, *Room Service*, produced in 1937 by George Abbott. The play was by John Murray and Allan Boretz, who just might be two thirds of the typographically challenged 'Boratz, Dietz, Murra,' authors of one of the discarded 'Day at the Races' outlines for Thalberg. The play was a hit, which must be barely comprehensible to anyone who views the screen version hacked out by Morrie Ryskind.

There is, from our point of view, a special interest in seeing Groucho, Chico and Harpo playing to an already fixed script, instead of the characters they had played so far. The piece has its obvious biographical echoes, with its tale of a bankrupt stage producer trying to put on a play while hanging on to the hotel rooms his troupe is staying in long enough to get a cheque from a backer. In the play, Binelli, the character played by Chico, is the director, but this is not as clear in the film. Harpo plays a character called Faker, who has one great moment, falling pretend dead out of a closet with a stage knife through his heart. The whole *mélange* includes a hotel manager who is Groucho's brother-in-law, a manic troubleshooter for the owners who wants everyone evicted, a crazy Russian waiter who wants a part in the show, the naïve author from Oswego who turns up for room and glory, an extremely young Ann Miller with whom the author falls in love, an idiot from the 'We Never Sleep' collection agency, in pursuit of the author's unpaid-for type-writer, an irate doctor, the harassed backer, a desperate turkey, and Lucille Ball, going through the paces as a go-getting secretary-cum-actress.

The three Marx Brothers are cooped up, not only by the script, but by the set, almost solely the hotel room, with a couple of corridors and alleyways for relief. At one point the young author, Davis, played by Frank Albertson, says, 'Gee, I never got arrested before for writing a play. I guess they'll take my fingerprints', to which Chico replies, truthfully, 'They got mine.' And soon after, as Harpo enters, Groucho (as producer Miller), comments: 'Well, the quartet is complete; what do we do now, sing Sweet Adeline?' But even these invocations of real life and old glories cannot lift *Room Service* from its doldrums.

In the original play, with Sam Levene, Philip Loeb and Teddy Hart in the main roles, the dialogue was somewhat more robust, with 'God damn it!' rather than 'Jumping butterballs', and Davis's play named 'Godspeed' rather than 'Hail and Farewell'. But the substitutes make little difference. There is an interest in seeing Groucho and Chico underplay their roles, with Groucho softer and more vulnerable than usual, and Chico playing, for the first time, not an idiot, but the fixer he was in real life. The director, William Seiter, was a veteran Keystone Kopper who had been directing movies on the conveyor belt since 1918. In 1933 he was at the helm of Laurel and Hardy's feature, *Sons of the Desert*. In 1938 alone, he directed four films. (Veteran crazy-comedyist Gregory La Cava was wooed, according to the *New York Times*, to take on the picture, but he clearly thought better of it.) The producer was Pandro S. Berman who, according to the memories of swimming star Esther Williams, was the only man in Hollywood who ate spaghetti with his bare hands.

Groucho had a soft spot for *Room Service*, which he considered a risk that had paid off, but it did demonstrate a problem that would plague him from then on. The more Groucho yearned to take on different roles, that would challenge him and extend his range as an actor, the more it was clear that audiences wanted him to play only one role, that of Groucho. From his experiment in *Twentieth Century*, through to his sallies into stock in the 1950s, he found his status as an icon set irrevocably, a mask that he couldn't tear off. In the end, he capitulated to it, but not without continuing bursts of rebellion. The one alternative sphere in which he could break through and still keep his audience – before television – was in his writing. His only achieved foray into screenwriting, with young Norman Krasna, entitled *The King and the Chorus Girl*, was produced and directed at Warner Brothers by Mervyn Le Roy in 1937. A thinly veiled satire on King Edward VIII's affair with Mrs Simpson, it was dubbed 'the season's silliest movie' by *Life* magazine, and sniffed at in England as an example of poor taste.

316

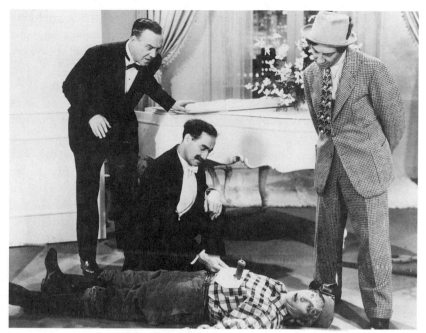

Room Service: is it foul play, or just the script?

One of the incidental pleasures of *Room Service* is a scene in which Groucho, Chico and Harpo, having persuaded the young author, Davis, to play dead in the hotel room so they can't be thrown out, stand above him singing: 'One last wee cheerio, to my friend they're calling back home . . .' – Harpo resplendent in a coal miner's cap with flickering flame. The author's play within the film, 'Hail and Farewell', climaxes with the Russian waiter proclaiming histrionically at the victory of the miners' strike that has apparently been proceeding below decks as the farce flowed upstairs: 'For this, Washington and Lincoln lived, and although I speak to you with a foreign accent, still I speak for a newer, a freer America!' – a speech delivered over Harpo's dead body, with the stage knife still thrust in his heart.

As *Room Service* was released, in September 1938, across the ocean, British Prime Minister Neville Chamberlain was meeting Adolf Hitler in Berchtesgaden, to hammer out the 'Munich Agreement' that would deliver Czechoslovakia to German rule, the German Reich having already annexed Austria. On 10 November, in Germany, officially inspired riots took place against Jews. The *Kristallnacht* – 'night of the broken glass' – brought home the fear sensed by Harpo in Berlin in 1933 and heralded the beginning of a new age of terror. The clowns were to be ever more eclipsed, and the legacy of Washington and Lincoln soon put to its most severe test. On the whole, though, America was in denial. A few commentators, such as Aleck Woollcott, had denounced fascism over the airwaves, but for most Americans, Europe's squabbles were far away, and in Hollywood, furthest away of all.

MGM was still courting the Marx Brothers, but they were playing hard to get, announcing another two-picture deal with RKO, the first to be, again, *Of Thee I Sing*. This never happened, and Groucho and Chico turned back to radio, signing up to an all-star round table discussion programme, sponsored by Kellogg's, called *The Circle*. Aleck Woollcott was in the show, with Basil Rathbone, Noël Coward, Merle Oberon and Boris Karloff. This passed the time neutrally into 1939.

But MGM was too good a catch to be ignored for long. By the spring of 1939, outlines and synopses were being turned in to the studio for the next Marx movie, first entitled *A Day at the Circus*.

The earliest outline was by Harpo's friend, Ben Hecht, and is only a little different from the plot line of the eventual movie: a rich showman, Joe Marlowe, has died leaving his circus to his son, the circus Strong Man, and the Three Marx Brothers, 'his associates as clowns and ringmasters'. The Strong Man plots to take it all, in cahoots with his sweetie, Pauline. There is a Mrs Chippendale, society dame, who gets the circus show against her will for her assembled upper-crust guests. There are eels in the bathtub, elephants in the living room, an escaped gorilla and everything we might expect from another Brothers versus Dumont imbroglio. Ben Hecht, eeled out, dropped away early, but Arthur Sheekman, in concert with another young and new screenwriter, Irving Brecher, produced a similar salad, with the pompous butler Whitcomb and the film-version Dumont, Mrs Dukesbury, already *in situ*.

Brecher was a brash New Yorker who had started out as a jobbing journalist, while sending in a stream of gags to Walter Winchell's column. Then he placed an ad in *Variety* which became famous: 'Berle-proof Gags For Sale – So Bad Even Berle Won't Steal Them.' Comedian Milton Berle, unable to resist such *chutzpah*, hired him immediately. Scripting for Berle's radio shows led on to Hollywood – via Mervyn Le Roy – and Groucho. The Marx Circus assignment was Brecher's third screenplay, after a pot-pourri, *New Faces of 1937*, and *School for Scandal* (1938).

318

By the summer, Brecher had produced, with Dore Schary, an unwieldy 143-page script which was then whittled down pretty sharply. The Thalberg scheme of on-the-road vaudeville rehearsal tours was scrapped, and the show went straight from script to studio.

At the Circus has universally been seen as a falling off; a sign, if *Room Service* were not enough, of the end of the age of Heroic Marxism. A sign of the times was the fact that Buster Keaton, ever more distant from his own days of glory, was employed by MGM to think up sight gags for Harpo. This embarrassment, at least, was not credited. But *At the Circus,* viewed today, with an eye for the tradition of film clowning, is, as was described in its time by *Variety*: 'Long on typical crazy antics of the Marxians, decidedly short on story or logic . . . with plenty of roustabout tumbling interwoven.' Returning to the familiar characters in their familiar circular battles was, nevertheless, a sound commercial move, despite the complaint of some critics, like Howard Barnes in the *New York Herald-Tribune,* that 'the Marx Brothers have almost none of the split-second timing that marked their great films of the past'.

At the Circus is appreciably slower than earlier films, but so was almost everything else in Hollywood, by 1939. As Joe Adamson has written: 'The Age of Heroic Comedy was over all around . . . Lloyd made *Professor Beware,* looked at *Professor Beware,* and quit. The Laurel and Hardy product of 1939, *Blockheads,* was hardly even worth the effort . . . There was nothing left but disintegration, demoralization, heartbreak, and Abbott and Costello.'

Surely not as bad as all that, yet! (As Adamson admits, W. C. Fields's last classics, *The Bank Dick* and *Never Give a Sucker an Even Break,* were still to come.) But there is no doubt that the fast, crackerjack pace of the great 1930s talkie comedies had slowed to a stately waltz.

At the Circus was produced by man-of-all-trades Mervyn Le Roy and directed by Eddie Buzzell, himself an old vaudeville hand. His career had begun, much like the Marx Brothers', with Gus Edwards, in 'Kid Kabaret' of 1912, another juvenile act, which introduced another Eddie, Eddie Cantor (George Jessel was another alumnus). The Brothers, at the time, were touring 'Fun in Hi Skule', but Buzzell finally caught up with them on a shared bill with *On the Mezzanine,* nine years on. After vaudeville, Buzzell became a star in musical comedies such as *The Gingham Girl* and *The Desert Song.* Buzzell was to direct the Marx Brothers' next film too, *Go West,* offering his comments about the experience in an interview with the *Brooklyn Eagle*:

'If I ever direct them a third time, I'll know the worse about my sanity . . .'

says Buzzell. 'The first Marx Brother picture I did was *At the Circus*. I left the following day for a long, leisurely jaunt through Europe to regain my composure . . . It isn't the director alone who suffers during a Marx production . . . for the cameraman also has his troubles. Wildness has no confines and the Marxes are wild. They never hit the spots they are supposed to in a moving shot . . . It isn't that they don't know any better or are not co-operative. It's just that their comedy is spontaneous . . . The camera boys tell me they once tried to solve the problem by using three cameras. One was supposed to stay with Harpo, another with Groucho, and a third with Chico, but the names confused them, and when the rushes were shown, they had all "caught" Harpo . . .'

It's good to know the Brothers were not tamed, even in 1939. *At the Circus* still has a number of mint delights, including Groucho's fourth on-screen song since Captain Spaulding, the immortal 'Lydia the Tattooed Lady' ('When her robe is unfurled she will show you the world / If you step up, and tell-her-where, / For a dime you can see Kankakee or Paree, / Or Washington crossing the Delaware . . .'). On the distaff side, the film contains perhaps the most painful of love tunes, the drippy 'Two Blind Loves', sung by Kenny Baker and Florence Rice. For the defence, we might point out a vintage Chico piano routine (though the prosecution could cite Harpo's solo in another embarrassing black jive vignette) and Margaret Dumont shot out of a cannon (though only by optical special effects).

One vignette that has always been missing from the picture is a scene introducing Groucho's legal-eagle character, J. Cheever Loophole, in a breach-of-promise trial, in which he himself turns out to be the culprit. This was shot but cut, presumably for length, and disappeared until resurrected (only on paper, with dialogue and stills) in *The Freedonia Gazette*, in 1984:

DEFENDANT'S ATTORNEY: Your Honor, the plaintiff's counsel has introduced no evidence other than this affidavit with half the pages missing.
GROUCHO: Well, affa-davit is better than none.

Well, just about. At the end of this vanished scene, Loophole dashes out of the courtroom, to be confronted by 'a quartette of Postal Telegraph boys' waving a telegram, from Chico, urging him to come and rescue the circus. But this odd glimpse of distant past messaging the present was left on the cutting-room floor.

Also left out – but at the script stage – all references, forbidden by the censor, Joseph Breen, to 'monkey glands' – as per scene where 'Loophole,

At the Circus: reunited by popular demand.

addressing the very old, shrivelled gentleman sitting with the young girl at the table, says: "Just mail them a dollar and they'll send you a monkey gland in a plain white envelope." This will automatically delete the further pointing up of this business when Loophole uses dialogue that is not in the finished script, "If you mail them five dollars I think they'll send you the whole monkey."' But, as usual, it is difficult to figure out what on earth the censor is talking about.

The picture, as it ends, does give us one properly surreal, almost Dalían moment. As the circus performs for Margaret Dumont's delighted four hundred society snooties, and the escaped gorilla pursues the villain, Carter, over the high wire, the classical symphony orchestra, conducted by the high-falutin' French maestro Jardinet, playing away on the bandstand which Chico has cut loose from its shoreline mooring, floats out to sea, past an ocean liner: Art detached from Life's vital enjoyment, speaking only to its own self-regard.

On 24 June 1939, Groucho wrote to Arthur Sheekman: 'Our picture, "A Day at the Circus," is progressing rather rapidly considering that it's our picture . . . I believe it will be much better than I thought . . . though I must admit, in establishing an alibi, that I have seen very little of the rushes. I'm getting too old for rushes – the projection rooms, or at least the ones they give us, are either a long climb or in an air-conditioned cellar, and I've decided to wait until the picture plays the Marquis before seeing it.' On 27 October, he wrote again to Sheekman: 'The boys at the studio have lined up another turkey for us and there's a strong likelihood that we'll be shooting in about three or four weeks.'

This was not the best of times for Groucho, or his brothers, despite the fact that none of them any longer had any reason to fear destitution. Even Gummo was well entrenched now as a Hollywood agent, with a client list that would include Barbara Stanwyck, Robert Taylor, Lana Turner, and Glenn Ford. His son, Robert, described the life they led at 601 Beverly Drive, plush up against the stars: 'Next door to us were John Dean and Ann Shirley. Across the street was Robert Montgomery. Down the street was the Schnozz, Durante . . . In my class I had Wallace Beery's daughter, Carole-Ann. The class behind me I had . . . Eddie G. Robinson Junior, and so on, it was all around us . . .' Groucho's own son Arthur was still hitting the tennis balls, and Miriam was developing into quite the little radical, more attuned than many to the outbreak of war in Europe. But Groucho agonized inside. In June 1940, he wrote to Sheekman:

'I'm not able to sleep anymore. You probably ask, "Why can't he sleep? He has money, beauty, talent, vigor and many teeth" – but the possession of all these riches has nothing to do with it. I see Bund members dropping down my chimney, Commies under my bed, Fifth columnists in my closets . . .' The funny man with the fake moustache was in turmoil over the fate of his country, and no doubt the grisly state of the country his grandparents had emigrated from, the Germany his mother had always considered her Fatherland. War in Europe deepened Julius Marx's concerns with American democracy, leading him to suggest to Sheekman that he might vote for the Republican candidate Wendell Wilkie in 1940, as a protest against any President, even Roosevelt, holding power for a third term in office. 'I think the only reason Roosevelt wants to run again,' Groucho wrote his friend, 'is that it prevents Mrs Roosevelt from getting him alone. He can always say, "Eleanor, you know I'm crazy about your body, but I have to meet the Spanish ambassador tonight and discuss the Czechoslovakia situation.'

The Czechoslovakia situation was, however, well past discussing by then. In September, Groucho discussed the war himself, with Chaplin at Chasen's, in the context of Chaplin's latest picture, *The Great Dictator*, while noting in wonderment, in his regular missive to Sheekman, the unprecedented event of Chaplin's paying the cheque for a six-person meal.

By this time, the next Marx Brothers picture, the other 'turkey', was getting into production, after a long series of postponements. *Go West*, in fact, had been developed as a project by Thalberg, in parallel with *A Day at the Races*. The first outline was logged as early as 15 April 1936, by Bert Kalmar, Harry Ruby and William Slavens McNutt – not a Groucho pseudonym, but an MGM payroll scribe. A composite script by Bert Kalmar and Harry Ruby was ready on 19 August 1936. In this version, the Marx Brothers were entangled with a rodeo. But whatever nag they were riding, they were soon thrown right off, as the whole project was filed away on Thalberg's death.

There was a hit comedy western shot in 1936, but this was Laurel and Hardy's *Way Out West*. When MGM returned to the project after *At the Circus*, the studio executives must have decided, in time-hallowed form, that one box office success deserved another, and what was required was to more or less copy the plot of the Laurel and Hardy movie and transfer it to the Marx Brothers. Irving Brecher and Dore Schary were, once again, brought in to mix the brew.

This time round, the Brothers succeeded in getting MGM to revive the vaudeville tour gambit that had worked so well in Thalberg days. Brecher and Schary beavered on, and in March 1940 the show went on the road, playing 103 performances from Chicago to Detroit. This way at least Groucho and the writers could hone the script's best scenes, and avoid the flatness of the previous movie.

But the script kept on changing. In a section omitted by Groucho from the published version of his 5 September letter to Sheekman (black-pencilled when the letters were prepared for publication in 1967), Groucho complains: 'Our picture has become a garbage can for the studio. The *ingénue*, who is no Helen Hayes, happens, by an odd coincidence, to be William Powell's wife . . . Cummings, the producer, is, as you know, Mayer's nephew; the unit manager is Cummings's cousin and his assistant is a son of Bill Goetz, who happens to be Mayer's son-in-law. So you see the only ones in the picture who are not related to anyone except to each other are the Marx Brothers . . .'

Eventually the whole salad was scraped on to the set. The vaudeville tour rewrites paid off, up to a point. The opening scene of *Go West* ranks as one of the Brothers' best, from Groucho's entrance *à la* Captain Spaulding with a train of black porters – 'Any of you boys got change for ten cents?' 'No sir!' 'Well, keep the baggage!' – to a classic exchange between Groucho, Chico and Harpo, with Groucho thinking he's fleecing the two tenderfoots by selling them a hat and coat, a dollar apiece, while in fact they're fleecing

Go West: tenderfoots check out the native talent.

him by taking his nine dollars change for the same ten-dollar bill they keep recapturing from his back pocket. Best line – Groucho to Chico: 'You love your brother, don't you?' Chico: 'No, but I'm used to him.' By the end of the scene Harpo has slit open Groucho's pants, Chico has flimflammed Groucho with the same logic used by the Federal Reserve to explain the national deficit, and everyone is off, somehow, to the West.

The film then limps on, through the old story of the deed to Dead Man's Gulch the railroad crooks are bent on stealing, the old prospector's beautiful granddaughter (played by Diana Lewis), a puffy, not-so-young leading man, John Carroll, and a reprise by Walter Woolf King (né Lassparri) as the villain. The only memorable stuff en route is some banter in a stagecoach, some stereotyped guff with Indians incorporating Harpo's harp solo, and a bit of comic boozing with the hotel bar girls. Then, at the end, the second of *Go West*'s *pièces de résistance* is delivered, the spectacular sight gag of a train chase in which the Brothers chop up the train's own carriages and furniture to keep the engine stoked up, foiling the crooks and arriving in time to drive the Golden Spike. (Note the echoes of Buster Keaton's *The General*!)

By this time Groucho was ready to drive the spike into his own heart, but despite mediocre box office, the Brothers prepared almost immediately for their fifth, and last, movie for Metro-Goldwyn-Mayer: *The Big Store*, released 20 June 1941 – two days before the German armies invaded Russia. The original title for the project had been 'Step This Way'. But it was more a case of 'Abandon hope, all ye who enter here.'

For material, the Brothers had raided *Flywheel, Shyster and Flywheel*, episode fifteen, and roped in Nat Perrin to recast the story, though the script, when it finally came out of the mangle, was credited to Sid Kuller, Hal Fimberg and Ray Golden. Kuller and Golden had worked with the Ritz Brothers. All that remains of the original skit, though, are the names Flywheel and Ravelli and the concept of their being guards for a big department store. Margaret Dumont was brought in for her own Marxist swan-song, as Martha Phelps, widow of the late Hiram Phelps, Department Store King. The plotting involves a crooked manager determined the books shouldn't be looked at, a lantern jawed male lead, Tony Martin, as popular singer-bandleader Tommy Rogers, who is co-inheritor of the store, and his lady love, Joan, played by Virginia Grey. The whole *mélange* was directed clunkily by veteran Chuck Riesner who had, strange to note, worked with all the comedy giants – Chaplin, Keaton, Fields back in the 1920s, but seemed here to have been brained with a mallet before stepping on to the set.

There are some funny scenes: the office of Wolf J. Flywheel, Private Detective and Bodyguard ('Bloodhounds Transfused – Fingerprints Manicured'), with Harpo as all-in assistant Wacky, with his battered old jalopy inscribed 'Welcome Home Admiral Dewey, Hero of Manila', is vintage, with some splendid flimflamming of client Margaret Dumont, but it only whets the appetite for what might have been if *Flywheel* had been properly adapted to the screen. Would that Flywheel's ingenious suggestion, in the original radio skit, that the store should give away 'a piano free with every purchase over a dollar', had been transferred to the film! Instead we have a lot of tedious mayhem with a harassed Italian couple and their eighteen children getting entangled in the beds department, and Groucho's song, 'Sing as you Sell', which involves the entire staff of the store and appears to go on for all eternity.

Chico and Harpo perform a unique four-handed piano routine, and Harpo has a lush harp solo, played in eighteenth-century courtier's costume, with his reflection accompanying him on violins in a succession of mirrors – shades, very dim shades, of the mirror scene in *Duck Soup*. As Harpo and Chico are seen performing with the grand Tommy Rogers band in a lugubrious rendition of an atrocity entitled 'Tenement Symphony', we can see the final decline of the former anarchists into the role of accompanists for the very kind of established social routines they had spent their entire artistic life, to date, tearing down. *The Big Store* rounds out *Go West*'s miscasting of the Marx Brothers as happy-go-lucky, somewhat pathetic jesters to a world that has them pegged from the start.

At the end of *The Big Store* it is not the Brothers who get to drive in the Golden Spike, but the anonymous functionary of the Square Deal Finance Company, who gets to tow away Wolf Flywheel's car, for non-payment of twelve years' instalments – one for every year the Marx Brothers had spent making talkies up to that point. In total ignominy, Groucho, Harpo and Margaret Dumont are hauled off by the forces of Capital Triumphant, protesting and struggling vainly, out of frame . . .

Groucho, for one, had been predicting this outcome for quite a while, and in April 1941 went public with his disenchantment. MARX BROTHERS, SICK OF MOVIES, TO QUIT, headlined the *Herald*: Break Up Comedy Team of 20 Years –

> The Marx Brothers, who have been chasing blondes, tinkling harps and cracking wise on the screen ever since the movies became the talkies, announced today that they were sick of picture making, abandoning Hollywood and splitting up one of the most prosperous comedy teams in show business.
>
> 'When I say we're sick of the movies,' explained burnt-corked mustachioed Groucho, 'I mean the people are about to get sick of us. By getting out now, we're just anticipating public demand, and by a very short margin. Our stuff simply is going stale. So are we.'
>
> Groucho, therefore, will become a writer of humor and perhaps a radio performer; Chico will head a jazz band with Lou Holtz, and Harpo will return to Broadway to play in a straight drama with Alexander Woollcott, and perhaps, Noël Coward . . .
>
> 'I don't drink and I don't play the races and I can afford to quit now while the quitting is good,' reported Groucho. 'I've saved my money and I don't get any fun out of picture making any more. I haven't got that old zip; that old sparkle in the eye. And when you get to feeling like that, it's not fair to the people who pay their good money to see you.'

This was not yet to be the final reel, but the separation was already an established fact. Chico had been making plans in New York for his own band since the winter of 1940. 'It's like when I was a kid and learning to draw,' he told the *New York World-Telegram*, 'I'd start to draw a horse and it'd turn out to be a boat. It's the same way with this band. I don't know what direction we're going – whether Texas or New York – I don't know who the musicians will be, whether we'll work up a whole musical comedy or become part of somebody else's show, or whether we'll end up in vaudeville or nightclubs.'

One thing was sure, this future would not include Betty. The last straw for her had been Chico's casual affair with a young girlfriend of his own daughter. From then on, when Chico was at home, he would be living in a separate part of the house from his wife. Maxine reports the dark irony of this situation: when Arthur Gordon, Chico's old partner before he joined the family act, came to have dinner with Betty and Maxine, they heard a door slam in the house. 'What was that?' Gordon asked.

Betty replied: 'It's the phantom of Elm Drive.'

Harpo, on the other hand, was experiencing his best days of domestic bliss. Marriage to Susan Fleming had transformed him into what he himself termed the 'most normal man in Hollywood'. Where Chico couldn't give up his premarital chick chasing, Harpo underwent a personality mutation and became the perfect family man. Susan could not have children, and so Harpo began adopting them, beginning with Bill, continuing with Alexander, James Arthur, and Minnie. Bill Marx once said Harpo's house had four front windows, and his ambition was to have a child in each window, greeting him as he came home from work.

Work, more often than not now, seemed to be golf at the Hillcrest Club, with friends Al Jolson, Eddie Cantor, George Jessel, Jack Benny, George Burns, Milton Berle, and even one or two gentiles. Harpo became involved, peripherally, through Charles Lederer, with the crowd surrounding John Barrymore and W. C. Fields, though, as a non-drinker, he was not in their wassailing inner circle. Writer Gene Fowler was an occasional friend, and the eccentric painter, John Decker, in whose house on Bundy Drive the Fields-Barrymore axis revelled, painted his and his brothers' portraits in the manner of Gainsborough, Franz Hals and Rembrandt.

But Harpo never lost touch with the old Algonquin favourites. A nagging bit of business had been left unfinished between Harpo, George S. Kaufman and Alexander Woollcott. On 16 October 1939, the curtain had risen on what would become George Kaufman's most successful play since *Of Thee I Sing*. Co-written with Moss Hart, *The Man Who Came to Dinner* was the Algonquinites' most incestuous project; a fitting epitaph, if more like a stake driven through the heart of the ruthless wits of the Round Table. A famous whiplash-tongued broadcaster, Sheridan Whiteside, is passing through the house of a wealthy mid-western couple on a lecture tour when he slips on the ice and becomes confined in their home. As a monstrously unwelcome guest, Whiteside becomes the bane and plague of everyone he encounters, but cannot be dislodged. The character was openly and mischievously based on Woollcott himself who, unlike worthies of our less enlightened age, delighted in his transformation into stage fiction.

A minor character in the play, an actor friend of Whiteside's called Banjo, was openly based on Harpo. He barges in during the third act and immediately assaults Whiteside's nurse. In the original production, Whiteside was played by Monty Woolley, and Banjo by David Burns. At a later run, Woollcott himself took on the role of Whiteside, guying himself with ferocious vigour and glee. But in July 1941, at Kaufman's favourite Bucks County Playhouse, located at the playwright's refuge in New Hope, Pennsylvania, another dream casting of *The Man Who Came to Dinner* was realized: George S. Kaufman as Whiteside, Moss Hart as the Noël Cowardesque Beverly Carlton, and Harpo himself as Banjo.

The *New York Herald-Tribune*, on 29 July, logged the historic moment, noting that Harpo 'contributed some of the best features of his screen technique, including the constant use of his auto-horn cane, his grimaces and a penchant for chasing girls about the stage . . .' His first words, as he rushed in and swept up the screaming nurse, were:

'I love you madly – madly. Did you hear what I said – madly! Kiss me! Again! Don't be afraid of my passion. Kiss me! I can feel the hot blood pounding through your varicose veins!'

Harpo had spoken. Nothing could be the same way again.

ACT V

The Vanishing Species

In the Hollywood Victory Caravan: Julius Henry Marx and friends . . .

30

Custody of the Moustache

COMEDIAN VANISHING, GROUCHO MARX BELIEVES:
The comedian, said Groucho Marx, is a vanishing species, and unless
something is done about it topnotch funny men may becomes as scarce
as penguins in Papeete . . . The decline of vaudeville, said Marx, is one
of the major reasons for the scarcity of comics. 'Every comedian for the
past 10 years,' he said, 'has been kidded about the time he spent in
vaudeville. Which just goes to show how dead vaudeville really is. It's
been dead for years but its end is just catching up with radio . . .'

New York World Telegram, 10 June 1938

In May 1941, while the Marx Brothers were singing as they sold in *The Big Store*, German bombers were blitzing England's cities, culminating in a massive attack on London on 10 May. Prime Minister Winston Churchill, who was out of London, at Ditchley Park, recorded the events of the day in his memoirs:

> After dinner, news arrived of the heavy air raid on London. There was nothing that I could do about it so I watched the Marx Brothers in a comic film which my hosts had arranged. I went out twice to enquire about the air raid and heard it was bad. The merry film clacked on, and I was glad of the diversion.

The diversion was *Monkey Business*, with its appropriate chorus of 'Sweet Adeline' from kippered herring barrels. In a world drowning in blood, the crazy comedians were doing their duty – providing a needful spark of sanity.

Seven months later, the war came as close to California as it ever would, when Japanese bombers attacked the US fleet at Pearl Harbor, in Hawaii, on 7 December 1941. But even this was hardly enough to shake the movie colony off its poolside deckchairs. Three months later, Groucho wrote to his friend Arthur Sheekman about 'the indifference, the blasé attitude and the smugness that seems to pervade this whole coast . . .', adding, in true Groucho style: 'And what servant trouble we're having! The local slaveys

331

have all become privy (ah, there's Mencken) to the fact that the defense industries offer much bigger salaries . . . I had no idea this was was going to disturb the luxury of my private life and I may have to write a letter to the London Times.'

Indeed, Groucho did no such thing. Instead, he and Harpo embarked on extended tours, with other show business stars, to entertain troops and workers at army camps, airfields, naval stations, arms factories, hospitals and ports from which US troops were launched towards the surreally named 'theatres' of war.

Harpo wrote about these enthusiastic GI crowds:

When I first appeared at an army camp, I had the weirdest feeling that I'd been there before. Then I realised why. It was like playing for the Russians all over again, only more so. These kids were starved for laughs, like the audiences in Moscow and Leningrad. The difference was that G.I.s didn't need plots or stories or reasons. They'd laugh at anything . . . While it lasted it was unbelievable. It was an entertainer's market. But for us on stage, it was also a time of deep heartbreak. I used to look out at the seas of young faces . . . and marvel that any of them could even crack a smile, knowing what they were going through and what they were headed for . . .

Harpo was prompted into reflecting on a Thornton Wilder story of a little girl who once asked the great playwright what a war was. 'A million men with guns go out and meet another million men with guns, and they all shoot and try and kill each other,' he had replied. 'But suppose nobody shows up?' asked the girl. To which Wilder had no answer. But the Marx Brothers had already answered her, in *Duck Soup*:

'It's too late, I've already paid a month's rent on the battlefield.'

Harpo not only travelled far and wide for the troops but was also addressing, in his own right, the challenge of the Marx Brothers' breakup. August 1941 saw him appearing with Aleck Woollcott in a summer stock production of a play called *The Yellow Jacket*, a Chinese fantasy written in 1911 by two Americans, Charles Hazelton and Harry Benrimo, played in the spirit of 'authentic' Chinese theatre. Woollcott was the Master of Ceremonies, Fay Wray played the leading lady, Chee Moo, and Harpo was the Property Man who spends the entire play silently handing props to the actors. He provides the ladder to heaven upon which Chee Moo climbs, and holds a red flag in front of a murder victim, to symbolize his demise from the stage. The play was produced by the North Shore Players and played in high school auditoriums and local halls in places like Marblehead, Massachusetts – until Pearl Harbor.

Chico, for his own part, launched his solo career one month after Pearl Harbor, having linked up with jazz band manager Ben Pollock, who had managed Benny Goodman, Glenn Miller, Artie Shaw and Jack Teagarden, at early phases of their careers. Chico's band included none of these, but assembled a group of solid musicians, names such as Marty Marcella and Bobby Clark on trumpets, George Wettling on drums, Johnny Frigo on bass fiddle, Bobby Miller on piano, along with three trombone and five sax players. The band was planned under the title of 'Chico Marx and his Ravellies', and was to follow a short series of solo radio sketches to be called 'Chico's Barber Shop'. The radio sketches never materialized, though they were to mutate, years later, into another medium. The band opened in Flatbush, Brooklyn, on 15 January 1942, moving on to the Windsor, Bronx and the Central, Passaic, NJ. Chico wrote about his début, in the *Billboard*:

'There I was, with sixteen other guys, but I certainly felt lonesome. Every fifteen seconds I'd think I was hearing Harpo blowing that automobile horn, and every other fifteen seconds I'd wish he was.'

Chico's band received lukewarm notices, since the only reason to attend was to see the world-famous Marx Brother performing fifteen minutes of his own inimitable piano solo. 'I love to work,' he told the *New York Times*, 'so I decided on the band and I'm just where I started thirty years ago, pounding the piano keys.'

Living an increasingly separate life, Chico was becoming a kind of ghost, not only in his own household, but in the world of show business that he had made his own. Instead of Groucho and Harpo, he had vocalist Siggy Lane, singing 'This Love Is Mine' and 'Dear Mom', while the band tootled 'Chattanooga Choo-Choo' and 'Deep in the Heart of Texas'. Siggy Lane was soon snatched up by the draft board, but a succession of other warblers followed. The band was accompanied by old-style vaudeville acts like 'The Manhattan Knights'. In a strange irony, Chico had regressed to the world of Uncle Al Shean, in his earliest days with the 'Manhattan Quartet'. As Paul Wesolowski wrote in *The Freedonia Gazette*:

By the end of the first few months, Chico had perfected his routine. Dressed in his familiar green hat and coat with yellow corduroys, he would shuffle out, give the band a downbeat, and shuffle off . . . [After the first numbers] Chico would come out . . . for a short monologue and then introduce 'Sugar' [singer Elisse Cooper], who would sing 'Don't

Sit Under the Apple Tree' . . . and 'I Dood it.' Then a novelty act [singer, dancer, acrobat] would be brought on. After that, Bobby Clark, band trumpeter, would come forward and sing a sentimental ballad, 'It ain't Necessarily So.' While Clark was singing and crying his heart out, Chico would sit on the edge of the bandstand eating a banana, in full view of the audience. [Due to wartime shortages, Chico was sometimes forced to use a carrot instead.] When Clark would pick up his trumpet and begin his solo, Chico would stuff the banana skin into the breast pocket of Clark's jacket . . .

The rest of the programme included a swing version of 'Pagliacci', more sentimental tunes with Chico making ironic remarks on the side, and then Chico's piano routines of the 'Beer Barrel Polka', 'Gypsy Love Song' and so on. In March, the band appeared in Cleveland, with the reviews noting, 'Sure-fire entertainment for the Palace's crowds . . . One of the big hits is the harmonica playing of Larry Adler . . . a gentleman of rare accomplishments [who] gave his own interpretation of "Blues in the Night," and played "Begin the Beguine . . ."' From Ohio the band expanded its tour further west, with one-night stands in Sheboygan, Oshkosh, Kenosha, Cedar Rapids, Sioux City. Reliving his roots, Chico was returning to the heyday, or hard days, of Minnie's boys, touching Los Angeles without lingering and heading back east, during the autumn of 1942. During that summer, he had also issued two records, with vocals by Siggy (now Ziggy) Lane and Skip Nelson. (The Hit label, numbers 7003 and 7004.) In October, the band opened a two-month engagement at the Blackhawk Café in Chicago, broadcasting highlights on a local radio show and drawing a crowd of 4,000 to a venue that was supposed to hold 500 persons.

The war intervened obliquely in Chico's life at this point, with fuel rationing forcing the band to remain in place, rather than travel, and to extend the Chicago run for two more months. It was a cold, freezing winter that year in the mid-west, as it was, in gruesome parallel, on the distant eastern front, where the German Reich was facing its first major setbacks, at Stalingrad. While German and Russian soldiers died in their hundreds of thousands in the snows of the Volga region, Chico warmed the American winter with his pistol-finger polkas.

Since Chico, unlike Groucho and Harpo, has left us no first-hand record, we have no open gateway into his inner life, apart from the memories provided by Maxine. He gave infrequent interviews, and wrote a small number of essays, about aspects of performing, the longest extant piece published in

334

Paramount's Press Book for *Horse Feathers*, about 'Making Fooling a Business'. Press puffs being suspect, as articles appearing under the performer's name were often written by publicists, it may have been Teet Carle, not Chico, who wrote:

> Frankly I don't know what comedy is. I've spent many a year as a comedian (I went on the stage back in the days when cornetists wore derbies instead of blowing into them) and still I don't know. I can tell you what people laugh at, or at least what they have laughed at. But I can't take a joke and state whether it will bring down the house or the curtain . . .
>
> All comedy, I hope to show if my lungs hold out, is based on humanness. So with the pun. Its basis is misunderstanding – and how often we are all victims of that! [Indeed! Chico then discusses pantomime, 'ad-libs' and original gags.] The primary use of the gag is by the 'ad lib' cracker, such as Will Rogers, Joe Frisco, Jack Benny, Frank Fay, William Collier, Jack Osterman, Julius Tannen and Phil Baker.
>
> Their greatest success, naturally, is confined to the stage, where they can make use of some local item or a celebrity who happens to be sitting in the audience. I do not mean that ad libbing cannot be practiced in motion pictures. But the screen is denied the local and somewhat the timely element. We must please the world and tastes change suddenly in these days.

Indeed they do. If this is Chico speaking, even through his ghost writer, we can sense a great yearning here for that vanished world when contact with the audience was the performer's daily drug. Chico, more than his brothers, was the man of the moment, a man whose taste for life was hyper-intense and immediate, giving little thought for the morrow and its unknown travails. Maxine remembers his exuberant physicality, the way he always leapt up the steps, two at a time. Susan, Harpo's wife, on the other hand, told Richard Anobile, in *The Marx Brothers Scrapbook*:

> Chico . . . liked to gamble and didn't care what it cost and what it would take away from his family . . . He didn't share the good things of the world with his family. He was always up and away . . . His enjoyment of gambling was to see if he could beat the odds. He didn't care to win; it wasn't important to him. Zep wants to have the odds in his favor. He's a good gambler and Chico was a bad gambler.

A lingering image, of the tough young street kid of 1890s New York, the eldest surviving son, living by his wits long before his younger brothers began to shuffle hesitantly towards the stage. Certainly his daughter, Maxine, did not find him unloving, but his love was like an uncontrollable force, a great tidal wave that engulfed all in its wake and then passed on, leaving the recipient reeling. His little essay of 1932 reveals two passions: the lore of the stage, and music, the abiding first love that he shared with his alter ego, Harpo. And so it may not be surprising that, reading between the lines of his life, we might conclude that Chico's most relaxed years were spent, not as a Marx Brother on the comic stage or screen, but as the show-business ghost, with his jazz band, traversing the hinterland of America while the world was falling apart overseas.

Brother Groucho, however, was having a tougher time answering the sixty-four-thousand-dollar question: what do you do when, at the age of fifty-plus, your best work, that established your fame and your fortune, lies behind you – but you are still full of the vim and vigour of life, searching for new challenges, despite the realization that the years past cannot be topped?

Harpo had entered his golden years, blissful in marriage, while Groucho's marriage was falling apart. Groucho said about the Brothers' breakup: 'We went our separate ways: I got custody of the mustache, Harpo kept the blond wig and Chico bought a new Buick.'

But Groucho's separation from his wife, which had been creeping up for several years, finally boiled over when, in June 1942, Ruth sued for divorce: 'Wife failed to see anything funny in Groucho jokes' said a headline of 29 June. 'His wife of 22 years, Mrs Ruth Marx, accused him of playing practical "jokes" which were "cruel and inhuman" and which caused "physical pain."' The couple had separated in December 1941, the press stated, after Groucho had told Ruth: 'This can't go on. We will just have to wind this thing up. Either you get a divorce or I will get one.' Said *The Herald*:

> The comedian did not contest the divorce, and a 31 page property settlement was filed with Judge Kauffman, providing for alimony payments of $10,000 per year for the next two years and 25 per cent of Marx's net income thereafter. The Marxes' two children, Arthur, 20, and Miriam, 15, were placed in joint custody of the couple . . .
> although Miriam will live with her father and Arthur will choose his residence. The comedian's legal name was given as Julius H. Marx in the divorce proceedings.

Ruth's alcoholism was not mentioned by the press, as both sides had evidently agreed to keep the sad secret concealed. Neither side cited infidelities, though Hector Arce claims a fling for Ruth with a dance instructor on the way back from their last Hawaiian vacation, and several short flings for Groucho while on run-up vaudeville tours. Groucho remained extremely touchy about the hints of physical abuse in Ruth's suit, and typically told Arce: 'I've never hit a woman except in self-defense.' Groucho's continual barbed remarks to Ruth, however, such as his insults about her 'concentration camp' food, and his put-downs of her intellectual shortcomings, were as painful as any actual blows.

Ruth would eventually remarry, in 1946, a stage manager and distant relation of her family, John J. Garrity. Groucho consoled himself, in the immediate trauma of the divorce, with the continuing sales of his second book, *Many Happy Returns*, which had been published in January, 1942. This was composed of a *mélange* of essays lampooning the Internal Revenue Service, including the deep-felt poetic sentiment: 'The more the moolah / You make in your racket / The quicker you go / In a higher bracket.' In the wake of Pearl Harbor, however, jokes about taxation, however sellable, were hardly uppermost in the mind.

Responding to the patriotic fervour, Groucho joined up in the spring on a morale-boosting junket across country under the title of the 'Hollywood Victory Caravan'. This was a special train, complete with dining room and barber shop, crammed chock-full of Hollywood's Who's Who: Cary Grant, Bing Crosby, James Cagney, Pat O'Brien, Claudette Colbert, Merle Oberon, Joan Bennett, Olivia de Havilland, Bob Hope, Laurel and Hardy, Bert Lahr. The tour opened in Washington on 30 April, after a big garden party at the White House with the President and Mrs Roosevelt, and closed in San Francisco on 19 May. Groucho developed a new unrequited crush, on Miss de Havilland, but she had eyes only for dashing director John Huston, who had an advantage over them all by being in uniform.

The entire Marx Brothers clan was now out west – Zeppo still managing his mainly theatrical agency, and Gummo well ensconced as one of Hollywood's most successful agents. Gummo was famed throughout the movie colony for his straight dealing, working with his clients often on a handshake basis alone. As his son Robert related:

'He had this large stable of stars, but his real forte was in writers, directors and producers, and that's where he had a huge pool of talent that he represented. No matter who I spoke to over the years, people that had known Dad in the business said to me that he was an incredibly honest man . . . whatever his word was, that was it, and his concept with his stars was, he had no contract with them neither, he said, look, if I represent you well, you'll stay with me, if you're unhappy with me, then leave. And he built a very nice business . . .'

Keeping brother Groucho in his own nice business was not proving all that easy. During 1942 he was a semi-regular on the 'Rudy Vallee Sealtest Show', which put food on the table, but provided little fodder for the soul. Groucho wrote to Arthur Sheekman of an offer of a role in an Offenbach operetta, *La Vie Parisienne*, but this came to nought. In July 1942, a month after his divorce, Groucho wrote to Sheekman about a new consolation:

'Dame Rumor hit it over the head. Head over heels is right . . . She's far too good for me but every man thinks that when he's enamoured . . . this girl had two years at Stanford and a year at UCLA. The only fly in the ointment is that she's 22 and I'm 97 . . . One day, without flinching, I told her how old I was. She said "Who cares?" and went on talking.'

But nothing seems to have come of this either. Groucho, December 1942, to Sheekman:

I am leading a quiet, sinless life. A good deal of my time is spent in the balcony or shelf of the Marquis Theater . . . I sit alone in the balcony, alternately smoking and sleeping. I used to sleep on Ruth's shoulder when we were married – now I don't even have that . . . This theater, by the way, is utterly devoid of nookie. There's a girl that comes every night but she stays in the box office, attempting to sell tickets. I have a hunch she's the manager's wife. You can be sure of one thing, Sheek, old boy, nookie will never die out. It's as old as the hills, particularly the kind I get . . .

In February 1943, Arthur Marx was married to Irene Kahn, daughter of Gus and Grace, Groucho's old song-writing friends. Groucho was left with doting daughter Miriam to keep him company at the Marquis. Gummo, however, was galloping to the rescue, with an offer from a new sponsor, Pabst Blue Ribbon Beer, for a half-hour show on CBS radio. As *Newsweek* remarked, after the show aired, late in March:

During this half hour, for a reputed $2,500 a week, the predatory Groucho leeringly quips with his vocalists, Virginia O'Brien and Donald Dickson. As host of a full-fledged variety show, he also has command of announcer Dick Joy, Robert Armbruster's orchestra and any guest star who has the stamina to stand up under a half-hour of Marxist dialectics. Among those already committed to the ordeal are Joan Bennett, Hedda Hopper, Lucille Ball and Charles Laughton.

Without Chico, Harpo or Zeppo, and courtesy of Gummo, Groucho was reinventing himself as a solo performer. It may have seemed, at the start, just a minor ploy to keep the wolf from the door, to afford those alimony payments, and to drown his sorrows and fears of loneliness in work. But fate decreed that Pabst Blue Ribbon Beer was to be the hops from which, in its own maturing process, an entirely new Marx brew would be distilled . . .

Of Thee I Sing – From 'Dear Mir' to
The Almost Last Hurrah . . .

All this has been okayed by the Hays Office, *Good Housekeeping* and the
survivors of the Haymarket Riots; and if times are ripe, this picture can
be the opening gun in a new worldwide disaster . . .

Groucho (letter to Warner Bros., 1946)

On 17 November 1941, Groucho wrote to his daughter Miriam's boyfriend,
Dick Comen, who had been inducted into the Navy and, Miriam had told
her father, was experiencing some age-old problems:

Dear Dick,
    I am reluctant to advise you about your life. I doubt whether I am
qualified to do that. I am constantly making mistakes of my own and
I'm sure I'll continue to do so as long as I live. However, you must snap
out of your dejection. You must also learn not to be surprised when you
encounter anti-Semitism. This has, to my knowledge, existed for at least
twenty centuries, but I'm sure that history will prove (despite the fact
that it still flourishes all over the world) that it is definitely decreasing.
Your case is not an isolated one . . . It is bigotry based on ignorance and
it will only be solved as the bigots become educated. Needless for me to
tell you, though I intend to, it is up to you to comport yourself in such a
manner that you will eventually gain their respect.

To Miriam, Groucho wrote, on 29 April, 1942, from the Mayflower Hotel,
Washington: 'Tomorrow we are having tea at the White House. I hope they
have pumpernickel.'
    Hollywood in the early 1940s was a land of make-believe in more ways
than one. The United States that was swept into war by the Japanese attack
on Pearl Harbor was a country split by major divisions on the central issue
of 'isolation' versus 'engagement'. Powerful forces opposed America's
entrance into the war, particularly against Nazi Germany. The pro-German
'Bund' was the foremost funnel for Nazi propaganda and propagandists.
But spies, and what were later to be termed 'fifth columnists', were not a

requirement of American isolationism. The fear of the 'Un-American foreigner', once the Catholic, then the Jew, and always the black, was a deeply ingrained force in American affairs. Traditional 'Americans' were also often anglophobes, reliving the War of Independence against the British Empire which was now, in the view of many, receiving a long-overdue comeuppance. Both Washington and Jefferson had warned about 'foreign entanglements', though what the founding fathers would have thought about the snuffing out of France was a point that got lost in the argument.

The Japanese attack led to another phenomenon, the internment of all persons of Japanese origin, whether they were US citizens or not. This caused many in Hollywood to lose their gardeners, rendering this policy highly unpopular with the élite. But involvement with the war in Europe also deepened the hostility of forces that had always been against the movie colony, and had been accusing it of poisoning the well springs of America, and in particular America's youth, from silent movie days, when the Fatty Arbuckle scandal had first galvanized the zealots of censorship and cultural control. Burton Wheeler, Montana Democratic Senator and stalwart of the America First Committee, lambasted the movie makers for conducting a 'violent propaganda campaign intended to incite the American people to the point where they will become involved in this war'. Senator Nye of North Dakota went further, stating that 'in each of these companies there are a number of production directors, many of whom have come from Russia, Hungary, Germany . . . [who are] interested in foreign causes'. A prominent American hero, Charles Lindbergh, was another mouthpiece of isolation, describing American Jews openly as the 'principal war agitators'.

Present-day commentators have seized on the Jewish angle, the overwhelming presence of first-generation Jewish immigrants at the head of the major studios – Louis B. Mayer, the Warner brothers, Harry Cohn, Samuel Goldwyn, Zukor and Lasky – to argue both that these moguls' assimilative ambitions created the Hollywood myth of an idealized melting-pot, and that their reluctance to stand out as Jews faced with Nazism led to the dearth of anti-Nazi films from Hollywood studios. This kind of analysis, unashamedly ethnocentric, but with a peculiar echo of traditional anti-Semitic claims, puts the cart before the horse. The American melting-pot dream was no more Jewish in origin than it was German, Polish, Irish, Italian or specific to any one immigrant group. (Only black Americans, for obvious racialist reasons, found their path to assimilation blocked.) Early Hollywood was a seething pot-pourri of émigrés of all nations. Chaplin, a non-Jew (but assumed by the Nazis to be Jewish because of his political sympathies) lampooned the Immigrant as the poverty-stricken tramp who yearns for respectability and acceptance only to kick it in the pants when it arrives. And the Marx Brothers, quintessential non-Jewish Jews, carried the archetypes of multi-ethnic vaudeville to the pinnacle of talkie comedy culture. 'This program', calls Groucho in *Animal Crackers*, 'comes to you from the House of David.' But it could equally have come from 'Smith Brothers Shredded Wheat' or the 'Wee Kirk of the Heather'. As Roscoe W. Chandler riposted to Chico who unmasked him as Abie the Fishman: 'Say, how did you get to be Italian?'

America is a state of becoming, where every individual can reinvent him or herself, where changing your name from Issur Danielovitch to Kirk Douglas is a *sine qua non* of the process. *E pluribus unum.*

But there is no doubt that in the 1940s Hollywood's Jews experienced a powerful jolt to their comfortable belief that, in Groucho's naïve words to Dick Comen, anti-Semitism 'is definitely decreasing', and the bigots would eventually become educated. It was not only the Jews who feared polarization and the underlying potential for ethnicity to undermine the American dream, as events in our own day can demonstrate. And so when America, and Hollywood, went to war in the 1940s, the melting-pot was the rallying cry.

The spirit of Hollywood, nevertheless, dreamed on, in the sun, under the tall palm trees. Groucho continued to tour army camps and navy bases through 1943 and 1944, while recording for Pabst Blue Ribbon. Miriam, sixteen going on seventeen, and a card-carrying radical in her own right, often visited backstage at the recording studio where Groucho was schmoozing with the other performers, his writers – Artie Stander, Fred Fox, Selma Diamond – and producer Dick Mack. (At one time there were twelve writers on the show.) During one visit Miriam met ex-Dead End Kid Leo Gorcey and his young wife, Kay, who swiftly became a close friend. The Gorceys' marriage was a farce, as Leo was a violent man whom Kay feared intensely. Miriam persuaded Groucho to take Kay into his house for her temporary protection. The consequences were not as Miriam had imagined. This time Groucho indeed fell head over heels in love, and Kay decided to divorce Leo Gorcey.

However, Groucho's abiding love during this period remained his rebellious teenage daughter. A typical letter, written while on tour, from Okmulgee, Oklahoma, is dated 17 July 1944:

Dear Gooch,
     Sunday morning in Okmulgee. It is a hundred and four this morning

342

and the only sounds are the buzzing of flies and the tolling of the church bells. I tried to take a walk down the main street, but there is no shade and after a block of aimless wandering past a few chain stores I ducked back to the comparative cool of the hotel.

I have had very little mail from you, three letters and a phone call. I hope, by the way, that the phone call and the wire have cleared up whatever confusion you had in your mind about my attitude concerning your job . . .

I have had an opportunity to do a little reading on this trip and finished two of Bemelman's books. The one is a sort of travelogue and though interesting, too much of it becomes a bore. The other one, however, *Now I Lay Me Down to Sleep*, a book of the month, is merely wonderful, and I want you to read it when I return. I think you will find this a little over your head in spots (yes, I know you have read Santayana but some of his allusions you cannot understand), but it's a great book . . . All my love to you and kisses and I am eager to see your beautiful but sulking face again.

Your Perspiring Padre.

These letters to Miriam (published by her in 1992), reveal a quite different Groucho from the wisecracking, put-downing, aphoristic curmudgeon of his other public and private letters to enemies and friends. By now he had relinquished Arthur to the worlds of tennis and matrimony, not to speak of the US Coast Guard, which claimed his services in 1942, and it was Miriam who became her father's intellectual companion. From a letter dated 18 October 1945:

Dear Mir,

You conclude by saying, 'What do you think of the world's plight and what about the London Council?' A scientist by the name of Oppenheimer testified yesterday before Congress that it was conceivable that in the very near future forty million people could be exterminated with a series of atomic bombings. I agree with you that Attlee is not distinguishing himself but you must realize that he inherited a tough problem from Churchill. Churchill is certainly lucky that he got out from under. Here's a nation that has been ravaged and semi-pauperized by this last war, a small island whose resources alongside of ours are minute – I don't think anyone could have done much better. The Labor Party after the last war inherited the same giant headache and they were finally thrown out by the Conservatives. This may well happen again.

The end of the war had caught Groucho in San Diego, on tour for the vaudeville-style testing of *A Night in Casablanca* (of which, more anon). It was a town 'full of sailors and mildewed buildings', as he wrote to Miriam a few days later, from Oakland: 'Armistice Day was really something in San Diego. The police feared the inevitable riots and closed everything. The result was it was impossible to get anything to eat, and if it hadn't been for the popcorn that was sold in the movie theatres, the whole town would have starved to death.'

Groucho had married Kay on 21 July 1945, one month after her formal divorce from her first husband, as reported by the *Los Angeles Times*:

> Without mustache or cigar or any of his film comedian brothers, but full of wisecracks, Julius (Groucho) Marx, 54, yesterday married Catherine Mavis Gorcey, 24, former wife of Dead End Kid Leo Gorcey and daughter of an Atlanta (Ga.) candy company executive.
>
> The marriage ceremony was performed by Justice of the Peace O. Benton Worley at 8152 Sunset Blvd., the home of the best man, Arthur Sheekman, and his wife, Gloria Stuart, film actress, who gave the bride away.
>
> Marx, who was divorced by his first wife, Ruth Marx, four years ago, said he was going to stay on his honeymoon 'until the Hollywood Stars win a ball game.' Later he said his next picture, filming of which starts in three weeks, will keep him in Hollywood.

Pabst Blue Ribbon had finally un-Grouchoed itself in January 1944, on the company's 100th anniversary. The reasons for this are not clear. Hector Arce reports two rumours: one that Groucho had rebuked the sponsor's young son during a billiards game at the boss's home with the unwise words: 'Fuck off, kid.' The other version was Groucho's own tale that he had got one of the older Pabst sons drunk on Miller's High Life, an unlikely process. However the rift had occurred, Groucho was left with only the army tours to occupy him professionally. Harpo was on tour separately, spending his leisure time building up his adopted family: baby Alexander, adopted in 1943; then James Arthur and Minnie, adopted in 1944, to join seven-year-old Billy.

The era of the Round Table had finally ended with the death of Alexander Woollcott. Aleck suffered a fatal heart attack on 23 January 1943, in the midst of a radio panel discussion on the civilian role in the war effort. He collapsed while in full throttle, attacking the isolationists and enemies of his hero, Roosevelt. Harpo wrote that, according to a CBS employee who was present, Woollcott's last gesture, as he was carried out on a stretcher, was to lift his big black floppy hat and place it over his face. His old friends, Harpo, Ruth Gordon, Neysa McMein, George Kaufman and all, gathered for the last time at the Algonquin.

'When you mourn something irreplaceable,' wrote Harpo, 'you don't mourn for the thing you lost. You mourn for yourself.'

The sirens, nevertheless, were calling. The Marx Brothers may have proclaimed the demise of their act, but no one wanted to attend the funeral. Deep in the wilds of Hollywood, where the tom-toms were still pounding out their litany of joy and merry-making, despite four years of war and draft boards, a producer named David Loew, son of MGM's co-founder, Marcus Loew (the one who was neither Metro nor Goldwyn nor Mayer) plotted the resurrection.

The Marxian Lazaruses were reluctant, but the catalyst, so the story goes, was Chico. Throughout the war years, Chico continued touring, taking time off only for a short illness in the winter of 1942–43 (during which Harpo stood in for him for one week at the Cleveland Palace), and a vacation in the summer of 1943. In October the 'Chico Marx Hollywood Revue' was playing the National Theatre in Louisville. In November he was in New Orleans with something called the 'Chico Marx Hollywood Cavalcade'. Everywhere he went Chico continued to indulge his after-hours pastime of gambling until, once again – as had occurred during the tour of *Animal Crackers* – he fell foul of gambling's not-so-hidden patrons, who began demanding their pay-off. If this did happen on tour, it makes sense to assume that Chico was in some trouble, since he could not count on the friendly credit he could obtain, up to a point, in his home town of Los Angeles. Unlike star-struck mobsters like Bugsy Siegel, these mid-west gangsters had little time for celebrities. On the other hand, if Chico were in real danger, it seems unlikely that Harpo or Groucho, despite the latter's vehement refusal to fund his brother's vice, would not chip in a few bundles of the folding stuff. Even Betty, though estranged, never turned against Chico and, according to Maxine, gave him half the $300,000 securities Groucho had handed her to protect herself from Chico's depradations. Of course, he lost it all.

But the legend that the Marx Brothers made their last two movies only to save Chico from the gangsters is another of those superficially attractive tales. Groucho, in particular, was aching for a return to movies, as his later solo appearances would show. On 23 September 1945, he wrote to Miriam: 'As you know, I am not particularly proud of my radio appearances, and only do it to keep my hand in and make a little money.' Harpo, too, was merely ticking over, and was in any case not the hardest of nuts to crack, if two out of three were weakening.

And so *A Night in Casablanca* was born.

One of the most familiar Marx Brothers stories is the almighty spat that *A Night in Casablanca* caused between the Marx Brothers and Warner Brothers, producers of that fine piece of cinematic bric-a-brac, *Casablanca*, starring Humphrey Bogart and Ingrid Bergman. Loew and his writer, Joseph Fields – *Ziegfeld Follies* veteran and son of the famous vaudevillian Lew Fields (Daisy Dumont's employer) – had concocted a spoof with characters called Humphrey Bogus and Lowan Behold. Getting wind of this *lèse-majesté*, Warner Brothers' legal department claimed the rights for the title name 'Casablanca'. Groucho's reply, on behalf of the whole Marx team, has become an oft-quoted classic:

Dear Warner Brothers:

Apparently there is more than one way of conquering a city and holding it as your own. For example, up to the time that we contemplated making this picture, I had no idea that the city of Casablanca belonged exclusively to Warner Brothers . . .

It seems that in 1471, Ferdinand Balboa Warner, your great-great-grandfather, while looking for a shortcut to the city of Burbank, had stumbled on the shores of Africa and, raising his alpenstock (which he later turned in for a hundred shares of the common) named it Casablanca.

I just don't understand your attitude. Even if you plan on re-releasing your picture, I am sure that the average movie fan could learn in time to distinguish between Ingrid Bergman and Harpo. I don't know whether I could, but I certainly would like to try.

You claim you own Casablanca and that no one else can use that name without your permission. What about 'Warner Brothers?' Do you own that, too? You probably have the right to use the name Warner, but what about Brothers? Professionally, we were brothers long before you were. We were touring the sticks as The Marx Brothers when Vitaphone was still a gleam in the inventor's eye, and even before us there had been other brothers – the Smith Brothers; the Brothers Karamazov, Dan Brothers, an outfielder with Detroit; and 'Brother Can You Spare a Dime?' . . .

This letter went on at some length (see *The Groucho Letters*) but did not mollify Warner's lawyers, who fired off another letter asking for the movie's plot line. Groucho topped himself with an even stranger note, describing his role in the movie as 'a Doctor of Divinity who ministers to the natives, and, as a sideline, hawks can openers and pea jackets to the savages along the Gold Coast of Africa'. Chico is 'working in a saloon, selling sponges to barflies who are unable to carry their liquor. Harpo is an Arabian caddie who lives in a small Grecian urn on the outskirts of the city . . . There are many scenes of splendor and fierce antagonism, and color, an Abyssinian messenger boy, runs riot. Riot, in case you have never heard, is a small nightclub on the edge of the town.'

This version was, in skewed fashion, not a bad description of the movie, as it turned out, but Warner Brothers requested clarification, resulting in a third Groucho missive: 'Since I wrote to you, I regret to say there have been some changes in the plot of our new picture, *A Night in Casablanca*. In the new version I play Bordello, the sweetheart of Humphrey Bogart. Chico and Harpo are itinerant rug peddlers who are weary of laying rugs and enter a monastery just for a lark. This is a good joke on them, as there hasn't been a lark in the place for fifteen years . . .' And so forth. 'This, as you see,' Groucho wrapped up, 'is a very skimpy outline. The only thing that can save us from extinction is a continuation of the film shortage.'

It has since been alleged that the above exchange was in fact a promotional stunt concocted by the publicists for the movie, though Warner Bros. took it seriously. As all is fair in love and Hollywood, the Marx Brothers proceeded to plan. The real sweetener for the Brothers (Marx, not Warner, Smith or Karamazov) was a revival of the pre-shooting vaudeville tour, which took place in the summer of 1945 despite being cut short by Groucho's wedding and by the August armistice with Japan. We can only imagine the synchronicity of the Marx Brothers romping about on stage in fez and baggy pants while the atomic bomb was being dropped on Hiroshima. Uncomprehending, Groucho could only respond to that cataclysmic event with silence.

As pre-production continued, Joseph Fields's jokes turned out to be pretty flat and a whole gaggle of new writers was drafted in. The names Tulina, Howard Harris, Sydney Zelinka were mentioned, as well as

347

Groucho and Brothers themselves. Back at the studio, Roland Kibbee, radio gag writer for Groucho, Fred Allen and Fanny Brice, was brought in to shore up the screenplay. The director, Archie Mayo, had already been assigned. The Marxes got along with him fine, as well they should, as he had a pedigree as long as your arm in helming pictures such as *Bordertown* (1935), *The Petrified Forest* (1936, with the real Humphrey Bogart), *Black Legion* (1937), *Charley's Aunt* (1941), with Jack Benny, and over fifty other titles. Strange to tell, though he lived until 1968, *A Night in Casablanca* (1946) was his next to last movie . . .

Another uncredited contributor to the Marxian couscous was the then cartoonist Frank Tashlin, swept up to provide sight gags for Harpo, and who was later to become one of the few rays of comic light of the 1950s (*The Girl Can't Help It, Will Success Spoil Rock Hunter?*, and those Jerry Lewis movies that were actually funny). Thus fortified, the Marxes swung into action.

Once again, many changes were made on the road from script to final screen version. One interesting omission was an opening sequence with Groucho – now renamed Ronald Kornblow, instead of Humphrey Bogus (maybe Warner Brothers' letters were not all flannel), running the Desert View Motel. According to this version, headed '3rd Partial Revision: September 5, 1945', the picture opens 'Exterior Desert, Day. Only sand and sky are visible. Camera slowly pans to a hand-painted sign sticking in the sand, reading:

Free Parking.

This is the 'DESERT VIEW MOTEL – OUT OF THE HIGH TENT DIS-TRICT'. Inside, another sign reads: 'PLEASE CLOSE YOUR TENT FLAP BEFORE LEAVING' –

Close shot – office: Groucho is revealed reclining on the mattress. He wears an ill-fitting white linen suit topped off by a red fez. Near him rests an elaborate oriental water-cooled pipe on which he is drawing, through a long corded tube. The pipe is rigged so that there is a cigar in the far attachment . . .
A giant Arab emerges from the tent marked "2" –

GROUCHO: Checking out, eh?
Veiled Arab girls emerge one by one from the tent –
GROUCHO (*signing them out*): And Mrs Shrak Abdullah! (*another girl emerges*) And Mrs Shrak Abdullah! (*another girl emerges*) And Mrs Shrak Abdullah!

This continues for a considerable number of Mrs Shrak Abdullahs, prompting Groucho's ticking off: 'Bungalow number 2, the bridal suite . . . Shark [sic] Abdullah and twenty-eight wives for twenty-seven days (correcting himself) . . . twenty-seven wives for twenty-eight days . . . I'd have charged you for an extra wife if you weren't on your toes – and it takes quite a man to be on his toes with twenty-seven wives. I'd be on my heels.' This last phrase is crossed out on the page and replaced with – 'You were almost charged up – with twenty-eight wives. A guy's got to be charged up to have twenty-eight wives. That'll be a hundred and forty francs.' The Arab pays and stalks off. Groucho: 'I don't envy him. Remember, every one of those wives has a mother!'

Groucho then finds a spare wife left sobbing in the bridal tent. He consoles her: 'Men are ten cents a dozen.' She says: 'He'll come back for me.' Groucho: 'Well, he'd better hurry. Remember, the management is not responsible for wives left over thirty days.' He adds, passionately: 'Don't be a fool, come away with me.' Girl: 'I'll never leave here. I'm a part of Africa, and Africa is a part of me.' Groucho: 'Well, at least I'm seeing the best part of Africa.'

But, alas, none of this is in the movie. Nor is Chico's account of his camel taxicab rates:

A Night in Casablanca: Frederick Giermann as Kurt, Lisette Verea as Beatrice, Sig Ruman and an elf.

CHICO: Twenty francs for a camel with two lumps, and ten francs for a
camel with one lump.
GROUCHO: What do you charge for a camel with no lumps?
CHICO: A camel with no lumps is a horse.

Instead of all this offensively promising orientalist folderol, we have, in
the movie, an overwhelming emphasis on the spoof plot line of a villainous
Nazi, Heinrich Stubel, played by Sig Ruman (new spelling, same
apoplectic face), trying to take over the Hotel Casablanca where he and his
cronies have hidden looted treasures before the end of the war. Groucho is
the sucker brought in to manage the hotel by the French Governor and the
heavily unshaven policeman Captain Brizzard (Groucho; 'I've seen five o-
clock shadow but this is ridiculous'). Chico is unimaginatively named
Corbaccio and Harpo is Rusty, Sig's abused valet. Charles Drake and Lois
Collier moonlight as the young lovers, though they do not, mercifully, sing.
The one who does sing is Lisette Verea as the Nazi's moll Beatrice Reiner,
beating out a Kalmar, Ruby and Ted Snyder song: 'Who's Sorry Now?'

Well, almost everybody, it seems. Groucho's letters to Miriam, during
shooting, show him ill at ease at having to cross the picket line of studio
workers who were on strike at the time to force the producers to accept their
union. Groucho was a supporter of union rights, but his bread was buttered
on the other side. Added to this, some of Miriam's young radical friends had
joined the picket line in solidarity. Groucho's letters to Miriam are full of politics (such as the comments on Churchill and Attlee quoted earlier) and comments on movies he has enjoyed, such as the recent release *Mildred Pierce* and
the Gershwin biopic *Rhapsody in Blue*. Miriam sends her father a prose piece
on Mrs Roosevelt and Groucho replies, refusing to judge her literary efforts.
While still shooting, Groucho is apparently moonlighting on 'The Dinah
Shore Show', unwilling to cut off his radio contacts. On 24 November he
writes to Miriam about his exhaustion with the rigours of movie making:

> I want a rest when I complete this. I want to sit down and read, and
> sleep and listen to music and go to the movies and arise when I please,
> not at the whim of some stupid bastard known as a unit manager, who
> apparently gets a sadistic delight on summoning actors to the set six
> hours before they are needed. Well, it will soon be over and some day it
> will all seem like a bad or a good dream, depending on whether it is a
> good picture or not.

In early December the film was finished and viewed, at a length of two hours: 'Archie Mayo says it's one of the best pictures he's seen, but, oh boy, can Mayo be wrong.' In early January the film was previewed at Huntington Park, at one hour and fifty-three minutes, with what Groucho termed 'a semi-juvenile audience, the kind that all the theatres seem to get on Friday nights . . . They laughed a bit, but mostly at Harpo. Either they didn't understand my stuff or they weren't amused. We are taking twenty minutes of dead stuff out of it . . . David Loew agrees with us that Mayo turned in an extremely inept piece of directing, but that's over now and can't be remedied . . .'

Groucho professed himself terribly depressed at this preview – 'We worked so long and hard on this, and thought we had it so solid and tight, and then to see reams of it emasculated by that fat idiot, well it was heart rending . . . I am sure that it will be better than *The Big Store*, but it will never be another *Night at the Opera*.'

Desperate cutting reduced the film to the ninety-three minutes we now have. Groucho's judgement stands the test of time: *A Night in Casablanca* is far below the Marx Brothers' peaks, but not as low as the bargain basement of *The Big Store* or the ground floor of *Room Service*. The Brothers are back, in good wisecracking spirits, if slowed down by age, a certain depleted energy, and Mayo's stolid stewardship.

There are, nevertheless, some fruity moments: Frank Tashlin's sight gags for Harpo included the classic, 'Say what do you think you're doing, holding up the building?' – upon which Harpo lets go and the wall comes down; Harpo blowing bubbles through a pair of eyeglasses, and pulling out an enormously long cork from a wine bottle; lifting the flame from a candle and nibbling at it; eating the teacup, and so on; Chico's 'Drive Yourself Camel' or 'Chameau à Piloter Soi-Même'; Groucho's echoes of *Cocoanuts*: 'The staff? Assemble the guests, I'll tell 'em what I expect of them!' and other *bons mots*: 'Join me!' 'Why, are you coming apart?' Ogling Beatrice's waggling behind: 'That reminds me, I must get my watch fixed.' The scene where Harpo and Chico pile tables and chairs on the nightclub dance floor to get tips from the queuing patrons, as Groucho, mincing along with Beatrice, comments, 'This place has a wonderful floor show, too bad it doesn't have a floor.'

Chico constantly interrupting Groucho's tryst with Beatrice is a faded echo of *A Day at the Races*: 'Hey boss, you got a woman in there?' 'She lives here!' 'Yeah, but you don't, she'll have to get you out!' Other Cocoanutty hotel jokes stir the juices: 'You've been in your room three and a half hours and your trunks haven't arrived? Well, put your pants on, nobody'll know the difference.' And the reception desk routine with the haughty elderly couple whom Groucho insults after the man, Smythe, has arrogantly called him 'clerk': 'Sir, you may not be aware of it, but I am President of the Moroccan Laundry Company!' 'You are?' ripostes Groucho, tearing his chemise from under his jacket, 'Well, take this shirt and have it back Friday!' And the *coup de grâce*: 'Sir, this lady is my wife. You should be ashamed!' Groucho: 'If this lady is your wife, *you* should be ashamed!'

In all, Groucho's demeanour in the film is as a much harsher, more denigrating purveyor of insults than he ever was in the Kaufman–Ryskind, Kalmar–Ruby scripts. The lope is more wolflike, the roué really is ageing. And of course, poor Lisette Verea cannot really stand in for the combination Thelma Todd and Margaret Dumont that she is called upon to play. Of the old gang, only Siggy Ruman (with or without the two 'n's), is in top form, surpassing himself as the inept and spluttering Stubel, whose toupee covering his tell-tale scar is whisked into Harpo's vacuum cleaner. The penultimate scene, in which the three brothers continually unpack the Nazi's trunks and move his clothes from bag to table to closet and back, driving him crazy, is vintage Marxism. It's too slow, but it exploits to the full the Marxes as the three imps of a well-deserved retribution. The final scene, in which they fly a plane into the jailhouse, is marred by very unspecial effects.

The longest of all Chico-Harpo guess-the-words routine; a Chico piano solo – 'We're gonna play a classical number, we're gonna play the second movement from the Beer Barrel Polka' – Chico tickling the keys effortlessly while standing up and scratching his rear; Harpo alone with a harp in the concealed treasure room, playing to a Rembrandt blonde – what more do we want? Harpo looks old, showing his age – fifty-eight, though he still claimed fifty-three – through the make-up. Even the silent imp cannot defeat Time.

At the end, it may, despite the tackiness, be appropriate for Harpo to be piloting a battered Dakota aircraft, an icon of the war just ended, to a brief moment of flight – even shorter, perhaps, than the original Wright Brothers' hop – before diving back into the ground. ('Look, no hands! Aaaargghhhh!') The lost treasure may have been found, but something else eluded the Brothers. At the last moment, when the movie's young lovers embrace clumsily, Beatrice, the redeemed villainess, looks on wistfully, sighing: 'If a thing like that could only happen to me!' – as the satyr's leer gathers on the three brothers' faces, and they take off, chasing her, under the end credits, through the mock Casablancan crowds.

It was so much funnier when they were younger, sassier, as when Chico stated brashly in the theatre manager's office of *On the Mezzanine*: 'I no speaka da very good English, but I'm full of pep and I got the ambish!'

But the clock, pitilessly, kept ticking on.

32

Solo Dreams

TAXI DRIVER: Who perchance will pay my fare?
GROUCHO: (*to waiter at drive-in restaurant*): Give this man his fill of meat
and drink and add it to his taxi fare.
WAITER: And to whom may I ask should I charge it?
GROUCHO: To experience!

A Girl in Every Port (1952)

When *New York Times* writer Mary Morris interviewed the Marx Brothers on the set of *A Night in Casablanca*, Groucho told her:

The ideal life for me is to sleep until 10, brood until about noon, breed until 12:30, then be driven to work by a liveried chauffeur and treated gently. Then I wouldn't be so irascible. I'd welcome a little velvet instead of the canvas gloves and brass knuckles used in this business. They rout a guy out of bed at 6 in the morning. I leave a call – no, I set the alarm and it clangs and frightens me so I throw back my electric blanket . . . the only product I've signed a testimonial for that I use. In the morning you just have the toast brought in and put under the covers. It's the toast of the town, that toast!

One of the gag writers had warned Miss Morris she would not find Groucho in a good mood that day. '"The greatest ad-lib oral wit of our time,"' she wrote, 'is inclined to be moody, and now that he's "famous for his comment," he suffers from being with people who constantly expect him to live up to his reputation. He has a deep-seated feeling of insecurity about his talent, and consequently is "very modest for a comedian."'

But Groucho had other, more general reasons for his unease in the movie business, complaining to his interviewer that movies were 'in a static condition'. They don't show life as it really is – 'Women don't have babies in the movies – just knit. The movies don't recognise any real heavies in the world. You don't dare make a joke that implies there's anything wrong with Franco. The poor public is smothered under tons of goo. No wonder it's sometimes a shock to face life in the raw . . .'

Mary Morris wrote:

The trouble, he said, extended much further than the censorship people
. . . the producers and distributors' greatest fear was the fear they
wouldn't make money. They were 'made of jelly and crawl into the
walls when presented with a picture like *The Negro Soldier*.'

The only solution, he feels, is to own a whole theater chain special-
ising in grown-up movies. 'I don't want to go always to see the pictures
the four-year-olds like. In the publishing business, they make books for
people of different tastes. Everyone, including the four-year-olds, don't
have to like Proust, Huxley, Isherwood.'

He feels that the theater and books are the only mediums in which
one can say what one wants to say without restrictions. He'd like to go
back to the theater in a show that would allow him to use his humor to
make political comment. He's talked with writers about doing a picture
around the idea of the Marx Brothers in Washington but the difficulties
are rather overwhelming . . .

I said he sounded pretty serious.

'I'm a serious man with a comic sense but I don't see why, if you hit
one note and are successful, you must stick to that all your life. I've had
enough of those scenes climbing out of the window or hiding in the
closet when the husband comes home and finds the girl on the bed.
There are other facets to be explored . . .'

A similar desire for movies to reflect the world differently was expressed
by no less an insider than Darryl F. Zanuck, even before the war had ended:

When the boys come back from the battlefields overseas, you will find
they have changed. They have learned things in Europe and the Far
East. How other people live . . . I recognise there'll always be a market
for Betty Grable and Lana Turner and all that tit stuff. But they're
coming back with new thoughts, new ideas. . . . We've got to start
making movies that entertain but at the same time match the new climate of the times. Vital, thinking men's blockbusters. Big-theme films.

But this was wishful thinking. The troubles on the picket lines at MGM,
Warner Brothers and other studios during the making of *A Night in
Casablanca* were symptoms of a wider conflict which was about to precipi-
tate the happy denizens of Hollywood into their most profound crisis, and
make 'thinking men's blockbusters' into the most unlikely dreams that
money could buy. The strike, which had been called by the Conference of

Studio Unions under the leadership of left-winger Herb Sorrell, was opposed by the Screen Actors' Guild, whose new president was thespian Ronald Reagan, then only beginning the long march that would take him across the political borders to the far Republican right. Republican candidates had just won a majority in both the Senate and the House in the elections of 1946, resulting in the invigoration of the until-then moribund House Un-American Activities Committee, which acquired a new zealous chairman, Republican J. Parnell Thomas. Other red-blooded Americans to join the hunt were Los Angeles lawyer Richard M. Nixon and the Senator from Wisconsin, Joseph McCarthy. The target of the new inquisitors was, implicitly, the entire Rooseveltian New Deal, whose champion had died on 12 April 1945, bequeathing the Democratic Party and the Presidency to Vice-President Harry Truman. Truman, who was able to stomach the dropping of two atomic bombs on Japan, would have no problem inaugurating wide-ranging 'loyalty' tests on all government employees, to fit in with the 'anti-communist' crusade.

If the New Deal as a whole was a tough nut to crack, Hollywood left-wingers and liberals were a soft pistachio, with a marshmallow coating. And they were much better value for money for publicity-hungry politicians. The investigation of subversion in Hollywood began in May 1947 and led to a number of 'friendly witnesses', such as Robert Taylor and Ginger Rogers's mother, testifying to the extreme danger of communist infiltration into tinseltown. Mrs Rogers's daughter's role as a dupe in the pro-Russian weepie *Tender Comrade* (1943) figured largely in the discussions. Nineteen other putative witnesses, the 'unfriendly' ones, gathered in Los Angeles to consider their responses if called before the Committee: Herbert Biberman, John Howard Lawson, Dalton Trumbo, Alvah Bessie, Lester Cole, Edward Dmytryk, Robert Rossen et al. Some of them were Communist Party members, others merely freethinkers; both categories were anathema to the inquisitors. Ten of the nineteen were Jewish. Their eventual decision was to stonewall the Committee by evading its questions without actually refusing to answer; a strategy that was to lead to charges of contempt and the jailing of the famous 'Hollywood Ten'. To bolster their position, a supporting group, the Committee for the First Amendment, was formed, at the instigation of directors John Huston and William Wyler, to protect freedom of speech. The big names who joined this latter group included Humphrey Bogart, Frank Sinatra, Gene Kelly, Katharine Hepburn, Rita Hayworth, producers Walter Wanger, William Goetz and Jerry Wald, writers George S. Kaufman and Archibald MacLeish, and Groucho Marx.

Groucho's political views were, as we have seen, more often aired in private than in public, as his letters to Miriam attest. From 15 March 1946:

I think the American people are on to Churchill. He was repudiated by his own Labor Party in England, he's been an imperialist all his life and he has no standing today in war politics. He was a wonderful aid to England during the war. He keeps yowling about Russia but you notice that he never mentions India or all the British territory that they controlled throughout the war. As you know, I am not anti-English or anti-Russian, I'm trying to be an American and the only thing I'm interested in is what is good for America.

But the liberal view of what was good for America, and that of the Un-American Activities Committee's and the FBI's, were in drastic conflict. Groucho may not have been the most far-sighted of political animals, but he could sense the pressures that had for a long time been building on those in Hollywood who might be considered red-minded rather than red-blooded, not to speak of the inquisitors' anti-Semitic tinge. These were not people to whom you could suggest going into the water up to the knees — they insisted on total immersion or nothing.

Unbeknownst to Groucho, the FBI were keeping tabs on his political life, as his confidential FBI file reveals. Revived by researcher Jon Wiener in *The Nation* in 1998, the file includes a report, dated 1 December 1953 (LA 100-46665), which cites allegations by a 'rank and file member' of the Communist Party in San Diego County that Groucho 'contributes heavily' to the Party. The report itself casts doubt on this source, and Groucho's 'Dear Mir' letters indicate pretty clearly that he had no time for the CP. But his involvement with the First Amendment Committee, the Hollywood Democratic Committee, Russian War Relief and opposition to Fascist Spain were cited, as well as later allegations concerning his radio and TV show, *You Bet Your Life* (of which, more anon). The file cites a *Daily Worker* article of 1934 praising Groucho as a person of impeccable 'working class origin' and noting his support of Tom Mooney, a prominent socialist trade union leader, falsely jailed in 1916 for a bomb outrage in California. Last but not least, Groucho was also linked with a 1930s 'New Declaration of Independence', which called for 'the immediate breach of all economic relations with Germany'. FBI director J. Edgar Hoover, however, took no action on these matters, perhaps sensing that Groucho's imaginary bite was a lesser threat than his bark.

*

Chico and Harpo, meanwhile, were keeping an even lower profile, politically, in the run-up to these dangerous times. Chico, as evidenced by Mary Morris's interview, was as politically literate as a circus elephant whose chief concern is feeding times. Neither war nor cold peace deflected Chico from continuing to tour his dance bands, as shown by a clipping from *Variety* of 24 July 1946:

> Roxy, N.Y., Chico Marx, Jane Pickens, Debonairs, Harold Barnes, John Guelis, Jess Renna, Varsity 8, Roxyettes, Paul Ash House Orch: 'Centennial Summer.' Well-blended mixture of music, terping and comedy makes the bill here this sesh a pleasant enough midsummer divertissement, but one that has nothing the customers will go out and talk about . . . Marx does well with his zany piano work but his act disappoints, probably because there's none of the comedy associated with him and his two brothers. He tries hard to pull off some gags but most of them fall flat. He's dressed in his Italian costume and, naturally, plugs his accent all the way.
>
> Teeing off with his standard 'Beer Barrel Polka,' he devotes the rest of the time he's on to kidding with the band. Violinist he brings down from the orch to do an assist on 'Gypsy Love Call' steals his thunder. Marx doubles with the band's pianist on a burlesqued version of the 'Mexican Hat Song,' with the two of them running around the stool as they switch parts.

Running around and around the piano stool was not getting Chico anywhere, but it neatly symbolizes the fact that Chico had nowhere else to go. Unlike Groucho, the character Chico had created thirty-five years earlier, from 'Fun in Hi Skule' to 'Home Again', had too narrow a range to make it easy to contemplate any full-blown screen role on his own. Out of fashion and out of date, he continued to be – just Chico. No longer the family man, and a slowly fading echo of the great seducer of the past.

In November 1946, Maxine, working to carve out a place for herself as a screen and radio actress (her first film role was in one of Basil Rathbone's Sherlock Holmes movies, in 1942), married James H. (Shamus) Culhane, then a director of animation at the Walter Lantz studio. Culhane recalled his first meeting with Chico, in a Japanese restaurant he had chosen, in the hope that the bill would not devastate his meagre funds. The great comedian greeted his new son-in-law-to-be perfunctorily and settled down to study his racing guide. 'He was in the process of losing a million dollars on horses,' Culhane wrote. 'It looked like hard work.' He continued:

When the kimono-clad waitress came, Chico waved the menu away. 'Just bring me a medium steak with French fries.' The waitress almost popped her obi. The manager came, and one could tell by the way he fussed and bowed that he recognised Chico.

They, of course, had no steak and potatoes, but if Mr. Marx would kindly wait, the chef would send someone to the nearest steakhouse. Chico agreed, and the manager went off, his face saved. He wouldn't have to commit hara-kiri.

At the end of the meal, Chico asked the impecunious animator to drop him off at a party at Pickfair, Mary Pickford and Douglas Fairbanks's mansion. But he was clearly not going there to reduce it to the shambles of Rittenhouse Manor. Those days were over, and Signor Emanuel Ravelli had long been tamed. Maxine recalled that Chico liked his prospective son-in-law, but kept tormenting him with endless Irish jokes: "'If I hear another Pat and Mike story,'' Shamus told me after one night out with Chico and Mary, "I'm going to throw something at your father.''"

Mary was Mary Dee (aka Mary DiVithas) a young actress whom Chico had met in 1942 and who had become his constant companion, although they would not be married until 1958. Mary Dee bore a strong resemblance to Betty as she had been twenty years earlier, a coincidence that caused Betty a great deal of pain. Still, Betty and Chico did not divorce until just before his second marriage. Perhaps Chico still wanted to keep all his options open, to pretend that he could keep the dice rolling for the impossible jackpot to be won.

Early in 1947, while performing in Las Vegas, Chico suffered a mild heart attack which caused him to retire temporarily from his performances. He returned to convalesce in Hollywood. But Chico couldn't afford to stay retired for long.

Harpo, on the other hand, could afford to do as he wished. Having become the complete family man, he cultivated his growing children like a zealous gardener tending his prize tulips. Lined up on the lawn for a TV photocall, each member of his brood carried their own beeping horn. But Harpo's permanent childhood was, at least in part, a subterfuge; for he, like Groucho, had his own ideas about the outside world. This part of Harpo's life has remained virtually unknown, and was directly connected to his close friendship with screenwriter Ben Hecht.

Hecht, in the welter of Hollywood Jewish *angst* about the War and the Nazi persecution of German and European Jews, had become the most outspoken voice for the militant Zionism of the anti-British Irgun Zvai Leumi (National Military Organisation), whose representative in the United States was Peter Bergson. Bergson had bearded Hecht in his room at the Algonquin Hotel and convinced him that the Jewish plight required not just verbal protest, but active help for the fight to establish a Jewish State in Palestine. Bergson and his colleagues, Samuel Merlin and Mike Ben-Ami, had shrewdly zeroed in on Hecht as a passionate enthusiast who would rally to the cause where other Hollywood grandees would be cautious. After initial reluctance to become involved in any political cause at all, let alone an armed 'Revolution' in Palestine, Hecht became the Irgun's main fundraiser in America, convincing such non-Jewish Jews as David O. Selznick and Ernst Lubitsch to sponsor his 'Committee for a Jewish Army of Stateless and Palestinian Jews'. As the war progressed, and the contours of the Nazi Holocaust began to emerge, Hecht became more and more involved in finding cash for Irgun arms, and more significantly, in funding the grand scheme of landing thousands of Jewish refugees aboard rickety ships on the shores of Palestine, in defiance of the British colonial regime. One of these ships even bore his name, the immigrant ship *Ben Hecht*.

Harpo Marx, alone of the brothers, had had a direct glimpse of the consequences of Nazism at its inception in Germany, in November 1933, en route to Leningrad and Moscow. The shop windows daubed with '*Jude*' and the terribly cowed and frightened Jewish storekeepers were images that stuck in his mind. While there was no immigrant ship *Harpo Marx*, Harpo was extremely sympathetic to his friend's efforts, and shunted various sums of money his way. This kind of support was by its nature clandestine, as not only was it contrary to declared US support for Britain's colonial policies, but also to the mainstream American Zionist organizations, who took the position that armed opposition to the British was terrorism, and counter-productive to the Jewish cause in Palestine. (The Arab cause in Palestine was, in those days, either invisible or viewed, as in Hecht's eyes, as an adjunct of British imperial policy.) Harpo's continued sympathies with the Zionist cause were reflected, years later, by the donation of his harp to the Rubin Academy of Music and Dance in Jerusalem.

But Marxism cannot, for long, reside in politics! Harpo's ambitions, in the immediate aftermath of the Second World War, were concentrated on his domestic front, with the continuation of his regular guest appearances, and the glimmer of an idea, to be developed with Ben Hecht, of a movie which would be a solo vehicle for him. The original story was tentatively titled *The*

Sidewalk. This would mutate into the most unhappy *Love Happy*, positively the last movie in which the Marx Brothers ever appeared together.

The first mention of this project occurs in one of Groucho's letters to Miriam, dated 17 May 1947, in which Groucho says: '[The script] is good but still needs a lot of fixing. Now if they can get a studio to put money in it, he [Harpo] will be set for the beginning of a new career. Oh, I forgot: Chico too is in it.'

By this time the Marx tribe had been joined by Melinda, the child of Groucho's marriage to Kay, who was born on 14 August 1946, and Steve, his son Arthur and daughter-in-law Irene's firstborn, who arrived on 8 May 1947. The circumstance of Groucho's first grandchild being only a year younger than his own new daughter did not appear to bother him, though it was obviously a difficult situation for both Arthur and Miriam, who had to endure endless letters recounting how cute and bubbly Groucho's new baby was.

Meanwhile Zeppo and Gummo had continued to run their joint agency, each with his separate list of clients. Zeppo, however, had been steadily losing interest in show business, and was casting his eye about for other prospects. Recalling his old love of tinkering with vehicles and machines, Zeppo joined up with a machinist at RKO studios, named Marman, to form an engineering company, manufacturing coupling devices for aircraft. Little is known of this wartime enterprise, but it was said that one of their devices was used to hold the first atomic bombs in place, an ultimate Marxism that is beyond irony. By 1949, Zeppo was to divest himself of all his interests in the agency, and abandon show business for good.

Gummo remained a full-time agent, now representing Groucho along with all his other Hollywood clients. As Paul Wesolowski wrote, Gummo could serve 'as what Groucho called "a buffer between me and the rest of America." If Groucho wanted to reject an offer for any reason, Gummo could send the rejection letter, making it seem that he, not Groucho, had nixed the deal. The producers could imagine that Groucho would have accepted the offer if he had only known about it, and wouldn't hold it against him.'

In late 1946, however, Groucho accepted one offer that, he hoped, would launch him in a new direction, resuming his career in motion pictures but as a solo star. The vehicle of his comeback was to be a musical in glorious Technicolor and to co-star the latest comet to hit Hollywood, the 'Brazilian Bombshell' – Carmen Miranda, alias Maria do Carmo Miranda da Cunha.

The movie was to be called *Copacabana*, but turned out not to be in Technicolor after all. Groucho wrote to Miriam: 'What the critics will call it is something to conjure with.' 'I am sure,' he wrote to her in another letter, 'it will be one of the worst movies of the new season.' And that was even before he met the Brazilian Bombshell! Some days later he wrote that he had just seen one of her previous pictures and 'my heart sank. In addition to looking like a dressed up bulldog, she sings each song the same as the preceding one, and to top it off, she is supposed to feed me [lines] in the picture, and I didn't understand a goddamned word she uttered.'

In the event, Groucho had less to worry about from La Miranda than from the script, which was essentially ludicrous and totally inappropriate to his character. The melancholy *mélange* had been perpetrated by a gaggle of writers which included, officially, Allan Boretz, Howard Harris and Laszlo Vadnay, with additional dialogue by Sydney Zelinka and, according to Groucho, Walter de Leon, and his old pal Charlie Lederer, who tried to inject some funny lines. These might include the moment when Groucho hands the cloakroom attendant Carmen's mink coat with the comment: 'Take good care of this and at ten o'clock give it a saucer of milk', or his riposte to the question, 'Why are you always chasing women?' – 'I'll tell you as soon as I catch one.' Other exchanges: 'How would you like to see your name in lights?' 'Why, are you an electrician?' 'No, but I've got some good connections' (eyebrows wiggle), are best consigned to the Outbins of History

The plot, such as it was, had Groucho as Lionel Q. Devereux, Carmen's fiancé of ten years and partner in her act. (They needed five writers to come up with that name.) Being the worst actor in the business, and so poor he has to steal the performing monkey's peanuts and the performing seal's fish, he decides to become Carmen's agent instead. He eventually gets her a gig at the Copacabana Club, but only at the price of adding to the bill the fabulous but non-existent Mademoiselle Fifi, whom the manager of the club really wants. So, La Miranda has to don a veil and become the French-Oriental *chanteuse*, as well as herself, engendering much confusion and changes of costume and accent which, the writers hoped, would engender a great deal of mirth. Suffice to say that the amusement meter does not hover very high, though Groucho does his best to be Groucho with no other brother to spark off against.

The result is as if Ronald Kornblow of the Hotel Casablanca had married Beatrice Reiner, and was trying to sell her talents to Colonel Heinrich-Sig-Ruman-Stubel. But, alas, there is no Sig Ruman. Instead there are Abel Green of *Variety* and the famous New York columnist Louis Sobol appearing as themselves. The Copacabana was a very real New York nightclub, featuring top acts such as Frank Sinatra, Dean Martin, Jerry Lewis and Nat 'King' Cole. This might potentially have made the movie notable, but alas none of these luminaries so much as shows a cufflink, and La Miranda's signature fruit gear reigns supreme. Kay, Groucho's new wife, appeared in a small bit part.

As things turned out, despite his fears, Groucho got on well with his co-star, finding her 'charming to work with, unspoiled and unaffected'. As an old trouper, Groucho could not fail to respond to the plight of another thespian trapped, as he was, by the expectations conjured by an invented self. (Although she could hardly be an object of pity since, as Groucho noted to Miriam, she followed the movie by singing in a café in Florida for 14,000 smackers a week.) Variously touted as an Argentine, Mexican or Brazilian, Carmen Miranda was in fact a Portuguese national brought up in Brazil, who had become a star of radio, movies and stage, before being brought to America to join the Broadway musical *Streets of Paris*. Her speciality was hot and sassy, with lots of bananas on top. It was not a bad idea to mate her with Groucho, but the material was simply not up to snuff.

On viewing the rushes, Groucho wrote: 'I look like a cross between my father, Mephistopheles, and an opium peddler on the Mexican border.' Given his low expectations, however, he thought the movie was turning out rather well. He got to sing a Kalmar and Ruby song, 'Go West, Young Man', surrounded by a posse of cowgirls – 'If you can't get a seat on the subway, Go west young man' – while cheering himself on from the audience: two Grouchos for the price of one. But even two late-blooming Grouchos were no match for the glories of the past. Sam Coslow produced and wrote Miranda's songs, and Alfred E. Green, who was no slouch at all, and had directed Mary Pickford, John Barrymore, Edward G. Robinson and the biopic *The Jolson Story*, was at the helm. The film seemed to have seeped into his karma though, as his last recorded movie feature, in 1954, was entitled *Top Banana*.

One thing was sure about *Copacabana*: it could hardly furnish any evidence of un-American activities for the committee about to sit in judgement over Hollywood – unless the scene of Groucho evading the cops by leaving with the line, 'I just remembered I forgot to pay my income tax', and the puzzled response after he's left: 'There's something phony about that guy', might be deemed disrespectful to the Internal Revenue Service. The film was popular with audiences, and set fair for profit, so that Groucho was even approached to make another picture with Miranda. But, he decided, once was enough.

Groucho was keen to return to another pet project, a play, *Time for Elizabeth*, which he had co-written with Norman Krasna, a young writer who had already carved out a strong career in Hollywood. Krasna had won the Academy Award for his original screenplay of *Princess O'Rourke*, which he also directed, in 1943. Other Krasna screenplays included Fritz Lang's *Fury* (1936), *Mr and Mrs Smith* and *The Devil and Miss Jones* (both 1941) and *White Christmas* (1944).

Krasna and Groucho had been working for some years on their play, which had been inspired by a magazine advertisement of an old man standing with a young girl beside a yacht, with the caption: 'You too can live like this on $200 a month.' After many versions it had mutated into a rather mild satire of an old washing-machine company man retiring with his wife to a life of leisure and boredom in Florida, only to realize he pines for the old job. Krasna was to direct the play, which would finally open on Broadway in September 1948. Groucho was originally supposed to star but, as he was by then committed elsewhere, the authors had to make do with Otto Kruger, a great-nephew, it appears, of the South African Boer leader Paul Kruger.

The cause of Groucho's unavailability for the stage in 1948 was his renewed commitment to radio. A year earlier, appearing with Bob Hope in a *Walgreen Radio Special* in April 1947, Groucho's ad-libbing had impressed a young producer called John Guedel, who had his own show, 'People Are Funny', featuring Art Linkletter as the MC. Guedel sensed in Groucho a deep frustration with reading material – particularly poor material – from scripts, and his perhaps unacknowledged desire to break out into something more spontaneous and free. Instead of working with professionals, wouldn't Groucho's wisecracking talent be enhanced by contact with ordinary people? Guedel suggested to Groucho something that might have appeared ridiculous at the time: that he should become a quizmaster in a new quiz show Guedel was working to set up.

Groucho's initial reluctance was only skin deep. In fact, he was ready and willing to return to radio, where he never needed to rise at six in the morning to go to the studio where 'a bald-headed makeup man with halitosis slaps a cold wet sponge on my map and applies what he calls Max Factor pancake'. He was only afraid that producer Guedel would be unable to sell him in a medium at which he had struck out four times.

He need not have worried. Guedel knew both his medium and his market. He had his own strategy. Instead of selling to the networks, he sold to the clients. Al Gellman, president of the Elgin-American Compact

Company, remembered Groucho from *The Cocoanuts*, with great affection. With Elgin in the bag, Guedel sold the show to the smallest of the networks, the American Broadcasting Company. On 27 October 1947, the first show aired on ABC.

The day before, 26 October, another radio programme, 'Hollywood Fights Back', was broadcast by the Committee for the First Amendment, challenging the Un-American Activities Committee's inquisition. The main speaker was the novelist Thomas Mann – one of the many famous exiles from Nazi Germany who had found refuge in California, beside the dream factory – voicing his fears of a new-old nightmare:

'Spiritual intolerance, political inquisitions, and declining legal security, and all in the name of an alleged "state of emergency," . . . that is how it started in Germany. What followed was fascism, and what followed fascism was war.'

A clarion call, of sorts, for Rufus T. Firefly to rise to his anarchic defence of liberty. But Firefly was dead, and in his place his creator, Groucho, had, in the nick of time, found his own refuge.

'Is It Sad Or High-Kicking?'

'I find television very educational. The moment somebody turns it on, I go
into the library and read a good book.'

Groucho

You Bet Your Life ran as a radio programme for three years, and as a radio and
television transmission for another eleven and a half years, ending on 29
June 1961. The programme was so successful that its format was recycled,
and continued, with the comedian Bill Cosby, in the early 1990s.

It was due to *You Bet Your Life* that the story of the Marx Brothers segues
into the story of Groucho, entertainer *par excellence*, twentieth-century icon,
and the most recognizable face in show business after, or even before,
Charlie Chaplin's tramp. Precisely because Groucho resisted the idea of
appearing – even for the radio audience – in his screen costume of greasepaint moustache and frock-coat, but accepted co-director Bernie Smith's
proposal that he should at least grow a real moustache instead, Groucho was
able to become known to millions as himself: the Groucho in your living
room, rather than an outdated mask. The Marx Brothers had conquered the
stage, and taken a lien on the talking picture as soon as it had sprung into
life, but Groucho alone, despite the early *Flywheels* with Chico, was able to
master the broadcast mass media. When Groucho began broadcasting on
television in 1950 there were just over three million TV sets in the United
States. Five years later there were 32 million. All the fans of the Marx
Brothers movies – even if each watched their idols' films six hundred times
over on the screen – would not equal the number of viewers who would
watch *You Bet Your Life* on one night at its peak, in 1957.

I confess, I made up that last statistic, but the point stands. Groucho provided the continuity that enabled TV viewers to recognize the Brothers
when their movies appeared on television, and to make the link between
these ancient marvels and the man who was still very much alive and
kicking on the stage at Carnegie Hall, in 1972.

The first radio show which aired on 27 October 1947, at 5 p.m. (West
Coast time) on a Monday afternoon, was a rough diamond. Groucho was

introduced by one Jack Slattery, and crackled on with the words: 'Folks, this is just as new to me as it is to you. I've never done one of these shows before. I only came in tonight because I heard they were giving away one thousand dollars in cash. Now I find out I'm the one who gives it away . . . Who's the first to play You Bet Your Life?'

The familiar format was already in place: two contestants, chosen beforehand and paired by the producers, had to answer questions either in chosen categories, or in general knowledge, for an escalating cash prize, bolstered by the secret word which, when uttered by a contestant, would jack them directly to the big cash questions. The signal deployed when the secret word was spoken was an obnoxious wooden duck, descending from the flies. (As Chico, of course, enquired: 'Why a duck? Why a-no chicken?') The duck was apparently Groucho's idea, and it bore, of course, his signature moustache and spectacles.

Groucho's ad-libs, which so delighted the audience, derived from a scripted basis, constructed by the show's writers, Bernie Smith, Hy Freedman, Howard Harris and Ed 'Doc' Tyler. From the start, the show was pre-recorded, so that editing became crucial to its success. The slickness of the show led to rumours, in later years, that it was rehearsed beforehand, but it was important for the show's impact that Groucho did not meet the contestants ahead of time. What did occur was a rigorous weeding-out of the prospective candidates, by means of long interviews by the researchers, so that those appearing were a known quantity by the time they stepped on the set. The basic idea was an extension of Guedel's previous show, 'People Are Funny', built on the now ubiquitous notion that ordinary people, as well as celebrities, could provide as much entertainment, if not more, than professional actors – and at a much lower cost.

People from all walks of life and of all ethnic origins appeared on the show. At one point the sponsors, the DeSoto motor company, who had taken over when the show transferred to the NBC network, went into a tailspin because the supervisor, Bernie Smith, had paired a white girl with a black man. Smith went ahead anyway. Band leader Jerry Fielding ran into similar flak when he engaged a black musician, Buddy Collette, to join the whites – on radio! This ran counter to the segregation that was exemplified by separate black and white musicians' unions. These tiny, pathetic revolutions were the most that could be expected for the times.

Groucho's greatest successes came from ordinary contestants, like the bubbly Yugoslav Anna, who seemed to have married two husbands, both called Badovnic (not simultaneously!), or an amateur Mexican dancer,

Ramiro Gonzalez Gonzalez, who responded to Groucho's suggestion that they might set up an act as the Two Hot Tamales – 'No, we would call it Gonzalez Gonzalez and Marx', to which Groucho answered: 'That's great billing. Two people in the act and I get third place.'

Groucho's collaborator in this enterprise was a well-chosen young straight man, George Fenneman, who began by reading the show's commercials, and then became the butt of endless ribbing by the star. Fenneman had been born in Beijing, China, to a travelling American businessman, and Groucho kidded him endlessly about this, inquiring after his lost laundry and deploying other mildly offensive slurs. Fenneman bore these with good-natured equanimity, earning him Groucho's highest soubriquet as 'the male Margaret Dumont'. In one show, Fenneman descended from above instead of the wooden duck, suspended by wires. From the humble start of 'And now a word from our sponsor', he became a major asset to the show, the nice guy who could always be embarrassed, as by Groucho calling him out to be paired with an eager young woman who would then be told by the leering host that her on-stage partner was a married man with three children. (In the 1950s Fenneman branched out to become the narrator's voice of the police show, *Dragnet*, the one who intoned: 'Names have been changed to protect the innocent . . .')

Early television, in particular, was prudish to a degree that would have puzzled even Margaret Dumont herself. Offcuts of the show reveal Groucho, having perpetrated a joke that might be considered the slightest bit risqué, then making a clip-clip-clip scissors gesture with his fingers, knowing that that segment would never make it on air. Exchanges such as:

GROUCHO: Are you sure your husband hasn't lost some of his buttons in this laundry?
WOMAN: I don't think he ever lost his buttons in the laundry, but he lost his pants at the wedding.
GROUCHO: That's a little premature, isn't it?

Or the lady who told Groucho that her husband was on twenty-four-hour call with his job, prompting: 'He's on twenty-four hour call and you've got ten kids?' Lady: 'He gets home in between calls.' Groucho: 'Imagine if he had a job around the house.'

Clip clip clip.

Sheer madness. But the sponsors were, as ever, perfect cowards. In 1953, the House Un-American Activities Committee, still going strong, though close to the Last McCarthy Hurrah, subpoenaed the bandleader Jerry

Radio days: 'That's me, Groucho Marx', with George Fenneman.

Fielding as a member of a 'Front' organization during the war. Having seen the treatment of the defiant Hollywood Ten, who had served their jail sentences for defying the committee, Fielding, like everyone else, invoked the Fifth Amendment, refusing to answer any questions about his past. But merely being named was enough for oblivion. Fielding left the show on a mere hint from director Robert Dwan and then found that not one of his colleagues returned his calls from then on. This included Groucho who, as we now know from his disclosed FBI records, could have been formally accused of association with many of the same liberal groups during the war. It was a silence of which Groucho was thoroughly ashamed and, years later, as an old man, he tried to mollify Fielding. But Fielding would not respond. In the early 1950s, everyone knew on which side the bread was buttered, and the sponsor's cowardice was paramount. Groucho's FBI file reveals that the Bureau had in fact received a number of letters to J. Edgar Hoover from people complaining about Groucho's 'communist' bias as the presenter of the show, and asking the famous G-man what he was going to do about it. But once again, Hoover let Groucho alone.

You Bet Your Life had migrated from its first home at ABC to the larger CBS network in October 1949, and climbed to number six in the radio ratings. A battle between CBS and NBC for the television rights was won by NBC after Groucho was hustled by a CBS executive with the line: 'You're a Jew and I'm a Jew. We should stick together. You can't afford to sign with NBC.' This was not the way to woo Groucho, who had an old-fashioned distaste for this kind of pleading, especially as the supplicant chose to make his plea in his brother Gummo's bathroom.

The transition from one well-paid post to another was, however, not the only matter affecting Groucho in 1949, as another long-term project, which had bumbled along without resolution for several years, had eventually come to fruition. Nineteeen forty-nine, such a good year for Groucho, was to go down in infamy in Marxian circles as the year of the completion of *Love Happy*.

After nearly two years, the script Ben Hecht had written for Harpo, *The Sidewalk*, later renamed *Diamonds in the Sidewalk*, had finally mutated into an actual screenplay, prepared by Frank Tashlin and Mac Benoff, to be produced by United Artists. The record shows that the Executive Producer was none other than Mary Pickford, co-founder of the studio. Perhaps Chico's schmoozing at Pickfair had paid off, though the petite *grande dame* of Hollywood denied all knowledge of the film thereafter.

Director David Miller had been set to start the ball rolling as early as March 1948, but producer Lester Cowan, who had driven both W. C. Fields and Mae West to distraction in their joint movie *My Little Chickadee* in 1940, managed to get the project pushed back over five months. Shooting commenced in August, about the same time that the Brothers' uncle, Al Shean, died in New York (12 August), cutting the last but one link of the Marxes with their nineteenth-century Schoenberg roots. The Brothers could not attend the funeral, but sent red roses to cover the coffin. Aunt

Hannah, however, was present at the funeral. She was now the only surviving sibling of Minnie Schoenberg and would live to be ninety years old.
The last living child of Dornum, she may well, assuming she inherited
grandfather Levy's vigour in old age, have been spry enough to see her
nephews' movie swansong . . .

The experience of shooting *Love Happy* was dire. One day during the
long-drawn-out production, reported Joe Adamson, a shaken Harpo came
home to his wife Susan and told her: 'Do you know what I just did today? I
stood over Lester Cowan, trembling with rage, and I said, "I hate you! I hate
you! I think you are the vilest man in the whole world. I spit on you!" And
I spit on him!' If such a soul as Harpo could be reduced to this, imagine the
impact on less tolerant mortals.

Harpo's pain was so great that he never so much as hinted at the existence
of *Love Happy* in his 1961 book, *Harpo Speaks*. The Brothers, and many of
their fans, preferred to blot it out of living memory. From the beginning,
things were not going Harpo's way, as the studio agreed to finance the film
only if the other two brothers would appear in it, making it a full-blown
Marx Brothers vehicle. Chico, in any case, badly needed the money. Eager
to return to work after his 1947 heart attack, he had resumed a gruelling
tour of his piano act, even venturing as far as Australia in the early spring of

Chico entertaining in Australia, 1948.

1948. By the summer, he was back and ready for his last movie role.

Groucho reluctantly agreed to appear in the movie 'for a brief bit'. In the event, he provided the movie's linking narration and loped on in a couple of barely relevant scenes. When the movie finally reached the screen in March 1950, the plot line made very little sense, and appeared to have been hammered together by the Ritz Brothers on amateur night in the Catskills. Groucho is Sam Grunion, private dick, who has been tracking the stolen Romanov diamonds for eleven years – 'through the Khyber Pass, over the Pyrenees, round the Cape of Good Hope and into Gimbel's basement' – ending up with a troupe of sad sack actors, 'struggling to put on a show' who, the plot forgets, have nothing to do with the diamonds until they're found by their mute mascot, Harpo, who has inadvertently picked them up in a can of sardines, in which they have been hidden by the evil wholesalesman, Throckmorton, and his boss, the slinky Madame Egilichi. Harpo is in love with Maggie Philips, played by Vera-Ellen, but she is in love with Mike, the show's primo ballerino. Chico is Faustino the Great, looking for a job as usual.

Well, there's not much sense to the plot of *Horse Feathers* either. But *Horse Feathers* was base metal alchemized to gold, whereas *Love Happy* is a case of golden talents being turned to scrap. While all fingers of blame point to the detested Lester Cowan, it is still incomprehensible how a talent like Frank Tashlin could have turned out such sludge. Sight gags such as Harpo being searched and divested of a huge number of objects – dummy legs, a barber's pole, a 'Rosebud' sled, and even a dog – from his magic raincoat, fall flat in the leaden context. Somewhere in the story, Hecht's original idea of Harpo as an ageless sprite, an imp of a pre-moral and primeval existence, like Kipling's Puck, mutated into a mentally retarded tramp, a fool unaware even of his own foolishness, soft-headed rather than soft-hearted. At the age of sixty-one, even Puck had to show his wrinkles to the world. It is a terrible sight, as Harpo, evading the crooks who are chasing him for the jewellery, rushes across the fake rooftops, while lighted signs for Bulova watches, Kool cigarettes and Mobil gas attest to the product placement resorted to by the producers when the film began to run out of funds. Only one of these signs is used dramatically, when Harpo is seen astride a series of flying horses which flick on and off, as if carrying him higher and higher, perhaps trying to escape the film altogether. But even Harpo had to come down to earth.

Other consolations include Leon Belasco as the violin-playing creditor Lyons, joining Chico for the only reconstruction in any Marx Brothers movie of the early 'rathskeller' act performed by Chico and Lou Shean before 1911. Chico: 'You noodle with that and I'll macaroni with this.' And there is the moment for which the film is most famous, a brief scene in detective Grunion's office, when a hitherto un-noted blonde actress slides in to tell Groucho: 'Some men are following me.' 'Really? I can't understand why!' ripostes Groucho, eyebrows working overtime. Such was the fourth screen clip of Marilyn Monroe. Several girls were tested for the part, with Groucho unerringly casting the winner, proving that there was nothing wrong with his eyesight at the age of fifty-nine.

Oddly enough, the *New York Times* gave *Love Happy* a good review, commending its 'helter-skelter entertainment' and 'pot-pourri of mirth' – proving that some cinema critics should see their optician more regularly. Encyclopaedist Glenn Mitchell reports that in Great Britain the film was banned for a while, due to the uncredited but widely known involvement of Ben Hecht, whose exploits in Palestine did not endear him to Her Majesty's Government. It was eventually released in 1951.

Rather than continue to spit on Lester Cowan, Harpo chose to distance himself from the agony of the production by joining Chico on a short special appearance in London, in June 1949. Topping the bill at the Palladium, the two brothers were back in their element, reprising bits and pieces from their films and shows. As *Variety* reported: 'The Marx Bros.' act . . . embraces their complete bag of tricks. There is the inevitable opening with Harpo chasing a screaming blonde and from then on there is 50 minutes of unrestrained tomfoolery which takes in a game of poker, a piano duet and, of course, the solo on the harp.'

The Times wrote: 'What makes these great clowns is this combination of fun and fantasy with something else, a mixture of worldly wisdom and naïveté, of experience but also of an innocence never altogether lost, of dignity and absurdity together, so that for a moment we love and we applaud mankind.' The conservative *Daily Telegraph*, on the other hand, turned a sour face, commenting that 'within the limits of the footlights they are only partially amusing'.

Perhaps so. But blissful it must have been for those who, in the hot summer of 1949, in austere post-war Britain, looked upon the jangling echoes of the act that had first found its madcap format early in the second decade of the century, two world wars before, on the stages of the American hinterland. For any veterans of El Alamein and the Blitz who might have sat in the Palladium, it would have been a sobering thought to ponder that the veterans who could have seen those first performances would have been the survivors of the Spanish-American, or even the Civil War itself.

In Groucho's book, co-written with Hector Arce, about his quiz show, *The Secret Word Is Groucho*, published in 1976, he recalls a favourite anecdote, about those old-time days:

'A man goes up to the box office in a small town. "What's playing tonight?" he asks.

'"Tickets are one dollar," the man at the box office replies.

'"I'll take one," the fellow says. "But tell me, what is it – sad or high-kicking?"'

That, said Groucho, was all of show business. But if the Marx Brothers' exit from the movies was sad, no one would deny that the act we will remember was the high-kickingest of them all.

Twilight of the Gags, *or* 'Wife Failed to See Anything Funny in Groucho Jokes'

Life – is so peculiar,
It's so cold you turn blue,
But then the next day could be sunny
So you get sunstroke or flu.
When you're a helpless baby
There's nothing to do but cry,
And when you finish living,
There's nothing to do but die,
And in the years between times,
There's nothing to ask but why?
Life – is so peculiar – don't know why we even try . . .

Groucho and Bing Crosby in *Mr Music* (1950)

Groucho was to make two more movies as a solo star, *Double Dynamite* in 1951 and *A Girl in Every Port* in 1952. In 1950 he made a guest appearance in a Bing Crosby musical, *Mr Music*, with a brief vaudeville double act and song (by Johnny Burke and James Van Heusen) which provide a tantalizing glimpse of yet another might-have-been. Groucho and Bing merge effortlessly together, consummate professionals doing what comes naturally, with grace and ease, in a movie that contains little else that's memorable.

Double Dynamite was a strange concoction out of Howard Hughes's RKO stable, starring Jane Russell and Frank Sinatra as two bank clerks waiting to get married, but Frankie, poor boy, feels they just can't afford it. Groucho, as Emil Keck, a wisecracking, poetry-quoting waiter, suggests that they rob a bank, but Frankie is too clean-cut to take this tip. Instead he takes a tip on a sure-fire win at the races, given him by a crook he has saved from being beaten up in the street by two rivals. Frankie keeps winning money on the horses, the bank is short of a similar sum of money because of an internal fraud, Frankie is suspected, and so on and so forth. In the end it turns out that the adding machine in the bank made the mistake.

The film was, in fact, shot in the winter of 1948, concurrent with

Groucho's bit part in *Love Happy*, but Hughes, perhaps unclear as to why he should be releasing a film that did not in fact reveal Miss Russell's cleavage to any profitable degree, despite the suggestive title, held it back for over two years. Groucho was miscast in the film and that's all there is to it. Sample dialogue: Sinatra: 'Do we have to have poetry?' Groucho: 'It goes with the lunch.' Groucho and Sinatra sing 'The nicest people we know / Are the people who get their faces on dough.' The prosecution rests.

Groucho, however, failed to learn his lesson and signed up for a second RKO lucky dip, this time co-starring with William Bendix. They play two sailors whose career as scam artists has been temporarily interrupted by a spell in the brig. Bendix has been left $1,450 by an aunt and has bought a horse – shades of Hi-Hat – a useless nag called 'Little Aaron' which has a twin called 'Little Shamrock' who is a demon on the track. All you need to do is switch the horses and – you get the picture. The sub-plot involves beautiful, pouting young Jane Sweet (Marie Wilson), who is in love with young horse trainer Bert (Don de Fore). Director-writer was Chester Erskine, the script based on a story, 'They Sell Sailors Elephants', by one Frederick Hazlitt Brennan. Perhaps it was the 'Elephants' in the title that attracted Groucho – echoes of Captain Spaulding, long lost beyond the Limpopo.

In an article in *Holiday* magazine in April 1952, S. J. Perelman recorded his experiences in flying out from New York to visit Groucho on the set of *A Girl in Every Port*, describing the scene in his inimitable fashion:

> The set to which I was directed, a faithful replica of a battleship, hummed with activity; hordes of extras in navy blue were absorbed in scratch sheets . . . and high on a camera parallel, two associate producers, arms clasped about each other, were busily examining their pelts for fleas. Groucho, as was his wont, was in the very thick of the mêlée. He was sprawled blissfully in a director's chair, having his vertebrae massaged by Marie Wilson, a young lady whose natural endowment caused a perceptible singing in the ears. I promptly drew up a chair next to her and confided that I too was suffering from a touch of sacroiliac, but the fair masseuse appeared to be hard of hearing . . .
>
> 'Well,' [Groucho asked] 'what's the chatter on Broadway?' In a few incisive phrases, I summed up recent developments there, such as Olga Nethersole's resounding success in Sappho, the razing of Hammerstein's Victoria, and the emergence of A. Toxen Worm as leading drama critic, and, to bolster his spirits, revealed that Milton Berle's TV show had a much larger following than his own. He was visibly pleased. 'Let's get

together before you leave town,' he said, wringing my hand warmly. 'I'd like you to poison some moles in my lawn.' At this juncture, the lunch gong pealed, and leaving an effigy of himself with Miss Wilson to rub until his return, Groucho bore me off to the commissary . . .

[Jump cut] . . . 'All right, settle down everybody – this is a take!' bawled the director. 'Hit the wind machine, and remember, Groucho, bend down into his ear and plead with him.' A hush fell over the turbulent sound stage, technicians exchanged a last crisp monosyllable, and the transparency screen behind the set lit up to reveal half a dozen race horses plunging towards us. In front of them, in jockey's silks, sat Marx and Bendix on two amazingly lifelike steeds molded of rubber. As the machinery underneath them began churning, the horses came alive; their necks elongated, manes and tails streamed in the breeze . . . The riders plied their mounts with whip and endearments, straining forward into the camera to steal the scene from each other . . .

A few minutes afterward, rid of his makeup and in jaunty spirits, Groucho met me at the door to his dressing room. The picture was finished, and he was at last free to resume his passionate avocation, the collecting and cross-fertilization of various kinds of money.

[And later, after a final lunch at Romanoff's –] . . . 'My boy,' he said, and his voice shook slightly, 'a very wise old man once said that there are two things money cannot buy – nostalgia and friendship. He died in the poorhouse. Don't forget to square that tab on the way out.' He gripped my hand hard and was gone, a gallant freebooter who had made his rendezvous with Destiny. As his skulking, predatory figure faded from view, wreathed in chicanery, I bowed my head in tribute. 'Adieu, Quackenbush,' I whispered. 'Adieu, Captain Spaulding. No man ever buckled a better swash.' Then, through a mist of tears, I soberly signed his name to the check and went forth to a workaday world.

Groucho's penchant for cross-fertilizing various kinds of money was never better served than in this period. His deal with NBC Television for *You Bet Your Life* guaranteed him a minimum sum of $263,200 annually for ten years, which included $4,800 per week for every week the programme was on the air, with an $800-per-week annual pay hike, and a whopping 38 per cent of the net profits. Producer John Guedel was in for a mere $98,700 annually. This would suit Groucho nicely, particularly as the fallout from his turbulent domestic life was about to call for double doses, not of dynamite, but of alimony. Julius H. Marx's first marriage had taken twenty years to fail, but the second unravelled in much faster motion and this time it was Groucho who filed for divorce, in April 1950. No less an eminence than gossip columnist Louella Parsons announced on 7 April that:

> Groucho Marx admitted that he and his wife, the former Kay Gorcey, have separated and he will file for a divorce. However, there seems to be a slight difference of opinion as to what actually caused the family rift.
>
> Groucho says it's career trouble, and that his wife wants to return to singing and dancing, but Kay, who has been married to the comedian for the past five years, told me: 'It isn't true that I want a career. I can't stand Groucho's friends.'

On 14 April Groucho petitioned the Superior Court in Los Angeles, charging his wife with 'extreme cruelty' and asserting she had caused him 'grievous mental suffering'. He told Judge Edward R. Brand that Kay 'never took care of the house, and was completely indifferent to her surroundings. In fact, it was necessary for me to run the house . . . order the meals, see that the help stayed in line, and all the things like that.'

Gummo supported Groucho's petition, testifying that Mrs Marx's conduct 'made the famed funnyman "gloomy, morose and nervous,"' a condition he was, in fact, quite capable of producing on his own. Kay, it appears, having escaped the physical abuse of her first husband, Leo Gorcey, was ill-equipped to deal with the kind of verbal barrage that had driven Groucho's first wife, Ruth, to despair. Groucho's mask slipped a little when he told the judge that 'worst of all, she didn't seem to think he was much of a comedian, noting that she was able to stand going to his radio show only twice in three years'. This echoed the complaint headlined at the time of Groucho's divorce from Ruth: 'Wife Failed to See Anything Funny in Groucho Jokes.'

As Groucho and Kay had signed a prenuptial agreement, Groucho was bound to pay $134,215 in alimony over the following ten years, and also $1,300 a year to support three-year-old Melinda, whose custody was granted to Kay. Three years later, Groucho won back custody of Melinda, then six years old, owing to Kay's 'illness', a euphemism for the alcoholism that, as with Ruth before her, had become her refuge. In 1954, Groucho married Eden Hartford, a Beverly Hills model he had met on the set of *A Girl in Every Port*, who was herself on her second marriage. They were married on 17 July in Sun Valley, Idaho, by Justice of the Peace O. R. Hunt, with the only witness, according to the *Los Angeles Examiner*, being 'the comedian's 7-year-old daughter, by a former marriage, Melinda.'

Groucho's troubled relationships with his wives and children were to be a continuing source of distress . By the beginning of the 1950s Miriam had become a habitual drinker. In 1949, at the age of twenty-two, she had barely survived a car crash caused by stalling on railway tracks in Massachusetts while driving under the influence of alcohol.

Groucho's firstborn, Arthur, appeared secure in his marriage to Irene Kahn, though they too would divorce some years later, and Arthur would remarry Lois, ex-wife of Irene's brother Donald, somewhat against Groucho's idea of propriety. Arthur was soon to embark on his own career as a writer. In 1954 the first of a series of eight articles about his father's life and career began appearing in the *Saturday Evening Post*. Later they became a hardback book, *Life with Groucho*, which was a runaway success. The serialization, however, did not go ahead smoothly. Groucho, despite having read Arthur's text and okayed the humorous footnotes that appeared at the bottom of the pages under his own name, confronted his son with a denunciation of the manuscript as 'scurrilous . . . you've made me out to be some kind of ogre – and a cheap one at that'. Stunned by this reaction, Arthur continued with his publication plans, undaunted by threats of legal action from his own father. In the event, Groucho was bluffing, playing out the endgame of control over a son who had long been carving out his own path in life. Instead of writs, he instructed his lawyer to hand Arthur a copy of the manuscript containing his own objections, which would have omitted almost half the book. Arthur accepted these, then dumped the amended galley proofs in the rubbish bin and sent his own uncorrected version to the magazine. On publication, Groucho did not say a word.

Melinda, being only seven, had no opportunity to resist her father's wish to mould her to his will. Groucho's letters to Miriam reveal how much he doted on the child, as he had doted on his first two children well into their teenage years. But he had, for some reason, discerned in her childish pranks a budding talent for show business, and kept bringing her into his television shows to co-star at his side. In one TV special they sang the duet of 'Anything you can do, I can do better', and then skipped offscreen together, Groucho-style. In one very uncomfortable episode of *You Bet Your Life*, he asked her straight-faced if she was married. But the child was unable to express to her all-powerful father her deep embarrassment at these moments and her total lack of desire for a performing life.

Groucho's third marriage, to Eden, was to last for fifteen years, until 1969, when she, too, was to divorce him, citing his 'uncontrollable temper'

Home comforts with Eden Hartford-Marx.

and 'hostile and abusive moods'. She claimed that Groucho, then seventy-three years old, knocked her down and threatened her several times, 'belittling and ridiculing' her in front of guests, relatives and servants. Melinda, twenty-two, had by then flown the coop.

But in 1955, after a year of marriage, Eden provided an idyllic picture to *The American Weekly*, describing the moment she was introduced to

Groucho with her sister Peggy, Groucho asking her other sister, Dee, who was in the movie: 'Give me the rundown on these two. Which one's married and which isn't?'

'I have never seen anyone read as much as Groucho,' Eden told the magazine. 'He reads magazines and books of every kind and marks things he thinks are particularly interesting for me to read . . . Groucho's eight year old daughter Melinda always has several of her friends over on weekends so we have a fairly crowded, active and noisy back yard.'

Groucho had moved several times in the previous few years, having left the small bungalow in West Los Angeles he had bought during the war for a larger house, number 1277 Sunset Plaza Drive, from which most of the letters to Miriam were written, and then moved again, with Kay, to a two-storey, sixteen-room villa in Beverly Hills with a billiard room and a citrus orchard in the grounds. Here Eden moved in, describing their life together in Norman Rockwell-like hues:

> While Groucho is napping, I paint. I am a very enthusiastic amateur painter. Groucho approves of my hobby and likes to have me hang some of my portraits in our home. He has no interest in trying to paint himself . . . Often on Saturday nights Arthur, Groucho's son, and his wife Irene come to dinner. [Arthur was nine years older than Eden.] After dinner they play piano while Groucho accompanies them on his guitar. I must admit it's a pretty good combo . . .
>
> Groucho tries his hand at most of the repairs around the house, but usually comes around to calling the repairman. He was never so happy as when he put a washer in his bathroom sink and it worked. However, now the cold water runs hot and the hot tap runs cold . . .
>
> 'Groucho hates to waste money. He'll put in an expensive swimming pool, but make sure an electric light doesn't burn unnecessarily. He'll complain about the price of food but have champagne for dinner. He'll drive around the block three times to avoid a parking lot fee, but he bought me a beautiful mink coat for Christmas without me even hinting. I guess you would call him a little eccentric, but I like him that way . . .

Stands to reason. The idyll continued, but soon afterwards Eden talked Groucho into selling his citrus grove villa and building a luxury new house of glass and stone which cost, according to Arthur Marx, $300,000, paid in full, as Groucho didn't believe in mortgages. Groucho acquiesced because he understood why Eden didn't want to stay in the home of his ex-wife. The new mansion had a sunken bathtub and round bedroom with a circular bed.

Groucho was also persuaded to buy a second home in Palm Springs, where he could be near Harpo and Gummo. Zeppo too had moved down to Palm Springs, after his own divorce from his wife Marion which was granted her on the usual grounds of cruelty, in Las Vegas in May 1954.

Zeppo dropped out of sight, in Palm Springs, living off his profits from his engineering enterprises, mainly a large pay-off received from the Aeroquip Corporation for the sale of his joint company, Marman Products. The only public record of his activities reveals the persistence of his unlucky attraction for lawsuits. In 1952, police had been called to a street brawl with film producer Alex Gottlieb, allegedly over a gambling debt claimed by Gottlieb. In 1953, an epic lawsuit was launched by Zeppo's neighbour at North Beverly Drive, oil executive Mortimer Singer, claiming $300,000 damages on the grounds that Zeppo and Marion's nine-year-old son, Timmy, had thrown a rock at his eight-year-old daughter and injured her eye. This saga dragged on for three years and ended, at the other side of Zeppo's divorce and decampment to Palm Springs, with little Timmy being cleared at a cost of $22,500 compensation for the injured girl, Denise. Within three weeks of the settlement, in May 1957, Zeppo was involved in a punch-up at the Mocambo nightclub, over a girlfriend, Lillian Sherlock. ZEPPO MARX TRADES BLOWS IN STRIP BOUT, the *Los Angeles Times* reported gleefully. In his late fifties, Zeppo appeared to settle for a life as a somewhat jaded playboy and gambler, his only financial link with his brothers consisting of a 6,000-acre citrus farm under the burning desert sun which they purchased together.

Both Gummo and Harpo were living quieter lives. Gummo had slowly wound up his agency, selling some of his interests to the MCA company and others to William Morris. In 1952, his son Robert served in the Korean War, and offered to take over the agency on his return. According to Robert, Gummo sold the agency partly to prevent his son from becoming 'trapped' in a show business career. He continued to represent his brothers, arranging television appearances for Chico and Harpo, and controlling Groucho's deals. But as a businessman he had wound up his career, and retired with his wife Helen to Palm Springs.

'I built them a house down there,' his son Robert told me. 'I was in the building business at the time . . . and they retired there, he became a golfer.'

'It's a long time for a retirement,' I suggested to Robert.

'A long retirement, right . . . Dad was not a super-energetic guy . . . he was quiet, reserved and easygoing . . . he would get up in the mornings, he would read his paper, he would do a little with his investments . . . We had a ranch, big grapefruit ranch that the boys bought into as a tax deal, and he would go down and take a look around there for a little bit, he'd come back, he'd have lunch at the Tamarisk Country Club – he was one of the people who had started that . . . and he would play golf, and that evening they would socialize, and that was what he wanted to do . . .'

'The fascinating thing', I suggested, 'is that the brothers were so close, and yet very different in temperament . . .'

Robert Marx: 'Very different. Absolutely. Zeppo was tight like a string. He was constantly taut. Groucho was that way. Harpo was very laid-back like Gummo . . . Chico was on his knees throwin' dice all the time. Or somethin'!'

Or somethin' . . . For Chico and Harpo, the post-movie years were indeed very different. Harpo had wasted little money, spending what he had on his home and family, allowing Gummo to take care of his earnings. An early TV report on the Harpo Marxes at home – Edward R. Murrow at 'El Rancho Harpo' – shows Harpo, Susan and their kids fooling around on the porch, Harpo in his wig replying to all questions with his old horn.

According to Bill Marx, Harpo continued to play the harp every day of his life. He took up painting, remembering the advice of Algonquinite Neysa McMein, producing still lifes and landscapes which he gave to charities and scattered all over the country.

'He went through different phases,' said Bill. 'There was his wonderful curiosity for colour, he would go through a colour period, he would go through a shapes period, he would go through a scenic period . . . always waffling between representational, traditional perspectives and some primitive, or he'd put 'em together, but . . . there was always something just off centre that made you say, hey, there's a wonderful quirkiness here . . .'

But Harpo's main love continued to be music. Bill Marx: 'He always told my Mom, Bill has gotten me out of the key of C. Because when I first started working with him as his arranger, conductor . . . Dad and I had a great affinity for the element of harmony. And he would sit at his harp and I would give him some chords to play on the harp and arrange pieces of music that were very intricate, because they required unusual harmonic structures, and he loved that.' We have already mentioned Harpo's love for Gershwin, Ravel and Debussy. Later on, said Bill, 'he started talking about Schoenberg and then later electronic stuff and all of the new wave . . . But in those days . . . he loved Prokofiev and Stravinsky . . . it was pretty unconventional and – Scriabin was another person that he loved . . . we shared that together . . . I would play the piano and Dad would play the harp and we'd play little tunes together . . .'

Both Harpo and Chico continued to make public appearances, and carved out a small niche for themselves in the early days of television, though nowhere as spectacularly as Groucho's triumphs. Chico, in fact, made the first appearance on TV of any of the brothers, in NBC's 'Texaco Star Theatre' in October 1948. It was a sixty-minute show with Milton Berle and Joe Philips, and Chico 'noodled around' with the routine that would end up in *Love Happy*. Another shot, in January 1949, just after that movie had wrapped, was an abortive pilot for a series called 'Papa Romani' in which he played the avuncular owner of an ice cream shop. This character returned in a year-long series called *The College Bowl*, which put him in a campus setting. It ran to twenty-six shows, only clippings of which seem to have survived.

Harpo's first TV appearance was in the NBC Comedy Hour, in November 1951, with Donald O'Connor, Yvonne De Carlo and Roger Price (according to Marxian enthusiast Jay Hopkins, who has posted an exhaustive list of Marx Brothers TV slots on the Internet). Both Harpo and Chico continued to make guest appearances of this sort four or five times a year, on average, through the 1950s. A recent TV compilation programme, *The Unknown Marx Brothers*, also cites a series of commercials: one by Harpo and Chico for Creamy PROM, an oleaginous hair product; and Harpo in five surreal vignettes for Labatt's Beer, which seem to have been designed by an anonymous budding Salvador Dalí.

In 1952, Harpo reprised his role as the Property Man in *The Yellow Jacket*, for the Pasadena Playhouse. In 1955, he could be seen in an episode of *I Love Lucy*, as himself, reprising the famous *Duck Soup* mirror scene with Lucille Ball. In 1957 he appeared, again as himself, in an episode of CBS TV's 'Playhouse 90', *Snowshoes: A Comedy of People and Horses*, with Barry Sullivan and John Carradine. In the same year Groucho revived his own co-authored *Time For Elizabeth*, at summer stock theatres in New Jersey and Rhode Island, with himself in the lead role of Ed Davis, and Eden Marx playing a small part. His appearance in summer stock, Groucho told the Philadelphia *Sunday Bulletin* (18 August 1957), was a prelude to doing the play as a ninety-minute TV special for NBC (a prize that did not come his way, in fact, until 1964). After that, Groucho said, 'I'll probably be doing one special a year. I'll still continue to do You Bet Your Life, but I'll do the special, too.'

'As a legitimate actor?' asked the *Bulletin*.

'"No actors are legitimate," snapped Groucho. "But it will be acting – not as Groucho."

'"Will there always be a Groucho?"

"'There'll always be a Groucho, just as there will always be an England – although lately, England hasn't been doing so well.'"

Nineteen fifty-seven was a watershed year for a couple of other reasons, too. It was the year in which director Irwin Allen starred all three Marx Brothers, Groucho, Chico and Harpo, in their very last movie to feature all three. Adapting Hendrik Van Loon's encyclopaedic *The Story of Mankind*, Allen matched the folly of the project itself with the even greater folly of casting the brothers individually, in different episodes, rather than together: Harpo was apple-struck Isaac Newton, Chico was a monk talking to Columbus and Groucho, as Peter Minuit, bought Manhattan from the Indians. You can't get a more Grouchoesque name than Hendrik Van Loon, but even that didn't help this prize turkey.

The second milestone that year was the only appearance ever of all five Marx Brothers on the same broadcast – and only the second time in history that they had been on stage together: Groucho, Chico, Harpo, Gummo and Zeppo, guesting on an NBC chat show,'Tonight: America After Dark', for host Jack Lescouli, on 18 February.

Chico in particular was facing lean times; in May 1957 he was forced to file for Social Security in Santa Monica. In November, columnist Drew Pearson revealed that Chico was being pursued by the tax authorities for $77,564, a sum he could not dream of paying. His brothers put up an instalment of $25,000 and Chico pledged any annual sum he might earn over $7,000 to the Revenue men. They were not expecting a windfall. On 22 August 1958 Chico married Mary Dee (DiVithas), five days after his official divorce from Betty. Only Gummo and Harpo, of the brothers, attended the wedding. Groucho was absent on a trip to Europe, with Eden and Melinda, taking in the visit to Dornum described by TV director Robert Dwan earlier in our saga.

Groucho, Chico and Harpo were to appear together for the last time in 1959 in another CBS show, *The Incredible Jewel Robbery*. A thirty-minute piece directed by veteran movie helmer Mitchell Leisen, and hosted by Ronald Reagan, who was destined for greater things, it was by all accounts beyond sadness. Strictly pantomime roles for Chico and Harpo were capped by a brief appearance by Groucho at the end, saying: 'We aren't talking till we see our lawyer.' A wise decision they would have done well to implement.

Sporadic guest appearances continued nevertheless. In April 1960, Groucho fulfilled one of his long-cherished dreams by starring in NBC's Bell Telephone Hour production of Gilbert and Sullivan's operetta *The Mikado*, as Ko-Ko, the Lord High Executioner ('I've got a little list / I've got a little list / Of society offenders who might well be underground / Who never would be missed . . .'). Helen Traubel, Dennis King and Stanley Holloway co-starred. Another tantalizing production, later in that year, was an episode of the *June Allyson Show*, entitled *Silent Panic*, starring Harpo. He played a deaf-mute, working as a 'mechanical man' in a department store window, who witnesses a murder but can't communicate what he saw to the police. Harpo's painted clown face, with its deathly pallor, and his inability to do what the old Harpo could achieve so easily with a few well-chosen whistles and mime, show that writer Arthur Dales understood something both about the nature of Harpo's clown mask and the inevitable entropy of the post-Marx Brothers world which had degraded it. Harpo's anguish, as he gesticulates wildly at the uncomprehending cops, who tag him as a half-wit, highlights the painful absence of his interpreter, Chico. The killers could safely commit their crime in front of Harpo because, in the world in which we lived – the world of atomic fear and cold war; on the brink of the Vietnam War and the assassination of John F. Kennedy (an event to be witnessed itself by so many dumbstruck Harpos) – we had all lost the ability of reading his face, of understanding his language.

Groucho alone survived and flourished in the television age because he had, through loathing and fatigue, rather than great prescience, abandoned his mask, and reappeared as himself, as Groucho, in fact – as Julius Henry Marx. This was the man, not the image, punning, quipping and stinging his way into everyman and everywoman's living room. Thus, stripped naked – with added barnacles like the great Jewish whale, unharpooned by all the gentile Ahabs – Julius could stand alone, as an entire personality, rather than as one third, or one fourth, or one fifth, of an organic, multi-faceted, schizophrenic and totally invented whole.

But there was still one more transformation, one more trick up the sleeve of the Marxian frock-coat, that could be achieved, to keep the show on the road.

What Price Pumpernickel? – The Marxist Manifestos
or Beyond the Ghosts

Honk! Honk!

Harpo

In 1959, Groucho published his autobiography, *Groucho and Me*. In 1961, Harpo clocked in to the Marxian author's club, trumping his brother with a whopping 450 pages of his own version, *Harpo Speaks*, co-written with Rowland V. Barber. In 1963, Groucho published another book of humorous essays, under the title *Memoirs of a Mangy Lover*, and in 1965, his literary ego was given a massive boost by a request from the Library of Congress that he donate his personal letters to their prestigious collection. This bequest resulted in a compilation, *The Groucho Letters*, edited by Arthur Sheekman and published in 1967.

These books and compilations provide a unique personal perspective on the lives of the Marx Brothers, and of Groucho's own personality in particular. Groucho had, of course, been publishing his essays since 1923, when his earliest pieces appeared in Franklin P. Adams's column *The Conning Tower*. *The New Yorker*, the *Saturday Evening Post*, the *New York Times*, *Colliers*, *Liberty* and other magazines and journals published most of the pieces that would later turn up in his three books of compilations. Groucho's first book, *Beds*, in 1930, was, as we have seen, also serialized, just before its launch, in four parts in *College Humor*. It coined one of his best, if lesser known, *bons mots*: 'It isn't politics that makes strange bedfellows. It's matrimony.'

A great deal of argument has taken place about the extent of ghost-writing – particularly of the early essays – in Groucho's work, mainly by his young friend Arthur Sheekman. Note the claim that Sheekman, rather than Groucho, wrote *Beds*. Robert Bader, compiler of the later book of Groucho essays (*Groucho Marx and Other Short Stories and Tall Tales*, 1992), has established that Groucho had in fact lent his name to some of Sheekman's own pieces, when Sheekman found it difficult to get published, and this led to the later confusion of authorship. The earliest letter in the Groucho Marx box of letters at the Library of Congress is a missive to Sheekman, on the letterhead of the Hotel Muehlbach in Kansas City, dated 3 September 1930 and querying: 'Have you done any work on the piece? If you have, send it along, and I'll take a whack at it. Show business is still thriving on the road, and we are rolling in everything but money . . . I understand the herring is excellent in Cleveland. Cordially, Groucho.'

The first chapter of *Beds* – 'Essay on the Advantage of Sleeping Alone' – a blank page with an editor's footnote: 'The author neglected to write anything for this chapter', would seem to be pure Groucho. Albeit not much happened in these Beds, not even the strange matrimonial contretemps that formed the backbone of his friend James Thurber's own fantasies in prose and cartoon form. Thurber's classic, *Is Sex Necessary?*, had been published in 1929, and included such chapter headings as 'How To Tell Love from Passion', 'What Should Children Tell Parents?' and 'Frigidity In Men'. Thurber was a much weirder and, dare one say, better writer than Groucho, whose use of a joke was often to circumvent, rather than explore, the depths of a problem. Thurber found strange and fantastic angles from which to view some point of trivia, such as his discussion of the 'Feminine Types', like the 'Quiet Type' observed on the bus:

> I resolved to put the matter to her quite frankly, to tell her, in fine, that I was studying her type and that I wished to place her under closer observation. Therefore, one evening, I doffed my hat and began.
>
> 'Madam,' I said, 'I would greatly appreciate making a leisurely examination of you, at your convenience.' She struck me with the palm of her open hand, got up from her seat, and descended at the next even-numbered street – Thirty-sixth, I believe it was.

Now Groucho:

> I have noticed that when a man first gets married, he is always the first one in bed – because he wants to warm the bed for his bride. After he has been married five years, he still gets into bed first – but for a different reason. He does it to avoid winding the clock, turning off the radiator and lights, and seeing to it that the maid is well covered.

There speaks a man who has occupied quite a number of beds in a dual, rather than single occupancy, despite Groucho's later description of *Beds* as 'a book about people not fucking'. Both Thurber and Marx were occupying the trenches of the familiar post-war (1914–18 vintage) 'battle of the sexes' which also heavily influenced the artistic milieu of W. C. Fields, and so many others. Both were working, in different styles, in a vein of American middle-class essay that became pőpularized not only by Thurber but by their contemporaries Robert Benchley and S. J. Perelman, to both of whom Groucho has been compared – and we have already discussed his debt to George S. Kaufman. The sexual battleground, and other human foibles, are observed at a certain distance, with a conscious striving for the impact of style, rather than substance. The Algonquinite barbs, the shafts of wit, are the ends, not the means of the exercise. At the finale of *Beds*, Groucho recalls the quip of Wilson Mizner, the most barbed of all New York raconteurs, who recalled 'his embarrassment when he first came into the world, and found a woman in bed with him . . . I wasn't embarrassed,' says Groucho.

In this middle-class world, Groucho was of course an impostor. Just as, to some extent, Thurber was too, a fragile creature from Mars observing the incomprehensible antics of Man and Womankind. But Thurber was a sub-urbanite in the Big City, whereas Groucho, like his brothers, was a genuine street arab, a child of immigrants who had elbowed his way to the table and was determined to get his just desserts, not to speak of the entrée.

Those humble beginnings, though, imbued Julius Henry Marx with a definite sense of inferiority when it came to his trespassing on the domain of the 'men of letters' he admired. Painfully aware of his lack of formal educa-tion, he is always, as noted before, the first to put himself down, even ahead of his put-downs of others. 'Why should anyone buy the thoughts and opin-ions of Groucho Marx?' he asks in the opening pages of *Groucho and Me*. 'I have no views that are worth a damn, and no knowledge that could possibly help anyone.' A couple of pages later, he continues the preliminary work of setting up defences: 'Nowadays things have to be merchandized. You can't just write a book and expect the public to rush out and buy it unless it's a classic. I could write a classic if I wanted to but I'd rather write for the little people. When I walk down the street I don't care a hoot if people point a finger at me and say, "Look at him, he just wrote a classic!" No, I'd rather have them say admiringly, "What a trashy writer! But who else today gives away a fried egg and a bag of corn with each copy of his book?"'

The irony is that Groucho did indeed write a classic, and did, of course, want people to recognize him for it, but he always armoured himself for failure. The joy of *Groucho and Me* was that it was Groucho's own story, true or false, told in his own voice, and without the ghostly hand of a collaborator, although some portions of the book were, again, revisions of previously published pieces. By definition, readers of Groucho's books were, and are, people who are drawn to them because they are by Groucho, a pre-existing, larger-than-life figure, subsuming old Julius Henry Marx. None of us care about the fried egg.

When Groucho's letters were published, the fans discovered yet another side of old Julius. Composed of letters written mainly from the 1940s onwards, these revealed a man as barbed in private as he could be in public, but in a freer, less encumbered style. Some of the letters, like the exchange with Warner Brothers over *A Night in Casablanca*, were the public Groucho, but most, to friends like Arthur Sheekman, Goodman Ace, Norman Krasna, Fred Allen, Harry Ruby and others were the true anarchic voice of Julius:

To Goodman Ace, 25 November 1953:

Dear Goodman:
    I have always heard that if one stayed long enough in Port Said the whole world would pass before him. This is a God damned lie. The whole world passes before you if you have a room on the 5th floor of the Muehlback Hotel, facing one of Katz's numerous drugstores. The din that a small, corrupt city can raise between the hours of 1 p.m. and 10 a.m. is indescribable, certainly by me . . . Every bus, streetcar, vendor, hawker, factory whistle, blows and clangs at full blast . . . The concerted din that rolls past Katz's drugstore can make a 5-grain Seconal hang its head in shame. This city sneers at barbiturates. Having tried everything else, I finally crawled under the bed and rooted for the atomic bomb . . .

Some of Groucho's correspondents gave as eloquent as they got. Fred Allen, in particular, excelled at his signature mode of writing without capital letters. One of his letters, not included in the published book, is a typical tribute from one irascible ex-vaudevillian and present broadcasting star to another:

June 19th, 1953:
    ernest zachow, jr. of portland, maine, is one of your listeners and he is not afraid to come right out and say so. ernest came right out and said so while he was under oath during the murder trial of mrs. evangelyne m. cooper.
    mrs cooper had claimed that ernest, your listener, had tapped her husband, lancelot cooper, in the cranial area with a cleaver. the jury gave short shrift to mrs. cooper and her testimony. those twelve men, good and true, knew that a man who listens to your program is not the type of man who goes around with a bare meat cleaver hitting women's

husbands in the cranial area. the jury found mrs. cooper guilty and your listener, ernest zachow, was dismissed and warned by the judge to leave the y.m.c.a. a little earlier in the future since your show starts at 9 p.m . . . now that you know what one of your listeners has been doing in recent weeks it might be well to give some thought to what some of your other fans are doing . . .

'fred allen' was the recipient of various Groucho confidences, such as his rather peevish reaction to son Arthur's serialized 'My Old Man Groucho' memoirs:

To Fred Allen, 11 October 1954:

Are you reading the pieces about me in the S.E. Post? I had no idea I was such a nut . . .

And again, on 22 November:

It seems to me I come off as quite a nut in this book . . . I realize now I've been crazy all these years without being aware of it.

Indeed, Groucho was having to come to terms with the fact that life in the post-atomic bomb age was rather baffling for an old vaudevillian funster – letter just before Christmas Eve, to Allen: 'As I lay there in bed with a hot water bottle on my dogs, an electric blanket covering my hairy chest and half a dozen assorted antibiotics tossing around inside of me, I wondered what the hell the world was coming to . . . The medics can now stretch your life out an additional dozen years but they don't tell you that most of these years are going to be spent flat on your back while some ghoul with thick glasses and a matted skull peers at you through a machine that's hot out of "Space patrol" . . .'

Little did Groucho know that these idly typed letters would, when published, complete his transformation from an old ham to an icon, proving that the rebellious, maverick soul was innate, that the act had taken over, and Groucho and Julius had merged, and become one. As for Fred Allen's worries about his friend's fans' behaviour, he need not fret, as they were fairly sober, in the main, and included people from all walks of life, the eminent and the mundane. The poet T. S. Eliot, in a famous exchange in 1963, wrote to Groucho that he had one Grouchian portrait hanging on his wall, and another on his desk. As Groucho was due to visit England the following year, Eliot invited him and his wife for dinner. Eliot was in fact quite ill at the time (he died in 1965), so the occasion might well have been less than side-splitting. Groucho recorded his experiences in England to one of his young fans, TV's Dick Cavett, who had asked him if he had been following the antics of another foursome newly arrived upon the entertainment scene. On 16 September 1964 he wrote:

> Yes, I did see the Beatle movie in London. My wife and daughter, both of whom are considerably younger than I am (in fact my wife claims she is younger than my daughter) had a fine time at the movie. Halfway through, I wandered to the men's room and suddenly found myself in a pub across the street, drinking nut brown ale and singing 'The Whiffenpoof Song' to a stunned and incredulous crowd . . . My criticism of the Beatles picture is that it is sans jokes. Lunacy is not necessarily comedy . . .

The letter ended with a tribute to a young stand-up comedian he had discovered in New York – Woody Allen. Groucho had long become a father figure to younger entertainers to whom he often paid a generous attention, encouraging talent wherever he perceived it genuinely cropping up.

By 1961, if we wind the reel back a piece, two Marxes were literary veterans, as Harpo's book was published – by the same house that had published *Groucho and Me*, Bernard Geis Associates, in which Groucho had a five per cent interest. Harpo's book was launched with a grand party at the Algonquin Hotel, attended by such luminaries as Ben Hecht, Bennett Cerf and the visiting Irish playwright Brendan Behan, who had some months before revealed that, according to his researches, James Joyce had referred to the Marx Brothers in his stupendous novel *Finnegans Wake*: 'The three lipoleum Coyne Grouchin down in the living detch.' Groucho wondered whether Joyce might have visited the United States in 1923 and seen *I'll Say She Is*. (He had not, but somewhere along the line, he had mined the vein.) The guests at Harpo's party were provided with Harpo wigs and beeping horns, just to add to the atmosphere. Harpo told a reporter from the *New York Herald Tribune* that 'Groucho wrote every word of his book. I didn't write a word of mine. Books is not my racket.'

In fact, Harpo had spent many months with his co-writer, Rowland V. Barber, who had cut his teeth on *TV Guide* profiles, and over a period of three years, he had written copious notes which Barber then had to organize, with an ear for Harpo's distinctive voice, which of course few members of the general public had ever heard. Bill Marx, in an afterword to a later reprint of the book, described the voice: 'Even softer than Groucho's, although he had the same Upper East Side accent, with the same lyrical, fractured vowels.

"Turkey" became "takey," "hamburger" "hambaiger." "Oil" became "erle,"' as in 'getting up aily tamarra mawning to erl up before going out on the golf cawss.'" Answering the phone: 'Yeaaaaaah? This is Haaaa-po.'

Barber performed a heroic job, given Harpo's admitted confusion over dates, and the old birth date shift, which played havoc with the chronologies. But Harpo's voice does emerge, vivid and poignant, with a much more detailed picture than Groucho provided of the hectic and hairy vaudeville days.

To Don Ross of the *Herald Tribune*, Harpo related his present pride in his family and his home in Palm Springs: "'Mrs Marx," he said proudly, "was elected to the board of the unified school districts of Palm Springs. They have eight schools." . . . He paints a lot. "I am a realistic painter," he said, "to me a tree is a tree." . . . Can the world expect any more books from the Marxes, Harpo was asked. "Not from me," he said. "But maybe Chico will write one. That man is one of the world's biggest gamblers." Harpo looked at his watch. "You know what he's doing now? He's at the Friars in Beverly Hills playing pinochle or bridge or gin. If he isn't there he's playing golf. But wherever he is he's gambling. I think there's a book there.'"

But it was never written. Harpo spoke to Don Ross at the end of April 1961. Within a few days, Chico was booked in to the Cedars of Lebanon hospital in Los Angeles for what a Hollywood press agent called 'chest congestion'. In fact, it was his second heart attack. Groucho, Harpo and Maxine gathered round his bed. After a short hospital stay he was allowed home, to be with his wife, Mary Dee, though still in the constant care of a nurse.

Maxine recounts that she saw her father one more time:

I kissed him hello. He was quiet for a moment. Then he said, 'I wish I were Groucho so I could help you out.'

I looked into his eyes. 'I wouldn't exchange you for anybody.'

His nurse came in. 'Mr. Marx, is it time for us to brush our teeth?'

'Later; nurse,' he said.

She left the room.

'Is it time to brush our teeth?' he mimicked. 'Is it time to drink our juice? Who does she think we are, anyway?'

He still hadn't lost his sense of humor.

Before I left that day, Chico said: 'Remember, honey, don't forget what I told you. Put in my coffin a deck of cards, a mashie niblick, and a pretty blonde.'

On 11 October 1961, at ten-thirty a.m., Chico died.

Coughing in the Night, *or* Lingering Past the Late Show

DRIFTWOOD: But listen, it's a contract, isn't it?

FIORELLO: Oh, sure.

DRIFTWOOD: We've got a contract?

FIORELLO: You bet.

DRIFTWOOD: No matter how small it is.

FIORELLO: Hey, wait – wait! What does this say here? This thing here?

DRIFTWOOD: Oh, that? Oh, that's the usual clause. That's in every contract. That just says, uh, it says: If any of the parties participating in this contract is shown not to be in their right mind, the entire agreement is automatically nullified.

FIORELLO: Well, I don't know.

DRIFTWOOD: It's all right. That's in every contract. That's what they call a sanity clause.

FIORELLO (*shaking his head triumphantly*): You can't fool me. There ain't no Sanity Claus.

A Night at the Opera (1935)

Thursday, 12 October 1961, The Citizen News:

Marx Brothers Weep for Chico.

BEVERLY HILLS – The Marx Brothers, who gave so much laughter to the world, wept today over the death of brother Chico, a heart attack victim at the age of 70 [*sic*].

Chico, the wild piano-playing Italian-dialect member of the zany act, died in his Beverly Hills home with a nurse and his wife, Mary, at his side . . .

As funeral arrangements were being made at Forest Lawn Memorial Park in nearby Glendale the usually glib, sarcastic Groucho was only able to say, 'Please, I can't talk about it now.' Harpo, who never said a word in their act, said quietly, 'Everyone will miss Chico.'

Though he was the eldest of the five brothers – the others being Gummo and Zeppo – the lively, irreverent Chico was always a cause of concern to the rest of the family . . .

Groucho had once said, remembering Minnie: 'I still hear her voice as she talked to a family friend about us. "Sam can cough all night and I never hear him," she said. "But if one of my boys coughs just once, I'm wide awake."'

Now that we know that the first Marx Brother to die was Manfred, at the age of seven months, of a sudden influenza, we can appreciate that statement more fully. Who would Manfred have been? What madness might have been unleashed by the Six Marx Brothers, compounded on stage and screen? Or might Minnie have been less desperate to thrust the survivors forward? Leo, loved to distraction, realizing his allure but also determined to carve his own path in a hard world full of loaded dice, learned to tickle the piano keys for a living, while his zest for life explored darker corners. Ahdie, the good-natured second living son, was in no hurry to get anywhere in his wanderings through the streets and odd jobs of Manhattan. Julius was *der Eifersuchtige* – the jealous one, the complicated birth, the third son, for whom there was much less attention; the one who used to say, 'Our mother treated us all equally – with contempt'; the boy who was always more ambitious. Milton was the sickly one, who needed to be closely nurtured, the so reluctant entertainer. Herbert, the late addition, the afterthought, always felt the weight of those four other living brothers, and a dead one, bearing down on him.

And Pauline, Hannah's daughter, adopted by Minnie? The elder 'sister', or embryonic Maggie Dumont, passed on into marriage and oblivion . . . Might there have been a different show?

The Marx Brothers did not want to die. This might seem a ridiculous thing to say, but other performers were more ready. Chaplin prepared himself for the death of the clown almost as soon as he had concluded, reluctantly, that the age of the talkie was permanent. By *Monsieur Verdoux*, in 1947, he had degraded the clown into Bluebeard, the serial murderer of his wives, who went off to the guillotine in his final moments, goading his executioners with the promise, 'I shall see you all very soon.' Then, in *Limelight*, in 1952, he made sure the audience could see, without subterfuge, the clown himself dying on the stage; not just the metaphorical 'death' feared by all performers, but the thing itself, ashen and painful. And once Calvero, alias Charlie the Tramp, was dead, Chaplin could live his life, albeit in exile.

The Marx Brothers had decided to kill their act, but they remained in thrall to the characters they had created. Only Groucho, as we have seen, escaped, courtesy of *You Bet Your Life*, into a new successful orbit. Chico continued to plough his furrow, as *The Cocoanuts'* Willie the Wop, long after the character had ceased to have any *raison d'être* on its own, once the band had stopped playing. Harpo, occasionally donning his old raiment, for charity or fun, if for little profit, joined him on the road until quite late in the day, playing final gigs in places like Las Vegas and Reno, but always complaining to Maxine: 'I can't talk sense to your father. He just laughs at me, or worse, agrees to lay off the wild nights and then goes ahead and does what he wants to do. I can't control it, Maxine, and I don't want to hear about it any more.' But the brothers continued to prop up Chico, until his own heart could no longer do the job.

The last project the Marx Brothers – Groucho, Chico and Harpo – embarked on together was a still-born television series, *Deputy Seraph*. Filming of a pilot began soon after the transmission of the cack-handed *Incredible Jewel Robbery* in March 1959. Chico and Harpo were cast as angels who helped earthly matters along, bringing lovers together, foiling criminal plots, and all the usual things angels do. Groucho, the 'Deputy Seraph', was on hand to undo their misdeeds. The producer and co-author, Phil Rapp, shot seventeen minutes of uncut material. Long thought lost, this footage was found and clips included in the 1993 programme, *The Unknown Marx Brothers*. Chico's health was so obviously bad that the producers found him uninsurable, and the project collapsed for lack of backing. Despite Paul Wesolowski's brave claims that the salvaged footage is a treat for Marxists, the fragments have a melancholy air that is only deepened by the realization of how close both Chico and Harpo were to true celestial status. The record shows Chico made one more TV appearance, on 10 October 1960, playing a 'Championship Bridge' game with partner Ivan Erdos against John Gerber and Edith Kemp. He lost.

Harpo continued to appear on guest slots, after his last 'starring' role in December 1960 as the mechanical man in *Silent Panic*. He promoted his book, and clowned around, guesting, for one night only in May 1961, on Groucho's own show. His last television appearances were on the *Red Skelton Show*, and an ABC 'musicale' special, in September and October 1962. Then, in January 1963, at a fund-raising concert for symphony orchestras at the Pasadena Civic Center, performing with folk singer Allan Sherman, Harpo announced his formal retirement. Asked to come forward and speak by Sherman, he astounded and delighted his audience by talking at great length, unleashing a stream of tales and anecdotes that seemed to be never ending. Then he walked off the stage, for ever.

Harpo had suffered his first, mild heart attack in May 1959. Several more 'retirement' attacks occurred until he decided that idleness was too dangerous and took up the harp and the wig again. He painted constantly, and submitted reluctantly to being taken care of by his children. 'It was almost', Bill Marx told me, 'as if I had become his Dad, without being his Dad . . . we all come full circle . . .' But Harpo's mind was restless. Gummo might have enjoyed retirement for the past decade, but Harpo discovered, as he wrote, somewhat cryptically, 'I was different from most people. Most people have a conscious mind and a subconscious. Not me. I've always operated on a subconscious and a sub-subconscious . . .'

Well, it becomes clearer if beeped. By the summer of 1964, Harpo was faced once again with a worsening heart condition. Gummo suggested a new surgical procedure, a heart bypass operation, which might free up his clogged valves. This kind of thing was less common and more hazardous then than it is now, over three decades of medical progress later. Despite his wife's misgivings, Harpo signed up for the operation. Admitted to Mount Sinai Hospital in Los Angeles on 26 September, Harpo was operated on for 'vascular surgery, suffering from an aneurysm of the aorta'. The operation appeared to have gone well, but at six-thirty p.m. on Monday 28 September, he suffered a seizure, and all efforts to revive him failed. Time of death was announced as eight-thirty-nine p.m.. His wife Susan and two of his sons were at the bedside. Groucho, Gummo and Zeppo were not present.

Harpo's last reported public appearance had taken place one month before, in Palm Springs, 'at a dinner honoring Police Chief Gus Kettering'. The report does not state whether, when the Chief shook Harpo's hand, a shower of hotel crockery and silver cascaded out of the guest's sleeves. But the silver trumpets, nevertheless, sounded somewhere.

Arthur Marx said the only time he had seen his father, Groucho, weep was when Harpo died.

If losing Chico was the loss of the tactile, musical hand of the Brothers, Harpo was the heart, torn out and buried. Services, at the Groman Mortuary, were private, and only the close family attended.

Harpo left an estate worth one million dollars, to his wife and four children. But Harpo's legacy cannot be measured in money. As with the greats of silent comedy – Chaplin, Keaton and Lloyd – never was silence more eloquent.

And then there were three. Zeppo, on his citrus farm in Palm Springs, had remarried, on 18 September 1959, in Las Vegas. His new wife was Barbara Blakely, variously described as ex-fashion model and ex-show girl. He was fifty-eight and she was twenty-nine. Was Zeppo still trying out the footsteps of Groucho? A previous engagement, to the even younger model Diane Davis, aged either twenty-two or nineteen – depending on the newspaper you read – had been extremely short-lived. '"She wants to sing," the 57 year old talent agent said from his Palm Springs home. "But out here in the desert there is no one who can hear her. Let's just say we had a friendly personality clash."'

Zeppo continued to be dogged by legal wrangles, primarily a little difficulty with a Federal Grand Jury in Terre Haute, Indiana, concerning a tax-dodging betting syndicate. Although the syndicate had grossed millions, Zeppo convinced the jury he had made only peripheral bets over the telephone from Palm Springs or Las Vegas. Zeppo drew the last packed house of his life to answer the stern query of how he got the syndicate's phone number with: 'You can ask any little girl coming out of a kindergarten in Las Vegas, and she'll tell you how to find a bookie.' There speaks Chico's brother!

But Zeppo had clearly not given up entirely on his engineering ventures, since as late as 1969 he was reported by *Variety* to have patented, with California engineer Albert D. Herman, 'a double wrist watch that checks on the wearer's heart, sounding an alarm if something goes wrong'. Too late for Chico and Harpo both.

Gummo remained in retirement. And so there were not three, but one Marx Brother left, still active in the field in which they had started out over sixty years before.

Groucho prepared, after Harpo's death, to resume a project he had set in motion during his trip to England in the summer of 1964. As early as 1958, BBC television producers had expressed an interest in acquiring the British rights for *You Bet Your Life*. Groucho had flown over to London but had annoyed the BBC by demanding a fee to be interviewed. Six years later, there were friendlier overtures, from the rival broadcaster, the ITV network. As a sample, Groucho was first invited to guest on the ITV show, *The Celebrity Game*, aired on 12 June 1964, with Angry Young Novelist Kingsley Amis, actress Susan Hampshire, and Beatles manager Brian Epstein. In the interval between this appearance, dining with Mr and Mrs T. S. Eliot, and singing the 'Whiffenpoof' song in the pub after leaving the screening of the Beatles' *A Hard Day's Night*, Groucho signed a deal with the Rediffusion company for a thirteen-week British series, with an option for a further thirty-nine weeks.

Groucho returned to London to record the shows in the summer of 1965. Robert Dwan and Bernie Smith flew in with him to join the crew of British writers, Brad Ashton, Mike Sharland and John Wells, who had been engaged by Rediffusion's Head of Entertainment, Elkan Allan, to provide the Limey angle for the show. But the programme was a total bomb. Groucho couldn't bridge the chasm between American and British (or rather English) English and found himself completely lost for *bons mots*. During a warm-up, he tried to tell the tale of the woman who went into the druggist for a dime's worth of chaffing powder. 'Walk this way, please,' says the druggist. 'If I could walk this way, I wouldn't need the powder.' But the audience understood neither 'druggist', nor 'chaffing powder', nor 'dime'. Once he had groped for 'chemist', 'talcum' and 'shilling', the joke had died, and been laid to rest in Waukeegan.

The only advice the British writers could give Groucho and his cohorts was to 'make the show dirtier', since to British ears, even in those tasteful days, American TV humour was 'fit only for choirboys'. But the whole soufflé failed to rise. To make matters worse, Groucho took to affecting what he thought was a 'cockney' accent, which only made the audience's teeth grate. Rediffusion's miserly rewards for contestants did not help either, prizes ranging from £1 to £150, with dumb-bells who couldn't even answer the easy questions ('Who's buried in Grant's tomb?' for America, and 'For whom is the Victoria Monument named?' in the UK) being sent off with a premium bond and a cigar.

Clearly, the whole idea was misconceived. Groucho's repartee in *You Bet Your Life* was based on his gut knowledge of his audience, their quirks and their foibles. Britain and America were still two nations divided by a common language, and the Atlantic was still an ocean between. In any case the audience, which expected the quick-fire wisecracking of *The Cocoanuts* or *Animal Crackers*, could not warm to this ageing, slowed-down, quiet and laconic man. Perhaps, ironically, he was too English for them. But that might be a paradox too far.

Before Groucho left for England, another Marxian milestone was carved on 17 April 1965, when ABC transmitted its *Hollywood Palace* show, hosted by Groucho, with special guest star Margaret Dumont. Melinda Marx and South African singer Miriam Makeba also appeared in this show, but the dusky diva did not, apparently, participate in the Groucho-Maggie reprisal of 'Hooray for Captain Spaulding, the African Explorer'. It was Maggie's last appearance, an appropriate ghost, as she had died on 6 March, a few days after the show had been recorded. She had eked out a career of sorts, after the Marx Brothers, having appeared in a total of forty-four films in roles that included cameos for W. C. Fields, Laurel and Hardy, Danny Kaye, Red Skelton and even, heaven forfend, Abbott and Costello, having to endure being covered in soot by Lou's incompetent vacuum cleaner salesman. In her last movie, *What a Way To Go!* (1964), co-starring with Shirley MacLaine, Paul Newman, Dean Martin, Gene Kelly and Dick Van Dyke, she regained some of her dignity as MacLaine's self-centred mother, who pushes poor Shirley towards marriage with rich Dino, while Shirley prefers the ordinary Dick. Maxine Marx reports a lunch with the great lady in which Maggie told her, 'Those boys ruined my career! . . . Nobody took me seriously as a dramatic actress, they always thought they saw Groucho peeking out from behind my skirt.'

But like many showbiz dissimulators, she had to live with her own invention, to the bitter end. No one knew that, in 1965, when she died, she was eighty-three, not seventy-six years of age.

After publication of *The Groucho Letters*, Groucho's fame rocketed to new heights, boosted further by a key retrospective of Marx Brothers films at the Museum of Modern Art in New York. Groucho, Harry Ruby and Maxine attended the opening night on 18 April 1967.

On the brink of the watershed year of 1968, at a time of campus radicalism and rebellion, of youth and 'hippie' culture, and a new disdain for the establishment and all its works, the Marx Brothers had become icons and precursors, as if they were the Founding Fathers of a new dispensation, rather than the culmination of a hidden heritage of old vaudevillian fun. A generation whose opinion makers no longer dressed in suits nor lunched at the Algonquin, but devoured junk food or macrobiotic seeds, and dressed in T-shirts and ragged jeans, was well attuned to accepting a mixture of politics, transgressive behaviour, art – high and low, from Picasso to Popeye – movie models, graphic art, cartoons, music, the wild dance of personal desires and public ideals. Chico and Harpo might be gone, and Zeppo and Gummo lost in the background, but Groucho was still around, acerbic as ever, unwilling to suffer any foolishness but his own, disdainful of all cant and pretension, a living symbol of rebellion against the high and the mighty, with his cigar and moustache intact, and those sceptical, eyebrow-wiggling, come-on eyes.

In a moment of madness in 1968, Groucho agreed to play a bizarre role in a film directed by Otto Preminger, *Skidoo*, which tried to plug into the new Age of Aquarius by means of an absurd tale of gangsters converted to the ideals of peace, love and dropping acid. Preminger later claimed to have taken some tabs to help him understand his characters, but that merely seems to have made a bad movie into a complete turkey. Groucho played the mastermind referred to as 'God', operating from a fortified yacht and made up to look like what the old Groucho might have resembled had he been dosed with cocaine for a week and then pickled in formaldehyde. Groucho told the *New York Times*, in March 1970:

> I only did five days' work on the picture, you can't blame me. It had Gleason too, you know. I was lousy. When I say I was lousy . . . I wasn't any worse than the rest of the cast. But they gave me a lot of money and I only worked five days. I played God. Jesus, I hope God doesn't look like that.

But Groucho was determined not to find out, for some time. Nineteen sixty-nine saw another retrospective event, this time of his domestic life, with yet another marriage falling apart. Eden Hartford-Marx sued for divorce on the familiar grounds of 'extreme cruelty', alleging that her husband had an 'uncontrollable temper, was hostile and abusive and ridiculed her in the presence of family, friends, guests and servants'. She demanded a 'reasonable share' of their estimated $3-million-plus 'community property', asked the court to evict the miscreant from their $350,000 home at 1083 Hillcrest Road, Beverly Hills, and also asked for $3,500 monthly support pending trial. Her attorney was the soon-to-be-famous Marvin Mitchelson. Two months later Groucho's daughter, Melinda, filed for divorce in Juarez, Mexico, from her own husband, a Hollywood producer, after only three months of marriage (prompting the Grouchoesque comment that 'the bride got custody of the wedding cake'). Melinda had been travelling for a long time in Europe and elsewhere, and Groucho had, at one point, become so concerned at her lack of contact with him that he had hired detectives to track her down, round several capes of good hope, over the Pyrenees and then, not into Gimbels' basement but to a kibbutz in Israel, where a short-lived and farcical engagement to a fellow kibbutznik was played out to a flurry of press curiosity which, luckily for both father and daughter, soon died down.

Groucho retained the house in Hillcrest Road, but had to pay Eden her alimony and continue to reflect on the injuries his world fame, and his own shortcomings, were inflicting on those nearest to him. In December 1969, the court finally awarded Eden property worth close to $1 million including half the proceeds from the prospective sale of their home, which did not take place. (For the pedants: $21,000 alimony, $337,000 from Groucho's TV residuals and 50 per cent of the $350,000 house.)

But Groucho remained Groucho. He was not going to stay alone in the

house with nothing but a hot water bottle for long. Old friends and colleagues continued to rally round, and he could bask in the recognition not
only of his peers but of the new generation whose music and manners he
could neither appreciate nor comprehend. The older generation were not
stinting in their praise either. He liked to tell the tale of the day he was
walking in Wilshire Boulevard, and a couple passed him, the woman then
turning back to touch him on the shoulder and say, 'You're Groucho? Don't
die, just keep right on living.'

That was one request Groucho was glad to grant. In 1970, the stage production of Arthur Marx's musical about the Brothers' early years, *Minnie's
Boys*, co-written with Robert Fisher and produced by Arthur Whitelaw,
opened at the Imperial Theatre in New York. Groucho had been closely
involved with this project since 1968. He enjoyed this fantasy of the early
vaudeville years, and was instrumental in persuading the producers to cast
Shelley Winters as Minnie. Unfortunately, she couldn't sing, but then nei
ther could Minnie, which was not a handicap in real life – unlike Broadway.
The show lost money, and closed after eighty performances. Arthur and
Groucho retired to lick their respective wounds.

Groucho and his friends, the self-styled 'Geezer Club', continued to
meet, with some regularity, at Nate'n'Al's Deli in Beverly Drive. Harry
Ruby, Arthur Sheekman, Nunnally Johnson and other survivors were the
members. Groucho, while continuing to obey the injunction to live, was
not in good health, and was suffering from arteriosclerosis. In 1971, he suffered a mild stroke, from which he seemed to recover fairly rapidly. It didn't
prevent him from continuing to flirt with young girls, who would be taken
out to lunch and cuddles. But the days of priapic leaping were long over.
Later that summer, however, he was introduced to a young Canadian
woman who had trained for the theatre and played a number of small roles
on the New York stage, but had just flown out to California, looking for she
knew not what. What she found was Groucho.

Her name was Erin Fleming.

Groucho and Erin became a running saga that was to tip over into scandal,
and drag Groucho, his son and daughters, his brothers, relatives and
friends, and the voracious press and public, into a frenzy of allegations and
counter-allegations, blighting his final years. Pro-Erin and anti-Erin camps
sprang up, with daggers drawn, and recriminations that even engulfed
Groucho's biographer, Hector Arce, who came on the scene when the battle
was in full sway.

Erin might have appeared to Groucho as yet another candidate in the line of pretty girls who might fulfil the roles his fantasy required. He had married three women of generally similar temperament, whose unquestioning devotion took a steady hammering as they became the butt of his often bullying wit. W. C. Fields quipped famously about a woman: 'She drove me to drink – it's the only thing I'm indebted to her for.' Groucho's wives had the inverse experience, and didn't end up thanking him for it. But all three were vulnerable to his shafts. Erin was not, it appears, the vulnerable type, and by the time she met him, Groucho was a much diminished figure, both physically and mentally. Soon after she began dating him, and then taking on her chief role as his secretary and general manager, he suffered a second, more serious stroke, and from then on his speech was slow and slurred, and his mental agility began to be impaired.

So soon after his divorce from Eden, and at the age of eighty-one – by now Groucho was admitting his real age – he could not be taken seriously as a suitor, but it is clear that he fell under the spell of Erin's charm, her looks and her dynamic capacity to take charge of his affairs. Brought in to organize and answer his mailbag of thousands of fan letters from around the world, she soon realized the potential for Groucho to make a major comeback into the show-business world. He might not be able to sing very loudly, or dance, or host a TV show, but his mere appearance, with minimum effort, could be made into a major event. The try-out of a one-man show, at Iowa State University, where Groucho was fêted by pom-pom-swirling cheerleaders, led to a triumphant evening at Carnegie Hall in New York. This was followed by a gruelling but satisfying trip to Cannes, France, to be fêted at a gala screening of A Night at the Opera and given a medal as a Commander of the Order of Arts and Letters, something Rufus T. Firefly might have had a thing or two to say about.

Just before his trip east, Groucho had attended another special event, the awarding of an honorary Oscar for Charles Chaplin, in April, by the industry that had allowed him to be harassed into exile twenty years before. Chaplin, who had not set foot in America since 1952, met Groucho at his reception and had the following words of advice for his contemporary who had first seen him on the stage in Canada playing a young British hooligan: 'Keep warm.' He was, after all, eighteen months older than Groucho.

Now everyone was getting medals, perhaps for simply surviving so long. In September Groucho suffered his severe stroke, but Erin told the press he had been hospitalized due to being 'overwrought at the killing of the 11 Israelis at the Olympics'. This inaugurated a pattern of Erin down-playing

An actor reflects at twilight – with Erin Fleming.

major setbacks in Groucho's health. A prospective concert at the Dorothy Chandler Pavilion in Los Angeles was postponed until December. It was the last rerun of the Carnegie Hall programme, showing excerpts from the movies, *Animal Crackers*, *A Day at the Races*, *Horse Feathers* etc., followed by Groucho, accompanied by Marvin Hamlisch on the piano, singing a medley of old toons, including Irving Berlin's least favourite song, 'Stay Down Here Where You Belong', an anti-intervention ditty of the First World War, and Gus Kahn's 'Oh, How That Woman Could Cook', a nice tribute to Minnie, who couldn't. Sound recordings of the Carnegie Hall show reveal a Groucho in fine, if somewhat quavering, fettle, still with impeccable comic timing. The songs are interlaced with family reminiscences, all the old tales of Chico and Uncle Julius Schickler, with a sideline comment on 'our adopted sister, Polly . . . She wasn't a bad lookin' girl,' said Groucho, 'but her rear end stuck a way out. You could play pinochle on her rear end.' Thus was Pauline consigned to her posterity.

This was Groucho's last hurrah as a performer, though there would be some scattered guest appearances afterwards. Nineteen seventy-three was a slack year, during which Groucho gave a series of long taped interviews to a young writer, Richard Anobile, who had proven his Marxist bona fides by publishing an illustrated book of Marx Brother quotations, *Why A Duck?* This was to become a collaborative book, *The Marx Brothers Scrapbook*, which would cause tears and recriminations. Anobile, as noted earlier, included all of Groucho's salty and uncensored expressions, four-letter words and ribald or insulting comments on friends and family, which Groucho, in his fragile state, had not intended for publication. In the event, he appeared to have cleared the galleys for publication without properly reading them, and then tried, unsuccessfully, to have an injunction placed on the book at the last minute.

Erin's involvement in this case, as in every other, was as Groucho's chief, and only, arbiter and guardian. From the summer of 1974, the relationship between Erin and Groucho was witnessed, from the inside, by a young film student, Steve Stoliar, who had been engaged by Erin to answer the accumulating fan mail that she had, in fact, left to gather.

Stoliar was one of the legions of stalwart Marx fans who had come to Erin's attention by the diligence with which he bombarded Universal Pictures – who had acquired the rights to the old Paramount movies – with requests to acquire and re-release *Animal Crackers*, which had fallen into copyright limbo owing to the expiration of its licence. When Universal finally bent to the will of the fans, *Animal Crackers* was a runaway success, and Groucho was almost trampled to death by fans and police horsemen at its première in New York. Stoliar's determination to get Groucho's autograph resulted in an offer of a job, as archivist and organizer of memorabilia, working at the house in Hillcrest Road.

Stoliar described his feeling at entering his idol's house as the feeling 'when Dorothy opens her door into Munchkinland and everything turns to Technicolor'. But his starry-eyed innocence did not last very long. Groucho's household, at that time, consisted of a maid, Agnes, a friendly cook, Martha Brooks, a gardener and a succession of personal nurses. Erin Fleming, in fact, did not live in the house, but had a residence of her own very close by. She was, however, the mistress of the household, and jealous of any trespass on her domain.

The main conflict was over the relationship between Groucho, Erin and Groucho's son, Arthur, and his daughters, Miriam and Melinda. Miriam was undergoing a series of alcohol rehabilitation cures, Melinda was a very occasional visitor and a long-standing tension remained between Groucho and his writer son. Stoliar, who recounted his tale of Groucho's last two years in a memoir, *Raised Eyebrows*, published in 1996, became more and more concerned at the erratic nature of Erin's stewardship of Groucho, and her determination to present his children as uncaring ogres. Zeppo, an occasional visitor, was a rare ally of Erin's, appreciative of Groucho's luck, at his age, in having such an attractive companion. Erin was, in fact, not as young as she made herself out to be, having recently breasted thirty, but that still gave her a good half-century advantage over Julius Henry Marx!

Stoliar writes:

After asking what Groucho was like, people usually want to know about Erin. This is a complex subject and one about which I have mixed feelings . . . I usually begin by saying that whatever they've heard about her is probably true, however flattering or damning or contradictory it may appear.

If they heard that she came along at a time when Groucho was alone, his last wife having left him, his children having found other priorities, and that Erin picked him up, dusted him off and devoted herself tirelessly to helping him go out a living legend, that was true . . .

And if they heard that she was extremely hard to get along with, given to wild mood swings, abusive to Groucho – at least verbally and possibly physically – and that she made his final years a rougher ride than they needed to have been, sadly that was true as well.

The Groucho that Stoliar found was not always alone, as a steady stream of old friends kept visiting. His grandson Andy, Arthur's son, was constantly around, too, as were a *mélange* of Erin's own Hollywood friends, such as actors Bud Cort and Sally Kellerman. Journalist and writer Lyn Erhard, alias Charlotte Chandler, who had interviewed Groucho for *Playboy* magazine in March 1974, was present for long periods, taping long rambling reminiscences by Groucho and friends Morrie Ryskind, George Seaton, George Burns, Nat Perrin, Jack Benny et al., as well as new admirers like Elliott Gould and Woody Allen. Another outsider, Hector Arce, was talking with Groucho and Erin about a proposed book on Groucho's radio and TV show *You Bet Your Life*, which would be published as *The Secret Word Is Groucho*, in 1976. This led to another planned collaboration, a large coffee-table book of Groucho's treasure trove of photographs, with Groucho's own notes, that would become *The Groucho Phile*. The project of a full biography of Groucho, by Arce, emerged in this context. At first Erin was delighted at this new tranche of Grouchomania, but soon enough, Arce too would become embroiled in her eternal war against Groucho's children, who were becoming increasingly concerned at her power over their ailing and very rich father.

Groucho himself, the centre of all this attention, was seen by Stoliar as a frail old man often bewildered by the whirlwind of emotions around him, sometimes flashing out with shafts of the old wit, as to an interviewer:

REPORTER: Do you enjoy being called a living legend?
GROUCHO: Yes.
REPORTER: Why?
GROUCHO: Because I'm dead.
REPORTER: You're going to be eighty-five soon. How does it feel?
GROUCHO: Sixty-nine felt better.

In an interview with Bill Cosby, who asked him if he believed in 'life after death', Groucho replied: 'I have serious doubts about life before death, the way we're going now.' (*Pause.*) 'I believe in death during life, and so does everyone watching this show.' Cosby, digging himself a deeper hole: 'Do you have any unfulfilled wish?' Groucho: 'Yes, I'd like to terminate this interview as soon as possible.'

In April 1974, Groucho had received an honorary Academy Award, handed to him by Jack Lemmon, who had handed Chaplin his own Oscar in 1972. Groucho made a brief speech, saying: 'I only wish Harpo and Chico could have been here – and Margaret Dumont, who never understood any of our jokes. She used to say, "Julie, what are they laughing at?"' But Maggie Dumont only smiled, from the grave. At another awards ceremony, the Student Academy Awards, in June 1976, Groucho, in the audience rather than on the podium, kept interrupting the speaker, who tried to maintain his serious purpose: 'Now then, these young filmmakers –' 'What about the old filmmakers?' called Groucho. '– will take their place –' 'They're not gonna take *my* place!'

Indeed they were not. But matters were coming to a head at home, with Erin's behaviour alienating more and more of Groucho's friends and assistants, and her impatient and intemperate outbreaks becoming more frequent, so that, when Groucho couldn't come up with a funny anecdote about *A Night at the Opera* for his dinner guests, Erin became enraged, yelling at him: 'You stupid, senile old bastard!' Maxine Marx, who was present at one such outburst, recalled to me her sense of shock and revulsion. Perhaps feeling she had gone too far, Erin suddenly insisted that Groucho should make peace with his children, and Arthur and his wife Lois began to visit. Miriam spoke to her father on the telephone from one of her rehabilitation centres. In January 1977 Melinda came to visit, but this only sparked off further outbursts from Erin. Soon after, Groucho fell and fractured his hip. Hospital tests showed he had suffered another stroke some time before, an incident that had been denied by Erin. Alarmed by this evidence of neglect, Arthur Marx finally took legal action to have himself declared Groucho's legal guardian, with the Bank of America overseeing Groucho's finances.

At this point the Groucho Marx affair broke out into lurid press headlines. A paranoid Erin, believing Arthur had planted bugging devices in the house, hired two private detectives to search the premises. They found no bugs, but they did find a grocery bag containing twenty-nine syringes, in a storm drain. Reporting this to Erin, the two detectives were ordered by her to bury the suspicious articles in the yard. Instead they took them to the Beverly Hills police who found residual traces of the barbiturate Nembutal on the syringes.

And the rest is Hollywood hysteria: THREAT TO GROUCHO MARX'S LIFE CLAIMED; POSSIBILITY OF MARX DEATH PLOT PROBED; MARX'S MANAGER THREATENED TO KILL 2, COURT TOLD, and so forth. Where Chico and Harpo's last years had been private, allowing the brothers their dignity, Groucho's last months were a public inferno, with the subject of all the sound and fury shuttled in and out of hospital wards, mostly oblivious of the tawdry drama played out around him. Worst of all, there were no jokes. Arthur's attorneys claimed in court that Erin was a danger to Groucho's life, and one of his nurses, sacked by Erin, testified that Erin had, on at least one occasion, given him a tranquillizer so that she could go out with her friends. Evidence was heard of Erin's verbal abuse and violent shaking of Groucho. The two detectives hired by Erin testified that when they confronted her after they had handed in the syringes to the police, she had said to both of them: 'I'm going to kill you.' On the other hand, Zeppo testified that Groucho was in love with Erin, and that removing her from his side would probably kill him. The court appointed Groucho's old friend Nat Perrin to be his legal guardian on a temporary basis, and when he was too exhausted to carry out this task, Groucho's grandson Andy was appointed in his place.

On Thursday, 21 April 1977, Gummo died in Palm Springs. He was known to be extremely upset at Groucho's predicament and had been lonely and melancholy since the death of his wife Helen the year before. A spokesman for the Eisenhower Medical Center announced his death 'of natural causes'. Zeppo was quoted as saying, 'I guess his heart just gave out.'

Few but the immediate family noted the death of the unknown Marx Brother, who had left the stage in 1918, nearly sixty years before. He slipped away as quietly as he had lived, in his retirement, for the past two decades. The world's slowest whirlwind dancer had finally hung up his taps. He left no movies to record his contribution, but only the memories of his gentle good nature. He had lived to the full, in his own quiet way, his long life of eighty-five years.

Groucho was not told of Gummo's death. Nat Perrin told the *Los Angeles Herald-Examiner*, on 29 April, that Groucho was not even aware of the fierce court battle fought over him. 'I think his real, deep enjoyment in life comes from seeing his old buddies,' Perrin said. 'You can't carry on a real conversation [but friends can] get some messages to him by conversing with his nurse.' In an ironic symbol of the old meeting the new, Attorney Douglas Dalton, representing Erin Fleming, was also representing another client, Roman Polanski, up before the same Santa Monica court in a sex and drugs case. The vultures could have a field day.

On 22 June, Groucho was discharged from Cedars-Sinai Hospital to go home but was rushed back a day later as he was unable to swallow food or liquids. On the 25th another ex-cook, John Ballow, testified against Erin, describing how she would smack Groucho at the dinner table, or when he was unable to sign his cheques properly, because of his shaky signature. Ballow claimed Erin had often coaxed Groucho to adopt her, and was constantly disparaging about his son and daughters, calling Melinda 'that hippy tramp'. 'Many times he got so upset', Ballow said, 'he almost, well, tears would come to his eyes.'

Two weeks later Erin testified, having filed a deposition of 912 pages, denying everything alleged against her. She said that, in her recent visit to Groucho in hospital, he had told her, 'You are the woman I love. I want you to stay with me.'

On 27 July, Erin's lawyer agreed to Andy Marx being appointed Groucho's permanent guardian, with the Bank of America overseeing the estate. Groucho remained in hospital, visited regularly by Erin, by Arthur and Lois Marx, and Andy. At one point in mid-August, Andy told Steve Stoliar, Groucho whispered to a nurse approaching with a thermometer, 'What do you want?' 'We have to see if you have a temperature,' said the nurse. 'Don't be silly,' whispered Groucho, 'everybody has a temperature.' This was, it appears, Groucho's last joke.

On 16 August, Elvis Presley died, causing massive press excitement and speculation. In January 1935, when Elvis had been born, the Marx Brothers were awaiting script revisions of *A Night at the Opera*, having already been through two and a half careers, from vaudeville to film. But the representatives of two very different generations of show business shared the week of their extinction, as Groucho died three days after the 'king', on 19 August. Arthur, Lois and Andy watched him slip away, at seven-fifteen p.m. The immediate cause of death was recorded as pneumonia.

Groucho died exactly a century, plus fifteen days, from the day when his grandfather, Levy Schoenberg, first set foot in the United States, on 4 August 1877.

Among the many obituaries, Alden Whitman in the *Los Angeles Times* wrote:

Groucho Marx was an illusion in death. He was not what he seemed on the surface. Underneath was a human being vastly more complicated and more interesting than the cardboard cutout that got into print. He hinted at his inner turmoils when he replied to a fan who remarked how pleased he was to meet the famous Groucho. "I've known him for years," Marx said, "and I can tell you it's no pleasure."'

Well, it certainly was for us.
Hello, I must be going.
And then there was one.

Zeppo learned of his last remaining brother's death on the evening news, having been cut off by the rest of the family because of his strong support for Erin Fleming's case. He continued to express this support to the press, while Groucho's family and friends gathered to memorialize Julius Henry Marx. Zeppo was now alone, as his wife since 1959, Barbara, had divorced him in 1973. (She went on to marry Frank Sinatra, in 1976.) Zeppo's love life, however, continued, dogged by even more lawsuits. A court in Indio, near Palm Springs, ordered him to pay $20,690 to one Jean Bodul, thirty-seven, estranged wife of 'reputed mob figure James Fratianno', for beating her about the face and head in an incident in April 1973, in the driveway of the Tamarisk Country Club. Judgment was passed in November 1978. Zeppo was seventy-seven years old. To the breathless press, Zeppo said he wasn't bothered by the money as much as by the slur on his reputation. 'The Marx Brothers never had a reputation for beating women. This was the first time I've been in court in my life.'

During 1979 Zeppo developed lung cancer. He continued to enjoy his Palm Springs social life, and fishing trips off the coast on a commercial fishing boat he had bought for summer excursions. Girlfriends, who were later named in his will, continued to come and go. In August 1979 the BBC aired his last interview, conducted by Barry Norman, from which I have quoted earlier in our tale.

NORMAN: Groucho always said you were the wittiest of the Marx Brothers. Tell us about Zeppo Marx.

ZEPPO: Oh, well now you want me to make a joke or something.

NORMAN: No, I didn't mean that. Did you feel that you wanted . . .

ZEPPO: Yes, I wanted to be a comedian and there wasn't an opportunity for me to be a comic. It was a very difficult time at the finish getting funny stuff for three boys, Groucho and Chico and Harpo . . . I felt frustrated because I couldn't do the things that I was thinking up for them to do, and rightly so. I didn't resent it at all, but every time I walked out on the stage I felt I was cheating, because I wasn't doing a good job. So I just got up and quit . . . I wanted to be on my own so I went out.

NORMAN: Do you miss your brothers?

ZEPPO: Oh yes. I miss Gummo very much because he lived down here and we were together every day . . . Of course you miss your family and when you get older you have some people that you're bound to miss. So (*chuckles*) you have to do the best you can. But it's hard to think about the kind of feeling that you had with these brothers and your friends.

From the *Los Angeles Times*, 1 December 1979:

Zeppo, the Marx brother who got the girl but never the gags, died of lung cancer early Friday at Eisenhower Medical Center in Palm Springs. The last survivor of the five famous brothers was 78 . . . Memorial services are scheduled for 2 p.m. Sunday at Wiefels and Sons Mortuary, Palm Springs. The body is to be cremated.

And then there were none.

The war raged on, nevertheless, over Groucho's ghost. The Bank of America sued Erin Fleming for $400,000 the executors claimed had been fraudulently taken by her from the estate. Erin counter-sued for moneys owing to her as Groucho's manager. This case was pending for five years. Meanwhile, in May 1982, the urn containing Groucho Marx's ashes in Eden Memorial Park in the San Fernando Valley was mysteriously stolen from its crypt and found, a few hours later, intact, at Mount Sinai Memorial Park in Glendale. This was, the police claimed, the second time that crypt had been opened and the urn removed, though they did not elaborate. Perhaps the thieves had read of the macabre snatching of Charlie Chaplin's coffin from his grave at

Vevey, Switzerland, in March 1978, by two unemployed East European blackmailers. Chaplin had died in December 1977, five months after Groucho. Thus the era of the comic giants just about came to an end. Buster Keaton had died in 1966, and Harold Lloyd in 1971. Only Mae West, of all the movie greats, outlived the Marx Brothers, hanging on until 1980.

The temporary thieves of Groucho's ashes were never found. Erin Fleming's case was heard in January and February 1983, in Santa Monica. This time Erin's erratic behaviour was so extreme that she was ordered by the judge to undergo a psychiatric evaluation. She was found to be 'severely mentally ill', but was still ordered to pay the Bank of America over $400,000 in compensatory damages and punitive charges. This was reduced to half the amount, but the verdict itself was upheld on appeal, in 1987. By this time legal costs had eaten away large amounts of the estimated $2 million value of Groucho's estate, comprising cash, property and stocks in A. T. & T., General Motors and Texaco.

Erin Fleming disappeared. In 1995 Steve Stoliar, preparing his book about Groucho's last years, conducted a search for any subsequent press mention of her name. He found an item from the *Los Angeles Times*, of 13 June 1990: 'Erin Fleming Arrested With Gun'. She had been held after walking into the West Hollywood Sheriff's office at eleven p.m., with a loaded .357 Magnum revolver in her bag.

Subsequent reports located her in the psychiatric ward of the County-USC Medical Center in 1992. Later, in 1993, Stoliar was sent a copy of a letter she had fired off to celebrities such as Dick Cavett, claiming to be a victim of lawyers' conspiracies. Sightings in 1998 found her in more settled circumstances, in recovery from her traumatic years.

Whatever her mental state when she met Groucho, it seems clear that Erin Fleming could not comprehend the consequences of attaching herself to, and then trying to control, a person of such fame and celebrity as Groucho Marx. Groucho may have seemed a frail old man, witty and amusing, and so he was, a man of flesh and blood. But he was also a receptacle for the affections and fantasies of millions of people who thought they knew him through the powerful echoes of his image on the movie screen, and on TV. No matter how closely we pick over the details and minutiae of his life and work, the famous artist remains – despite the hubris and presumption of the biographers – in his own right, an enigma. What was it like to be Groucho, a figure who seemed to be known by so many, a public icon, the property of the masses, the object of so many people's eager desire to be amused, transported and entertained; and at the same time to be the private person, the father who loved, not wisely, nor even perhaps too well, but in his own individual, ornery fashion; the brother of his equally famous brothers; the son of Samuel and Minnie Marx; the grandson of Sophie and Levy Schoenberg, alias Levy Funk, that strong-armed ventriloquist of Lower Saxony, the umbrella maker who had embarked, one hundred years before, upon his journey to a new, unknown land?

And where lie the roots of that jongleur wandering, deep in the obscure past? Is there a never-never land, from which the jokes mysteriously flow, and to which the jokesters' spirits return?

Dick Cavett, remembering Groucho, told the press eulogizers of a birthday greeting Groucho had once sent an unidentified friend:

'If you keep having birthdays, you'll eventually die. Love, Groucho.'

Now there's a man who understood reality, both wisely, and too well.

The Legacy

On 16 August 1955, the *Los Angeles Times* ran a somewhat sad story:

GROUCHO'S TWIN'S HERE BUT HE'S NOT LAUGHING

A. M. Ezekiel, an optometrist from Jakarta, Indonesia, set out on a world trip last month to study optical operations in various lands. But he keeps getting sidetracked.

People keep thinking he's Groucho Marx.

It's no different in Los Angeles yesterday when he sought to interest a reporter in his mission. He wound up waggling his eyebrows and puffing a cigar in the best Marxian manner.

Ezekiel said that even in Jakarta, Indonesia's capital, he is occasionally greeted by cries of 'Hey, Groucho!' when sighted in the street.

'But I pay no attention to this silly business,' said Ezekiel, 'and when I showed some friends a picture of Groucho that had been sent me, they mistook Groucho for me . . .'

Ezekiel figures it will be about five more months before he completes his tour and gets back to Jakarta, and to his own identity.

The cinema, that robust child of photography, was the first art form to preserve time in a capsule; a mechanical form that both records a moment, or a process, of reality, and also its illusion, a narrative dream. Hollywood's greatest moment of self-realization, of articulating this idea, might be in Billy Wilder's *Sunset Boulevard*, when the ageing Gloria Swanson views herself in her youth. We can all, of course, watch our family snapshots or videos, but not as recorded by Erich von Stroheim. 'You're Norma Desmond. You used to be big,' marvels young William Holden. 'I am big,' snaps the actress, 'it's the pictures that got small.'

The Marx Brothers have survived, and got even bigger, despite the fact that the pictures got smaller and smaller, till they could even be shrunk to the size of the five-inch TV sets on the back of airline seats, or even smaller, to wristwatch TVs. The Brothers have proved, however, that it is not size, but depth that matters – the depth of memory reworked, and of a rare transference from one generation's esteem to another's. How many other comedians can have cracked up twelve-year-old Sid Perelman in 1916 and other twelve-year-olds eighty years later? The Marx Brothers, like all comedians, always insisted that all they were trying to do was to make a living by making other people laugh. They were not trying to comment on society, attack social mores, subvert the populace against received wisdoms, 'deconstruct' language, or turn the world upside down. They were not 'seeing the greatest potential for personal expression as existing outside of any structured relationship', nor did they perceive the denouement of *Duck Soup* as pushing the Brothers 'outside of narrative, essentially outside of causality and continuity, with no hope of assimilating them back again', as some current analysts enthuse. They were simply fooling around. But it is precisely in this pure idea of 'fooling around' that they achieved their deepest, most profound impact.

Why the Marx Brothers? Why-a no chicken? Why-a no Ritz Brothers, or Olsen and Johnson, or the Three Stooges? As I observed about W. C. Fields, funny is in the eye of the beholder, and no one who thinks a comedian unfunny will be persuaded to laugh even under threat of torture. The statement 'They make me laugh', or 'I just don't think they're funny' is the full stop of the argument. Social commentators and medical personnel might make the argument that laughter is good for you, but as some of them also tell me watching *Nightmare on Elm Street* is a cathartic experience, I think we should leave science aside. We may note, on the other hand, Woody Allen's testimonial to the therapeutic value of watching the Marx Brothers, when the neurotic Elliot in *Hannah and her Sisters* explains how viewing their movies made him appreciate life even if it was devoid of logic or meaning.

This is, at root, a story about culture; about how certain characters and their antics, and dialogue, become a part of a kind of collective semi-demi-consciousness (honk honk) and seem, from the screen, to speak for us. The clown, as ever, dares what we do not dare, and insults the king, even when in his employ. The British comedian Spike Milligan once tried to articulate what Laurel and Hardy meant for him: when they first walked out on the screen, he said, I knew they were my friends. In his foreword to the British edition of *Harpo Speaks*, Milligan wrote of the Marx Brothers: 'Later, when I started to write comedy, it was their influence that moulded my style. Sanity was out, logic was out, creative lunacy was in.' (And indeed Spike Milligan's *Goon Show* scripts, with Peter Sellers et al., are like Harpo's stream-of-sub-consciousness made verbal.) But, as I have tried to tease out, there was a great deal in the Brothers' comedy, both in their characters and in their writers' dia-logue, that beat out their music to the rhythm of their own inner logic, of their life story, of their heritage, both in terms of family and profession, and that was, not the confusion of madmen, but the rebellion of the sane in the confusing world of the deranged. The Brothers' *folie de grandeur*, after all, is their stubborn insistence on trying to make sense of a senseless world. As Chico concludes unerringly: 'This painting was stolen by left-handed moths!'

Groucho's famous wisecracks, like his riposte to the Friars' Club: 'Please accept my resignation. I don't care to belong to any club that will have me as a member', and to *Confidential Magazine*: 'Gentlemen, If you continue to publish slanderous pieces about me, I shall feel compelled to cancel my subscription', reflect, to many, straightforward truths about the cussedness of ordinary human behaviour. All the more ironic, to Groucho Marx, that words he threw out as no more than casual afterthoughts reverberate as profound witticisms, while the stuff he laboured over, line by line, often ended on the cutting room floor.

Like so many, I am a fan. But as I view once again my Marx Brothers videos, fine-combing for gestures, lines and nuances, I fancy, after this long quest, that I can discern the 'real' Marx Brothers hiding behind those masks and costumes – Minnie and Sam's boys who never grew up. Their real heritage: from Minnie, a desperate need to rise up, out of the subsuming, teeming mass, to make their individual mark, forcefully and – if need be – ruthlessly, but with a wild, devil-may-care abandon; and from Frenchy/Samuel/ Simon Marx, a kind of confident humanity, an authentic acceptance of the absurdity of life – almost, paradoxically, self-effacing: Dr Hackenbush's knowledge of his limits, but his total and even reckless refusal to let this get him down. On and on the siblings bicker, vying for parental attention as they tutsi-frutsi each other, like Chico and Groucho, or collaborating, like Chico and Harpo, in their own secret childhood language; Zeppo, the little brother, frozen out; Gummo, the fifth, spare wheel.

And striding behind them, their own Paul Bunyan, the Primal Ancestor, the axe-wielding Levy Schoenberg, alias Funk, son of Abraham and Schontje Weiler, husband of the melodious harpist Fanny, unsung artisans of the flatlands of Dornum, daring people to come forth and have their heads chopped off, so that the showman could re-attach them as new.

Out of fact, and into legend – cartoon figures, icons, timely metaphors.

In Robert Coover's complex novel, *The Public Burning*, set in the last days before the execution of the alleged atom-bomb spies Julius and Ethel Rosenberg, the Marx Brothers make a fictive entrance amid a long line of real personalities subsumed by the author in his narrative: Harpo, as Ethel Rosenberg, is at the centre of the masque in Times Square, sitting in the electric chair, writing furious letters to Groucho who, as Julius Rosenberg, wisecracks with the executioner, Chico:

CHICO: If you don' talk, Mr. Roastenburg, we gonna givva you da chair!
GROUCHO: Okay, don't bother to wrap it, I've got my car.
CHICO: I mean you gotta sit in dat chair and face-a da music!
GROUCHO: Face the music! That's why you call it Sing Sing, hunh?

As Coover's co-opted Marx Brothers clown about, and the clock ticks down towards the atom spies' execution and the degradation of America's love affair with illusions, 'Uncle Sam' – alias Sam Slick, the Yankee Peddler – 'comes hurrying out, bobbing his stern white brows and imitating Groucho's famous stiff-backed ass-to-the-ground stride, to garner the last burst of laughter and applause . . .'

Uncle Sam playing Groucho: what could better reflect the true absurdity of self-serving, phoney patriotism – as Coover's modern-day lynch mob presses on, 'The Star-Spangled Banner' playing, towards the high-voltage catharsis of the darker side of the American Dream.

Out of legend, and into our everyday lives: Groucho's insistent voice, letting everyone at the party know the host is wearing no clothes, continues a tradition as universal as Cervantes and Rabelais, and as American as Mencken and Mark Twain. The Marx Brothers have become our modern model of the age-old troubadours of liberty and romance – transcending society's capricious rules and strictures – and yanking off the Emperor's trousers for good measure, just so that reality can be seen in a much clearer light.

But only in the theatre can the heads be re-attached, and only in the movies can the clowns be immortal. Cue *I Pagliacci*:

Vanno laggiu,	(They go over there
Verso un paese strano	To a strange country
Che sognan forse	Of which perhaps they dream,
E che cercano in van,	And which they seek in vain,
Ma I boemi del ciel	But heaven's bohemians
Seguon l'arcano poter	Follow the mysterious power
Che li sospinge.	That drives them.)

And make that five hard-boiled eggs.

'Hello, we must be going!' Hail and farewell!

Acknowledgements

A repeated accolade to Paul Wesolowski, Number One Fan and keeper of the archival flame in New Hope, Pennsylvania. Heartfelt thanks to members of the far-flung Marx family, to Miriam Marx Allen, Bill Marx and Robert Marx in California, and to Maxine Marx in New York, who have given of their time and sanity and endured my 'Why-a-duck' queries, with a wave of goodwill towards Arthur Marx, who has endured a lifetime of smart-alecks burrowing around the old plantation. Joe Adamson, pioneer Marxist, has always been gracious with his time and expertise. A further thanks to David Rothman, volunteer genealogist, whose skeptical interrogation of old documents could put any Special Prosecutor to shame. Much kowtowing to all the usual suspects in archives east and west: to Rod Bladel and staff at the Billy Rose Theatre Collection at the New York Public Library for the Performing Arts; Scott Curtis and staff of the Special Collections division of the Margaret Herrick Library of the Academy of Motion Picture Arts and Sciences in Los Angeles; Geraldine Duclow and staff of the Theatre Collection at the Free Library of Philadelphia; staff of the Motion Picture, Manuscript Division and Rare Books Department at the Library of Congress, Washington, DC; staff of the Family History Archive at the Temple of Jesus Christ of the Latter Day Saints in Los Angeles, who understood that I could never be a member of a club which would have me as a member; staff at the Brooklyn Public Library, the Schubert Archive, New York, the British Film Institute Library and Westminster Reference Library, London. Thanks also to Jean-Michel Bouhours and staff at the Centre Georges Pompidou's cinema service. More hosannahs to the one and only Miles Kreuger, keeper of the Institute of the American Musical in Los Angeles, Anthony Slide, Walter Donohue, Rick Mitz, Paul and Kalinka Rothman, Oren Moverman, Glenn Mitchell, Michael Pointon, Joel Finler, Ian Gibson, Armond Fields, Frank Ferrante, Eileen Naseby, Don and Maya Peretz, and, hey now, it's Mairi again – stuck with Hugo Z. Hackenbush for two years. Free vouchers for a week each at the Standish Sanatorium will be available in the foyer.

The FBI and the Marx Brothers

The Federal Bureau of Investigation releases personal and public interest files when requested under the Freedom of Information/Privacy Act. What emerges from such a request often reveals more about the FBI's enormous appetite for keeping files than about these files' subjects, and highlights the Bureau's historical obsession with the merest hint of left-wing values. Much of the material consists of newspaper cuttings or gossip reported by agents from various sources. Personal details, ages, even the spelling of names can be inaccurate. In Groucho's case, as discussed in Chapters 32 and 33, there is no mystery in his inclusion among the thousands of US citizens listed as being involved in protests and activities against fascism in Europe, or in support of Republican Spain, or boycotts of Nazi Germany, not to speak of his open involvement in the protests against the excesses of the House Un-American Activities Committee.

Nevertheless, the FBI did not neglect the other Marx Brothers. Having requested files on both Harpo and Chico Marx, I was hoping to find some enlightenment about Harpo's 1933 Moscow visit, and possibly Chico's connections on the gambling scene. The trawl, however, does not cast light on either. In Harpo's file, there are two items. One is a cutting from the socialist magazine *The Worker*, from July 1947, citing Harpo's support for a new, non-profit, inter-racial hospital, and his arrangement of a benefit for the cause, which featured stars such as Edward G. Robinson, Frank Sinatra, George Burns and boxing champion Joe Louis. Close friendships with Paul Robeson and Lena Horne are also cited. "'The hospital's a wonderful way to combat prejudice,'" Harpo is quoted as stating, 'his big eyes sparkling with enthusiasm.' The item, headed 'Healing Without a Color Line' is duly recorded on 4 August 1947 and denoted 'Clipped at the Seat of Government'.

The other item on Harpo, which also mentions Gummo, lists financial assets in connection with investments in two Las Vegas hotels, the Casa Blanca and the Riviera, in 1953. Harpo's total cash investment was $55,000 and Gummo's $36,000. Harpo's net worth at this point is down as $485,013.49 in property and cash and Gummo's as $355,292.54. The papers are on file due to tax investigations of applicants for gambling licences in the said hotels. At some point Harpo and Gummo's interests in the hotels were dissolved, but it is difficult to work out the details as much of the document I have received is blacked out, the Bureau's normal procedure when names other than those on the formal FIA request are cited. Nothing shedding official light on Harpo's funding or fund-raising for Ben Hecht's revolutionary activities in Palestine has emerged.

The file on Chico Marx is largely a fat dossier on the 'Dibble and Dabble' copyright infringement case as detailed in Chapter 29. As this was a Federal prosecution it is not surprising that the file exists, but what may be a little odd is Bureau chief J. Edgar Hoover's personal interventions in the case. On 20 March 1937, to the 'Special Agent in Charge, Los Angeles: Re: GROUCHO MARX – COPYRIGHT. Dear Sir, The Bureau file in the above entitled case indicates that this case is not receiving prompt investigative attention in your district. This matter should be placed in line for early investigative attention and you should submit a report to the Bureau at the earliest possible date.' And again, on 23 July 1937, to the same recipient: 'Dear Sir, The Bureau desires that it be advised as to the exact status of the case at the present time. Very truly yours, John Edgar Hoover, Director.'

As this was a plain misdemeanour case, Hoover's interest can raise eyebrows. Was the Director's personal authority required in every single Federal case in 1937? There is nothing in the files to indicate interest in Groucho or Chico prior to this date, though the Groucho file does cite the *Daily Worker*'s praise for him in 1934 (see Chapter 32). Perhaps the very name 'Marx' lit a red bulb in the zealous guardian's head. Be that as it may, the file contains reports, details of the case, telegrams to head office reporting the highlights and numerous newspaper cuttings. It also includes the almost illegible copies of the original 'Dibble and Dabble' script and that of Al Boasberg, showing that Boasberg had indeed used entire chunks of the plaintiffs' work pretty much word for word. As Boasberg had died before the case was heard, it was Groucho and Chico who took the fall.

The only other entry under 'Chico Marx' is a rather typical piece of malicious gossip from one Colonel Justin G. Doyle, tendered to the FBI Director in Indianapolis on 1 June 1951, referring to an incident in 1941, when Colonel Doyle was a Morale Officer assigned to accompany the 'Flying Show', 'a USO Troup consisting of various big name movie and radio stars, on a trip through the Caribbean Theatre of Operations'. The main fly in this ointment was the presence of John Garfield, who was already under suspicion of being redder in his politics than in his patriotic veins (or maybe because his original name was Julius Garfinkle; Julius was not a popular name with the FBI, and we hadn't even reached Julius Rosenberg yet!). Colonel Doyle quotes his own contemporary report:

On November 12, 1941 during the performance at the theater at 'Waller Field', Fort Read, Trinidad, (blacked out) one of the actresses came to me during the performance and told me that she did not care what CHICO MARX said in the company of show people, but she thought it was terrible for him to be 'crabbing' about things before soldiers and that he was in the ante room doing it then. I immediately went to the dressing room where there were several soldiers present. I had them leave eventually and casually. During this time I did not hear anything unusual.
November 13, 1941, in a hotel room at Miami, Florida, I hear Mr. OLIVER HARDY and Mr. STAN LAUREL refer to Mr. GARFIELD and Mr. CHICO MARX in a disparaging way as the two Communists.
I have heard that Mr. JOHN GARFIELD was mentioned in connection with the investigation some time ago, of Hollywood actors contributing to Communistic activities. From my observation and association with them it is recommended that these two actors be excluded from any further camp shows.
JUSTIN G. DOYLE, Major, Infantry, Assistant Morale Officer.

The 1951 report is filed with the recommendation: 'This information is being furnished by this office for informational purposes only, and no further investigation is to be conducted in Indianapolis unless advised to the contrary.' A year later, Garfield was dead of a heart attack, after several years of persecution by HUAC agents and the downward curve of both his personal life and his career.

The suggestion that Chico, of all the Marx Brothers the least political and least left-wing, should none the less be cited for such transgressions, and perhaps simply his friendship with a subversive suspect, shows how deep the paranoia of the sentinels of morale could seep, though Chico was not, in fact, excluded from further shows for troops. Piquant, too, that an idle remark by Laurel and Hardy should be thought worthy of note in the cause of national security.

The FBI's attentions did not, it seems, have any impact on the Marx Brothers' careers, but are indicative of the extent to which all those of Hollywood's denizens who might be classified as mavericks, renegades, social climbers, Jews, non-whites, opponents of racism and bigotry, or simply critics of the status quo and government policy, were considered potential enemies of the state, therefore meriting a watchful eye.

Marx-Schoenberg Family Tree

Abraham Schönberg *m.* Schöntje Weiler (Dornum, Prussia)

Levy Schönberg 1823–1920 *m.* *1851* Fanny Sophie Solomons 1829–1901

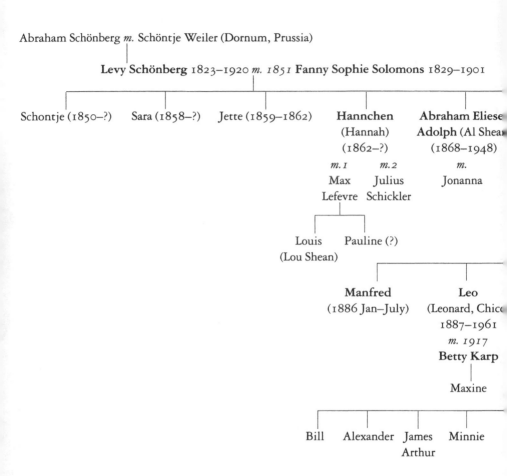

Schontje (1850–?)   Sara (1858–?)   Jette (1859–1862)   Hannchen   Abraham Eliese
                                                           (Hannah)   Adolph (Al Shea
                                                           (1862–?)   (1868–1948)
                                                        m. 1   *m. 2*   *m.*
                                                        Max   Julius   Jonanna
                                                     Lefevre Schickler

                                              Louis   Pauline (?)
                                           (Lou Shean)

                                                    Manfred   Leo
                                                (1886 Jan–July) (Leonard, Chic
                                                                 1887–1961
                                                                 m. 1917
                                                                 Betty Karp

                                                                    Maxine

                            Bill   Alexander James   Minnie
                                                Arthur

422

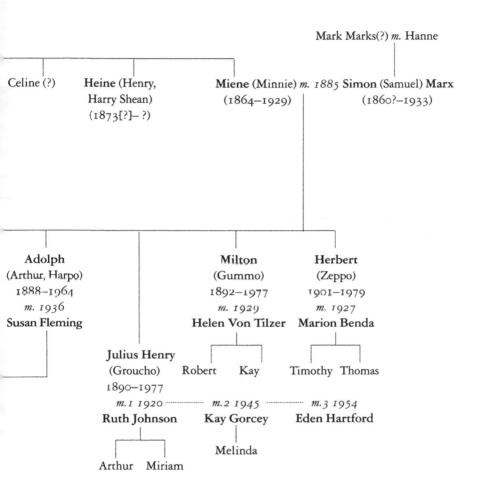

Mark Marks(?) *m.* Hanne

Celine (?)   Heine (Henry,   Miene (Minnie) *m. 1885* Simon (Samuel) Marx
              Harry Shean)   (1864–1929)   (1860?–1933)
              (1873[?]– ?)

Adolph   Milton   Herbert
(Arthur, Harpo)   (Gummo)   (Zeppo)
1888–1964   1892–1977   1901–1979
m. 1936   *m. 1929*   *m. 1927*
Susan Fleming   Helen Von Tilzer Marion Benda

              Julius Henry
              (Groucho)   Robert   Kay   Timothy   Thomas
              1890–1977
              m.1 1920 ············· *m.2 1945* ············· *m.3 1954*
              Ruth Johnson   Kay Gorcey   Eden Hartford

                                             Melinda
              Arthur   Miriam

423

Chronology

Levy Schoenberg (grandfather), born 1823, Dornum, Prussia.
Fanny Schoenberg-Solomons, born 1829, Bruchhausen, Prussia.
Minnie Schoenberg (mother), born 1864, Dornum, Prussia.
Abraham Elieser Adolph Schoenberg (a.k.a. Al Shean), born 1868, Dornum, Prussia.
Simon Marx (Marrix?) (father), born 1860 (?), Strasbourg (?), Alsace, France.

1877, 4 August – first arrival of Levy Schoenberg, with daughter Hannah, in NYC.
1879, 9 August – second arrival of Levy Schoenberg in NYC, with Fanny, Minnie, Adolph and Heinie.

Pauline 'Marx' (daughter of Hannah Schoenberg), born January 1885.
Manfred Marx, born January 1886, NYC, died 17 July 1886.
Leo (Leonard, Chico) Marx, born (22?) March 1887, NYC.
Adolph (Arthur, Harpo) Marx, born 23 November 1888, NYC.
Julius Henry (Groucho) Marx, born 2 October 1890, NYC.
Milton (Gummo) Marx, born 23 October 1892, NYC.
Herbert (Zeppo) Marx, born 25 February 1901, NYC.
[Sam Marx (apocryphal?) possibly born 1902, died???]
Fanny Schoenberg dies 10 April 1901.

1904–1905 – first appearances of Julius (Groucho), singing in church halls.
Summer 1905 – first professional show for Julius, with Leroy Trio.
Sometime in 1905 (?) – Milton (Gummo) in ventriloquist act with Uncle Heinie (performing as Harry Shean).
November 1905–January 1906: Julius with Lily Seville, touring.
April–June 1906: Julius in Gus Edwards' 'Postal Telegraph Boys'.
August–November 1906: Julius in 'Man of Her Choice'.
Spring, summer 1907: Julius and Milton (Gummo) in Ned Wayburn's School of Vaudeville.
June–December 1907: Julius, Milton and Mabel O'Donnell in Ned Wayburn's Nightingales (a.k.a. The Three Nightingales.)
January–June 1908: The Three Nightingales under Mama Minnie's management.
June 1908–September 1909: Julius, Milton, Adolph (Harpo) and Lou Levy as The Four Nightingales. Touring the boondocks, west and south.
October 1909–January 1910: Marxes settle in Chicago. Minnie Schoenberg becomes Minnie Palmer.

424

February–May 1910: Minnie Palmer's Six Mascots: with Minnie and Aunt Hannah.

Summer, autumn 1910: 'The Mascots' – probably without Aunt Hannah or Lou Levy.

1910–1911: Leonard (Chico) with Arthur Gordon as Gordoni and Marx.

January 1911: The Three Marx Brothers (Julius, Milton and Arthur) and Company.

June 1911–September 1912: The Three Marx Bros. in 'Fun in Hi Skule'.

Summer 1911–May 1912: Leonard (Chico) and Lou Shean as Marx and Shean.

May–August 1912: Leonard with George Lee.

September 1912–September 1914: Four Marx Brothers – Leonard, Julius, Arthur and Milton, with company, in 'Mr Green's Reception'.

September 1914–August 1918: Four Marx Brothers in 'Home Again'.

March 1917: Leonard marries Betty Karp.

October–November 1918: Four Marx Brothers in 'The Street Cinderella'.

October 1918: Milton (Gummo) leaves the act to join the US Army. Herbert (Zeppo) replaces him for final performances of 'The Street Cinderella'.

December 1918: Four Marx Brothers – Leonard, Julius, Arthur and Herbert, revert to 'Home Again'.

February 1919: 'The Marx Brothers Revue', quickly named 'N'Everything', runs to December 1920.

4 February 1920: Julius (Groucho) marries Ruth Johnson.

20 February 1920. Death of Levy (Louis) Schoenberg.

February 1921–August 1922: Four Marx Brothers in 'On the Mezzanine Floor' – later renamed 'On the Balcony'.

June 1922: British tour of 'On the Balcony' and 'Home Again'.

Autumn 1922: Marx Brothers shoot lost silent film – 'Humor Risk'.

September 1922–March 1923: Four Marx Brothers in Shubert vaudeville unit – 'Twentieth Century Review'. Bankrupt in Indianapolis, 7 March.

29 May 1923: Philadelphia opening of the Four Marx Brothers in their first full-length show, 'I'll Say She Is'.

19 May 1924: 'I'll Say She Is' opens at Casino Theatre on Broadway. Runs into 1925.

October 1925–November 1927: 377 performances of 'The Cocoanuts' by George S. Kaufman and Morrie Ryskind.

12 April 1927: Zeppo marries Marion Benda.

23 October 1928: New York opening of Animal Crackers by George S. Kaufman and Morrie Ryskind. Total 171 performances.

16 March 1929: Gummo marries Helen Von Tilzer.

3 May 1929: Première of Marx Bros.' first film – The Cocoanuts.

13 September 1929: Death of Minnie Marx-Schoenberg.

24 October 1929: The Wall Street crash – beginning of Groucho's insomnia.

29 August 1930: New York Première of film Animal Crackers.

February–March 1931: The Marx Brothers move to Hollywood.

28 November 1932–22 May 1933: Groucho and Chico broadcast 26 episodes of 'Flywheel, Shyster and Flywheel', for NBC Radio's 'Five Star Theatre'.

11 May 1933: Samuel (Simon) 'Frenchy' Marx dies in Los Angeles.

28 September 1936: Harpo marries Susan Fleming.

Filmography

Humor Risk (or **Humorisk**) (1920?)
Unknown length. Lost silent film.
Director: Dick Smith (alleged!). *Screenplay*: Jo Swerling.
Cast: Villain: Groucho Marx. Detective (Watson): Harpo Marx. Italian: Chico Marx. Damsel: Mildred Davis.

Too Many Kisses (1925)
Produced by Famous Players Lasky. Silent.
Director: Paul Sloane. *Screenplay*: Gerald Duffy, from the story 'A Maker of Gestures' by John Monk Saunders. *Photography*: Hal Rosson.
Cast: Richard Gaylord Jr: Richard Dix. Yvonne Hurja: Frances Howard. Julio: William Powell. Flapper: Alyce Mills. Village Peter Pan: Harpo Marx.

The Cocoanuts (1929)
96 minutes.
Released by Paramount Famous Lasky, 3 August 1929. Presented by Adolph Zukor and Jesse L. Lasky. *Producer*: Monta Bell. *Associate Producer*: James R. Cowan. *Directors*: Robert Florey and Joseph Santley. Adapted by Morrie Ryskind from the musical play and book by George S. Kaufman (and Morrie Ryskind). *Music and lyrics*: Irving Berlin. *Musical Director*: Frank Tours. *Choreographers*: Chester Hale and Maria Gambarelli. *Photography*: George Folsey. *Art Director*: Ernst Fegte. *Editor*: Barney Rogan.
Cast: Hammer: Groucho Marx. Harpo: Harpo Marx. Chico: Chico Marx. Jamison: Zeppo Marx. Mrs Potter: Margaret Dumont. Polly Potter: Mary Eaton. Bob Adams: Oscar Shaw. Penelope: Kay Francis. Yates: Cyril Ring. Hennessey: Basil Ruysdael. Bell Captain: Sylvan Lee. Dancing Bellhops: Gamby-Hall Ballet Girls and Allan K. Foster Girls. Lifeguard: Barton MacLane.

Animal Crackers (1930)
98 minutes.
Released by Paramount Publix Corp., 29 August 1930. *Director*: Vincent Heerman. *Screenplay*: Morrie Ryskind; from the musical play and book by George S. Kaufman and Morrie Ryskind. *Music and lyrics*: Bert Kalmar and Harry Ruby. *Music arranger*: John W. Green. *Photography*: George Folsey. *Art Director*: Ernst Fegte. *Recording Engineer*: Ernest F. Zatorsky. *Continuity*: Pierre Collings.

426

Cast: Geoffrey T. Spaulding: Groucho Marx. The Professor: Harpo Marx. Emanuel Ravelli: Chico Marx. Jamison: Zeppo Marx. Mrs Rittenhouse: Margaret Dumont. Arabella Rittenhouse: Lillian Roth. Roscoe W. Chandler: Louis Sorin. Mrs Whitehead: Margaret Irving. Hives: Robert Greig. Parker: Hal Thompson. Grace Carpenter: Kathryn Reece. Inspector Hennessy: Edward Metcalfe. Footmen: The Music Masters. Girl: Ann Roth.

Monkey Business (1931)
77 minutes.
Released by Paramount Publix Corp., 19 September 1931. *Associate Producer*: (uncredited) Herman Mankiewicz. *Director*: Norman McLeod. *Screenplay*: S. J. Perelman and Will B. Johnstone, with additional dialogue by Arthur Sheekman. *Assistant Director* (uncredited): Charles Barton. *Photography*: Arthur L. Todd.
Cast: Stowaways: Groucho, Harpo, Chico and Zeppo Marx as themselves. Lucille Briggs: Thelma Todd. Alky Briggs: Harry Woods. Joe Helton. Rockliffe Fellowes. Mary Helton: Ruth Hall. Captain: Ben Taggart. First Officer: Tom Kennedy. Officer: Otto Fries. Manicurist: Evelyn Pierce. Madame Swempski: Maxine Castle. Gangster: Leo Willis. Passenger on ship and man on dock: Samuel 'Frenchy' Marx.

Promotional Trailer: The House that Shadows Built (1931)
Reconstruction of opening sequence of 'On the Mezzanine', with Groucho, Chico, Harpo, Zeppo and George Lee (?).

Horse Feathers (1932)
68 minutes.
Released by Paramount Publix Corp., 19 August 1932. *Producer* (uncredited): Herman Mankiewicz. *Director*: Norman Z. McLeod. *Screenplay*: Bert Kalmar, Harry Ruby, S. J. Perelman and Will B. Johnstone. *Additional dialogue* (uncredited): Arthur Sheekman. *Music and lyrics*: Bert Kalmar and Harry Ruby. *Dance Director*: Harold Hecht. *Photography*: Ray June. *Sound*: Eugene Merritt.
Cast: Professor Quincy Adams Wagstaff: Groucho Marx. Pinky: Harpo Marx. Baravelli: Chico Marx. Wagstaff Jr: Zeppo Marx. Connie Bailey (college widow): Thelma Todd. Jennings: David Landau. Biology Professor: Robert Greig. Mullen: James Pierce. MacHardie: Nat Pendleton. Retiring President: Reginald Barlow: Other Professors with Beards: Edward J. LeSaint, E. H. Calvert. Bartender: Edgar Dearing. Man at Bar: Vince Barnett. Man at Slot Machine: Syd Saylor. Peggy: Florine McKinney. Cop: Ben Taggart. Connie's maid: Theresa Harris.

Hollywood on Parade (1932)
Paramount short.
Promotional one-reeler with Groucho, Harpo and Chico along with Skeets

Gallagher, Eddie Lambert and his Orchestra, Lois Wilson, Claire Windsor, Ivan Lebedeff, Vivian Duncan and Fifi D'Orsay.

Hollywood on Parade (1933)
Paramount short.
Promotional one-reeler, romping on the lot with Chico Marx, W. C. Fields, Buster Crabbe, Earl Carroll Girls, etc.

Duck Soup (1933)
70 minutes.
Released by Paramount Productions Inc., 17 November 1933. *Director*: Leo McCarey. *Screenplay*: Bert Kalmar and Harry Ruby, with additional dialogue by Arthur Sheekman and Nat Perrin. *Songs*: Bert Kalmar and Harry Ruby. *Music Advisor*: Arthur Johnston. *Photography*: Henry Sharp. *Art Directors*: Hans Dreier and Wiard B. Ihnen. *Recording Engineer*: H. M. Lindgren. *Editor*: LeRoy Stone.
Cast: Rufus T. Firefly: Groucho Marx. Pinky: Harpo Marx. Chicolini: Chico Marx. Bob: Zeppo Marx. Mrs Gloria Teasdale: Margaret Dumont. Ambassador Trentino: Louis Calhern. Vera Marcal: Raquel Torres. Lemonade man: Edgar Kennedy. Failed spy: Leonid Kinsky. Zander: Edmund Breese. Ministers of Finance: William Worthington and Davison Clark. Judges: George McQuarrie, Fred Sullivan and Eric Mayne. Prosecutor: Charles B. Middleton. Palace Guard: Dale van Sickel. Harpo's horse: Blanca. (*Note: Copyright records list Harpo's character as 'Brownie' {!}*)

A Night at the Opera (1935)
96 minutes.
Released by MGM, 15 November 1935. *Executive Producer* (uncredited): Irving Thalberg. *Director*: Sam Wood. *Screenplay*: George S. Kaufman and Morrie Ryskind. *Story*: James Kevin McGuinness. *Uncredited Screenwriters*: Al Boasberg, Harry Ruby, Bert Kalmar, George Seaton, Robert Pirosh and George Oppenheimer. *Music*: Herbert Stothart. *Dance Director*: Chester Hale. *Photography*: Merritt B. Gerstad. *Art Directors*: Cedric Gibbons and Ben Carre. *Set Decorator*: Edwin B. Willis. *Wardrobe*: Dolly Tree. *Sound*: Douglas Shearer. *Songs*: 'Alone', music by Nacio Herb Brown, lyrics by Arthur Freed, 'Cosi-Cosa', music by Bronislau Kaper and Walter Jurmann, lyrics by Ned Washington. *Film Editor*: William LeVanway.
Cast: Otis B. Driftwood: Groucho Marx. Tomasso: Harpo Marx. Fiorello: Chico Marx. Mrs Claypool: Margaret Dumont. Herman Gottlieb: Siegfried Rumann. Rosa: Kitty Carlisle. Ricardo Baroni: Allan Jones. Rodolpho Lassparri: Walter Woolf King. Captain: Edward Keane. Detective Henderson: Robert Emmet O'Connor. Steward: Gino Corrado. Engineer: Frank Yaconell. Engineer's assistants: Billy Gilbert, Jack Lipson. Bearded Aviators: Leo White, Jay Eaton and Rolfe Sedan. Lift operator: Otto Fries. Opera performers: Rita and Rubin,

Luther Hoobyar, Rodolfo Hoyos, Olga Dane and James J. Eoolf. Sign Scraper: Harry Tyler. Whistling double for Harpo Marx: Enrico Ricardi.

La Fiesta De Santa Barbara (1935)
19 minutes.
MGM promotional short, with The Gumm Sisters (including Judy Garland), The Spanish Troubadors, etc., and, in the audience, Warner Baxter, Chester Conklin, Gary Cooper, Andy Devine, Ida Lupino, Buster Keaton, Harpo Marx, et al.

Yours for the Asking (1936)
68 minutes.
Released by Paramount, 24 July 1936. *Producer*: Lewis E. Gensler. *Director*: Alexander Hall.
Cast: George Raft, Dolores Costello Barrymore, Ida Lupino, Reginald Owen. Among the extras: Charles Ruggles and Groucho Marx.

Hollywood – The Second Step (1936)
10 minutes.
An MGM Miniature, released 5 December 1936. *Director*: Felix F Feist, *Narrator*: Carey Wilson. With Chico Marx and Maureen O'Sullivan as themselves.

The King and the Chorus Girl (1937)
94 minutes.
Released by Warner Bros., 27 March 1937. *Producer/Director*: Mervyn LeRoy. *Screenplay*: Norman Krasna and Groucho Marx. With Fernand Gravet, Joan Blondell, Edward Everett Horton, Alan Mowbray and Mary Nash.

A Day at the Races (1937)
109 minutes.
Released by MGM, 11 June 1937. *Producers* (uncredited): Irving Thalberg, Sam Wood and Lawrence Weingarten. *Associate Producer*: Sam Spiegel. *Director*: Sam Wood. *Screenplay*: Robert Pirosh, George Seaton, George Oppenheimer and (uncredited) Al Boasberg. *Music*: Bronislau Kaper and Walter Jurmann. *Lyrics*: Gus Kahn. *Musical Director*: Franz Waxman. *Choreography*: Dave Gould. *Photography*: Joseph Ruttenberg. *Art Directors*: Cedric Gibbons and Stan Rogers. *Sets*: Edwin B. Willis. *Sound*: Douglas Shearer. *Wardrobe*: Dolly Tree. *Film Editor*: Frank E. Hull.
Cast: Dr Hugo Z. Hackenbush: Groucho Marx. Stuffy: Harpo Marx. Tony: Chico Marx. Mrs Upjohn: Margaret Dumont. Dr Steinberg: Siegfried Rumann. Gil: Allan Jones. Judy Standish: Maureen O'Sullivan. Morgan: Douglas Dumbrille. Whitmore: Leonard Ceeley. Flo Marlowe: Esther Muir. Sheriff: Robert Middlemass. Jockey: Frankie Darro. Detective: Pat Flaherty. Singers: Ivie Anderson and the Crinoline Choir. African-American performers: The Three

Chocolateers, Plantation Boys, Four Hot Shots, Ben Carter, Darby Jones, Dorothy Dandridge, Gus Robinson and Buck Woods.

Sunday Night at the Trocadero (1937)
20 minutes.
Released by MGM, 2 October 1937. *Director*: George Sidney. With Reginald Denny, George Hamilton's Music Box, etc., and guest stars Robert Benchley, Eric Blore, June Collyer, Bert Wheeler, Mr and Mrs Groucho Marx.

Room Service (1938)
78 minutes.
Released by RKO Radio Pictures, 30 September 1938. *Production Supervisor*: Pandro S. Berman. *Director*: William A. Seiter. *Screenplay*: Morrie Ryskind, from the stage play by John Murray and Allan Boretz. *Photography*: J. Roy Hunt. *Art Directors*: Van Nest Polglase and Al Herman. *Sets*: Darrel Silvera. *Music Director*: Roy Webb. *Sound*: John L. Cass. *Editor*: George Crone.
Cast: Gordon Miller: Groucho Marx. Faker Englund: Harpo Marx. Harry Binelli: Chico Marx. Christine Marlowe: Lucille Ball. Leo Davis: Frank Albertson. Hilda Manney: Ann Miller. Wagner: Donald MacBride. Joseph Gribble: Cliff Dunstan. Hogarth: Philip Loeb. Sasha: Alexander Astro. Dr Glass: Charles Halton. Jenkins: Philip Wood.

At the Circus (1939)
87 minutes.
Released by MGM, 20 October 1939. *Producer*: Mervyn LeRoy. *Director*: Edward Buzzell. *Screenplay*: Irving Brecher, early drafts (uncredited) by Ben Hecht, Arthur Sheekman and Dore Schary. *Music Director*: Franz Waxman. *Songs*: Harold Arlen, lyrics by E. Y. Harburg (including 'Lydia, the Tattooed Lady'). *Dance Director*: Bobby Connolly. *Director of Photography*: Leonard M. Smith. *Art Directors*: Cedric Gibbons and Stan Rogers. *Sets*: Edwin B. Willis. *Costumes*: Dolly Tree, Valles. *Sound*: Douglas Shearer.
Cast: J. Cheever Loophole: Groucho Marx. Punchy: Harpo Marx. Pirelli: Chico Marx. Mrs Dukesbury: Margaret Dumont. Jeff Wilson: Kenny Baker. Julie Randall: Florence Rice. Peerless Pauline: Eve Arden. Goliath: Nat Pendleton. John Carter: James Burke. Professor Atom: Jerry Marenghi. Whitcomb: Barnett Parker. In Gibraltar's skin: Charles Gemora. Jardinet: Fritz Feld.

Go West (1940)
80 minutes.
Released by MGM, 6 December 1940. *Producer*: Jack Cummings. *Director*: Edward Buzzell. *Screenplay*: Irving Brecher and (uncredited) Dore Schary, early drafts by Bert Kalmar, Harry Ruby and J. Slavens McNutt. *Director of Photography*: Leonard Smith. *Art Directors*: Cedric Gibbons and Stan Rogers. *Sets*: Edwin B. Willis. *Costumes*: Dolly Tree and Gile Steele. *Music Director*:

Georgie Stoll. *Songs*: Roger Edens, Bronislau Kaper and Charles Cadman, lyrics by Gus Kahn. *Sound*: Douglas Shearer.
Cast: S. Quentin Quale: Groucho Marx. Rusty: Harpo Marx. Joe Panello: Chico Marx. Terry Turner: John Carroll. Eve Wilson: Diana Lewis. Red Baxter: Robert Barrat. Beecher: Walter Woolf King. Lulubelle: June MacCloy. Saloon girls: Iris Adrian, Joan Woodbury. Indian Pete: Mitchell Lewis. Dan Wilson: Tully Marshall.

The Big Store (1941)
83 minutes.
Released by MGM, 20 June 1941. *Producer*: Louis K. Sidney. *Director*: Chuck Riesner. *Screenplay*: Sid Kuller, Hal Fimberg and Ray Golden, from a story by Nat Perrin. *Photography*: Charles Lawton. *Art Directors*: Cedric Gibbons and Stan Rogers. *Sets*: Edwin B. Willis. *Music Director*: Georgie Stoll. *Songs*: Hal Borne and Ben Oakland, lyrics by Sid Kuller, Hal Fimberg, Milton Drake and Artie Shaw. *Dance Director*: Arthur Appell. *Sound*: Douglas Shearer. *Editor*: Conrad A. Nervig.
Cast: Wolf J. Flywheel: Groucho Marx. Wacky: Harpo Marx. Ravelli: Chico Marx. Martha Phelps: Margaret Dumont. Grover: Douglas Dumbrille. Tommy Rogers: Tony Martin. Joan Sutton: Virginia Grey. Fred Sutton: William Tannen. Peggy Arden: Marion Martin. Kitty: Virginia O'Brien. Giuseppi: Henry Armetta. Detective: Dewey Robinson. Finance man: Charles Lane.

Screen Snapshots No. 2 (1943)
One-reel short.
Released by Columbia, September 1943. *Director*: Ralph Staub. With Groucho Marx and Carole Landis.

Stage Door Canteen (1943)
132 minutes.
Released by United Artists, 12 May 1943. *Director*: Frank Borzage. Wartime star vehicle featuring practically every member of actor's equity (with Yehudi Menuhin added) including Johnny Weissmuller, Gypsy Rose Lee and Harpo Marx.

Screen Snapshots Number 8 (1943)
10 minutes.
Columbia Pictures. With Groucho, Harpo and Chico Marx, Gene Autry, Tyrone Power, Kay Kyser and the Ritz Brothers.

The All-Star Bond Rally (1945)
Two-reeler.
Released by 20th Century Fox. Featuring Bing Crosby, Linda Darnell, Betty Grable, Bob Hope, Carmen Miranda, Fibber McGee and Molly, and Harpo Marx.

431

A Night in Casablanca (1946)

85 minutes.

Released by United Artists, 10 May 1946. *Producer*: David L. Loew. *Director*: Archie L. Mayo. *Screenplay*: Joseph Fields and Roland Kibbee. Uncredited sight gags by Frank Tashlin. *Director of Photography*: James Van Trees. *Production Designer*: Duncan Cramer. *Sets*: Edward Boyle. *Music*: Werner Janssen, song 'Who's Sorry Now?' composed by Ted Snyder, lyrics by Bert Kalmar and Harry Ruby. *Sound*: Frank Webster. *Editing*: Gregg C. Tallas and Grace Baughman.

Cast: Ronald Kornblow: Groucho Marx. Rusty: Harpo Marx. Corbaccio: Chico Marx. Heinrich Stuebel: Sig Ruman. Beatrice Rheiner: Lisette Verea. Pierre: Charles Drake. Annette: Lois Collier. Captain Brizzard: Dan Seymour. Galoux: Lewis Russell. Kurt: Frederick Giermann. Emile: Harro Mellor. Spy: David Hoffman.

Copacabana (1947)

90 minutes.

Released by United Artists, 30 May 1947. *Producer*: Sam Coslow. *Director*: Alfred E. Green. *Screenplay*: Laslo Vadnay, Allan Boretz, Howard Harris and Sydney Zelinka. *Director of Photography*: Bert Glennon. *Production Designer*: Duncan Cramer. Song 'Go West, Young Man' by Bert Kalmar and Harry Ruby.

Cast: Lionel Q. Devereaux: Groucho Marx. Carmen Novarro: Carmen Miranda. With Steve Cochrane, Gloria Jean, Edgar Dearing, Dewey Robinson, Louis Sobol, Earl Wilson, Abel Green and Andy Russell as themselves.

Love Happy (1950)

85 minutes.

Released by United Artists, 3 March 1950. 'Presented' by Mary Pickford. *Producer*: Lester Cowan. *Director*: David Miller. *Screenplay*: Frank Tashlin and Mac Benoff, from an original draft by Ben Hecht, story by Harpo Marx. *Photography*: William C. Mellor. *Production Designer*: Gabriel Scognamillo. *Sets*: Casey Roberts. *Music and songs*: Ann Ronell. *Editors*: Basil Wrangell and Al Joseph.

Cast: Harpo: Harpo Marx. Faustino: Chico Marx. Sam Grunion: Groucho Marx. Maggie Phillips: Vera-Ellen. Madame Egelichi: Ilona Massey. Bunny Dolan: Marion Hutton. Alphonse Zoto: Raymond Burr. Throckmorton: Melville Cooper. Mr Lyons: Leon Belasco. Mackinaw: Eric Blore. Mike Johnson: Paul Valentine. Client in Grunion's office: Marilyn Monroe.

Mr Music (1950)

113 minutes.

Released by Paramount, 28 December 1950. *Producer*: Robert L. Welch. *Director*: Richard Haydn. *Screenplay*: Arthur Sheekman. *Cast*: Bing Crosby, Nancy Olson, Charles Coburn, Ruth Hussey, Robert Stack. Guest artists: Dorothy Kirsten, Peggy Lee, and Groucho Marx in musical number with Bing Crosby.

Double Dynamite (1951)
80 minutes.
Released by RKO Radio, December 1951. *Producer:* Irving Cummings Jr.
Director: Irving Cummings. *Screenplay:* Melville Shavelson, with additional dialogue by Harry Crane. From a story by Leo Rosten, based on a character created by Mannie Manheim. *Photography:* Robert De Grasse. *Art Directors:* Albert
S. D'Agostino and Field M. Gray. *Music:* Leigh Harline, songs by Sammy
Kahn and Jule Styne.
Cast: Mildred Goodhue: Jane Russell. Johnny Dalton: Frank Sinatra. Emil Keck:
Groucho Marx. With Don McGuire, Howard Freeman, Frank Orth, Harry
Hayden, William Edmunds, Russ Thorson, Joe Devlin and Claire Du Brey.

A Girl in Every Port (1952)
87 minutes.
Released by RKO Radio, January 1952. *Producers:* Irving Allen and Irving
Cummings Jr. *Director:* Chester Erskine. *Screenplay:* Chester Erskine, from the
story 'They Sell Sailors Elephants' by Frederick Hazlitt Brennan. *Director of
Photography:* Nicholas Musuraca. *Art Directors:* Albert S. D'Agostino and
Walter E. Keller. *Music:* Roy Webb.
Cast: Benny Linn: Groucho Marx. Tim Dunnevan: William Bendix. Jane Sweet:
Marie Wilson. Bert Sedgwick: Don DeFore. Garvey: Gene Lockhart.
Millicent: Dee Hartford. With Hanley Stafford, Teddy Hart, Percy Helton,
George E. Stone.

Will Success Spoil Rock Hunter? (1957)
94 minutes. Color, Cinemascope.
Released by 20th Century Fox, August 1957. *Producer/Director/Writer:* Frank
Tashlin. From the play by George Axelrod. *Photography:* Joe MacDonald.
With Tony Randall, Jayne Mansfield, Betsy Drake, Joan Blondell. Groucho Marx
as Georgie Schmidlapp.

The Story of Mankind (1957)
100 minutes. Technicolor.
Released by Warner Bros., 8 November 1957. *Producer and director:* Irwin Allen.
Screenplay: Irwin Allen and Charles Bennett, from the book by Hendrik Van
Loon. *Director of Photography:* Nicholas Musuraca. With Ronald Colman, Vincent
Price, Sir Cedric Hardwicke, Hedy Lamarr, Virginia Mayo, etc., etc., etc.
Groucho Marx as Peter Minuit. Harpo Marx as Isaac Newton. Chico Marx as
monk.

Skidoo (1968)
98 minutes. Technicolor-Cinemascope.
Released by Paramount, 16 December 1968. *Producer/Director:* Otto Preminger.
Screenplay: Doran William Cannon, from a story by Erik Kirkland. *Photography:*

Leon Shamroy. With Jackie Gleason, Carol Channing, Peter Lawford, George Raft, Cesar Romero. Groucho Marx as 'God'.

[Exhaustive filmography, bibliography, details of all the Marx Brothers television appearances, and much other Marxiana, can be found on the World Wide Web (Why a web? Why-a-no beak?) at www.whyaduck.com]

Marx Brothers Departures
Chico Marx: 11 October 1961.
Harpo Marx: 28 September 1964.
Gummo Marx: 21 April 1977.
Groucho Marx: 19 August 1977.
Zeppo Marx: 30 November 1979.

Notes on Sources

Abbreviations

ARCHIVES AND COLLECTIONS
AMPAS: Academy of Motion Pictures Arts and Sciences, Margaret Herrick Library, Los Angeles, California.
FHA: Family History Archive, Mormon Church, Los Angeles, California.
FLP: Free Library of Philadelphia Theatre Collection.
LCMD: Library of Congress, Manuscript Division, Washington DC.
LCMP: Library of Congress, Motion Picture Division, Washington DC.
LCRB: Library of Congress, Rare Books Department, Washington DC.
MK: Miles Kreuger, Institute of the American Musical, Los Angeles, California.
NYPA: New York Library of the Performing Arts, Billy Rose Collection, Lincoln Center, New York, NY.
PW: Paul Wesolowski Collection, New Hope, Pennsylvania

BOOKS
GM: Groucho Marx, *Groucho and Me.*
GWC: Maxine Marx, *Growing Up with Chico.*
GP: Groucho Marx and Hector Arce, *The Groucho Phile, An Illustrated Life.*
HS: Harpo Marx, *Harpo Speaks.*
MBS: Groucho Marx and Richard J. Anobile, *The Marx Brothers Scrapbook.*

NEWSPAPERS AND PERIODICALS
NYDM: *The New York Dramatic Mirror.*
NYT: *The New York Times.*
Note: Quotations from script dialogue unsourced below are transcribed from on-screen dialogue, from prints of the respective films.
Source dates are in US style – month–day–year.

Chapter 1

p.7 Census form: FHA.
p.8 'Thanks to the amazing spirit . . .' *HS*, p.19.
p.8 'In addition to the five brothers . . .' *GM*, p.19.
p.9 'There were ten mouths to feed . . .' *HS*, pp.19–20.
p.9 'His estate, when probated . . .' *GM*, p.36.
p.10 'a pretty good shape . . .' *GM*, p.21.

435

p.13 'with one trouser leg shorter . . .' *GM*, p.20.
p.14 'Frenchie always managed . . .' *HS*, p.20.
p.14 'What a cook he was! . . .' *Redbook Magazine*, 3/1933 (FLP).

Chapter 2

pp.16–17 'We drove from Amsterdam . . .' *Los Angeles Times*, 8.23.1977.
pp.18 'There are some people who swear . . .' Sara Hamilton, 'The Nuttiest Quartette in the World', *Photoplay Magazine*, July 1932.
p.18 'He met his future wife, Fanny . . .' Hector Arce, *Groucho*, G. P. Putnam's & Sons, 1979, p.19.
p.21 Census, 1880: FHA.
p.23 'Since neither my grandfather . . .' *GM*, p. 29.

Chapter 3

p. 26 'It's Ireland and Italy . . .' E. J. Kahn, *The Merry Partners, the Age and Stage of Harrigan and Hart*, Random House, NY, 1955, p.64.
p.26 'I am delightfulness to met you . . .' Armond Fields and L. Marc Fields, *From the Bowery to Broadway*, Oxford University Press, 1993, p.82.
p.26 'Was has gesachta? . . .' Douglas Gilbert, *American Vaudeville*, Whittlesey House, McGraw Hill, NY, p.73.
p.26 'He knows apoudt der Yiddish man . . .' *NYDM*, March 17 1900.
p.28 'a variety and music hall turn . . .' clippings, NYPA.
p.28 'My first role was in a drama . . .' clippings, NYPA.
p.29 'unable to pay off the mortgage of the farm . . .' clippings, NYPA.
p.29 'I started the famous Manhattan Comedy Four . . .' *Rochester Leader*, 2.11.1916, NYPA.
p.30 'Harpo attended lectures . . .' *HS*, p.16.
p.30 'The boys were really not . . .' Bill Marx, interview, 9.18.97.
p.31 'The hit of the evening . . .' *NYDM*, 4.20.1895.
p.31 'The Manhattan Four, one of the funniest . . .' *NYDM*, 8.31.1895.
p.31 'The pictures were thrown upon the screen . . .' *NYDM*, 7.4.1895.
p.31 'A Tin Wedding . . .' etc. FLP.
p.32 'CAPTAIN KIDD: A ship! . . .' etc., LCMD.
p.33 'COMMODORE: Now listen . . .' etc., LCMD.

Chapter 4

p.35 '"Schupkie!" he cried . . .' Kyle Crichton, *The Marx Brothers*, Wm. Heinemann, 1951, p.6.
p.36 'Give or take a few years . . .' *GM*, p. 19.
p.38 'School doesn't teach you . . .' *HS*, p.28.
p.39 'His "street smarts . . ."' *GWC*, p.3.

p.40 'just emerging from Abercrombie . . .' *GM*, p.64.
p.41 'My Dad never went through . . .' Bill Marx interview, loc. cit.
p.41 'I've been reading a book called . . .' *GM*, p.45.
p.43 'The can would be swung . . .' etc. *HS*, p.56.

Chapter 5

p.45 'I did an act with my uncle . . .' *MBS*, pp.19–20.
p.45 'The first real job I ever got . . .' *GP*, p.11.
p.46 'The show opened with . . .' *GP*, p.15.
p.46 'Leroy hadn't told us . . .' 'Bad Days are Good Memories', *Saturday Evening Post*, 8.29.1931.
p.46 'the most malevolent expressions . . .' *GM*, p.54.
p.47 'Lily Seville is a directly imported . . .' *Dallas Daily Times Herald*, 12.24.1905, PW.
p.47 'A pale, proud, English beauty . . .' caption, photo clipping, NYPA.
p.48 'Miss Seville is a typical . . .' *Dallas Morning News*, 12.25.1905, PW.
p.48 'Another act below the standard . . .' *Houston Chronicle*, 1.2.1906, PW.
p.48 'very high class as a study . . .' *San Antonio Light*, 1.7.1906, PW.
p.49 'School-days, school-days . . .' clippings, NYPA.
p.50 'boyish pranks at one another's expense . . .' *NYDM*, 5.5.1906.
p.50 'I went on the stage with . . .' *GP*, p.17.
p.51 'After betting all his earnings on himself . . .' *GWC*, p.7.
p.51 'better than handkerchiefs . . .' *GM*, p.65.
p.52 'Get out of here . . .' etc. *HS*, pp.85–93.
p.53 'I now regarded myself . . .' *HS*, p.93.

Chapter 6

p.54 'NED WAYBURN IS . . .' etc., *New York Sunday Telegraph*, 1.31.1904, NYPA.
p.55 'All pupils must wear . . .' clippings, NYPA.
p.55 'He uses a whistle now . . .' *The World*, 7.8.1906, NYPA.
p.55 'Yesterday was commencement day . . .' etc., *NJ Sun*, 4.14.1907, NYPA.
p.56 'Two clean-cut . . .' *NYDM*, 9.21.1907, PW.
p.57 'The larger of the youths . . .' *Variety*, 12.21.1907, PW.
p.57 'Phantastic Phantoms . . . it is a foolish thing . . .' *Milwaukee Sentinel*, 8.14.1907, NYPA.
p.58 'How those boys love to talk about her . . .' *Liberty*, 6.3.1933, NYPA.
p.59 'We played some pretty good theatres . . .' *MBS*, p.14.
p.59 'He was from Brooklyn . . .' Hector Arce, *Groucho*, p.67.
p.59 'While I was working at the nickelodeon . . .' *HS*, p.94.
p.59 '"I have a great idea," she said . . .' *GM*, p.68.
p.60 'A sea of hostile mocking faces . . .' *HS*, p.95.

Chapter 7

p.67 'crawled right up the legs . . .' *NY Post*, 11.18.1939, NYPA.
p.67 'A quartet of youngsters . . .' *Variety*, 6.6.1908, PW.
p.68 'spent a day in legendary Nagacdoches . . .' *The Freedonia Gazette*, No.17, winter 1986, p.9, PW.
p.70 'To the younger generation . . .' *Columbus Evening Dispatch*, 10.1.1916, PW.
p.70 'have been accosted, at the stage door . . .' ibid., 10.4.1916. PW.
p.70 'The German comedian is exceptionally clever . . .' *Variety*, 4.23.1910, PW.
p.72 'Where do you work-a, John? . . .' etc., *GWC*, p.11.
p.72 'Shean and Marx are quite new . . .' *Variety*, 10.7.1911, PW.

Chapter 8

p.74 'She had red hair . . .' etc., Groucho Marx, *Memoirs of a Mangy Lover*, Da Capo Press, NY, 1997, pp.3–4.
p.75 'A hot sport in New Orleans . . .' *GM*, opp. p.128.
p.75 'Gummo did not like the stage . . .' interview with Robert Marx, 1.22.1998.
p.76 'The frock coat was borrowed . . .' *GP*, p.18.
p.76 'a burlesque side . . .' *Saginaw Courier Herald*, 6.18.1911, PW.
p.77 'My Patsy Brannigan costume . . .' etc. *HS*, pp.108–109.
p.77 'Groucho: What is the shape of the world? . . .' Joe Adamson, *Groucho, Chico, Harpo & Sometimes Zeppo*, Coronet, 1976 (1973), p.49.
p.78 'When Gus Edwards' School Boys . . .' *Variety*, 2.24.1912, PW.
p.78 'the biggest musical instrument . . .' *HS*, p.123.
p.79 'His great loves in music . . .' interview with Bill Marx, loc. cit.
p.80 'Shean and Marx have separated . . .' *Variety*, 5.19.1912, PW.
p.80 'Minnie Palmer . . .' *Variety*, 5.25.1912, PW.
p.80 'has arranged to look after . . .' *Variety*, 6.1.1912.
p.80 'A new tabloid production . . .' *Variety*, 10.25.1912.

Chapter 9

p.83 'On a Pantages trip . . .' Fred Allen, *Much Ado About Me*, Atlantic Monthly Press, 1956, p.220.
p.84 'Milton Marx, one of the Marx Brothers . . .' *Clipper*, 5.24.1913, PW.
p.84 'the musical piece was written by the four boys . . .' *Battle Creek Enquirer*, 1.16.1913, PW.
p.84 'the smart doings and sayings . . .' *Kalamazoo Gazette*, 1.13.1913, PW.
p.85 'BEVY OF PEACHES . . .' *Kalamazoo Gazette*, 1.12.1913, PW.
p.87 '"Mr Green's Reception" is a Prime Pippin . . .' *Flint Daily Journal*, 17.1913, PW.
p.87 'Mr Green (who has miraculously lost . . .)' *HS*, p.119.
p.88 'a foolish aristocratic mamma . . .' *Kalamazoo Gazette*, 2.18.1913, PW.

p.88 'The Four Marx Brothers are shaking hands . . .' *Clipper*, 7.19.1913.

p.89 'My mother was always trying to get the boys . . .' quoted in *The Freedonia Gazette*, Winter 1981, p.5, PW.

p.90 'a big motor truck . . .' *Denver Times*, 11.26.1913, PW.

p.90 'Cold weather could not keep back . . .' *Clipper*, 1.17.1914, PW.

p.90 'Herbert Marx, youngest of . . .' *Clipper*, 1.24.1914, PW.

p.90 'having nine men to spare . . .' *Lansing State Journal*, 3.10.1914, PW.

p.90 'The Marx Brothers' show . . .' *Flint Daily Journal*, 3.13.1914, PW.

Chapter 10

p.91 'This merry little musical short . . .' *Variety*, 9.24.1914, NYPA.

p.92 'Al Shean and the Four Marx Brothers . . .' etc., *Clipper*, 7.4.1914, PW.

p.93 'lack of finished singing . . .' etc., quoted in *Clipper*, 1.2.1915, PW.

p.93 'why a man, who can evidently play . . .' *Brooklyn Eagle*, 5.3.1916, NYPA.

p.94 'Why Harpo Doesn't Talk . . .' etc., *Los Angeles Times*, 12.11.1948, AMPAS.

p.95 '(In the old) commedia dell'arte . . .' interview with Bill Marx, loc. cit.

p.95 'To recall with any degree of clarity . . .' S. J. Perelman, *Holiday Magazine*, April 1952, AMPAS.

Chapter 11

p.99 'Mr Shean has the more credible . . .' undated clipping, NYPA.

p.99 'The Four Marx Brothers . . .' *Flint Daily Journal*, 9.3.1915, PW.

p.101 'Our mother expected us . . .' *Columbus Daily Dispatch*, 10.1.1916, PW.

p.101 'who plays "Nondescripty" . . .' *San Antonio Light*, 11.18.1917, PW.

p.102 'The first morning on the farm . . .' Hector Arce, *Groucho*, p.94.

p.103 'It's a comfort to go into the theatre . . .' *Houston Press*, 11.17.1917, PW.

p.103 'The hole is . . .' *Clipper* (?), 2.15.1918, PW.

p.103 'A few short years ago . . .' *Utah Democrat*, 3.9.1918, PW.

p.104 'Minnie Palmer was served . . .' *Clipper*, 12.19.1914, PW.

Chapter 12

p.106 'an iron bed, a lumpy mattress . . .' *GM*, p.76.

p.106 'In Laredo . . .' *HS*, p.126.

p.107 'We played towns I would refuse . . .' *GM*, p.95.

p.107 'When we were living in Chicago . . .' *Redbook Magazine*, 1933 ibid., FLP.

p.108 'It seemed as if an army . . .' *GWC*, p.19.

p.109 'Their code of honor . . .' etc., *GWC*, p.21.

p.110 'I never did care about show business . . .' *MBS*, p.174.

p.110 'BBC: You came into the act . . .' etc., *The Freedonia Gazette*, Winter 1981, loc. cit

p.110 'Gummo felt that he was . . .' interview with Robert Marx, loc. cit.

p.III 'THE WISE DRUMMER . . .' PW.
p.III 'DEVIL: What's the matter . . .' LCMD.
p.112 'Groucho and Harpo bought second hand cars . . .' *MBS*, p.22.
p.112 '(Gummo) came out of the army . . .' etc., interview with Robert Marx, loc. cit.
p.113 'Julius Marx is developing . . .' *Variety*, 2.7.1919, PW.
p.113 'Julius has the role of Henry Hammer . . .' *Louisville Evening Post*, 2.23.1919, PW.
p.114 'There are several comely girls . . .' *Louisville Herald*, 2.24.1919, PW.

Chapter 13 – nil

Chapter 14

p.118 'My Fellow Countrymen . . .' Frederick Lewis Allen, *Only Yesterday*, Bantam Books, NY, 1946, p.30.
p.119 'To hell with the United States' ibid., p.62.
p.119 'It was Mothers' night . . .' *Variety*, 6.16.1920, PW.
p.120 'trendsetter to the nation . . .' Ann Douglas, *Terrible Honesty – Mongrel Manhattan in the 1920's*, Farrar Straus & Giroux, 1995, p.18.
p.120 'To lay in the wordly wisdom . . .' *The Vintage Mencken*, Vintage Books, NY, 1990, p.viii.
p.120 'For the habitual truth teller . . .' ibid., p.72.
p.121 'It is almost as safe to assume . . .' ibid., p.146.
p.122 '– I am Madam Vici . . .' etc. *Art in Vaudeville*, LCMD.
p.123 'the Timberg "crawl-off" . . .' *Variety*, 4.23.1952, NYPA.
p.123 'MANAGER: Come in . . .' etc., LCRB.

Chapter 15

p.129 'ZEPPO: I never considered . . .' *The Freedonia Gazette*, Winter 1981, p.7.
p.130 'I was working for Remick & Company . . .' interview courtesy of Anthony Slide.
p.130 'I must point out that . . .' Groucho Marx, *Memoirs of a Mangy Lover*, p.42.
p.131 'PLAYBOY: What was your first . . .' *Playboy Magazine*, March 1974, p.62.
p.131 'I was trying to fuck a girl . . .' *MBS*, p.39.
p.131 'A poor man's pet . . .' Groucho Marx, *Memoirs of a Mangy Lover*, p.31.
p.132 'We are gathered here to join this couple . . .' Arthur Marx, *My Life with Groucho*, Robson Books, 1988, p.34.
p.132 'They, in retaliation . . .' *GWC*, p.30.
p.133 'Chico, Zeppo and I . . .' etc., *Saturday Evening Post*, 8.29.1931, FLP.
p.134 'Leo Marx slipped in on skates . . .' *Variety*, June 1921, PW.
p.134 'I'd make up parodies . . .' *MBS*, p.40

p.135 'Non-stop entertainment . . .' *The Era*, June 21 1922.

p.136 'seems to be a little too trans-Atlantic . . .' *The Times*, June 27 1922.

p.136 'People began to hoot and whistle . . .' etc., *HS*, p.151.

p.137 'MARX BROS. UNIT FEATURE . . .' *Variety*, 9.22.1922.

p.137 'The Four Marx Brothers . . .' *Hartford Daily Courant*, 11.22.1922, PW.

p.138 'TEMPESTUOUS UNIT . . .' *Variety*, 12.1.1922, PW.

p.139 'Four Marx Brothers are headliners . . .' *Cleveland Press*, 1.30.1923, PW.

Chapter 16

p.141 'The suffering of the audience . . .' etc., Howard Teichman, *Smart Aleck – The Wit, World and Life of Alexander Woollcott*, William Morrow & Company, NY, 1976, p.83.

p.142 'His name is Woollcott . . .' ibid., p.63.

p.143 'The truth is that the Round Table . . .' Scott Meredith, *George S. Kaufman and his Friends*, Doubleday & Co., NY, 1974, p 159.

p.144 'Someday you'll realize, young man . . .' etc. *HS*, p.159.

p.145 'MARX BROS. IN STOCK . . .' *Variety*, 4.3.1923, PW.

p.145 'The Four Marx Brothers will head . . .' *Variety*, 5.3.1923, PW.

p.146 '"I'LL SAY SHE IS" HAS ' Philadelphia Public Ledger, 6.5.1923, Miles Kreuger, Institute of the American Musical.

p.147 'her personal victory . . .' *GM*, p.133.

p.147 'His jaunty and shameless . . .' clippings file, FLP.

p.148 'HARPO MARX AND SOME BROTHERS . . .' *New York Sun*, 5.20.1924, NYPA.

p.148 'Didn't the son-of-a-bitch . . .' etc. *HS*, p.168.

Chapter 17

p.151 'was probably the most undistinguished . . .' *GM*, p.127.

p.152 etc. quotations from *I'll Say She Is* script, from Miles Kreuger Collection, Institute of the American Musical, Los Angeles.

p.156 'Francois: Why don't you marry me . . .' *GP*, p.44.

Chapter 18

p.158 'My father acknowledged . . .' *GM*, p.131.

p.158 'more the hot sport type . . .' etc., *HS*, p.181.

p.159 'I'd like to take off my shoes . . .' Thomas Kunkel, *Genius in Disguise, Harold Ross of* The New Yorker, Random House, NY, p.79.

p.159 'a cowhand who'd lost . . .' ibid., p.82.

p.159 'Ross looks like . . .' Scott Meredith, *George S. Kaufman* etc., p.156.

p.159 'I loved him almost as much . . .' etc. *GWC*, p.36.

p.160 'Running, always trying to keep up . . .' *GWC*, p.39.

p.161 'the best originator . . .' Shamus Culhane, *Talking Animals and Other People*, Da Capo Press, NY, 1998 (first published 1986), p.295.
p.164 'satire is what closes . . .' Scott Meredith, *George S. Kaufman* etc., p.89.
p.164 'I'd as soon write . . .' ibid., p.267.
p.164 'I have never seen Mr Kaufman . . .' quoted in Hector Arce, *Groucho*, p.133.
p.165 'His habit of walking in his office . . .' Scott Meredith, loc. cit., p.68.
p.165 'in the throes of composition . . .' ibid., p.274.
p.165 'The admission fee was a viper's tongue . . .' *GM*, p.132.
p.165 'You couldn't say, "pass the salt" . . .' Scott Meredith, loc. cit., p.156.
p.166 'Harpo Marx belongs . . .' *The New Yorker*, 12.1.1928, FLP.
p.166 'October 17, Tuesday . . .' *By George, A Kaufman Collection*, St Martin's Press, NY, 1979, p.178.

Chapter 19

p.170 'creator of Uncle Remus . . .' Charlotte Chandler, *Hello, I Must be Going, Groucho & His Friends*, Abacus, UK, 1995 (1978), p.92.
p.170 'Groucho Marx, in fact, has proposed . . .' *New York Herald Tribune*, 1.20.1937, NYPA.
p.171 'It was on this very stage . . .' undated, Daisy Dumont clippings file, Shubert Archive, New York.
p.172 'The Marquis de St. Gautier needs money . . .' Daisy Dumont clippings, NYPA.
p.173 'She returned to the stage . . .' Margaret Dumont clippings file, FLP.
p.173 'actually believed that . . .' Charlotte Chandler, loc. cit., p.95.
p.173 'I strongly suspect . . .' Morrie Ryskind, *I Shot an Elephant in My Pyjamas*, Huntington House, 1994, p.68.
p.174 'Irving woke me up at five . . .' Laurence Bergreen, *As Thousands Cheer: The Life of Irving Berlin*, Hodder & Stoughton, 1990, p.248.
p.175 'I'll tell you what . . .' ibid., p.250.
p.176 'Morrie Ryskind and I once learned . . .' Scott Meredith, loc. cit., pp.278–9.
p.176 'BELLBOYS: We want our money . . .' etc., from *The Cocoanuts*, script in PW.
p.178 'AMERICA FOR AMERICANS . . .' NYPA.
p.178 'Go to Florida . . .' Frederick Lewis Allen, *Only Yesterday*, p.301.
p.179 'Schlemmer: You are now in . . .' etc., script in PW.
p.179 'In the height of the fury . . .' Frederick Lewis Allen, loc cit., p.310.
p.181 'Groucho (*as Harpo leaves*) . . .' PW, loc. cit.

Chapter 20

p.183 'VAUDE: What is your opinion . . .' quoted in *GP*, p.63.
p.184 '"What about my son" . . .' Arthur Marx, *My Life with Groucho*, p.60.

p.185 'I'm not going to forgive him . . .' *GWC*, p.46.
p.186 'Something I hadn't done since . . .' *HS*, p.193.
p.186 'Tell the driver . . .' etc., *HS*, p.194.
p.187 'You'll never be alone, Harpo . . .' *HS*, p.203.
p.187 'a bachelor-size summer estate . . .' etc., *HS*, p.211.
p.187 'was to get Harpo Marx's harp . . .' Howard Teichman, *Smart Aleck*, p.169.
p.188 'Harpo Marx pulled up to the boat . . .' ibid., p.172.
p.188 'dance around the court on his toes . . .' *HS*, p.223.
p.188 'a tall, skinny, red-faced old geezer . . .' *HS*, p.252.
p.189 'You may bring the books now . . .' *HS*, p.257.
p.189 'There is a little too much . . .' *Evening Post*, 10.24.1928, FLP.
p.189 'is the most steadily . . .' clipping, 10.24.1928, FLP.
p.191 'They are nihilists . . .' clipping, FLP.
p.192 'in a collaboration . . .' Morrie Ryskind, *I Shot an Elephant in My Pyjamas*, p.74.
p.192 'Groucho's great gift is . . .' *MBS*, p.79.
p.192 'Chico: You got everything . . .' etc., quotes from *Animal Crackers* script, PW.
p.194 'Girls were coming out of his office . . .' Hector Arce, *Groucho*, p.143.
p.198 'A short history of . . .' *The New Yorker*, 9.23.1929, NYPA.

Prologue:

p.201 'About the end of 1928 . . .' etc., S. J. Perelman, *Show Magazine*, 11.1961, reprinted in *Esquire*, 9.1981, NYPA.

Chapter 21

p.205 'Why are you so concerned . . .' Brian Taves, *Robert Florey, the French Expressionist*, The Scarecrow Press, Metuchen NJ, 1987, p.113.
p.205 'What was there to rehearse . . .' etc., ibid., p.114.
p.205 'I had five cameras . . .' *MBS*, p.117.
p.206 'The Marx Brothers gave me . . .' etc., Brian Taves, loc. cit., p.114.
p.206 'Florey had an eye . . .' ibid., p.117.
p.209 'The underlined word . . .' etc., MPPDA files, AMPAS.
p.210 'Eliminate the word . . .' etc., ibid., AMPAS.
p.212 'Marx, this is a fast rider . . .' *GM*, p.148.
p.212 'Don't tell me you've never heard of Goldman Sachs? . . .' *GM*, p.150.
p.212 'All his life he had been striving . . .' Arthur Marx, loc. cit., p.97.
p.213 'He tried sleeping on his back . . .' ibid., p.101.
p.213 'probably worth a medium-sized bag . . .' etc., *HS*, p.278.
p.213 'I was one of the luckiest citizens . . .' etc., *HS*, p.281.
p.214 'The Crazy House . . .' etc., interview by Anthony Slide with Victor Heerman.
p.214 'I said, "Hell, I've seen the Marx Brothers "' etc., ibid.

Chapter 22

p.221 'Instead of buying my *Beds* . . .' etc., quoted in Robert Bader, *Groucho Marx & Other Short Stories & Tall Tales*, Faber & Faber, 1993, p.xv.

p.221 'Some of us are greatly indebted . . .' Groucho Marx, *Beds*, Farrar & Reinhart, NY 1930, p.34.

p.222 'My career on the stage . . .' quoted in the *The Freedonia Gazette*, May 1980, p.6.

p.222 'Twas the night before Christmas . . .' Arthur Marx, loc. cit., p.109.

p.223 'This delightful quartette . . .' clipping in *MBS*, p.143.

p.223 'the almost insolent carelessness . . .' ibid., p.145

p.224 'FIRST: The Corporation . . .' *The Freedonia Gazette*, Winter 1981, p.14.

p.224 'We piled aboard the Santa Fe . . .' *GM*, p.166.

p.225 'the kind of village . . .' Howard Teichman, *Smart Aleck*, p.267.

p.226 'Will you accept three hundred per week . . .' Ben Hecht, *Child of the Century*, Simon & Schuster, NY, 1954, Signet, 1995, p.435.

p.227 'May I come in . . .' etc., Hector Arce, *Groucho*, p.184.

Chapter 23

p.229 'The studios are large enclosures . . .' *NYT*, 11.29.1931.

p.229 'Hollywood is very unsure . . .' *NYT*, 12.13.1931.

p.232 'plugged songs with George Gershwin . . .' *Time*, 9.13.1943, AMPAS.

p.232 'I'm sorry you asked how . . .' *The Groucho Letters*, Sphere Books, London, 1969 (1967), p.147.

p.232 'the rowdies and bums . . .' *MBS*, p.154.

p.237 'Now you know the way, Mrs Feibleman . . .' *Monkey Business* file, AMPAS.

p.238 'They are exactly like . . .' etc., quoted in Joe Adamson, loc. cit., p.160.

p.239 '*muchos desiertos* . . .' Salvador Dalí, Marx Bros. script file, Dept. of Cinema, Musée National d'Art Moderne, Centre Pompidou, Paris.

p.239 'The Marx Brothers are the typical . . .' clippings, NYPA.

p.239 'refusal of any rational image . . .' Buñuel interview, BBC *Arena*, 1984.

p.241 'Jimmy, a young Spanish aristocrat . . .', Dalí: Marx Bros. script, loc. cit. (Transcription by Felix Fanes of Fundacio Gala-Salvador Dalí, Figueras, Spain.)

p.242 'autobiographies, riding . . .', Hal Roach Studios press release, 1932, AMPAS.

p.242 'Did he call you harsh . . .' *L. A. Herald*, 3.2.1934, AMPAS.

Chapter 24

p.244 'The 1931 Nut Crop . . .' etc., Press Books, LCMP.

p.245 'Harpo Marx is now a sizeable . . .' 7.7.1931, clippings, NYPA.

p.246 'Big mop red curly hair . . .' *HS*, p.290.

p.249 'certain necessities of life . . .' *Los Angeles Examiner*, 8.19.1932, AMPAS.

p.250 'He is seventy-two years old now . . .' *Redbook Magazine*, 3/1933, loc. cit.

p.250 'I attribute their success . . .' *New York World Telegram*, 8.17.1932, NYPA.

p.250 'The Fifth Brother, by Gummo Marx . . .' courtesy of Robert Marx.

Chapter 25

p.253 'Look, I explain it to you . . .' LCMD.

p.254 'I suppose I ought to begin with Marconi . . .' Tower Radio, 7.1934, from Michael Barson, *Flywheel, Shyster & Flywheel*, Pantheon Books, NY.

p.255 'JUDGE: Counsellor Flywheel . . .' etc., quotes from Barson, loc. cit., p.71.

p.255 'What do you get an hour . . .' etc. ibid., p.6.

p.256 'JONES: Ravelli, then you didn't . . .' ibid., p.11.

p.256 'JUDGE: Gentlemen of the jury . . .' ibid., p.73.

p.256 'GROUCHO: Emanuel Ravelli . . .' ibid., p.150.

p.257 'Taxes? Hey, I got a brudder . . .' ibid., p.91, Episode 8.

p.257 'I know how to make a pair of pants last . . . ibid., p.133, Episode 11.

p.257 'GROUCHO: Ravelli, what are you singing . . .' ibid., p.18.

p.257 'Chico, will you stop muttering . . .' ibid., p.164, Episode 13.

p.258 'If we don't sell the Essolube . . .' ibid., p.61

p.258 'Mr Ravelli, your case interests me . . .' ibid., p.67

p.259 Paramount contract, in *The Freedonia Gazette*, Summer 1982 and Winter 1982.

p.260 'Regarde, papa . . .' GWC, p.79.

p.260 'Samuel Marx, 72, dies . . .' *New York World-Telegram*, 5.12.1933, NYPA.

Chapter 26

p.262 'The Yellow Man's burden . . .' Howard Teichman, *Smart Aleck*, p.159.

p.263 'It is almost impossible . . .' *The Vintage Mencken*, p.146.

p.263 'I am certainly happy . . .' *Love, Groucho; Letters from Groucho Marx to his Daughter Miriam*, edited by Miriam Marx Allen, Faber & Faber, 1992, p.33.

p.264 'This is the most devastating . . .' ibid., p.81

p.264 'He lay down on the couch . . .' *NYT*, 1.27.1946, NYPA.

p.265 'Reds Invite Harpo Marx . . .' *NYT*, 11.19.1932, NYPA.

p.266 'A large, soggy man . . .' GM, p.182.

p.267 'TRENTINO: My dear Mrs Teasdale . . .' etc., 'Cracked Ice', 'temporary script' January 6 1932 (*sic* for 1933), by Harry Ruby, Bert Kalmar and Grover Jones, AMPAS.

p.270 'McCarey: I don't like it . . .' *Cahiers du cinéma*, No.7, January 1967, PW.

p.270 'another truckload of hilarious . . .' *Motion Picture Herald*, 11.11.1933, AMPAS.

p.270 'Practically everyone wants a good laugh . . .' *Variety*, 11.28.1933, AMPAS.

p.270 'Name the Four Marx Sisters . . .' Press Books, LCMP.

p.271 'Harpo Marx is on his way . . .' ibid., LCMP.

p.272 'Inside, behind half empty counters . . .' *HS*, p.301.

p.272 'four hundred knives . . .' *HS*, p.302.

p.273 'Leningrad: In Broadway's own . . .' *Los Angeles Examiner*, 12.19.1933, AMPAS.

p.273 'a strenuous day in which he had told . . .' *Los Angeles Times*, 12.31.1933, AMPAS.

p.273 'The only time I ever played . . .' *HS*, p.328.

p.274 'so that if the bell rang . . .' Robert Conquest, *The Great Terror*, Penguin Books 1971, p.610.

p.274 'Bourgeois or proletarian . . .' *Los Angeles Times*, 1.20.1934, AMPAS.

p.274 'I suppose a good ballet star . . .' clippings, NYPA.

p.275 'MRS TEASDALE . . .' etc., 'Cracked Ice' script, loc. cit., AMPAS.

Chapter 27

p.276 'The Four Marx Brothers took a 25 per cent . . .' *New York Herald Tribune*, 3.31.1934, NYPA.

p.277 'singing waiters with red noses . . .' *The Freedonia Gazette*, Vol.1, No.4, p.8, PW.

p.278 'The important fact that . . .' *Variety*, 8.23.1934, NYPA.

p.279 'I was a little annoyed by this . . .' *MBS*, p.203.

p.280 'When Thalberg returned . . .' *GM*, p.180.

p.281 'the greatest tenor in Italy . . .' MGM scripts, *A Night at the Opera* files, AMPAS.

p.281 'widow of the enormously wealthy . . .' etc., ibid.

pp.283–5 'In the huge office of . . .' etc. quotes from ibid.

p.286 'Once he was established . . .' etc., Scott Meredith, *George S. Kaufman & His Friends*, p.525.

p.286 'the noise, laughter, music and mating calls . . .' Morrie Ryskind, *I Shot an Elephant in My Pyjamas*, p.109.

p.286 'Temporary Incomplete Screenplay . . .' etc., MGM scripts, loc. cit., AMPAS.

p.287 'When the talkies came in . . .' *The Freedonia Gazette*, summer 1987, p.7, PW.

p.288 'We went to Salt Lake City . . .' *The Freedonia Gazette*, winter 1984, p.4, PW.

p.288 'As soon as a show . . .' *MBS*, p.207.

p.289 'Groucho: And two hard-boiled eggs . . .' MGM scripts, loc. cit., AMPAS.

p.291 'they filed with the probate court . . .' Otto Friedrich, *City of Nets*, University of California Press, 1997 (1986), p.168.

p.291 'Sam Wood was a hell of a nice guy . . .' interview for *The Freedonia Gazette*, Winter 1983, p.7, PW.

p.294 'I remember one of the scenes . . .' ibid.

p.294 'the particularly American issue . . .' Raymond Durgnat, *The Crazy Mirror: Hollywood Comedy & the American Image*, Faber & Faber, 1969, p.151.

p.296 'The contract routine is one of the few . . .' Joe Adamson, loc. cit., p.287.

Chapter 28

p.298 'Care should be taken to avoid offense . . .' etc., MPPDA files, AMPAS.

p.299 'Laughs on a high frequency . . .' *Variety*, 12.11.1935, AMPAS.

p.300 'I beg your pardon . . .' *GM*, p.243.

p.301 'Hey, Spencer . . .' *GWC*, p.91.

p.301 'Our family had fallen into . . .' *GWC*, p.98.

p.301 'Norman was playing deaf to Zeppo's . . .' *GP*, p.113.

p.302 'To me there are two common . . .' clipping, 9.9.1933, FLP.

p.303 'A squashed fedora . . .' *HS*, p.387.

p.303 'Mrs Marx was happily confident . . .' clipping, 11.6.1936, FLP.

p.304 'a fair sized town . . .' etc., MGM script files, *A Day at the Races*, AMPAS.

p.306 'The little brown fella . . .' *MBS*, p.206.

p.308 etc. Race track scene – MGM files, loc. cit., AMPAS.

Chapter 29

p.313 'After Thalberg's death . . .' *GM*, p.188.

p.314 'Do I have to get my head shaved . . .' *NY Herald Tribune*, 4.16.1937, NYPA.

p.314 'What's the limit we can get , . .' *Daily News*, 10.30.1937, AMPAS.

p.314 'We might take it to . . .' *Los Angeles Examiner*, 4.13.1938, AMPAS.

p.318 'his associates as clowns . . .' etc., MGM script files, *At the Circus*, AMPAS.

p.318 'Berle-proof Gags for sale . . .' Irving Brecher 'Biography', Paramount press release, November 1951, AMPAS.

p.319 'the Marx Brothers have almost none . . .' *NY Herald Tribune*, 11.17.1939, AMPAS.

p.319 'The Age of Heroic Comedy . . .' Joe Adamson, loc. cit , p. 349.

p.319 'If I ever direct them . . .' *Brooklyn Eagle*, 2.2.1941, NYPA.

p.320 'Defendant's Attorney . . .' *The Freedonia Gazette*, Winter 1984, p.8.

p.320 'Loophole, addressing the very old . . .' MPPDA files, AMPAS.

p.321 'Our picture, *A Day at the Races* . . .' Groucho Marx letters, LCMD.

p.322 'The boys at the studio . . .' ibid., LCMD.

p.322 'Next door to us was . . .' interview with Robert Marx, loc. cit.

p.322 'I'm not able to sleep anymore . . .' June 12 1940, Groucho Marx letters, LCMD.

p.322 'I think the only reason Roosevelt . . .' July 1 1940, ibid., LCMD.

p.323 'Our picture has become a garbage can . . .' September 5, 1940, ibid., LCMD.

p.326 'The Marx Brothers, who have been chasing . . .' Herald, 4.10.1941, AMPAS.

p.327 'It's like when I was a kid . . .' *New York World Telegram*, 11.27.1940, NYPA.

p.327 '"What was that?" Gordon asked . . .' *GWC*, p.143.

p.328 'contributed some of the best features . . .' etc., *New York Herald-Tribune*, 7.29.1941, NYPA.

447

Chapter 30

p.331 'After dinner, news arrived . . .' quoted in *GP*, p.183.

p.331 'The indifference, the blasé attitude . . .' Groucho Marx letters, LCMD.

p.332 'When I first appeared at an army camp . . .' etc., *HS*, p.416.

p.333 'There I was, with sixteen other guys . . .' quoted in *The Freedonia Gazette*, November 1979, PW.

p.333 'I love to work . . .' *NYT*, 1.15.1942, NYPA.

p.333 'By the end of the first few months . . .' *The Freedonia Gazette*, loc. cit., p.15, PW.

p.334 'Sure-fire entertainment . . .' *Cleveland Press*, 3.28.1942, NYPA.

p.335 'Frankly I don't know . . .' Paramount Press Books, LCMD.

p.335 'Chico liked to gamble . . .' *MBS*, p.179.

p.336 'We went our separate ways . . .' *GP*, p.193.

p.336 'Wife failed to see anything funny . . .' *Los Angeles News* (?), 6.29.1942, AMPAS.

p.336 'The comedian did not contest . . .' *Los Angeles Herald*, 7.15.1942, AMPAS.

p.337 'I've never hit a woman except . . .' Hector Arce, *Groucho*, p.287.

p.337 'The more moolah/You make . . .' Groucho Marx, *Many Happy Returns*, Simon & Schuster, NY, 1942.

p.337 'He had this large stable of stars . . .' interview with Robert Marx, loc. cit.

p.338 'Dame Rumor hit it over the head . . .' Groucho Marx letters, 7.27.1942, LCMD.

p.338 'I am leading a quiet, sinless life . . .' 12.16.1942, ibid., LCMD.

p.338 'During this half hour . . .' *Newsweek*, 4.5.1943, NYPA.

Chapter 31

p.340 'Dear Dick, I am reluctant to advise . . .' *Love, Groucho*, edited by Miriam Marx Allen, p.9.

p.340 'Tomorrow we are having tea at the White House . . .' ibid., p.11.

p.341 'violent propaganda campaign . . .' Otto Friedrich, *City of Nets*, p.51.

p.341 'in each of these companies . . .' ibid., p.51.

p.341 'principal war agitators . . .' ibid., p.51.

p.342 'Dear Gooch, Sunday morning in Okmulgee . . .' *Love, Groucho*, p.13.

p.343 'Dear Mir You conclude by saying . . .' ibid., p.31.

p.344 'full of sailors and . . .' ibid., p.18.

p.344 'Without mustache or cigar . . .' *Los Angeles Times*, 7.22.1945, AMPAS.

p.345 'When you mourn something irreplaceable . . .' *HS*, p.432.

p.346 'Dear Warner Brothers . . .' etc., quoted in Groucho Marx, *The Groucho Letters*, Sphere, 1969 (1967), pp.15–19.

p.348 'FREE PARKING . . .' etc., Marx Bros. scripts, *A Night in Casablanca* file, AMPAS.

p.350 'I want a rest when I complete this . . .' *Love, Groucho*, p.39.

p.351 'Archie Mayo says . . .' 12.18.1945, ibid., p.45.
p.351 'a semi-juvenile audience . . .' 1.14.1946, ibid., p.53.

Chapter 32

p.353 'The ideal life for me . . .' etc., *NYT*, 1.27.1946, NYPA.
p.354 'When the boys come back . . .' Otto Friedrich, *City of Nets*, p.179.
p.356 'I think the American people are on to . . .' *Love, Groucho*, p.66.
p.357 'Roxy, N.Y., Chico Marx . . .' *Variety*, 7.24.1946, NYPA.
p.357 'He was in the process of losing . . .' Shamus Culhane, loc. cit., p.289.
p.358 '"If I hear another Pat and Mike story . . ."' *GWC*, p.168.
pp.358–9 Harpo and Zionism – information from Bill Marx, Paul Wesolowski and Ben Hecht, *Child of the Century*.
p.360 '(The script) is good but still needs . . .' *Love, Groucho*, p. 120.
p.360 'as what Groucho called "a huffer , . ."' *The Freedonia Gazette*, Winter 1987, p.12, PW.
p.361 'I am sure it will be one of the worst movies . . .' 10.3.1946, *Love, Groucho*, p.95.
p.361 'my heart sank . . .' 10.23.1946, ibid., p.98.
p.362 'charming to work with . . .' etc., November 1946, ibid., p.103.
p.363 'a bald-headed makeup man with halitosis . . .' 1.15.1947, ibid., p.110.
p.364 'Spiritual intolerance, political inquisitions . . .' Otto Friedrich, *City of Nets*, p.321.

Chapter 33

p.366 'Folks, this is just as new to me . . .' Groucho Marx with Hector Arce, *The Secret Word is Groucho*, G. P. Putnam's & Sons, NY, 1976, p.31.
p.367 'No, we would call it Gonzalez . . .' ibid., p.80.
p.367 'Groucho: Are you sure your husband . . .' ibid., p.204.
p.367 'He's on twenty-four hour call . . .' ibid., p.206.
p.369 'You're a Jew and I'm a Jew . . .' ibid., p.50.
p.370 'Do you know what I just did today . . .' Joe Adamson, *Groucho, Harpo, Chico and Sometimes Zeppo*, p.407.
p.372 'helter-skelter entertainment . . .' *NYT*, 4.8.1950, quoted in Glenn Mitchell, *The Marx Brothers Encyclopedia*, B. T. Batsford, London, 1996, p.148.
p.372 'The Marx Bros. act embraces . . .' *Variety*, 6.29.1949, NYPA.
p.372 'What makes these great clowns . . .' quoted in *NYT*, 6.21.1949, NYPA.
p.372 'within the limits of the footlights . . .' ibid.
p.373 'A man goes up to the box office . . .' *The Secret Word Is Groucho*, p.64.

Chapter 34

p.375 'The set to which I was directed . . .' *Holiday Magazine*, 4/1952, AMPAS.

p.377 'Groucho Marx admitted . . .' etc., *Los Angeles Examiner*, 4.7.1950, AMPAS.

p.377 'extreme cruelty . . .' etc., *Los Angeles Times*, 4.15.1950, AMPAS.

p.377 'never took care of the house . . .' etc., *Herald Express*, 5.12.1950, AMPAS.

p.377 'worst of all, she didn't seem to think . . .' *Daily News*, 5.12.1950, AMPAS.

p.378 'the comedian's 7-year-old daughter . . .' *Los Angeles Examiner*, 7.18.1954, AMPAS.

p.378 'scurrilous you've made me out to be . . .' Arthur Marx, *My Life with Groucho*, p.194.

p.378 'uncontrollable temper . . .' etc., *Citizen-News*, 1.8.1969, AMPAS.

p.380 'Give me the rundown on these two . . .' etc., *The American Weekly*, 9.4.1955, NYPA.

p.381 'ZEPPO MARX TRADES BLOWS . . .' *Los Angeles Times*, 5.31.1957, AMPAS.

p.381 'I built them a house . . .' interview with Robert Marx, loc. cit.

p.382 'He went through different phases . . .' etc., interview with Bill Marx, loc. cit.

p.383 'I'll probably be doing one special . . .' *Philadelphia Sunday Bulletin*, 8.18.1957, FLP.

Chapter 35

p.387 'Have you done any work . . .' Groucho Marx letters, LCMD.

p.387 'I resolved to put the matter . . .' James Thurber and E.B. White, *Is Sex Necessary?*, Dell, 1950 (1929), p.84.

p.387 'I have noticed . . .' Groucho Marx, *Beds*, p.35.

p.388 'his embarrassment when he first came . . .' ibid., p.48.

p.388 'Why should anyone buy . . .' *GM*, p.12.

p.388 'Nowadays things have to be merchandized . . .' ibid., p.14.

p.389 'To Goodman Ace . . .' *The Groucho Letters*, p.235.

p.389 'ernest zachow, jr., of portland . . .' Groucho Marx letters, LCMD.

p.390 'Are you reading the pieces about me . . .' *The Groucho Letters*, p.78.

p.390 'It seems to me I come off . . .' ibid., p.78.

p.390 'As I lay there in bed . . .' ibid., p.81.

p.391 'Yes, I did see the Beatle movie . . .' Groucho Marx letters, LCMD.

p.391 'The three lipoleum coyne . . .' somewhere in *Finnegans Wake*. Go look!

p.391 'Groucho wrote every word . . .' *New York Herald Tribune*, 4.30.1961, AMPAS.

p.391 'Even softer than Groucho's . . .' *HS*, p.482.

p.392 '"Mrs Marx," he said proudly . . .' etc., *New York Herald Tribune*, loc. cit.

p.392 'I kissed him hello . . .' *GWC*, p.175.

Chapter 36

p.393 'Marx Brothers Weep for Chico . . .' *Citizen-News*, 10.12.1961, AMPAS.

p.394 'I still hear her voice . . .' Groucho Marx with Hector Arce, *The Secret Word is Groucho*, p.150.

p.395 'I can't talk sense to your father . . .' *GWC*, p.170.

p.396 'It was almost . . .' interview with Bill Marx, loc. cit.

p.396 'I was different from most people . . .' *HS*, p.466.

p.396 'vascular surgery . . .' etc., clippings, AMPAS.

p.397 '"She wants to sing . . ."' *Los Angeles Times*, 12.30.1958, AMPAS.

p.397 '"You can ask any little girl . . ."' clipping, 7.10.1959, AMPAS.

p.397 'a double wrist watch . . .' *Variety*, 2.19.1969, AMPAS.

p.398 'Walk this way, please . . .' etc., *Los Angeles Times*, 7.18.1965, AMPAS. Also information in *The Freedonia Gazette*, Summer 1981, PW.

p.400 'I only did five days' work . . .' *NYT*, 3.1.1970.

p.402 'overwrought at the killing of . . .' *Variety*, 9.15.1972, AMPAS.

p.404 'when Dorothy opens her door . . .' Steve Stoliar, *Raised Eyebrows*, General Publishing Group, Los Angeles, 1996, p.41

p.405 'After asking what Groucho was like . . .' ibid., p.69.

p.406 'Reporter: Do you enjoy being called . . .' ibid., p.112.

p.406 'life after death . . .' Cosby interview, clip in *The Unknown Marx Brothers*, 1993.

p.406 'I only wish Harpo and Chico . . .' Hector Arce, *Groucho*, p.451.

p.406 'Now then, these young filmmakers . . .' Steve Stoliar, loc. cit., p.202.

p.407 'THREAT TO GROUCHO MARX . . .' clippings, AMPAS, 16–20 April 1977.

p.408 'I think his real, deep enjoyment . . .' *Los Angeles Herald Examiner*, 4.29.1977, AMPAS.

p.408 Ballow testimony, *Los Angeles Times*, 6.26.1977, AMPAS.

p.408 'What do you want . . .' Steve Stoliar, loc. cit., p.261.

p.409 'Groucho Marx was an illusion in death . . .' *Los Angeles Times*, 9.4.1977, AMPAS.

p.409 'reputed mob figure . . .' etc., *Variety*, 11.20.1978, AMPAS.

p.410 'Groucho always said you were . . .' BBC interview quoted in *The Freedonia Gazette*, Summer 1982, p.9, PW.

p.410 'Zeppo, the Marx brother who got the girl . . .' *Los Angeles Times*, 12.1.1979, AMPAS.

p.411 'severely mentally ill . . .' *Los Angeles Herald Examiner*, 2.4.1983, AMPAS.

p.411 'Erin Fleming arrested with gun . . .' quoted in Steve Stoliar, loc. cit., p.276.

p.412 'If you keep having birthdays . . .' *Los Angeles Times*, 8.21.1977, AMPAS.

Epilogue

p.413 'GROUCHO'S TWIN HERE . . .' *Los Angeles Times*, 8.16.1955, PW.

p.416 'CHICO: If you don't talk . . .' etc., Robert Coover, *The Public Burning*, Grove Press, New York, 1998 (1977), pp.455, 456.

Select Bibliography

It is conventional wisdom that there are dozens of books published about the Marx Brothers, but most of them are celebratory volumes, pictorial descriptions of their films and monographs in various film book series. The key books published to date are of two kinds: autobiography and compilations. The only originally researched biographical study of any of the Marx Brothers to date has been Hector Arce's *Groucho*, published by G. P. Putnam's & Sons in 1979 and reprinted in Perigee paperback in 1980. Sources and information unavailable to Arce, who has sadly died, have been since incorporated into the Marxian story.

The two autobiographies, Groucho's *Groucho and Me*, first published by Bernard Geis Associates in 1959, and Harpo's *Harpo Speaks* (co-written with Rowland Barber) first published by Bernard Geis Associates/Random House in 1961, remain the key personal accounts of the Marx Brothers on their own lives. Of the two, Harpo's is the more detailed tale of the Marxes' childhood, given the chronological conundrums discussed in my own text. Groucho also, as has been told, published several more books (some co-written), listed below, and dozens of short essays and articles. Forty-seven of these are included in Robert S. Bader's compilation, *Groucho Marx and Other Short Stories and Tall Tales*, first published by Faber & Faber in 1993.

Of the many compilations, two are of central importance: *The Groucho Phile*, co-written by Groucho and Hector Arce and first published by Galahad Books in 1976, contains a treasure trove of photographs from Groucho's own collection and a much more accurate account of his career than he presented in 1959. *The Marx Brothers Scrapbook*, by Groucho Marx and Richard J. Anobile, first published by Darien House in 1973, also contains excellent pictorial arcana, and much important oral evidence, though the integrity of the text has been challenged by other Marx Brothers scholars. Mistakes in transliteration of names and places have been often cited. Personally, I have had a dog-eared copy of the paperback for years, which has given me great pleasure.

The only book-length account of the Marx Brothers' early life and family tales is Kyle Crichton's notorious – and rare – *The Marx Brothers*, first published by Doubleday & Co. in 1950. This is, as I have noted, largely fictional, though it, too, has entertained me on rainy nights.

Books by sons and daughters of the Marx Brothers, which I have cited, include Arthur Marx's books, listed below, Maxine Marx's unique memoir, *Growing Up with Chico* (first published by Prentice Hall in 1980), and Miriam Marx Allen's book of Groucho letters, *Love, Groucho*, first published by Faber & Faber in 1992.

Personal accounts by people close to Groucho in the final decade of his life include the reliable Steve Stoliar's *Raised Eyebrows* (General Publishing Group, 1996), and the somewhat more capricious *Hello, I Must Be Going* by Charlotte Chandler (first published by Doubleday & Co. in 1979).

Joe Adamson's *Groucho, Harpo, Chico and Sometimes Zeppo* (phew! what a mouthful!), first published by Simon & Schuster in 1973, remains the best of the analyses of the Brothers' films to date, though it does not detail the Marxes' stage career. Adamson's book was written before Marx historian Paul Wesolowski began compiling his voluminous archive, and the author promises an imminent update.

Glenn Mitchell's *The Marx Brothers Encyclopedia*, published by B. T. Batsford in 1996, provides much detailed pleasure, particularly regarding the Brothers' little-known British tours, and other vintage Marxiana.

Books published by French, German and other fans of the Brothers are less known to your Anglocentric author, but attest to the abiding interest in the Marx Brothers in many parts of the globe. Those who have not watched *A Night at the Opera* dubbed in German on satellite television have not fully lived.

The General Selection

Adamson, Joe, *Groucho, Harpo, Chico and Sometimes Zeppo* (detailed above).
Alion, Yves, *Les Marx Brothers*, Edilig, Paris, France, 1985.
Allen, Fred, *Much Ado About Me*, Little, Brown and Company, 1956.
Allen, Frederick Lewis, *Only Yesterday*, Bantam Books, NY, 1946.
Anobile, Richard J., *Why a Duck?* (compilation), Darien House, NY, 1971.
– *Hooray for Captain Spaulding!* (compilation), Darien House, 1974.
– with Groucho Marx, *The Marx Brothers Scrapbook* (detailed above).
Arce, Hector, *Groucho* (detailed above).
– and Groucho Marx, *The Groucho Phile* (detailed above).
– and Groucho Marx, *The Secret Word is Groucho*, Berkeley Medallion Books, NY, 1976.
Bader, Robert (ed.), *Groucho Marx & Other Short Stories & Tall Tales* (detailed above).

Barson, Michael (ed.), *Flywheel, Shyster & Flywheel, the Marx Brothers' Lost Radio Shows*, Pantheon Books, NY, 1988.
Benayoun, Robert, *Les Frères Marx*, Seghers, Paris, France 1980.
– *Les Marx Brothers ont la parole*, Editions du Seuil, France 1991.
Bergan, Ronald, *The Life and Times of the Marx Brothers*, The Green Wood Publishing Company, London, 1992.
Bergman, Andrew, *We're in the Money; Depression America & Its Films*, New York University, 1971; Elephant Paperbacks, Chicago, 1992.
Chandler, Charlotte, *Hello, I Must Be Going – Groucho and his Friends* (detailed above).
Crichton, Kyle, *The Marx Brothers* (detailed above).
Culhane, Shamus, *Talking Animals and Other People*, Da Capo Press, NY, 1998.
Durgnat, Raymond, *The Crazy Mirror – Hollywood Comedy and the American Image*, Faber & Faber, London, 1969.
Eyles, Allen, *The Marx Brothers, Their World of Comedy*, Zwemmer, London, 1966.
– *The Complete Films of the Marx Brothers*, Citadel Press, NY, 1992.
Finler, Joel W., *The Hollywood Story*, Octopus Books, 1988.
Flamini, Ronald, *Thalberg, the Last Tycoon and the World of MGM*, Crown Publishers, NY, 1994.
Florey, Robert, *Hollywood d'hier et d'aujourd'hui*, Editions Prisma, Paris, 1948.
Friedrich, Otto, *City of Nets; a Portrait of Hollywood in the 1940's*, University of California Press, 1997.
Gabler, Neil, *An Empire of Their Own: How the Jews Invented Hollywood*, Crown Publishers, NY, 1988.
Gehring, Wes D., *The Marx Brothers: a Bio-bibliography*, Greenwood Press, Westport, CT, 1987.
– *Groucho Marx and W. C. Fields, Huckster Comedians*, University Press of Mississippi, Jackson, 1994.
Gilbert, Douglas, *American Vaudeville*, McGraw Hill/Whittlesey House, NY, 1940.
Hecht, Ben, *A Child of the Century*, Simon & Schuster, NY, 1954.
Hoppe, Ulrich, *Die Marx Brothers*, Wilhelm Heyne Verlag, München, 1985.
Jenkins, Henry, *What Made Pistachio Nuts? Early Sound Comedy & the Vaudeville Aesthetic*, Columbia University Press, 1992.
Kyro, Ado, *Le Surréalisme au cinéma*, Arcanes, Paris, France, 1953.
Laurie, Joe, Jr. and Abel Green, *Show Biz from Vaude to Video*, Henry Holt & Co., 1951.
– *Vaudeville, from the Honky Tonks to the Palace*, Henry Holt & Co., 1953.
Louvish, Simon, *Man on the Flying Trapeze: The Life and Times of W. C. Fields*, Faber & Faber, London; W. W. Norton & Co., NY, 1997.
Maltin, Leonard, *The Great Movie Comedians, From Chaplin to Woody Allen*, Crown Publishers, NY, 1978.
– *Movie Comedy Teams: The Marx Brothers*, Signet Books, NY, 1970.
Marx, Arthur, *Life with Groucho*, Simon & Schuster, NY, 1954.
– *Not as a Crocodile*, Harper & Brothers, NY, 1958.
– *Son of Groucho*, David McKay, NY, 1972.

– *My Life with Groucho*, Robson Books, London, 1988.

Marx, Groucho, *Beds*, Farrar & Rheinhart, NY, 1930.

– *Many Happy Returns*, Simon & Schuster, 1942.

– *Groucho and Me* (detailed above).

– *Memoirs of a Mangy Lover*, Bernard Geis Associates, NY, 1963.

– *The Groucho Letters*, Simon & Schuster, NY, 1967.

– with Richard J. Anobile, *The Marx Brothers Scrapbook* (detailed above).

– with Hector Arce, *The Groucho Phile* (detailed above).

– with Hector Arce, *The Secret Word Is Groucho*, Berkeley Medallion Books, NY, 1976.

Marx, Harpo with Rowland Barber, *Harpo Speaks* (detailed above).

Marx, Maxine, *Growing Up with Chico* (detailed above).

Marx Allen, Miriam, *Love, Groucho* (detailed above).

Mast, Gerald, *The Comic Mind, Comedy and the Movies*, University of Chicago Press, 1979.

Mencken, H. L., *The Vintage Mencken*, gathered by Alistair Cooke, Vintage, NY, 1990.

Meredith, Scott, *George S. Kaufman and his Friends*, Doubleday & Co., NY, 1974.

Meryman, Richard, *Mank: The Wit, World and Life of Herman Mankiewicz*, William Morrow & Company, 1978.

Mitchell, Glenn, *The Marx Brothers Encyclopedia* (detailed above).

Perelman, S. J., *The Most of S. J. Perelman*, Simon & Schuster, NY, 1958.

– *The Last Laugh*, Simon & Schuster, NY, 1981.

Robinson, David, *The Great Funnies: A History of Film Comedy*, E. P. Dutton & Co., NY, 1969.

Ryskind, Morrie with J. M. Roberts, *I Shot an Elephant in My Pyjamas: The Morrie Ryskind Story*, Vital Issues Press, 1994.

Stein, Charles W., *American Vaudeville as Seen by its Contemporaries*, Knopf, NY 1984.

Stoliar, Steve, *Raised Eyebrows* (detailed above).

Teichman, Howard, *George S. Kaufman, an Intimate Portrait*, Atheneum, NY, 1972.

– *Smart Aleck: The Wit, World, and Life of Alexander Woollcott*, William Morrow & Company, NY, 1976.

Thurber, James and E. B. White, *Is Sex Necessary?*, Harper & Brothers, NY, 1929.

– *The Years with Ross*, Little Brown & Co., NY, 1959.

Wolf, William, *The Marx Brothers*, Pyramid Communications, NY, 1975.

Woollcott, Alexander, *While Rome Burns* (essays), Grossett & Dunlap, NY, 1934.

Zimmerman, Paul D. with Burt Goldblatt, *The Marx Brothers at the Movies*, G. P. Putnam's & Sons, NY, 1968.

Magazine

The Freedonia Gazette, published intermittently by Paul Wesolowski, New Hope, Pennsylvania.

Index

461

465